CATEGORY SPECIFICITY IN
BRAIN AND MIND

Brain Damage, Behaviour and Cognition:
Developments in Clinical Neuropsychology
Titles in Series

Category specificity in brain and mind

Edited by

Emer M. E. Forde
Neurosciences Research Institute, Aston University, UK

and

Glyn W. Humphreys
Behavioural Brain Sciences Unit, University of Birmingham, UK

First published 2002 by Psychology Press
27 Church Road, Hove, East Sussex, BN3 2FA

Simultaneously published in the USA and Canada
by Psychology Press
29 West 35th Street, New York, NY 10001

Psychology Press is part of the Taylor & Francis Group

© 2002 Psychology Press

Typeset in Times by RefineCatch Limited, Bungay, Suffolk
Printed and bound in Great Britain by
Biddles Ltd, Guildford and King's Lynn
Cover design by Joyce Chester

British Library Cataloguing in Publication Data
A catalogue record for this book is available from the British Library

Library of Congress Cataloging-in-Publication Data
Category specificity in brain and mind/[edited by] Emer M.E. Forde and
Glyn W. Humphreys.
      p.   cm.—(Brain damage, behaviour, and cognition)
   Includes bibliographical references and index.
   ISBN 1–84169–290–5 (hbk.)
   1. Human information processing.   2. Differentiation
(Cognition)   3. Categorization (Psychology)   4. Form perception.
5. Visual perception.   6. Neuropsychology.   I. Forde, Emer M.E.,
1970– II. Humphreys, Glyn W.   III. Series.

RC386.2.C283   2002
616.8—dc21   2001058924

ISBN 1–84169–290–5

For
Patrick, Elizabeth and Glyn

Contents

List of contributors

Dr Martin Arguin, Groupe de Recherche en Neuropsychologie Expèrimentale, Département de Psychologie, Université de Montréal, C.P. 6128, Succ. Centre-Ville, Montréal, Quebec, H3C 3J7, Canada.

Professor Alfonso Caramazza, Department of Psychology, William James Hall, Harvard University, 33 Kirkland Street, Cambridge, MA 02138, USA.

Dr Howard Chertkow, Lady Davis Institute, 3755 Côte St Catherine Road, Montreal, Quebec, H3T 1E2, Canada.

Mr George Cree, Department of Psychology, University of Western Ontario, London, Ontario, N6A 5C2, Canada.

Dr Joseph T. Devlin, Centre for Functional Magnetic Resonance Imaging of the Brain, University of Oxford, John Radcliffe Hospital, Headley Way, Headington, Oxford OX3 9DU, UK.

Dr Emer Forde, Neurosciences Research Institute (Psychology), Aston University, Aston Triangle, Birmingham B4 7ET, UK.

Professor Karl Friston, Wellcome Department of Cognitive Neurology, Institute of Neurology, Queen Square, London WC1N 3BG, UK.

Professor Guido Gainotti, Servizio di Neuropsicologia Università Cattolica–Policlinico Gemelli, Largo A. Gemelli 8, 00168 Rome, Italy.

Dr Peter Garrard, Institute of Cognitive Neuroscience, Alexandra House, 17 Queens Square, London WC1N 3BG, UK.

Professor Rochel Gelman, Rutgers Center for Cognitive Science, 172 Freylinghuysen Road, Piscataway, NJ 08854–8020, USA.

Ms Marissa Greif, Department of Psychology, Yale University, PO Box 208205, New Haven, CT 065208205, USA.

Professor John Hodges, Medical Research Council Cognition and Brain Sciences Unit, 15 Chaucer Road, Cambridge CB2 2EF, UK.

Professor Glyn Humphreys, Department of Psychology, University of Birmingham, Edgbaston, Birmingham B15 2TT, UK.

Professor Remo Job, Dipartimento di Psicologia dello Sviluppo, Via Venezia 6, 35100, Padova, Italy.

Professor Frank Keil, Department of Psychology, Yale University, 2 Hillhouse Avenue, PO Box 208205, New Haven, CT 065208205, USA.

Ms Nancy Kim, Department of Psychology, Yale University, PO Box 208205, New Haven, CT 065208205, USA.

Professor Koen Lamberts, Department of Psychology, University of Warwick, Coventry CV4 7AL, UK.

Dr Matthew Lambon Ralph, Department of Psychology, University of Manchester, Manchester, UK.

Dr Alyssa Lafosse, Department of Psychology, 405 Hilgard Avenue, Franz Hall, UCLA, Los Angeles, CA 90024, USA.

Professor Ken McRae, Department of Psychology, University of Western Ontario, London, Ontario, N6A 5C2, Canada.

Professor Jean Mandler, Department of Cognitive Science D-015, University of California San Diego, La Jolla, CA 92093, USA.

Dr Helen Moss, Department of Experimental Psychology, University of Cambridge, Downing Street, Cambridge CB2 3EB, UK.

Professor David Plaut, Departments of Psychology and Computer Science, Center for the Neural Basis of Cognition, Carnegie Mellon University, 4400 Fifth Avenue, Pittsburgh, PA 15213, USA.

Dr Cathy Price, Wellcome Department of Cognitive Neurology, Institute of Neurology, Queen Square, London WC1N 3BG, UK.

Professor M. Jane Riddoch, Behavioural Brain Sciences Centre, University of Birmingham, Edgbaston, Birmingham B15 2TT, UK.

Dr Timothy Rogers, Department of Psychology, Center for the Neural Basis of Cognition, Carnegie Mellon University, 4400 Fifth Avenue, Pittsburgh, PA 15213, USA.

Dr Laurie Santos, Department of Psychology, William James Hall, Harvard University, 33 Kirkland Street, Cambridge, MA 02138, USA.

Professor Giuseppe Sartori, Dipartimento di Psicologia Generale, Piazza Capitaniato 3, 35100, Padova, Italy.

Ms Laura Shapiro, Department of Psychology, Whitehead Building, Goldsmiths College, University of London, New Cross, London SE14 6NW, UK.

Dr Kaveri Subrahmanyam, Department of Child and Family Studies, California State University, Los Angeles, CA 90032, USA.

Professor Lorraine Tyler, Department of Experimental Psychology, University of Cambridge, Downing Street, Cambridge, CB2 3EB, UK.

Dr Christine Whatmough, Lady Davis Institute, 3755 Côte St. Catherine Road, Montreal, Quebec, H3T 1E2, Canada.

Professor Stefano Zago, Istituto di Psicologia, Via Saffi 15, 61029, Urbino, Italy.

Series preface

From being an area primarily on the periphery of mainstream behavioural and cognitive science, neuropsychology has developed in recent years into an area of central concern for a range of disciplines. We are witnessing not only a revolution in the way in which brain–behaviour–cognition relationships are viewed, but a widening of interest concerning developments in neuropsychology on the part of a range of workers in a variety of fields. Major advances in brain-imaging techniques and the cognitive modelling of the impairments following brain damage promise a wider understanding of the nature of the representation of cognition and behaviour in the damage and undamaged brain.

Neuropsychology is now centrally important for those working with brain-damaged people, but the very rate of expansion in the area makes it difficult to keep up with findings from the current research. The aim of the *Brain Damage, Behaviour and Cognition* series is to publish a wide range of books that present comprehensive and up-to-date overviews of current developments in specific areas of interest.

These books will be of particular interest to those working with the brain-damaged. It is the editors' intention that undergraduates, postgraduates, clinicians, and researchers in psychology, speech pathology and medicine will find this series a useful source of information on important current developments. The authors and editors of the books in this series are experts in their respective fields, working at the forefront of contemporary research. They have produced texts that are accessible and scholarly. We thank them for their contribution and their hard work in fulfilling the aims of the series.

CC and GH

Sydney, Australia and Birmingham, UK

Series Editors

Preface

Both the functional organisation of cognitive processes such as perception, memory and language, and their anatomical organisation in the human brain have long been central topics in psychology, physiology, and philosophy. One of the most basic of these cognitive processes, essential to the survival of all species, is the ability to recognise other animals and objects. Although effortless for most people, the processes that underlie our ability to recognise and name objects are complex and probably involve a number of hierarchically organised stages. For instance, to recognise an object we must be able to extract information about its overall shape, size, and constituent parts. We must match this information to stored memories of the visual properties of objects and perhaps derive information about associated non-visual properties (e.g. is it dangerous? is it edible?), and, finally, we must access its name. Patients with selective impairments in object recognition and naming have provided invaluable clues into the organisation of the underlying cognitive processes. Particularly fascinating are patients with object recognition and naming impairments restricted to one category of object. Typically, patients with these "category-specific" impairments have difficulty in naming living things but not non-living things, although there have also been a few reports of patients with the reverse pattern (see Forde & Humphreys [1999] Humphreys & Forde [2001] for reviews). In *Category specificity in brain and mind* we aim to address a number of fundamental questions raised by studies of patients with these impairments. For instance, what processes are involved in the recognition of visually presented objects? Have we evolved category-specific visual recognition systems that can be selectively damaged following brain injury? How do we acquire and, subsequently, organise our conceptual knowledge about living and non-living things? What are the core features or defining properties of different categories of object? How can we model object recognition and naming in order to capture the patterns of deficits found after brain damage?

Patients with category-specific impairments were first documented in the neuropsychological literature over half a century ago. Nielsen (1946) described one patient, Flora D, who had particular problems in recognising living things and another, CHC, who had problems in recognising non-living things. Flora D and CHC also had different patterns of neurological damage. Flora D's lesion included damage to the left occipital lobe and CHC to the right temporal and right occipital lobes and, consequently, Nielsen (1946, p. 186) argued that "one occipital lobe [the left[1]] may serve in recognition of animate objects while the other [the right] serves for inanimate ones". Nielsen's hypothesis—that category-specific impairments emerge after brain damage because we have separate category-specific recognition systems in brain and mind—is arguably the most intuitive and parsimonious explanation for these cases. Indeed, this view is currently shared by a number of neuropsychologists and articulated in some detail in two of the chapters in this book (Santos & Caramazza, Chapter 1; Sartori, Job & Zago, Chapter 2), although the precise anatomical areas Neilsen outlined have been shown to be incorrect by more detailed patient analysis (Gainotti, Chapter 14) and by studies using functional imaging (Price & Friston, Chapter 15).

Our book opens with the two chapters in which Santos and Caramazza (Chapter 1) and Sartori, Job, and Zago (Chapter 2) defend the idea of category-specific neural recognition systems using recent neuropsychological data. In particular, Santos and Caramazza outline their 'domain-specific theory' and argue that we have evolved three separate semantic systems for the recognition of animals, plants, and non-living objects, respectively. This chapter raises a number of important questions that are subsequently addressed by the authors. For example, is there any good reason why the human brain should have evolved separate semantic systems for animals, plant life, and non-living things? Is there any evidence for category-specific recognition systems in other mammals? Sartori, Job, and Zago (Chapter 2) also suggest that we have separate systems for the recognition of living and non-living things. However, they suggest that visual recognition systems diverge at stages preceding access to semantic knowledge and propose that the stage of accessing visual memories (i.e. accessing a 'structural description system') might be categorically organised. One important prediction from these chapters is that, if we have evolved separate recognition systems for

---

[1] Insertions in square brackets made by the present authors.

different categories of object, young infants should have an innate predisposition to distinguish between these categories. In Chapters 11–13, some leading developmental psychologists address this question (Mandler, Chapter 11; Subrahmanyam, Gelman & Lafosse, Chapter 12; Keil, Kim & Greif, Chapter 13).

A radically different explanation for category-specific impairments was outlined in a seminal paper by Warrington and Shallice (1984), which provided the catalyst for an intense interest in this topic over the past 25 years. Warrington and Shallice described four patients with category-specific impairments in recognising living things. Patient JBR, for example, had profound difficulties in recognising pictures of living things, such as animals, fruit, and vegetables, despite having relatively normal recognition of non-living things, such as furniture, tools, and clothing. Interestingly, however, when Warrington and Shallice extended the range of categories tested, they found that JBR also performed poorly with food items, precious stones, musical instruments, and types of cloth, indicating that his impairment did not conform to a neat dichotomous dissociation between living and non-living things. As a result, Warrington and Shallice suggested that JBR's problem did not reflect an impairment to a neural system dedicated to recognising living things. Instead they argued that category-specific impairments arise because different types of information are needed to recognise different categories of object. In particular, they argued that sensory information is primarily important in differentiating between living things, whereas functional information (e.g. information about how objects are used) is important in differentiating between non-living things. Warrington and Shallice (1984, p. 849) suggested that "a semantic system based on functional specifications may have evolved for the identification of inanimate objects" and that this semantic system would be independent from a sensory semantic system. This "sensory/functional" hypothesis has arguably been the most widely accepted explanation for category-specific impairments in recent years. Indeed, it is outlined as the "standard view" against which other hypotheses are tested in almost all of the chapters in this book. Some of the authors provide neuropsychological cases (e.g. Humphreys, Riddoch & Forde, Chapter 3), normative data (McRae & Cree, Chapter 8), computational modelling (Rogers & Plaut, Chapter 9) and lesion data (Gainotti, Chapter 14) consistent with this theory. In contrast, others argue that it is no longer a tenable idea (Santos & Caramazza, Chapter 1; Sartori et al., Chapter 2; Moss, Tyler, & Devlin, Chapter 5).

In addition to the "domain-specific" and "sensory/functional" theories outlined above, there are now a number of other important explanations for category-specific impairments. For example, Arguin (Chapter 4) and Humphreys et al. (Chapter 3) stress the contribution of similarity between categorically related exemplars in explaining the observed patterns of deficits. They suggest that category-specific impairments for living things can emerge because these items belong to categories that have perceptually similar exemplars. In Chapter 10, Lamberts and Shapiro demonstrate how an exemplar-based model of categorisation can simulate category-specific impairments for living things on the basis of this similarity principle. This chapter provides an interesting comparison with the chapter by Rogers and Plaut (Chapter 9), who describe how a connectionist model of semantic memory can simulate category-specific effects (see also Moss et al., Chapter 5). In contrast to accounts that stress the importance of visual information for differentiating between living things, Moss et al. propose that the recognition of living and non-living things does not depend on accessing any particular type of property. Instead, they argue that all kinds of stored knowledge are represented in a single homogenous semantic system and that category-specific effects emerge because the underlying structure of this stored knowledge differs for living and non-living things (the "conceptual structure" account). They propose that living things share significantly more correlated features and have fewer distinctive features than non-living things. As a consequence, random damage to stored knowledge leads to category-specific recognition impairments for living things, except at the most severe levels of damage. Consistent with this idea, McRae and Cree (Chapter 8) provide a substantial database of normative data demonstrating that living things do have more correlated features and fewer distinctive features than non-living things. McRae and Cree's study is particularly useful because few studies have investigated category-specific effects in normal subjects. The authors demonstrate how the properties control subjects use to describe objects from different categories can give us a window on the underlying structure of stored semantic information, and how this breaks down in patients with category-specific naming impairments.

One reason for the diversity in the explanations for category-specific impairments might be that these patients do not form a homogenous group and, as a result, no single theory can account for all of the available neuropsychological data (see Humphreys et al., Chapter 3; Keil et al., Chapter 13, for elaborated discussion of this point). Indeed, it is becoming increasingly apparent that category-specific impairments can emerge from damage to different levels of the object recognition and naming system. For example, Arguin (Chapter 4) and Moss et al. (Chapter 5) provide examples of patients with category-specific impairments for living things following damage to different levels of the object naming system, namely to visual processing and to stored semantic knowledge, respectively. Explaining category-specific impairments following brain damage is thus a complex issue. Future studies that define the loci of patients' impairments within the object recognition and naming system will be useful in determining the factors that affect the recognition of living and nonliving things at each stage of the naming process. An example of this approach is provided by Garrard, Lambon Ralph, and Hodges (Chapter 6), who investigated whether patients with selective and progressive impairments to semantic memory showed category-specific impairments in recognition and naming tasks. These patients can be used to investigate a number of important questions. For instance, does degradation to semantic memory necessarily affect one category of objects more than another? Alternatively, does decline of semantic knowledge concerning one type of property (say, visual knowledge) affect recognition of one category more than another? Do category-specific impairments for living and non-living things emerge following different levels of damage to the semantic system? Similar questions are discussed by Whatmough and Chertkow (Chapter 7), who provide a comprehensive review of the literature on category-specific effects in patients with Alzheimer's disease.

In the final two chapters, Gainotti (Chapter 14) and Price and Friston (Chapter 15) provide overviews of the brain regions that are involved in the recognition and naming of different categories using lesion data and functional neuroimaging techniques, respectively. These chapters not only address the important question of what (if any) brain regions are specialised for living and non-living things but they are also useful for testing predictions from the competing theoretical accounts of category-specific impairments outlined in earlier chapters.

Category specificity in brain and mind provides a comprehensive and up-to-date review of the most influential theories concerning how we acquire and organise our knowledge about different categories of object. The chapters have been written by leading international researchers in each field and the research reviewed spans a number of disciplines, including cognitive psychology, developmental psychology, neuropsychology, functional brain imaging, and computer modelling. Although researchers in each of these areas have been interested in understanding category-specificity in brain and mind for many years, it is only now that ideas from these different perspectives are beginning to converge. The chapters in the book illustrate that, although we have learnt many facts about category-specificity in brain and mind over the past few decades, great controversy remains over a number of fundamental questions. We look forward to future research that addresses these questions and that contributes to the ultimate quest of neuroscientists—to unravel the mysteries of brain and mind.

Emer Forde and Glyn Humphreys

CHAPTER ONE

The domain-specific hypothesis

A developmental and comparative perspective on category-specific deficits

Laurie R. Santos and Alfonso Caramazza
Harvard University, Cambridge, MA, USA

CATEGORY-SPECIFIC DEFICITS: AN INTRODUCTION

Understanding the nature of semantic category-specific deficits might provide one avenue for discovering the organisation of semantic knowledge in the brain. Since the early 1980s, when Warrington and colleagues (Warrington, 1981; Warrington & MacCarthy, 1983; Warrington & Shallice, 1984) described their fascinating cases in detail, a wealth of data has shown that knowledge of living things can be impaired largely independently of knowledge of non-living things (e.g. Basso, Capitani, & Laiacona, 1988; Hillis & Caramazza, 1991; Laiacona, Capitani, & Barbarotto, 1997; McCarthy & Warrington, 1988; Sheridan & Humphreys, 1993; Silveri & Gainotti, 1988; see Forde & Humphreys, 1999, for a review). Similarly, neuropsychologists have identified a number of cases of disproportionate impairment of the category of non-living things relative to the category of living things (Hillis & Caramazza, 1991; Sacchett & Humphreys, 1992; Warrington & McCarthy, 1987).[1]

What do these patterns of semantic impairment suggest about the structure of knowledge in the brain? At first glance, the double dissociation between the living and non-living categories would seem to imply that our

---

[1] In this article we are only concerned with category-specific *semantic* deficits. We will not consider cases of category-specific *agnosia* (see Chapters 3 and 4 for reviews of such cases).

knowledge of everyday objects is organised in the form of at least two distinct semantic categories. None the less, very few researchers have embraced this categorical view of semantic knowledge. Most neuropsychologists have preferred reductionist, non-categorical accounts of these deficits (e.g. Caramazza, Hillis, Rapp, & Romani, 1990; Moss, Tyler, Durrant-Peatfield, & Bunn, 1998; Warrington & Shallice, 1984; see Caramazza & Shelton, 1998, for an exception). These non-categorical accounts appeal to the notion that semantic space is not uniform; similar kinds of things tend to share similar properties and thus features tend to co-occur more often within a category than across categories. If the properties of similar kinds of things do cluster together in semantic space, it is possible that damage to one area of semantic space will produce disproportionate impairments for different kinds of things. In this way, reductionist accounts argue that category-like deficits can emerge from a non-categorical, feature-based organisation.

Two broad classes of reductionist account have been proposed. Until recently, the dominant view was the sensory/functional (SF) account, first proposed by Warrington and Shallice (1984; see also Farah & McClelland, 1991; Gainotti & Silveri, 1996; Silveri & Gainotti, 1988). The SF theory makes two basic assumptions. The first is that semantic knowledge is organised into a set of modality-specific subsystems: the visual and the functional/ associative subsystems. The visual subsystem stores information about the visual–semantic properties of objects (e.g. chairs have backs; horses have tails). The functional/associative subsystem stores information about an object's function and other non-sensory properties of objects (e.g. pianos are for playing; cows give milk). The second assumption is that visual and functional/associative properties are not equally important for the meaning of living and non-living things. Instead, visual semantics is more central to the meaning of living things than is functional/associative semantics, and functional/associative semantics is more important than visual semantics in determining the meaning of non-living things. Given these assumptions, category-specific deficits for living things could result from damage to the visual semantic subsystem, whereas category-specific deficits for non-living things could result from damage to the functional/associative semantic subsystem. Thus, on this view, the selective impairments experienced in cases of category-specific deficits result not from damage to different semantic categories *per se*, but from damage to different modality-specific conceptual systems.

The basic intuition motivating the SF theory of category-specific deficits is not without merit. For example, several researchers have argued that colour is especially important in the identification of fruits (e.g. Santos, Hauser, & Spelke, 2001; Warrington & McCarthy, 1987) and that visual features, more generally, are crucial for the identification of animate objects (e.g. Keil, Smith, Simons, & Levin, 1998). However, the fact that particular visual features (e.g. colour, motion patterns) are especially salient in identifying objects of different semantic categories does not imply that conceptual knowledge is organised by modality. Perhaps the principal role of these salient properties is simply to draw attention to the objects that possess them (Caramazza & Shelton, 1998; Keil et al., 1998; Santos, Hauser, & Spelke, 2001). Conceptual knowledge of objects involves considerably more than the features that might be salient for their quick categorisation. This knowledge includes information that is not directly or easily accessible through the senses (e.g. the properties "edible" and "dangerous"). Thus, whether or not conceptual knowledge is organised by modality does not follow in any obvious way from the fact that objects might have salient perceptual properties that distinguish among semantic categories. Rather, the issue is an empirical matter, and the evidence shows that the SF theory fails to account for the principal facts of semantic category-specific deficits.

The SF theory makes two predictions about the nature of category-specific deficits. One prediction is that semantic category-specific deficits should occur in clusters that reflect the assumption that certain modalities are more salient for some categories than for others. For example, as visual properties are presumably most salient for specifying the meaning of animate and inanimate biological kinds, these categories should always be damaged together (on some accounts this will also include musical instruments). The other prediction is that category-specific deficits for living things will necessarily co-occur with a deficit in processing visual semantic properties, and that selective deficits for non-living things will necessarily co-occur with a deficit in processing functional/associative semantic properties of objects. That is, the SF account predicts that impairments for kinds of information (visual or functional/associative) and types of semantic categories (living and non-living) necessarily co-occur. However, both predictions have been disconfirmed. There are multiple reports of patients with category-specific deficits that are more fine-grained than the living–non-living distinction. For example, Hart, Berndt, and Caramazza (1985) reported a patient with severe impairment for the category of fruit and vegetables, but not for animals or artefacts (see also Farah & Wallace, 1992), and Caramazza and Shelton (1998) reported a patient with severe difficulty with animals, but not with fruit and vegetables or artefacts. Equally problematic for the SF account are recent reports showing that, contrary to expectations derived from this theory, category-specific deficits do not necessarily co-occur with modality-specific impairments (Caramazza & Shelton, 1998; Laiacona et al., 1993, 1997; Lambon Ralph, Howard, Nightingale, & Ellis, 1998; Moss et al., 1998; Samson, Pillon, & De Wilde, 1998). For example, patient EW (Caramazza & Shelton, 1998), who presented with a severe deficit in naming animals, was equally impaired in processing the visual and functional/associative properties of these objects and performed normally with the visual attributes of non-animals, including fruit and vegetables. Thus, despite its popularity, the SF theory simply does not account for the facts of semantic category-specific deficits (see Caramazza & Shelton, 1998, for a detailed criticism).

The other class of reductionist theories of category-specific deficits does not assume a modality-based organisation of conceptual knowledge in the brain. These theories simply assume that members of a semantic category have many more properties in common than do objects from different semantic categories. The Organised Unitary Content Hypothesis (OUCH) is an example of these theories (Caramazza et al., 1990; for other variants see, Devlin, Gonnermann, Andersen, & Seidenberg, 1998; Moss et al., 1998; Riddoch, Humphreys, Coltheart, & Funnell, 1988). The two core assumptions of OUCH-type theories are that semantic properties are not distributed uniformly across categories but tend to cluster together *independently* of their modality, and that objects within a category share many more properties than do objects across categories (Keil, 1989; Keil et al., 1998; Rosch et al., 1976). That is, conceptual space is "lumpy". For example, animals are generally capable of particular types of motion, they have particular types of shapes and odours, they are made of certain kinds of stuff, they produce certain kinds of noises, and they are found in particular types of environments. This example illustrates both core assumptions of the OUCH-type accounts: objects within a category share many semantic features, and the semantic features tend to be highly intercorrelated. Damage to a part of the brain that represents a "lumpy" region of semantic space will result in a category-specific deficit.

Theories of this type can account for the two major facts of category-specific deficits: they correctly predict that the deficits can involve fine-grained distinctions, like those for animals versus fruits and vegetables (e.g. Hart et al., 1985), and that the deficits are not (necessarily) associated with selective impairment to a modality-defined type of knowledge (e.g. Caramazza & Shelton, 1998). However, although the OUCH-type models can explain the patterns of data that have been observed in patients with category-specific deficits, they nevertheless fail to account for expected but missing patterns of data. Why have neuropsychologists observed so many patients with selective impairment for the category of living things but no clear cases of selective impairment for the category of furniture or vehicles? In other words, why are some areas of semantic space repeatedly damaged and not others? OUCH-type theories are silent on this important question.

Faced with this issue, Caramazza and Shelton (1998; Caramazza, 1998; Shelton & Caramazza, 2000) raised the possibility of a very different organisation of semantic knowledge, one that is explicitly categorical in nature. This categorical approach, the domain-specific hypothesis, argues that semantic knowledge is organised, in part, in the form of a small number of distinct semantic categories and thus category-specific deficits can in principle reflect damage that is restricted to a specific category. Patients with a disproportionate impairment for living things, the domain-specific account argues, have damage primarily to the brain regions that represent the categories of animate and inanimate biological kinds, while those who display a disproportionate impairment for non-living things have relative sparing of those brain areas.

The domain-specific account is based in part on the notion that the categories that can be damaged selectively are those that were most salient during our phylogenetic past. These domains, Caramazza and Shelton (1998) have argued, were built-in by natural selection to quickly solve important and computationally complex survival problems (e.g. finding food, avoiding predators). One such domain is our knowledge of the living animate domain,[2] a domain likely to have been salient over primate evolution for distinguishing predators and prey, locating conspecifics, etc. As reviewed above, neuropsychologists have identified many cases of selective impairment of the category of living things. A second candidate for an evolutionarily salient domain is the category of naturally occurring food objects (see Rozin, 1990; Santos, Hauser, & Spelke, 2001). Accordingly, there is some evidence that the category of fruit and vegetables can be selectively impaired (e.g. Hart et al., 1985). A third phylogenetically salient category might involve tools. Unlike the previous two domains, which are likely to be phylogenetically quite ancient, the domain of tools has become important in primate evolution only fairly recently. As such, this category could take one of two forms. One possibility is that tools represent a recently acquired domain-specific knowledge system in primate evolution. Alternatively, the domain of inanimate living objects, more generally, could be phylogenetically older and consist of a "default" category of objects; in other words, the domain of inanimate non-living objects deals with objects that are not animals or foods. This default domain could have guided our primate ancestors in reasoning about non-living objects (e.g. rocks that would serve as landmarks) that were relevant over primate evolution, and could have been appropriated more recently in the human species for reasoning about the artefactual domain. Regardless, as

---

[2] There is some evidence that the living animate category can be further divided into the categories of conspecific and non-conspecific (see Shelton, Fouch, & Caramazza, 1998). Prosopagnosics, for example, demonstrate that the category of human faces can be selectively impaired. In addition, there is evidence for dedicated neural mechanisms for the processing of conspecific faces in human adults (Kanwisher, McDermott, & Chun, 1997) and in non-human animals (see Perrett & Mistlan, 1990; Perrett et al., 1985, 1992). There is also evidence that the system for recognition of faces comes on-line early in development in humans (Johnson & Morton, 1991) and in non-human primates (Mendelsohn, Haith, & Goldman-Rakic, 1982; Rodman & Nace, 1997). Similarly, young infants begin to reason about human faces in a special way even as newborns (see Meltzoff & Moore, 1995). Finally, there is some evidence that knowledge of body parts can be damaged or spared selectively (Shelton et al., 1998).

mentioned above, current evidence suggests that our knowledge of inanimate non-living objects can be independently damaged in cases of category-specific deficits (Hillis & Caramazza, 1991; Sacchett & Humphreys, 1992; Warrington & McCarthy, 1987).

The domain-specific theory, therefore, accounts for the fact that only a few selected categories can be independently impaired following brain damage. Unlike reductionist accounts, the domain-specific theory does explain why certain patterns of impairment are not observed; *only* those domains that were important in human evolutionary history will be represented in highly specialised brain regions and, therefore, can be selectively impaired following brain damage. This account thus makes the prediction that there will be a restriction on the number and types of categories that can be selectively damaged.

To date, the domain specificity view has received scant attention in the field of neuropsychology. None the less, the domain-specific hypothesis, like the OUCH-type reductionist models, is entirely consistent with the empirical facts about category-specific deficits. The domain-specific hypothesis correctly predicts that the deficits observed after brain damage will be restricted to a limited set of categories: those broad domains that were salient over our phylogenetic history. It also accounts for the fact that we fail to observe modality-specific deficits and impairments to highly restricted categories (e.g. furniture). Furthermore, the notion of domain-specific semantic organisation has had enormous impact in various areas of the cognitive sciences (see Hirschfeld & Gelman, 1994, for a review). Cognitive developmentalists, for example, have widely embraced the notion of domain-specific constraints on knowledge acquisition (Carey & Spelke, 1994; Hirschfeld & Gelman, 1994; Keil, 1989). Similarly, those studying animal cognition have accepted the notion that many different species possess domain-specific recognition systems to solve species-specific computational problems (e.g. finding appropriate food, avoiding certain classes of predators, mate selection, navigation strategies; see Hauser, 2000, for a review).

For these reasons, we will argue that the domain-specific view of semantic knowledge organisation deserves further consideration. If nothing else, the hypothesis has great heuristic value as an alternative to the more popular OUCH-type theories, thereby encouraging the articulation of more precise claims about the organisation of conceptual knowledge. To this end, in this chapter we will explore the organisation of conceptual knowledge from developmental and comparative perspectives, emphasising the way in which domain-specificity has shaped these fields. We will review recent research in the fields of cognitive development and the evolution of cognition, and suggest that adults, young infants, and several non-human primate species share important characteristics in processing information from different domains. Specifically, we will argue that infants and non-human primates distinguish between three broad domains of objects: animate entities, food objects,[3] and artefacts. These distinctions provide clues about the developmental and evolutionary history of the organisation of semantic knowledge and might shed light on the nature of category-specific deficits.

A BRIEF DESCRIPTION OF THE DOMAIN-SPECIFICITY APPROACH

Before launching into these two different approaches it is important to first return to the notion of domain-specificity and outline the theory underlying this approach. The domain-specific approach assumes that cognition is not mediated by a set of general computational mechanisms capable of tackling any cognitive problem; instead, it assumes that the mind is made up of a suite of specialised processing systems each geared towards analysing specific types of information. As Hirschfeld and Gelman (1994 p. xiii) put it: "domain specificity is the idea that all concepts are not equal, and that the structure of human knowledge is different in important ways across different content areas". Our knowledge of an artefact, for example, is likely to consist of our understanding of its intended design (Bloom, 1996), information about its form and the relation to its function (Landau, Smith, & Jones, 1998a; Madole, Oakes, & Cohen, 1993), and knowledge of the types of actions people perform with it (Brown, 1990; Meltzoff, 1995). Our understanding of an animal, in contrast, could consist of information about its outer visual features such as colour and surface markings (Keil, 1989; Keil et al., 1998), its pattern of motion (Gelman, 1990; Premack, 1990), and its inner structure (Keil, 1989; Simons & Keil, 1995), but also whether it is dangerous and where it is typically found.

Another main tenet of the domain-specificity view is that the content areas that make up human cognition are not random; the domains that compose human cognition are geared towards solving problems that have been relevant in our evolutionary history (see Sperber, 1994). Such problems are likely to be those that are cognitively complex, universal in a species, and necessarily learned quickly and without error. For example, the task of finding food is one that is phylogenetically quite ancient (Rozin, 1990). All animals must find things to eat, and must also avoid things that are inedible or poisonous. Similarly, despite the fact that learning to find appropriate foods is a complex cognitive task (involving navigation, categorisation, etc.), the

---

[3] The categories of "food" and "inanimate living object" have been treated as distinct categories in investigations of category-specific deficits, but they have often been conflated into a single category in investigations of domain-specific knowledge. It would be interesting to see if infants and/or non-human animals make distinctions between artificial foods (e.g. cookies) and natural foods (e.g. apples).

window for learning how to find food is very brief. If the task of finding food is not learned quickly, it can lead to starvation. In addition, finding food can be a dangerous activity. The cost of error is high and could potentially result in death. Faced with these odds, natural selection is likely to favour specific cognitive mechanisms that solve the task accurately and efficiently over more domain-general mechanisms that take time to learn and sometimes lead to errors.

Therefore, if domain-specificity accounts are correct then the domains of knowledge that make up human cognition are likely to be those that were most salient in primate evolution (or earlier) and most costly in terms of survival and reproductive success. This hypothesis predicts that the domain-specific distinctions that humans possess should be shared by closely related primate species whose cognitive mechanisms serve similar functions evolutionarily. Similarly, because natural selection is likely to favour domain-specific mechanisms for problems that have a narrow window of learning, one would predict that these distinctions should emerge early and consistently in human ontogeny, without need for much experience. Do domain-specific distinctions follow this pattern? Do children, human infants, and non-human primates share some features of our adult domain-specific reasoning?

DOMAIN-SPECIFIC DISTINCTIONS IN CHILDREN

There is now much evidence to suggest that children attend to broad distinctions between domains from a very early age.[4] One of the more important distinctions young children make concerns living versus non-living entities. Four-year-old children understand that, unlike non-living things, living objects are capable of growth (Gelman & Wellman, 1991; Rosengren, Gelman, Kalish, & McCormick, 1991).[5] Rosengren and colleagues (1991) found that children accurately predict that older animals are typically bigger, but do

---

[4] Mandler (see Chapter 11) also proposes that early semantic knowledge is organised categorically. None the less, she does not agree with our suggestion of an evolutionary basis for these initial distinctions. Instead, she argues that the particular categories that emerge early do so because they are the ones that are most salient in ontogeny, i.e., the ones that infants most easily acquire given their sensory capabilities and natural predispositions. However, this view leaves unanswered the question of *why* human infants are ready to pick up on *these* particular distinctions. This question, we argue, can be answered best using an evolutionary framework.

[5] There is much controversy in the field of cognitive development regarding when children develop a notion of biology. Some have argued that an adult-like understanding of biology does not emerge until about 7 years of age (see Carey, 1985, 1994). Others, however, have argued that children have some sophisticated notions of living kinds by about the fourth year of life (see Keil, 1989, 1994). Although this issue of conceptual change in the domain of biology is still unresolved, it remains clear that young children and even infants (see Spelke, Phillips, & Woodward, 1995; Chapter 11; Mandler & McDonough, 1993, 1996) make some important distinctions between objects in the animate and inanimate domains.

not predict the same kinds of size changes for artefacts. In addition, Gelman and Wellman (1991) showed that children recognise that animals and plants have an innate potential for growth; 4-year-old children accurately predict that seeds will grow into larger, visually different plants but that small artefacts will not change over time. Young children also understand that the properties that are important for living kinds differ from those that are typically important for non-living objects. By 5 years of age, children begin to realise that the properties that are most relevant to animals (e.g. outside markings, number of inside parts) are different than those that are relevant to machines and artefacts (e.g. shape and size) (Keil et al., 1998). Taken together, it seems that children make some distinctions between non-living things on the one hand and living creatures, like plants and animals, on the other.

In addition, children seem to make some distinction between animate and inanimate living kinds. Gelman, Coley, and Gottfried (1994) review evidence that young children recognise that animals, unlike plants, are capable of moving on their own. They showed 4-year-old children videos of animals, plants, and artefacts moving across a stage in one of two ways: either the object was carried by an experimenter or moved on its own. Children were much less likely to attribute external causes of movement (e.g. "the experimenter moved him", etc.) to animate objects. This was true even in cases where the experimenter was involved in the motion. It appears that children recognise that only animate objects can move without being propelled by another object.

Keil and colleagues (Keil 1989, 1994; Keil et al., 1998) have used these differences in children's understanding of different domains to suggest that children have different "modes of construal" for different domains of objects. When children reason about animate objects, he argues, they adopt an essentialist stance. Essentialism, put simply, is the idea that natural kinds have a non-readily observable causal structure that makes them what they are. Older children believe that animals maintain their identity over gross perceptual changes. Keil (1989), for example, told children stories about raccoons whose fur and tail were transformed by a doctor and made to look like that of a skunk. Second graders recognise that this skunk-looking raccoon is still a raccoon despite that fact that it perceptually resembles a skunk. In contrast, when viewing artefacts, children adopt a more teleological mode of construal (Keil, 1994; Keil, Levin, Richman, & Gutheil, 1999). Children seem to understand that the features of artefacts are the way they are not because of an underlying essence, but because a human designer built them that way (see Bloom, 1996; Bloom & Markson, 1996).

Children also seem to attend to domain distinctions when learning new words. As many studies have now demonstrated, children show a shape bias in word learning (Landau, Smith, & Jones, 1988, 1998a,b). That is, they will generalise a new object label to other objects of the same shape as the one they originally heard named, even if the new objects differ substantially in size, texture, or colour. Recent research suggests, however, that children's shape bias is not universal. In fact, children are biased to generalise by shape only for domains in which the feature of shape is actually relevant to category membership. For example, although 3- and 4-year-old children demonstrate a robust shape bias when learning artefact labels, they show a colour and texture bias when learning labels for novel food objects (Lavin & Hall, 1999; Santos, Miller, & Hauser, 1999). Santos et al. (1999) argued that children attend to colour and texture when learning words for food objects because substance features, like colour and texture, are more important for differentiating between different types of foods. Similarly, children also modify their shape bias when learning the names of novel animate objects. Jones, Smith, and Landau (1991) found that children pay more attention to colour and texture when generalising labels given to small toys with eyes. Such studies demonstrate that young children are already attending to distinctions between the animate, artefact, and food domains, and use these distinctions when learning labels for new objects.

DOMAIN-SPECIFIC DISTINCTIONS IN INFANTS

Other recent evidence suggests that the domain-specific knowledge children display during word learning is in place long before children utter their first words. Recent work using non-linguistic paradigms indicates that humans begin to make important distinctions between the artefact, animate, and food domains even in infancy. Jean Mandler and her colleagues provided an impressive demonstration of early conceptual knowledge in 14-month-old infants (Mandler, 1988; Mandler & McDonough, 1993, 1996; see Chapter 11 for a review). Mandler and colleagues used an imitation procedure in which an experimenter modelled a certain action with a target object. The target object was either a vehicle (e.g. toy truck) or an animal (e.g. stuffed dog). They then provided children with exemplar objects from the same and different domains. They found that 14-month-olds generalise "drinking" and "sleeping" actions only to objects in the animal domain and "giving a ride" and "being keyed" actions only to objects in the vehicle domain. Such generalisations seem to be constrained solely by boundaries of the object domain and not by overall perceptual similarity between objects; for example, a dog "drinking" was generalised to a perceptually dissimilar bird but not to an equally perceptually dissimilar aeroplane. These results suggest that, by 14 months of age, infants already distinguish between animals and artefacts.

Infants also distinguish between the types of motion that animate and inanimate objects demonstrate. Alan Leslie and colleagues (Leslie, 1982, 1994; Leslie & Keeble, 1987) examined what infants understood about the motions of inanimate objects using an expectancy violation procedure. The expectancy violation procedure presents infants with "magical" unexpected events that violate a principle of the physical or social world. If infants notice this violation, they are expected to look longer at the unexpected event than at a control non-magical event. Thus, duration of looking can be used as an indicator of knowledge. This type of paradigm has been used successfully with human infants for over a decade (see reviews in Baillargeon, 1995; Spelke, 1985, 1991), and has more recently been applied to non-human primates (see Hauser & Carey, 1998, for a review). Leslie and Keeble (1987) employed just such a procedure to examine whether infants, like adults, perceived physical causality. They presented infants with a launching event (see Michotte, 1963) in which a moving ball collided with another ball. By 6 months of age, infants predict that a second stationary ball will move if, and only if, the moving ball first contacts it. In other words, inanimate objects such as a ball do not move on their own, but only move when propelled to move by an external agent or other moving object (see Baillargeon, 1995). This principle has been labelled the "contact principle" and is thought to be one of the infant's core principles about physical object motion (Spelke, 1991; Spelke, Breinlinger, Macomber, & Jacobson, 1992).

More recent work suggests that infants also make distinctions about which types of objects are subject to the contact principle. One signature of animate objects is that they can move without being propelled by external agents. Spelke, Phillips, and Woodward (1995) found that infants recognise this distinction at an early age. By 9 months of age, infants realise that people, unlike blocks and balls, can move without being contacted by an external agent. In addition, infants recognise that animate objects can take different paths of motion than inanimate physical objects (see Gelman, 1990, for a review). Infants realise that animate objects can begin moving on their own and can take curvilinear paths (Gelman, 1990), and typically move in ways that are consistent with their goals (Gergely, Nadasdy, Csibra, & Biro, 1995; Meltzoff, 1995; Premack & Premack, 1995; Woodward, 1998).

In conclusion, within the first year of life, infants make simple, yet important, distinctions about the motions of objects in different domains and their causally-related features. These domain-specific distinctions mimic the three broad content areas that can be independently damaged in cases of category specific deficits. In addition, they emerge quite early in development and presumably without the need for much experience.

DOMAIN-SPECIFIC KNOWLEDGE IN NON-HUMAN PRIMATES

As mentioned earlier, the domain-specific account suggests that distinctions between domains should be geared towards solving important phylogenetic problems and thus, might be evolutionarily ancient (see Pinker, 1997; Sperber,

1994). As such, it predicts that the domain distinctions found in humans should be shared with some of our closest primate relatives (see Hauser, 2000; Hauser & Carey, 1998). Do non-human primates make the same distinctions among animate objects, artefacts, and foods as human adults and children?

Non-human primates, like all other animals, must categorise the objects in their environment in order to interact with them appropriately. One of the most important categories for primates to master is the difference between what is edible and what is inedible. As one might expect, non-human primates in the wild possess a considerable amount of knowledge about the foods that they eat, the time different food objects are found, and the location of ripe foods (Menzel, 1997). More interestingly, perhaps, non-human primates' understanding of the living, inanimate natural world extends beyond the realm of edible objects. Wrangham and colleagues (Huffman & Wrangham, 1994; Wrangham & Goodall, 1989; Wrangham & Nishida, 1983) discovered that chimpanzees use certain species of plants for medicinal purposes. Huffman and Wrangham (1994) reported that chimpanzees in several geographically separate populations swallow leaves of certain non-nutritious plants during times of high parasitisation. Although the leaves contain no nutritional value and are highly unpalatable, they are thought to cure intestinal parasites (Wrangham & Goodall, 1989). Similarly, Mahale chimpanzees have been observed chewing the pith of the bark of bitter plant species when they appear ill (Huffman & Wrangham, 1994). Local tribes use these same plants when curing indigestion or stomach parasites.

Naturally living non-human primates also appear to have some knowledge about inanimate non-living objects. Many non-human primates naturally use tools in the wild (McGrew, 1992) and in captivity (Visalberghi & Tomasello, 1998; Visalberghi & Trinca, 1989) and some even manufacture and modify their tools (Matsuzawa, 1994; Tomasello & Call, 1997). Chimpanzees, perhaps the most extensive non-human tool users, use stone anvils and hammers to crack oil palm nuts (Boesch-Ackermann & Boesch, 1993; Matsuzawa, 1994), they fish into thick termite mounds with small sticks (Goodall, 1986), they build nests (McGrew, 1992), and they tear pieces of bark as shoes for climbing up prickly tree trunks to obtain berries (Alp, 1997).

In addition to these naturalistic observations, many experimental studies have demonstrated that non-human primates can be trained to form categories like animals, food, and artefacts (see Thompson, 1995, for a review of training studies). None the less, although these experimental studies have demonstrated that non-human primates show sensitivity to important distinctions between domains, it is difficult to assess the degree to which these abilities reflect the animals' naturally evolved capacities as opposed to being the result of extensive training. More recently, however, those who study non-human primates in the laboratory have adopted a more direct comparative approach, and have begun using the same tasks developed for human infants and children to ask questions about non-human primates' understanding in different domains (Hauser, 2000; Hauser & Carey, 1998). These tasks allow for direct comparisons between humans and non-human animals and get around the problems with training that plague many classic operant categorisation paradigms.

When examined using these "spontaneous" tasks, non-human primate species manifest some of the same domain distinctions as human infants and children. First, non-human primates seem to make some very broad distinctions between living and non-living entities, specifically between the motion of animate and inanimate objects. Santos and colleagues (Santos, 1997; Santos, Schecter, & Hauser, unpublished data) used an expectancy violation paradigm like that of Leslie and Keeble (1987) to examine tamarins' understanding of contact. They found that tamarins, like 6-month-old human infants, expect a toy car to begin rolling only if it is first contacted by another moving car. Tamarins recognise that inanimate, artefact-like objects (e.g. small toy cars) do not move on their own and must be contacted by another object before being set in motion. They also seem to respect this no-action-at-a-distance principle when operating tools. Tamarins trained on a task in which they must pull a cloth to retrieve a food reward recognise that food must be on top of the cloth, and thus actually contacting the cloth, in order to achieve successful retrieval (Hauser, Kralik, & Botto-Mahan, 1999; see Willatts, 1999, for a similar experiment with human infants).

Like infants, however, tamarins do not expect all objects to conform to the contact principle. Hauser (1998) used an expectancy violation paradigm to examine whether tamarins think some types of object are capable of self-propelled motion: moving on their own without first being contacted by another object (see Premack, 1990). Hauser presented tamarin subjects with a box with a clear front. The box was divided into two chambers that were connected through a hole in the centre. Hauser then placed an object in the left chamber of the box, lowered a screen for a few seconds, and then raised it to reveal one of two test events. In the first event, the object remained in the original chamber prior to placing the screen in position. In the other test event, the object had been moved to the other chamber of the box. Hauser found that tamarins looked longer when an artefact-like object (a moving clay toy) or a food object (a pile of fruit loops cereal) appeared to move to the other side of the box. In contrast, tamarins did not look longer when a live frog or a live mouse was revealed in the other side of the box. This pattern of results suggest that tamarins recognise that only animate creatures, like mice and frogs, can move to a new location on their own. Like infants, it seems that tamarins distinguish between the animate and inanimate objects and the types of movement of which they are capable.

In addition to expecting different kinds of objects to move differently, non-human primates make important distinctions between the properties that are relevant and irrelevant for objects from different domains. Hauser and colleagues have done an extensive series of studies investigating the properties that non-human primates attend to when choosing between different artefact-like objects in a tool-use task (Hauser, 1997; Hauser et al., 1999; Santos, Miller, & Hauser, unpublished data). In the original series of studies, Hauser first trained tamarins to use a blue cane to pull out-of-reach food. After training, the features of the tool were changed and subjects were given a choice between a tool with a new colour and a tool with a new size, or between a tool with a new shape and one with a new texture. Hauser found that, without any further training, tamarins spontaneously disregarded changes in colour and texture and reliably chose these canes over those with novel shapes and sizes. Hauser et al. (1999) replicated this experiment using a cloth-pulling task and, again, found that tamarins spontaneously disregarded colour and considered shape properties to be most important to the functionality of the tool.

Santos, Miller, and Hauser (unpublished data) used an expectancy violation paradigm to examine a similar question in a more inexperienced population, a group of semi-free-ranging rhesus macaque living on the island of Cayo Santiago, Puerto Rico (see Rawlins & Kessler, 1987). They presented subjects with an L-shaped stick pushing a grape down a ramp. After habituating subjects to this event, they then changed either the colour of the tool or its shape. They found that inexperienced rhesus monkeys looked longer when the tool changed shape than when it changed colour. Taken together, this evidence suggests that, like human children, tamarins and rhesus macaques attend to the functional property of shape and disregard irrelevant properties like colour.

Like children, however, monkeys' selective attention to shape seems to be restricted to the domain of artefacts. Santos, Hauser, and Spelke (2001) used a social facilitation paradigm to examine the features to which the same population of rhesus monkeys attend when reasoning about food objects. In these studies, an experimenter ate a novel object (e.g. pink sphere) and then presented the subject with a choice of two objects to eat. These objects differed from the model object on one dimension (e.g. pink cube versus green sphere). Without training, subjects selectively chose food items of the same colour over those of the same shape. In other words, subjects spontaneously generalised the edibility of a novel object using the feature of colour over the feature of shape. Thus although non-human primates attend specifically to the features of shape during a tool use task, they find colour to be a more important property of foods. These results suggest that not only do non-human primates distinguish between the food and artefact domains, they also possess some understanding of the properties that are relevant to each.

In summary, non-human primates in the wild and in captivity seem to reason differently about three broad domains of objects: animate objects, artefacts, and foods. These distinctions correspond to the domain-specific distinctions that children initially attend to and coincide with the independent dissociations observed in cases of category-specific impairments.

DEVELOPMENTAL AND COMPARATIVE PERSPECTIVE ON SEMANTIC KNOWLEDGE

The three major domain distinctions that infants and non-humans take into account—animate entities, inanimate but living food objects, and artefacts—mimic the three major categories that can be selectively damaged in category-specific deficits (see Caramazza, 1998, for a review). One interpretation for this coincidence, consistent with the domain-specificity account, is that semantic knowledge in primates is organised in (at least) three distinct, broad categories that reflect ontogenetically—and evolutionarily—salient distinctions. These distinctions are shared across primates and are built-in to the human mind as adaptations for solving computational problems that reoccur throughout evolutionary history.

An alternative account, one that is consistent with the reductionist class of models, suggests that all human and non-human primates share these three domain distinctions because the properties of each domain are highly inter-correlated and reflected directly in the environment that is shared by all three groups. For example, all primates observe animate objects taking goal-directed paths and generating self-propelled motion (Premack, 1990). All primates learn that the palatability of certain foods change as substance properties, like colour and texture, change. The fact that the structure of the environment and the features that co-occur for a given domain are the same across the three groups suggest that a similar semantic organisation could be constructed by virtue of similar experiences.

How then can we distinguish between the domain-specificity view of semantic knowledge on the one hand and the OUCH-type accounts on the other? Do the two views make any different predictions about the acquisition of semantic knowledge? One such prediction has to do with the importance of shared experience in the development of consistent and universal domains of knowledge. The OUCH-type accounts of domain-specific reasoning in children and primates rest on the idea that the structure of the environment is similar in human and non-human primates. In other words, the broad set of features that tend to co-occur for a given domain in the experience of a human adult also tend to occur together in the experience of the human infant and many primate species. The question then becomes: is this a safe assumption? Infants, for example, have had far less experience with entities from all domains than adults. Infants do not begin to make the edible/inedible distinction until about the first year of life (Rozin, 1990), and thus do not share the wealth of experience that adult humans have with the problems associated with reasoning about foods. None the less, as reviewed above, children seem to reason differently about the domain of food objects from a rather young age, and share some adult-like assumptions about the properties of food objects despite their vast differences in experience with solid food (Santos et al., 1999). Likewise, because their motor systems are slow to develop, infants have far less experience manipulating artefacts than adults, and thus their early knowledge of artefacts is likely to be based more on the visual features of these objects than is that of adults. This suggests that the types of perceptual features that make up children's knowledge of artefacts should, in theory, differ considerably from those that compose adults' knowledge. None the less, children's reasoning about the motions of physical objects and artefacts is quite adult-like, even, in some cases, from a few months of age (Baillargeon, 1995; Spelke, 1991; Spelke et al., 1992). Furthermore, infants' knowledge of animate objects is typically limited to conspecifics, and perhaps to some minimal experience with non-human animals (e.g. pets). This would suggest that their experience of animate objects would be impoverished relative to that of adults[6] and thus that the structure of their knowledge would be quite different. None the less, very young infants seem to share adults' assumptions about animate motion (Gelman, 1990). In the animate domain, as in the domain of foods and artefacts, glaring differences in children's experience do not seem to map onto the emergence of different types of categories in semantic space, as the reductionist models might predict.

The case for non-human primates sharing the same experience as adult humans becomes even more implausible. Cotton-top tamarins and rhesus macaques, the two species reviewed in this paper, have never been observed using tools in the wild. Consequently, their experience with artefacts is rather minimal, especially relative to that of a human child or a human adult. None the less, they share some basic adult human assumptions about the artefactual domain. For example, primate non-tool-users, like experienced human adults, understand that global shape is important for categorising inanimate non-living objects. Similarly, they recognise that colour and surface properties are irrelevant for an artefact's function (Hauser, 1998; Hauser et al., 1999). Is it safe to assume, then, that their minimal experiences with the properties of artefacts are sufficient to generate property correlations in semantic space that are similar to our own?

---

[6] Even indigenous people with vastly more experience with animals seem to reason about animate kinds in the same way as inexperienced westerners (Atran, 1990, 1998). Specifically, all people appear to believe that living things possess a causal structure or essence. In addition, all cultures, regardless of experience, classify different kinds of species in a hierarchical framework and use this hierarchy as an inductive framework for making assumptions about similarities and differences across species.

While the assumption of shared experience across non-human primates and human infants strains the scenario of semantic knowledge acquisition proposed by reductionist theories, it is by no means a decisive blow. One could easily imagine that although the experiences of non-human primates and human infants differ at the surface level, enough of primate experience is shared at a deep level to preserve the domain distinctions observed in all three groups. In other words, although non-human primates and infants have different levels of experience in the three domains, the world has enough of a statistically reoccurrent domain-specific structure for category-like structure to emerge anyway.

The two models make another set of alternative predictions about primate semantic knowledge and its early emergence. The OUCH-type accounts of semantic knowledge rely on the fact that the initial differences between domains must be perceptually derived. According to this view, early knowledge is derived from domain-general mechanisms that pick up on the readily observable features of all objects and organise this knowledge in a semantic space in which correlated features tend to cluster together. This view of semantic knowledge acquisition, unlike the domain-specific view, makes the prediction that the features that give rise to domain-specific distinctions must be—at least initially—based on observable perceptual properties. Does a child's early domain-specific knowledge consist mostly of perceptual information? The answer to this question is not an unequivocal yes. Although young children clearly possess some understanding of the perceptual features typically associated with different domains, much evidence now suggests that children seem to develop abstract principles about specific domains before they recognise the specifics associated with those principles (see Wellman & Gelman, 1988; also Chapter 11). By 4 years of age, children recognise that artefacts and animals have different insides (e.g. Gelman et al., 1994), yet they don't seem to have a concrete notion about what these different insides will look like until they are about 7 years of age (Simons & Keil, 1995). In other words, children understand that these two domains will have different insides without any understanding of or experience with the specific properties associated with these different insides. Similarly, children appear to reason about domain-specific phenomena for which they have no direct perceptual evidence. Even though the perceptual features of growth are not easily or directly observable (consider the time-scale of a seed growing into a full-grown plant!), children seem to understand that growth is a phenomenon specific to animate things. Similarly, children know about growth-related transformations (e.g. tadpole to a frog) before they understand the sequence of perceptual changes associated with those transformations. In short, children appear to reason with abstract, conceptual principles before they recognise the concrete perceptual features associated with these principles. This abstract-to-concrete knowledge shift may hold true for non-human primates as well. Rhesus monkeys, for example, recognise that shape is more critical for the functioning of an artefact before they have an understanding of which particular aspects of shape are crucial for a given function (Santos, Miller, & Hauser, unpublished data). These examples suggest that some aspects of domain-specific knowledge in children and non-human primates emerge as abstract principles before they are understood on the basis of observable concrete properties. Similarly, it suggests that conceptual knowledge might not be derived solely from directly observable perceptual phenomena, as the reductionist accounts would suggest. Instead, this finding is more consistent with the domain-specificity view: some more abstract category-specific distinctions are in place at the outset, and the acquisition of concrete perceptual information comes with experience.

CONCLUSIONS FOR CATEGORY-SPECIFIC IMPAIRMENTS

We have argued that the domain-specific view of semantic knowledge deserves greater consideration in the field of neuropsychology. It provides a plausible alternative to OUCH-type accounts of category-specific deficits. Not only is the domain-specific hypothesis consistent with the empirical observations of category-specific deficits, but it also satisfactorily explains the acquisition of semantic knowledge in human children and the aspects of human semantic knowledge that are shared with non-human animals.

ACKNOWLEDGMENTS

The writing of this chapter was supported in part by NIH grants NS 22201 and DC 04542 to AC and an NSF predoctoral fellowship to LRS. The authors would like to thank Marc Hauser, Jean Mandler, Emer Forde, Glyn Humphreys, and Kimiko Domoto-Reilly for their insightful comments on this manuscript.

REFERENCES

Alp, R. (1997). "Stepping-sticks" and "seat-sticks": New types of tools used by chimpanzees in Sierra Leone. *American Journal of Primatology, 41*, 45–52.

Atran, S. (1990). *Cognitive foundations of natural history: Towards an anthropology of science.* Cambridge: Cambridge University Press.

Atran, S. (1998) Folk biology and the anthropology of science. *Behavioral and Brain Sciences, 21*, 547–611.

Baillargeon, R. (1995). Physical reasoning in infancy. In M.S. Gazzaniga (Ed.), *The cognitive neurosciences* (pp. 181–204). Cambridge, MA: MIT Press.

Basso, A., Capitani, E., & Laiacona, M. (1988). Progressive language impairment without dementia: A case with isolated category specific semantic defect. *Journal of Neurology, Neurosurgery & Psychiatry, 51*, 1201–1207.

Bloom, P. (1996). Intention, history, and artefact concepts. *Cognition, 60*, 1–29.

Bloom, P., & Markson, L. (1998) Intention and analogy in children's naming of pictorial representations. *Psychological Science, 9*, 200–204.

Boesch-Achermann, H., & Boesch, C. (1993). Tool use in wild chimpanzees: New light from dark forests. *Current Directions in Psychological Science, 2*, 18–21.

Brown, A. (1990). Domain-specific principles affect learning and transfer in children. *Cognitive Science, 14*, 107–133.

Caramazza, A. (1998). The interpretation of semantic category-specific deficits: What do they reveal about the organisation of conceptual knowledge in the brain? *Neurocase, 4*, 265–272.

Caramazza, A., Hillis, A.E., Rapp, B.C., & Romani, C. (1990) The multiple semantics hypothesis: Multiple confusions? *Cognitive Neuropsychology, 7*, 161–189.

Caramazza, A., & Shelton, J.R. (1998). Domain-specific knowledge systems in the brain: The animate-inanimate distinction. *Journal of Cognitive Neuroscience, 10*, 1–34.

Carey, S. (1985). *Conceptual change in childhood*. Cambridge, MA: MIT Press.

Carey, S. (1994). On the origin of causal understanding. In D. Sperber, D. Premack, & A.J. Premack (Eds.), *Causal cognition: A multidisciplinary debate* (pp. 268–308). Oxford: Clarendon Press.

Carey, S., & Spelke, E.S. (1994). Domain-specific knowledge and conceptual change. In L.A. Hirschfeld & S.A. Gelman (Eds.), *Mapping the mind: Domain specificity in cognition and culture* (pp. 169–200). Cambridge: Cambridge University Press.

Devlin, J.T., Gonnerman, L.M., Andersen, E.S., & Seidenberg, M.S. (1998). Category-specific semantic deficits in focal and widespread brain damage: A computational account. *Journal of Cognitive Neuroscience, 10*, 77–94.

Farah, M.J., & McClelland, J.L. (1991). A computational model of semantic memory impairment: Modality specificity and emergent category specificity. *Journal of Experimental Psychology: General, 120*, 339–357.

Farah, M.J., & Wallace, M.A. (1992). Semantically-bounded anomia: Implications for the neural implementation of naming. *Neuropsychologia, 30*, 609–621.

Forde, E.M.E., & Humphreys, G.W. (1999). Category-specific recognition impairments: A review of important case studies and influential theories. *Aphasiology, 13*, 169–193.

Gainotti, G., & Silveri, M.C. (1996). Cognitive and anatomical locus of lesion in a patient with a category-specific semantic impairment for living beings. *Cognitive Neuropsychology, 13*, 357–389.

Gelman, R. (1990). First principles organise attention to and learning about relevant data: Number and the animate-inanimate distinction as examples. *Cognitive Science, 14*, 79–106.

Gelman, S.A., Coley, J.D., & Gottfried, G.M. (1994). Essentialist beliefs in children. In L.A. Hirschfeld & S.A. Gelman (Eds.), *Mapping the mind: Domain specificity in cognition and culture* (pp. 341–365). Cambridge: Cambridge University Press.

Gelman, S. A., & Wellman, H. (1991). Insides and essences: Early understandings of the non-obvious. *Cognition, 28*, 213–244.

Goodall, J. (1986). *The cimpanzees of Gombe*. Cambridge, MA: Belknap Press.

Gergely, G., Nadasdy, Z., Csibra, G., & Biro, S. (1995). Taking the intentional stance at 12 months of age. *Cognition, 56*, 165–193.

Hart, J., Berndt, R.S., & Caramazza, A. (1985). Category specific deficit following cerebral infarction. *Nature, 316*, 439–440.

Hauser, M.D. (1997). Artifactual kinds and functional design features: What a primate understands without language. *Cognition, 64*, 285–308.

Hauser, M.D. (1998). A non-human primate's expectations about object motion and destination: The importance of self-propelled movement and animacy. *Developmental Science, 1*, 31–38.

Hauser, M.D. (2000). *Wild minds: What animals really think*. New York: Henry Hold Publishers.

Hauser, M.D., & Carey, S. (1998). Building a cognitive creature from a set of primitives:

Evolutionary and developmental insights. In D. Cummins & C. Allen (Eds.), *The evolution of mind* (pp. 51–106). Oxford: Oxford University Press.

Hauser, M.D., Kralik, J., & Botto-Mahan, C. (1999). Problem solving and functional design features: Experiments on cotton-top tamarins (*Saguinus oedipus*). *Animal Behaviour, 57,* 565–582.

Hillis, A.E., & Caramazza, A. (1991). Category-specific naming and comprehension impairment: A double dissociation. *Brain and Language, 114,* 2081–2094.

Hirschfeld, L.A., & Gelman, S.A. (1994). *Mapping the mind: Domain specificity in cognition and culture.* Cambridge: Cambridge University Press.

Huffman, M.A., & Wrangham, R.W. (1994). Diversity of medicinal plant use by chimpanzees in the wild. In R.W. Wrangham, W.C. McGrew, F.B.M. de Waal, & P.G. Heltne (Eds.), *Chimpanzee cultures* (pp. 129–148). Cambridge: Harvard University Press.

Johnson, M.H., & Morton, J. (1991). *Biology and cognitive development: The case for face recognition.* Oxford: Blackwell.

Jones, S.S., Smith, L.B., & Landau, B. (1991). Object properties and knowledge in early lexical learning. *Child Development, 62,* 499–516.

Kanwisher, N., McDermott, J., & Chun, M.M. (1997) The fusiform face area: A module in human extrastriate cortex specialised for face perception. *Journal of Neuroscience, 17,* 4302–4311.

Keil, F. C. (1989). *Concepts, kinds, and cognitive development.* Cambridge, MA: MIT Press.

Keil, F. C. (1994). The birth and nurturance of concepts by domains: The origins of concepts of living things. In L.A. Hirschfeld & S.A. Gelman (Eds.), *Mapping the mind: Domain specificity in cognition and culture* (pp. 234–254). Cambridge: Cambridge University Press.

Keil, F.C., Levin, D.T., Richman, B.A., & Gutheil, G. (1999). Mechanism and explanation in the development of biological thought: The case of disease. In D. L. Medin & S. Atran (Eds.), *Folkbiology* (pp. 285–319). Cambridge, MA: MIT Press.

Keil, F.C., Smith, W.C., Simons, D.J., & Levin, D.T. (1998). Two dogmas of conceptual empiricism: Implications for hybrid models of the structure of knowledge. *Cognition, 65 (2–3),* 103–135.

Laiacona, M., Barbarotto, R., & Capitani, E. (1993). Perceptual and associative knowledge in category specific impairment of semantic memory: A study of two cases. *Cortex, 29,* 727–740.

Laiacona, M., Capitani, E., & Barbarotto, R. (1997). Semantic category dissociations: A longitudinal study of two cases. *Cortex, 33,* 441–461.

Lambon Ralph, M.A., Howard, D., Nightingale, G., & Ellis, A.W. (1998). Are living and non-living category-specific deficits causally linked to impaired perceptual or associative knowledge? Evidence from a category-specific double dissociation. *Neurocase, 4,* 311–338.

Landau, B., Smith, L.B., & Jones, S.S. (1988). The importance of shape in early lexical learning. *Cognitive Development, 3,* 299–321.

Landau, B., Smith, L., & Jones, S. (1998a). Object shape, object function, and object name. *Journal of Memory and Language, 38,* 1–27.

Landau, B., Smith, L., & Jones, S. (1998b). Object perception and object naming in early development. *Trends in Cognitive Science, 2,* 19–24.

Lavin, T., & Hall, G. (1999). *Perceptual properties and children's acquisition of words for solids and non-solids.* Poster presented at the biennial meeting for the Society for Research in Child Development. Albuquerque, NM.

Leslie, A.M. (1982). The perception of causality in infants. *Perception, 11,* 173–186.

Leslie, A.M. (1994). ToMM, ToBy, and Agency: Core architecture and domain specificity. In L.A. Hirschfeld & S.A. Gelman (Eds.), *Mapping the mind: Domain specificity in cognition and culture* (pp. 119–148). Cambridge: Cambridge University Press.

Leslie, A.M., & Keeble, S. (1987). Do six month old infants perceive causality? *Cognition, 25,* 265–288.

Macario, J.F. (1991). Young children's use of colour and classification: Foods and canonically colored objects. *Cognitive Development, 6*, 17–46.

McCarthy, R.A., & Warrington, E.K. (1988). Evidence for modality-specific meaning systems in the brain. *Nature, 334*, 428–430.

McGrew, W.C. (1992). *Chimpanzee material culture: Implications for human evolution.* Cambridge: Cambridge University Press.

Madole, K.L., Oakes, L.M., & Cohen, L.B. (1993). Developmental changes in infants' attention to function and form-function correlations. *Cognitive Development, 8*, 189–209.

Mandler, J.M. (1988). The cradle of categorisation: Is the basic level basic? *Cognitive Development, 3*, 247–264.

Mandler, J.M., & McDonough, L. (1993). Concept formation in infancy. *Cognitive Development, 8*, 291–318.

Mandler, J.M., & McDonough, L. (1996). Drinking and driving don't mix: Inductive generalization in infancy. *Cognition, 59*, 307–335.

Matsuzawa, T. (1994). Field experiments on use of stone tools by chimpanzees in the wild. In R.W. Wrangham, W.C. McGrew, F.B.M. de Waal, & P.G. Heltne (Eds.), *Chimpanzee cultures* (pp. 351–370). Cambridge: Harvard University Press.

Meltzoff, A.N. (1996). Understanding the intentions of others: Re-enactment of intended acts by 18-month-old children. *Developmental Psychology, 31*, 838–850.

Meltzoff, A.N., & Moore, M.K. (1995). Infants' understanding of people and things: From body imitation to folk psychology. In J.L. Bermudez, A. Marcel, & N. Eilan (Eds.), *The body and the self* (pp. 43–70). Cambridge, MA: MIT Press.

Mendelsohn, M.J., Haith, M.M., & Goldman-Rakic, P.S. (1982). Face scanning and responsiveness to social cues in infant rhesus monkeys. *Developmental Psychology, 18*, 222–228.

Menzel, C. (1997). In A. Whiten and R. Byrne (Eds.), *Machiavellian intelligence II: Extensions and evaluations* (pp. 207–239). Cambridge: Cambridge University Press.

Michotte, A. (1963). *The perception of causality.* Andover: Metheun.

Moss, H.E., Tyler, L.K., Durrant-Peatfield, M., & Bunn, E.M. (1998). "Two eyes of a see-through": Impaired and intact semantic knowledge in a case of selective deficit for living things. *Neurocase, 4*, 291–310.

Perrett, D.I., Hietane, J.K., Oram, M.W., & Benson, P.J. (1992). Organization and functions of cells responsive to faces in the temporal cortex. *Philosophical Transactions of the Royal Society of London, B, 335*, 23–30.

Perrett, D.I., & Mistlin, A.J. (1990). Perception of facial attributes. In W.C. Stebbins & M.A. Berkeley (Eds.), *Comparative perception: Complex signals* (pp. 187–215). New York: Wiley.

Perrett, D.I., Smith, P.A., Potter, D.D., Mistlin, A.J., Head, A.S., Milner, A.D., & Jeeves, M.A. (1985). Visual cells in the temporal cortex sensitive to face view and gaze direction. *Philosophical Transactions of the Royal Society of London, B, 223*, 293–317.

Pinker, S. (1997) *How the mind works.* New York: W. W. Norton & Co.

Premack, D. (1990). The infant's theory of self-propelled objects. *Cognition, 36*, 1–16.

Premack, D., & Premack, A.J. (1995). Intention as psychological cause. In D. Sperber, D. Premack, & A.J. Premack (Eds.), *Causal cognition: A multidisciplinary debate* (pp. 185–199). Oxford: Clarendon Press.

Rawlins, R.G., & Kessler, M.G. (1987). *The Cayo Santiago macaques: History, behavior, and biology.* Albany, NY: SUNY Press.

Riddoch, M.J., Humphreys, G.W., Coltheart, M., & Funnell, E. (1988). Semantic systems or system? Neuropsychological evidence re-examined. *Cognitive Neuropsychology, 5*, 3–25.

Rodman, H.R., & Nace, K.L. (1997). Development of neuronal activity in cortical regions underlying visual recognition in monkeys. In N.A. Krasnegor, G.R. Lyon, & P.S. Goldman-Rakic (Eds.), *Development of the prefrontal cortex: Evolution, neurobiology, and behavior* (pp. 167–190). Baltimore: Paul H. Brooks Publishing Co.

Rosch, E., Mervis, C.B., Gray, W.D., Johnson, D.M., & Boyes-Braem, P. (1976). Basic objects in natural categories. *Cognitive Psychology, 8*, 382–439.

Rosengren, K.S., Gelman, S.A., Kalish, C.W., & McCormick, M. (1991). As time goes by: Children's understanding of growth in animals. *Child Development, 62*, 1302–1320.

Rozin, P. (1990). Development in the food domain. *Developmental Psychology, 26*, 555–562.

Sacchett, C., & Humphreys, G. W. (1992). Calling a squirrel a squirrel but a canoe a wigwam: A category-specific deficit for artefactual objects and body parts. *Cognitive Neuropsychology, 9*, 73–86.

Samson, D., Pillon, A., & De Wilde, V. (1998). Impaired knowledge of visual and non-visual attributes in a patient with a semantic impairment for living entities: A case of a true category-specific deficit. *Neurocase, 4*, 273–290.

Santos, L.R. (1997). *Precursors to a theory of mind: Insights from a non-human primate.* Honors thesis. Harvard University.

Santos, L.R., Hauser, M.D., & Spelke, E.S. (2001). Representations of food. Recognition and categorisation of biologically significant objects by rhesus monkeys (*Macaca mulatta*): The domain of food. *Cognition 82(2)*, 127–155.

Santos, L.R., Miller, C.T., & Hauser, M.D. (1999). *Knowledge of functionally-relevant features for different objects kinds.* Poster presented at the Biennial Meeting for the Society for Research in Child Development. Albuquerque, NM.

Shelton, J.R., & Caramazza, A. (2000). The organisation of semantic memory. In B. Rapp (Ed.), *A handbook of cognitive neuropsychology: What deficits reveal about the human mind/brain* (pp. 423–443). Philadelphia, PA: Psychology Press.

Shelton, J.R., Fouch, E., & Caramazza, A. (1998). The selective sparing of body part knowledge: A case study. *Neurocase, 4*, 339–351.

Sheridan, J., & Humphreys, G.W. (1993). A verbal–semantic category-specific recognition impairment. *Cognitive Neuropsychology, 10*, 143–184.

Silveri, M.C., & Gainotti, G. (1988). Interaction between vision and language in category-specific semantic impairment. *Cognitive Neuropsychology, 5*, 677–709.

Simons, D.J., & Keil, F.C. (1995). An abstract to concrete shift in the development of biological thought: The insides story. *Cognition, 56*, 129–163.

Spelke, E.S. (1985). Preferential looking methods as tools for the study of cognition in infancy. In G. Gottlieb & N. Krasnegor (Eds.), *Measurement of audition and vision in the first year of post-natal life: A methodological overview* (pp. 37–61). Norwood, NJ: Ablex Publishing Corporation.

Spelke, E.S. (1991). Physical knowledge in infancy: Reflections on Piaget's theory. In S. Carey & R. Gelman (Eds.), *The epigenesis of mind: Essays on biology and cognition* (pp. 37–61). Hillsdale, NJ: Lawrence Erlbaum Associates, Inc.

Spelke, E.S., Breinlinger, K., Macomber, J., & Jacobson, K. (1992). Origins of knowledge. *Psychological Review, 99*, 605–632.

Spelke, E.S., Phillips, A.T., & Woodward, A.L. (1995). Infants' knowledge of object motion and human action. In D. Sperber, D. Premack, & A.J. Premack (Eds.), *Causal cognition: A multidisciplinary debate* (pp. 44–78). Oxford: Clarendon Press.

Sperber, D. (1994). The modularity of thought and the epidemiology of representations. In L.A. Hirschfeld & S.A. Gelman (Eds). *Mapping the mind: Domain specificity in cognition and culture* (pp. 39–67). New York: Cambridge University Press.

Tomasello, M., & Call, J. (1997). *Primate cognition.* New York: Oxford University Press.

Thompson, R.K.R. (1995). Natural and relational concepts in animals. In H.L. Roitblat & J. Meyer (Eds.), *Comparative approaches to cognitive science. Complex adaptive systems* (pp. 175–224). Cambridge, MA: MIT Press.

Visalberghi, E., & Tomasello, M. (1998). Primate causal understanding in the physical and psychological domains. *Behavioural Processes, 42*, 189–203.

Visalberghi, E., & Trinca, L. (1989). Tool use in capuchin monkeys: Distinguishing between performance and understanding. *Primates, 30*, 511–521.

Warrington, E. (1981). Neuropsychological studies of verbal semantic systems. *Proceedings for the Royal Society of London, B, 295*, 411–423.

Warrington, E.K., & McCarthy, R. (1983). Category specific access dysphasia. *Brain, 106*, 859–878.

Warrington, E., & McCarthy, R. (1987). Categories of knowledge: further fractionations and an attempted integration. *Brain, 110*, 1273–1296.

Warrington, E.K., & Shallice, T. (1984). Category specific semantic impairments. *Brain, 107*, 829–854.

Wellman, H.M., & Gelman, S.A. (1988). Children's understanding of the non-obvious. In R.J. Sternberg (Ed.), *Advances in the psychology of human intelligence: Vol. 4* (pp. 99–135). Hillsdale, NJ: Lawrence Erlbaum Associates, Inc.

Willatts, P. (1999). Development of means-end behavior in young infants: Pulling a support to retrieve a distant object. *Developmental Psychology, 35*, 651–667.

Woodward, A.L. (1998). Infants selectively encode the goal object of an actor's reach. *Cognition, 69*, 1–34.

Wrangham, R.W., & Goodall, J.G. (1989). Chimpanzee use of medicinal leaves. In P.G. Heltne & L.A. Marquardt (Eds.), *Understanding chimpanzees* (pp. 22–37). Cambridge, MA: Harvard University Press.

Wrangham, R.W., & Nishida, T. (1983). *Aspilia* spp. leaves: A puzzle in the feeding behavior of wild chimpanzees. *Primates, 24*, 276–282.

CHAPTER TWO

A case of domain-specific semantic deficit

Giuseppe Sartori, Remo Job
Università degli studi di Padova, Padova, Italy

Stefano Zago
Università degli studi di Urbino, Urbino, Italy

INTRODUCTION

People carry various kinds of knowledge about concepts. For example, if you think of a dog, you will recall perceptual information (is four-legged, furry, barks), functional information (is used for hunting, guarding), associative information (is man's best friend, likes to chase cats) and encyclopaedic information (is a mammal, of different breeds). Moreover, knowledge refers to specific conceptual categories, such as living and non-living things, body parts, proper names. In addition, knowledge is accessible from different input modalities (pictures, written words, spoken words, sound, touch or smell). Our long-term memory, responsible for the representation of the encyclopaedic knowledge of the world and the meaning of words and concepts, is usually called "semantic memory", a notion first used by Quillian (1968) and further specified by Tulving (1972) (even if the issue was previously the focus of attention for many philosophers; see Eco, 1997). Semantic memory is often characterised in terms of what distinguishes it from "episodic memory", which is the explicit recollection of facts that occurred at a particular time and place in one's personal past, including their spatio-temporal relationship. It is precisely the lack of specific temporal and/or autobiographical information that characterises semantic memory. In remembering facts such as the capital city of Italy or the colour of an elephant, we have no awareness of the episodes during which these facts were acquired. The differentiation between semantic memory deficits and classic amnesic syndromes is motivated by the different nature of these two types of disturbances. The term "amnesia" is usually applied solely to disorders involving events or episodes whereas, in the case of pathology of semantic memory, it is the general knowledge, rather than specific recollections with their spatiotemporal framework, which is assumed to be impaired. Semantic memory also differs from the lexical system (i.e. the union of the words known to each and every speaking person) as semantic memory also concerns information acquired in other ways, such as via the sense of smell or touch.

Neuropsychological studies of patients and functional neuroimaging work on normal subjects have been useful sources of data for addressing issues about the organisation of conceptual–semantic knowledge in the human brain, and the discovery that different semantic categories can be selectively disrupted supports the notion that our semantic memory could be categorical in its organisation (Caramazza & Shelton, 1998, and see Chapter 1). The most frequently reported category-specific deficit is impaired knowledge of animals and foodstuffs with preserved knowledge of man-made objects. In this chapter, we a review an extensive study of an Italian patient, Michelangelo, who developed a severe and stable deficit for biological categories following infection by herpes simplex encephalitis. The investigations were carried out between 1984 and 1994. The main aims of the study were to address the following questions:

(1) Is the impairment a real category-specific deficit?
(2) Does the deficit reflect a difficulty in gaining access to semantic knowledge or is it caused by degradation of semantic memory?
(3) Is the disorder found in all modalities?
(4) What is the stage(s) of cognitive processing that is responsible for the selective semantic damage?
(5) Are specific loci of the brain critically involved in the representation of the disrupted semantic category?

MICHELANGELO: CASE HISTORY

In May 1984, Michelangelo was a 38-year-old man with 10 years of formal education. He was working as clerk in the health service of a town in northeastern Italy when he suddenly developed temporospatial disorientation and a severe anterograde amnesia. Initially, these symptoms were incorrectly interpreted as a consequence of an alcoholic syndrome. A few days post-onset he was admitted to the Neurological department. His EEG was normal but a CT scan showed bilateral low attenuation areas in the anterior temporal region. An increase in intratecal herpes antibodies was found via serial analysis of the liquor and serum (Pandy's reaction ++++) and the diagnosis of herpes simplex virus encephalitis was made. He was immediately treated with acyclovir.

Basic neuropsychological testing

At an initial neuropsychological examination, conducted at the bedside, Michelangelo was alert and co-operative. He presented with comprehension problems, a severe anomia, an anterograde amnesia and lack of awareness. He made a rapid recovery, although the anterograde amnesia and a category-specific deficit for living things remained unchanged. More formal examinations were performed 20 days post-onset. Table 2.1 gives a summary of Michelangelo's standard neuropsychological results. Michelangelo scored normally on a short-term verbal memory task but showed a severe anterograde amnesia. Performance on the retrograde memory test of public events, developed by Costa, De Renzi, and Faglioni (1989), was clearly related to the time since the onset of his brain damage. When tested on four-alternative forced-choice questions about events that happened in 1983–1984, he scored 12.5% correct (mean of controls = 79)

TABLE 2.1

Michelangelo's general neuropsychological assessment conducted 20 days post-onset in 1984

	Score
General Intelligence	
WAIS	
Verbal IQ	82
Performance IQ	76
Overall IQ	78
Progressive Coloured Matrices 47	31/36
Visuoperceptual abilities	
Poppelreuter Test (limited to non-living things)	10/10
Warrington Test	
Usual	19/20
Unusual view	17/20
Language	
Token Test	33/36
Memory	
Wechsler Memory Scale (IQ)	57
Digit Span	6
Warrington's Recognition Memory	
Words (n = 50)	38/50
Faces (n = 50)	26/50
Test of retrograde amnesia	period 1983–1984 12% (controls = 79%)
	period 1966–1967 50% (controls = 73.3)
Apraxia	
Oral apraxia	20/20
Ideomotor apraxia	72/72

whereas for events that happened in 1966–1967 his accuracy was 50% (mean of controls = 73.3). On the Warrington's (1984) Recognition Memory Test, there was a deficit both for faces and for words. Phonological and syntactic aspects of language were well-preserved so that speech was fluent without phonemic paraphasias. His reading and writing capabilities were also preserved. No apraxic impairments were detected. On visuo-perceptual tests he was correct in identifying overlapping figures in Poppelreuter's Test and in identifying objects seen from unusual views. These data rule out the presence of a low-level visual processing deficit. His performance on Raven's Coloured Progressive Matrices was better than average (31/36).

Impairment in naming animals and vegetables

In January 1985 Michelangelo was presented with the Snodgrass and Vanderwart (1980) set of line drawings and was able to correctly name 17/54 (31%), 11/31 (35%), and 131/175 (75%) of animals, vegetables, and objects, respectively. Although Michelangelo's poor naming was not restricted to animals and vegetables, his performance was worse for these categories than for man-made objects. Michelangelo is a particularly interesting case because he was an active member of the WWF (World Wildlife Fund, now the Worldwide Fund for Nature) and an underwater diver, and, according to his wife and colleagues, he was able to identify huge numbers of mammals, fish, and birds premorbidly. The Snodgrass and Vanderwart's (1980) set was administered again in December 1989 and the results showed a similar pattern over time (Figure 2.1). The Snodgrass and Vanderwart (1980) line

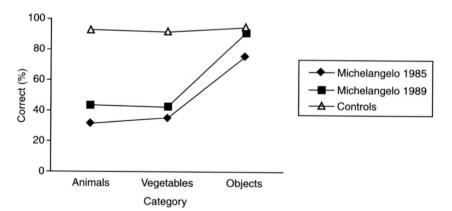

Figure 2.1. Performance of the control group and Michelangelo (in 1984 and 1989) on the Snodgrass and Vanderwart (1980) set. (Note the recovery to normal levels on objects observed in 1989.)

drawings do not convey information about colour or texture, and these properties might well be important for recognition (Price & Humphreys, 1989). Colour could be particularly important for the identification of living things (Sheridan & Humphreys, 1993; Warrington & McCarthy, 1987). Consequently, two other picture-naming tasks were administered in 1985 to assess the influence of surface properties of objects, such as colour and texture. One set of coloured pictures was taken from Ladybird Books. Control subjects performed equally well across categories (mean correct = 61/61 objects, 19.7/20 animals and 38.7/39 vegetables) but Michelangelo was much poorer at naming animals (9/20) than objects (47/61) (Fisher $P < .001$). With the Snodgrass and Vanderwart set he showed an advantage for objects over vegetables but this was not confirmed with the second set of stimuli (29/39 correct for vegetables) (Fisher $P = .47$) and he was significantly worse with animals compared to vegetables ($P = .02$). In a further set of 48 photographs of animals, Michelangelo correctly named only 16/48 (33%). Control subjects scored an average 42.7/48 (89%) correct and Michelangelo's performance was markedly below the worst control in naming animals (control range 41–44), even when stimuli were presented as photographs. In summary, the cardinal feature of Michelangelo's naming impairment was a severe and persistent inability to name exemplars from the category of living things, a pattern that appeared similar to the post-encephalitis patients originally reported by Warrington and Shallice (1984).

Demonstration of the knowledge deficit

A patient who can no longer answer a question such as 'Does the giraffe have a long neck?' could have lost the representation of this fact. Alternatively, the representation might still be present but the procedures by which it is accessed are impaired. Various empirical criteria have been proposed to differentiate between a deficit of "storage" and a deficit of "access" (see Rapp & Caramazza, 1993; Shallice, 1988; Warrington, 1975; Warrington & McCarthy, 1983; Warrington & Shallice, 1979). A storage deficit should show at least the following characteristics:

(1) The patient must fail consistently on the same items in different administrations of the same test. In the case of an access deficit the same overall accuracy would be expected but different items could be named on different occasions.
(2) The patient's performance should show item-specific consistency across tasks that tap the same underlying knowledge.
(3) Benefits from phonemic cueing in naming accuracy should be absent.

We now consider how well Michelangelo's performance fits these criteria.

Consistency over time. Between January 1985 and August 1990 Michelangelo was asked to name the same set of 40 black and white drawings (20 objects: 10 animals and 10 vegetables) eight times (Job, Miozzo, Sartori, & Zago, 1991). Half of the pictures in each category were correctly named in a session preceding the first one and the other half were not. All the pictures were taken from Snodgrass and Vanderwart's (1980) set. The first six presentations were given in the period between January 1985 and April 1985. There were three testing sessions once a week for three weeks, and three sessions in February, March, and April 1985. The final two testing sessions were in September 1988 and in August 1990. The results are summarised in Table 2.2. The results show a high consistency in naming between different sessions even when these sessions were carried out months or even years apart. Named items continue to be named and unnamed items generally continue to be unnamed, although a few began to be named in the course of time.

Consistency across tasks.   Animals and vegetables from the previous set were presented for verbal definition and five independent judges were asked to rate Michelangelo's definitions. If at least 4/5 judges could recognise the concept Michelangelo's response was scored as correct. Michelangelo scored 11/20 correct on both the picture naming and the verbal definition tasks and was consistent for 18/20 items across the two tasks.

Effects of phonemic cueing in naming accuracy.   In many studies on category specificity the investigations have been restricted to naming. Consequently, these reports are not necessarily relevant for understanding the organisation of the semantic memory *per se*, as the impairment may be at the lexical level or to some aspect of its interface with semantics (Farah & Wallace, 1992). For example, the case studied by Hart, Berndt, and Caramazza (1985) showed a category-specific deficit limited to the names of fruits and vegetables in picture naming and in naming to verbal descriptions. This patient could, however, correctly match a word to the appropriate picture. This was taken as evidence that conceptual/semantic knowledge was preserved, despite the patient's inability to select the names of the pictures. However, Hillis and Caramazza (1995) argued that a category specific deficit in naming pictures and words, "would not be predicted by damage at the level of the phonological output lexicon, as there is no theoretical reason for assuming that the output lexicon would be organised by category".

A number of authors have argued that a category-specific impairment in picture naming cannot be considered as a non-ambiguous indication of a semantic memory disturbance and a patient with a clear semantic deficit should show difficulties in a number of tasks, such as picture naming, verbally describing the characteristics of objects, choosing the correct attribute among alternatives in visual or verbal presentations and drawing from

TABLE 2.2
Consistency of the responses in naming black and white pictures

		Time of test							
		Jan 85	Jan 85	Jan 85	Feb 85	Mar 85	Apr 85	Sep 88	Aug 90
Correctly named items									
(1)	Barrel	+	+	+	−	+	+	+	+
(2)	Bus	+	+	+	+	+	+	+	+
(3)	Cup	+	+	+	+	+	+	+	+
(4)	Envelope	+	+	+	+	+	+	+	+
(5)	Fence	+	+	+	+	+	+	+	+
(6)	Frying pan	+	+	+	+	+	+	−	+
(7)	Guitar	+	+	+	+	+	+	+	+
(8)	Mountain	+	+	+	+	−	+	+	+
(9)	Sled	+	+	+	+	+	+	+	+
(10)	Traffic light	+	+	+	+	+	+	+	+
(11)	Chicken	+	+	+	+	+	+	+	+
(12)	Cow	+	+	+	+	+	+	+	+
(13)	Dog	+	+	+	+	+	+	+	+
(14)	Snake	+	+	+	+	+	+	+	+
(15)	Tiger	+	+	+	+	+	+	−	+
(16)	Asparagus	+	+	+	+	+	+	−	+
(17)	Corn	+	+	+	+	+	+	+	+
(18)	Grapes	+	+	+	+	+	+	+	+
(19)	Mushroom	+	+	+	+	+	+	+	+
(20)	Pear	+	+	+	+	+	+	+	+
Incorrectly named items									
(1)	Anchor	−	−	−	+	−	+	−	+
(2)	Axe	−	+	+	+	−	−	−	+
(3)	Box	−	+	+	+	+	+	+	+
(4)	Bow	−	−	−	−	−	+	−	−
(5)	Crown	−	−	−	+	−	+	+	+
(6)	Kite	−	+	+	+	+	+	−	+
(7)	Rollerskate	−	−	−	−	−	−	−	+
(8)	Rolling-pin	−	+	+	−	+	−	−	+
(9)	Salt shaker	−	+	+	+	+	+	−	−
(10)	Thimble	−	−	−	−	−	−	−	−
(11)	Bear	−	−	−	−	−	−	−	−
(12)	Camel	−	−	−	−	−	−	+	−
(13)	Kangaroo	−	−	−	−	−	−	+	+
(14)	Ostrich	−	−	−	−	−	−	−	−
(15)	Penguin	−	−	−	+	+	+	−	−
(16)	Carrot	−	+	+	−	+	+	+	+
(17)	Onion	−	−	−	+	+	−	+	−
(18)	Pepper	−	−	−	+	−	+	−	−
(19)	Pineapple	−	−	−	−	−	−	−	−
(20)	Tomato	−	−	−	−	−	−	+	−

+, Correctly named; −, incorrectly named.

memory. Sartori et al. (Sartori, Miozzo, Zago, & Job, 1991; Sartori, Job, & Coltheart, 1993a) studied the case of Dante, a post-encephalitic patient with a word-finding category-specific deficit for animals. Naming was much easier for him when given a phonemic cue (the first sound of the word). Furthermore, he was capable of accessing structural knowledge about the animals that he was unable to name (e.g. in object decision and in part–whole matching tasks). These data were interpreted as evidence that his naming defect for animals was not due to a loss of knowledge but rather to a category-specific naming difficulty. Farah and Wallace (1992) also reported a patient with good access to semantics but poor naming of fruit and vegetables. They argued that the patient had a specific impairment in name retrieval as opposed to a recognition or semantic impairment for living things. These reports illustrate that, although a naming impairment can be a good starting point for isolating category-specific semantic deficits, the investigations should not be limited to naming alone; patients exist with category-specific naming deficits and should not be confused with patients who have category-specific impairments to semantic memory (see Forde et al., 1997, for an alternative view). Sartori et al. (1993a) evaluated the effects of phonemic cueing on Michelangelo's naming ability. After failing to name a picture, he was given a phonemic cue (the initial phoneme of the correct name) and then asked to produce the correct name with the help of this cue. His naming accuracy for animals was 47% without cueing and 53% with cueing, and for objects was 94% both with and without cueing. Thus, Michelangelo could not significantly benefit from phonemic cueing. Sartori et al. (1993a) argued that sensitivity to phonemic cueing distinguishes between a naming deficit that arises within the phonological output lexicon (impaired access to a representation in this lexicon being aided by the partial phonological information provided by a phonemic cue) and a naming deficit that is caused by an impairment within the semantic system (a difficulty there would not be aided by providing non-semantic cueing). Thus, the cueing data are consistent with the hypothesis that Michelangelo's naming impairment is semantic in origin.

Is the category-specific disorder in naming a side effect?

A number of authors have suggested that the category-specific effects observed in patients are not real but a side-effect arising from a number of confounding variables, such as the name frequency, visual complexity, and visual familiarity of the to-be-named pictures (Funnel & Sheridan, 1992; Stewart, Parkin, & Hunkin, 1992). These authors claimed that non-living things are named more accurately than living things because, when we randomly choose a set of stimuli, animals are more likely to have lower name frequencies, be less familiar and more visually complex pictures than non-living things. Michelangelo was evaluated on various occasions to assess whether his difficulty in naming living things disappeared when these variables were taken in account. In 1989 he was given a set of 64 pictures (32 living things and 32 non-living things) matched for picture familiarity, picture complexity, and name frequency. Michelangelo named 46.9% living things and 93.8% non-living things. Of Michelangelo's 18 naming errors, 6 were visual and semantic (that is, the response was an item that was similar in appearance and in meaning to the target, such as naming lemon as "orange" or squirrel as "rabbit"), 1 was a visual error, and 1 was an omission. In 1993 a second test was administered (Sartori, Miozzo, & Job, 1993c). Michelangelo was presented with two sets of pictures (animals and objects) matched for familiarity, visual complexity, and name frequency. He named 12/40 (30%) of the animals correctly and 28/40 (70%) of the objects, showing again that the category effect was reliable when name frequency, visual complexity, and familiarity were controlled.

Funnell and De Mornay Davies (1996) made an important point in arguing that category-specific deficits for living things might be explained by familiarity if this variable not only included the frequency but also the quality of an individual's interaction with an item. For instance, some items like lions are as familiar as cats in one sense but the familiarity that comes from direct interaction is missing. Consistent with this idea, Funnell and De Mornay Davies reported a case of a professional musician who had a category-specific recognition impairment for living things but showed normal performance with musical instruments. This was an interesting pattern because musical instruments are often reported to be as impaired as animals in patients with category-specific impairments for living things (e.g. Forde et al., 1997). This objection, however, does not apply to Michelangelo. As mentioned previously, he was an active member of WWF, he used to take people on bird-watching tours, was a fisherman and an underwater diver. His familiarity with animals could be considered to be at the highest level possible but he, none the less, developed a profound deficit for biological items.

In conclusion, the existence of genuine category-specific recognition and/or naming effects has been challenged by a number of authors. While it might be true that, for some patients, the effects disappear when the stimuli are carefully matched on a number of confounding variables, there is ample evidence that the category-specific effects are reliable in other patients. Michelangelo seems to be one of the patients whose deficits have survived several attempts at proving their artificiality. In particular, he can be considered a clear case to which Funnell and De Mornay Davies's (1996) objection does not apply. He was very familiar with animals and his familiarity involved all sensory modalities but, none the less, he presented with a severe and lasting impairment with animals.

Degradation of stored knowledge

We have argued that Michelangelo has a deficit to stored knowledge about living things and, in the next section, we assess whether this impairment involved all aspects of these items. When asked open-ended questions such as "What is the visual appearance of an ostrich?", Michelangelo answered "It has four legs . . . big ears . . . a thick tail". This example typifies Michelangelo's responses with questions about the visual appearance of animals. He provided features that were indeed characteristic of animals, but he could not report the specific features of a given animal. However, when we evaluated Michelangelo's knowledge about the non-visual properties of animals, his performance was better. For example, he was able to sort pictures of ferocious and non-ferocious animals, to match an animal's sound to its name and to match a verbally presented environment to the name of a given animal (e.g. to match desert with camel). Thus it is clear that Michelangelo had not lost all his knowledge of living things. In the next series of tests we assessed his visual/perceptual knowledge in more detail.

Tests of stored visual knowledge

Tasks with visual input

Part–whole matching task.   In this task, Michelangelo was presented with a set of 16 animals and 50 objects. Each of the 66 trials consisted of a target object with a part missing plus drawings of 2 (in the case of objects) or 4 (in the case of animals) choices for the missing part. The patient's task was to choose which part was correct for the target object (see also Riddoch & Humphreys [1987] for use of this task). For example, for the animals, the target might be a headless body with four alternative heads. The isolated parts were magnified (×4) to avoid guessing on the basis of perceptual cues (see Figures 2.2 and 2.3). The position of the target was varied over the stimulus set and targets were only presented once. Michelangelo scored 5/16 (31%) correct with living things and 41/50 (82%) correct with non-living things. His performance was significantly more impaired with living than non-living things than control subjects (mean = 14.7/16, SD = 1.2 for living things; mean = 44/50, SD = 1.5 for non-living things).

Reality decision task.   Michelangelo was asked to judge if a given picture was of a real object or an unreal object (for use of this task, see also Kroll & Potter, 1984; Riddoch & Humphreys, 1987). The test consisted of 48 pictures: 24 were real things (16 animals, 8 inanimate objects) and 24 were of unreal things constructed by joining appropriate parts from two real items to produce plausible but non-existent non-animal and non-objects. The test was designed to assess Michelangelo's ability to access perceptual knowledge

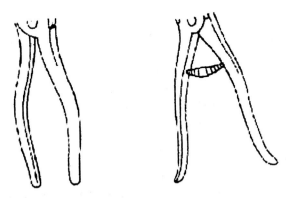

Figure 2.2.   Part–whole matching for non-living things.

Figure 2.3.   Part–whole matching for animals.

specific to a particular animal or inanimate object. Michelangelo performed normally with the inanimate stimuli (8/8 and 7/8 with the real and unreal objects, respectively; control mean = 7.4/8 (SD = 1.7) and 7.2/8 (SD = 1.3) for real and unreal objects, respectively). In contrast, he made a large number of errors with the animals, all consisting in wrongly accepting an unreal animal as a real one (he scored 16/16 for real and 4/16 for unreal animals, respectively). His performance with animals was impaired compared to a group of control subjects, who scored a mean of 14.4/16 (SD = 0.8) and 14.2/16 (SD = 1.5) for real and unreal animals, respectively.

Tasks with neither visual input nor visual output

Perceptual properties decision task.   To verify whether Michelangelo's deficit in processing information about the visual properties of objects also occurred in the verbal domain, he was asked to judge if a verbally presented perceptual attribute was characteristic of a given concept. For example, he was asked to judge the veracity of the following statements: "A motorcycle has a rear view mirror", "A motorcycle has a steering wheel", "A rabbit has long ears", "A rabbit has a curved beak". There were 20 names (10 animals and 10 inanimate objects) and each name was presented 8 times (4 times with correct attributes and 4 times with incorrect attributes). Michelangelo performed normally with inanimate stimuli (71/80 correct; control mean = 72.6/80, SD = 2.9) but was impaired with animals (48/80 correct; control mean = 69.5/80, SD = 4.1). It is important to note that the Michelangelo's performance in this test was similar to the tasks in which pictures were used. This pattern of results is consistent with the idea that stored knowledge of perceptual attributes might be interrogated from both visually and verbally presented stimuli and with the hypothesis that Michelangelo had an impairment to stored visual knowledge for living but not for non-living items.

Tasks with visual output

Drawing from memory.   In this task, Michelangelo was asked to draw from memory an object or an animal when given a spoken name. Some examples of Michelangelo's drawings are given in Figure 2.4. His drawings of animals showed the same types of error that characterised his performance in other tasks tapping visual/perceptual knowledge (e.g. incorrectly combining animals' parts and a lack of specific structural features). In contrast, his drawings of inanimate objects, although imperfectly executed, did not contain incorrect perceptual attributes. As in other cases (e.g. Lambon Ralph, Howard, Nightingale, & Ellis, 1998), Michelangelo's drawings of animals showed a "prototype effect" with most items drawn as a skeleton of a very prototypical animal, such as a horse or a dog.

Figure 2.4. Drawing from memory of animals and objects. (Note that although objects are drawn with many details and are clearly recognisable, animals seem to be variants of a "four-legged animal".)

Tests of stored non-visual knowledge

We have shown that Michelangelo's ability to access visual knowledge about living things was impaired and, in the next experiment, we assessed his knowledge of the functional/encyclopaedic properties of animals that he could and could not name. To do this we used a forced-choice task similar to that developed by Warrington (1975). For each item, Michelangelo was presented with questions concerning six non-visual semantic properties and asked to select the correct response from two or three choices. The questions tapped knowledge of the following features:

(1) Superordinate category (Is x a bird, a mammal, or a member of another category?)
(2) Usual habitat (Does x have an Italian or a foreign habitat?)
(3) Type of food eaten (Is x carnivorous, herbivorous, or omnivorous?)
(4) Ferocity (Is x ferocious or not?)
(5) Domesticity (Is x domestic or not?)
(6) Edibility (Is x edible or not?).

The task was administered twice on different sessions held 1 week apart. In one session, Michelangelo was presented with the spoken names of the items and in the other session he was presented with the pictures of the items (Job, Miozzo, & Sartori, 1994). His performance with verbal presentation was good (Table 2.3) and there was no difference for named and unnamed items when they were presented verbally ($t(5) = 1$, $p = .36$). However, named items were responded to more accurately than unnamed items when these items were presented as pictures ($t(5) = 4.3$, $p = .007$). Unnamed items yielded poorer performance when presented as pictures than when presented as words ($t(5) = 3.61$, $p = .02$). Thus, Michelangelo performed above chance on functional/encyclopaedic attributes about animals he could not name. It could be that functional/encyclopaedic knowledge for unnamed animals is preserved better than visual knowledge. To evaluate this, we administered another version of a perceptual features verification task that distinguished between named and unnamed items. We presented Michelangelo with 40 animals, 20 of these were named in a previous session and another 20 were not. Each item was presented verbally on two occasions, once with a

TABLE 2.3
Michelangelo's results on a functional attributes verification task for animals

	Picture		Word	
	Named	*Unnamed*	*Named*	*Unnamed*
Category	100	85	100	85
Habitat	90	80	95	90
Food	95	60	80	75
Ferocity	95	80	85	95
Familiarity	100	85	95	90
Edibility	75	65	85	85
Mean	93	76	90	87

Chance level of performance was 33% for Category and Food and 50% for the other attributes.

perceptual feature that was correct and once with a perceptual feature that was incorrect. The perceptual features included specific parts (e.g. horns), shape (e.g. short tail) and texture (e.g. has stripes). Michelangelo was better at this task with those items that he had previously named (82% correct) compared to unnamed (58% correct). We propose that degradation to semantic knowledge underlay his failure in both naming and feature verification, i.e. Michelangelo had a specific deficit to a component of semantic memory that stores visual knowledge and this deficit impaired his performance when visual information was probed, regardless of the modality of the stimulus. Because Michelangelo could retrieve functional/contextual attributes for unnamed items (Table 2.3), we propose that visual knowledge is stored at least partially independently from non-visual knowledge (for similar proposals, see Basso, Capitani, & Laiacona, 1988; Chertkow, Bub, & Caplan, 1992; De Renzi & Lucchelli, 1994; Farah, Hammond, Metha, & Ratcliff, 1989; Forde et al., 1997; Goldenberg, 1992; Powell & Davidoff, 1992; Sartori et al., 1993; Sartori & Job, 1988; Silveri & Gainotti, 1988).

EXPLAINING CATEGORY-SPECIFIC IMPAIRMENTS: THE "PERCEPTUAL–FUNCTIONAL" THEORY

A number of authors have proposed that a deficit for living things could be the consequence of the differential importance of perceptual and functional information in the identification of living and non-living things (e.g. see Chapter 3; Warrington & Shallice, 1984). For instance, Warrington and Shallice (1984) suggested that non-living objects have distinctive perceptual and functional characteristics (e.g. the ball is round and is used in a football game) but that living things tend to have less distinctive functional attributes and are differentiated primarily on the basis of their perceptual features. Interestingly, Farah and McClelland (1991) showed that in definitions of animals, there were eight visual properties for every one functional property, whereas in the case of non-living objects the ratio of visual to functional properties was 1.4:1 (for a critique of this study, see Caramazza & Shelton, 1998). This imbalance is consistent with the idea that perceptual features are particularly important for recognising animals and that generalised damage to perceptual knowledge can lead to more difficulty in recognising living compared to non-living things. The assumption is that non-living things can also be defined on the basis of their functional features and consequently would not be as vulnerable when perceptual knowledge is impaired. However, some data inconsistent with this theory were collected from Michelangelo. Michelangelo was asked to identify the features that could be used to distinguish between two known items and he was able to perform this task as well as control subjects for both living and non-living things. He generated appropriate perceptual and functional distinguishing features for 12/12 pairs

TABLE 2.4
The number of perceptual and functional features generated to
distinguish between pairs of items

	Michelangelo	Control mean (SD)	Control range
Objects			
Functional	4	6.8 (1.4)	5–8
Perceptual	8	4.6 (1.2)	3–6
Vegetables			
Functional	1	1.8 (2.69)	0–9
Perceptual	6	10.3 (2.67)	4–12
Animals			
Functional	0	1.5 (1.02)	0–3
Perceptual	6	7.9 (2.07)	1–10

of man-made objects, 7/12 vegetables and 6/12 animals (Table 2.4). These data clearly show two things:

(1) Warrington and Shallice's (1984) hypothesis that normal subjects rely more heavily on perceptual features to distinguish between animals was confirmed. Control subjects used 5 times more perceptual than non-perceptual features in distinguishing pairs of animals whereas for objects they used 1.5 times more non-perceptual than perceptual features.

(2) Michelangelo's category-specific recognition impairment for living things was not due to a generalised non-categorical impairment to perceptual knowledge because he used a similar pattern of functional and perceptual features to distinguish between concepts. Warrington and Shallice's (1984) perceptual/functional theory predicts that, when distinguishing among pairs of similar items, patients with a general-ised impairment to perceptual knowledge would generate a signifi-cantly lower number of perceptual features compared to controls. In Michelangelo's case this prediction did not hold for non-living objects, vegetables, or animals. On the contrary, he generated more perceptual features than controls when distinguishing between pairs of objects. This finding is consistent with other data recently collected on patients with category-specific impairments. For example, Lambon Ralph et al. (1998) observed that their patient DB did not show any difference between perceptual and functional attributes in a feature verification task despite showing a clear impairment for animals with respect to objects in picture naming tasks (see also Caramazza & Shelton, 1998; Laiacona, Capitani, & Barbarotto, 1997; Moss, Tyler, Durrant-Peatfield, & Bunn, 1998). A second patient, IW, studied by Lambon

Ralph et al. (1998) had an impairment to perceptual knowledge compared to functional/associative knowledge. According to the perceptual/functional hypothesis, we should expect this case to show a greater impairment for animals but IW was slightly better at matching definitions to names of animals than to non-living things. This pattern can be considered as strong evidence against the perceptual/functional theory of category specificity.

EXPLAINING CATEGORY-SPECIFIC IMPAIRMENTS: THE "CROWDING" THEORY

The "crowding theory" proposes that category-specific impairments for living things are not due to an impairment to knowledge about the category of living things *per se* but rather they are a consequence of higher within-category structural similarity for animals than for man-made objects (see Chapters 3 and 4; Humphreys, Riddoch, & Quinlan 1988; Riddoch & Humphreys, 1987). According to this account, an impairment in visually based access to semantic information will tend to impair recognition of items from living categories. In addition, there may be difficulties for certain categories of non-living things if there are high levels of perceptual overlap between the exemplars (e.g. musical instruments, cars; Forde et al., 1997). We tested this theory by presenting Michelangelo with sets of animals (birds, crustaceans, fish, insects, mammals, molluscs, and reptiles) and non-living things that had visually similar exemplars (boats, carriers, guns, buildings, vehicles, vessels). A group of control subjects rated the within-category visual similarity of the items and only pictures matched for within-category visual similarity were included in the final set (see Sartori et al., 1993). Michelangelo's category specific deficit for animals remained even when he was presented with non-living things that had the same level of within-category similarity as animals.

Devlin, Gonnerman, Anderson, and Seidenberg (1998) outlined a variation of this "crowding theory" and developed a computational model that explicitly distinguished between perceptual and functional features but not between categories (see Chapter 5; Tyler, Durrat-Peatfield, Levy, Voice, & Moss, 1996). The authors asked normal subjects to produce features of concepts and then analysed the correlations between features for living and non-living things. The average number of perceptual features produced for living items was higher than for non-living things and more functional features were produced for non-living things. Furthermore, living things had fewer unique distinguishing features and more intercorrelated properties than non-living things. Devlin et al. (1998) showed that random damage to their connectionist model resulted in a major impairment for living things. This demonstrated that category-specific effects in patients could arise as a consequence of the larger number of intercorrelated features for living things. However, as mentioned above, Michelangelo was not impaired with visually similar non-living things (e.g. as boats, guns, buildings) that presumably have as many intercorrelated features as animals. According to Devlin et al. (1998), these subcategories of non-living things should show a similar pattern of impairment to living things. Animals and non-living things that have numerous visually similar neighbours should all be recognised on the basis of distinguishing features. For instance, a robin might be distinguished from other birds by activation of the uncorrelated distinguishing feature 'red-breast'. Similarly, a Porsche Carrera Cabrio can be distinguished from the Porsche Boxter by the shape of its back. To test this variation of the crowding theory in more detail, Michelangelo was given 36 pairs of words that referred to known items that were similar and asked to explain the difference between the two concepts in each pair (see Sartori & Job 1988, task 18). There were 12 animal pairs (e.g. tiger–leopard), 12 fruit/vegetable pairs (e.g. strawberry–gooseberry) and 12 pairs of non-living things (e.g. cup–bowl). The similar items had many common intercorrelated features and very few distinctive features, and we assumed that the ratio of highly intercorrelated features to less intercorrelated features was similar across categories. Michelangelo's performance was similar to control subjects with pairs of non-living things but well below the worst control for vegetables and animals. For example, for animal pairs, the worst control identified correctly a distinguishing feature in 10/12 occasions while Michelangelo scored 6/12 correct. This suggests that his category-specific impairment was not due to a widespread and general impairment to distinguishing features, as he was able to access these properties for non-living things.

ARE SPECIFIC BRAIN REGIONS CRITICALLY INVOLVED IN CATEGORY-SPECIFIC IMPAIRMENTS?

Many of the patients who have been reported with a category-specific deficit for living things have recovered from herpes simplex encephalitis, a disease that typically causes bilateral inflammation and necrosis in the inferior and medial parts of the temporal lobes and the orbito-frontal cortex (De Renzi & Lucchelli, 1994; Laiacona et al., 1997; Pietrini et al., 1988; Sartori et al., 1993b; Sheridan & Humphreys, 1993; Silveri & Gainotti, 1988; Sirigu, Duhamel, & Poncet, 1991; Stewart et al., 1992; Warrington & Shallice, 1984). The localisation of this lesion is thought to result from the proximity of these areas to the route of entry of the virus in the brain (Davis & Johnson, 1979) or from a particular affinity of the virus for the adult limbic cortices (Damasio & Van Hoesen, 1985). However, non-herpes patients have also been reported with deficits for living things: for example, patients with closed head injury (Farah et al, 1989; Farah, McMullen, & Meyer, 1991; Laiacona, Barbarotto, & Capitani, 1993), vascular accidents (Forde et al., 1997), slowly progressive degenerative diseases (Basso et al., 1988; Barbarotto, Capitani, Spinnler, & Trivelli, 1995), antibody-mediated paraneoplastic syndrome (Hart & Gordon, 1992), and developmental disturbances (Temple, 1986). What stands out in most of these cases is that they seem to have damage involving the middle and lower parts of the temporal lobes (with a preference for the left side) thus mimicking the herpes lesion. As observed by Patterson and Hodges (1995), it is important to note the rarity of reports of selective semantic memory loss resulting from cerebrovascular accidents. This might be because the area that appears to be most crucial for semantic memory is supplied by both the middle and posterior cerebral arteries: dual vascular territory strokes are unusual and are likely to produce multiple cognitive deficits. Gainotti and co-workers (see Chapter 14; Gainotti, 2000; Gainotti, Silveri, Daniele, & Giustolisi, 1995) reviewed the neuroanatomical correlates of category-specific patients and hypothesised that the anteromesial and inferior parts of the temporal lobes play a critical role in the storage and retrieval of semantic knowledge for living items, because these are represented in a more visual fashion. On the contrary, man-made artefacts, which are mainly bound to knowledge based on manual use and concrete utilisation of objects, are represented in the dorsolateral convexity (frontoparietal regions, especially in the left hemisphere), where motor and somatosensorial functions are mainly represented. These areas correspond broadly to the site of radiologically identified lesions on the cases having a selective deficit for non-living things (Gainotti et al., 1995). There is, however, limited imaging data on these patients and there are some reported exceptions to this pattern. For example, GP, a patient studied by Cappa et al. (1998) had a lesion in the anterior part of the left temporal lobe. A number of functional neuroimaging studies relevant to this issue have also been conducted (for a review, see Chapter 15). For example, Sergent, Otha, and McDonald (1992) asked subjects to make categorical judgements to living and non-living things and measured the brain activity for each category using positron emission topography (PET). Living things were associated with bilateral activation of the inferior occipital temporal areas, whereas non-living things activated a number of areas, including the dorsal lateral frontal cortex, with a preference for the left hemisphere. These results are consistent with the observations made in brain-injured patients and were interpreted as favouring the existence of two different cerebral systems for the recognition of living and non-living things, respectively. Martin, Wiggs, Ungerleider, and Haxby (1996) have verified this pattern of activation in normal subjects during a naming task with animals and tools. Both types of stimuli generated bilateral activity of the ventrotemporal regions and Broca's area. However, while the naming of animals activated the left medial occipital lobe (centred on the calcarine sulcus), naming tools activated the left middle temporal gyrus and left premotor regions. In a further study, Damasio et al. (1996) identified the lesions in patients with category-specific disorders and measured the brain activity (using PET) of control subjects when naming items taken from three categories of stimuli: (i) faces of well-known people; (ii) animals; and (iii) tools. A deficit in face naming was correlated with altered blood flow in the left temporal pole; a deficit in naming animals correlated with inferotemporal (mostly anterior) lobe activation and a deficit in man-made object naming correlated with more posterior inferotemporal regions. Sartori and Umiltà (2000) have, however, discussed in length why these data cannot be considered as a valid source of evidence for a cognitive and neural model of category specificity. For instance, there are some potential problems with the logic used in functional imaging studies (e.g. the subtractive methodology, see Chapter 15) and none of the PET studies reported above have taken into account the various confounding variables that could cause a spurious category effect when designing the experimental stimuli and tasks. Consequently, any difference in localisation found between living and non-living things could be due to a difference in localisation of visual routines required for distinguishing between highly visual similar items versus less visually similar items (although see Moore & Price [1999] for an attempt to separate category from visual similarity).

One of the few experiments that successfully controls for within-category visual similarity was reported by Perani et al. (1995). These authors required their subjects to decide whether pairs of pictures were instances of the same object (e.g. a cow in two different positions) or different objects (e.g. a racket and a carpet-beater). The recognition of animals was associated with bilateral activation of the inferior occipital temporal areas, whereas the recognition of objects activated a vast number of areas including the dorsal lateral frontal cortex, with a preference for the left hemisphere. In this task, the "same" items were visually different exemplars of an object; "different" items were visually similar. Consequently, the difference in brain localisation for animals and objects could not come from a greater reliance on visual discrimination routines for animals than for man-made objects. Thus, this study provides further evidence for a domain-specific theory of semantic memory.

To summarise, there is evidence from both lesion studies and functional neuroimaging for the idea that retrieving knowledge from different semantic categories involves different regions of the cerebral cortex. In particular, the neuroimaging data suggests that the inferotemporal areas are crucial for processing living things (however, see Chapter 15).

CONCLUSIONS

We have reviewed a number of accounts of category specific-deficits, including: (i) the idea that category-specific impairments do not exist when confounding factors, such as familiarity and visual complexity, are properly controlled; (ii) the perceptual/functional theory; (iii) visual crowding explanations; and (iv) a genuine categorical organisation of knowledge. We propose that the data reported on Michelangelo is inconsistent with the first three explanations for the following reasons.

The first hypothesis claims that there is no genuine category-specific effect to be explained (Funnell & Sheridan, 1992; Stewart et al., 1992). However, Michelangelo showed a robust impairment for animals on a number of occasions when naming line drawings, coloured pictures, and photographs, even when living and non-living items were matched carefully (Sartori, Miozzo & Job, 1993c). For some patients, careful matching has reduced the category effect but in Michelangelo it persisted and, more importantly, it had the same magnitude (a clear 40% difference in favour of non-living things) in naming tasks with both non-matched and carefully matched stimuli. Furthermore, this difference was stable over time; the magnitude of the category effect was similar in 1984 and in 1989.

The second hypothesis emphasises the importance of certain attribute types for the differentiation between exemplars within a category. Some authors (e.g. Farah & McClelland, 1991; Warrington & Shallice, 1984) have suggested that living things are primarily differentiated from one another on the basis of how they look, whereas artefacts tend to have specific functions. According to this theory, random damage to perceptual features in a semantic network (not organised by category) is likely to give rise to an impairment with living items because perceptual features are more important for their identification than they are for the identification of man-made objects. This perceptual/functional theory predicts that patients with category-specific recognition impairments for living things would be poorer at retrieving visual compared to functional information, irrespective of category. The data collected on Michelangelo are inconsistent with this explanation. Our patient was clearly impaired with perceptual knowledge but only for animals. The functional/perceptual hypothesis has a corollary. If we take two artefacts (e.g. rifle–pistol) that are functionally similar and ask a patient with a deficit for living things to identify the difference between the two concepts then the patient should also show an impairment on this task, because objects that are functionally similar can be distinguished only via the perceptual features. Widespread non-category-specific impairment to visuoperceptual knowledge should lead to difficulties distinguishing between two objects irrespective of the fact they belong to the category of non-living things (functional features are of no help in this case). Surprisingly, Michelangelo's performance on this task was well within the normal range, indicating that perceptual knowledge for artefacts was intact and that he did not have a generalised impairment to perceptual knowledge (Sartori & Job, 1988).

The third explanation claims that category-specific impairments for living items arise from the fact these items tend to have many more features in common than non-living things. In the first version of this theory, Riddoch and Humphreys (1987) suggested that the category effect arose because animals share more visual features than artefacts and belong to more structurally similar categories. Recently, a variation of this explanation was proposed by Devlin et al. (1998), who suggested that animals have fewer distinctive features, more common (perceptual) features and more intercorrelated features than non-living things. According to this hypothesis, animals are more vulnerable following brain damage because they have few distinctive features. Experiments conducted on Michelangelo, however, permit us to rule out this explanation. Michelangelo did not show any impairment in detecting distinctive features for objects belonging to sets of visually similar non-living things, such as different types of car or buildings. His problem was not widespread damage to distinctive features but was restricted to categories of living things.

In our first report on Michelangelo, we proposed that he had an impairment to a category- (or domain-) specific visual knowledge system (Sartori & Job, 1988). After extensive further testing this explanation has survived and seems still the most plausible explanation for Michelangelo's performance. Caramazza and Shelton (1998; see Chapter 1) have outlined an evolutionary explanation for the development of such a system. In particular, they suggested that evolutionary pressures have led to specialised, distinct neural substrates for three broad categories of knowledge (animals, plants, and artefacts). There are other reasons why biological categories should have an evolutionary history different to artefacts. Artefacts change rapidly over time with the evolution of culture and the time-frame for such changes is very different to that for natural evolution. These ideas are not, however, essential to our domain-specific hypothesis and the idea remains valid whether or not we agree with the evolutionary explanation.

REFERENCES

Barbarotto, R., Capitani, E., Spinnler, H., & Trivelli, C. (1995). Slowly progressive semantic impairment with category specificity. *Neurocase, 1*, 107–119.

Basso, A., Capitani, E., & Laiacona, M. (1988). Progressive language impairment without dementia: a case study with isolated category-specific semantic defect. *Journal of Neurology, Neurosurgery and Psychiatry, 51*, 1201–1207.

Cappa, S.F., Frugoni, M., Pasquali, P., Perani, D., & Zorat, F. (1998). Category specific naming impairment for artefacts: a new case. *Neurocase, 4*, 391–397.

Caramazza, A., & Shelton, J.R. (1998). Domain-specific knowledge systems in the brain: the animate–inanimate distinction. *Journal of Cognitive Neurosciences, 10*, 1–34.

Chertkow, H., Bub, D., & Caplan, D. (1992). Constraining theories of semantic memory processing: evidence from dementia. *Cognitive Neuropsychology, 9*, 327–365.

Costa, M., De Renzi, E., & Faglioni, P. (1989). Un questionario italiano per lo studio della memoria retrograda. *Archivio di Psicologia, Neurologia e Psichiatria, 50*, 735–755.

Damasio, H., Grabowski, T.J., Tranel, D., Hichwa, R.D., & Damasio, A. (1996). A neural basis for lexical retrieval. *Nature, 380*, 499–505.

Damasio, A., & Van Hoesen, G.W. (1985). The limbic system and the localization of herpes simplex encephalitis. *Journal of Neurology, Neurosurgery and Psychiatry, 48,* 297–301.

Davis, L.E., & Johnson, R.T. (1979). An explanation for the localization of herpes simplex encephalitis. *Annals of Neurology, 5,* 2–5.

De Renzi, E., & Lucchelli, F. (1994). Are semantic systems separately represented in the brain? The case of living category impairment. *Cortex, 30,* 3–25.

Devlin, J.T., Gonnerman, L.M., Andersen, E.S., & Seidenberg, M.S. (1998). Category-specific semantic deficits in focal and widespread brain damage: a computational account. *Journal of Cognitive Neuroscience, 10,* 77–94.

Eco, U. (1997). *Kant e l'ornitorinco.* Milano: Bompiani.

Farah, M.J., Hammond, K., Metha, Z., & Ratcliff, G. (1989). Category specificity and modality specificity in semantic memory. *Neuropsychologia, 27,* 193–200.

Farah, M.J., & McClelland, J. (1991) A computational model of semantic memory impairment: modality specificity and emergent category specificity. *Journal of Experimental Psychology: General, 120,* 339–357.

Farah, M.J., McMullen, P.A. & Meyer, M.M. (1991). Can recognition of living things be selectively impaired? *Neuropsychologia, 29,* 185–193.

Farah, M.J., & Wallace, M.A. (1992). Semantically bounded anomia: implications for the neural implementation of naming. *Neuropsychologia, 30,* 609–621.

Forde, E.M.E., Francis, D., Riddoch, M.J., Rumiati, R.I., & Humphreys, G.W. (1997). On the links between visual knowledge and naming: A single case study of a patient with a category-specific impairment for living things. *Cognitive Neuropsychology, 14,* 403–458.

Funnell, E. & De Mornay Davies, M.P. (1996). JBR: A reassessment of concept familiarity and a category specific disorder for living things. *Neurocase, 2,* 461–474.

Funnell, E., & Sheridan, J. (1992) Categories of knowledge? Unfamiliar aspects of living and non-living things. *Cognitive Neuropsychology, 9,* 135–153

Gainotti, G. (2000). What the locus of brain lesion tells us about the nature of the cognitive defect underlying category-specific disorders: a review. *Cortex, 36,* 539–559.

Gainotti, G., Silveri, M.C., Daniele, A., & Giustolisi, L. (1995). Neuroanatomical correlates of category-specific semantic disorders: a critical survey. *Memory, 3,* 247–264.

Goldenberg, G. (1992). Loss of visual imagery and loss of visual knowledge – A case study. *Neuropsychologia, 30,* 1081–1090.

Hart, J. Jr, & Gordon, B. (1992). Neural subsystem for object knowledge. *Nature, 359,* 60–64.

Hart, J., Bernt, R.S., & Caramazza, A. (1985). Category-specific naming deficit following cerebral infarction. *Nature, 316,* 439–440.

Hillis, A.E., & Caramazza, A. (1991). Category-specific naming and comprehension impairment: A double dissociation. *Brain, 114,* 2081–2094.

Hillis, A.E., & Caramazza, A. (1995). The compositionality of lexical semantic representations: Clues from semantic errors in object naming. *Memory, 3,* 333–358.

Humphreys, G.W., Riddoch, M.J., & Quillian, P.T. (1988). Cascade processes in picture identification. *Cognitive Neuropsychology, 5,* 67–103.

Job, R., Miozzo, M., Sartori, G., & Zago, S. (1991) *On not being able to learn at 50 what you knew as a child: a longitudinal study of a brain-damaged patient.* EST's Longitudinal Networks Summing-up Conference, Budapest, March 21–23.

Job, R., Miozzo, M., & Sartori, G. (1993). On the existence of category-specific impairments. A reply to Parkin and Stewart. *The Quarterly Journal of Experimental Psychology, 46,* 511–516.

Job. R., Miozzo, M., & Sartori, G. (1994). Quando chiamare la sedia 'tavolo' è rilevante per i modelli semantici. Dati neuropsicologici e l'architettura funzionale della memoria semantica. *Archivio di Psicologia, Neurologia e Psichiatria, 55,* 96–120.

Kroll, J.F., & Potter,M.C. (1984). Recognising words, pictures, and concepts: A comparison of lexical, object, and reality decision. *Journal of Verbal Learning and Verbal Behaviour, 23,* 39–66.

Laiacona, M., Barbarotto, R., & Capitani, E. (1993). Perceptual and associative knowledge in category specific impairment of semantic memory: A study of two cases. *Cortex, 29,* 727–740.

Laiacona, M., Capitani, E., & Barbarotto, R. (1997). Semantic category dissociations: A longitudinal study of two cases. *Cortex, 33,* 441–446.

Lambon Ralph, M.A., Howard, D., Nightingale, G., & Ellis, A.W. (1998). Are living and non-living category-specific deficits causally linked to impaired perceptual or associative knowledge? Evidence from a category-specific double dissociation. *Neurocase, 4,* 311–338.

McCarthy, R.A., & Warrington, E.K. (1990). The dissolution of semantics. *Nature, 343,* 599.

Martin, A. Wiggs, C.L. Ungerleider, L.G., & Haxby, J.V. (1996). Neural correlates of category-specific knowledge. *Nature, 379,* 649–652.

Moore, C.J., & Price, C. (1999) A functional neuroimaging study of the variables that generate category specific object processing differences. *Brain, 122,* 943–962.

Moss, H.E., Tyler, L.K., Durrant-Peatfield, M., & Bunn, E.M. (1998). Two eyes of a see-through: impaired and intact semantic semantic knowledge in a case of selective deficits for living things. *Neurocase, 4,* 291–310.

Parkin, A.J., & Stewart, F. (1993). Category-specific impairments? No. A critique of Sartori et al. *Quarterly Journal of Experimental Psychology, 46,* 505–509.

Patterson, K., & Hodges, J.R. (1995). Disorders of semantic memory. In: A.D. Baddeley, B.A. Wilson, B.A., & Watts, F.N. (Eds.), *Handbook of memory disorders.* Chichester: John Wiley.

Perani, D., Cappa, S.F., Bettinardi, V., Bressi, S., Gorno-Tempini, M., Matarrese, M., & Fazio, F. (1995). Different neural systems for the recognition of animals and man-made tools. *NeuroReport, 6,* 1637–1641.

Pietrini, V., Nertempi, P., Vaglia, A., Revello, M.G., Pinna, V., & Ferro-Milone, F. (1988). Recovery from herpes simplex encephalitis: Selective impairment of specific semantic categories with neuroradiological correlation. *Journal of Neurology, Neurosurgery and Psychiatry, 51,* 1284–1293.

Powell, J., & Davidoff, J. (1995). Selective impairments of objects knowledge in a case of acquired cortical blindness. *Memory, 3,* 435–461.

Price, C.J., & Humphreys, G.W. (1989) The effects of surface detail on object categorisation and naming. *Quarterly Journal of Experimental Psychology, 41A,* 797–828

Quillian, M.R. (1968). Semantic memory. In: M. Minsky (Ed.), *Semantic information processing.* Cambridge, MA: MIT Press.

Rapp, B.C., & Caramazza, A. (1993). On the distinction between deficits of access and deficits of storage: A question of theory. *Cognitive Neuropsychology, 10,* 114–142.

Riddoch, M.J., & Humphreys, G.W. (1987). Visual object processing in optic aphasia: A case of semantic access agnosia. *Cognitive Neuropsychology, 4,* 131–185.

Sacchett, C., & Humphreys, G.W. (1992). Calling a squirrel a squirrel but a canoe a wigwam: A category specific deficit for artefactual objects and body parts. *Cognitive Neuropsychology, 9,* 73–86.

Sartori, G., & Job, R. (1988). The oyster with four legs: a neuropsychological study on the interaction of visual and semantic information. *Cognitive Neuropsychology, 5,* 105–132.

Sartori, G., Job, R., & Coltheart, M. (1993a). The organisation of object knowledge: Evidence from neuropsychology. In D.E. Meyer & S. Kornblum (Eds.), *Attention and performance XIV: Synergies in experimental psychology, artificial intelligence, and cognitive neuroscience.* Cambridge, MA: MIT Press.

Sartori, G., Job, R. Miozzo, M., Zago, S., & Marchiori, G. (1993b). Category specific form knowledge deficit in a patient with herpes simplex virus encephalitis. *Journal of Clinical and Experimental Neuropsychology, 15,* 280–299.

Sartori, G., Miozzo, M., & Job, R. (1993c). Category-specific naming impairments? Yes. *The Quarterly Journal of Experimental Psychology, 46,* 489–504.

Sartori, G., Miozzo, M., Zago, S., & Job, R. (1991) *Category-specific word finding impairment.* Presented at the 29th Annual Meeting of the Academy of Aphasia, Rome, October 13–15.

Sartori, G., & Umiltà, C.A. (2000). How to avoid the fallacies of cognitive subtraction in brain imaging. *Brain and Language, 74*, 191–212.

Sartori, G., Zago, S., & Miozzo, M. (1990). *Selective impairment of perceptual knowledge: further investigation.* Presented at the European Brain and Behaviour Society Workshop in Cognitive Neuroscience, Padua, May 24–26, 1990.

Sergent, J., Otha, S., & MacDonald, B. (1992). Functional neuroanatomy of face and object processing. A positron emission tomography study. *Brain, 115*, 15–36.

Shallice, T. (1988). Specialisation within the semantic system. *Cognitive Neuropsychology, 5*, 133–142.

Sheridan, J., & Humphreys, G.W. (1993). A verbal-semantic category-specific recognition impairment. *Cognitive Neuropsychology, 10*, 143–184.

Silveri, M.C., & Gainotti, G. (1988). Interaction between vision and language in category-specific semantic impairment. *Cognitive Neuropsychology, 5*, 677–709.

Sirigu, A., Duhamel, J.R., & Poncet, M. (1991). The role of sensori-motor experience in object recognition. A case of multimodal agnosia. *Brain, 114*, 2555–2573.

Snodgrass, J.G., & Vanderwart, M. (1980). A standardised set of 260 pictures: Norms for name agreements, image agreements, familiarity, and visual complexity. *Journal of Experimental Psychology: Human Learning and Memory, 6*, 174–215.

Stewart, F., Parkin, A.J., & Hunkin, N.M. (1992). Naming impairments following recovery from herpes simplex encephalitis: Category specific? *The Quarterly Journal of Experimental Psychology, 44*, 261–284.

Temple, C.M. (1986). Anomia for animals in a child. *Brain, 109*, 1225–1242.

Tyler, L.K., Durrant-Peatfield, M.R., Levy, J.P., Voice, J.K., & Moss, H.E. (1996). Distinctiveness and correlations in the structure of categories: Behavioural data and a connectionist model. *Brain and Language, 55*, 89–91

Tulving, E. (1972) Episodic and semantic memory. In E.Tulving & W. Donaldson (Eds.), *Organisation of memory.* New York: Academic Press.

Warrington, E.K. (1975). The selective impairment of semantic memory. *Quarterly Journal of Experimental Psychology, 27*, 635–657.

Warrington, E.K. (1984). *Recognition memory test.* Windsor, UK: NFER-Nelson.

Warrington, E.K., & McCarthy, R.A. (1987). Categories of knowledge: Further fractionation and an attempt at an integration. *Brain, 110*, 1273–1296

Warrington, E.K., & Shallice, T. (1979) Semantic access dyslexia. *Brain, 102*, 43–63

Warrington, E., & Shallice, T. (1984). Category-specific semantic impairments. *Brain, 107*, 829–854.

CHAPTER THREE

The principle of target–competitor differentiation in object recognition and naming (and its role in category effects in normality and pathology)

Glyn W. Humphreys, M. Jane Riddoch
Behavioural Brain Sciences Centre, University of Birmingham, UK

Emer M.E. Forde
Neurosciences Research Institute, Aston University, Birmingham, UK

INTRODUCTION

For both normal subjects and patients with selective brain lesions, objects belonging to some categories can be particularly hard to recognise and/or to name (for reviews see Caramazza, 1998; Forde, 1999; Forde & Humphreys, 1999; Humphreys & Forde, 2001; Saffran & Schwartz, 1994). Numerous accounts have been offered to explain why these differences in recognition and naming occur, illustrated by the other chapters in this book and discussed in some detail below. In this chapter, we propose that category effects can be determined by a principle of information processing that we term target–competitor differentiation. We argue that processes of response selection, in general, require that target stimuli be differentiated sufficiently from competitors. Differentiation operates dynamically, across time, and concurrently at different levels of representation; in this way, processing at one level can constrain differentiation at other levels. Thus one given process (e.g. name selection) can be facilitated by recruiting information from different sources if it aids the differentiation between a target and its competitors. We argue that differentiation for name selection can draw on various types of information, including functional associations as well as perceptual contrasts between stimuli, and that the differentiation process has pervasive effects on both the nature of our stored representations and on the processes recruited when different tasks are performed. We discuss the implications of target–competitor differentiation for object recognition and naming in both normality and pathology, and the relations between our account and other proposals in the literature.

OBJECT RECOGNITION AND NAMING, AND TARGET–COMPETITOR DIFFERENTATION

We begin by reviewing the processes involved in visual object recognition and naming, in part because these processes usefully illustrate the role of target–competitor differentiation in response selection, and in part because many examples in the literature draw on recognition and naming tasks. We do not wish the points we make, however, to be limited to one modality or one set of processes. We contend that the principle of target–competitor differentiation determines processing across different modalities and a large variety of tasks (although the nature of the differentiation process itself will vary as a function of the sensory representation of stimuli and the kinds of information needed for task performance).

Consider the task of naming a line drawing of a fox—a common enough test used to probe recognition and naming in many neurological patients. One minimal (indeed simplistic) account of this task is that it calls on three processes: (i) the computation of a perceptual description of the stimulus; (ii) the matching of this description with a memory representation of the object; and (iii) the retrieval of a name associated with the perceptual representation of the stimulus in memory. However, even were these the only processes involved, the efficiency with which they are achieved will be determined by a wide variety of factors. These factors will lead to differences between how quickly a fox might be named when compared with other moderately common objects (e.g. a tin opener).

To illustrate the factors that determined object naming we take each putative process in turn, starting with the computation of a perceptual description.

Computing perceptual descriptions

This process almost certainly does not happen in a single step, but rather takes place dynamically, over time. There are consequences of this. For instance, low-spatial-frequency components in an image are processed more rapidly than high-spatial-frequency components (Sergent, 1987), so that the global shape of an object (expressed in the low-spatial-frequency components) may be realised more rapidly than the local details (conveyed by high-spatial-frequency components). The likelihood that each local part of an object is coded at any given time also varies, with more parts being coded as processing time lengthens (Lamberts & Freeman, 1999). Thus different types of information will emerge across time, and this emerging information can be used continuously to gain access to the memory representation of the object (Lamberts & Freeman, 1999; Riddoch & Humphreys, 1987a). The way that perceptual descriptions are computed over time constrains the naming process. The quality of the perceptual information available will also impact on access to memory. Line drawings are relatively impoverished representations of objects, whereas real objects have colour, texture, depth, and physical size information available, and these other properties can be realised in a perceptual description and used to access memory representations.

Now consider the process of matching the perceptual description to a stored memory representation. There are two issues we wish to highlight here: the effects of perceptual similarity on this matching process, and the form that the memory representation may take (itself depending on factors such as perceptual similarity).

Matching to memory

The impact of perceptual similarity.   Objects vary in their perceptual similarity relative to other objects. A fox has a similar perceptual structure to other animals—a dog, a wolf, a cat, a sheep, a horse, and so forth. The similarity is based partly on global shape, partly on local parts (e.g. the shape of the tail). Now, in accessing memory on the basis of a perceptual description, representations of stimuli with similar perceptual structures also become activated, as well as the representation of the target. This is evidenced by the effects of visual similarity on the errors people make when identifying and acting on objects under deadline conditions, and by effects of similarity on object categorisation under time pressure (see Lamberts & Freeman, 1999; Rumiati & Humphreys, 1998; Vitkovitch & Humphreys, 1991). Also, as information about global shape and local parts can emerge over different time courses, so the memory access process might be sensitive to contrasting forms of similarity over time. If global shape is computed early-on, then similarity of global shape may initially be conveyed, with similarity determined by common local parts emerging later in time.[1]

A task such as object naming requires that a unique label is applied to an object, distinguishing this "target" from others. For such a task, activation in the representations of objects other than the target provides competition for the target gaining access to its unique label. The greater the competition, the longer it will take to derive the unique label (see Humphreys, Lamote, & Lloyd-Jones, 1995, for some simulations). If objects from different categories

---

[1] Another view is that local parts are computed independently over time (see Chapter 10; Lamberts & Freeman, 1999). Early-on, then, similarity will be based on the few parts computed (even if global shapes differ). Effects of similarity of global shape may then only occur later in time, when more parts are computed and overlap across all the parts may determine similarity.

vary in their perceptual similarity with one another, then this will impact on their naming times; objects will be more difficult to name if they belong to categories with high levels of perceptual similarity. However, perceptual similarity need not always have a detrimental impact on performance. For tasks that draw on information that is common to category members, perceptual similarity should have a positive effect because activation across different object representations can be mapped onto the same response. Other things being equal, then, when similarity is high, there will be more evidence for this response than when similarity is low and fewer representations are activated.

Humphreys, Riddoch, and Quinlan (1988) derived measures of perceptual similarity between objects in two ways. They had subjects list the number of common parts across different categories of object, and they also computed the amount of contour overlap between category members based on the outlines of standardised and size-normalised drawings of objects. This last procedure gives one measure of the similarity of global shape, whereas listings of common parts may reflect the similarity of more local parts. Humphreys et al. found that, on both measures, living things tended to have higher levels of perceptual similarity, relative to other members of the same category, than non-living things. Lamberts & Shapiro (see Chapter 10) report similar findings from ratings of perceptual similarity, and from a study merely requiring same–different responses based on physical identity—it is harder to reject as "different" two randomly paired living things than two randomly paired non-living things. Based on the factor of perceptual similarity alone, then, we might expect differences between living things and non-living things across a range of tasks requiring object processing. In particular, access to individual names should be slower for living things than for non-living things. This has been found in studies with normal subjects (Humphreys et al., 1988; Snodgrass & Yuditsky, 1996). Similar evidence has even been found in studies of discrimination learning with monkeys. Gaffan & Heywood (1993) found that the monkeys took longer to learn individual responses associated with pictures of living things than with pictures of non-living things, with the category effect increasing as the number of stimuli in the set increased. This work provides converging evidence for the idea that living things have high levels of perceptual overlap, that impacts negatively on tasks in which responses have to be linked to individual category members.

On the other hand, access to common information across category members should be faster for living than for non-living things. This too has been shown in studies measuring superordinate classification decisions and the time to access common functional properties of objects (Humphreys, Price, & Riddoch, 1999; Riddoch & Humphreys, 1987a; Tyler & Moss, 1997). Now, it could be argued that the advantage for living things in tasks such as superordinate classification is due to their belonging to relatively well-formed (and well-known) "natural" categories, whereas non-living things belong to arbitrary categories. Responses to living things are faster because they have stronger associations with their category labels. There is some reason for arguing this, and classification responses to living things are faster than to non-living things even when words are presented, when effects of physical similarity should be lessened. Nevertheless, the advantage for living things is increased when stimuli are presented pictorially (Job, Rumiati, & Lotto, 1992). These results are consistent with the effects of perceptual similarity on matching to memory.

The nature of stored knowledge.   In addition to the impact of perceptual similarity on the online processing of objects, we suggest that it will have additional effects on the nature of our stored knowledge. In particular, consider the point we raised above, concerning the effects on recognition and naming of perceptual information additional to object shape—such as colour, texture, and size. For objects that have high levels of overlap in form, these additional perceptual cues might be very useful for differentiating a target from its competitors; there is empirical evidence for this assertion. The time to name and categorise objects is faster if congruent colour and texture cues are present (e.g. in photographs and coloured drawings), and this effect is larger for living things than for non-living things (Price & Humphreys, 1989; Tanaka & Presnell, 1999). Because of the useful role played by these additional cues in the identification of living things, the cues could come to be "weighted" within our stored representations, and more strongly weighted for living than for non-living things. In most learning algorithms there is a process of "credit assignment", with stronger reinforcement for information that leads to successful response selection (see Rumelhart, Hinton, & Williams [1986] for one example). Due to credit assignment, the "weights" that make up the stored representations for living and non-living things will differ. It also turns out to be the case that one "type" of living thing will tend to have the same colour and texture whenever encountered—bananas will be yellow, cabbages green, zebras striped, foxes rust-coloured, and so forth. This is not the case for many non-living things (objects such as telephone booths and taxis, which do tend to have the same colour in the same city, are the exception rather than the rule). Thus colour and texture do not only help to differentiate a living thing from its competitors, they are also reliable cues; they can be diagnostic of the identity of living things (Tanaka & Presnell, 1999). For this reason, too, colour and texture might be more strongly weighted in the representations of living things than in those of non-living things. The main point to come away with is that properties such as perceptual similarity will affect not only online access to memory but also the nature of the memory representations themselves (which properties are strongly weighted, which are not).

Name retrieval (and name learning)

Having matched an object to memory, we must remember the arbitrary label associated with the particular object in order to assign it a name. At first sight, this would appear to be a matter of simple stimulus–response learning. Once the shape, colour, and other diagnostic properties of a fox are learned, an associative link can be set up so that we give the stimulus the name "fox". The effectiveness of this link could depend on factors such as the frequency of occurrence of the name (Jescheniak & Levelt, 1994), and names that occur frequently should develop stronger weights between their stored perceptual memories and their names.

However, several new issues arise at this juncture. One is whether name selection requires that perceptual processing is completed before selection is begun, or whether selection is more continuous, being constrained directly as perceptual (and other) properties of objects are processed over time. This is the question of whether name selection is continuous or discrete. We return to this question after first considering the kinds of stored knowledge that may facilitate name selection.

To address this second issue, consider the topic of generalisation. How do we know to give a different picture of a fox the same label? Two general approaches to this question have been suggested. One is to store more memory representations, so that we maintain multiple perceptual templates for objects, each of which may be associated with the same name (Edelman & Duvdevani-Bar, 1997; Tarr & Bulthoff, 1995). Another is to store a more abstract representation that captures what we might think of as the "perceptual essence" of a fox—this will specify features that are invariant across different occurrences of the object (perhaps its overall volumetric shape or the shape and relative positions of its parts; see Biederman [1987]; Marr [1982]). This single representation may then be linked to the appropriate name ("fox").

We are not committed to either of these views of stored perceptual representations, but the argument about the "essence" of the fox does allow us to broaden the notion of memory representation beyond the domain of perception. For example, let us return to our earlier example of a tin opener. Tin openers, even more than foxes, come in many shapes, sizes, and colours (Figure 3.1). The "perceptual essence" of a tin opener is relatively hard to define. On the other hand, tin openers all perform the same function: they cut into a tin and they can be used in a rotating action to open the tin. The "essence" of a tin opener is perhaps not its shape, which can vary considerably across exemplars, but its function. To assign an object the name "tin opener", it could be useful to draw on learned associations with the actions that are performed with it—differentiating between the target and its competitors using functional as well as perceptual information. This example

Figure 3.1.   Example tin openers, with perceptually different structures.

illustrates that the idea of differentiation applies to more than the use of perceptual information to enable an object to be linked to a unique response; we hold that non-perceptual, associative knowledge is recruited if it facilitates the process.

   If non-perceptual information can be drawn upon in object naming, then the naming process could be determined by more than an association between a stored perceptual representation of an object and its name (and by more than the three simple processes we initially suggested—computing a perceptual description, accessing a perceptual memory, and retrieving a name). Indeed, the link between perceptual knowledge and a name could normally be modulated by functional and other forms of associative (non-perceptual) information, to help differentiate between objects. The involvement of non-perceptual knowledge can have general utility for learning object names, as children acquire a vocabulary. Generalisation of a name across different learning encounters will depend on those aspects of the environment that stay constant. While this might often be the perceptual characteristics of an object, it is not necessarily the case. Generalisation of the name "tin opener" might well come about not through seeing two exemplars that are visually rather different but by seeing the two objects being used in the same way. Indeed, some evidence for a strong role of functional information in vocabulary learning was reported by Humphreys and Riddoch (1999), in a case study of a child with learning difficulty. They had the child learn names to tools under two conditions: (i) the tools were presented along with contextual information consistent with where the object would be found (e.g. a picture of a knife shown alongside a table with a place setting); (ii) the tools were presented along with a gestured action by the experimenter (e.g. a cutting action, for the knife). On each presentation of the object, the child was told its name. After the learning trials, the child was presented with pictures of the target objects and she was asked to remember the names. Humphreys and Riddoch found that name learning was substantially better when the tools were initially seen concurrently with their actions than when seen concurrently with their contexts. This suggests that knowledge about the actions linked to the objects could facilitate both name learning and retrieval, perhaps by helping to differentiate between the different tools.

Having associative knowledge modulate name retrieval will also be useful in another way for learning names, because this knowledge can be used to link perceptual representations with names across different learning situations. For instance, in one situation a name might be linked to a verbal description about the activity of an animal ("the fox has been hunting the chickens again!"). In another, a child might see the animal carrying out that very function (the fox, hunting chickens). The functional knowledge about the object will enable associations to be established between the perceptual memory (what the fox looks like) and the name (/fox/), although the child did not experience the two together. For instance, by means of Hebbian learning, reactivation of the same functional knowledge on the second occasion will partially activate the perceptual description or the name (whichever is not available at the time), enabling the weights to this knowledge to increase too (see Pulvermuller [1999] for a discussion of the role of Hebbian learning in this context). The factors that determine name learning, and their relation to category effects in naming, are dealt with in Chapters 11, 12 and 13.

This argument, for a modulatory role of functional (and perhaps other forms of associative) knowledge in object naming, is consistent with the majority of evidence on naming in normal subjects and in brain-lesioned patients. As we have pointed out, when normal subjects have to name objects within a response deadline, they often make errors that are visually related to the objects (Vitkovitch & Humphreys, 1991; Vitkovitch, Humphreys, & Lloyd-Jones, 1993), However, the errors are rarely only visually related; far more frequently the errors are both visually and semantically related (e.g. reflecting another object that is visually related to the target, but also from within the same category; fox—dog; tin opener—bottle opener). This is consistent with a set of visual competitors initially being activated, but with this set constrained by semantic information derived from the target. In addition, if there were direct links between stored perceptual descriptions and names, not modulated by associative knowledge, then we would expect there to be patients with poor associative knowledge but who can still name objects (who could name a picture of a fox but not know that it is a wild animal that hunts). The evidence for this, at least at present, is weak (Hodges & Greene, 1998, although see Brennen, Danielle, Fluchaire, & Pellat, 1996).

Now, if name selection is influenced by functional as well as perceptual information derived from objects, models need to be clear on how this joint influence might come about. One important question was raised at the beginning of this section; does name selection operate as a discrete process, after access to perceptual and functional knowledge has been completed, or does selection operate continuously over time? To our mind, there is much to be said for having processing operate continuously between levels. For instance, in a model with continuous processing, perceptual similarity will constrain access to functional knowledge in a direct way, rather than functional knowledge being derived solely from the object that "wins" the competition for access to perceptual memory. We have suggested that objects with similar perceptual structures gain fast access to common functional representations, and we have noted empirical evidence consistent with this (Humphreys, Riddoch, & Price, 1997; Tyler & Moss, 1997). This is in accord with information being transmitted between perceptual and functional representations in a continuous fashion, and continuous processing could well be a means for gathering biologically relevant information quickly. Such a continuous approach can also explain why visual as well as semantic similarity determines naming errors under deadline conditions (mentioned earlier; Vitkovtich et al., 1993). Functional and name information for objects is constrained by the initial set of visual competitors activated by perceptual descriptions as they are computed over time.

PERCEPTUAL AND FUNCTIONAL KNOWLEDGE ACROSS DIFFERENT CATEGORIES

We have argued that generalisation of names is dependent on which properties of an object are relatively constant across different situations and exemplars, and which properties are variable. These properties will also change across object categories. As indicated by our examples of the fox and the tin opener, the perceptual properties of living things tend to be relatively constant; the perceptual properties of non-living things less so. The functional properties of non-living things, however, might be relatively constant. In addition to this, an important point is that these constant, functional properties of non-living things can also uniquely specify the name of the object. Only a tin opener opens tins! For this reason, the functional properties of non-living things might be strongly weighted within the representations linking the objects to their names. For living things, perceptual properties might carry relatively more weight, given their utility for generalisation. Of course, there is likely to be even finer gradations of knowledge representation than this. For example, the kinds of perceptual knowledge that are weighted may differ for animals, fruits, and vegetables—depending on the similarity of their perceptual structure (e.g. colour and texture may be more important for fruits and vegetables, which tend to have highly overlapping forms). Similarly, the particular functional associations that are weighted strongly will vary across non-living things. Tools should have particularly strong associations with hand actions, vehicles with motion, etc. There should be a gradation of weightings across different types of perceptual and non-perceptual knowledge that determines the representations of different object classes, and individual objects within these classes.

According to the principle of differentiation for response selection, there is a second reason for the stronger weighting of perceptual than functional knowledge for the naming of living things (additional to its utility for generalisation). This relates to the way that perceptual similarity constrains object recognition. We argued earlier that living things tend to be more similar than non-living things, both in terms of their overall global shapes and in terms of their common parts. Given the way that perceptual descriptions are derived over time, the initial retrieval of non-perceptual (associative, functional) knowledge from living things is likely to be driven by common global information. This common input will produce rapid access to shared forms of knowledge (e.g. that the animal eats, breathes, runs etc.), and will delay access (because of competition) to more precise associative and functional knowledge. Hence the functional knowledge that is accessed early-on might not provide the differentiation needed for naming. Because of factors such as credit assignment in learning, functional knowledge will not be strongly reinforced for naming; rather, reinforcement should be based on those perceptual attributes that eventually differentiate both relevant functional and name information.

Warrington and Shallice (1984) were among the first to argue that perceptual and functional knowledge might be differentially important for the identification of living and non-living things. Subsequently, Farah and McClelland (1991) gathered listings of the properties by asking subjects to mark the visual and functional attributes in dictionary definitions of living and non-living things. For living things they found that far more visual attributes than functional attributes were marked. In contrast, roughly equal numbers of visual and functional attributes were marked for non-living things. This supports the idea that perceptual properties are more strongly weighted than functional properties in the representations of living things, whereas this bias is reduced for non-living things. Caramazza and Shelton (1998) criticised Farah & McClelland's method, pointing out that the definition of "functional attribute" (what is the object used for?) reduced the assignment of functional attributes to living things, because their functional attributes concern self-generated activities (eating, breathing, running), not their use as instruments. However, other investigators have attempted to overcome these problems by having subjects themselves list properties for objects, and largely similar findings have resulted. McRae, de Sa, and Seidenberg (1997), for example, found that, whereas sensory properties were listed with roughly equal frequency for living and non-living things, there were significantly more non-sensory features (e.g. used for carpentry, worn by women) for non-living things (see also Chapter 8). The nature of our representations seems to differ for living and non-living things. The contrasting representations can be linked to the process of differentiation for naming, especially when considered within the context of generalisation and credit assignment in learning.

TASK EFFECTS REVISITED

Effects of modality

We have proposed that effects of perceptual similarity will vary according to the task that subjects are asked to do. Tasks requiring assignment of separate responses to individual category members (such as naming) will be negatively affected by perceptual similarity; tasks requiring common responses to made to category members (such as superordinate classification) will be positively affected. To the extent that different categories vary in their perceptual similarity, then "category effects" will emerge.

Our discussion has been confined to the consideration of object recognition and naming. But what if words rather than objects are presented, and subjects are asked to answer questions about the properties of the objects that the words correspond to? Quite diverse views have been expressed in the literature about the impact of input modality on accessing knowledge about objects. Some authors have argued that different memory stores represent knowledge about objects, according to the modality of the input stimulus—there are separate stores of perceptual knowledge accessed by objects and by words, separate stores of functional knowledge accessed by objects and by words, and so forth (e.g. McCarthy & Warrington, 1994; Warrington, 1975; see Riddoch, Humphreys, Coltheart, & Funnell [1988] for some discussion). Other authors have argued that the same knowledge is accessed across different modalities, so that (for example) the same store of perceptual knowledge will be called upon if the task requires verification of the perceptual properties of an object, both when objects and when words are presented (e.g. to answer a probe such as the word "red?", when given either the word "fox" or a black and white line drawing of a fox) (Beauvois, 1982; Caramazza, Hillis, Rapp, & Romani, 1990; Riddoch et al., 1988; Shallice, 1988). Our view is close to the latter. But, in addition, we propose that some forms of knowledge can be recruited even when a task does not apparently require that knowledge. One example of this is object naming. We have suggested that object naming can recruit functional associations that an actor has with objects, and that this functional information can help differentiate between a target and its competitors to facilitate name retrieval. However, as illustrated by our initial, simple three-process account, object naming does not logically require access to any other stored knowledge besides a perceptual memory and a name.

This same argument will hold for other tasks. Take questions that address associative knowledge about animals, such as "do penguins live in cold climates?". We have pointed out that perceptual representations capture the "essence" of many individual living things, because: (i) these representations enable generalisation to occur in naming; and (ii) perceptual differentiation is necessary to retrieve detailed functional as well as name information about living things, so that perceptual information will be strongly weighted in learning. Consequently, perceptual representations might be recruited even when associative questions are asked about such stimuli. The recruitment of perceptual representations is less likely when the same questions are asked about non-living things, because strongly weighted functional representations should then support task performance.

Data from studies using functional brain imaging are relevant to these claims. Several investigators have evaluated the brain regions that are activated when subjects name tools, comparing performance either to when they name living things (e.g. animals) or relative to "lower level" baseline tasks (e.g. passive viewing of non-object stimuli). Martin, Wiggs, Ungerleider, and Haxby (1996), in a PET study, found that naming tools selectively activated the left middle temporal gyrus and the left inferior region—areas very similar to those activated when subjects name actions associated with objects (Martin et al., 1995) or when they imagine grasping objects (Decety et al., 1994). Overlap in left inferior frontal areas between tasks involving the naming of tools and verb generation to tools has also been reported (e.g. Grabowski, Damasio, & Damasio, 1998; Grafton, Fadiga, Arbib, & Rizzolatti, 1997). These results are consistent with the idea that activating information about object use and the associated motor action is important for naming tools.

Studies relevant to the issue of whether the same knowledge sources are activated by words and pictures as input have been conducted by Chao, Haxby, and Martin (1999) and by Thompson-Schill, Aguirre, D'Esposito, and Farah (1999). Thompson-Schill et al. (1999) had subjects answer yes–no questions about the visual and functional properties of living and non-living things, and fMRI was used to assess whether a region of interest in the left fusiform gyrus was activated in each condition, relative to a baseline condition in which nonsense auditory stimuli were presented. The left fusiform gyrus was chosen as the area of interest because previous studies have shown that it is involved in representing the visual properties of objects (D'Esposito et al., 1997; Martin et al., 1995). Thompson-Schill et al. found that there was a significant interaction between category (living versus non-living) and type of question (visual versus functional). The left fusiform gyrus was activated only by the questions requiring retrieval of visual knowledge for non-living things; however, it was activated by *both* the visual and functional questions for living things. This suggests that visual knowledge is recruited even when functional knowledge must be retrieved for living things.

Chao et al. (1999) have also reported overlapping activation within the lateral fusiform gyrus both when animals are named from pictures and when subjects name and retrieve meanings from words (e.g. to answer the question, "forest animal?" with the word "deer"). There was also overlap across modalities for tools, but in different areas—the middle fusiform gyrus and middle temporal gyrus. The regions implicated in the study by Chao et al. have previously been linked to the processing of form (lateral fusiform gyrus) and motion (middle fusiform and temporal areas) (Bonda, Petrides, Ostry, & Evans, 1996; Ungerleider & Haxby, 1994). Hence the findings are consistent with specific forms of knowledge being drawn on to different degrees when accessing stored knowledge about living and non-living things, and that these forms of knowledge are organised around brain regions associated with visual/perceptual coding and action. That brain areas are recruited to facilitate the differentiation between target representations and their competitors is further indicated in a PET study by Gerlach, Law, Gade, and Paulson (1999), who had subjects carry out object decision tasks with living and non-living things and varied the difficulty of the task by manipulating the similarity of the non-objects to real objects. They found that living things activated larger areas within the right inferior temporal and anterior fusiform gyri than non-living things, and, importantly, that this effect increased when the non-objects were structurally similar to real objects. Gerlach et al. argue that the right inferior temporal and anterior fusiform activations reflect the degree of perceptual differentiation needed for objects to access stored visual memories. The amount of differentiation required is increased for living things compared with non-living things.

One other interesting point is that Chao et al. (1999) reported some variation within the categories of living and non-living items (e.g. between houses, tools, and chairs). This in turn suggests that varying kinds of knowledge are important in the representation of each type of stimulus (e.g. houses, although non-living, are not associated with activation of the middle temporal gyrus, which is linked to movement). More discussion of the evidence on category effects from studies of functional imaging is provided by Price and Friston in Chapter 15.

Top-down processing for naming: The Hierarchical Interactive Theory (HIT)

We argued ealier that there can be differences between the information recruited during the processing of living and non-living things, with these differences emerging as a function of the modality of presentation (e.g. with perceptual knowledge being drawn on for living things, even with verbal input). We have also argued, prior to this, that perceptual knowledge is likely to play a more dominant role in the naming of living things than in the naming of non-living things. We now wish to return to this last issue, to consider this dominant role for perceptual knowledge in more detail.

As a result of the way in which perceptual descriptions are derived over time, the earliest (global) information derived from living things will tend to be shared across category members. Assignment of an individual response to such stimuli will thus be contingent on the encoding of sufficient perceptual cues to differentiate the target from its competitors. There are two ways in which this might occur. One is that name assignment simply waits until perceptual coding is completed, in a bottom-up manner. We presume that this will also delay access to precise functional information. An alternative is that, following a first pass in processing, additional perceptual information is recruited in a top-down manner to help differentiate between stimuli. This latter view asserts that more perceptual information might actually be derived to name an object than to derive functional information about it.

A PET study completed by Price et al. (1996) is relevant to this issue. They had subjects perform four tasks: (1) name (coloured) objects; (2) name the colour of non-objects (matched to the object for complexity); (3) say "yes" to the coloured objects (the object baseline); and (4) say "yes" to the coloured non-objects (the non-object baseline). They argued that the contrast between the two baseline conditions (say "yes" to objects and non-objects) can reveal areas involved in object recognition (activated by objects but not by equally complex non-objects). The brain regions mediating name retrieval could be indicated by the contrasts between the two naming conditions (conditions 1 and 2) relative to the two "say yes" baselines (both the naming tasks required retrieval of a stored phonological label associated with the visual stimulus). Of most relevance here, though, is the interaction based on the difference between the object naming condition and its baseline (conditions 1 minus 3) relative to that between the non-object colour naming condition and its baseline (conditions 2 minus 4). This interaction indicates areas associated with retrieving the names of known objects from vision. Price et al. found that this interaction was linked to selective activation of the left inferior and posterior temporal lobe. They concluded that this region is particularly involved in name retrieval for known objects, and it is more activated in name retrieval than in object recognition alone. The same area has also been found to be activated more by animals than by tools (Martin et al., 1996; Perani et al., 1995). We suggest that, to name animals, there needs to be greater top-down activation of perceptual knowledge relative to when the task involves naming tools.

This argument for top-down recruitment of extra perceptual information, for naming, has been articulated in the "Hierarchical Interactive Theory" (HIT) of object recognition and naming recently presented by Humphreys and Forde (2001). This theory has two main assumptions: (i) that there exists a hierarchy of stored representations that are activated en route to object naming. This hierarchy incorporates stored associative and functional knowledge in addition to stored perceptual descriptions (Figure 3.2); and (ii) that activation of the representations can take place in a top-down as well as a bottom-up manner. In the arguments presented here, we have tried to illustrate how, for living things in particular, top-down recruitment of perceptual knowledge emerges from the principle of differentiation between target and nontarget representations, for name assignment.

RELATIONS TO OTHER ACCOUNTS

Our proposals are similar to several other accounts of category-specific differences in object processing. For example, several authors have argued that perceptual and functional knowledge vary in their importance for the recognition of, respectively living and non-living things (Warrington & Shallice, 1984). These accounts, like our own, hold that the recognition of living things will be selectively disrupted by damage to stored perceptual representations, whereas recognition of non-living things will be associated with damage to stored functional knowledge (see Farah & McClelland, 1991, for simulations). The principle of perceptual differentiation provides one way of understanding how the selective importance of perceptual and functional knowledge may come about for different categories.

Another related approach is provided by the Organised Unitary Content Hypothesis (OUCH) model of semantic memory, suggested by Caramazza et al. (1990). OUCH does not differentiate different types of stored knowledge; both perceptual and functional (action-related) properties are said to be stored within a single semantic system. The model assumes, however, that salient parts of objects directly activate corresponding functional attributes in semantic memory (e.g. the prongs and handle of a fork activate corresponding associative knowledge of object usage). This direct activation of action-related information from the parts of the object leads to privileged access to semantic memory for objects relative to words (cf. Potter & Faulconer, 1975). In addition, non-living things can benefit particularly from this because they enjoy a higher degree of correlation between their perceptual and functional features. De Renzi and Lucchelli (1994) made a similar

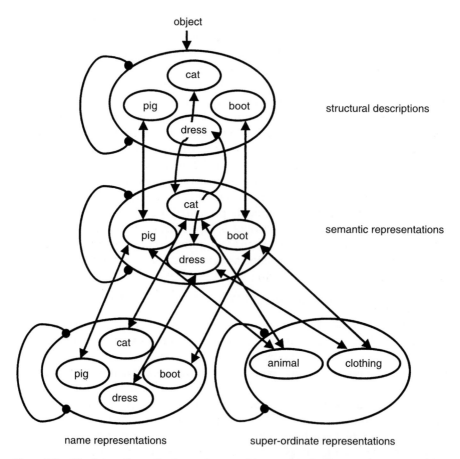

Figure 3.2.   The interactive activation and competition model of object naming proposed by Humphreys et al. (1995). → indicates excitatory links and ─● inhibitory links. This model incorporates two of the basic principles of the HIT framework: functionally isolatable subsystems (e.g. separating perceptual knowledge about objects [in the structural description system] from other forms of stored knowledge), and interactive processing (top-down as well as bottom-up).

argument, suggesting also that, for non-living things, perceptual and functional knowledge could interact. Hence functional cues could "help specify hypotheses on the nature of the stimulus" (DeRenzi & Lcchelli, 1994, p. 20). This process should be unavailable for living things, which have few links between perceptual and functional knowledge.

Both De Renzi and Lucchelli's account and the OUCH model emphasise the importance of correlations *between* perceptual and functional properties of objects. Other authors, though, have postulated that correlations *within* sets of sensory and/or functional features are also useful for object recognition. McRae et al. (1997; see Chapter 8), using feature lists generated by normal subjects, have pointed out that, for living things, a smaller set of common features captures more of their listed properties than is the case for non-living things. They argue that correlations between the small set of features are useful for retrieving common information relevant to living things (e.g. their category, their common functional properties), but not for deriving individual name responses—much as we have argued from the principle of differentiation. Moss, Tyler, and colleagues (Durrant-Peatfield, Tyler, Moss, & Levy, 1997; Moss, Tyler, Durrant-Peatfield, & Bunn, 1998; Moss, Tyler, & Jennings, 1997; Tyler & Moss, 1997) take a related position, but they highlight one further factor: the contrast between features correlated across category members and those that distinguish between category members. For living things, the correlated perceptual features are associated with common biological functions, which do not distinguish individual exemplars. The distinctive perceptual features of living things, on the other hand, individuate these stimuli but tend not to be related to the functional capabilities of the objects. In contrast to this, non-living things have distinctive perceptual features that are correlated with their function in terms of action (e.g. the serrated edge of a saw, the prongs of a fork). These differences in how correlated and distinctive features link to object function will lead to item-specific functional information being easier to recover for non-living things (and, we might add, to stronger weighting of functional attributes in the representations of non-living things).

Another similar argument to our own concerning top-down (re-entrant) activation comes from Damasio (1989, 1990), who proposed that object naming involves reciprocal excitation between representations that specify perceptual knowledge about objects and "convergence zones" that store the combinatorial relations between the features linked to each object (drawing together knowledge from different modalities). Activation of a convergence zone can generate reactivation of perceptual knowledge stores until a pattern of synchronised neuronal firing is achieved, when response selection might take place. Although similar in spirit, our account provides more detail on the kinds of knowledge that might be drawn upon to differentiate name selection for different classes of object, on how re-entrant activation might be more a feature of naming than categorisation tasks, and on how visual perceptual processing in particular constrains access to stored knowledge. Also similar in spirit to the general idea of differentiation for response selection is the account offered by Warrington and McCarthy (1987). These authors suggested that stored knowledge about objects is represented in "channels" for particular sensory and motor modalities. Object recognition would be achieved by retrieving information from the various channels in which the different properties and associations of objects were stored, so that some unique pattern of activation could be achieved, representing the individual exemplar.

SPECIFIC PREDICTIONS

Similar to the other accounts in the literature that we outlined in the last section, our proposals lead to the conclusion that there should be privileged retrieval of detailed functional and naming information for non-living things, whereas there should be advantages for living things when tasks require access to functional information that is common across category members. We agree, too, that information about the co-occurrences of both perceptual and functional features are likely to play an important part in establishing and structuring our knowledge representations during learning. For any Hebbian learning process, co-occurrences of perceptual and functional features will lead to the development of strong connection weights between their representations; fast access to common category information is thus continuously reinforced for living things. Also, to the extent that distinctive features predict item-specific functions and names, then these features will be reinforced for response selection for individual exemplars.

Our account differs from all of the above, though, in stressing not only the importance of different forms of knowledge representation, but also the dynamic time-course of processing and how different knowledge representations may be recruited over time (and even in a top-down manner). There are several implications, and we outline five here.

(1) Because of the online effects of perceptual similarity, category differences should be increased when stimuli are presented as pictures relative to when they are presented as words, even though words should activate perceptual representations of living things to some degree (see Humphreys et al., 1997).

(2) As a result of our assumption of continuous processing underlying differentiation, effects of perceptual similarity should be "carried through" to influence name selection and not just (for example) access to perceptual or functional knowledge.

(3) It should be the case that category effects based on perceptual similarity emerge in patients who have no deficits in stored knowledge but whose impairment is in deriving appropriate perceptual descriptions for objects. Such impairments can exacerbate "normal" effects of perceptual similarity on accessing stored memories.

(4) Following the assumption of a hierarchy of stored representations, object recognition and naming should fractionate in ways that leave access to some forms of stored knowledge intact although access to other forms of knowledge are impaired. An example is that, if a lesion

affects the retrieval of associative and functional knowledge, a patient might still show evidence of accessing perceptual knowledge from vision (see Figure 3.3, p. 75).

(5) Certain forms of knowledge (e.g. perceptual knowledge, for living things) will need to be activated more in tasks that require individual responses to be selected for exemplars (e.g. in naming) than in tasks that require access to common responses (e.g. categorisation).

How well do these assertions stand up to the empirical data from both normal and disordered object processing?

Pictures and words

Some evidence indicating that category differences can be larger with pictures than with words was discussed earlier, when we pointed out that the advantage in superordinate categorisation for living things relative to non-living things is larger with pictures than with words as stimuli (Humphreys et al., 1999; Job et al., 1992). An event-related potential (ERP) study by Kiefer (2001) also suggests that differences between living and non-living things can be exaggerated with pictures, although some effects can also be found with words. Kiefer asked subjects to judge whether a superordinate category "probe" stimulus (presented either verbally or by means of two pictures from the chosen category) matched a target stimulus (presented either as a name or a picture). Differences in early ERP components emerged for living and non-living targets (after about 160–200ms), but were restricted to when pictorial presentations were used. Such early effects are consistent with there being more elaborated perceptual processing of pictures of living things than non-living things. There were also differences between the categories on later ERPs, with living things producing a reduced N400 component over occipitotemporal (bilateral) areas and non-living things a similar reduction over frontocentral (left hemisphere) sites. Differences in this particular component of the ERP (the N400) over frontocentral sites have previously been documented in contrasts between action verbs and concrete nouns (Dehaene, 1995; Pulvermuller, Preissl, Lutzenberger & Birbaumer, 1996), consistent with the frontocentral changes reflecting the retrieval of associated action knowledge. These differences in the later ERP component in Kiefer's study were found with both words and pictures as stimuli. The late effects can be interpreted in terms of living and non-living things drawing on contrasting forms of associative knowledge, which is stored in different brain regions, for both verbal and pictorial stimuli alike. These category differences in accessing associative knowledge occur in addition to category differences in perceptual processing found only with pictures.

Effects of perceptual similarity on name selection

Humphreys et al. (1988) separated sets of objects according to whether they were "structurally similar" in relation to other members of the category or whether they were "structurally dissimilar"—the structurally similar items being living things and the structurally dissimilar items primarily non-living things (although members of the category "body parts" were also structurally dissimilar). Structural similarity was based on measures of overall contour overlap and the number of parts listed in common across category members (as mentioned earlier). Normal subjects were then required to name sets of structurally similar or dissimilar items that could also vary in the frequency of occurrence of their names. Name frequency was chosen as a factor likely to reflect differences in the efficiency of name selection. Humphreys et al. found that naming times were faster for structurally dissimilar items with high name frequencies that for the other sets of items, and that structurally similar items showed few effects of frequency on naming times (see also Snodgrass & Yuditsky, 1996). To account for the results, Humphreys et al. proposed that structurally dissimilar items gained relatively rapid access to stored perceptual and associative memories, so that the frequency of their name became a rate-limiting factor on naming time. In contrast, access to perceptual and associative memories provided the rate-limiting factor in name retrieval for structurally similar items, limiting effects of a variable at the stage of name selection. For instance, if perceptual differentiation is sufficiently long, then both high and low frequency names could be preselected by the time that the earlier process is completed. The data are consistent with name selection being constrained by perceptual differentiation. The results were simulated by Humphreys et al. (1995) using an interactive activation and competition and framework. In this framework naming was achieved by competition between name representations activated continuously from visual and semantic representations.

The data from studies of naming to deadline, which we have already noted, are also in line with perceptual similarity directly affecting name selection (because errors are confined to sets of items that are visually similar to targets). Vitkovitch et al. (1993), using a deadline procedure, also showed that, for a given target object, the "spread" of incorrect names across subjects was greater with living than with non-living things. A fox might be misnamed as a dog, a cat, a horse, a donkey, and so forth. A tin opener might be misnamed as bottle opener, but little else. This suggests that a larger set of names is activated by the visual properties of living things than of non-living things, so that there is a wider candidate set for errors in name selection.

Finally, data on the effects of surface detail on object recognition and naming fit with the idea that perceptual variables can impact at a name retrieval stage. Earlier, we pointed out that surface information might be more important for living things than for non-living things because: (i) it can help to differentiate between sets of perceptually similar exemplars; and (ii) surface cues are more consistent for living than for non-living things (i.e. surface cues are more diagnostic of their identities). Studies by Davidoff and Ostergaard (1988) and Price and Humphreys (1989) showed that effects of colour are more pronounced on object naming than on categorisation, with Price & Humphreys also demonstrating that effects of surface detail in general were larger on living than on non-living things (see also Tanaka & Presnell, 1999). The enhanced effects on naming could occur because colour information is itself directly associated with a name (Davidoff & Ostergaard, 1988), or because it helps reduce the candidate set of names activated from the perceptual properties of objects by facilitating perceptual differentiation (Price & Humphreys, 1989). Moore and Price (1999) report evidence from a PET study that converges with the perceptual differentiation account. They showed less activation in regions of the inferior and posterior temporal lobe, associated with high-level visual processing, when subjects named coloured relative to black and white drawings. We suggest that better perceptual differentiation reduces competition for name selection, in line with the dynamic processing account we have outlined.

Category effects in patients without deficits in stored knowledge

There is clear evidence that some patients have selective difficulties in identifying stimuli from particular categories because they have impaired stored knowledge about the affected items. Some patients, for example, are poor at drawing objects from memory items from the affected category (Sartori & Job, 1988); they might also be unable to assign a name to a verbal definition of an object, or to answer questions about the object's functional as well as perceptual properties (e.g. Caramazza & Shelton, 1998; Funnell & de Mornay Davies, 1996; Laiacona, Barbarotto, & Capitani, 1993; Samson, Pillon, & de Wilde, 1998; Sheridan & Humphreys, 1993). We consider such deficits in the final section of the chapter. For now, though, we draw attention to patients who also find some classes of object more difficult to identify than others but who still seem to have intact stored knowledge about the objects. This was reported to be the case for an agnosic patient, HJA, by Riddoch and Humphreys (1987b). Though HJA had a problem in recognising many common objects by sight, this impairment was worse for living than for non-living things. Despite his recognition problem, HJA showed good stored knowledge for living things when initially tested; he could provide detailed definitions and accurate drawings from memory (often better than control subjects!). It is difficult to attribute the category-specific recognition deficit for HJA to a loss of stored knowledge. On the other hand, HJA does have a variety of other visual perceptual impairments that could lead to poor differentiation within classes of living thing that have similar perceptual structures (Riddoch & Humphreys, 1987b).

One other interesting point relates to the arguments we have made about the implications of differentiation processes for learning. Riddoch et al. (1999) retested HJA some 16 years after the stroke that generated the recognition problems in the first place. On the retests there was evidence for deterioration of HJA's stored knowledge about the perceptual properties of objects. For example, his drawings from memory had become more difficult for independent observers to identify and his definitions listed fewer visual attributes. Furthermore, the decrease in the number of visual attributes produced by HJA was greater for living than for non-living things (Riddoch et al., 1999), and this was matched by an increase in his production of non-visual functional attributes.

These retest results fit with the idea of continued updating of our memories based on interactions with objects. Because of his visual processing deficit, HJA's long-tem visual memory appears to have deteriorated over time. We speculate that this affected living things more because long-term visual representations need to remain finely tuned to differentiate between these (perceptually similar) items and because visual attributes are strongly weighted in their stored representations.

Cases such as HJA demonstrate that impaired perceptual processes can be sufficient to generate abnormally strong category effects in patients (see also Chapter 4). We take this as strong evidence in favour of our approach. On the other hand, it is important to note that other patients with apparently impaired processing of the visual properties of objects do not necessarily find living things harder to recognise than non-living things. For example, Humphreys and Rumiati (1998) reported data from a probable Alzheimer's disease patient with poor perceptual knowledge for objects. She was impaired at object decision and she made visual naming errors when objects were misidentified. Lambon Ralph, Howard, Nightingale and Ellis (1998) documented a patient who was impaired at matching objects to definitions that stressed visual rather than functional properties of objects; she was also impaired at producing perceptual features in her own definitions. For this patient, naming tended to be even worse for artefacts, although there was good performance on object decision.

Given that impaired perceptual processing seems sufficient to generate category effects, the challenge is to explain why it does not necessarily generate them (or indeed can generate trends for worse performance for non-living things).[2] Humphreys and Forde (2001) discuss various possibilities, including the idea that different forms of perceptual deficit could generate problems that are selective for non-living rather than living things. For example, a perceptual deficit for living things could emerge if patients are able to encode only global representations that are unelaborated with more local details (see Boucart & Humphreys [1992]; and Humphreys, Riddoch, & Quinlan [1985] for evidence of this with HJA). In contrast, a perceptual deficit for non-living things could be generated if patients process parts in isolation from one another, as many non-living things can be decomposed into parts that have little meaning outside the more global context of the object. We suggest that it will be important to understand the nature of the perceptual deficits that disrupt the recognition of different kinds of object. For now, though, we conclude that the process of perceptual differentiation can be disrupted in some patients and that this, in itself, can produce category differences in object recognition and naming.

Hierarchical breakdown in recognition and naming

Although we are argue that the processes mediating object recognition and naming operate dynamically over time, so that perceptual and functional knowledge can differentiate name retrieval, we also maintain that there is a hierarchy of stored representations—perceptual memories, functional and associative knowledge, names (see Figure 3.2). Perceptual descriptions of objects first activate perceptual memories, before this activation is transmitted through to representations of functional knowledge and names. One of the values of this approach is that it can help to explain patients who seem to be able to gain selective access to some but not all memories about objects. Riddoch and Humphreys (1987c) first reported a dissociation between intact performance on difficult object decision tasks and impaired access to other types of stored knowledge in patients. Their object decision task required discrimination between pictures of real objects and pictures of non-objects (of equal perceptual complexity and perceptual "goodness") created by interchanging the parts of real objects. Discrimination between objects and perceptually good non-objects seems likely to depend on access to stored knowledge. Despite their patient (JB) showing good discrimination on this task, Riddoch and Humphreys found that he was poor at matching associatively

---

[2] It is interesting that the patients reported by Humphreys and Rumiati (1998) and Lambon Ralph et al. (1998) appeared to have reasonably intact early visual processing and to have either a deficit in accessing visual memory or in using visual memories to retrieve other forms of knowledge. In fact, Lambon Ralph et al. report good object decision performance in their patient, which is consistent with visual access to stored perceptual knowledge being achieved. Such patients seem rather different in kind from a patient such as HJA, who has a frank deficit in encoding perceptual descriptions.

related objects. Similar results have been reported now on several occasions (Breedin, Saffran, & Coslett, 1994; Hillis & Caramazza, 1995; Humphreys & Riddoch, 1999; Riddoch & Humphreys, 1987c; Sheridan & Humphreys, 1993; Stewart, Parkin, & Hunkin, 1992). It appears that such patients can access perceptual memories (to distinguish objects and non-objects) but have impaired access to associative knowledge. Other patients seem to have good access to associative and functional knowledge about objects, but still to have poor name retrieval (e.g. Kay & Ellis, 1987). These patterns of dissociation can be accounted for in terms of a hierarchical model of memory access to perceptual and then to associative/functional and then to name representations.

Top-down (re-entrant) processing of perceptual information for naming

In addition to the evidence from PET for increased activation of the regions of posterior, inferior occipitotemporal cortex in object naming as opposed to recognition tasks (e.g. Price et al., 1996), neuropsychological data are consistent with the argument for top-down recruitment of perceptual knowledge for naming. There have been reports of a number of patients in the literature who appear to have selective deficits in name retrieval, which are also selective for living things (e.g. Farah & Wallace, 1992; Forde et al., 1997; Hart, Berndt, & Caramazza, 1985; Humphreys et al., 1997). In all the cases, the patients were particularly poor at naming fruit and vegetables; however, they were able to sort fruit and vegetables into separate categories despite being poor at naming individual exemplars. This result is interesting because fruit and vegetables have similar perceptual structures, so this categorisation is probably not based on crude visual features. From this result, some authors have concluded that the lesions arises after access to semantic knowledge has taken place (Farah &Wallace, 1992; Hart et al., 1985). Forde et al. (1997), however, tested how much their patient (SRB) knew about the visual properties of the objects he could not name. They had SRB: (i) carry out object decisions with fruit, vegetables and fruit–vegetable non-objects; (ii) draw objects from memory; (iii) answer questions about visual and functional properties of objects; and (iv) produce names to perceptual and functional definitions. They found that, although he had good functional knowledge, SRB was impaired at retrieving perceptual knowledge. This was found both with verbal questions and when he made fine-grained decisions to visual stimuli (as in object decision). An example of SRB's drawing from memory is shown in Figure 3.3a. Forde et al. concluded that, although the behavioural deficit was more pronounced in naming than in categorisation, the functional lesion affected perceptual knowledge. They suggested that SRB could access sufficient semantic knowledge to discriminate between fruit and vegetables but that he was impaired at activating perceptual knowledge further, to enable the stimuli to be differentiated sufficiently for naming to take place.

Further evidence for a link between visual processing and name retrieval deficits was reported by Humphreys et al. (1999), who presented evidence from a second patient, DM, which was similar to that found with SRB (Figure 3.3b). In addition, they required DM to name line drawings that were degraded with light visual lines. These lines produced a marked disruption to DM's naming. Nevertheless, she remained able to describe many functional and associative properties of the objects. Humphreys et al. suggest that the visual information derived bottom-up from the stimuli was sufficient to retrieve semantic properties, but that DM too was impaired at reactivating perceptual knowledge for naming. This problem was exacerbated by adding "visual noise" (the lines) to the stimuli.

Both SRB and DM had posterior lesions affecting medial extrastriate regions of the left hemisphere. Medial extrastriate regions have also been

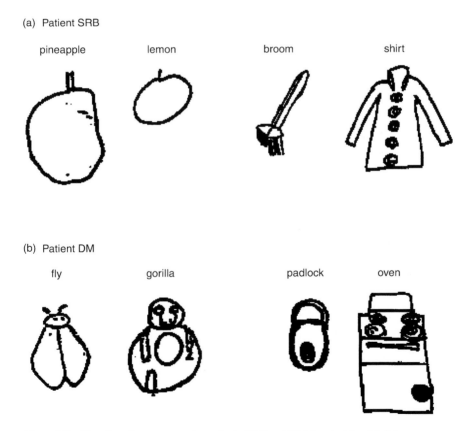

(a) Patient SRB

pineapple   lemon   broom   shirt

(b) Patient DM

fly   gorilla   padlock   oven

Figure 3.3.   Drawings from memory by patients SRB and DM (see text for details).

reported to be more activated by living than by non-living things in some PET studies of object naming (Martin et al., 1996) and these areas again probably mediate visual processing (Ungerleider & Haxby, 1994). The lesion data point to the naming deficits reflecting impaired visual rather than postsemantic processing.

Category-specific "naming" deficits have not only been noted for living things. Cappa et al. (1998) and Silveri et al. (1997) have reported apparent naming problems that were more severe for non-living things. For example, the patients could perform picture–word matching even when they could not name the objects involved. However, picture–word matching is a relatively insensitive task and it can be carried out at high levels by agnosics with clear deficits in accessing stored knowledge from vision (Riddoch & Humphreys, 1987b). Hence, we need to be cautious in interpreting these findings. In addition, there remain relatively few patients with deficits for non-living things when compared with patients impaired for living things. It would be useful to have some data here, in which the knowledge of the patients is probed in more detail. Nevertheless, we note that this idea of top-down (re-entrant) processing need not be confined to perceptual knowledge in the case of living things, and there might be similar activation of functional knowledge in order to modulate name competition between non-living objects. Damage to this process should lead to patients being able to make categorisation responses to stimuli while showing a selective naming impairment.

A SUMMARY AND ACCOUNT OF OTHER FORMS OF CATEGORY-SPECIFIC DEFICIT

We have tried to specify ways in which the differentiation approach to object recognition and naming relates to other accounts of category-specific deficits in patients, and ways in which our approach lends itself to novel, specific predictions. Starting from a general principle of information processing, we have articulated an account that can accommodate many of the results from the behavioural literature and from studies of the functional anatomy of object processing. We have also tried to outline how the approach can capture particular forms of category-specific deficit found in the neuropsychology literature, including patients without impairments of stored knowledge and patients who appear to have naming deficits for just some object categories.

In accounting for patients with apparent category-specific naming problems, we have argued that there could be relatively subtle deficits in the types of knowledge (perceptual, functional) needed to differentiate the target from competitors at a name level. Many patients, however, present with much clearer category-specific deficits in recognition (and not just naming). For example, patients can be very poor at performing object decisions for items from the affected categories (Caramazza & Shelton, 1998; Sartori & Job,

1988), consistent with a substantial deficit in visual perceptual knowledge. To date, patients with deficits in perceptual knowledge have been more impaired at identifying living things than non-living, which fits with the idea that perceptual knowledge is strongly weighted for the representation of these items.

Other patients, however, can demonstrate intact object decision performance for living things and yet still be impaired at retrieving functional knowledge about the objects both from vision and from verbal description ("Do penguins come from cold climates?") (Laiacona, Capitani, & Barbarotto, 1997; Sheridan & Humphreys, 1993). Good object decision performance suggests that the deficit occurs after visual access to perceptual knowledge has taken place. This should not be taken to mean that perceptual knowledge can be retrieved from other modalities, however. Recall patient JB documented by Riddoch and Humphreys (1987c), who could discriminate objects from non-objects in object decision but who remained deficient at matching associatively related objects. JB was also extremely impaired at drawing from memory, when given names. Riddoch and Humphreys suggested that the problem in vision, when going from intact perceptual knowledge to functional/associative knowledge, was actually bidirectional. JB could not retrieve visual knowledge from the names of objects, so his drawings were very impaired. Now, to the extent that perceptual knowledge captures the "essence" of many living things (see sections on object recognition and naming, p. 52, and on target–competitor differentiation, pp. 52–56), it is even possible that poor retrieval of perceptual knowledge (even from a name) will in turn disrupt decisions about the functional properties of these items. This would help to explain why some patients have deficits for functional as well as visual properties of living things (Humphreys & Forde, 2001). Other patients, who can retrieve perceptual knowledge from a name, might have their deficit confined to vision (a uni-directional dissociation; e.g. Riddoch & Humphreys, 1993).[3] An alternative possibility is that patients have impairments in functional knowledge that are indeed specific to living things. For instance, there might be particular kinds of association (e.g. with eating) that help to differentiate living things and that, like other types of functional knowledge (e.g. for hand actions, with tools) can be impaired. In this last case, patients will be impaired at retrieving functional knowledge about living things from names as well as from vision.

Our arguments have primarily been confined to the advantages for non-living over living things, found both in many patients and also in normal observers (depending on the differentiation required for name retrieval). However, as already noted both here and in the other chapters in this volume, patients can also present with deficits in the recognition of non-living things. Our account of these last deficits matches that made by perhaps the majority

---

[3] Or indeed confined to whichever input modality was lesioned.

of other authors (see section on relations to other accounts, p. 65)—these deficits are probably linked to lesions to functional knowledge, which normally helps to differentiate between non-living things (Cappa et al., 1998; Hillis & Caramazza, 1991; Sacchett & Humphreys, 1992; Warrington & McCarthy, 1983, 1987, 1994). It is interesting in this respect to note Warrington and McCarthy's (1987) finding that the impairment was most evident with "small manipulable objects", as if the functional knowledge lost pertained to associations with hand actions and object usage. Whether other, finer-grained, breakdowns can occur needs to be explored in more detailed tests of such patients.

CONCLUSIONS

We conclude that the principle of differentiation for response selection provides a useful framework for understanding both how object processing normally operates and how it can be disrupted by damage to selective parts of the recognition and naming system. In both normality and pathology, object category is a pervasive influence on the efficiency of recognition and naming. The principle of differentiation accounts both for how online processing differences can emerge between classes of objects and for how contrasting stored representations will be formed. Deficits in patients can reflect both disorders of online processing (e.g. due to impaired perceptual analysis) and deficits in knowledge representation and retrieval.

ACKNOWLEDGEMENTS

This work was supported by grants from the European Union, the Medical Research Council and the Wellcome Trust.

REFERENCES

Beauvois, M.F. (1982). Optic aphasia: A process of interaction between vision and language, *Philosophical Transactions of the Royal Society, B289*, 35–47.
Biederman, I. (1987). Recognition-by-components: A theory of human image understanding. *Psychological Review, 94*, 115–147.
Bonda, E., Petrides, M., Ostry, D., & Evans, A. (1996) Specific involvement of human parietal systems and the amygdala in the perception of biological motion. *Journal of Neuroscience, 16*, 3737–3744.
Boucart, M., & Humphreys, G.W. (1992). The computation of perceptual structure from collinearity and closure: Normality and pathology. *Neuropsychologia, 30*, 527–546.
Breedin, S.D., Saffran, E.M., & Coslett, H.B. (1994). Reversal of the concreteness effect in a patient with semantic dementia. *Cognitive Neuropsychology, 11*, 617–660.
Brennan, T., Danielle, D., Fluchaire, I., & Pellat, J. (1996). Naming faces and objects without comprehension. *Cognitive Neuropsychology, 15*, 93–110.
Cappa, S.F., Frugoni, M., Pasquali, P., Perani, D., & Zorat, F. (1998). Category-specific naming impairment for artefacts: A new case. *Neurocase, 4*, 391–397.

Caramazza, A. (1998). The interpretation of semantic category-specific deficits: What do they reveal about the organisation of conceptual knowledge in the brain? *Neurocase, 4,* 265–272.

Caramazza, A., Hillis, A.E., Rapp, B.C., & Romani, C. (1990). The multiple semantics hypothesis: Multiple confusions? *Cognitive Neuropsychology, 7,* 161–189.

Caramazza, A., & Shelton, J.R. (1998). Domain specific knowledge systems in the brain: The animate–inanimate distinction. *Journal of Cognitive Neuroscience, 10(1),* 1–34.

Chao, L.L., Haxby, J.V., & Martin, A. (1999). Attribute-based neural substrates in posterior temporal cortex for perceiving and knowing about objects. *Nature Neuroscience, 2,* 913–919.

Damasio, A.R. (1989). Time-locked multiregional retroactivation: A systems-level proposal for the neural substrates of recall and recognition. *Cognition, 33,* 25–62.

Damasio, A.R. (1990). Category-related recognition defects as a clue to the neural substrates of knowledge. *Trends in Neuroscience, 13(3),* 95–98.

Davidoff, J.B. & Ostergaard, A.L. (1988). The role of colour tasks in categorical judgements. *Quarterly Journal of Experimental Psychology, 40A,* 533–544.

Decety, J. Perani, D., Jeannerod, M., Bettinardi, V., Tadary, B., Woods, R., Mazziotta, J.C., & Fazio, F. (1994). Mapping motor representations with positron emission tomography. *Nature, 371,* 600–602.

Dehaene, S. (1995). Electrophysiological evidence for category-specific word processing in the normal human brain. *NeuroReport, 6,* 2153–2157.

De Renzi, E., & Lucchelli, F. (1994). Are semantic systems separately represented in the brain? The case of living category impairment. *Cortex, 30,* 3–25.

D'Esposito, M., Detre, J.A., Aguire, G.K., Aslop, D.C., Tippett, L.J., & Farah, M.J. (1997). A functional MRI study of mental image generation. *Neuropsychologia, 35,* 725–730.

Durrant-Peatfield, M.R., Tyler, L.K., Moss, H.E., & Levy, J.P. (1997). *The distinctiveness of form and function in category structure: A connectionist model.* Proceedings of the 19th Annual Cognitive Science Conference, University of Stanford. Hillsdale, NJ: Lawrence Erlbaum Associates, Inc.

Edelman, S., & Duvdevani-Bar, S. (1997) A model of visual recognition and categorisation. *Philosophical Transactions of the Royal Society, B352, 1191–1202.*

Farah, M.J., & McClelland, J.L. (1991). A computational model of semantic memory impairment: Modality specificity and emergent category specificity. *Psychological Review, 120,* 339–357.

Farah, M.J., & Wallace, M.A. (1992). Semantically bounded anomia: Implications for the neural implementation of naming. *Neuropsychologia, 30(7),* 609–621.

Forde, E.M.E. (1999). Category specific recognition impairments. In G.W. Humphreys (Ed.), *Case Studies in the Neuropsychology of Vision.* Hove, UK: Psychology Press.

Forde, E.M.E., Francis, D., Riddoch, M.J., Rumiati R., & Humphreys, G.W. (1997). On the links between visual knowledge and naming: A single case study of a patient with a category-specific impairment for living things. *Cognitive Neuropsychology, 14(3),* 403–458.

Forde, E.M.E., & Humphreys, G.W. (1999). Category-specific recognition impairments: A review of important case studies and influential theories. *Aphasiology, 13(3),* 169–193.

Funnell, E., & de Mornay-Davies, P.D. (1996). JBR: A re-assessment of concept familiarity and a category specific disorder for living things. *Neurocase, 2,* 461–474.

Gaffan, D., & Heywood, C.A. (1993). A spurious category-specific visual agnosia for living things in normal human and nonhuman primates. *Journal of Cognitive Neuroscience, 5(1),* 118–128.

Gerlach, C., Law, I., Gade, A., & Paulson, O.B. (1999) Perceptual differentiation and category effects in normal object recognition: A PET study. *Brain, 122,* 2159–2170.

Grabowski, T.J., Damasio, H., & Damasio, A.R. (1998) Premotor and prefrontal correlates of category-related lexical retrieval. *Neurimage, 7,* 232–243.

Grafton, S.T., Fadiga, L., Arbib, M.A., & Rizzolatti, G. (1997) Premotor cortex during observation and naming of familiar tools. *Neuroimage, 6*, 231–236.

Hart, J., Berndt, R.S., & Caramazza, A. (1985). Category-specific naming deficit following cerebral infarction. *Nature, 316*, 439–440.

Hillis, A.E., & Caramazza, A. (1991). Category-specific naming and comprehension impairment: A double dissociation. *Brain, 114*, 2081–2094.

Hillis, A.E., & Caramazza, A. (1995) Cognitive and neural mechanisms underlying visual and semantic processing: Implications from 'optic aphasia'. *Journal of Cognitive Neuroscience, 7*, 457–478.

Hodges, J.R., & Greene, J.D.W. (1998) Knowing about people and nursing them: Can Alzheimer's disease patients do one without the other? *Quarterly Journal of Experimental Psychology, 51A*, 121–134.

Humphreys, G.W., & Forde, E.M.E. (2001). Hierarchies, similarity and interactivity in object recognition: On the multiplicity of 'category-specific' deficits in neuropsychological populations. *Behavioral and Brain Sciences, 24*, 453–509.

Humphreys, G.W., Lamonte, C., & Lloyd-Jones, T. J. (1995). An interactive activation approach to object processing: Effects of structural similarity, name frequency and task in normality and pathology. *Memory, 3*, 535–586.

Humphreys, G.W., Price, C., & Riddoch, M.J. (1999). From objects to names: A cognitive neuroscience approach. *Psychological Research, 62*, 118–130.

Humphreys, G.W., & Riddoch, M.J. (1999). Impaired development of semantic memory: Separating semantic from structural knowledge and diagnosing a role for action in establishing stored memories for objects. *Neurocase, 5*, 519–532.

Humphreys, G.W., Riddoch, M.J., & Price, C. (1997). Top-down processes in object identification: Evidence from experimental psychology, neuropsychology and functional anatomy. *Proceedings for the Royal Society, Series B, 352*, 1275–1282.

Humphreys, G.W., Riddoch, M.J., & Quinlan, P.T. (1985) Interactive processes in perceptual organization: Evidence from visual agnosia. In M.I. Posner & O.S.M. Marin (Eds.), *Attention and performance XI*. Hillsdale, NJ: Lawrence Erlbaum Associates, Inc.

Humphreys, G.W., Riddoch, M.J., & Quinlan, P.T. (1988). Cascade processes in picture identification. *Cognitive Neuropsychology, 5*, 67–103.

Humphreys, G.W., & Rumiati, R. (1998). When joys come not in single spies but in battalions: Within category and within modality identification increases the accessibility of degraded semantic knowledge. *Neurocase, 4(2)*, 111–126..

Jescheniak, J-D., & Levelt, W.J.M. (1994) Word frequency effects in speech production: Retrieval of syntactic information and of phonological form. *Journal of Experimental Psychology: Learning, Memory and Cognition, 20*, 824–843.

Job, R., Rumiati, R., & Lotto, L. (1992). The picture superiority effect in categorisation: Visual or semantic? *Journal of Experimental Psychology: Learning, Memory and Cognition, 18(5)*, 1019–1028.

Kay, J., & Ellis, A.W. (1987) A cognitive neuropsychological case study of anomia: Implications for psychological models of word retrieval. *Brain, 110*, 613–629.

Kiefer, M. (2001) Perceptual and semantic sources of category-specific effects in object categorization: Event-related potentials during picture and word categorization. *Memory and Cognition, 29*, 100–116.

Laiacona, M., Barbarotto, R., & Capitani, E. (1993). Perceptual and associative knowledge in category specific impairment of semantic memory: A study of two cases. *Cortex, 29*, 727–740.

Laiacona, M., Capitani, E., & Barbarotto, R. (1997) Semantic category dissociations: A longitudinal study of two cases. *Cortex, 33*, 441–461.

Lamberts, K., & Freeman, R.P.J. (1999) Categorization of briefly presented objects. *Psychological Research, 62*, 107–117.

Lambon Ralph, M., Howard, D., Nightingale, G., & Ellis, A.W. (1998). Are living and non-living category-specific deficits causally linked to impaired perceptual or associative knowledge? Evidence from a category-specific double dissociation. *Neurocase, 4*, 311–338

McCarthy, R., & Warrington, E.K. (1994). Disorders of semantic memory. *Philosophical Transactions of the Royal Society of London, 346*, 89–96.

McRae, K., de Sa, V.R., & Seidenberg, M.S. (1997). On the nature and scope of featural representations of word meaning. *Journal of Experimental Psychology, General, 126(2)*, 99–130.

Marr, D. (1982). *Vision: A computational investigation into the human representation and processing of visual information.* San Francisco: W.H. Freeman.

Martin, A., Haxby, J.V., Lalonde, F.M., Wiggs, C.L., & Ungerleider, L.G. (1995). Discrete cortical regions associated with knowledge of colour and knowledge of action. *Science, 270*, 102–105.

Martin, A., Wiggs, C.L., Ungerleider, L.G., & Haxby, J.V. (1996). Neural correlates of category-specific knowledge. *Nature, 379*, 649–652.

Moore, C.J., & Price, C. J. (1999). A functional neuroimaging study of the variables that generate category-specific object processing differences. *Brain, 122(5)*, 943–962.

Moss, H.E., Tyler, L.K., & Jennings, F. (1997). When leopards lose their spots: Knowledge of visual properties in category-specific deficits for living things. *Cognitive Neuropsychology, 14(6)*, 901–950.

Moss, H.E., Tyler, L.K., Durrant-Peatfield, M.R., & Bunn, E.M. (1998). 'Two eyes of a see-through': impaired and intact semantic knowledge in a case of a selective deficit for living things. *Neurocase, 4(4/5)*, 291–310.

Perani, D., Cappa, S.F., Bettinardi, V., Bressi, S, Gorno-Tempini, M., Matarrese, M., & Fazio, F. (1995). Different neural systems for the recognition of animals and man-made tools. *NeuroReport, 6*, 1637–1641.

Price, C.J., & Humphreys, G.W. (1989). The effects of surface detail on object categorisation and naming. *Quarterly Journal of Experimental Psychology, 41A*, 797–828.

Price, C.J., Moore, C.J., Humphreys, G.W., Frackowiak, R.S.J. & Friston, K.J. (1996). The neural regions sustaining object recognition and naming. *Proceedings of the Royal Society of London, Series B, 263*, 1501–1507.

Potter, M.C. & Faulconer, B.A. (1975). Time to understand pictures and words. *Nature, 253*, 437–438.

Pulvermuller, F. (1999) Words in the brain's language. *Behavioral and Brain Sciences, 9*, 253–336.

Pulvermuller, F., Preissl, H., Lutzenberger, W., & Birbaumer, N. (1996) Brain rhythms of language: Nouns vs. verbs. *European Journal of Neuroscience, 8*, 937–941.

Riddoch, M.J., & Humphreys, G.W. (1987a). Picture naming. In G.W. Humphreys & M.J. Riddoch (Eds.), *Visual object processing: A cognitive neuropsychological approach.* London: Lawrence Erlbaum Associates Ltd.

Riddoch, M.J., & Humphreys, G.W. (1987b).A case of integrative visual agnosia. *Brain, 110*, 1431–1462.

Riddoch, M.J., & Humphreys, G.W. (1987c). Visual object processing in optic aphasia: A case of semantic access agnosia. *Cognitive Neuropsychology, 4(2)*, 131–185.

Riddoch, M.J., & Humphreys, G.W. (1993). The smiling giraffe. In R. Campbell (Ed.), *Mental lives.* Oxford: Blackwell.

Riddoch, M.J., Humphreys, G.W., Coltheart, M., & Funnell, E. (1988). Semantic system or systems? Neuropsychological evidence re-examined. *Cognitive Neuropsychology, 5*, 3–25.

Riddoch, M.J., Humphreys, G.W., Gannon, T., Blott, W., & Jones, V. (1999). Memories are made of this: The effects of time on stored visual knowledge in a case of visual agnosia. *Brain, 122*, 537–559.

Rumelhart, D.E., Hinton, G.E., & Williams, R.J. (1986). Learning internal representations by error propagation. In D.E. Rumelhart & J.L. McClelland (Eds.), *Parallel distributed processing: Explorations in the microstructure of cognition: Vol. 1.* Cambridge, MA: MIT Press.

Rumiati, R.I., & Humphreys, G.W. (1998). Recognition by action: Dissociating visual and semantic routes to action in normal observers. *Journal of Experimental Psychology: Human Perception and Performance, 24,* 631–647.

Sacchett, C., & Humphreys, G.W. (1992). Calling a squirrel a squirrel but a canoe a wigwam: A category-specific deficit for artefactual objects and body parts. *Cognitive Neuropsychology, 9,* 73–86.

Saffran, E.J., & Schwartz, M. F. (1994). Of cabbages and things: Semantic memory from a neuropsychological point of view: A tutorial review. *Attention and Performance, 15,* 507–536.

Samson, D., Pillon, A., & De Wilde, V. (1998). Impaired knowledge of visual *and* nonvisual attributes in a patient with a semantic impairment for living entities: A case of a true category-specific deficit. *Neurocase, 4(4/5),* 273–290.

Sartori, G., & Job, R. (1988). The oyster with four legs: A neuropsychological study on the interaction of visual and semantic information. *Cognitive Neuropsychology, 5(1),* 105–132.

Sergent, J., (1987). Information processing and laterality effects for object and face perception. In G.W. Humphreys & M.J. Riddoch (Eds.), *Visual object processing: A cognitive neuropsychological approach.* London: Lawrence Erlbaum Associates Ltd.

Shallice, T. (1988) *From neuropsychology to mental structure.* Cambridge: Cambridge University Press.

Sheridan, J., & Humphreys, G.W. (1993). A verbal–semantic category-specific recognition impairment. *Cognitive Neuropsychology, 10(2),* 143–184.

Silveri, M.C., Gainotti, G., Perani, D., Cappelletti, J.Y., Carbone, G., & Fazio, F. (1997). Naming deficit for non-living items: Neuropsychological and PET study. *Neuropsychologia, 35,* 359–367.

Snodgrass, J.G., & Yuditsky, T. (1996). Naming times for the Snodgrass and Vanderwart pictures. *Behavioural Research Methods, Instruments and Computers, 28,* 516–536.

Stewart, F., Parkin, A.J., & Hunkin, N.M. (1992). Naming impairments following recovery from herpes simplex encephalitis. *Quarterly Journal of Experimental Psychology, 44A,* 261–284.

Tanaka, J.W., & Presnell, L.M. (1999) Color diagnosticity in object recognition. *Perception and Psychophysics, 61,* 1140–1154.

Tarr, M.J., & Bulthoff, H.H. (1995) Is human object recognition better described by geon structural descriptions or by multiple views? Comment on Biederman and Gerhardstein (1993). *Journal of Experimental Psychology: Human Perception and Performance, 21,* 1494–1505.

Thompson-Schill, S.L., Aguirre, G.K., D'Esposito, M., & Farah, M.J. (1999). A neural basis for category and modality specificity of semantic knowledge. *Neuropsychologia, 37,* 671–676.

Tyler, L., & Moss, H. (1997). Functional properties of concepts: Studies of normal and brain-damaged patients. *Cognitive Neuropsychology, 14(4),* 511–545.

Ungerleider, L.G., & Haxby, J.V. (1994) 'What' and 'where' in the human brain? *Current Opinions in Biology, 4,* 157–164.

Vitkovitch, M., & Humphreys, G.W. (1991) Perseverative responding in speeded naming to pictures: It's in the links. *Journal of Experimental Psychology: Learning, Memory and Cognition, 17,* 664–680.

Vitkovitch, M., Humphreys, G.W., & Lloyd-Jones, T. (1993). On naming a giraffe a zebra: Picture naming errors across different categories. *Journal of Experimental Psychology: Learning, Memory and Cognition, 19,* 243–259.

Warrington, E.K., (1975). The selective impairment of semantic memory. *Quarterly Journal of Experimental Psychology, 27,* 635–657.

Warrington, E.K., & McCarthy, R. (1983). Category-specific access dysphasia. *Brain, 106,* 859–878.

Warrington, E.K., & McCarthy, R. (1987). Categories of knowledge: Further fractionations and an attempted integration. *Brain, 110*, 1273–1296.

Warrington, E.K., & McCarthy, R. (1994). Multiple meaning systems in the brain: A case for visual semantics. *Neuropsychologia, 32(12)*, 1465–1473.

Warrington, E.K., & Shallice, T. (1984). Category-specific semantic impairment. *Brain, 107*, 829–854.

CHAPTER FOUR

Visual processing and the dissociation between biological and man-made categories

Martin Arguin
Département de psychologie, Université de Montréal and Centre de recherche, Institut Universitaire de Gériatrie de Montréal, Canada

INTRODUCTION

The observation and detailed characterisation of selective impairments affecting particular cognitive areas in brain-damaged individuals can be used to inform the anatomical and functional architecture of normal cognition. Among the most striking forms of selective impairments to have been documented by neuropsychology since the mid-1980s are those that selectively affect the processing of objects from particular semantic categories while sparing objects from other categories. Most often, the semantic boundary that separates the affected categories from those that are spared distinguishes between biological and non-biological (i.e. man-made) items. In this chapter, we will review evidence from cases with category-specific visual recognition impairments that are attributable to a deficit in visual rather than semantic processing. Evidence from these studies will be used to speculate on the organisation of the visual system in the intact brain and on how this organisation interacts with the differing features of biological and non-biological semantic categories to eventually produce categorical effects in visual object recognition.

In the first papers to appear on category specific impairments, the dissociations between biological and non-biological categories in brain-damaged patients were more or less taken as an *a priori* sign that the functional deficit concerned semantic memory. For example, as an argument against the possibility that the category-specific deficits they observed in their patients were due to visual problems, Warrington and Shallice (1984 p. 847) stated that "category specificity findings are very difficult to explain in terms of some form of visual processing deficit". McCarthy and Warrington (1988 p. 428) added "for a category specific deficit to arise in the first place it is necessary that the information should have already been categorised along a semantic dimension". From these postulates it appeared unlikely, or even impossible, that presemantic deficits, such as those affecting vision, could ever result in category-specific impairments.

This view soon had to be revised, however, with the publication of cases with category-specific impairments that were quite clearly the consequence of deficits concerning visual processing rather than semantic memory. As a shorthand, we will refer to these cases as suffering from category-specific visual agnosia, or CSVA. To properly understand the investigations that were conducted on these cases, and to assess their possible implications for visual processing, we will first present an overview of current basic assumptions about the organisation of the visual recognition system.

VISUAL OBJECT PROCESSING

Although surface features such as colour might facilitate visual object recognition to some degree for object classes possessing characteristic surface properties, such as biological objects (Humphrey, Goodale, Jacobson, & Servos, 1994; Price & Humphreys, 1989; Wurm, Legge, Isenberg, & Luebker, 1993), it appears that the most fundamental information for visual object recognition is shape (Biederman & Ju, 1988; Marr & Nishihara, 1978). Shape processing is a complex issue and its intricacies are beyond the scope of this chapter (see Feldman & Richards [1998] and Hoffman & Singh [1997] for recent reviews). Most authors agree on a broad division of visual processes involved in visual object recognition along two main sequential stages, and this simple division will be sufficient for the present purpose.

The first stage is that of perceptual encoding, which is concerned with registering the properties of the image projected on the retina and in constructing an adequate perceptual representation of seen objects. One main function of this processing stage is to discriminate between visual objects. It is widely assumed that this stage is responsible for performance in perceptual discrimination or perceptual judgement tasks. Brain-damaged individuals with so-called apperceptive agnosia (Lissauer, 1890/1988) or visual form agnosia (Benson & Greenberg, 1969; Milner & Heywood, 1989), for instance, would suffer from a deficit at the stage of perceptual encoding.

The second visual processing stage is that of structural descriptions, i.e. a long-term memory store holding information on the visual appearance of objects. Such a memory system is assumed to be required to insure object constancy, i.e. the stability of object recognition across changes in the retinal position of the image, its size, orientation, viewpoint, etc, and to mediate the arbitrary mappings between the visual appearance of a particular instance of an object and central representations of its meaning (Marr, 1982). Activation of structural descriptions is generally agreed to be the basis for performance in such tasks as object decisions, where observers must distinguish between visual instances of real objects and those of invented or meaningless objects (e.g. made of juxtaposed parts taken from distinct real objects; Figure 4.1). As will be described below, most patients with CSVA suffer from a deficit affecting the stage of structural descriptions.

Beyond visual processing, two other stages must be assumed for a complete account of visual object recognition. One is semantic memory, which is a long-term store holding our knowledge of the meanings of objects. Along with other authors (e.g. Coltheart et al., 1998; Humphreys, Lamote, & Lloyd-Jones, 1995; Humphreys, Riddoch, & Quinlan, 1988), we will assume that the information that is kept in semantic memory pertains mainly to non-sensory information (often referred to as functional, associative, or encyclopaedic object properties), such as what an object is for, what it does, where it lives, etc, and that sensory information is stored in modality-specific and code-specific memory systems such as structural desciptions in the case of vision. This implies, among other things, that one must refer to the structural description system to answer verbal questions about specifically visual properties of objects (e.g. "do cats have pointed ears?"). In visual object recognition, access to semantic memory, which permits the assignment of meaning to the stimulus, is via the structural description system. Finally, from semantic memory it is possible to access phonological representations of object names to permit the naming of visually presented objects.

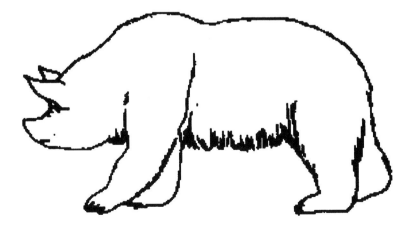

Figure 4.1. Example of a negative item that might be used in the object decision task.

Neuropsychological evidence indicates that both semantic memory and phonological representations can be selectively affected by brain damage and, in some instances, these deficits can result in category specific impairments.

One final but crucial assumption regarding the organisation of the visual recognition system is that the stages involved interact with one another in a cascaded fashion (McClelland, 1979), meaning that the flow of information between successive stages is continuous and independent of whether any stage has settled into a stable solution. One key implication of this is that variables that specifically affect separate stages of processing might neverthe-less have interactive effects on performance (Humphreys et al., 1995). As will be seen, this property is important for accounting for the observations described below.

CATEGORY-SPECIFIC VISUAL AGNOSIA (CSVA)

Possibly the first CSVA patient to have been reported in the neuro-psychological literature is HJA, who showed poorer performance in the visual recognition of biological than non-biological objects (Riddoch & Humphreys, 1987a; see also Riddoch et al., 1999). This patient was impaired in the integration of the local visual features of objects into a global unit, although he retained good knowledge of the visual and semantic properties of objects (Humphreys & Riddoch, 1987; Riddoch & Humphreys, 1987a). This means that HJA's visual recognition disorder, as well as its category specificity, were a function of a visual deficit affecting perceptual encoding, and not of an impaired semantic memory. It appears the case of HJA has gone relatively unnoticed in the literature on category-specific impairments, possibly because of the emphasis that was placed on a detailed characterisa-tion of his visual deficit rather than on its category specificity, which remained relatively unexplored. Other reports of brain-damaged individuals with category specific visual recognition impairments caused by a preseman-tic deficit soon followed, however.

Apart from HJA, there are nine other cases of category-specific impair-ments that are quite clearly attributable to functional damage preceding the semantic system.[1] These are, in alphabetical order: ELM (Arguin, Bub, & Dudek, 1996b; Dixon & Arguin, 1999; Dixon, Bub, & Arguin, 1997, 1998; Dudek, Arguin, & Bub, 1994; Dudek, Arguin, Dixon, & Bub, 1997); Felicia (De Renzi & Lucchelli, 1994); Helga (Mauri et al., 1994); Giuletta (Sartori et

---

[1] Several other brain-damaged cases with category-specific impairments reported in the litera-ture could possibly fit within this group. However, either their impairments are complicated by word comprehension impairments, suggesting a semantic memory deficit, or the testing con-ducted was insufficient to point unambiguously to a presemantic visual deficit as the cause of these impairments.

al., 1993a); IL (Arguin et al., 1996a); JB (Humphreys et al., 1988; Riddoch & Humphreys, 1987b); LH (Farah, Hammond, Mehta, & Ratcliff, 1989; Farah, McMullen, & Meyer, 1991; Etcoff, Freeman, & Cave, 1991); Michelangelo (Mauri et al., 1994; Sartori, Coltheart, Miozzo & Job, 1995; Sartori & Job, 1988; Sartori, Miozzo, & Job, 1993b); and SRB (Forde et al., 1997).

Several important generalisations can be made from these patients. Each of them shows an impairment that is either selective to biological objects (animals, fruit and vegetables, plants, insects, etc.) or is significantly greater for these categories than for non-biological objects. In addition, in cases where this has been documented, patients can often report the superordinate category (e.g. animal) of visual objects they fail to identify by their basic level names (e.g. cat). One important point to note is that the disorder is often accompanied by a recognition impairment for some categories of man-made objects, in particular musical instruments and makes of car (see also Basso, Capitani, & Laiacona, 1988; Damasio, 1990; Farah, 1991; Humphreys & Riddoch, 1987b; Warrington & Shallice, 1984). Thus, although the biological/non-biological distinction is a convenient shorthand to refer to the categories that are affected versus those that are spared, it appears it does not completely account for the dissociations that are observed (see, however, Caramazza & Shelton, 1998). This suggests that some fundamental object property that is not captured by the distinction between biological and man-made objects may be involved in, and perhaps responsible for, these dissociations. We will return to this issue later.

Another important trait that is common to most patients with CSVA is that their brain damage can involve the inferior temporal lobe of either the left or right hemisphere, or it can be bilateral. These lesions are often caused by herpes simplex encephalitis. With respect to lesion localisation, exceptional cases are JB, who showed a left parieto-occipital lesion, and Helga, who suffered from Alzheimer's dementia and showed diffuse cortical atrophy on CT scan.

One key feature in the above cases is that, as far as their investigators could determine, visual perceptual encoding functions were normal. This is at variance with HJA, who was clearly impaired at this level. Rather, a central issue in the more recent cases was access to stored structural descriptions. Access from vision is assessed by tests such as the object decision task, where subjects have to discriminate between pictures of real versus unreal (invented) but plausible objects. Access from language is assessed by object recognition from a verbal description or by probe questions about the structural properties of an object referred to by its name. All the above cases show some form of impairment affecting the retrieval of stored visual information specific to biological objects. Except for JB, all of them show impaired retrieval of stored visual knowledge for biological objects from both visual and verbal input, thereby suggesting functional damage to the structural description system. In the case of JB, access to structural descriptions from vision was normal but was impaired from a verbal input. This suggests that the deficit in JB concerns the links between structural descriptions and semantic memory.

In striking contrast to their performance in tests probing stored knowledge of the structural properties of biological objects, all of these patients perform either normally or at least significantly better on similar tasks using man-made objects. The evidence also suggests intact or relatively spared semantic memory in these cases because they demonstrate at least adequate non-sensory knowledge of both biological and non-biological objects.

One obvious question that must be asked with respect to the above CSVA cases is "what are the features of the visual recognition system and/or the differences between biological and non-biological objects that would be sufficient to account for the categorical dissociations observed?". Several propositions have been put forward to answer this question.

Accounts of CSVA[2]

Visual recognition in general is to some degree affected by factors such as the frequency or the visual complexity of the item or our familiarity with it. From this, Stewart, Parkin, and Hunkin (1992) as well as Funnell and Sheridan (1992), argued that, when left uncontrolled, such factors could artifactually cause performance dissociations between the processing of biological and man-made objects. In support of this argument, Stewart et al. (1992) reported patient HO, who was poorer at the visual identification of pictures of biological than non-biological items. However, when items from these broad categories were matched carefully according to name frequency, visual complexity, and familiarity (Snodgrass & Vanderwart, 1980), no residual effect of semantic category remained in the visual identification performance of the patient. A similar study was reported by Funnell and Sheridan (1992) whose patient, SL, exhibited a dissociation between biological and man-made objects that was, in fact, entirely determined by differences in familiarity. The explanation of the biological/non-biological dissociation as an artifact of uncontrolled trivial factors defended by Funnell and Sheridan (1992) and by Stewart et al. (1992) does not apply to the CSVA cases listed above, however. Indeed, in each of these cases, the dissociation between visual recognition performance for biological and man-made items remains when the effects of frequency, familiarity, and complexity are either controlled or partialled out by regression analysis.

---

[2] This review is by no means exhaustive. Its main purposes are to highlight the different directions authors have taken in reasoning about the possible causes of category-specific impairments and to review what appear as the most relevant alternatives in the context of CSVA. The reader should consult Forde and Humphreys (1999) for a current discussion of the various accounts of category specific impairments.

If the categorical dissociation observed in a particular brain-damaged patient cannot be the trivial consequence of uncontrolled factors such as those discussed by Stewart et al. (1992) and by Funnell and Sheridan (1992), it is tempting to believe that the biological and man-made items used in testing are comparable in every possible respect, save the semantic category they belong to. Such a belief inevitably leads to the assumption that category-specific impairments can be explained only by a categorically organised perceptual processing system. Sartori and Job (1988) have defended such a possibility to account for the category specificity of the visual agnosia of their patient, Michelangelo (see also Caramazza, 1998; Caramazza & Shelton, 1998; Samson, Pillon, & De Wilde, 1998; for similar views regarding patients with category-specific impairments caused by a deficit of semantic memory). More precisely, the argument proposed by Sartori and Job is that a component of Michelangelo's structural description system that was specialised for the representation of biological objects has been damaged whereas the component concerned with non-biological objects was spared. While this explanation does fit the patient's data, no independent evidence can be cited to support such a categorical organisation of the structural description system. This reduces the explanation proposed to little more than a redescription of the data.

Rather than implicating exclusively the functional architecture of the visual system in the search for an explanation of category-specific effects in CSVA, other authors have also considered the possibility that the very nature of our knowledge of biological and non-biological objects differ. Certainly, the most widely cited such account is that of Warrington and Shallice (1984; but see also Warrington & McCarthy [1987] and Damasio [1990] for variants thereof) who argued that our knowledge of biological objects is more heavily based on sensory than functional properties whereas the opposite would be true of man-made objects. Because of this asymmetry, selective loss of knowledge of sensory properties (such as in most cases of CSVA) would result in greater recognition impairments for biological than non-biological objects. Empirical support for the central premises of Warrington and Shallice's (1984) theory has been provided by Farah and McClelland (1991) and by McRae, de Sa, and Seidenberg (1997). Notably, subjects in these studies reported more sensory than functional properties for terms referring to biological objects. These observations have been contested by Caramazza and Shelton (1998), however, on the grounds that the definitions of what should stand as a "functional" property that were used by previous authors were too narrow to fully capture the breadth of our non-sensory knowledge of biological objects. Caramazza and Shelton (1998) also provided an informal report of data suggesting there is no difference in the number of sensory and functional properties for biological objects if a broader notion of what should stand as a functional property is used. Tyler and Moss (1997) as well as Moss, Tyler, Durrant-Peatfield, and

Bunn (1998) concur and argue that if one takes into account non-sensory features such as to see, to breathe, to move, etc, there is no shortage of functional features that can be attributed to biological objects.

Another approach to account for CSVA is to seek objective differences between biological and non-biological categories that are more fundamental than the factors discussed by Stewart et al. (1992) and Funnell and Sheridan (1992), and which might interact with particular sensitivities of the visual recognition system in order to produce category specific impairments. In particular, we might note that biological objects are caused by evolution. This means that taxonomically related biological categories will share a large part of their genetic background, and therefore that they will most often have similar visual forms. No such constraint exists for man-made objects, which are manufactured to meet a particular function. This function is the main determinant of their shape (see also De Renzi & Lucchelli [1994] for a related argument) and man-made objects of the same superordinate category (e.g. furniture, tools) might differ substantially in their precise function. This implies that categorically related man-made items might show large differences in their visual appearances. Empirical support for such inferences has been reported by Humphreys et al. (1988), who showed that most semantically related biological objects are more visually similar with each other than non-biological objects, as measured by the numbers of rated common parts and amount of contour overlap. Congruently, McRae et al. (1997) found that normal observers report a greater frequency of co-occurring properties, among them visual properties, between biological than non-biological objects. This suggests that biological items not only share large numbers of their visual features with each other, as shown by Humphreys et al. (1988), but also that they frequently share combinations of visual properties. Moss et al. (1998) as well as Devlin, Gonnerman, Andersen, and Seidenberg (1998) and Gonnerman, Andersen, Devlin, Kempler, and Seidenberg (1998) have all argued similarly and have added that biological items possess fewer distinctive properties, i.e. properties that would uniquely identify them relative to any other object, than man-made items (see also Gaffan & Heywood [1993] for related arguments).

Obviously, the processing demands imposed on the perceptual encoding and structural description stages of visual object recognition will be greater if the items presented are more similar to one another or, alternatively, less distinct. Indeed, such conditions might require a greater level of detail in perceptual analysis, more time to perform relevant discriminations, or even possibly the activation of special visual processes not required otherwise. The above observations can therefore contribute to a satisfactory account of CSVA that makes no appeal to assumptions of fundamental differences between our internal representations of biological and non-biological classes. They might also explain why difficulties in the visual identification of musical instruments and of car makes are often observed in CSVA, as these object categories contain some highly visually similar items.

In support of the role of visual similarity as a determinant of categorical effects in visual object recognition, Humphreys et al. (1988) as well as Gaffan and Heywood (1993), showed that neurologically intact observers perform more poorly in tasks requiring the identification of biological than man-made objects. In fact, as reported by Gaffan and Heywood (1993), even monkeys find it more difficult to discriminate between biological than non-biological items. Clearly, then, some fundamental visual difference exists between both object classes that has a significant impact on the operation of our visual system. Further and more direct support for the role of similarity in the category specificity of CSVA has been reported recently in a study of Forde et al. (1997) in the case of SRB. Forde et al. showed that SRB's visual object naming performance is more strongly determined by the amount of contour overlap (i.e. visual similarity) among objects than by the semantic category (biological versus non-biological) of the item. Furthermore, they report that the category specificity of SRB's agnosia is cancelled in a task where visually presented dogs and cars must be identified at a subordinate level, a task that requires the processing of visual information in a great level of detail for both categories.

Critical appraisal[3]

One important point that must be emphasised regarding the current account of CSVA is that its key explanatory factor is not just visual similarity by itself, but rather within-category similarity; that is, the visual similarity between objects that belong to the same semantic category. Interestingly, when cast against the assumed organisation of the visual recognition system, we note that within-category similarity actually refers to two separate processing stages, one interested in visual shape (i.e. perceptual encoding or structural descriptions), the other in object meaning (semantic memory). In other words, with respect to the stages involved in visual object recognition, within-category similarity does not stand as a single factor but rather as the inter-action of two separate factors, namely, visual similarity and semantic relatedness. That interactive effects can occur between two factors that act on separate processing stages is not entirely obvious (McClelland, 1979; Stern-berg, 1969, 1998). However, evidence from neurologically intact observers suggests that such interactions do indeed occur in visual object recognition (Humphreys et al., 1988; Vitkovitch, Humphreys, & Lloyd-Jones, 1993). These findings argue that the successive stages involved in visual object rec-ognition interact with one another in a cascade manner (as described earlier;

---

[3] Some of the issues raised here are elaborated on later in this chapter.

Humphreys et al., 1995; Lloyd-Jones & Humphreys, 1997) and perhaps more importantly in the present context, they maintain the validity of the "within-category similarity" account of CSVA.

Although, from the above discussion, the problem of CSVA might appear to have been solved, the studies reported so far still suffer from two key limitations. One of them is the exclusive reliance, in visual recognition tasks, on stimuli that refer to real-world objects. In such stimuli, visual shape and meaning are intrinsically tied and each object is unique in various ways, many of which might be unknown to the experimenter (e.g. personal experiences with particular objects). One problem this poses is that the notion of inter-active effects of shape similarity and of semantic proximity proposed by the "within-category similarity" account of CSVA cannot be explored fully and that some of its underlying assumptions remain untestable. Indeed, it is prac-tically impossible to entirely dissociate visual similarity from semantic prox-imity effects using real-world objects. In addition, with such stimuli, one can never be sure that the object categories used (e.g. visually similar versus dis-similar) do not differ on basic aspects such as the type of visual features that define their shapes. In fact, it has been argued that some types of category-specific impairments take their source in the differing kinds of visual features that define the shapes of objects from various semantic categories (Etcoff et al., 1991). Another problem the exclusive reliance on real-world objects poses is that it is extremely difficult to avoid a degree of circularity between the dissociations observed and the principles that are invoked to account for them. Indeed, clear proof for a theory requires the experimental manipulation of specific key factors that are uncontaminated by other vari-ations, and an examination of their effects. In most studies of CSVA, this is simply not done and the explanations proposed for the semantic category dissociations observed must remain *post hoc*. That is, investigators retro-spectively invoke some difference between the spared and impaired semantic categories to account for the observed dissociation without actually being able to provide an experimental test of the effect of that difference. One notable exception to this rule is the study of SRB by Forde et al. (1997), which managed to demonstrate that within-category visual similarity had a greater impact on recognition performance than the biological/man-made distinction.

Another important limitation is that most studies of CSVA are limited in their characterisation of the impairments suffered by the patients. In particu-lar, studies systematically attempt to localise the functional deficit within a broadly defined model of visual object recognition such as that outlined at the beginning of this chapter. They fail, however, to further specify the nature of the disorder affecting the damaged processing stage or connection. In the end, this means that studies of CSVA teach us little about the organisation of the visual object recognition system that we do not already know or assume.

In most cases, then, studies of CSVA are akin to investigations into unusual experimental preparations provided by nature designed to test particular notions about the structure of the world and about independently derived hypotheses on the organisation of the visual system.

There is, however, evidence from one particular case of CSVA that we believe offers some significant advances with respect to the limitations noted here. This case is that of ELM, who has been studied over a period of almost 10 years and who has been the subject of several reports (Arguin et al., 1996b; Dixon & Arguin, 1999; Dixon et al., 1997, 1998; Dudek et al., 1994, 1997). The evidence from these investigations is congruent with the notion of "within-category similarity" as a major factor in explaining CSVA. These, however, provide a complete exploration of the visual similarity by semantic relatedness interaction that is quite unique in both neuropsychology and cognitive psychology. They also provide fundamental indications about the way in which our visual system represents shape that leads to specifications on the notion of visual similarity.

INVESTIGATIONS OF ELM

ELM was an anglophone man born in 1928 who had to retire from his employment as a dispatcher. In 1982, he suffered a first ischaemic cerebral lesion deep in the right mesiotemporal lobe. This left him with mild nominal dysphasia and memory impairment that disappeared some months later. A second neurological episode occurred in 1985 and the CT scan conducted then evidenced bilateral inferior temporal lesions, with the left hemisphere damage substantially more voluminous than that on the right (see Arguin et al., 1996a, Figure 1). The investigations of his visual agnosia that are discussed below were conducted between 1988 and 1996.

Initial studies of ELM were conducted at the Montreal Neurological Institute by Matthew Decter, in collaboration with doctors Daniel Bub and Howard Chertkow (Decter, 1992). These revealed the presence of colour agnosia, surface dyslexia and dysgraphia, severe prosopagnosia, and a visual object recognition deficit specific to biological objects. On the line drawings of Snodgrass and Vanderwart (1980), for instance, ELM made 61% errors with biological objects but only 12% with man-made objects. Regression analyses showed that this asymmetry across semantic categories was not a function of confound variables such as familiarity or complexity. It is noteworthy that most of his errors to man-made objects on the Snodgrass and Vanderwart (1980) images concerned musical instruments, which he persistently failed to recognise despite being an amateur musician himself; he also showed major problems in recognising makes of cars. Despite having difficulties in providing the basic level name of biological objects he attempted to identify visually, ELM was consistently able to provide its superordinate category. Studies aimed at specifying the locus of functional impairment showed intact visual perceptual encoding. Notably, the patient was capable of visually recognising man-made objects from unusual viewpoints and was very comfortable at driving his car. Other tests, however, pointed to a damaged structural description system leading to impaired retrieval of stored structural information specific to biological objects. In the object decision task, for instance, ELM was at chance with pictures of animals (error rate of 41%) but excellent with man-made objects (error rate of 7%). On verbal questions probing stored knowledge about the visual appearances of biological objects, he was similarly impaired (45% errors on two-alternative forced-choice questions). By contrast, he did much better on a similar test probing non-sensory knowledge of the same items (error rate of 15%). In summary, then, ELM showed a pattern of cognitive impairments that was, as far as object recognition was concerned, highly similar to that of most other CSVA patients and which appeared to take its source in an impaired structural description system.

Shape processing

The following studies reported by Arguin et al. (1996b) focused on an attempt to provide a more detailed characterisation of the visual shape representation deficit of ELM. This began with a study of the confusion errors the patient made between fruits and vegetables in matching line drawings of these objects to their auditory names (picture–word matching; Arguin et al., 1996b, experiment 1). The use of fruits and vegetables in this experiment was motivated by the fact that these items were the most visually simple that ELM had difficulty recognising visually, and therefore that shape-based errors with such stimuli would be much easier to interpret than with visually complex biological items like animals or insects. ELM's errors on mismatching trials in this experiment were highly instructive. These errors were heavily concentrated on pairs of items that shared prominent visual shape features with each other. The most notable visual property that determined the errors was elongation. Thus, elongated items (e.g. cucumber and banana) were very often confused with one another and rounded objects (e.g. onion and apple) were confused among themselves. Errors on negative picture–word pairs involving an elongated and a rounded item almost never occurred. Another shape property that appeared determinant was tapering. Thus, negative pairs of items such as pear–lemon, which appear to have been pinched on one or both ends to produce tapered extremities, led to frequent errors. By contrast, there appeared to be no semantic constraint on errors on negative trials. Fruits were readily confused with vegetables, domestic items were confused with exotic ones, fruits that grow on trees were confused with others that grow in bushes, etc. These observations are congruent with the notion that visual similarity, not semantic proximity, is the first determinant of visual recognition errors in CSVA. It was further proposed that ELM's errors on mismatching picture–word pairs were largely determined by the existence of common prominent shape features among items, along with an incapacity to take into account the inconsistency between them on other aspects of their shapes. For instance, it was quite clear that ELM's frequent acceptation of the picture–word pair cucumber–banana was due to their common degree of elongation. However, had he been capable consistently to consider at the same time that cucumbers are typically straight whereas bananas are curved, he would never have accepted such a negative match. From this, it was hypothesised that ELM's main deficit was in processing the full complement of features that are required to uniquely specify the shape of a particular object, i.e. to reliably distinguish it from any other item that has some shape features in common with it. This hypothesis, referred to as that of a shape integration impairment, was tested in a series of subsequent experiments.

To gain full control over the visual properties of the stimuli used and to avoid the arbitrary constraints imposed by the shapes of real-world objects in this investigation of shape processing in ELM, the subsequent studies by Arguin et al. (1996b) made use of computer-generated two-dimensional (2D) synthetic shapes. These stimuli were filled ellipsoids whose shapes were defined parametrically along the dimensions of elongation (or aspect ratio; defined as the ratio of major over minor axes), curvature (perpendicular to the major axis), and tapering (along the major axis). The rationale for using these particular dimensions, as well as the details of the method used for generating these shapes, can be found in Arguin et al. (1996b). Examples of shapes that can be produced using this scheme are illustrated in Figure 4.2. The feature values of the stimuli aligned along the horizontal axis vary on elongation, items aligned along the vertical axis vary on curvature, and those on the depth axis differ on tapering.

In one picture–word matching experiment using such synthetic stimuli, items had shapes resembling some idealised fruits and vegetables (Arguin et al., 1996b, experiment 2). In other respects, the paradigm was highly similar to that used in the preceding picture–word matching experiment. The results confirmed one implication of the hypothesis of a shape integration deficit in ELM, namely that error rates on negative trials should decrease with the number of shape features by which the object referred to by the word differed from the picture presented. Thus, ELM accepted negative picture–word pairs on 43.5% of trials if items differed from each other by only one shape feature. However, pairs differing on two shape features were accepted as matching on 25% of trials and those differing along the three shape dimensions of elongation, curvature, and tapering led to an error on only 8.3% of trials. The most significant advances in the study of shape processing in ELM were achieved,

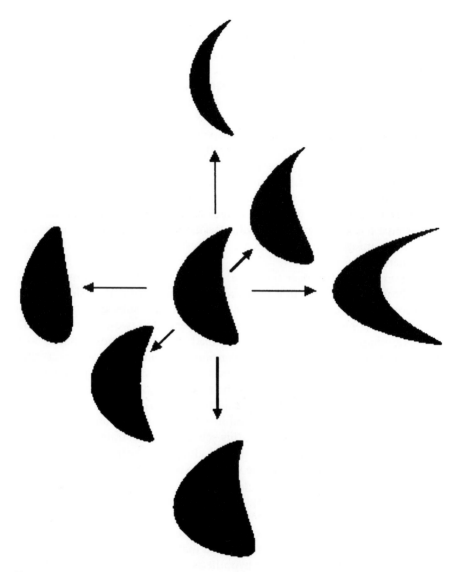

Figure 4.2.   Illustration of the dimensions used to define the shapes of stimuli in Arguin et al. (1996b).

however, in tasks where the stimuli used made no explicit reference to the visual appearances of real-world objects.

Possibly the most crucial experiment for a characterisation of the shape-processing deficit in ELM was one where he was required to learn unique and arbitrary associations between sets of four shapes and particular spatial locations on a computer screen (Arguin et al., 1996b, experiment 4). In a first, learning, phase of the experiment, ELM was exposed to each stimulus of a set placed at its respective corner on the computer screen and asked to remember each shape–location assignment. In a second, test phase, each shape was shown individually at the centre of the computer screen and ELM was simply asked to point to its previously assigned location. In this experiment, two classes of stimulus sets were used. One was called " single dimension sets", and was made of items whose shapes varied either on elongation, curvature, or tapering, but whose values on the other two dimensions remained constant, thereby rendering them irrelevant. This organisation of single dimension sets is illustrated in Figure 4.3a, which shows the locations of each stimulus within a 2D shape space. For instance, the single dimension "elongation" shape set was made of items differing from each other by their feature value on the dimension of elongation, whereas stimuli all were

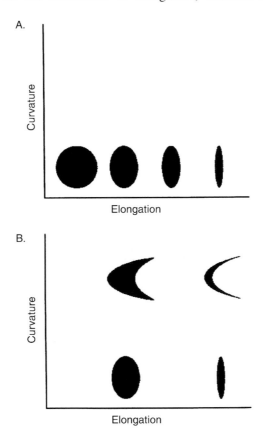

Figure 4.3. Example of stimuli from a single dimension set (A) and a conjunction set (B) along with their respective locations within a two-dimensional shape space.

assigned identical feature values on the dimensions of curvature and tapering. The second class of stimulus sets was called "conjunction sets". Shapes in a conjunction set varied along two dimensions (elongation and curvature, elongation and tapering, or curvature and tapering) in such a way that each item of a set had the same feature value as another item on one of those dimensions, and the same feature value as a third item on the other dimension (Figure 4.3b). All items shared the same feature value on the irrelevant dimension. For instance, the four shapes constituting the "elongation/ curvature" conjunction set were produced by crossing two feature values on the dimension of elongation with two feature values on the dimension of curvature; all items shared the same value on curvature. With this stimulus arrangement, the unique identification of a particular item within a conjunction set required the processing of a conjunction of the critical shape features as otherwise, confusions would occur between items that shared feature values with one another. By contrast, proper processing of the single critical feature dimension was sufficient for accurate performance with single dimensions sets. In a patient like ELM, who was assumed to have difficulty in processing combinations of shape features (i.e. shape integration deficit), it was expected that performance would suffer with conjunction relative to single dimension sets. The results supported this prediction, with ELM making about twice as many errors with conjunction shape sets (56.7%) as with single dimension sets (29.2%). The distribution of errors made by ELM with conjunction sets was also congruent with the notion of a shape integration impairment. Thus, on 91.2% of his errors with conjunction sets, ELM pointed to the location of an item that shared one critical feature with the target. In other words, it was extremely rare for ELM to confuse items from conjunction sets that had no property in common on one of the critical dimensions.

Crucially, the conjunction effect observed in the above shape–location learning experiment cannot be accounted for simply on the basis that shapes from conjunction sets were less distinct from one another than those from single dimension sets; in fact, the opposite was true. Thus, the feature values used to construct items from conjunction sets were quite extreme (e.g. straight versus sharply curved) and the differences between these feature values were as great as or greater than just about any feature value difference that existed among shapes from single dimension sets (see Figure 4.3). For instance, in conjunction sets involving the dimension of curvature, curvature differences were as great as the total range of curvature values covered in the "curvature" single dimension set. Congruent with this view, Dixon et al. (1997, experiment 1) later showed that neurologically intact individuals rated shapes from single dimension sets as more visually similar among themselves than those from conjunction sets. What these observations mean is that ELM's particular difficulty with conjunction sets in the shape–location task was not a function of the overall discriminability between shapes, but rather of the fact that specific pairs of items in these sets shared shape features along dimensions that were at the same time critical to distinguish among objects, something that did not exist in single dimension sets.

A subsequent experiment corroborated this interpretation and showed that ELM's deficit was not one of perceptual encoding, but rather that it concerned the stored representations of object shapes or access to these memory representations (Arguin et al., 1996b, experiment 5). This experiment assessed perceptual encoding while placing minimal demands on memory for visual shapes and used exactly the same stimulus sets as the previous shape–location task. Thus, on every trial, a single target shape was shown at the centre of a computer screen for 1 second. Then, following a blank delay of 1 second, the four stimuli of the set the target belonged to were displayed simultaneously for an unlimited duration, each at a randomly determined corner of the computer screen. ELM's task was simply to point to the shape that matched the previously displayed target. In this experiment, ELM made a single error out of 240 trials with shapes from conjunction sets (0.004% errors) but made an error on 8.8% of trials with single dimension sets, a difference that was highly significant. This result demonstrated the greater difficulty of perceptual discriminations among items from single dimension sets and confirmed that the deficit exhibited by ELM with conjunction sets in the previous shape–location experiment concerned the integration of features defining the shapes of objects held in memory.

The observations obtained from ELM with synthetic shapes confirmed inferences based on his initial testing, namely that his deficit affected the structural description stage of visual processing. Most importantly, however, they also provided a detailed description of this deficit, which can be characterised as one affecting the integration of features defining the shapes of objects held in memory. That such a deficit led to CSVA affecting particularly biological objects is congruent with the notions discussed in the preceding sections, according to which this disorder is largely a function of the greater visual similarity between biological objects than between man-made objects. The concept of visual similarity that was highlighted by the results of Arguin et al. (1996b), however, dissociates from one referring to overall discriminability among shapes, as defined by the Euclidian distance separating items in a perceptual shape space (e.g. Garner, 1974; Shepard, 1991). Rather, these results indicated that the relevant definition of visual similarity is according to whether or not items share features with one another on critical dimensions that determine their shapes.

Interaction of shape by semantic processing

Even for the theories discussed above that implicate visual similarity as a key element in explaining visual recognition impairments specific to biological objects, some additional factor seems to be required for a complete account of this type of disorder. In the context of visual object recognition, the concept of similarity requires a reference group that specifies what a particular target object is similar to. The relevant reference group for all of the visual similarity theories of CSVA discussed above is always made of objects that belong to the same semantic category as the target. The reasons why this is so are not always transparent, however. One clear and explicit statement that has been made in this regard is by Riddoch, Humphreys, and their collaborators (Forde et al., 1997; Humphreys et al., 1988, 1995; Riddoch & Humphreys, 1987b). For these authors, the reason why the reference group against which visual similarity is assessed is made of objects of the same category is because the visual object recognition system operates in cascade. This implies the occurrence of interactive effects of factors that tap separate processing stages, notably those concerned with the visual shape of an object (i.e. perceptual encoding and structural descriptions) and those concerned with its meaning (i.e. semantic memory). Thus, what their theory predicts is that increased visual similarity between objects will cause some uncertainty on the representation of the target at the stages processing its shape. This uncertainty will then be transmitted to semantic memory, where it will be magnified if the items that are visually similar to the target are also semantically related to it. In other words, the prediction is for an overadditive interaction of visual similarity and semantic proximity, such that the effect of visual similarity will be exclusive to, or much greater for, semantically related objects than for items that belong to separate semantic categories. A complementary hypothesis suggested by Arguin et al. (1996b) that could contribute to the interaction of visual similarity with semantic proximity is that of feedback from semantic memory to structural descriptions, which could help separate the shape representations of visually similar items if they are semantically very distinct from one another.

Decisive tests of the predicted interaction between visual similarity and semantic proximity are extremely difficult to produce if the visual stimuli used make explicit reference to real-world objects. Attempts of partial tests of this interaction in CSVA patients have been made by Forde et al. (1997), as described earlier, as well as by Arguin et al. (1996b, experiment 6). The visual and semantic properties of real-world objects are inextricably tied, however, and the contribution of each of these factors can hardly be separated completely. One way to escape this difficulty is to devise a new kind of paradigm where the links existing between the visual shape of an object and its meaning become entirely under the control of the experimenter. Such a paradigm, affording a full exploration of the visual similarity by semantic relatedness interaction, has been developed by Dixon et al. (1997), who have applied it to ELM.

As described at the beginning of this chapter, it is widely assumed, both in cognitive psychology and neuropsychology, that the links within the object recognition system between the visual shape and the name of an object are not direct, but rather that they are mediated by semantic memory. In terms of the present purpose, this means that if one were able to force the links between the shape of an item and an arbitrary name it has been assigned to pass through a particular conceptual representation in semantic memory, it would become possible experimentally to manipulate the semantic value of a visually presented item independently of its shape. This is what Dixon et al. (1997) attempted.

The initial paradigm that was developed was one where the subject was asked to learn arbitrary associations between a visual shape and a particular sound that referred to an object that was recognisable by the subject. In the test phase, a visual shape was then shown by itself and the subject was asked to provide its name. In their experiment 2, for instance, Dixon et al. (1997) asked ELM to learn to associate the sounds of a leaf-blower, of water being poured into a glass, of a motorcycle, and of a telephone ringing, with each of a set of four distinct shapes. In the test phase, ELM was then required to indicate whether the single shape presented was the "leaf-blower", the "water", the "motorcycle", or the "telephone". The sounds used corresponded either to semantically related or unrelated objects and the shape sets tested within this paradigm were single-dimension or conjunction sets, such as defined by Arguin et al. (1996b; see earlier).[4] In support of the assumptions underlying the paradigm, results showed that the semantic relatedness of the objects referred to by the sounds indeed had an effect on ELM's performance, with semantically related sounds leading to poorer performance. Most importantly, the results showed an interaction between the effects of shape set (single dimension versus conjunction) and semantic relatedness (close versus distant). Thus, the effect of semantic relatedness was absent with single-dimension shape sets, which also produced smaller error rates than conjunction shape sets. The effect of semantic relatedness was very large with conjunction sets, however. For instance, in the second half of the experiment, ELM made 41.14% errors with the semantically related conjunction sets, but no error at all with semantically unrelated conjunction sets. A subsequent experiment (experiment 3) using the same paradigm showed that the

---

[4] As in Arguin et al. (1996b), shapes from single-dimension sets were less discriminable from one another than those from conjunction sets. The results, described later, again support a definition of visual similarity in terms of shared shape features among objects rather than Euclidian distance between objects in shape space.

shape-by-semantics interaction was independent of whether the sounds used referred to biological or man-made objects. This indicated that what controlled ELM's visual identification performance was indeed the combined factors of visual similarity among shapes (in terms of whether or not they shared critical features) and semantic relatedness, not the biological versus non-biological distinction *per se*.

However, the most remarkable finding from ELM came from an extension of the shape–sound paradigm described earlier, where object sounds were simply replaced by auditory object names (Dixon et al., 1997, experiment 4). Thus, ELM was first asked to learn specific shape–name associations and was then tested with shapes shown individually, to which he had to respond with their assigned names. Strikingly, this rather elementary procedure was sufficient to attach the meaning referred to by the name to a simple visual shape that had no prior association with this semantic content (this was revealed to be true not only in ELM, but also in neurologically intact controls; Dixon et al., 1997, experiment 6). Indeed, the results from the shape–name task replicated those from the shape–sound paradigm. Those observations were then extended in another experiment using the shape–name paradigm with single-dimension and conjunction shape sets along with name sets that varied parametrically in their semantic relatedness (Dixon et al., 1997, experiment 5). The results showed no effect whatsoever of semantic relatedness on ELM's performance with single-dimension sets (error rates with these stimuli averaged between 10% and 20%). Thus, the correlation between his error rates with single-dimension sets and the degree of semantic proximity among the names used was .06. In sharp contrast, the error rates with conjunction sets increased very markedly (from about 0% to 66%) and linearly with an increased semantic relatedness between the names. The correlation between error rates with conjunction sets and semantic relatedness was .81. Again, this effect of semantic relatedness with conjunction sets of shapes was independent of the biological versus man-made distinction.

The above experiments show unambiguously that ELM's visual object recognition performance is controlled jointly by the existence of shared shape features among objects that must be distinguished and by their semantic relatedness. Specifically, the stimulus context that is disproportionately problematic for ELM in a visual recognition task is one where the processing of conjunctions of shape features is required to uniquely identify items that are closely related in terms of their assigned semantic content. Given the differing properties of biological and man-made objects discussed previously, these observations from ELM can account for the category selectivity of the patient's visual agnosia without the need to assume fundamental differences in the way biological and non-biological categories are represented. These results also fit with the fact that, within the realm of man-made objects, ELM has (as have several other CSVA cases) major difficulties in the visual recognition of musical instruments and makes of cars; categories that also comprise objects that are highly similar in shape. The joint effect of visual similarity and semantic proximity also applies to ELM's profound difficulties with face recognition. In an extension of the shape–name paradigm, Dixon et al. (1998) asked ELM to learn unique and arbitrary associations between visually presented (unknown) faces and famous people's names that referred to semantically related or unrelated individuals. ELM's performance was profoundly impaired (up to 60% errors) with sets of visually similar faces that were assigned semantically related names. By contrast, his performance was at a level indistinguishable from that of matched controls if visually similar faces were assigned semantically unrelated names or if visually very distinct faces received the names of related famous persons.

Legitimate questions still remain however, relative to the implications that can be derived from the studies of patient ELM. One such question is whether the notion of shared shape features, as well as its interactive effect with semantic proximity, remains relevant with respect to other individuals. Indeed, although it was possible to document the properties of ELM's visual recognition impairment in great detail, the possibility remains that the functional architecture that was documented is quite unusual, for reasons related to particular features of either the patient's brain damage or his development. Another question pertains to the properties of a visual recognition system that are required to account for the joint effects of shared shape features and semantic relatedness. In principle, the structure of the visual recognition system argued for by Humphreys, Riddoch, and their collaborators (Forde et al., 1997; Humphreys et al., 1988, 1995; Riddoch & Humphreys, 1987b) appears relevant. However, the currently existing implementation of this model (Humphreys et al., 1995) is based on local object representations in the shape domain, i.e. the shape of an object is represented "holistically" by a single processing unit in the model. This organisation appears incompatible with shared shape features as the index of visual similarity to which ELM was particularly sensitive, as opposed to Euclidian distance between object representations in shape space. Indeed, the effect of shared shape features such as demonstrated by ELM (and in other instances as well, see later) suggests that visual shapes are represented as distributed collections of discrete features and that a particular integration operation is required to distinguish reliably between items that have critical shape features in common (see Arguin et al., 1996b; for an elaborated discussion of this issue). We may therefore ask whether it is possible to achieve the interactive effects of semantic relatedness and visual similarity in a model where the shape of an object is explicitly defined over a set of distributed, discrete features. The next two sections will address these issues in turn.

GENERALISATION OF IMPLICATIONS FROM ELM

Sensitivity to shared critical features among shapes that must be discriminated, as well as to the semantic relatedness of labels assigned to them, are not exclusive to ELM. Other instances of such effects have been observed. Possibly the most relevant case is that of patient IL, who showed CSVA due to brain damage produced by herpes simplex encephalitis (Arguin et al., 1996a). Following his recovery, IL complained of major memory problems—initially claiming no recollection of his past life, a problem that partially resolved afterwards—as well as prosopagnosia and visual object agnosia. On matched sets of line drawings of biological and man-made objects from the Snodgrass and Vanderwart (1980) set, he made 65% errors on biological items but only 20% with man-made items. Like most other CSVA cases, IL's visual perceptual encoding was intact but he showed major difficulties in accessing stored structural descriptions of biological objects, both from vision (46% errors with animals and 48% errors with fruit and vegetables in the object decision task) and from verbal questions (45% errors on two-alternative forced-choice questions). His performance in these tasks was substantially better with man-made objects (28% errors on object decisions; 10% on verbal questions). His semantic memory appeared relatively spared and his performance on verbal questions probing non-sensory knowledge did not vary as a function of whether they concerned biological or non-biological objects (15% errors in both conditions).

IL was tested on the shape–name learning paradigm where semantically related or unrelated names were assigned arbitrarily to items from single dimension or conjunction shape sets that were made of four stimuli each. Although IL performed very poorly in this task (overall error rate of 57%), his results nevertheless revealed an interactive effect of shape set by semantic relatedness of the same form as that previously observed in ELM. Thus, IL's performance was unaffected by semantic relatedness with single dimension shape sets (59% and 53% errors with semantically related and unrelated labels, respectively). However, his performance with conjunction shape sets was much worse if items were assigned semantically related (74% errors) rather than unrelated (43% errors) labels. These results constitute a replication of the previous key findings from ELM (Arguin et al., 1996b; Dixon et al., 1997). Additionally, they also support the account of CSVA based on the joint effects of shared shape features and semantic proximity, as well as its implications for the organisation of the visual object recognition system.

Another category of brain-damaged patients with whom the shape–name learning paradigm has been applied with interesting results are those with dementia of the Alzheimer's type (DAT; Dixon & Arguin, 1999). Such patients frequently suffer difficulties in visual object recognition and a number of reports suggest that these difficulties are greater with biological than man-made objects (Daum, Riesch, Sartori, & Birbaumer, 1996; Mazzoni et al., 1991; Silveri, Daniele, Giustolisi, & Gainotti, 1991). Dixon and Arguin (1999) tested DAT patients using the shape–name learning paradigm where each of a set of three shapes was paired arbitrarily with a particular object name. One class of shape sets was made of items that shared multiple features among themselves so that the processing of conjunctions of shape features was required for unique identification (conjunction sets). The other class of stimulus sets was made of items that could be distinguished from all the others by the processing of a single shape feature (single-feature sets). Name sets were semantically related or not and were made of terms referring either to biological or man-made objects. Over their two experiments, Dixon and Arguin (1999) found no effect of the biological/non-biological distinction in the terms used but main effects of shape set and of semantic relatedness of the names. Thus, error rates were about doubled with conjunction relative to single-feature shape sets as well as with semantically related relative to unrelated names. Irrespective of the implications these results might have regarding particular clinical features of DAT or the apparent category speci-ficity of visual recognition deficits in this disorder, the observations of Dixon and Arguin (1999) clearly show that shared-shape features and semantic relatedness are major determinants of performance in individuals other than ELM.

Shared-shape features also affect perceptual encoding in neurologically intact individuals. Arguin and Saumier (2000) had normal observers perform visual searches for predetermined target shapes that differed from distractors either by a single feature or by a conjunction of features. For instance, in the single-feature condition the target could be defined relative to distractors by its unique value on the shape dimensions of elongation or curvature. In the conjunction condition the target had the same value as some distractors on the dimension of elongation and the same value as other distractors on the dimension of curvature, thus requiring the processing of combinations of shape features for accurate target detection. Results showed markedly slower search rates in the conjunction than the single-feature condition and separate control experiments demonstrated that the discriminability of the targets and distractors was effectively equated across these conditions. Thus, the slower search rates in the conjunction condition are specifically attributable to the fact that processing combinations of shape features was essential in this con-dition whereas this was not required in the single-feature condition. These observations demonstrate that sensitivity to shared-shape features in visual performance extends beyond ELM and that it is a property of the intact visual perceptual encoding system.

MODELLING THE INTERACTION BETWEEN
SHARED-SHAPE FEATURES AND
SEMANTIC RELATEDNESS

The theory of visual object recognition proposed by Humphreys, Riddoch, and their collaborators (Forde et al., 1997; Humphreys et al., 1988, 1995; Riddoch & Humphreys, 1987b) appears capable of producing the interactive effects of visual similarity and of semantic proximity that are required to account for category-specific effects in CSVA. The implemented version of this theory, however, is based on local representations of object shapes, a property that contradicts the findings cited above from ELM, IL, DAT patients, and neurologically intact observers. These argue instead for distributed representations of object shapes that are made of collections of discrete features that must be integrated when objects share shape features with one another.

To account for the observations made in patient ELM, Dixon et al. (1997; see also Dixon et al., 1998, Dixon & Arguin, 1999) have proposed an alternative model where shape representations are based on collections of discrete features. This model was largely inspired by the ALCOVE model, which was initially proposed as an account of various visual categorisation data (Kruschke, 1992). The system of Dixon et al. (1997) encodes visual shapes through a series of input nodes, each coding a feature value defining the item on a particular shape dimension. Activation from these input nodes is then transferred to a hidden layer that represents exemplars as points in a multidimensional psychological space. This psychological space acts as a long-term memory that has the dual responsibility of coding stored properties about objects on both visual and semantic dimensions. The hidden exemplar layer connects to output units responsible for the production of responses identifying a particular target shape applied on the input units. Two key features largely determine the operation of the model. One is the assumption of a limited pool of attentional resources in the connections between input and hidden units (Nosofsky, 1986). Thus, if a particular condition requires the processing of multiple shape dimensions for correct discriminations among objects (as in conjunction shape sets), the overall attention pool is divided across these dimensions. Less attention is therefore available for each relevant stimulus dimension than if correct performance can be supported by the processing of a single stimulus dimension. In that case, all of the attentional resources can be directed to that dimension and none is allocated to the irrelevant dimensions. The other major feature of the model is that activation within the hidden layer is not an all-or-none matter, but rather is a graded function of the similarity between the exemplars stored in this long-term memory and the stimulus presented on the input layer. Specifically, it was assumed that activation in the hidden layer falls off exponentially as the similarity between the stimulus values coded at input and in the hidden layer decrease. The rate of this fall-off of activation is a function of a specificity parameter that controls the selectivity of units in the hidden layer. The simulations conducted by Dixon et al. (1997) using this model replicated the effect of shared-shape features shown by ELM in the shape location task as well as the interactive effects of shared-shape features and semantic relatedness in the shape–name task (the latter result was also found in IL [Arguin et al., 1996a] as discussed earlier). These observations were produced by decreasing the selectivity of units in the hidden layer, without affecting the connections between input and hidden exemplar units or the attention weights that modulate their function. Crucial to the production of the above results is the fact that the hidden exemplar layer codes both visual and semantic properties of known objects. Impairment of this level of processing by reducing the selectivity of units therefore renders the network overly sensitive to both visual similarity and semantic proximity. As these two factors affect the same level of processing, they will also interact with one another (Sternberg, 1969, 1998), thus replicating the results of ELM in the shape–name task. However the very feature of Dixon et al.'s (1997) model that appears crucial in simulating the findings from ELM is also problematic. Indeed, the long-term memory store that is assumed to be impaired in ELM codes both visual and semantic knowledge of objects. This predicts an impairment affecting stored visual as well as semantic object properties. This assumption is contradicted by the dissociation exhibited by ELM (as well as by other CSVA patients) between impaired access to stored structural descriptions but intact semantic knowledge.

A more recent series of simulations (Rzempoluck, Bub, & Arguin, 1998) have been conducted using a trainable cascade connectionist network with an architecture very similar to that of Dixon et al. (1997). The major innovation, however, was that two (instead of just one) hidden layers were used, one representing stored knowledge of object shape and the other semantic properties. This architecture is highly consistent with that described at the beginning of this chapter and appears entirely compatible with the occurrence of dissociations between the structural descriptions and semantic memory stages. Simulations of ELM's and IL's performance in the shape–name task were conducted on this model following selective damage to the connections between the input nodes, which code feature values on specific shape dimensions, and the first hidden layer, which corresponds to the structural descriptions stage. Results showed the same interactive effects of shared-shape features and of semantic relatedness as exhibited by ELM and IL, even while the model codes these two factors at separate processing stages.

CONCLUSIONS

This chapter has reviewed the literature on visual object recognition impairments attributable to a presemantic deficit and that are specific to biological object categories. Several authors concur that such impairments are not a function of a categorically organised visual object recognition system but rather that they reflect the greater visual similarity of objects within biological than man-made categories. In particular, it has often been assumed that the greater within-category similarity for biological objects renders them more difficult to dissociate from each other and, therefore, more susceptible to the effects of brain damage. The studies of patient ELM that are reviewed above have provided the first controlled experimental demonstration that visual similarity and semantic proximity do indeed jointly determine visual object recognition performance in category-specific visual agnosia. These investigations have implications that extend beyond the particular case of ELM. Notably, results have argued for distributed representations of object shapes that are made of collections of discrete features. Support for this assumption has been found in patient IL (who is another case suffering from CSVA), DAT patients, and neurologically intact observers. Finally, we report computational models that are capable of replicating the interactive effects of visual similarity and semantic proximity documented in patients ELM and IL while implementing a distributed code for shape representation.

ACKNOWLEDGEMENTS

The present work was supported by a grant from the Natural Sciences and Engineering Research Council of Canada to Martin Arguin. Thanks to Daniel Saumier for his technical assistance and for stimulating discussions on category specific deficits. Martin Arguin is Chercheur-boursier of the Fonds de la Recherche en Santé du Québec.

REFERENCES

Arguin, M., Bub, D., Dixon, M., Caillé, S., & Fontaine, S. (1996a). Shape integration and semantic proximity effects in visual agnosia for biological objects: a replication. *Brain and Cognition 32*, 259–261.

Arguin, M., Bub, D., & Dudek, G. (1996b). Shape integration for visual object recognition and its implication in category specific visual agnosia. *Visual Cognition, 3*, 221–275.

Arguin, M., & Saumier, D. (2000). Conjunction and linear separability effects in visual shape encoding. *Vision Research, 40*, 3099–3115.

Basso, A., Capitani, E., & Laiacona, M. (1988). Progressive language impairment without dementia: a case with isolated category specific semantic defect. *Journal of Neurology, Neurosurgery, and Psychiatry, 51*, 1201–1207.

Benson, D.F., & Greenberg, J.P. (1969). Visual form agnosia: A specific defect in visual discrimination. *Archives of Neurology, 20*, 82–89.

Biederman, I., & Ju, G. (1988). Surface versus edge-based determinants of visual recognition. *Cognitive Psychology, 20*, 38–64.

Caramazza, C. (1998). The interpretation of semantic category-specific deficits: What do they reveal about the organization of conceptual knowledge in the brain? *Neurocase, 4*, 265–272.

Caramazza, A., & Shelton, J. (1998). Domain-specific knowledge systems in the brain: The animate-inanimate distinction. *Journal of Cognitive Neuroscience, 10*, 1–34.

Coltheart, M., Inglis, L., Cupples, L., Michie, P., Bates, A., & Budd, B. (1998). A semantic subsystem of visual attributes. *Neurocase, 4*, 353–370.

Damasio, A.R. (1990). Category-related recognition defects as a clue to the neural substrates of knowledge. *Trends in Neuroscience, 13*, 95–98.

Daum, I., Riesch, G., Sartori, G., & Birbaumer, N. (1996). Semantic memory impairment in Alzheimer's disease. *Journal of Clinical and Experimental Neuropsychology, 18*, 648–665.

Decter, M. (1992). *Multiple representation of object concepts: Evidence from category-specific agnosia*. Unpublished Master's dissertation, McGill University, Montreal, Canada.

De Renzi, E., & Lucchelli, F. (1994). Are semantic systems separately represented in the brain? The case of living category impairment. *Cortex, 30*, 3–25.

Devlin, J.T., Gonnerman, L. M., Andersen, E.S., & Seidenberg, M.S. (1998). Category specific semantic deficits in focal and widespread brain damage. A computational account. *Journal of Cognitive Neuroscience, 10*, 77–94.

Dixon, M., & Arguin, M. (1999). Shape set dimensionality versus structural distance effects in a patient with category-specific visual agnosia. *Brain and Cognition, 40*, 101–104.

Dixon, M., Bub, D., & Arguin, M. (1997). The interaction of object form and object meaning in the identification performance of a patient with category-specific visual agnosia. *Cognitive Neuropsychology, 14*, 1085–1130.

Dixon, M., Bub, D., & Arguin, M. (1998). Semantic and visual determinants of face recognition in a prosopagnosic patient. *Journal of Cognitive Neuroscience, 10*, 362–376.

Dudek, G., Arguin, M., & Bub, D. (1994). Human integration of shape primitives. In C. Arcelli, L.P. Cordella, and G.S. di Baja (Eds.), *Aspects of Visual Form Processing* (pp. 188–198). River Edge, NJ: World Scientific.

Dudek, G., Arguin, M., Dixon, M., & Bub, D. (1997). Coding simple shapes for recognition and the integration of shape descriptors. In M. Jenkins & L. Harris (Eds.), *Computational and Psychophysical Mechanisms of Visual Coding* (pp. 44–60). New York: Cambridge University Press.

Etcoff, N. L., Freeman, R., & Cave, K.R. (1991). Can we lose memories of faces? Content specificity and awareness in a prosopagnosic. *Journal of Cognitive Neuroscience, 3*, 25–41.

Farah, M.J. (1991). Patterns of co-occurrence among the associative agnosias: Implications for visual object representation. *Cognitive Neuropsychology, 8*, 1–19.

Farah, M.J., Hammond, K.M., Mehta, Z., & Ratcliff, G. (1989). Category-specificity and modality-specificity in semantic memory. *Neuropsychologia, 27*, 193–200.

Farah, M.J., & McClelland, J.L. (1991). A computational model of semantic memory impairment: Modality specificity and emergent category specificity. *Journal of Experimental Psychology: General, 120*, 339–357.

Farah, M.J., McMullen, P.A., & Meyer, M.M. (1991). Can recognition of living things be selectively impaired? *Neuropsychologia, 29*, 185–193.

Feldman, J., & Richards, W. (1998). Mapping the mental space of rectangles. *Perception, 27*, 1191–1202.

Forde, E.M.E., Francis, D., Riddoch, M.J., Rumiati, R., & Humphreys, G.W. (1997). On the links between visual knowledge and naming: A single case study of a patient with a category-specific impairment for living things. *Cognitive Neuropsychology, 14*, 403–458.

Forde, E.M.E., & Humphreys, G.W. (1999). Category-specific recognition impairments: A review of important case studies and influential theories. *Aphasiology, 13*, 169–193.

Funnell, E., & Sheridan, J. (1992). Categories of knowledge? Unfamiliar aspects of living and nonliving things. *Cognitive Neuropsychology, 9*, 135–153.

Gaffan, D., & Heywood, C.A. (1993). A spurious category-specific visual agnosia for living things in normal human and nonhuman primates. *Journal of Cognitive Neuroscience, 5*, 118–128.

Garner, W.R. (1974). *The Processing of Information and Sructure*. Potomac, MD: Lawrence Erlbaum Associates, Inc.

Gonnerman, L.M., Andersen, E.S., Devlin, J.T., Kempler, D., & Seidenberg, M.S. (1998). Double dissociation of semantic categories in Alzheimer's disease. *Brain and Language, 57*, 254–279.

Hoffman, D.D., & Singh, M. (1997). Salience of visual parts. *Cognition, 63*, 29–78.

Humphrey, G.K., Goodale, M.A., Jacobson, L.S., & Servos, P. (1994). The role of surface information in object recognition: Studies of a visual form agnosic and normal subjects. *Perception, 23*, 1457–1481.

Humphreys, G.W., Lamote, C., & Lloyd-Jones, T.J. (1995). An interactive activation approach to object processing: Effects of structural similarity, name frequency, and task in normality and pathology. *Memory, 3*, 535–586.

Humphreys, G.W., & Riddoch, M.J. (1987a). *To See but not to See: A Case Study of Visual Agnosia*. Hillsdale, NJ: Lawrence Erlbaum Associates, Inc.

Humphreys, G.W., & Riddoch, M.J. (1987b). On telling your fruit from your vegetables: A consideration of category-specific deficits after brain damage. *Trends in Neurosciences*, 10, 145–148.

Humphreys, G.W., Riddoch, M.J., & Quinlan, P.T. (1988). Cascade processes in picture identification. *Cognitive Neuropsychology, 5*, 67–103.

Kruschke, J.K. (1992). ALCOVE: An exemplar-based connectionist model of category learning. *Psychological Review, 99*, 22–44.

Lissauer, H. (1890). Ein fall von Seelenblindheit nebst einem Beitrage zur Theorie derselben. *Archive fur Psychiatrie, 21*, 222–270. Translated in Jackson, M. (1988). Lissauer on agnosia. *Cognitive Neuropsychology, 5*, 157–192.

Lloyd-Jones, T.J., & Humphreys, G.W. (1997). Perceptual differentiation as a source of category effects in object processing: Evidence from naming and object decision. *Memory and Cognition, 25*, 18–35.

McCarthy, R.A., & Warrington, E.K. (1988). Evidence for modality-specific meaning systems in the brain. *Nature, 334*, 428–430.

McClelland, J.L. (1979). On the time relations of mental processes: An examination of systems of processes in cascade. *Psychological Review, 86*, 287–330.

McRae, K., de Sa, V.R., & Seidenberg, M.S. (1997). On the nature and scope of featural representations of word meaning. *Journal of Experimental Psychology: General, 126*, 99–130.

Marr, D. (1982).*Vision*. San Fancisco: Freeman.

Marr, D., & Nishihara, H. K. (1978). Representation and recognition of the spatial organization of three-dimensional shapes. *Proceedings of the Royal Society of London, B200*, 269–294.

Mauri, A., Daum, I., Sartori, G., Riesch, G., & Birbaumer, N. (1994). Category-specific semantic impairment in Alzheimer's disease and temporal lobe dysfunction: A comparative study. *Journal of Clinical and Experimental Neuropsychology, 16*, 689–701.

Mazzoni, M., Moretti, P., Lucchini, C., Vista, M., & Muratorio, A. (1991). Category-specific semantic disorders in Alzheimer's disease. *Nuova Rivista di Neurologia, 61*, 77–85.

Milner, A.D., & Heywood, C.A. (1989). A disorder of lightness discrimination in a case of visual form agnosia. *Cortex, 25*, 489–494.

Moss, H.E., Tyler, L.K., Durrant-Peatfield, M., & Bunn, E.M. (1998). Two eyes of a see-through: Impaired and intact semantic knowledge in a case of selective deficit for living things. *Neurocase, 4*, 291–310.

Nosofsky, R.M. (1986). Attention, similarity, and the identification-categorization relationship. *Journal of Experimental Psychology: General, 115*, 39–57.

Price, C.J., & Humphreys, G.W. (1989). The effects of surface detail on object categorization and naming. *Quarterly Journal of Experimental Psychology, 41A*, 797–828.

Riddoch, M.J., & Humphreys, G.W. (1987a). A case of integrative visual agnosia. *Brain, 110*, 1431–1462.

Riddoch, M.J., & Humphreys, G.W. (1987b). Visual object processing in optic aphasia: A case of semantic access agnosia. *Cognitive Neuropsychology, 4*, 131–185.

Riddoch, M.J., Humphreys, G.W., Gannon, T., Blott, W., & Jones, V. (1999). Memories are made of this: The effects of time on stored visual knowledge in a case of visual agnosia. *Brain, 122*, 537–559.

Rzempoluck, E., Bub, D.N., & Arguin, M. (1998). *A computational model of visual processes in context-specific visual agnosia.* Unpublished technical report, University of Victoria, Canada.

Samson, D., Pillon, A., & De Wilde, V. (1998). Impaired knowledge of visual and nonvisual attributes in a patient with a semantic impairment for living entities: A case of a true category-specific deficit. *Neurocase, 4*, 273–290.

Sartori, G., Coltheart, M., Miozzo, M., & Job, R. (1995). Category specificity and informational specificity in neuropsychological impairment of semantic memory. In C. Umiltà & M. Moscovitch (Eds.), *Attention and Performance XV* (pp. 537–550). Cambridge, MA: MIT Press.

Sartori, G., & Job, R. (1988). The oyster with four legs: A neuropsychological study on the interaction of visual and semantic information. *Cognitive Neuropsychology, 5*, 105–132.

Sartori, G., Job, R., Miozzo, M., Zago, S., & Marchiori, G. (1993a). Category-specific form-knowledge deficit in a patient with herpes simplex virus encephalitis. *Journal of Clinical and Experimental Neuropsychology, 15*, 280–299.

Sartori, G., Miozzo, M., & Job, R. (1993b). Category-specific naming impairments? Yes. *Quarterly Journal of Experimental Psychology, 46A*, 489–504.

Shepard, R.N. (1991). Integrality versus separability of stimulus dimensions: From an early convergence of evidence to a proposed theoretical basis. In G.R. Lockhead & J.R. Pomerantz (Eds.), *The Perception of Structure: Essays in Honor of Wendell R. Garner* (pp. 53–71). Washington DC: American Psychological Association.

Silveri, M.C., Daniele, A., Giustolisi, L., & Gainotti, G. (1991). Dissociation between knowledge of living and nonliving things in dementia of the Alzheimer type. *Neurology, 41*, 545–546.

Snodgrass, J.G., & Vanderwart, M.A. (1980). Standardised set of 260 pictures: Norms for name agreement, image agreement, familiarity, and visual complexity. *Journal of Experimental Psychology: Human Learning and Memory, 6*, 174–215.

Sternberg, S. (1969). The discovery of processing stages: Extensions of Donders' method. *Acta Psychologica, 30*, 276–315.

Sternberg, S. (1998). Discovering mental processing stages: The method of additive factors. In D. Scarborough & S. Sternberg (Eds.), *Methods, Models, and Conceptual Issues: An Invitation to Cognitive Science* (Vol. 4, pp. 703–863). Cambridge, MA: MIT Press.

Stewart, F., Parkin, A.J., & Hunkin, N.M. (1992). Naming impairments following recovery from herpes simplex encephalitis. *Quarterly Journal of Experimental Psychology, 44A*, 261–284.

Tyler, L., & Moss, H. (1997). Functional properties of concepts: Studies of normal and brain-damaged patients. *Cognitive Neuropsychology, 14*, 511–545.

Vitkovitch, M., Humphreys, G.W., & Lloyd-Jones, T.J. (1993). On naming a giraffe a zebra: Picture naming errors across different object categories. *Journal of Experimental Psychology: Learning, Memory, and Cognition, 19*, 234–259.

Warrington, E.K., & McCarthy, R. (1987). Categories of knowledge: Further fractionations and an attempted integration. *Brain, 110*, 1273–1296.

Warrington, E.K., & Shallice, T. (1984). Category specific semantic impairments. *Brain, 107*, 829–854.

Wurm, L.H., Legge, G.E., Isenberg, L.M., & Luebker, A. (1993). Color improves object recognition in normal and low vision. *Journal of Experimental Psychology: Human Perception and Performance, 19*, 899–911.

CHAPTER FIVE

The emergence of category-specific deficits in a distributed semantic system

Helen E. Moss, Lorraine K. Tyler and Joseph T. Devlin
Department of Experimental Psychology, University of Cambridge, UK

INTRODUCTION

Patients with category-specific semantic deficits—a greater impairment for one domain or category of concepts than another—have played a key role in the development of theories of the organisation of conceptual knowledge in semantic memory. The most widely debated dissociation has been that between knowledge of living and non-living things, and this will be the focus of the current chapter. Numerous reports in the neuropsychological literature suggest that brain damage can disrupt knowledge of living things to a significantly greater extent than non-living things in some patients, whereas in other, albeit rarer, cases the reverse pattern is found (Barbarotto, Capitani, Spinnler, & Trivelli, 1995; Basso, Capitani, & Laiacona, 1988; Caramazza & Shelton, 1998; De Renzi & Lucchelli, 1994; Farah, Hammond, Mehta, & Ratcliff, 1989; Forde et al., 1997; Laiacona, Capitani, & Barbarotto, 1997; McCarthy & Warrington, 1988; Moss, Tyler, Durrant-Peatfield, & Bunn, 1998; Pietrini et al., 1988; Sacchett & Humphreys, 1992; Sartori & Job, 1988; Silveri & Gainotti, 1988; Warrington & McCarthy, 1987; Warrington & Shallice, 1984; for a review see Forde & Humphreys, 1999).

The simplest account of selective semantic impairments is that the behavioural dissociations between different categories of knowledge are a direct reflection of the underlying organisation of the conceptual system, implying that there are distinct, independent stores for each category of information (Goodglass, Klein, Carey, & Jones, 1966). An important recent development of this account suggests that certain domains of knowledge, such as animal and plant life, have their own dedicated neural systems as a result of their importance in evolutionary terms (Caramazza & Shelton, 1998).[1] These neural systems can be independently affected by focal brain damage, so resulting in truly selective deficits. An influential alternative has been the sensory/functional account developed by Warrington and colleagues (McCarthy & Warrington, 1988; Warrington & McCarthy, 1987; Warrington & Shallice, 1984). This suggests that the first-order organising principle in semantic memory is not category or domain of knowledge, but type of semantic property. It is argued that semantic memory is fractionated into separate stores for sensory/perceptual information and for functional (sometimes referred to as associative) information. Living things concepts are claimed to be more dependent on perceptual properties, and therefore more severely affected by damage to the perceptual subsystem, whereas the reverse tends to be true for non-living things, with greater impairments resulting from damage to the store of functional information.[2]

The domain-specific account and the sensory/functional account have been influential but both have their limitations. The sensory/functional account has recently been challenged by reports of patients who have living things deficits without an accompanying deficit for perceptual properties (Laiacona et al., 1997; Lambon Ralph, Howard, Nightingale, & Ellis, 1998; Moss et al., 1998), or who have poor knowledge of perceptual properties without an accompanying deficit for living things (Lambon Ralph et al., 1998). The domain-specific account predicts that there should be a strong association between focal lesions in specific regions of the brain and the domain of knowledge that is impaired. While there is some support for this link, with bilateral medial temporal damage often associated with impairments for living things and left frontoparietal damage with deficits for artefacts (Gainotti, Silveri, Daniele, & Giustolisi, 1995) there are certainly exceptions, and there are also reports of patients with category-specific deficits in the context of diffuse rather than focal brain damage (Gonnerman, Andersen, Devlin, & Seidenberg, 1997; Silveri, Danieli, Giustolisi, & Gainotti, 1991; Moss & Tyler, 2000). Functional neuroimaging studies also provide mixed results, with some reports suggesting regional specialisation for domains or categories of knowledge (Martin, Wiggs, Ungerleider & Haxby,

---

[1] The term "category" is used inconsistently in the literature. We will use the term "domain" to refer to the higher level distinction between living and non-living things, and reserve "category" for groups within those domains such as animals, fruit, tools, and vehicles.

[2] Other accounts have been put forward in the literature in which the deficit for living things is explained in terms of their lower familiarity (e.g. Funnell & Sheridan, 1992), greater visual complexity (e.g. Gaffan & Heywood, 1993) or some other "difficulty" factor. However, this kind of account cannot accommodate the reverse pattern of a greater deficit for non-living objects, and so we do not discuss them further here.

1996; Perani et al., 1995) and others more consistent with a unitary distributed semantic system (Devlin et al., 2000, 2002) or with organisation based on attribute type (e.g. motion/visual form) rather than domain *per se* (e.g. Chao, Haxby, & Martin, 1999; Mummery, Patterson, Hodges, & Price, 1998). Even if there are dedicated neural systems for certain domains of knowledge, the domain-specific account does not elucidate the organisation of information *within* domain-specific stores and so cannot explain the different patterns of breakdown of conceptual knowledge across domains that we discuss later in this chapter.

A NEW APPROACH: CONCEPTUAL STRUCTURE AND THE STRUCTURE OF CONCEPTS

We have recently begun to develop a new account of conceptual representation and category-specific deficits by bringing together theoretical insights and data from different disciplines with the aim of providing an integrated framework in which to model normal and disordered conceptual systems. At the heart of our approach is the investigation of the internal structure of concepts of different types, and hence we refer to it as the "conceptual structure account" (Durrant-Peatfield, Tyler, Moss, & Levy, 1997; Moss & Tyler, unpublished data; Tyler et al., 1996; Tyler, Moss, Durrant-Peatfield, & Levy, 2000). This account is fundamentally different from those outlined above in that we do not assume any explicit fractionation of semantic memory along either category/domain- or property-type boundaries. Rather, we suggest that there is a single, highly distributed network, in which all concepts are represented as patterns of activation over many nodes corresponding to semantic properties or "microfeatures". Damage to this kind of unitary, distributed system can potentially affect one category of concepts more than another because similar concepts are represented close together in semantic space— they have overlapping patterns of activation (for related similarity-based models, see Caramazza, Hillis, Rapp & Romani, 1990; also Dixon, Bub, & Arguin, 1997; Forde et al., 1997; Humphreys, Riddoch & Quinlan, 1988).

On the conceptual structure account, not only do similar concepts tend to activate overlapping sets of semantic features, but there are also systematic differences in the internal structure of concepts in different categories and domains. The central tenets of the account are that: (i) each concept has a specific structure, which is determined by the set of features it activates and the relations among those features; (ii) concepts in different categories and domains have characteristically different internal structure; and (ii) random, global damage throughout the system will affect concepts in different ways, as a function of their internal structure. Following McRae, de Sa, and Seidenberg (1997) and Devlin, Gonnerman, Andersen, and Seidenberg (1998) we claim that correlation is a key relation among semantic properties. Properties are correlated to the extent that they frequently occur together in concepts, such that the presence of one predicts that presence of the other. For example, the properties of "having eyes" and "being able to see" are very strongly correlated because they always occur together and do not occur separately. The significance of correlation is that in a distributed connectionist system, correlated properties support each other with mutual activation (Devlin et al., 1998). This means that strongly correlated properties are more resilient to damage within the semantic system than those that are more weakly correlated. Hence, different patterns of correlation among properties within a concept will lead to different patterns of loss and preservation of information, given the same degree of overall damage.

We claim that the structure of concepts in the living and non-living domains differs in systematic ways. The conceptual structure account addresses a criticism of earlier unitary, distributed models, such as OUCH (Organised Unitary Content Hypothesis; Caramazza et al., 1990), which was that such models are so flexible that they can explain any pattern of deficit, and are therefore theoretically unhelpful (Caramazza & Shelton, 1998). By developing very specific claims about conceptual structure, we are able to constrain the power of the account and make falsifiable predictions, thus overcoming this kind of objection. Our starting point was to base our theoretical assumptions about conceptual structure on well-supported claims in the psychological literature. First, living things (and most typically, animals) have many properties and many of these are shared among all members of a category (e.g. all mammals breathe, move, have eyes, can see, have live young, eat, and so on). Moreover, these shared properties co-occur frequently and so are strongly correlated (Keil, 1986, 1989; Malt & Smith, 1984). Living things also have distinctive properties that are informative in distinguishing one category member from another (e.g. "having stripes" versus "having spots"), although these tend to be correlated weakly, or not correlated at all, with other properties and so are vulnerable to damage. Artefacts have fewer properties in total, and they tend to be relatively more distinctive, with a smaller pool of information shared across all members of a category.

Another key aspect of the conceptual structure model, and the major difference from other correlation based models that have implemented some of the same fundamental assumptions (e.g. Devlin et al., 1998; McRae et al., 1997) is that we incorporate a set of claims about the relations between form (perceptual properties) and function in the living and non-living domains. These claims are again based on psychological research, drawing particularly heavily on the developmental literature, which investigates how children learn the relations among properties of concepts. We claim that an essential aspect of conceptual structure is the pattern of correlations between form and function (Tversky & Hemenway, 1984). Our argument goes as follows: if a perceptual form is consistently observed performing a function, then a system that is sensitive to co-occurrences will learn that a specific form implies a specific function (Madole, Oakes, & Cohen, 1993; Mandler, 1992). The nature of these form–function relations distinguishes between living things and artefacts. Artefacts have distinctive forms, which are consistently associated with the functions for which they were created (De Renzi & Lucchelli, 1994; Keil, 1986, 1989; see also Caramazza et al.'s [1990] claim of privileged relations among properties for a similar view). Artefacts are generally designed to perform a single distinctive function so that their form is as distinctive as the function. In contrast, living things tend to "do" similar things and they tend to resemble each other, thus they share many features. Individual variations in form tend not to be functionally significant (e.g. "a lion's mane"). Even so, living things (like artefacts) also have form–function correlations. But whereas the form–function correlations for artefacts involve distinctive properties, for living things it is the shared properties (e.g. "eyes", "legs") that are involved in form–function correlations (e.g. "eyes-see"; "legs-move"). We refer to these as biological functions (for further detail see Durrant-Peatfield et al., 1997; Tyler et al., 2000; Tyler & Moss, 1997).

In summary, the internal structure of concepts in the broad domains of living things and artefacts differ in that living things have more properties overall, more shared properties and more correlations among shared properties than do artefacts, while artefact structure is typically characterised by strong correlations between small sets of distinctive form and function properties. Because correlated properties support each other with mutual activation, distinctive properties of artefacts will be more resistant to damage than those of living things, while the reverse will tend to be the case for shared properties. Unlike the sensory/functional account, we are not claiming that functional information is more important for artefacts than for living things, but rather that there is a difference across domains in the *kind* of functional information that is most strongly correlated—and therefore most robust to damage. Living things have many, very important functional properties, but the most important ones concern their biological activities and are frequently shared across most or all members of a category, rather than their intended use or purpose in relation to human beings (Tyler & Moss, 1997).

The conceptual structure model comprises a set of claims about the nature of a central, distributed conceptual system and, as such, is applicable only to category-specific effects that arise as a result of damage to this system. Several researchers have suggested that the category-specific deficits of certain patients arise from damage outside of the conceptual system, in either: (i) a presemantic structural description system (Forde et al., 1997; Sartori, et al., 1993); or (ii) a postsemantic lexical system (Damasio, Grabowski, Tranel, Hichwa, & Damasio, 1996; Hart, Berndt, & Caramazza, 1985). In the former case, this would give rise to deficits in recognising visually presented objects or pictures for items with a high degree of structural similarity, while in the latter case problems would be manifest in tasks requiring the production of lexical labels for objects. At this stage in its development, the conceptual structure account is not tied to specific claims about the nature of the object recognition and lexical output processes that must clearly be a part of any complete cognitive theory. The scope of the current model is to characterise the structure of the conceptual system itself, and to accommodate data from those patients whose category-specific behaviour arises from an impairment located within the conceptual system rather than pre- or post-semantic processes—as revealed by pervasive deficits within one category or domain of knowledge, not restricted to any specific modality of input or output.

CONCEPTUAL STRUCTURE: A COMPUTATIONAL SIMULATION

The first phase of our research within the framework of the conceptual structure account was to implement our representational assumptions in a small-scale computational model and to simulate the effects of random damage. It is essential for our approach to demonstrate that random damage to a distributed semantic system can, in principle, have differential effects on conceptual representations that vary systematically in their internal structure in the ways outlined above, and to determine the patterns of behaviour that may result from these differential effects.

Our main representational claims were implemented in a simplified way in a smallscale connectionist model (Durrant-Peatfield et al., 1997; Tyler et al., 2000) in which concepts were represented by sets of "functional" and "perceptual" properties.[3] The properties were either shared (active for all members of a category) or distinctive (active only for a single concept). We constructed 16 concepts (or "semantic vectors") of which eight corresponded to living things and eight to artefacts. Within each domain we simulated two categories of four vectors each, such that the concepts with a category shared a proportion of their semantic properties. The proportion of shared to distinctive properties was higher for the living things than for the artefacts. The domains of artefacts and living things were further distinguished by the manner in which functional properties were correlated with perceptual properties. Specifically, the shared perceptual properties of living things (e.g. "has legs") were correlated with shared biological functions (e.g. "can move"), whereas distinctive perceptual properties (e.g. "a tiger's stripes") were not

---

[3] "Perceptual" and "functional" are in quotes, because in reality the features in this model were unnamed abstractions. Throughout the discussion of the model, we refer to named features such as "has legs" but these are just examples to illustrate the structure of the vectors in a more concrete way.

correlated with any other properties. In contrast, the eight artefacts had few shared, correlated properties and it was the distinctive perceptual properties (e.g. "has a serrated edge") that were strongly correlated with a specific function (e.g. "used for cutting").

After training a connectionist autoassociator on the 16 semantic vectors, the connections between layers were randomly chosen and progressively "lesioned" to simulate widespread damage to the system. For each level of lesioning, a percentage of connection weights (from 10% to 100%) were set to zero. We then evaluated the model's ability to correctly reproduce the semantic pattern for each item in the training set on its output layer, at each level of lesioning. Our predictions about the behaviour of the lesioned model were based on the assumption that loss of distinctive properties leads to errors in reproducing the correct target pattern, and that correlations protect properties in proportion to the strength of the correlation. So, we predicted that initially the model would make errors in correctly "identifying" living things because damage would have affected the vulnerable distinctive properties. We also predicted that mapping errors for living things would tend to be members of the same category because shared properties for living things are robust to damage due to their greater density of correlations. In contrast, we predicted that distinctive properties of artefacts would be preserved because they are correlated, allowing more accurate identification of the concept until the most severe levels of damage.

This was indeed what we found (Durrant-Peatfield et al., 1997; Tyler et al., 2000). For artefact concepts, the distinctive form–function correlations were preserved, enabling individual artefact concepts to be distinguished from each other. In contrast, the distinctive properties of living things were less well preserved whereas shared properties were robust to damage. Thus lesioning tended to make living things concepts hard to distinguish from each other while preserving their category membership. The model exhibited a selective deficit for living things, except at the most severe levels of lesioning. At this point, artefacts became more difficult to identify than living things, because severe damage overwhelmed both the shared properties and form–function-correlated properties of artefacts, leaving only the densely intercorrelated, shared biological functional correlations of living things. At this extreme level of damage, overall performance was very poor, but the remaining shared properties favoured living things over artefacts, giving them a small but significant advantage. The main results are presented in Figure 5.1.

In summary, the computational simulation demonstrates how the internal structure of concepts in terms of the patterns of correlation among properties produces differential effects of random damage through the system. Selective deficits for living things emerged at most levels of lesioning severity, but greater deficits for artefacts can arise on rare occasions when damage is

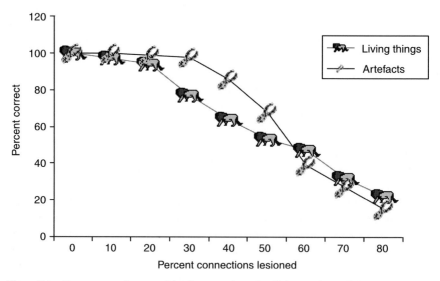

Figure 5.1. Percentage of correct-identity mappings for living and non-living things in the connectionist model as a function of lesion severity (percentage of connections set to zero). Adapted from Tyler et al. (2000).

particularly severe.[4] The model also simulates loss and preservation of particular kinds of semantic properties for items in the different domains as well as the overall dissociation—patterns of performance that can be directly tested in behavioural tests with semantically impaired patients (this is discussed later). We acknowledge that the model is small and over-simple, in that it includes only 16 artificially constructed concepts. Nevertheless, these vectors straightforwardly instantiated our major representational assumptions, which have also been supported by evidence from empirical studies of people's conceptual knowledge, as described in the following section.

CONCEPTUAL STRUCTURE: EMPIRICAL EVIDENCE SUPPORTING THE REPRESENTATIONAL ASSUMPTIONS

In the conceptual structure account we make a number of claims concerning the structure of concepts and how this differs across the living and non-living domains. As outlined above, these claims were based on findings in the

---

[4] This prediction contrasts with that of the Devlin et al. (1998) model, where artefact deficits were seen only at the mildest level of damage, followed by living things deficits damage, which was more severe. The difference in the two models is due to the pattern of form–function correlations in our conceptual representations, based on our specific theoretical claims, which were not instantiated in the Devlin et al. model.

psychological and developmental literature. We have also been able to examine these assumptions more directly in a large-scale normative study of the properties generated for a set of concepts by unimpaired young adults (Moss et al., unpublished data). Although property generation is a metalinguistic task and cannot provide a completely transparent window onto people's mental representations of concepts, it can give a good indication of the properties that people can readily retrieve and at least approximates their underlying conceptual knowledge. We asked 45 people to list the properties of 93 basic level concepts, taken from the categories of animals, fruit, tools, and vehicles. Items were matched for familiarity as far as possible across the living and non-living domain according to the ratings in the MRC database (Coltheart, 1981). The mean familiarity rating was 5.1 for living things and 5.16 for non-living things, t (68) < 1. Familiarity was also matched over the two categories within each domain (animals and fruit, 4.98 and 5.25, respectively, t (37) = 1.39, p > .1: tools and vehicles, 5.38 and 4.94, respectively, t (29) = 1.55, p > .1). Within the constraints of matching for familiarity, we chose as many exemplars as reasonably possible in order to provide a good estimate of conceptual structure within the category.

Once the properties had been compiled, we carried out a set of analyses to determine the distributional statistics for each domain, focusing on the variables relevant to the conceptual structure account. First we calculated the distinctiveness of each feature—this measures the amount of information that a feature provides about an object's identity. As in Devlin et al. (1998) the distinctiveness of a property is one over the number of words that property occurs in. Each property has a distinctiveness value associated with it ranging from one (highly distinctive) to zero (not distinctive). We then calculated the mean distinctiveness value for each concept as the average distinctiveness of each feature within the concept. As predicted, the mean distinctiveness of features within artefact concepts (.73) was significantly greater than for living things (.64; t (89) = 3.6, p < .01). The corollary of this finding is that living things had reliably more shared properties than artefacts, defining a shared property as one which was generated for more than one concept (a mean of 15 shared properties for living things and 8 for artefacts: (t (89) = 10.9, p < .001).

The analyses also showed that living things concepts had more properties overall (mean = 17.7 versus 11.3, t (89) = 10.67, p < .001) and more pairs of properties that were significantly correlated with each other (where the cutoff level for significance was α = .05; mean = 115 versus 47, t (89) = 9.95, p < .001). Finally, where there were significant form–function correlations (e.g. has "a blade"–"is used for cutting"), these were significantly more distinctive for non-living things than for living things (mean = 0.56 versus 0.46, t (89) = 8.5, p < .001), which is consistent with the hallmark claim of the conceptual structure account, that the distinctive properties of artefacts tend to be correlated in form–function relations, while for living things it is primarily the shared biological functional and perceptual properties that are correlated with one another.

In addition to the systematic differences across the living and non-living domains, we also found that there were interesting differences between the categories within each domain, i.e. between fruit and animals and between tools and vehicles. For example, the form–function correlations for tools were significantly more distinctive than those for vehicles, as well as those for the living things, whereas they were less distinctive for fruit than for animals. Differences across individual concepts within categories and across categories within domains are entirely consistent with our account, because all the key variables are continuous, rather than all-or-none. In spite of this variation, the domain-level differences were still significant, and in the predicted directions. This is the essential result for our prediction that damage to the system can affect the living and non-living domains in different ways.

Nevertheless, certain categories might be more or less typical of their domains and so different degrees of impairment over categories could also emerge. It should therefore be possible to generate more fine-grained predictions concerning the expected patterns of behaviour for specific categories within the living and non-living domains. At present, these predictions are more speculative than those at the domain level, as we do not yet have an implemented computational model of conceptual structure for specific categories. Our predictions are based on the distributional statistics from the property norm study, which showed that although the predicted differences over domains were generally true, there was also considerable variation across categories within domains. These data suggest that our claims about the living and non-living domains are most faithfully reflected by the categories of animals and tools, respectively, because animals have many shared, correlated properties with relatively few distinctive properties, whereas tools have little shared information and strong correlations among pairs of highly distinctive form and function properties. Therefore, we predict that the domain differences outlined above will all be most apparent if we compare data for animals versus tools. In addition, we predict that the concepts in the category of fruit (and vegetables) will be among the most vulnerable at all levels of damage because they are close together in semantic space and have very few, poorly correlated distinctive properties as well as fewer shared properties than other living things, such as animals. Within the artefact domain, vehicles pattern more closely with living things in some respects than do other artefacts such as tools, in that they have more shared, correlated properties. This leads to the prediction that, at severe levels of damage, it is tools that will most clearly show the predicted disadvantage for artefacts, due to their small number of shared, correlated properties. Figure 5.2 shows a schematic representation of the predicted effects on the four categories at increasingly severe levels of

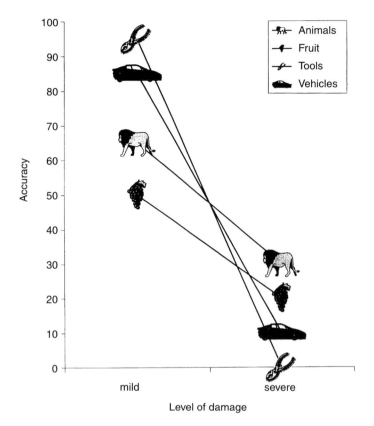

Figure 5.2.   Hypothetical patterns of deficit for animals, fruit, tools, and vehicles as a function of severity of impairment.

damage. This is an attempt to make the predictions concrete, although it is of course an oversimplification, because these effects will be modulated by many other variables such as concept familiarity, modality of input and output and the precise demands of the task. We present the current discussion as specula-tion, which might encourage further refinement of category-level predictions and lead to studies that can address these issues.

CONCEPTUAL STRUCTURE: NEUROPSYCHOLOGICAL EVIDENCE

A number of predictions are generated by the conceptual structure account. First, we expect that deficits for living things will frequently occur, as a result of both mild and moderate levels of damage to the semantic system, due to the vulnerability of the distinctive properties of living things concepts. Given that distinctive properties are necessary to uniquely identify concepts and to distinguish among them, loss of this information will disrupt performance on the majority of semantic tasks, including naming, matching, and property decisions. Critically for our account, the disproportionate loss of distinctive information for living things is predicted to occur even when damage is diffuse or patchy, for example in dementia of the Alzheimer's type (DAT) or generalised cerebral atrophy. Deficits for artefacts are predicted to be rarer, because the distinctive properties are more strongly correlated with each other. It is only at the most severe levels of damage, when the system has essentially lost all distinctive information, that living things will be at a slight advantage, due to the greater number of shared, correlated properties that can support at least some comprehension of living things concepts. In this context it is also important to note that a general prediction made by our account is that dissociations among living and non-living things will tend to be graded rather than all or none, because there will be different degrees of loss of properties across the domains rather than selective damage to independent stores of information.

Second, we predict a characteristic pattern of loss and preservation of semantic properties of different kinds. Distinctive properties of living things should be most vulnerable to loss, while shared information is highly robust. For artefacts, the difference between shared and distinctive information will be less marked, because shared properties will be relatively less robust (as they are fewer and less densely correlated) and distinctive properties will be relatively more robust (as they are more strongly correlated, especially in form–function correlations). We should be able to test this prediction directly by probing patients' knowledge of the shared and distinctive properties of concepts in different categories and domains. The pattern of loss and preservation of distinctive/shared information will also interact with the demands of different kinds of semantic tasks. Those that require intact distinctive properties will be most impaired for living things—including picture naming and word–picture matching with close category foils—while those that can be performed using shared information—such as category level sorting—should be less impaired for living things. The predictions of the conceptual structure account concerning the expected patterns of feature loss can be contrasted with the predictions of the sensory/functional account—that living things deficits will be associated with greater loss of perceptual than functional properties. The conceptual structure account does not predict a perceptual/functional dissociation, assuming that distinctiveness is held constant over these feature types. In the following sections we examine the evidence pertinent to these two sets of predictions, both from our own patient studies and from cases reported in the literature.

Domain dissociations and severity of damage

The computational simulation of the conceptual structure account revealed an interaction between severity of damage throughout the semantic system and the direction of impairment. Living things were more impaired at most levels of damage, but when damage was very severe and overall performance very inaccurate, living things had a slight advantage over artefacts. We suggest that this is due to the large number of highly intercorrelated shared properties for living things, which is the only information that can withstand this degree of damage, allowing a small percentage of living things trials to be correct (see Moss & Tyler [2000] for further details). This interaction means that the conceptual structure account can accommodate the double dissociation between living things and artefacts, with the proviso that artefact deficits are associated with the most severe semantic impairments, while mild or moderate impairments should generally produce deficits for living things. However, as will be discussed later it is not necessarily a simple matter to compare the severity of the semantic deficit across patients.

It is certainly the case that deficits for living things are much more frequently observed in general than artefact deficits, as is clear from the number of reported cases in the literature. Examination of reported results also confirms the prediction that selective deficits are rarely all-or-none but are a matter of degree, with performance in the "preserved" domain frequently below the normal range. For example, JBR (Warrington & Shallice, 1984), Michelangelo (Sartori & Job, 1988) Giulietta (Sartori et al., 1993), NV (Basso, Capitani, & Laiacona, 1988), and RC (Moss et al., 1998) all show performance below the control range for non-living things, as for well as living things, for several tasks. In some patients, the graded effect is more apparent on some tasks than others, with performance for the preserved category within the normal range for certain tasks such as word–picture matching, but still falling below the normal range for the more demanding tasks like picture naming (e.g. EW, Caramazza & Shelton, 1998). One or two other patients in the literature do seem to show a highly selective deficit (MF, Barbarotto et al., 1995; KR, Hart & Gordon, 1992), although for some it is not clear to what extent performance in the "preserved" category falls within or below the control range, as this is not reported (e.g. KR, Hart & Gordon, 1992). Nevertheless, performance is not truly selective for the vast majority of patients.

The most controversial issue is whether the small number of cases of selective deficit for artefacts that have been reported in the literature do indeed have very profound semantic impairments. It is possible that this was the case for the two patients reported by Warrington and McCarthy (1983, 1987). VER and YOT had severe global dysphasia and so only matching to sample techniques was possible. However, it is difficult to assess the severity of the semantic impairment given the profound production and comprehension impairments. Moreover, materials in these studies were not matched for familiarity and other variables that we now know may be important in determining the level of accuracy. Other patients reported to have deficits for the artefact domain do not seem to have particularly profound deficits (JJ, Hillis & Caramazza, 1991; CW, Sacchett & Humphreys, 1992).[5] At this stage we are not sure whether it is possible to account for these individual patients within our framework without weakening our assumptions. In the conceptual structure account we adopt the radical stance of attempting to account for dissociations in terms of purely random damage throughout the semantic system. However, it has also been demonstrated that even in a purely distributed system with no predefined category boundaries, similar concepts with overlapping patterns of activation will be represented close together in "lumpy" semantic space (Caramazza et al., 1990; Small, Hart, Nguyen, & Gordon, 1995; Zorzi, Perry, Ziegler, & Coltheart, 1999). Networks are self-organising, and members of a category could be captured by the same hidden units. This suggests that it would be possible for focal damage affecting specific clusters of microfeatures or hidden units to have disproportionate effects on individual categories, over and above the general patterns predicted by the structural characteristics of concepts in those categories. It is possible that occasional artefact deficits could arise at mild levels of damage in this way.

Several reports have suggested that there might be category-specific impairments in patients with DAT (e.g. Silveri et al., 1991) although data from group studies are mixed, and no clear interaction of the direction of category-specific deficits with severity of semantic disorder has emerged (Garrard, Patterson, Watson, & Hodges, 1998; Gonnerman et al., 1997). In general it is difficult to evaluate relative severity and extent of brain lesion across different patients, whether recovering from herpes simplex encephalitis (HSE) or cardiovascular accident (CVA), or those with progressive deficits, because comparable tests and data are rarely reported. It is not clear how to define the appropriate criteria of severity, particularly for patients with more wide-ranging cognitive and/or linguistic impairments.

A more promising approach is to carry out longitudinal studies of individual patients with progressive semantic disorders, which enables us to track the nature of category-specific effects over the course of the disorder. Longitudinal studies of two DAT patients are reported by Gonnerman, Andersen, and Kempler (1997). One patient showed a consistent deficit for living things, whereas the other showed a deficit for artefacts, although this was not

---

[5] Other intriguing reports of artefact deficits exist, but as only picture naming was tested, it is not clear to what extent these were cases of category-specific anomia rather than semantic deficits *per se* (e.g. Tippet, Glosser, & Farah, 1996; Silveri, et al., 1997).

significant at most of the testing sessions. It is possible that the former patient would have progressed to show the predicted artefact deficit, but it was not possible to carry out further testing, presumably due to the more widespread cognitive deficits associated with DAT. The pattern for the latter patient is unclear.

In a recent study we were able to investigate the nature of semantic impairments during the progression of the disorder for a patient with a generalised cerebral atrophy but whose cognitive functions in other domains were less compromised than those of DAT patients at comparable levels of semantic impairment.[6] ES showed a marked deficit for artefacts only at a late stage of the disorder, as predicted by our model. Earlier in the disease she either showed no difference between living things and artefacts or, in some tasks, a deficit for living things (Moss & Tyler, 2000). For example, we asked ES to name the set of Snodgrass and Vanderwart (1980) pictures at five time slices during the progression of her illness. Although ES was initially better at naming artefacts, by the final time slice her naming of artefacts had declined to the point where her accuracy was lower than for living things, as shown in Figure 5.3. This gave rise to a significant domain by time interaction, even

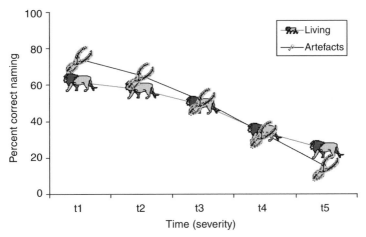

Figure 5.3. Naming performance over time for patient ES on the Snodgrass and Vanderwart (1980) picture set. The time axis runs from t1 (August, 1994) to t5 (December, 1996). Reprinted from Moss and Tyler, 2000, with permission from Elsevier Science.

---

[6] ES was initially diagnosed as having semantic dementia because of her impairment of naming and comprehension in the context of good everyday memory and orientation. This diagnosis was later revised to generalised cerebral atrophy. ES clearly had cognitive deficits other than a breakdown of conceptual knowledge, but these remained quite stable over the 2 years of our study, while her conceptual knowledge declined steadily. For example, ES's scaled scores were 21 and 19 on the verbal and performance components of the WAIS test in September 1994, and were well maintained at 17 and 22 respectively over a year later.

when factors such as familiarity and age of acquisition of the items were partialed out. A similar pattern was found in other tasks, including semantic priming, property verification, and generation of definitions, demonstrating that this was a semantic effect, rather than pure anomia.

A similar pattern has also begun to emerge for a second progressive aphasic patient, AA, with a similar progressive decline in semantic knowledge (Moss & Tyler, 2000). We tested AA's naming on a new set of colour pictures of living things (animals, insects, fruit, and vegetables) and artefacts (vehicles, toys, clothing, and tools), carefully matched for familiarity and other potentially important variables (Bunn, Tyler, & Moss, 1998). As shown in Figure 5.4, AA also showed a significant interaction of domain and time, over three time slices in a period of about 18 months, when factors such as familiarity and picture complexity were taken into account (logistic regression: Wald = 6.9, $p < .005$). By the fourth time slice, however, AA's performance had deteriorated dramatically and the difference was no longer apparent.[7] Again, a similar pattern was observed in other tasks, although the interaction did not reach significance.

Our computational simulation of domain dissociations as a function of severity of damage also highlighted that the nature of errors should change over time for the different domains. Specifically, the loss of distinctive information for living things should lead to within-category errors for living things

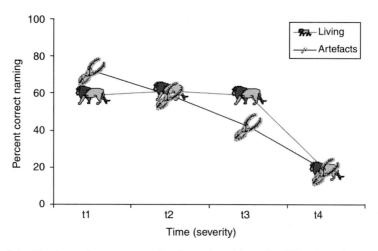

Figure 5.4. Naming performance over time for patient AA on the CSL colour photograph set (Bunn et al., 1998). The time axis runs from t1 (April, 1997) to t4 (October, 1998).

---

[7] We would have predicted an advantage for living things over artefacts to still be apparent at t4. However, it was very difficult to test AA at this point and significant attentional deficits interfered with her naming performance.

at an early point in the progression of the disorder. However, cross-category or cross-domain errors should be very rare, because of the well-preserved shared properties. Shared information for artefacts is less robust, and so errors could cross category, and even domain, boundaries when damage is severe. For example, shared properties of tools, such as "has a handle" and "is small" are not as numerous or densely intercorrelated with other properties as are the shared properties of animals (e.g. "has legs", "breathes", "has eyes", "can see"). Therefore, these properties are more vulnerable to loss, so allowing the system to sometimes misidentify a tool as a vehicle, for example, because the mismatching shared properties like "has a handle" are no longer present to help the system settle into the correct general pattern for some kind of tool. Our claim is not that cross-category errors are necessarily very common for artefacts, but rather that they will be more likely than for living things, for which between-category errors should hardly ever occur, even in the most severe deficits. This was the pattern demonstrated by the simulation, as shown in Figure 5.5.

There is some evidence for this pattern in longitudinal studies of picture naming performance. Hodges, Graham, and Patterson (1995) report a detailed breakdown of the naming errors of a semantic dementia patient, JL, over a period of 18 months. For living things, JL makes progressively more category-coordinate and superordinate errors, but he never produces a name that crosses categories (e.g. animal/fruit) or domains. However, for artefacts, occasional cross-category (e.g. "paintbrush"–"piece of vehicle") and even cross-domain (telephone–animal) errors emerge at the later time slices.

We have carried out a similar analysis of the naming errors for one of the progressive aphasic patients mentioned above. AA did not produce a single cross-category or cross-domain error for living things until the last test session, when there were two such responses out of 69 items ("rabbit"–"the boys"; "cauliflower"–"camel"). For artefacts, in contrast, occasional cross-domain errors (e.g. "skittles"–"orange") were produced, even at the first test session when she was already significantly impaired and, by the last two sessions there were eight and six such errors, respectively, including such striking examples as "pram"–"banana", "table–umbrella" and "book–candle".[8] Although the absolute numbers of cross-category and cross-domain errors are small, there appears to be a consistent tendency for such errors to be produced in greater numbers for artefacts than living things, and to increase over time, as predicted by our account. Moreover, a similar pattern can be observed in AA's word–picture matching data. In this task, the experimenter says a word aloud and the patient has to point to the pictured target from an array of four pictures containing the target (e.g. "lion"), a

---

[8] We have not been able to analyze the data for ES in the same way as her naming errors were almost always circumlocutions or no responses, rather than an incorrect item name.

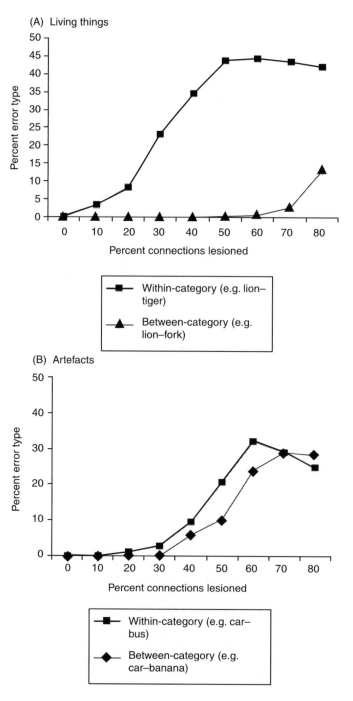

Figure 5.5. Percentage of within- and between-category errors in the computational model as a function of lesion severity (percentage of connections set to zero) for (A) living things and (B) artefacts. Adapted from Tyler et al. (2000).

within-category foil (e.g. "tiger") and two foils from a category within the other domain (e.g. "car" and "bus"). Errors are coded as within-category (e.g. "lion"–"tiger") or between-category (e.g. "lion"–"bus"). This is comparable to the task simulated in our computational model. As shown in Figure 5.6, AA's pattern of errors closely matches that predicted by the simulation. She shows more within-category errors than between-category errors for living things from the first test session onwards. She makes fewer errors overall for artefacts, and these errors are as likely to be between-category as within-category.

Patterns of loss and preservation of properties within domains

The conceptual structure account predicts that patients with deficits for living things will have impaired knowledge of distinctive relative to shared properties, but with relatively good preservation of distinctive knowledge for artefacts. We have reported precisely this pattern of knowledge for patient RC, who developed a semantic deficit following an HSE infection in 1992 (Moss et al., 1998). Preliminary tests revealed that RC had a significantly greater impairment for living things than artefacts. For example, he was able to name 49% of the artefacts in our colour picture set but only 10% of living things. Similarly, he scored 88% correct for artefacts and 67% correct for living things in a word–picture matching task that contained within-category foils. We compared RC's knowledge of distinctive and shared information for the two domains in a property verification task. He was asked say "yes" or "no" to spoken property questions. Half of the properties were distinctive—they were true of only one or a few members of a category ("Does a zebra have black and white stripes?") and the other half were shared by all members of the category ("Does a zebra have eyes?"). We also varied whether the questions concerned a perceptual or functional property of the concept. Control subjects were between 85 and 100% accurate in all conditions. RC showed a highly selective deficit for the distinctive properties of living things (55% correct), with scores of around 80% correct for all other conditions, including the shared properties of living things. Consistent with the conceptual structure account, RC showed no difference in accuracy for perceptual and functional properties. This is problematic for the sensory/functional account on which we would expect a patient with a clear-cut deficit for living things to have relatively greater problems with perceptually based properties. We also reported that RC's preserved knowledge of shared properties of living things supported his ability to do well in certain tasks where distinctive properties were not necessary. For example, when asked to sort living things by category (animals versus fruit) he was able to do this very well, and in fact, slightly better than the equivalent task for artefacts (vehicles versus tools). He was

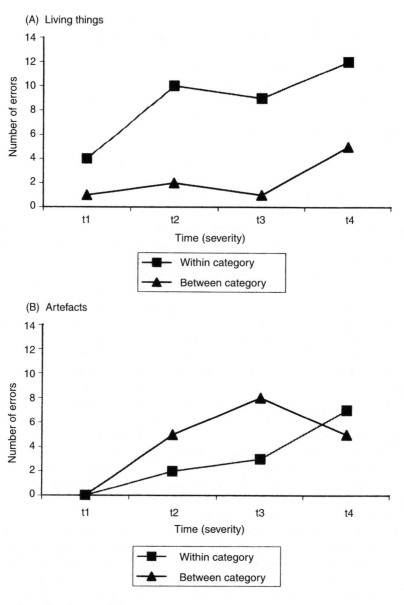

Figure 5.6. Number of within- and between-category errors over time for patient AA in a word–picture matching task for (A) living things and (B) artefacts.

also able to score 96% correct on a word–picture matching task in which the within-category foil was removed and replaced with one from a different category within the same domain.

A similar pattern of relatively preserved knowledge of shared properties and impaired knowledge of distinctive properties of living things has recently been reported for a patient, EW, who has a category-specific deficit for animals (Caramazza & Shelton, 1998). For most other patients in the literature, the appropriate contrasts between distinctive and shared information are not tested, so we cannot determine whether there is a particular problem with the distinctive properties of living things. However, in several reports, there are hints that this is the case. For example, Sartori and Job (1988) asked their patient, Michelangelo, to fill in the missing parts of incomplete drawings; they remark " the patient knows that he has to add parts of a superordinate category ... he adds fins to fishes, wings to birds, and horns to certain animals, but he has great problems in distinguishing, e.g. the horn of a rhinoceros from the antlers of a deer".

We have recently devised a new test of property knowledge to further investigate knowledge of shared and distinctive information. We selected 20 living things (10 animals and 10 fruit) and 20 artefacts (10 tools and 10 vehicles) and presented them each with four different true properties; these were either functional or perceptual, shared or distinctive. The distinctiveness of each property was determined by our property generation study described earlier. For each property we calculated the percentage of concepts within the category that had been attributed with that property. A property was counted as distinctive if it had been given for less than 50% of the category members (much less than 50% in most cases) and as shared if given for more than 50% of members (again, nearer to 100% for most properties). Concepts across domains were matched for frequency, familiarity, imageability, and objective age of acquisition (see Table 5.1). An equal number of false properties were created for each condition (shared/distinctive × functional/perceptual) by pairing concepts with properties from other items (e.g. "cat"—"does it have a curly tail?" / "cat"—"does it have wheels?").

We have carried out this test with RC and four other patients with relatively greater deficits for living than non-living things following HSE infection. We have discussed three of the patients in detail in earlier papers (JBR, Bunn et al., 1998; RC, Moss et al., 1998; SE, Moss, Tyler, & Jennings, 1997). Brief case details for each patient are given in the Appendix (p. 146). The same test was carried out with a control group of twelve normal subjects between the ages of 59 and 73 years.[9]

---

[9] The control group are older than all the patients except for SE. However, we do not envisage that a younger control group would show qualitatively different responses in this task which does not involve any reaction time component.

TABLE 5.1
Characteristics of stimuli in the property knowledge test

	Living things mean	Artefacts mean
Concept frequency[a]	23	24
Concept familiarity[b]	5.3	5.4
Imageability[b]	6.4	6.2
Objective age of acquisition (months)[c]	44	48
Distinctiveness (%)		
Distinctive properties	13	13
Shared properties	88	74

[a] CELEX (Baayen, Pipenbrook, & Guilikers, 1995).
[b] MRC database (Coltheart, 1981) and our own ratings.
[c] Morrison, Chappell, and Ellis (1997).

As shown in the Appendix, the HSE patients vary in terms of the overall severity of their semantic impairment and in degree of impairment for living things relative to non-living things. Nevertheless, all patients show a significant dissociation in at least one task. JBR and RC show the most marked dissociations, with significant impairments for living things in all three tasks shown (picture naming, naming to description, and word–picture matching). JH has an intermediate level of impairment, and also shows significant deficits for living things on all tasks. MW and SE show the mildest impairment, and the difference between living and non-living things reaches significance only in the picture naming task. However, we suggest that these patients do have a central semantic deficit (albeit mild) rather than a pure category-specific anomia. First, both show greater difficulty with the distinctive properties of living things in the current task (as discussed later). Second, we have documented SE's impairment for living things in tasks such as priming and property verification elsewhere (Moss et al., 1997).

We excluded the category of fruit from the main analysis because control subjects had difficulty with many of the distinctive properties of these items (mean accuracy only 73%) and so it is not clear that the properties chosen were familiar enough to provide a valid test for the patients. The results for the control group and the five patients are shown in Figure 5.7, which plots the percentage of correct responses for distinctive versus shared properties for animals, vehicles, and tools.

As can be seen in Figure 5.7, control subjects were able to respond accurately in all six conditions, with scores as follows: animals shared, mean = 97% (range = 87–100%); animals distinctive, mean = 93% (range = 86–100%); vehicles shared, mean = 98% (range = 95–100%); vehicles distinctive, mean = 96% (range = 86–100%); tools shared, mean = 99% (range = 92–100%); tools distinctive, mean = 97%, range = 88–100%). The patients showed varying degrees of difficulty on this task, with overall accuracy ranging from 70% for RC to 93% for MW. Four of the five patients showed a consistent pattern, with a selective deficit for the distinctive properties of animals relative to the non-living categories (tools and vehicles combined). This was the case for JBR ($\chi^2 = 16.6, p < .01$), SE ($\chi^2 = 5.2, p < .05$), MW ($\chi^2 = 3.37, 0.05 > p < .1$) and RC ($\chi^2 = 2.77, 0.05 > p < .1$). In contrast, these patients did not show any difference between animals and vehicles on the shared properties ($p > .1$ for all four patients). These results are consistent with the prediction of the conceptual structure account that the weakly correlated distinctive properties of living things such as animals will be particularly vulnerable to damage, and the densely correlated properties will be robust. For patients with the mildest degree of semantic loss (SE and MW), it is only the distinctive properties of animals that are impaired enough to fall below the control range, with the other three conditions preserved. The more severely affected patients, JBR and RC, show an exacerbation of the same pattern, with: (i) very low scores on the distinctive properties of animals, with accuracy falling at chance (40% and 49% correct for RC and JBR respectively); (ii) some degree of impairment for the distinctive properties of non-living things as well, although this is much milder for JBR (84%, and only a little below the control range); (iii) preservation of shared information for animals, vehicles, and tools, with accuracy still well within the normal range for both JBR and just below for RC.

In contrast, none of the patients showed a difference in accuracy of responses for perceptual as compared to functional properties, either for animals or for vehicles ($p > .05$ in all χ^2 tests). The sensory–functional theory suggests that deficits for living things are associated with greater loss of perceptual semantic properties because these are crucial for distinguishing among members of living things categories, such as animals. This prediction was not supported by these results.

We turn now to the one patient who did not show the selective deficit for distinctive properties of animals relative to vehicles in the current analyses. Unlike the other four, JH did not show a significant reduction in accuracy for animals relative to the combined non-living categories $\chi^2 = 1.8, p > .1$). Inspection of Figure 5.7 shows that this is because of her low score for the distinctive properties of tools (63%), which is no different to that for animals (57%, $\chi^2 < 1$). In contrast, she was accurate on the distinctive properties of vehicles (79%; vehicles versus animals, $\chi^2 = 3.06, p < .1$). We believe that this anomalous effect may be due to the specific circumstances of this patient, who was only 16 years old when she was taken ill with HSE and is now densely amnesic. It is likely that she is less familiar with some of the items in the tools category than the normal adult population (e.g. "axe", "chisel", "saw", "hammer").

Figure 5.7 also reveals a discrepancy between the two non-living categories

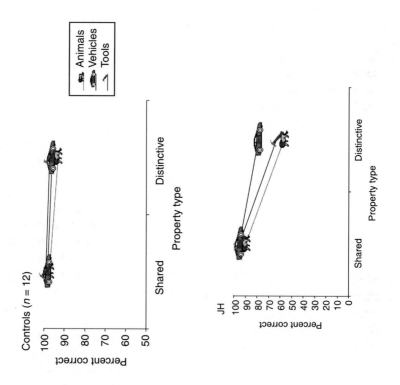

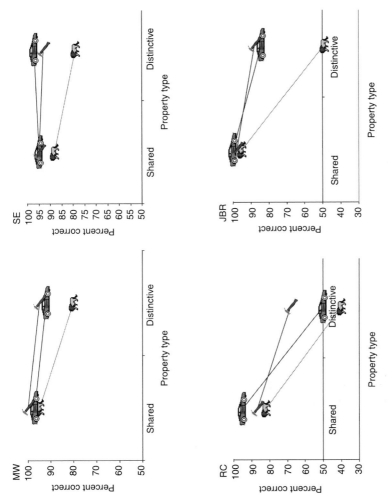

Figure 5.7. Percentage correct verification responses for shared and distinctive properties of animals, tools, and vehicles for control subjects and five HSE patients.

for patient, RC. In this case, the combined score for the distinctive properties of non-living things is significantly higher than that for animals, but it is clear that this effect is largely due to the category of tools (68% correct), while his scores for the distinctive properties of vehicles are really no better than for those of animals (50% versus 40%, respectively; $\chi^2 < 1$). This difference is consistent with the results of our property generation study, which suggested that tools are more typical of the non-living domain than are vehicles, in that they have fewer properties with more highly distinctive form–function correlations. Vehicles pattern with living things in some ways, because the correlated properties are not as distinctive. This may be the basis for RC's scores in the property knowledge task. We know from earlier studies that he has extensive damage to the semantic system, which primarily affects weakly correlated properties. In the current task, this leads to a deficit for the distinctive properties of vehicles as well as of animals. Nevertheless, the distinctive properties of vehicles are still somewhat more strongly correlated that those of animals, and so they are less vulnerable to loss in the more mildly impaired patients (SE, MW, and JBR).

GENERAL DISCUSSION

In this chapter we have given an overview of how the conceptual structure account of semantic representation explains category-specific deficits for living and non-living things. We have presented supporting data for the account, in terms of: (i) computational simulations of the predicted interactions of random damage and conceptual structure; (ii) distributional analyses of large-scale property generation norms that support the theoretical claims concerning the structure of concepts in the different domains; (iii) neuropsychological data from previously reported studies; and (iv) data from five HSE patients with living things deficits on a new property knowledge task that contrasts distinctive and shared properties across the domains. These studies show that the patients with living things deficits have disproportionate loss of distinctive properties of animals relative to non-living things, while knowledge of shared properties remains intact. Finally, a series of neuroimaging studies recently carried out in our laboratory provides a different kind of support for our account. In recent PET and fMRI studies, in which subjects carried out lexical decision and semantic categorisation tasks for sets of living and non-living things, closely matched according to familiarity, concreteness and length, we have found that there is activation of a large conceptual network for semantic tasks relative to baseline (e.g. letter detection or classification) with activation primarily in the left hemisphere involving the inferior and middle temporal gyri and the temporal pole. In none of these studies do we find any evidence of regional specialisation as a function of the living/non-living distinction or specific categories within those domains, including animals, fruit, tools, and vehicles, that is, there are no activations specific to either domain or category that reach significance when appropriately corrected for multiple comparisons (Devlin et al., 2000, 2002).

At this stage, the conceptual structure account is still a theory in development. We are currently working on a larger scale computational model, using the sets of properties generated for each concept in our property generation study as the basis for the conceptual representations. This will allow us to investigate the effects of damage in a more realistic model. We will also be able to compare the effects of damage on the individual categories within the broad domains of living and non-living things. The property norms suggest that categories within domains differ in important ways and this should lead to different patterns of damage in our model. Predictions will then be tested against the behavioural data of the neuropsychological patients in studies where theoretically important properties of carefully matched concepts in each category are contrasted. Future developments will also involve taking additional variables into account. Our current model includes the variables of distinctiveness and correlation, but we know from the psychological literature that there are other ways in which properties differ that may also be important determinants of conceptual structure—such as salience and of degree context-dependence (Barsalou, 1983; Medin & Shoben, 1988;). Similarly there are ways in which the concepts themselves differ, which we have not yet taken into account but that no doubt play an important part. For example, although it seems that the familiarity of concepts cannot be the full explanation of category-specific deficits, it is certainly the case that familiarity is an important additional variable, with the most familiar concepts in any category almost always the most likely to be preserved (Funnell & Sheridan, 1992; Stewart, Parkin, & Hunkin, 1992). Therefore, it is important to implement this variable in a complete model.

Finally, we acknowledge that our model in its current stage of development does not account for every patient with a deficit for living or non-living things reported in the literature. It is possible that some of these patterns will be more tractable to our model when we have developed it further along the lines described above. It is also worth noting that none of the other well-known alternative models provides a satisfactory model of the entire spectrum of neuropsychological data. For example, as we discussed above, we predict that artefact deficits will be associated with severe rather than mild deficits. There are at least two patients who seem to contradict this prediction, CW (Sacchett & Humphreys, 1992) and JJ (Hillis & Caramazza, 1991). But it is not only the conceptual structure account that runs into difficulty here. Patient JJ presents problems for the domain-specific account in which separate neural systems support each domain of knowledge; he has a deficit for artefacts, but is reported to have a left temporal lobe infarct, outside the "frontoparietal" region, which has frequently been claimed to be associated with the representation of artefact concepts. Moreover, JJ's deficit did not only extend to artefacts, but also to fruit and vegetables (effectively an isolated sparing of animal knowledge). This would imply a lesion to two separate semantic systems on the domain-specific account (one for plant life and the other for artefacts). Similarly, on the sensory–functional account, JJ would presumably be interpreted as having a deficit for functional information (resulting in the problem for artefacts) as well as for sensory information (resulting in the problem for fruit and vegetables), in which case it is not clear what kind of property knowledge would be intact to support his good knowledge of animals.

In summary, although there are many challenges to address, our research so far suggests that it might not be necessary to propose separate domain-based or property-based stores within semantic memory to account for selective semantic deficits, and that an approach that emphasises the structure of concepts in different domains and categories of knowledge provides a promising framework for future explorations.

ACKNOWLEDGEMENTS

This work was supported by a Wellcome Trust research fellowship to HM and an MRC programme grant to LKT. We are grateful to Rebekah Anokhina, Elaine Bunn, Mark Durrant-Peatfield, Paul de Mornay Davies and Stuart McLellan for their assistance with this research, and to all of the patients for their generous participation.

REFERENCES

Baayen, R.H., Pipenbrook, R., & Guilikers, L. (1995). The Celex Lexical Database (CD-ROM). Linguistic Data Consortium, University of Pennsylvania, Philadelphia, PA.

Barbarotto, R., Capitani, E., Spinnler, H., & Trivelli, C. (1995). Slowly progressive semantic impairment with category specificity, *Neurocase, 1*, 107–119.

Barsalou, L.W. (1983). Context-independent and context-dependent information in concepts. *Memory & Cognition, 10*, 82–93.

Basso, A., Captiani, E., & Laiacona, M. (1988). Progressive language impairment without dementia: A case with isolated category specific semantic impairment. *Journal of Neurology, Neurosurgery & Psychiatry, 51*, 1201–1207.

Bunn. E., Tyler, L.K., & Moss, H.E. (1998). Category-specific deficits: the role of familiarity re-examined. *Neuropsychology, 12(3)*, 367–379.

Caramazza, A., Hillis, A.E., Rapp, B.C., & Romani, C. (1990) The multiple semantics hypothesis: Multiple confusions. *Cognitive Neuropsychology, 7(3)*, 161–189.

Caramazza, A., & Shelton, J.R. (1998) Domain-specific knowledge systems in the brain: The animate-inanimate distinction. *Journal of Cognitive Neuroscience, 10*, 1–35.

Cardebat, D., Demonet, J-F., Celsis, P., & Puel, M. (1996). Living/non-living dissociation in a case of semantic dementia: A SPECT activation study. *Neuropsychologia, 34*, 1175–1179.

Chao, L.L., Haxby, J.V., & Martin, A. (1999). Attribute-based neural substrates in temporal cortex for perceiving and knowing about objects. *Nature Neuroscience, 2(10)*, 913–919.

Coltheart M. (1981). The MRC psycholinguistic database. *The Quarterly Journal of Experimental Psychology, 33A*, 497–505.

Damasio, H., Grabowski, T.J., Tranel, D., Hichwa, R., & Damasio, A. (1996). A neural basis for lexical retrieval. *Nature, 380*, 499–505.

De Renzi, E., & Lucchelli, F. (1994) Are semantic systems separately represented in the brain? The case of living category impairment. *Cortex, 30*, 3–25.

Devlin, J., Gonnerman, L., Andersen, E., & Seidenberg, M. (1998). Category-specific semantic deficits in focal and widespread brain damage: A computational account. *Journal of Cognitive Neuroscience, 10*, 77–94.

Devlin, J.T., Russell, R. P., Davis, M.H., Price, C.J., Wilson, J., Moss, H.E., Matthews, P., & Tyler, L.K. (in press). Susceptibility-induced loss of signal: Comparing PET and fMRI on a semantic task. *Neuorimage, 11(6)*, 589–600.

Devlin, J.T., Russell, R.P., Davis, M.H., Price, C.J., Moss, H.E., Jalal Fadili, M., & Tyler, L.K. (2002). Is there an anatomical basis for category specificity? Semantic memory studies in PET and fMRI. *Neuropsychologia, 40(1)*, 54–75.

Dixon, M., Bub, D.N., & Arguin, M. (1997). The interaction of object form and object meaning in the identification performance of a patient with category-specific visual agnosia. *Cognitive Neuropsychology, 14*, 1085–1130.

Durrant-Peatfield, M ., Tyler, L.K., Moss, H.E., & Levy, J. (1997). The distinctiveness of form and function in category structure: A connectionist model. In: M.G. Shafto & P. Langley (Eds.), *Proceedings of the Nineteenth Annual Conference of the Cognitive Science Society, Stanford University* (pp. 193–198). Mahwah, NJ: Lawrence Erlbaum Associates, Inc.

Farah, M.J., Hammond, K.M., Mehta, Z., & Ratcliff, G. (1989). Category-specificity and modality-specificity in semantic memory. *Neuropsychologia, 27(2)*, 193–200

Forde, E.M.E., Francis, D., Riddoch, M.J., Rumiati, R.I. & Humphreys, G.W. (1997). On the links between visual knowledge and naming: A single case study of a patient with a category-specific impairment for living things. *Cognitive Neuropsychology, 14*, 403–458.

Forde, E.M.E., & Humphreys, G.W. (1999). Category-specific recognition impairments: a review of important case studies and influential theories. *Aphasiology, 13(3)*, 169–193.

Funnell, E., & de Mornay Davies, P. (1996). JBR: A reassessment of concept familiarity and a category-specific disorder for living things. *Neurocase, 2*, 461–474.

Funnell, E., & Sheridan, J. (1992). Categories of knowledge: Unfamiliar aspects of living and non-living things. *Cognitive Neuropsychology, 9*, 135–153.

Gaffan, D., & Heywood, C.A. (1993). A spurious category-specific visual agnosia for living things in normal human and nonhuman primates. *Journal of Cognitive Neuroscience, 5*, 118–128.

Gainotti, G, Silveri, M.C., Daniele, A. & Giustolisi, L. (1995). Neuroanatomical correlates of category-specific impairments: A critical survey. *Memory 3/4*, 247–264.

Garrard, P., Patterson, K., Watson, P.C., & Hodges, J.R. (1998). Category-specific semantic loss in dementia of the Alzheimer's type. *Brain, 121*, 633–646.

Gonnerman, L., Andersen, E., Devlin, J., & Seidenberg, M. (1997) Double dissociation of semantic categories in Alzheimer's disease. *Brain and Language, 57*, 254–279.

Gonnerman, L.M., Andersen, E.S., & Kempler, D. (1997). Category-specific semantic impairments as a result of progressive semantic deterioration: Longitudinal data from Alzheimer's patients. *Brain & Language, 60*, 58–60.

Goodglass, H., Klein, B., Carey, P., & Jones, K. (1966). Specific semantic word categories in aphasia. *Cortex, 2*, 74–89.

Hart, J., & Gordon, B. (1992). Neural subsystems for object knowledge. *Nature, 359*, 60–64.

Hart, J., Berndt, R.S., & Caramazza, A. (1985). Categoy-specific naming deficit following cerebral infarction. *Nature, 316*, 439–440.

Hillis, A.E., & Caramazza, A. (1991). Category-specific naming and comprehension impairment: A double dissociation. *Brain & Language, 114*, 2081–2094.

Hodges, J.R., Graham, N., & Patterson, K. (1995). Charting the progression in semantic dementia: Implications for the organisation of semantic memory. *Memory, 3*, 463–496.

Humphreys, G.W., Riddoch, M.J., & Quinlan, P. (1988). Cascade processes in picture identification. *Cognitive Neuropsychology, 5*, 67–103.

Keil, F. (1986). The acquisition of living thing and artefact terms. In W. Demoupoulous & A. Marras (Eds.), *Language learning and concept acquisition: Foundational issues*. Norwood, NJ: Ablex.

Keil, F. (1989). *Concepts, kinds and cognitive development*. Cambridge, MA: MIT Press.

Laiacona, M., Capitani, E., & Barbarotto, R. (1997). Semantic category dissociations: A longitudinal study of two cases. *Cortex, 33*, 441–461.

Lambon Ralph, M.A., Howard, D., Nightingale, G., & Ellis, A. W. (1998). Are living and non-living category-specific deficits causally linked to impaired perceptual or associative knowledge? Evidence from a category-specific double dissociation. *Neurocase, 4*, 311–338.

McCarthy, R., & Warrington, E. (1988). Evidence for modality-specific meaning systems in the brain. *Nature, 334(4)*, 428–430.

McRae, K., de Sa, V., & Seidenberg, M. (1997). On the nature and scope of featural representations of word meaning. *Journal of Experimental Psychology: General, 126*, 99–130.

Madole, K., Oakes, L., & Cohen, L. (1993). Developmental changes in infants' attention to function and form–function correlations. *Cognitive Development, 8*, 189–209.

Malt, B.C., & Smith, E. (1984). Correlated properties in natural categories. *Journal of Verbal Learning and Verbal Behaviour, 23*, 250–269.

Mandler, J. (1992). How to build a baby II: Conceptual primitives. *Psychological Review, 99*, 587–604.

Martin, A., Wiggs, C., Ungerleider, L., & Haxby, J. (1996). Neural correlates of category-specific knowledge. *Nature, 379*, 649–652.

Medin, D.L., & Shoben, E.J. (1988). Context and structure in conceptual combination. *Cognitive Psychology, 20*, 158–190.

Morrison, C.M., Chappell, T.D., & Ellis, A.W. (1997). Age of acquisition norms for a large set of object names and their relation to adult estimates and other variables. *Quarterly Journal of Experimental Psychology, 50A*, 528–529.

Moss, H.E., & Tyler, L.K. (2000). A progressive category-specific semantic deficit for non-living things. *Neuropsychologia, 38*, 60–82.

Moss, H.E., Tyler, L.K., Durrant-Peatfield, M., & Bunn, E. (1998). "Two eyes of a see-through": Impaired and intact knowledge in a case of selective deficit for living things. *Neurocase, 4*, 291–310.

Moss, H.E., & Tyler, L.K. (2000). A progressive category-specific deficit for non-living things. *Neuropsychologia, 38*, 60–82.

Moss, H.E., Tyler, L.K., & Jennings, F. (1997). When leopards lose their spots: Knowledge of visual properties in category-specific deficits for living things. *Cognitive Neuropsychology, 14*, 901–950.

Mummery, C.J., Patterson, K., Hodges, J.R., & Price, C.J. (1998). Functional neuroanatomy of the semantic system: Divisible by what? *Journal of Cognitive Neuroscience, 10(6)*, 766–777.

Perani, D., Cappa, S.F., Bettinardi, V., Bressi, S., Gorno-Tempini, M., Matarrese, M., & Fazio, F. (1995). Different neural systems for the recognition of animals ands man-made tools. *Neuroreport, 6*, 1637–1641.

Pietrini, V., Nertempi, P., Vaglia, A., Revello, M.G., Pinna, V., & Ferro-Milone, F. (1988). Recovery from herpes simplex encephalitis: Selective impairment of specific semantic categories with neuroradiological correlation. *Journal of Neurology, Neurosurgery and Psychiatry, 51*, 1284–1293.

Sacchett, C., & Humphreys, G. (1992). Calling a squirrel a squirrel but a canoe a wigwam: A category-specific deficit for artefactual objects and body parts. *Cognitive Neuropsychology, 9*, 73–86.

Sartori, G., & Job, R. (1988). The oyster with four legs: a neuropsychological study on the interaction of visual and semantic information. *Cognitive Neuropsychology, 5*, 105–132.

Sartori, G., Job, R., Miozzo, M., Zago, S., & Marchiori, G. (1993). Category-specific form knowledge in a patient with herpes simplex virus encephalitis. *Journal of Clinical and Experimental Neuropsychology, 15(2)*, 280–299.

Silveri, M.C., Danieli, A., Giustolisi, L., & Gainotti, G. (1991). Dissociation between knowledge of living and nonliving things in dementia of the Alzheimer type. *Neurology, 41*, 545–546.

Silveri, M.-C., Gainotti, G., Perani, D., Cappelletti, J.-Y., Carbone, G., & Fazie, F. (1997). Naming deficit for non-living items: Neuropsychological and PET study. *Neuropsychologia, 35*, 359–367.

Silveri, M.C., & Gainotti, G. (1988). Interaction between vision and language in category-specific semantic impairment. *Cognitive Neuropsychology, 5(6)*, 677–709.

Small, S., Hart, J., Nguyen, T., & Gordon, B. (1995). Distributed representations of semantic knowledge in the brain. *Brain, 118*, 441–453.

Snodgrass, J.G., & Vanderwart, M. (1980). A standardised set of 260 pictures: Norms for name agreement, image agreement, familiarity and visual complexity. *Journal of Experimental Psychology: Human Learning and Memory, 6*, 174–215.

Stewart, F., Parkin, A.J., & Hunkin, N.M. (1992). Naming impairments following recovery from herpes simplex encephalitis: Category specific? *The Quarterly Journal of Experimental Psychology, 44A(2)*, 261–284.

Tippett, L.J., Glosser, G., & Farah, M.J. (1996). A category-specific naming impairment after temporal lobectomy. *Neuropsychologia, 34(2)*, 139–146.

Tversky, B., & Hemenway, K. (1984). Objects, parts and categories. *Journal of Experimental Psychology, 113*, 169–193.

Tyler, L.K., Durrant-Peatfield, M., Levy, J., Voice. J.K., & Moss, H.E. (1996) Distinctiveness and correlations in the structure of categories: Behavioural data and a connectionist model. *Brain & Language, 55(1)*, 89–92.

Tyler, L.K., & Moss, H.E. (1997). Functional properties of concepts: Studies of normal and brain-damaged patients. *Cognitive Neuropsychology, 14*, 426–486.

Tyler, L.K., & Moss, H.E. (1998). Going, going, gone? . . . Implicit and explicit tests of conceptual knowledge in a longitudinal study of semantic dementia. *Neuropsychologia, 6(12)*, 1313–1323

Tyler, L.K., Moss, H.E., Durrant-Peatfield, M., & Levy, J. (2000). Conceptual structure and the structure of concepts. *Brain and Language, 75(2)*, 195–231.

Warrington, E.K., & McCarthy, R. (1983). Category specific access dysphasia. *Brain, 106*, 859–878.

Warrington, E.K., & McCarthy, R. (1987). Categories of knowledge: Further fractionations and an attempted integration. *Brain, 110*, 1273–1296.

Warrington, E.K., & Shallice, T. (1984). Category specific semantic impairments. *Brain, 107*, 829–54.

Zorzi, M., Perry, C., Ziegler, J., & Coltheart, M. (1999). Category-specific deficits in a self-organizing model of the lexical–semantic system. In D. Heincke, G.W. Humphreys & A.C. Olson (Eds.), *Connectionist models in cognitive neuroscience*. London: Springer Verlag.

APPENDIX: BRIEF CASE DETAILS FOR THE SIX HSE PATIENTS INCLUDED IN THE PROPERTY KNOWLEDGE STUDY

RC (Moss et al., 1998)

RC is a 38-year-old right-handed man who had previously worked as a child-care assistant and was diagnosed as having HSE in 1992. An MRI scan in November 1997 identified bilateral damage to the temporal lobes extending from the lateral surface anteriorly, through the medial surface posteriorly (Brodmann's areas 28/38, the caudate nuclei, and the hippocampal regions). Damage was more extensive in the left hemisphere incorporating all the hippocampus and extending laterally in the left inferior temporal lobe (Brodmann's area 20).

JBR (Bunn et al., 1998)

JBR is a 41-year-old man who was diagnosed as having herpes simplex encephalitis at the age of 23. He was one of the four patients described by Warrington and Shallice (1984) and has subsequently been included in other studies of semantic memory (Funnell & Sheridan, 1992; Funnell & de Mornay Davies, 1996). An MRI scan in February 1996 revealed that the anterior halves of the temporal lobes were hypointense and this involved the medial and lateral temporal cortex to an equal degree. The entire right hippocampus was destroyed, while the posterior part of the left hippocampus was preserved. The amygdala was totally destroyed.

SE (Moss et al., 1997)

SE is a 67-year-old left-handed ex-railwayman who was diagnosed as having HSE in 1986. MRI imaging in 1993 showed gross destruction of the right temporal pole, uncus, hippocampus, parahippocampal gyrus, inferior and temporal lateral gyri to the level of the insula. There was little damage to the left hemisphere except for a small region of high signal on the T2-weighted sequence in the region of the uncus and the amygdala.

JH

JH is a 35-year-old right-handed woman who was diagnosed as having HSE at the age of 16. Visual inspection of an MRI scan in June 1998 revealed extensive bilateral damage to the temporal lobes affecting the superior, middle, and inferior gyri and extending from the occipitotemporal junction through to the temporal pole. This includes the medial temporal structures and extends into the insula and frontal operculum.

MW

MW is a 53-year-old former financial analyst who was diagnosed with HSE in 1983. Visual inspection of an MRI scan in April 1999 showed bilateral damage to the anteriomedial temporal lobes with some sparing of the hippocampal formation on the left. On the right, the damage is more extensive and encompasses the entire temporal lobe and some of the insula.[10]

TABLE 5.2

Background semantic memory tests for the five patients, comparing living and non-living things (per cent correct)

Patient	Task					
	Picture naming[a]		Naming to description[b]		Word–picture matching[a]	
	Living	Non-living	Living	Non-living	Living	Non-living
RC	10	49*	0	50*	67	88*
JBR	14	59*	10	77*	67	90*
SE	64	84*	77	93	98	100
JH	44	76*	30	60*	79	98*
MW	64	86*	63	73	92	100

[a] See Bunn et al. (1998) for details of the task and materials.
[b] See Moss et al. (1998) for details of the task and materials.
* significant at 0.05 in χ^2 analyses.

---

[10] We are grateful to Andrew Mayes for referring MW and JH to us.

CHAPTER SIX

Semantic dementia:
A category-specific paradox

Peter Garrard
Institute of Cognitive Neuroscience, London, UK

Matthew A. Lambon Ralph
University of Manchester, Manchester, UK

John R. Hodges
Addenbrooke's Hospital and MRC Cognition and Brain Sciences Unit, Cambridge, UK

INTRODUCTION

The occurrence of semantic deficits in which a patient's knowledge of objects from two broadly defined semantic categories (typically, biological kinds and man-made artefacts) is subject to contrasting degrees of impairment has been subject to a wide range of theoretical interpretations. One of the most influential of these accounts has proposed that such patterns of neuropsychological performance arise because of differences in the type of information that is most salient for the distributed cognitive representations of concepts in different semantic domains (Warrington & Shallice, 1984). In this formulation, visual attributes are held to be important to the task of distinguishing among exemplars of natural categories, while representations of artefacts are thought to be more heavily dependent on functional knowledge. For instance, according to this hypothesis, different types of fruit or breeds of dog are told apart mainly by virtue of their distinctive colours, shapes, sizes, surface markings, etc., whereas tools (e.g. different types of knives or saws) are distinguished in terms of their usage, and can differ markedly in appearance. That it is possible to produce an apparently category-specific effect, given these representational assumptions, by preferentially damaging a type of knowledge rather than a conceptual category, has been demonstrated convincingly in a connectionist framework (Farah & McClelland, 1991). The account has come to be known as the sensory–functional theory (SFT) (Caramazza, 1998; Caramazza & Shelton, 1998).

Other attempts at accounting for the phenomenon have focused on the possibility that the neural structures underlying semantically related objects are located together in separate cortical regions, allowing for the possibility of independent damage (Damasio, 1990). This explanation, however, fails to account for some apparently anomalous findings in the experimental literature. For example, body parts (a biological category with highly salient functional properties) tend to cluster with artefacts, whereas certain inanimate subgroups whose members are perceptually distinct but share a canonical function (e.g. fabrics, precious stones, and musical instruments) behave more like natural kinds (Warrington & McCarthy, 1987).

Some commentators have taken an altogether more sceptical line, arguing for the importance of psycholinguistic variables, such as concept familiarity and age of acquisition, in determining the vulnerability of different concepts (Funnell & Sheridan, 1992; Stewart, Parkin, & Hunkin, 1992). Although it is certainly true that the majority of reported cases have shown a selective impairment of knowledge relating to items in the less familiar domain of natural kinds (Basso, Capitani, & Laiacona, 1988; Farah, Hammond, Mehta, & Ratcliffe, 1989; Hart & Gordon, 1992; Hart, Berndt, & Carramazza, 1985; Hillis & Caramazza, 1991; McCarthy & Warrington, 1988; Pietrini et al., 1988; Sartori & Job, 1988; Sartori et al., 1993; Sheridan & Humphreys, 1993; Silveri & Gainotti, 1988; Silveri, Danilel, Giustolisi, & Gainotti, 1991; Warrington & Shallice, 1984), the fact that cases with the reverse advantage have also been reported (Hillis & Caramazza, 1991; Sacchett & Humphreys, 1992; Warrington & McCarthy, 1987) effectively excludes the possibility that differences in familiarity are the sole explanation of category-specific disorders (Shallice, 1988). None the less, the potential to create factitious category differences by ignoring the effects of non-semantic factors that vary systematically between domains was an important observation, and studies that claim to demonstrate category differences without taking such factors into consideration should be interpreted with some caution. It has also been shown that failure to recognise the contributions of extraneous neuropsychological factors can have the opposite effect, masking the presence of what would otherwise be genuine differences in performance between categories (Lambon Ralph, Howard, Nightingale, & Ellis, 1998). The selection of stimuli and statistical treatment of the associated variables has therefore come to be seen as being of central importance in the interpretation of data from this intriguing group of patients.

Turning to the cerebral lesion data relating to category-specific cases, an anatomical pattern is also evident: in those showing an advantage for artefacts over natural kinds, damage is often found in the temporal lobes, most commonly following herpes simplex virus encephalitis (HSVE) (Sartori &

Job, 1988; Sheridan & Humphreys, 1993; Silveri & Gainotti, 1988; War-rington & Shallice, 1984), whereas many of the cases showing an advantage for natural kinds over artefacts have damage in frontoparietal regions see Chapter 14 (Sacchett & Humphreys, 1992; Warrington & McCarthy, 1987). To tie these findings in with the SFT, it has been suggested that the temporal lobes might be important in the representation of higher-order visual knowledge, and frontoparietal regions perhaps more critical for the represen-tation of functional information (Gainotti, 1990). The fact that some patients with disproportionate impairment of natural-kinds categories due to tem-poral lobe damage have been shown to have more difficulty in both produc-tion and comprehension of perceptual information (De Renzi & Lucchelli, 1994; Silveri & Gainotti, 1988) provides a degree of empirical support for this idea. Other evidence, however, calls into question the association between category and knowledge type: several cases have been described with a rela-tive advantage for living things but no difference in their ability to answer questions relating to the visual or functional features of the same items (Caramazza & Shelton, 1998; Funnell & de Mornay Davies, 1996; Laiacona, Barbarotto, & Capitani, 1993; Lambon Ralph et al., 1998; Samson, Pillen, & de Wilde, 1998); and if it were permissible to argue from silence, then it would be reasonable to ask why no cases have been reported with a relative advan-tage for living concepts and disproportionate impairment of functional knowledge.

The appeal of this neuroanatomical interpretation of the sensory–functional account is, however, enhanced by its apparent convergence with experimental data on the dorsal and ventral "streams" of extrastriate visual processing (Mishkin, Ungerleider, & Macho, 1983). According to this dichot-omy, object recognition depends on a ventral pathway that incorporates the anterior–inferior portion of the temporal lobes, whereas dorsal projections, in inferior parietal regions, are important to the task of localising objects in space. A different, but related dissociation has been documented by Goodale, Milner, Jakobson, and Carey (1991): a patient with cortical damage second-ary to carbon monoxide intoxication was unable to make visual judgements about line orientation but could perform highly accurate visually guided hand movements in response to the same stimuli. The richness of corticocor-tical interconnections in the inferior parietal lobes has led to the hypothesis that this region serves a supramodal sensory function by which visuospatial, tactile and kinaesthetic information is integrated, and would therefore be a likely substrate for the representation of functional knowledge. More directly perceptual features (such as colour and shape) are believed to be separately represented in the temporal lobes. The findings of some more recent PET (Martin, Wiggs, Ungerleider, & Haxby, 1996; Mummery, Patterson, Hodges, & Wise, 1996), and fMRI (Thompson-Schill, Aguirre, D'Esposito, & Farah, 1999) activation studies are concordant with this idea that different types of knowledge are represented in anatomically separate regions (see Chapter 15).

The theoretical positions outlined above should be applicable to a wide range of cerebral pathologies and it is reasonable to ask what patterns of category-specific impairment might be expected in the syndrome of semantic dementia (SD). As will become apparent in the next section, the clinical and radiological features of this condition suggest that it provides an ideal neuro-anatomical and neuropsychological substrate for various aspects of the SFT to be tested.

SEMANTIC DEMENTIA (SD)

Semantic dementia is a syndrome resulting from a progressive but (at least in its early stages) focal neurodegenerative process. This process probably falls somewhere within the spectrum of Pick's disease (Kertesz, 1996) or fronto-temporal dementia (Snowden, Neary & Mann, 1996), but at any rate is not associated with the histological features of Alzheimer's disease (Hodges, Garrard, & Patterson, 1998). The syndrome is characterised by a loss of knowledge of facts, objects, and the meanings of words, with relative preser-vation of short-term (working) memory, day-to-day (episodic) memory, visuospatial skills and non-verbal problem solving (Hodges, Patterson, Oxbury, & Funnell, 1992; Snowden, Goulding, & Neary, 1989). Patients are thus well oriented and demonstrate good recall of recent life events, although their language difficulties often result in poor performance on bedside and formal tests of verbal memory. Verbal fluency scores are characteristically depressed in these patients and, when their performance on tests of category and letter fluency are compared, they typically score rather higher on the latter, which is the reverse of the normal pattern. Spontaneous speech can be superficially normal and the patients' fluent output, with its preserved syn-tactical structure and normal phonology and prosody, can obscure the fact that discourse is lacking in substantive content words. One clue to the diag-nosis might therefore be the frequency of word-finding pauses and the repeated use of generic expressions or circumlocutions, such as "stuff", "thing", or "one of those" (Bird, Lambon Ralph, Patterson, & Hodges, 2000). Frank errors, although rare, are almost always of the semantic vari-ety, manifested by the intrusion of semantically related words (e.g. "horse" for cow, or "window" for door; Hodges et al., 1992; Poeck & Luzzatti, 1988). Late in the course of SD the patient's vocabulary might be reduced to a few high frequency words or clichés, sometimes peculiarly appropriate to the condition (e.g. "I don't know what you're talking about" or "I don't under-stand at all"). Patients with SD invariably demonstrate profound anomia to both verbally and visually presented stimuli. Thus, neither asking the ques-tion "What do we call the small metal object carried on a ring and used to open doors?", nor showing a picture or photograph of a key, nor for that matter giving them a real key to hold, would result in the production of the appropriate verbal label. Finally, the problems encountered by SD patients are not confined to linguistically mediated tests: sorting of pictures according to some defined characteristic (e.g. size, country of origin, habitat, or diet), non-verbal tests of associative semantics and selection of a pictured concept on the basis of its characteristic sound are all performed at subnormal levels (Bozeat et al., 2000).

The phenomenon that is perhaps of greatest importance to the current chapter, however, is the nature of the concept definitions that are given by patients with SD. When invited to provide a definition of a particular concept with an instruction such as "tell me everything you know about a [e.g.] horse", the responses of these patients, despite appropriate prompting, are not only extremely impoverished, but usually dominated by information of a non-visual kind (Lambon Ralph et al., 1998; Parkin, 1993). For instance, when asked to provide a definition of a horse one of our patients, TR, responded entirely in terms of associative attributes, such as "you see them in the fields", or "they race them". For many of the items in our semantic test battery, particularly the less familiar animals, TR would deny any knowledge at all of the item in question, for example, "I don't know anything about a giraffe; I don't know what a giraffe is, I've never heard of it". For all the items he could define, however, whether from living or non-living categories, TR's descriptions were characterised by the same pattern of overwhelmingly associative information. The apparent lack of visual information was also present in other patients, albeit to a less dramatic extent, and the predominance of functional information has been noted in a systematic cross-sectional analysis of concept definitions (Lambon Ralph, Graham, Patterson, & Hodges, 1999).

What of the anatomical correlates of SD? In radiological terms, SD appears to be associated with profound focal atrophy of one or both temporal lobes, particularly the pole and inferolateral gyri (Garrard & Hodges, 2000; Hodges et al., 1998) (Figure 6.1). When the atrophy is asymmetric it is usually more severe on the left, but cases with selective right temporal lobe atrophy have also been described (Hodges et al., 1992; Barbarotto, Capitani, & Laiacona, 1996), with clinical and neuropsychological features that are at least superficially similar.

A recent quantitative study of the MRI scans of six SD patients has confirmed this anatomical association and showed, in addition, a correlation between the degree of semantic impairment and extent of atrophy at the left temporal pole (Mummery et al., 2000). With progression of the disease process, clinical evidence of frontal lobe dysfunction (usually behavioural and personality changes) invariably emerges and radiological appearances begin to reflect a more widespread pattern of cerebral atrophy. If studied early

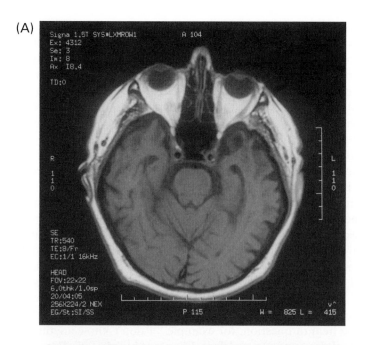

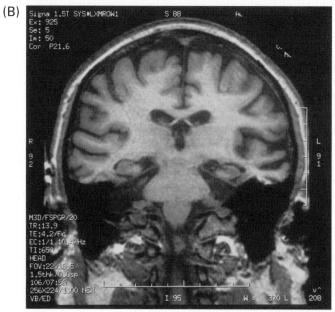

Figure 6.1. Representative axial (A) and coronal (B) T1-weighted MRI slices through frontal and temporal lobes of a patient with semantic dementia. Note the severely atrophic inferior gyrus and pole of the left temporal lobe.

154

enough, however, selective temporal lobe atrophy is a prominent feature in all of these patients.

The combination of selective temporal lobe atrophy and an apparent deficit in knowledge of the sensory aspects of concept definitions would appear to provide precisely the conditions under which a specific deficit in knowledge of living items might be expected to appear. Semantic dementia, however, accounts for only a fraction of the cases with category-specific impairment that have been described in the literature to date, and among the 40 or so published cases of SD, only six have been reported as showing a category-specific pattern (Barbarotto, Capitani, Spinnler, & Trivelli, 1995; Basso et al., 1988; Breedin, et al., 1994; Cardebat, Demonet, Celsis, & Puel, 1996; Lambon Ralph et al., 1999; McCarthy & Warrington, 1988); see Table 6.1 for further details. The absence of a category-specific difference is also apparent from studies that have focused on concept definition (Lambon Ralph et al., 1999) and non-verbal forms of assessment (Bozeat et al., 2000). Clinical and radiological information about the exceptional cases (i.e. those in whom a category-specific effect *has* been shown) is displayed in Table 6.1, below, from which it is also apparent that one case exhibited an advantage in the direction opposite to that predicted by the SFT.

There are a number of possible explanations for this apparent inconsistency between the impairment of sensory knowledge and the paucity of category-specific deficits observed in SD. First, patients with SD might vary on behavioural measures as a result of subtle differences in the distribution of cerebral atrophy within the temporal complex. Second, the supposed causal relationship between sensory knowledge and the cognitive representations of concepts from living categories might perhaps be no more than a conjunction of independent deficits. This possibility deserves consideration in the light of reported cases showing one deficit without the other (for two such cases and a review, see Lambon Ralph et al., 1998). Third, the degree of anomia present in SD, even at presentation, is often so severe that category differences on naming or generation of definition tasks may be masked by floor effects.

In support of the first possibility, the case reported by Barbarotto et al., (1996) showed a right-sided predominance of temporal atrophy and a degree of medial involvement that was unusually severe for SD, suggesting two candidate anatomical dimensions. Similarly, subtle abnormalities might not have been detected in the two earliest cases because of the insensitivity of CT in detecting temporal lobe changes. A similar variability in the incidence of category-specificity in a population of patients recovering from herpes simplex encephalitis had earlier been noted by the same authors (Barbarotto et al., 1996). A radiological analysis identified that the involvement of medial temporal structures in these patients was variable, but the authors were not able to demonstrate a systematic relationship between the presence of a category-specific pattern and involvement of any specific brain region. They

TABLE 6.1

Clinical, radiological, and neuropsychological details of the six published cases of semantic dementia with a category-specific deficit

Case ID	Clinical abstract	Strucural imaging (MRI unless otherwise stated)	Functional imaging (SPECT unless otherwise stated)	Neuropsychological assessment	Category-specific deficit	Factors controlled for
TOB Male 58 (McCarthy & Warrington, 1988; Parkin, 1993; Tyrell et al., 1990)	Deteriorating expressive language and comprehension 4 years; fluent speech with impoverished vocabulary; severe anomia; circumlocutions; impaired single-word comprehension	Left perisylvian atrophy (CT)	Hypometabolism in left posterior frontal, superior, middle and inferior temporal regions (PET)	WAIS, GNT, WAIS-R, PPT, Schonell Graded Word Reading Test, NART, Progressive Matrices, Oldfield's Naming Test, Peabody Picture Vocabulary Test	Definitions to spoken word: 30% correct for animals, 64% correct for inanimate objects, although normal on both categories with pictorial stimuli	Frequency
NV Male 73 (Basso et al., 1988)	Progressive word-finding and comprehension difficulties (especially for food items) over 5 years; fluent but circumlocutory speech	Bilateral inferior perisylvian atrophy (CT)	Not performed	Standardised tests of language, memory, praxis, and calculation, Weigl's test, verbal fluency, Snodgrass picture naming	Naming and word-picture matching of 10 animals and 10 fruit/vegetables consistently poorer than 10 inanimate objects and 10 items of furniture	Frequency
DM Male 56 (Breedin et al., 1994)	Difficulty remembering names and appointments; later difficulties restricted to semantic information; severe naming and single word comprehension deficits; surface dyslexia	Normal	Relative decrease in perfusion in left inferior temporal region relative to right	WAIS-R, RMT, BNT, PPVT, VOSP, PPT, functional similarity test, category synonymy test	Chance performance on category synonymy test for categories of animals, insects and musical instruments; above chance for non-living categories	Frequency

MF Male 54 (Barbarotto et al., 1995)	Progressive word-finding difficulties, problems with face recognition, word comprehension and writing 5 years; later personality change, obsession with food and religion	Diffuse atrophy, most marked in inferior and lateral aspects of right temporal lobe, including medial structures (hippocampus and parahippocampal gyrus)	Not performed	Standardised semantic battery, various formal tests of memory, attention, face perception and recognition, and praxis, Raven's progressive matrices	Naming, word–picture matching and feature questions on 30 living and 30 non-living items. Consistent advantage for non-living items across tests	Concept familiarity, frequency, prototypicality, visual complexity, name agreement, difficulty rating
GC Female 72 (Cardebat et al., 1996)	Progressive word-finding difficulties 4 years	Selective left inferior and medial temporal atrophy	Normal at rest; differential frontal activation during processing of animals and objects	WMS, WAIS, Benton face recognition test, Benton visual retention test, Rey Figure, Montreal–Toulouse 86 aphasia battery	Confrontation naming and word–picture matching: 3/40 and 3/20 for living; 16/38 and 16/20 for non-living categories	Not reported
IW Female 53 (Lambon Ralph et al., 1998)	Memory failure 2 years; word-finding difficulties for objects and people's names; impaired comprehension; surface dyslexia and dysgraphia	Left temporal lobe atrophy, especially pole and inferior region	Not performed	VOSP, BNT, Progressive Matrices, WAIS-R, RMT, Rey Figure, PPT, TROG, standardised semantic battery	Consistent advantage for animate categories in tests of picture naming, naming to definition, word–picture matching, and concept definition	Concept familiarity, age of acquisition, imageability, phoneme length, spoken frequency, visual complexity

did, however, hypothesise that a combination of medial and lateral temporal lobe damage may be necessary to produce a category-specific pattern.

The possibility of a role for medial temporal structures in the representation of different categories has also been suggested by one PET activation study of normal volunteers comparing verbal fluency for different semantic categories, in which an area of activation in the left medial temporal lobe was seen when subjects generated items from living, but not from non-living, categories (Mummery et al., 1996). If, as seems likely, concept representation necessitates the integration of stored information from segregated sensory modalities (Allport, 1985), then the multimodal projections to and from entorhinal cortex (Gainotti, 1990; Van Hoesen, Pandya, & Butters, 1972) would imply a central role for this region in the retrieval of semantic knowledge. Systematic variations in the featural structure of items belonging to different semantic domains (Garrard, Lambon Ralph, Patterson, & Hodges, 2001; McRae & Cree, this volume) may thus be of central importance to the vulnerability of different concepts.

It should be pointed out that although the occurrence category-specificity in the context of HSVE (a much more common condition) is also relatively rare, this disorder is much more anatomically and clinically heterogeneous than SD, and frequently causes communication problems that are too severe to allow more detailed testing of semantic memory. Neither of these arguments applies to SD, at least in the early stages, and any differences that do exist between individual cases must therefore be more subtle. It is difficult, however, to draw firm conclusions using a historical series of cases alone. Many of the early cases were reported in the literature because of their importance to understanding neurological rather than cognitive issues, and were not therefore studied in particular neuropsychological detail. Others were described before the importance of controlling for non-semantic variables was fully recognised, and might therefore have failed to discover a category advantage that was in fact present. It is therefore of interest to examine a prospectively recruited series of SD patients uniformly assessed using theoretically motivated neuropsychological instruments based on a consistent set of items. In the remainder of this chapter we will describe a set of results from just such a cohort of patients who have been recruited and studied in our department since 1992.

The cohort of SD patients in this study

SD is not a common clinical condition but, over a period of 8 years, eighteen patients with this syndrome have been seen in our department and have agreed to longitudinal neuropsychological testing and high-resolution neuro-imaging. Five of the patients died while under active follow-up and, in all of those whose brains were examined *post mortem*, spongiform degeneration, with or without the specific markers of Pick's disease (Pick bodies and Pick cells), was found. We present here the semantic memory test scores from a series of twelve of these patients and neuroradiological assessments on eight. All were tested on naming and comprehension of a consistent set of stimulus items, designed to detect category-specific differences.

All patients met the following diagnostic criteria for SD: (i) selective impairment of semantic memory causing severe anomia, impaired spoken and written single-word comprehension, reduced generation of exemplars on category fluency tests, and an impoverished fund of general knowledge about objects, people, and the meanings of words; (ii) relative sparing of other components of language output and comprehension, notably syntax and phonology; (iii) normal perceptual skills and non-verbal problem-solving ability; (iv) relatively preserved autobiographical and day-to-day (episodic) memory (Hodges et al., 1992).

Summary clinical and general neuropsychological data on each of the patients is given in Table 6.2. The patients in this group were selected because, early in the course of their evaluation, naming and word–picture matching scores were obtained using either all 260 items from the Snodgrass and Vanderwart corpus (earlier recruited patients), or a carefully selected subset of 64 of these stimuli, containing equal sets of living and non-living stimuli, matched on the basis of age-of-acquisition and familiarity (later recruited patients). The stimuli, together with their associated values, are listed in the Appendix (p. 180).

IS THE SEMANTIC DEFICIT IN SD CATEGORY SPECIFIC?

Figures 6.2 and 6.3 display the naming and spoken-word comprehension scores for natural kinds and artefacts achieved by each of the patients in the cohort on the age-of-acquisition-matched (Figure 6.2) and familiarity-matched stimulus sets (Figure 6.3).

Inspection of these scores reveals considerable variation between individual cases: four of the twelve patients (JL, BM, DG, and JC) showed an advantage for artefacts with some degree of consistency across tests and materials, whereas others (such as PS and SL) showed no clear effect. GC showed a sizeable advantage for natural kinds (on naming only) when the stimuli were matched for familiarity. Because of the small size of the individual sets being considered, however, none of the individual differences achieved statistical significance.

Because of the complex relationship between tests, matching variables, and semantic domain, formal analysis of each patient's performance was carried out using a regression analysis in order to determine the influence of domain, familiarity, and age of acquisition on the presence or absence of a

TABLE 6.2

Summary clinical and general neuropsychological data on each of the patients in the study cohort

Case ID	MS	PS	TR	BM	GC	JH
Age at onset (years)	62	55	53	47	56	56
Sex	Female	Female	Male	Male	Female	Female
Presenting symptoms	Word-finding difficulties; impaired comprehension of unusual words; some practical difficulties; subtle personality changes	Word-finding difficulties; impaired comprehension of spoken and written language	Insidious personality change; bizarre behaviour; change in social and eating habits; marked difficulties with face recognition	Difficulty remembering names of objects and people	Forgetting names of people, plants and trees; impaired comprehension of spoken and written language; personality change	Word-finding difficulties; impaired comprehension; personality change
Clinical features	Fluent, grammatical speech with marked anomia; impaired single word comprehension	Severe anomia; impaired comprehension of low frequency words; poor verbal fluency	Attentional impairment; anomia; single word comprehension problems; markedly reduced verbal fluency	Anomic, empty but grammatical speech	Fluent, grammatical but empty speech	Fluent, grammatical but empty speech; marked anomia; reduced verbal fluency
Raven's Coloured Progressive Matrices	nt	36	nt	31	nt	29
Rey Figure copy	22	32	35	36	36	31
RMT (faces)	22	18	nt	24	19	19
Digits forwards	3	4	5	7	6	4
TROG	69	74	71	80	80	67
Category fluency (animals/min.)	5	4	4	9	11	5
Letter fluency (FAS/min.)	6	5	2	6	11	6
PPT (pictures)	36	42	30	30	49	33
MRI appearance	Bilateral temporal lobe atrophy, more marked on the left	Atrophy of left superior, middle and inferior temporal gyri	Bilateral frontotemporal atrophy, most marked in the right temporal region	Bilateral temporal lobe atrophy, more marked on the right	Selective left temporal lobe atrophy	Selective left inferior temporal atrophy
SPECT appearance	Bilateral, mainly left frontotemporal hypoperfusion	Left temporal hypoperfusion	Bilateral symmetrical frontotemporal hypoperfusion	Patchy hypoperfusion: especially temporoparietal	Selective left temporal hypoperfusion	Left hemisphere hypoperfusion, mainly temporal

Case ID	DG	JL	SL	KH	DC	JC
Age at onset (years)	62	58	49	57	78	54
Sex	Female	Male	Female	Male	Female	Male
Presenting symptoms	Failure to recognise people; word-finding difficulties; subtle personality change	Forgetting names of people and places; loss of vocabulary; word-finding difficulties in conversation; visual agnosia; personality change	Forgetting names of people and objects for about 1 year; problems with concentration	Difficulty deriving semantic information from proper names; impaired understanding of low frequency words; circumlocutory naming; personality change	Forgotten words and names; word-finding problems; impaired comprehension, 2–3 years	Word-finding difficulties for 2–3 years; personality change
Clinical features	Fluent, grammatical empty speech; severe anomia: poor definitions; reduced verbal fluency; surface dyslexia	Fluent, grammatical speech with word-finding difficulties and semantic errors; surface dyslexia and dysgraphia	Fluent spontaneous speech with occasional grammatical errors; anomic; surface dyslexic; increased use of standard phrases	Mild anomia; poor famous face recognition; impaired single-word comprehension	Markedly reduced verbal fluency; severe anomia	Fluent grammatical language with word-finding difficulties; reduced category fluencies; anomic and mild single-word comprehension deficit; surface dyslexic and dysgraphic
Raven's Coloured Progressive Matrices	nt	29	30	35	nt	26
Rey Figure copy	24	34	30	36	32	27
RMT (faces)	13	25	49	20	nt	nt
Digits forwards	3	5	6	6	6	8
TROG	62	76	77	74	nt	77
Category fluency (animals/min.)	10	10	9	4	4	9
Letter fluency (FAS/min.)	9	8	9	6	3	8
PPT (pictures)	22	36	48	45	40	47
MRI appearance	Bilateral temporal lobe atrophy, more marked on the right	Bilateral temporal lobe atrophy, more marked on the right	Focal left temporal atrophy, particularly severe anteriorly	Predominantly right-sided temporal lobe atrophy	Generalised cerebral atrophy, particularly severe in left inferior temporal region	Generalised cerebral atrophy with marked involvement of temporal regions (including medial temporal lobes)
SPECT appearance	Bitemporal hypoperfusion, right more than left	Bilateral temporal hypoperfusion	Focal left temporal hypoperfusion	Focal right temporal lobe hypoperfusion	Focal left temporal lobe hypoperfusion	Hypoperfusion in left frontal and temporal regions

nt = not tested

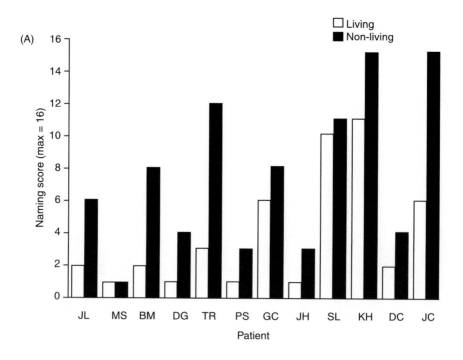

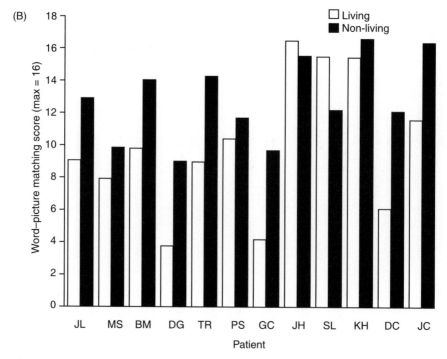

Figure 6.2. Scores (out of 16) on (A) naming and (B) spoken word-to-picture matching using equal sets of living and non-living stimuli matched for age of acquisition.

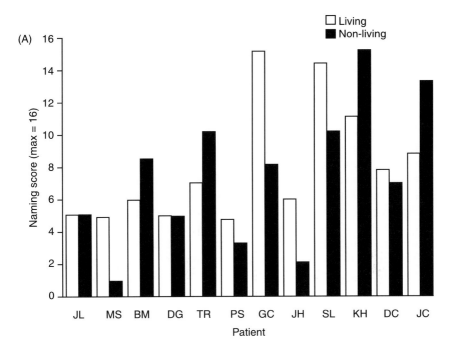

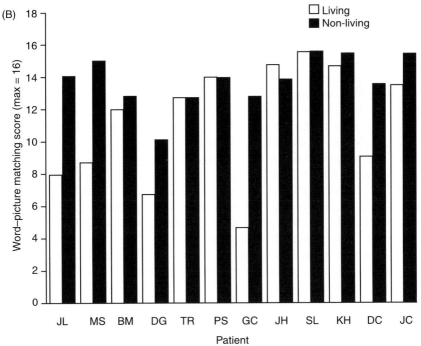

Figure 6.3. Scores (out of 16) on (A) naming and (B) spoken word-to-picture matching using equal sets of living and non-living stimuli matched for concept familiarity.

correct response on each item. This method was used by Barbarotto et al., (1995) in a single case study, and by Lambon Ralph et al., (1998) to analyse the determinants of correct naming responses in a group of eight SD patients. The latter study revealed consistent effects of familiarity and/or age of acquisition. Six of the eight patients studied by Lambon Ralph et al. (1998) are in the present group, so the set of patients considered was slightly smaller. Moreover, only naming responses were examined in that study, whereas the present data contains both naming and word–picture matching scores, which were analysed separately. The analyses are, however, limited to responses on 64 items (considerably fewer than the 132 considered by Lambon Ralph et al., 1998), and are therefore comparatively lacking in statistical power. Results of the individual regression analyses, as well as those of a linear regression of the group data, are presented in Table 6.3.

This survey of the individual performances of the patients in the group has revealed an inconsistent pattern, with category differences varying in magnitude, and even in direction, depending both on materials (those matched on familiarity versus those matched on age of acquisition) and method of assessment (naming versus word–picture matching). This variability suggests two further questions: first, is the tendency towards a category-specific pattern related to any measure of overall disease severity or degree of semantic impairment, as hypothesised by Gonnerman et al., (1997) and by Moss et al. (see Chapter 5)? Second, might a more consistent and statistically reliable picture be revealed by considering the patients in a cross-sectional fashion as a group?

In contrast to the Alzheimer's disease (AD) cohort analysed by Garrard, Patterson, Watson, and Hodges (1998) in relation to the first of these two questions, the number of patients considered here is small but, on the basis of data reported in Tables 6.2 and 6.3, it is clear that the performance of GC— the only patient to score more highly on the living than the non-living subset—is the highest scorer on a variety of non-semantic measures (e.g. Rey copy and letter fluency) and on the picture version of the Pyramids and Palm Trees Test (an index of overall semantic impairment). The other individuals whose performance on the semantic tests was significantly influenced by domain (JC, KH, JL, MS, and TR) are, however, evenly distributed amongst the range of scores on all these measures.

With respect to the second question, Figure 6.4 displays the mean probabilities of correct identification by the patient group of items from the natural kinds and artefacts sets, in each of the test conditions. Data from the two matched sets of items are shown separately. Word–picture matching, as expected, performed at a higher level than picture naming [$F(1,30) = 246.7$, $p < .001$], and in addition, overall performance was significantly better for non-living than for living items [$F(1,30) = 5.5$, $p < .05$]. There were no significant interactions. The familiarity-matched materials were identified

TABLE 6.3

Summary of individual logistic regression analyses incorporating three theoretically important predictor variables

					Patient ID									
	MS	PS	TR	BM	GC	JH	DG	JL	SL	KH	DC	JC	Group [F(3(df))]
A. Naming													
Model [χ²(3df)]	16.2**	23.3***	16.4****	12.8**	23.2***	24.4***	15.8**	16.8**	9.1*	13.8**	12.6**	23.0***	17.3***
Semantic domain			*		*					*		**	
Familiarity	*	*		*	**	**	*	*			*		***
Age of acquisition					*		*					*	**
B. Matching													
Model [χ²(3df)]	12.5**	10.5*	10.2*	14.4**	19.5***	5.4	9.2*	15.1**	8.0*	3.6	14.3**	13.0**	19.0***
Semantic domain	*				*			**					**
Familiarity		*		*				**	*				**
Age of acquisition	*			*									**

Semantic domain was entered as a categorical covariate, with living and non-living items coded as 1 and 0 respectively. The dependent variable is the response (correct or incorrect) to the item. With the exception of GC's naming, all significant effects of domain implied better performance on non-living items (i.e. regression coefficient (B)<0). Picture naming scores (A) and word–picture matching scores (B) were analysed separately.
*p<.05; ** p<.01; *** p<.001.

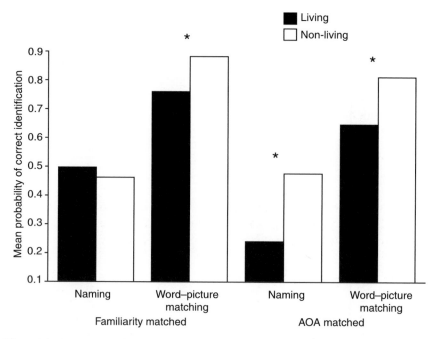

Figure 6.4.   Mean probabilities of correct identification of the living and non-living subsets of the two groups of stimuli ($p < 0.05$).

marginally but significantly better than the age-of-acquisition matched items [$F(1,30) = 4.7, p < .05$] but there was no interaction between matching criterion and test [$F(1,30) = 2.5, p > .05$]. The three-way interaction was significant, however, [$F(1,30) = 4.9, p < .05$]. When the responses to the two sets of items were considered separately a significant domain by test interaction emerged for the familiarity-matched [$F(1,30) = 6.5, p < .05$], but not for the age-of-acquisition-matched materials [$F(1,30) < 1$]. *Post hoc* comparisons, using Tukey's HSD test, revealed that all living–non-living differences were significant ($p < .05$), with the exception of those obtained from naming of the familiarity-matched materials.

Why should the reliability of the category difference seen in naming, but not in word–picture matching, vary in this way? The average scores achieved in the naming test would not favour the suggestion that this discrepancy arose because of floor effects. One possibility is that the two tasks are affected to different degrees, and perhaps for different reasons, by these factors. A more plausible, if prosaic, suggestion is that, in spite of careful matching of the test stimuli, the foils used in the word–picture matching tests (which were not explicitly matched across domain) might have been marginally more familiar for the non-living categories, producing a small, but spurious, advantage in this test. An analysis of the mean familiarity of all nine foils used on each word–picture matching trial (which consisted of the seven remaining category items together with two novel stimuli that did not otherwise appear as test items), confirmed this suspicion: there was a small but consistent difference between the living and non-living items in the familiarity matched subset on this measure (t-test, $p = .01$).

To summarise, a single case survey of eight patients with SD has revealed a number of individuals who demonstrate a relative domain advantage that is not completely explained on the basis of accessory variables, and some tendency for an advantage in favour of non-living items seemed almost invariable. The magnitude of this difference, however, and the extent to which it is genuinely attributable to membership of one or other domain, varied markedly between cases. When considered as a group, the overall trend that emerged from the pooled data was a marginally greater preservation of knowledge relating to non-living concepts. Again, however, it is worth emphasising that the difference was small—and in comparison to the size of the non-living advantage displayed by some of the post-HSVE cases, this finding is both striking and puzzling. To try to explain this category-specific paradox, we considered the possibility that our patient population was more heterogeneous than we originally thought, with cases differing from one another in some respect that was crucial to the production of category-specific differences. To address this issue retrospectively is difficult, but we were able to look for differences in the preservation of sensory versus functional knowledge in some of the more recently recruited cases, and in the distribution of cerebral atrophy using existing MRI scans.

COGNITIVE DIFFERENCES AMONG SD PATIENTS

To examine the possibility that the variations in performance could have been due to differences in the characteristics of the underlying knowledge, two of the patients from the cohort who were undergoing active testing (KH and SL) were reassessed using a test of naming to definition. These two patients were equivalent in terms of disease progression, semantic, and overall cognitive impairment (see Table 6.2), but had contrasting profiles in terms of category selectivity: while SL showed no overall effect of semantic domain, KH showed a consistent advantage for non-living items in all test conditions (see Figures 6.2 and 6.3), with domain emerging as a significant predictor of successful naming in the regression analysis (see Table 6.3). The naming to definitions test, which was based on the same 64 items as the other tests in the semantic battery, provides a verbal description to which the subject is required to produce the name of the described item. There were two descriptions for each item in the battery, one stressing the item's perceptual attributes, and the other its functional attributes. For instance, the word "camel" was sought using the "functional" question "What do we call the bad-tempered animal that is ridden in the desert, and can survive without water?", and by the "sensory" question "What do we call the large four-legged animal with hooves and one or two humps on its back?". Alternating sensory and functional questions were used for each item, followed by the remaining question for each item in the same order.

This method, which is designed to detect differences in impairment to sensory and functional information, has been used previously in the evaluation of patients with disproportionate semantic impairment for living items (Silveri & Gainotti, 1988). The patients who were reported in that study showed an interaction between category and question type, in that they had greater difficulty producing the names of living items when the questions stressed perceptual rather than functional attributes. The method has been criticised, however, on the grounds that the two types of question were not matched for difficulty and that functional attributes of, in particular, animals, were likely to represent rather low frequency information (Caramazza & Shelton, 1998). The present version of the test is less vulnerable to this criticism, because all questions were based on semantic features that had been generated in a feature norming project by cognitively normal individuals of comparable age and educational level to the cohort members (as discussed later). Although not formally matched for frequency, none of the attributes used in the definitions was of low production frequency. The numbers of living and non-living items correctly named by each subject in response to the perceptual and functional definitions are shown in Figure 6.5, together with the mean and 95% confidence limits achieved in each condition by a group of twenty normal controls (mean age = 72, SD = 4.8).

The influences of familiarity, age of acquisition, domain, question type, and the domain by question type interaction on correct name production were once again analysed using separate logistic regressions for each subject. Both regression equations were significant but the influence of individual variables varied markedly between the two subjects: whereas in the case of SL none was significantly predictive of correct naming, KH's responses were significantly influenced by age of acquisition, domain, and the domain by question type interaction, but not by question type alone. In other words, KH's performance was best for naming non-living things from definitions that were dominated by functional attributes. To examine this result in more detail, we returned to the feature norming data alluded to earlier.

This standardised set of semantic attributes for each of the battery items was assembled from a group of twenty normal volunteers (roughly matched for age and educational level to the AD patient group) in a feature norming procedure which is described in detail elsewhere (Garrard et al., 2000). A total of 869 unique attributes were generated to the stimulus words, many of which were associated with more than one item, making the total number of

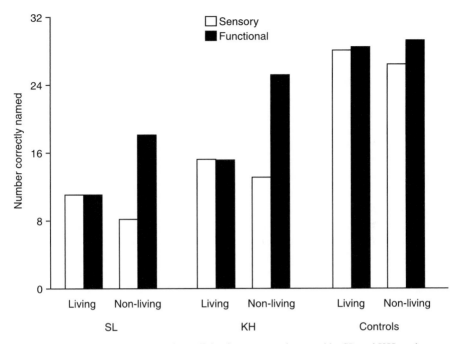

Figure 6.5. Numbers of living and non-living items correctly named by SL and KH, and mean scores achieved by a group of normal, age-matched controls, in response to verbal descriptions stressing perceptual and functional attributes.

concept–attribute pairs rather larger (2969). A large number of attributes had been generated by only one respondent and these were excluded from the set, leaving 618 unique attributes and 1657 concept–attribute pairs, each associated with a dominance value (defined as the proportion of subjects generating it in the test), and a distinctiveness value (defined as the proportion of concepts in the same category for which the attribute was generated). Attributes were classified as sensory, functional, encyclopaedic, or categorising, according to fixed criteria: sensory attributes (50.5% of the total) were those that could be appreciated in some sensory modality (e.g. "a tiger has stripes" or "a candle is long and thin"). Functional attributes (27.6%) were those that described an action, activity, or use, of an item (e.g. "a cat can catch mice", "an owl can fly", or "a suitcase can be carried"). Encyclopaedic attributes (14.7%) were those that described some other type of associative relationship (e.g. "a tiger is found in India", or "a spanner is kept in a toolbox"). Categorising features (7.2%) were those that placed the item in a superordinate category (e.g. "a dog is an animal").

Contemporary theoretical models of category-specific semantic impairments have variously emphasised the role of feature type (perceptual, functional, and encyclopaedic), feature distinctiveness, and feature intercor-relation in the representations of living and non-living concepts. Analyses of the distribution of attributes were therefore directed towards testing the assumptions of such models.

The raw numbers of features of each type were found to be distributed between the two conceptual domains in different proportions, with sensory features most numerous in both and a relatively greater disparity for living than for non-living concepts—a pattern reminiscent of Farah and McClelland (1991). The observed difference was, however, highly dependent on the inclusion or exclusion of encyclopaedic features—a point made by Caramazza and Shelton (1998).

With regard to distinctiveness, there was a striking asymmetry between the shared and distinctive features. More distinctive features of all types were associated with non-living concepts—a result also reported by McRae and Cree in Chapter 8—and the numbers of shared and distinctive features of living things (with the exception of the encyclopaedic subset) were approxi-mately equal. This result appeared to run counter to the hypothesis that visual features are crucial for distinguishing among living things (Warrington & McCarthy, 1987).

The analyses relating to feature intercorrelation showed that only around 10% of feature combinations were significantly intercorrelated, and that these were very largely made up of shared features. Even allowing for the possibility that the data were unrepresentative of semantic knowledge in its entirety, it is difficult to see how the influence of this subset of features could produce category dissociations of the magnitude of those described in the neuropsychological literature.

To examine the content of patients' conceptual knowledge about indi-vidual items we constructed lists of core features derived from the database, and asked subjects to produce as much information as possible about each item, presented in spoken word form. The test instruction was simply: "Tell me everything you know about a . . .", with encouragement to mention: (i) general ways of describing the item; (ii) the parts of the item; and (iii) things that the item can do or ways in which it can be used. The attribute set was used to quantify the patients' performance. Attributes associated with each item were listed on a score sheet, together with their dominance values. Credit was given for knowledge of an attribute if it was verbally generated during testing but, to overcome the output difficulties of the more anomic subjects, similar credit was given for non-verbal responses (e.g. gesturing, imitating, or pointing), using a lenient criterion of success. No time limit was imposed but attribute generation for each concept was terminated when the patient either indicated that he or she could think of no more to say, or began to repeat previously generated attributes. At this point, the patient was prompted to demonstrate knowledge of the remaining attributes on the score sheet, using probe questions that were specific (but never in the form of direct yes/no questions). For instance, if a patient had not mentioned spontaneously that a camel has a humped back, the question "what does a camel have on its back?" was asked. The acquisition of each patient's test data took place in a series of sessions (typically four or five) over a period of up to 2 months, each session lasting between 2 and 3 hours. The same procedure was carried out on twenty age-matched control subjects (although the testing time required was considerably shorter). The patients' attribute knowledge for each item was calculated as the proportion of the total number of attributes available for that item, with each attribute weighted by its dominance value.

The test was administered to a group of patients with mild or moderate Alzheimer's disease, as well as to four patients with SD, and proved to be a reliable and sensitive method of assessing semantic memory impairment. All patients achieved measurable scores on the test and not even the most mildly affected members of the AD group (in whom semantic impairment is recognised to be much milder than in patients with SD) scored at a level within the normal control range. In a number of cases, testing was repeated after an interval of 12 months and performance had declined appreciably, on both the spontaneous and prompted test conditions, in all of these individuals.

Figure 6.6 displays the mean proportions of the dominance-weighted totals of sensory, functional, encyclopaedic and categorising features

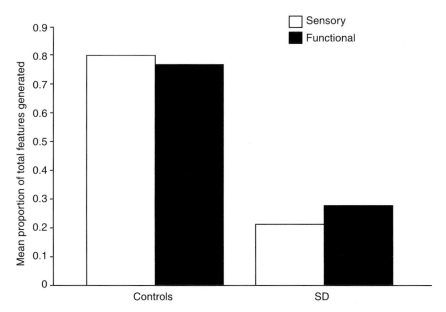

Figure 6.6.   Mean proportions of sensory and functional feature knowledge achieved on the 64 items in the semantic battery by four SD patients and twenty control subjects.

generated after prompting, by a group of four patients with SD (DG, TR, KH, and SL), compared with the control group. The result confirms the informal observation made earlier of an excess of functional and encyclo-paedic information in SD patients' concept definitions. The difference is clearly much less striking after normal production frequency is taken into consideration, and did not reach statistical significance. The result looked very similar when the number of features alone were considered (i.e. after removing the weighting factor of feature dominance).

Returning to our two paradigm cases, KH and SL, how, if at all, did the attribute knowledge of these two contrasting subjects differ? The results were disappointingly uniform: although their overall test scores were similar, as might be predicted from their equivalence in terms of disease progression, so too were their relative scores when broken down into sensory and functional/ associative information. Moreover, when the test items were split by semantic domain, neither case showed an interaction between domain and type of feature knowledge. This null result persisted even when the analysis was restricted to the patients' knowledge of attributes at the distinctive end of the spectrum. The same held true when the results of all four SD patients who were assessed in this way were included in the analysis: although the sensory feature knowledge was more impaired than functional in the two severely affected patients (DG and TR), their overall scores were too low to reveal any statistically significant difference.

A detailed quantitative analysis of the attribute knowledge associated with a set of test items did not, therefore, uphold the informal observation that patients with SD show a severe selective deficit in sensory knowledge. The same approach also failed to replicate the suggestion, based on the results of a naming to verbal description test, namely that two subjects who differed in their category-specific profile also differed in the extent to which their sensory feature knowledge was impaired.

This method of evaluation is, of course, open to a number of criticisms, including the relevance to this particular issue of the production frequency metric. In its present form, however, it has provided no support to the notion that a disproportionate deficit of sensory knowledge underpins the emergence of the category-specific pattern that is seen in some, but not all, SD patients.

NEUROANATOMICAL VARIABILITY AMONG SD PATIENTS

To look for patterns of neuroanatomical abnormality, all patients underwent high-resolution MR brain imaging within 3 months of clinical presentation. Images from the first eight patients to be recruited (except for those of JL [see Figure 6.1], which were unavailable) were examined systematically for any differences in the relative extent of atrophy in medial and lateral structures, in accordance with the hypothesis of Barbarotto et al., (1996). The process of formal assessment was modified before the later patients were recruited, as part of a separate, more comprehensive programme of quantitative radiological evaluation. Assessments were made with reference to a normal MRI scan, on two separate occasions using a 5-point, semi-quantitative scale, on which 0 represented normality and 5 severe atrophy.

The assessor was an experienced consultant neuroradiologist who was blind to the patients' neuropsychological findings and to the hypothesis in question. Cohen's kappa was used to quantify the extent of agreement between the two assessments.

Agreement between the two assessments was only moderate ($\kappa = 0.52$, $p < .001$) when all points on the rating scale were considered in the comparison, owing to predictable discrepancies of mostly single scale points. When the assessments were collapsed into just two categories (normal or mild atrophy only versus moderate or severe atrophy) the agreement improved ($\kappa = 0.62$, $p < .01$); there were five discrepant cases, all differing by just one scale point. These five cases were reassessed and assigned to one of the binary categories. Comparison of the results of these assessments (shown in Table 6.4), with the behavioural measures reported above, reveals that three of the patients with the largest advantage for artefacts aggregated over all four conditions (TR, BM, and DG), are the only cases with any marked degree of atrophy visible in the medial structures of the right temporal lobe. The other patient who showed this pattern (JL) was originally reported as showing disproportionate atrophy of the right temporal lobe (Hodges et al., 1992).

TABLE 6.4

Binary ratings of degree of temporal lobe atrophy on MRI scans from the seven patients whose scans were available for inspection. Separate ratings are given for the medial and lateral structures in right and left hemispheres

Patient	Hemisphere				Aggregated naming and matching scores	
	Left		Right			
	Lateral	Medial	Lateral	Medial	Living (/64)	Non-living (/64)
MS	+	+	+	–	19	28
PS	+	–	–	–	29	33
TR	+	–	+	+	29	51
BM	–	+	+	+	28	46
GC	+	+	–	–	27	41
JH	+	–	–	–	34	35
DG	+	–	+	+	17	29

+, moderate to severe atrophy; –, normal or mild atrophy

The photograph of JL's initial MRI scan strongly suggests involvement of the right medial temporal structures. By contrast, the two cases with the smallest aggregated artefacts advantage (JH and PS) are the only patients in whom no medial atrophy was seen in either hemisphere. Although the numbers are too small for significance testing, there is clearly a striking similarity between this pattern and that which is apparent in the case reported by Barbarotto et al. (1996).

Why should the medial temporal lobe be important to the production of a category-specific deficit? The precise anatomy and functional roles of medial temporal structures in humans are not fully understood, but the richness of cortical projections to this region suggests a possible role in cross-modal integration of sensory information relating to stored concept representations.

CONCLUSIONS

The studies and results we have discussed above showed that, as would be predicted by the SFT, the pattern of semantic memory impairment in a group of patients with the syndrome of SD was characterised by a trend towards category-specificity, with an advantage for artefacts over natural kinds. This trend was more apparent when the stimuli were matched for age-of-acquisition, and was attenuated in the naming test when items were matched for familiarity. A significant advantage for comprehension of artefacts over natural kinds persisted in both matching conditions, suggesting that neither factor was the sole explanation for the observed domain advantage. When scores from each of the eight cases were examined individually, the patterns of impairment were generally consistent, although in one case (GC) the reverse advantage (i.e. in favour of natural kinds) was seen on naming when the stimuli were matched for familiarity. When individual logistic regression analyses were performed, however, it became clear that semantic domain *per se* was not independently influencing these patterns of performance in all cases.

According to the SFT, the small but statistically significant advantage in favour of artefacts shown by this group of patients was secondary to selective impairment of the visual components of conceptual knowledge resulting from damage to temporal lobe structures (Silveri & Gainotti, 1988; Warrington & Shallice, 1984). Although the combination of inferolateral atrophy of one or both temporal lobes, and the apparently reduced production of sensory information in tests of concept definition, would both favour this explanation, our results do not support any aspect of this conclusion. In the first place, in comparison to some previously reported category-specific cases—particularly those resulting from HSVE (Sartori & Job, 1988; Sheridan & Humphreys, 1993; Silveri & Gainotti, 1988; Warrington &

Shallice, 1984)—the degree of dissociation shown by our SD cases was rather unimpressive. Second, not every case in our series showed a pattern that was in keeping with the predictions of the sensory–functional hypothesis; particularly striking was the advantage in favour of living things evinced by case GC—a pattern that was also seen in case IW, the SD patient reported by Lambon Ralph et al. (1998). Finally, athough a comparison of the cognitive factors contributing to the naming abilities of two contrasting cases, one with a category-selective pattern and the other without, showed an interaction between semantic domain and feature type in the former, this difference was not borne out in a more detailed analysis of attribute knowledge.

To account for these anomalies, we attempted to relate the presence of a category-specific pattern to the distribution of pathology within the temporal lobes. Semantic dementia is typically associated with damage to the inferolateral parts of the temporal lobes, and tends to spare the more medial structures (Hodges et al., 1998), whereas the damage in HSVE much more often involves both lateral and medial structures. This anatomical difference raises the possibility that the medial temporal lobe plays a crucial role in the production of category-specific effects. A previous examination of radiological appearances in a series of post-encephalitic patients, some of whom had category-specific impairments, did not support this hypothesis (Barbarotto et al., 1996), but it was later advanced as an explanation for one of the few published cases of category specificity in the context of SD (Barbarotto et al., 1995), in whom medial temporal structures were clearly involved, at any rate on the basis of visual inspection of the MRI brain scans. This case was also exceptional for the laterality of the atrophy which, unlike the majority of patients with SD, was more severe on the right side. These two observations provided a possible explanation for the inconsistency of category-specific patterns of performance among the patients in our cohort. Detailed morphometric analysis on the MRI scans of the present cohort of patients was not available but visual assessment of regions of interest identified significant atrophy of right medial temporal structures in the three cases with the largest artefacts advantage, and similar changes on the left in two others. It was also clear that the two cases who showed the smallest trend towards an advantage for artefacts (PS and JH) were exceptional in having no medial temporal involvement in either hemisphere.

There is other evidence compatible with the view that damage to medial temporal lobe structures may be crucial to the appearance of category specificity. Although there has been no systematic evaluation of the regional distribution of damage in any large group of HSVE patients, the importance of medial temporal structures can be supported by the study of large groups of patients with probable AD (Garrard et al., 1998; Gonnerman et al., 1997), all of whom have atrophy of medial temporal structures (Braak & Braak, 1991).

These studies argued for the existence of a subgroup of cases with a category-specific pattern. Garrard et al. (1998) also showed that such cases tended to be at a relatively advanced stage of disease progression, and therefore probably have additional pathology in other regions, suggesting that medial temporal lobe damage might be necessary, although not sufficient, for the emergence of category specificity.

In summary, therefore, our data have provided no support for the idea that a relatively selective loss of the visual or sensory aspects of conceptual knowledge underpins the emergence of an advantage for non-living over living kinds in patients with category-specific impairments. They have, however, provided limited support for a possible anatomical basis for category-specific patterns. Quantitative longitudinal imaging studies will be necessary to shed further light on the interaction of medial and inferolateral neocortical regions in diseases of the temporal lobe, and the use of these methods will form the basis for future studies of this fascinating yet elusive neuro-psychological phenomenon.

REFERENCES

Allport, D.A. (1985). Distributed memory, modular subsystems, and dysphasia. In S. Newman & R Epstein (Eds.), *Current perspectives in dysphasia*. Edinburgh: Churchill Livingstone.

Barbarotto, R., Capitani, E., & Laiacona, M. (1996). Naming deficits in herpes simplex encephalitis. *Acta Neurologica Scandinavica, 93*, 272–280.

Barbarotto, R., Capitani, E., Spinnler, H., & Trivelli, C. (1995). Slowly progressive semantic impairment with category specificity. *Neurocase, 1*, 107–119.

Basso, A., Capitani, E., & Laiacona, M. (1988). Progressive language impairment without dementia: a case with isolated category specific semantic defect. *Journal of Neurology, Neurosurgery and Psychiatry, 51*, 1201–1207.

Bird, H., Lambon Ralph, M.A., Patterson, K., & Hodges, J.R. (2000). The rise and fall of frequency and imageability: how the progression of semantic dementia impacts on noun and verb production in the Cookie Theft description. *Brain and Language, 73*, 17–49.

Bozeat, S., Lambon Ralph, M.A., Patterson, K., Garrard, P., & Hodges, J.R. (2000). Nonverbal semantic impairment in semantic dementia. *Neuropsychologia, 38*, 1207–1215.

Braak, H., & Braak, E. (1991). Neuropathological staging of Alzheimer-related changes. *Acta Neuropathologica, 82*, 239–259.

Breedin, S.D., Saffran, E.M., & Coslett, H.B. (1994). Reversal of the concreteness effect in a patient with semantic dementia. *Cognitive Neuropsychology, 11*, 617–660.

Caramazza, A. (1998). The interpretation of semantic category-specific deficits: What do they reveal about the organization of conceptual knowledge in the brain? *Neurocase, 4*, 265–272.

Caramazza, A., & Shelton, J.R. (1998). Domain-specific knowledge systems in the brain: The animate–inanimate distinction. *Journal of Cognitive Neuroscience, 10*, 1–34.

Cardebat, D., Demonet, J.-F., Celsis, P., & Puel, M. (1996). Living/non-living dissociation in a case of semantic dementia: A SPECT activation study. *Neuropsychologia, 34*, 1175–1179.

Damasio, A.R. (1990). Category-related recognition defects as a clue to the neural substrates of knowledge. *Trends in Neurosciences, 13*, 95–98.

De Renzi, E., & Lucchelli, F. (1994). Are semantic systems separately represented in the brain? The case of living category impairment. *Cortex, 30,* 3–25.

Farah, M., Hammond, K., Mehta, Z., & Ratcliffe, G. (1989). Category-specificity and modality-specificity in semantic memory. *Neuropsychologia, 27,* 193–200.

Farah, M.J., & McClelland, J.L. (1991) A computational model of semantic memory impairment: modality specificity and emergent category specificity. *Journal of Experimental Psychology: General, 120,* 339–357.

Funnell, E., & De Mornay Davies, P. (1996). JBR: A reassessment of concept familiarity and a category-specific disorder for living things. *Neurocase, 2,* 461–474,.

Funnell, E., & Sheridan, J. (1992). Categories of knowledge? Unfamiliar aspects of living and non-living things. *Cognitive Neuropsychology, 9,* 135–153.

Gainotti, G. (1990). The categorical organisation of semantic and lexical knowledge in the brain. *Behavioural Neurology, 3,* 109–115.

Garrard, P., & Hodges, J.R. (2000). Semantic dementia: Clinical, radiological and pathological perspectives. *Journal of Neurology, 247,* 409–422.

Garrard, P., Lambon Ralph, M.A., Hodges, J.R., & Patterson, K. (2001). Prototypicality, distinctiveness and intercorrelation: analyses of the semantic attributes of living and non-living concepts. *Cognitive Neuropsychology, 18,* 125–174.

Garrard, P., Patterson, K., Watson, P.C., & Hodges, J.R. (1998). Category specific semantic loss in dementia of Alzheimer's type: Functional–anatomical correlations from cross-sectional analyses. *Brain, 121,* 633–646.

Gonnerman, L.M., Andersen, E.S., Devlin, J.T., Kempler, D., & Seidenberg, M.S. (1997). Double dissociation of semantic categories in Alzheimer's disease. *Brain and Language, 57,* 254–279.

Goodale, M.A., Milner, A.D., Jakobson, L.S., & Carey, D.P. (1991). A neurological dissociation between perceiving objects and grasping them. *Nature, 349,* 154–156.

Hart, J., Berndt, R., & Caramazza, A. (1985). Category specific naming deficit following cerebral infarction. *Nature, 316,* 439–440.

Hart, J., & Gordon, B. (1992). Neural subsystems for object knowledge. *Nature, 359,* 60–64.

Hillis, A., & Caramazza, A. (1991), Category specific naming and comprehension impairment: A double dissociation. *Brain, 114,* 2081–2094.

Hodges, J.R., Garrard, P., & Patterson, K. (1998) Semantic dementia and Pick complex. In A. Kertesz, & D. Munoz (Eds.), *Pick's disease and Pick complex.* New York: Wiley Liss.

Hodges, J.R., Patterson, K., Oxbury, S., & Funnell, E. (1992) Semantic dementia: Progressive fluent aphasia with temporal lobe atrophy. *Brain, 115,* 1783–1806.

Howard, D., & Patterson, K. (1992). *Pyramids and Palm Trees: A Test of Semantic Access From Pictures and Words.* Bury St. Edmunds, UK: Thames Valley Publishing Company.

Kertesz, A. (1996), Pick complex and Pick's disease: The nosology of frontal lobe dementia, primary progressive aphasia, and corticobasal ganglionic degeneration. *European Journal of Neurology, 3,* 280–282.

Laiacona, M., Barbarotto, R., & Capitani, E. (1993). Perceptual and associative knowledge in category specific impairment of semantic memory: A study of two cases. *Cortex, 29,* 727–740.

Lambon Ralph, M.A., Graham, K.S., Patterson, K., & Hodges, J.R. (1999). Is a picture worth a thousand words? Evidence from concept definitions by patients with semantic dementia. *Brain and Language, 70,* 309–335.

Lambon Ralph, M.A., Howard, D., Nightingale, G., & Ellis, A.W. (1998). Are living and non-living category-specific deficits causally linked to impaired perceptual or associative knowledge? Evidence from a category-specific double dissociation. *Neurocase, 4,* 311–338.

McCarthy, R., & Warrington, E.K. (1988). Evidence for modality specific meaning systems in the brain. *Nature, 334,* 428–430.

Martin, A., Wiggs, C.L, Ungerleider, L.G., & Haxby, J.V. (1996). Neural correlates of category-specific knowledge. *Nature, 379*, 649–652.

Mishkin, M., Ungerleider, L.G., & Macko, K.A. (1983). Object vision and spatial vision: Two cortical pathways. *Trends in Neurosciences, 6*, 414–417.

Mummery, C.J., Patterson, K,, Hodges, J.R., & Wise, R.J.S. (1996). Generating "tiger" as an animal name or a word beginning with T: Differences in brain activation. *Proceedings of the Royal Society, 26*, 989–995.

Mummery, C.J., Patterson, K., Price, C.J., Frackowiak, R.S.J., & Hodges, J.R. (2000). A voxel based morphometry study of semantic dementia: Relationship between temporal lobe atrophy and semantic memory. *Annals of Neurology, 47*, 36–45.

Parkin, A.J. (1993). Progressive aphasia without dementia—a clinical and cognitive neuropsychological analysis. *Brain and Language, 44*, 201–220.

Pietrini, V., Nertempi, P., Vaglia, A., Revello, M., Pinna, V., & Ferro-Milone, F. (1988). Recovery from herpes simplex encephalitis: Selective impairment of specific semantic categories with neuroradiological correlation. *Journal of Neurology, Neurosurgery and Psychiatry, 51*, 1284–1293.

Poeck, K., & Luzzatti, C. (1988), Slowly progressive aphasia in three patients: The problem of accompanying neuropsychological deficit. *Brain, 111*, 151–168.

Sacchett, C., & Humphreys, G.W. (1992). Calling a squirrel a squirrel but a canoe a wigwam: A category specific deficit for artifactual objects and body parts. *Cognitive Neuropsychology, 9*, 73–86.

Samson, D., Pillon, A., & De Wilde, V. (1998). Impaired knowledge of visual and nonvisual attributes in a patient with a semantic impairment for living entities: A case of a true category-specific deficit. *Neurocase, 4*, 273–290.

Sartori, G., & Job, R. (1988). The oyster with four legs: A neuropsychological study on the interaction between vision and semantic information. *Cognitive Neuropsychology, 5*, 105–132.

Sartori, G., Job, R., Miozzo, M., Zago, S., & Marchiori, G. (1993). Category specific form–knowledge deficit in a patient with herpes simplex virus encephalitis. *Journal of Clinical and Experimental Neuropsychology, 15*, 280–299.

Shallice, T. (1988). *From neuropsychology to mental structure*. Cambridge: Cambridge University Press.

Sheridan, J., & Humphreys, G. (1993). A verbal semantic category specific recognition impairment. *Cognitive Neuropsychology, 10*, 143–184.

Silveri, M.C., Danilel, A., Giustolisi, L., & Gainotti, G. (1991). Dissociation between knowledge of living and non-living things in dementia of the Alzheimer type. *Neurology, 41*, 545–546.

Silveri, M., & Gainotti, G. (1988). Interaction between vision and language in category specific semantic impairment. *Cognitive Neuropsychology, 5*, 677–709.

Snowden, J.S., Goulding, P.J., & Neary, D. (1989). Semantic dementia: A form of circumscribed cerebral atrophy. *Behavioural Neurology, 2*, 167–182.

Snowden, J.S., Neary, D., & Mann, D.M.A. (1996) *Fronto-temporal lobar degeneration: Fronto-temporal dementia, progressive aphasia, semantic dementia*. Edinburgh: Churchill Livingstone.

Stewart, F., Parkin, A.J., & Hunkin, N.M. (1992). Naming impairments following recovery from herpes simplex encephalitis: Category-specific? *Quarterly Journal of Experimental Psychology, 44a*, 261–284.

Thompson-Schill, S.L., Aguirre, G.K., D'Esposito, M., & Farah, M.J. (1999). A neural basis for category and modality specificity of semantic knowledge. *Neuropsychologia, 37*, 671–676.

Tyrrell, P.H., Warrington, E.K., Frackowiak, R.S.J., & Rossor, M.N. (1990). Heterogeneity in progressive aphasia due to cortical atrophy: A clinical and PET study. *Brain, 113*, 1321–1336.

Van Hoesen, G.W., Pandya, D.N., & Butters, N. (1972). Cortical afferents to the entorrhinal cortex of the rhesus monkey. *Science, 175*, 1471–1473.

Warrington, E.K., & McCarthy, R.A. (1987). Categories of knowledge: Further fractionations and an attempted integration. *Brain, 110*, 1273–1296.

Warrington, E.K., & Shallice, T. (1984), Category specific semantic impairments. *Brain, 107*, 829–853.

APPENDIX: LIST OF STIMULI USED IN THE STUDY, WITH ASSOCIATED VALUES OF CONCEPT FAMILIARITY AND AGE OF ACQUISITION (A-o-a)

Natural kinds	Familiarity	A-o-a	Artefacts	Familiarity	A-o-a
Age-of-acquisition matched set					
Turtle	2.40	3.40	Spanner	2.72	4.75
Elephant	2.35	2.05	Hammer	3.48	2.45
Camel	2.08	2.75	Saw	2.92	2.55
Monkey	2.58	2.40	Screwdriver	3.42	3.45
Alligator	1.65	2.95	Axe	2.28	2.95
Kangaroo	1.92	3.05	Scissors	3.98	2.65
Rhinoceros	1.52	3.30	Paintbrush	2.78	2.50
Tiger	2.10	2.10	Pliers	3.38	4.35
Chicken	2.42	2.80	Candle	3.08	2.80
Peacock	2.05	3.60	Toothbrush	4.62	2.15
Eagle	2.42	3.20	Envelope	4.12	3.45
Duck	2.75	1.95	Glass	4.78	2.35
Ostrich	1.52	3.80	Plug	4.18	2.70
Penguin	1.70	3.05	Brush	3.80	2.30
Swan	1.97	2.50	Key	4.85	2.35
Owl	2.22	2.45	Comb	4.52	2.10
Mean	2.10	2.83	Mean	3.68	2.87
95% CI	1.90–2.30	2.54–3.13	95% CI	3.26–4.11	2.46–3.08
Familiarity-matched set					
Mouse	2.45	2.05	Helicopter	2.55	3.00
Squirrel	3.82	2.65	Bicycle	3.78	2.40
Dog	4.60	1.50	Aeroplane	3.78	2.30
Horse	3.55	1.85	Train	4.15	4.90
Rabbit	2.95	1.85	Bus	4.50	2.20
Frog	2.48	2.48	Sledge	2.80	3.10
Cat	4.22	1.50	Lorry	4.02	2.65
Cow	2.42	1.95	Motorbike	3.25	3.00
Apple	3.98	1.70	Piano	3.42	2.15
Pear	3.55	2.05	Suitcase	3.65	3.65
Banana	3.65	1.80	Watering can*	2.72	–
Tomato	3.78	2.25	Barrel	2.02	3.80
Orange	3.34	1.85	Toaster	4.08	3.45
Strawberry	3.32	2.55	Basket	2.18	2.65
Cherry	3.38	2.80	Stool	3.08	2.35
Pineapple	2.95	3.05	Dustbin*	4.08	–
Mean	3.40	2.10	Mean	3.38	2.97
95% CI	3.07–3.74	1.90–2.34	95% CI	2.94–3.81	2.53–3.42

* There were no age-of-acquisition norms associated with these items.

CHAPTER SEVEN

Category-specific recognition impairments in Alzheimer's disease

Christine Whatmough and Howard Chertkow
Bloomfield Center for Research in Aging, Lady Davis Institute for Medical Research, McGill University, Montreal, Canada

INTRODUCTION

Category-specific deficits were first reported in individual subjects who had suffered herpes simplex encephalitis (Sartori & Job, 1988; Silveri & Gainotti, 1988; Warrington & Shallice, 1984) and motor vehicle trauma (Riddoch & Humphreys, 1987). Since then similar deficits have been reported in single-case and group studies of subjects with Alzheimer's disease (AD). In this chapter, we examine these reports and consider how this phenomenon relates to the disease and what it can tell us about brain organisation of semantic memory. The neuropathology of AD involves the progressive formation of neurofibrillary tangles and neuritic plaques concentrated in the cortical regions involved in the highest order of cognitive function, the associative cortex (lateral temporal, parietal, and frontal lobes), as well as in the limbic system (in particular the hippocampus). Focal brain lesions have the potential of informing us about the functional organisation of cognition by demonstrating that certain brain processes can be dissociated from each other. In contrast, the gradual, progressive, and more diffuse loss seen in AD provides critical clues to the organisation of semantic memory through studies of the dedifferentiation of knowledge systems.

This chapter is organised into four sections. The first section presents the basic phenomenology of semantic loss and naming deficits in AD and relates in detail the findings of researchers during the last 15 years regarding category-specific loss in this disease. In the second section we examine the factors that have influenced the occurrence of these findings and present our own most recent research, which has sought to address ambiguities and difficulties in the literature. The third section briefly investigates two other inbalances that have been reported with regard to concept knowledge. The fourth section considers explanations which have been put forward regarding category-specific loss in AD, concluding with a discussion of what AD can tell us about brain function.

SEMANTIC MEMORY LOSS IN ALZHEIMER'S DISEASE

The primary memory deficit of subjects with AD is episodic memory loss. That is, AD subjects (hence ADs) fail to retain memories of the who, what, and where of daily events. For many subjects, however, from the onset of episodic memory loss, a progressive loss of semantic memory sets in. Semantic memory is that body of knowledge that concerns object recognition, concept comprehension, and eventless factual knowledge (e.g. that cats purr). The loss of semantic memory in ADs can be demonstrated by their poor performance on basic tests such as picture naming, object recognition from an array of semantic foils, and simple questioning about objects (Henderson, 1996; Hodges & Patterson, 1995; Hodges, Salmon, & Butters, 1992; Martin, 1992a; Martin, Brouwers, & Cox, 1985). Early on, the explanation for the anomia seen in ADs was that they had a peripheral problem (Bayles & Tomoeda, 1990; Nebes, 1989; Nebes, Martin, & Horn, 1984; Ober et al., 1986). Poor performance on semantic tests, however, can also be demonstrated in ADs who perform normally on tests that require good perceptual resources, such as word-to-picture matching with physically confusable distractors, judgement of line orientation, and lexical decision tests (Chertkow, Bub, & Caplan, 1992; Crowe, Dingjan, & Helme, 1997; Hodges et al., 1999; Huff, Corkin, & Growdon, 1986; Smith, Murdoch, & Chenery, 1989).

The centrality of a semantic deficit in picture naming in ADs stands in contrast to the phenomenon of anomia in brain-damaged individuals with aphasia, whose deficits are largely postsemantic, at the level of phonological access. This contrast is demonstrable in a number of ways. First, phonemic cueing is only minimally helpful to subjects with AD, suggesting that their problems are more profound than difficulty accessing an otherwise intact representation (Daum, Riesch, Sartori, & Birbaumer, 1996; Mauri, Daum, Sartori, & Riesch, 1994). Second, there is a good correspondence between the items that individual subjects name and cannot name, and performance on those same items using other semantic tasks which require a pointing or "yes–no" response (Chertkow & Bub, 1990a,b; Hodges et al., 1992). Third, some have found that to a large measure subjects fail or succeed on the same items in test–retest (Chertkow & Bub, 1990a,b). Finally, semantic cueing (e.g.

picture of a "lion"—cue: "It is like a tiger") is generally ineffective in naming tasks in AD except in the retrieval of the names of objects for which the patient can demonstrate some knowledge through probe questioning (Chertkow & Bub, 1990a,b).

Naming models usually propose that the sensorial input of an object must activate its semantic representation in order for the phonological form of the object to be accessed (Gordon, 1997). As indicated above, this model of "semantics" preceding "phonology" holds true in AD. However, Chertkow and Bub (1990b) have suggested that certain qualifications can be added to this. They suggest that it is only a subset of knowledge about an object that is necessary for naming its pictorial presentation. The ability to name an object does not alone guarantee that all or even most of the semantic knowledge normally associated with an object is retained. Chertkow and Bub extensively probed the intactness of semantic knowledge about animals in ten AD subjects, by means of questions requiring yes–no answers. They found that if an AD subject could name the picture of an animal (e.g. zebra), upon word presentation of the animal, the subject could also correctly answer questions that uniquely identified the animal (e.g. "Is a zebra striped?") and that if the subject could not answer identification questions then he or she could not name a picture of the animal. However, even for animals that subjects were able to name, there were many basic questions concerning the animal and specific to that which subjects answered incorrectly (e.g. "Do zebras live in Africa?", "Do they eat meat?"). How could such dissociations in intact and lost semantic memory best be conceptualised? Chertkow and Bub (1990b) used the conceptual framework preposed by Miller and Johnson-Laird (1976), who focused on the need for both perceptual and functional features to be present in order to generate mental routines for successful object identification. "Identification semantics" would refer to the knowledge (both perceptual and functional) that went into the identification of each concrete item (with picture naming acting as the marker for successful identification). "Associative semantics" would refer to all additional concept knowledge not immediately necessary for such identification. That this associative knowledge is the first to become lost in AD is suggested by the fact that subjects who could not answer identification questions usually failed to correctly answer associative questions as well. Associative semantics appears to be stored amodally so that if subjects could not retrieve knowledge from a printed form of the name, then they were no better when the object was presented in picture form. Access to "identification knowledge", however, did appear to be enhanced by a pictorial presentation of the animals.

The preservation of identification knowledge in the presence of lost associative knowledge in AD suggests that there is a certain hierarchy in the strength of different types of semantic information to resist the effects of the disease. This is further supported by the fact that even subjects who are unable to name objects can still identify the object from among an array of pictures from completely different categories (Chertkow et al., 1992; Daum et al., 1996; Hodges et al., 1992). For instance, a patient who cannot distinguish a zebra from a horse can still distinguish it from a table or a car. Bayles, Tomoeda, and Trosset (1991) have also demonstrated this point, although they contend that this shows that concept knowledge is not lost but only that certain tasks are more difficult (require more attention).

Some researchers (Cronin-Golomb et al., 1992; Knotek, Bayles, & Kaszniak, 1990; Montanes, Goldblum, & Boller, 1996; Nebes & Brady, 1988; Nebes & Halligan, 1995) have argued that experimental evidence in fact supports a basic preservation of the organisation of semantics in AD. For instance, Montanes et al. (1996) found that in a task requiring various levels of classification (superordinate: living–non-living; subordinate: birds–insects; attribute: domestic–foreign) there was a normal hierarchy in the order of difficulty. This order of difficulty was the same for ADs as for normal control subjects, with the effect of order being much greater in the ADs. Similarly, Cronin-Golomb et al. (1992) found that in tasks in which subjects judged the prototypicality of an object within a category, ADs responded similarly to normal elderly subjects. Although we would question this insistence on stressing the "normal organisation" of semantics in the face of inarguably large semantic impairments, it is true that factors such as familiarity, prototypicality, word frequency, and associative strength, which strongly affect the performance of normal subjects on semantic tasks, also influence the performance of AD subjects on similar tasks. In a meta-analysis of studies in which correct reaction times (RTs) of ADs were compared with those of elderly normal controls, Nebes and colleagues (Nebes & Brady, 1992; Nebes, Brady, & Reynolds, 1992) found that there is a general cognitive slowing in AD, with a linear increase in the difference between ADs and elderly normal controls as difficulty increases. Some researchers, however, have gone beyond the claim of a normal organisation of semantic memory in AD and claimed that semantic memory is in fact intact and that what we are witnessing in AD is a progressive loss of access to this knowledge. These claims are based on the evidence of implicit memory tests where ADs can show normal effects (Nebes, 1989; Nebes, Brady, & Huff, 1989). For instance, Nebes and Halligan (1996) found that ADs showed normal semantic priming effects to words presented aurally in sentences. We, along with others (Chertkow et al., 1994; Martin, 1992a,b), however, have found that some ADs display abnormally large semantic priming effects (hyperpriming), which argues that "preserved" priming cannot be taken as proof that a semantic system remains intact. The bulk of the evidence, we would contend, supports the position that ADs experience a deterioration of their semantic memory.

CATEGORY-SPECIFIC DEFICITS IN
ALZHEIMER'S DISEASE

It is in the context of investigating patterns of semantic loss that category-specific impairments in AD were first reported. Chertkow and Bub (1990a) investigated the semantic knowledge of a group of ten AD subjects on items from a variety of taxonomic categories by means of probe questions requiring yes–no answers. Although the overall accuracy rate was 87.3%, they noted that the subjects were considerably worse for the categories of animals, fruits and vegetables (mean accuracy = 68.2%) than for non-biological categories such as vehicles, furniture, or clothing. Since then, several researchers have specifically tested whether the semantic loss in AD is homogeneous across semantic categories, and the deficit most frequently reported involves poorer semantic knowledge about biological objects than about non-biological objects. More recently, interest has also turned to investigating whether there are imbalances in loss of knowledge with regards object words versus action words, and abstract versus concrete knowledge. We will first consider in detail the biological–non-biological data and briefly consider the other contrasts as they are relevant for the discussion.

One of the first group of researchers to specifically compare ADs' semantic knowledge for biological objects with that for non-biological objects was Silveri, Daniele, Giustolisi, and Gainotti (1991). They tested fifteen ADs, of whom six were classified as having mild semantic–lexical disorders and nine as having moderate disorders. The experimental tasks consisted of a confrontation naming test and an association test in which subjects indicated whether an auditorally presented word was related to a pictured object. The stimuli used were twenty coloured pictures from the living category (flowers, fruits, and animals) and twenty from the non-living category (toys, furniture, clothing, vehicles, and kitchen items). The items were matched for prototypicality and word frequency. Both subgroups of ADs were more impaired on the living items than on the non-living on both tasks, whereas the control subjects were at ceiling for both subsets of items on both tasks. The difference in naming scores for living and non-living objects was 22.5% for the mild ADs and 27% for the moderate ADs.

Tippett, Grossman, and Farah (1996) questioned whether the category effect that Silveri et al. (1991) had found was not a result of poor matching of stimuli on pertinent variables. To confirm this, they first tested a group of fourteen ADs on the list of items used by Silveri et al. (1991) and found, as they had, a category effect. They then tested the subjects on a second and third set of line drawings taken from Snodgrass and Vanderwart (1980). The second set was composed of living (animals, fruits, vegetables and body parts) and non-living objects matched pairwise for familiarity and word frequency, and in the third set ten animals were matched with ten non-living objects for familiarity, word frequency, and visual complexity. Here, their test group of ADs did not demonstrate any category-specific deficit. In fact, the more impaired subjects ($n = 5$) tended to be better in naming living items. Although this difference in results between sets could be attributable to better matching of stimuli, the ADs were also significantly more accurate on the second and third sets (mean accuracy = 71%) than the first set (mean accuracy = 64%), indicating that the stimuli in sets two and three were probably more familiar than those in set one where an effect of category was found.

Hodges et al. (1992) reported the performance of 22 ADs on tasks of fluency (e.g. name as many animals as possible in 60 seconds), picture naming, picture sorting according to three hierarchical levels, word–picture matching, and verbal definitions. They found no category effect when analysing the group results or, in the case of the picture naming task, in looking for differences in individual cases. Pictures from the living category were chosen from the subcategories of land animals, sea creatures, and birds and the stimuli from the man-made categories were household items, vehicles, and musical instruments.

Daum et al. (1996) found that in testing eight ADs there was a category effect in picture naming when items from the categories of animate (animals and vegetables) and inanimate (furniture, toys, or kitchen utensils) were matched for familiarity, visual complexity, and verbal frequency. This category effect remained even after a slight overall improvement with phonemic cueing (5–6%). The subjects were also more often correct in answering probe questions about objects from the inanimate than from the animate class, although Daum et al. failed to find a significant difference in the ADs' capacity to define subsets of these items. On semantic probe questions, the ADs were more accurate in answering yes–no questions about functional–associative features of the objects than they were about visual structural questions for both living and non-living items. The difference in scores between the two types of questions showed a tendency to be greater for the animate objects. In an object decision task subjects were presented with line drawings of real and unreal animals and real and unreal inanimate objects and asked to indicate which were real. The unreal drawings were constructed by substituting distinctive parts from one object with that of another such as an elephant's head on a horse's body. Although the ADs had higher scores on the inanimate objects than on the animate, they tended ($p = .11$) to accept more false animals as real than inanimate objects. The modest size of the group tested ($n = 8$) may explain the failure of the analysis to reach significance. In a forced choice preference task in which subjects were asked to indicate which of two objects they preferred, one real and one not, their performance improved considerably with subjects preferring the real animal more often than the unreal, even though in previous testing they had not been able to recognise it as a real animal.

Daum et al. (1996) found that there was only a slight improvement on the picture naming task when phonemic cues were provided and that cueing did not remove the category effect. This argues against a major phonological retrieval problem being the source of the category effects. However, the subjects' poor performance on definitions was at least in part due to aphasic problems, because they were frequently able to gesture the use of objects they could define only by a superordinate, and they could in some cases provide appropriate animal sounds for animals they could not otherwise define. This would indicate that they did have in part an output problem. However, here again, when the effects of the retrieval problems were taken into account, the category effect still remained.

Mauri et al. (1994) presented a case study of an AD patient, Helga. They compared her performance on eight semantic knowledge tests with that of a patient (Michelangelo) who had manifested a category-specific loss since suffering from herpes simplex encephalitis (HSE). Tasks administered took a variety of forms: visual to visual (i.e. pictorial presentation with pictorial response selection), visual to verbal, verbal to verbal, and verbal to visual. This varying of presentation and response mode allowed Mauri et al. to assess whether apparent category effects were a function of more peripheral mechanisms of input or output. Helga demonstrated a deficit in the knowledge of biological items (animals and vegetables) but also responded more poorly than normals to inanimate objects. On most tests her accuracy profile was similar to Michelangelo's. Helga demonstrated a dissociation in her ability to draw animate and inanimate objects: she could draw simple objects, such as a boat or a fork, but was unable to draw a spider. Helga also demonstrated spared non-visual knowledge about the animate objects, in that she was able to answer questions about whether an animal was alien, edible, tame or ferocious. A notable aspect about Helga as a case study was the fact that she had been a cook and yet she was poor at naming a set of pictures that included vegetables.

Laiacona, Barbarotto, and Capitani (1998) tested twenty-six ADs (eleven men and fifteen women) on a task of picture naming and conducted an item analysis in which category (living versus non-living), frequency, familiarity, prototypicality, name and image agreement, and visual complexity were entered into a linear regression model. They did not find accuracy for the living category to be significantly different from accuracy for the non-living category. They also found semantic and visuosemantic errors to be the most prevalent type of errors for both categories. They proceeded to take a multiple single case approach to the data. Using this method of analysis they found a category deficit to be present in eleven out of the twenty-six subjects, eight of whom showed the typical dissociation (better non-living than living) and three of whom displayed an atypical dissociation (opposite direction). Of particular interest was the fact that the majority of those demonstrating the typical dissociation (seven out of eight) were men and all three subjects showing the atypical dissociation were women. Further investigation by Laiacona et al. (1998) led them to conclude that the gender effect could best be described as a loss of knowledge for living objects in the presence of preserved knowledge of non-living objects in men. There was no indication that the non-living objects (tools, furniture, and vehicles) were particularly more related to males. The mean education level of the subjects in this study was 6 years, which is lower than in many other studies, but this factor does not appear to have interacted with the category effect.

Montanes, Goldblum, and Boller (1995, 1996) reported two studies in which they assessed category-specific deficits in AD subjects. In the 1995 study they found that subjects were worse at naming black and white pictures from the living category than the non-living category and that this was true for pictures of both low and high complexity. They then tested the subjects on colour pictures and found that there was no category effect but that, in fact, subjects were better at naming low-frequency vegetables than low-frequency vehicles and animals. This first study also showed that when pictures of both categories were rated to be of equal familiarity, both ADs and normal subjects obtained lower scores on pictures of high visual complexity, irrespective of the category (living or non-) than on pictures rated to be of low visual complexity.

Montanes et al. (1995) also found, however, that the test group was heterogeneous and that a subgroup of four subjects (out of twenty-five) was disproportionately worse on verbal tasks than on visuo-constructional tasks, and another subgroup of equal number was found with the opposite profile. The effects of category, frequency, and visual complexity were more likely to be brought out in the verbal deficit group. The 1996 Montanes study emphasised the qualitative similarity in performance between ADs and normal controls. They show that thirty-nine ADs were better in classifying living things than non-living things, as were normal control subjects. There was no advantage of pictures over words in classifying at either a subordinate level: sorting into classes of animals, birds, tools, vehicles, etc. or an attribute level: tame versus wild, fast versus slow moving.

Cronin-Golomb et al. (1992) tested eighteen ADs and eighteen elderly normal controls in tasks designed to evaluate whether their mental organisation of concepts was abnormal compared to controls. The same experiments also compared performance on sets of stimuli that were animate (animals, birds, insects) with those that were inanimate (furniture, musical instruments, and vehicles). Tasks included: fluency (e.g. name as many vegetables as possible), category ranking (e.g. which of the following is the most typical vegetable: carrot, onion, turnip?), and a category dominance task in which the RT of the subjects was measured (Is a carrot a vegetable? Is a turnip a vegetable?). They found that the ADs were less fluent and slower than the elderly normal controls but that they demonstrated the same overall pattern of sensitivity to category dominance. The only animate–inanimate deficit that they found that was specific to the ADs and not the elderly normal controls was their ability to correctly rank all three members of the animate triads according to typicality. They concluded that ADs demonstrate normal semantic organisation with a general retrieval deficit.

Gonnerman et al. (1997) were interested in characterising the semantic loss of AD and its relationship to categories of objects as the disease progresses. They examined this question both cross-sectionally and longitudinally. Their particular interest was to look at the size and direction of category specificity in relation to naming scores for biological objects. For theoretical reasons we will present later, they hypothesised that semantic knowledge for artefacts would decline at a steady rate whereas knowledge for biological objects would initially be maintained until, at some critical point, a massive loss of semantic knowledge for items from the biological category would occur. There would thus be a crossover in accuracy from initially poorer artefact naming, to subsequent poorer biological naming. The cross-sectional study of these researchers examined two groups of AD subjects with fifteen subjects each, using in each case different sets of stimuli. In Experiment 1, three of the five best responders were slightly better naming biological stimuli (fruits and vegetables) than artefacts (furniture, vehicles, clothing, and weapons). Of the remaining ten subjects, six were better in naming the artefacts. The results for Experiment 2 present individual results in a graph that orders the subjects according to their naming scores for biological items. Presented in this way, it is shown that of the five subjects with the highest scores in naming biological items, three were better in naming biological items than artefacts and that the remaining ten subjects were better on non-biologcal items. However, if the subjects' results are instead considered in order of overall (i.e. mean of biological and non-biological) scores, the pattern is less clear. It can be seen that the subjects with mild naming deficits can be better for either or neither category of items and the subjects with poorer scores show a definite biological deficit. The longitudinal studies consisted of testing two subjects at 6-month intervals, one over a 4-year period and the second over a 2-year period. These tests fail, however, to show the critical crossover point. Rather, one subject shows a consistent and large advantage of artefacts over biological items and the other drops off dramatically in artefact naming, only to present a similar dramatic decline in biological naming 6 months later.

Garrard, Patterson, Watson, and Hodges (1998) closely examined the hypotheses of Gonnerman et al. (1997), according to which there is an early advantage for biological items. They used an items analysis so that they could include familiarity as a covariate, and analysed category as a between-groups factor. Analysed in this fashion, they did not find a category-specific impairment in ADs based on an aggregate score of tests of naming. However, in a multiple single-case analysis, they found that there was a category effect in the same direction in both a high scoring group and a low scoring group with no interaction: that is, the category effect was not greater for one group or the other. They similarly found that there was no interaction if the subjects were median split by their Mini-Mental State Examination (MMSE) score (mean of 19.9 range of 2 to 30). In analyses carried out using a "semantic index", which included picture naming, word–picture matching, and naming to description, they did find a category effect that was larger in low MMSE group. In summary, in all of their group analyses, Garrard et al. (1998) found that category effects when present were in the same direction (i.e. better biological than artefacts). The few individual subjects who did show better performance on biological items than on artefacts were among the most severely impaired, which would not be expected according to the Gonnerman et al. hypothesis.

Summary of category-specific deficits in Alzheimer's disease

The general finding of several studies is that groups of ADs do on average perform worse on biological objects than on non-biological objects (Daum et al., 1996; Garrard et al., 1998; Laiacona et al., 1998; Mauri et al., 1994; Silveri et al., 1991) when tested with tasks requiring object identification or utilising verbal probes of semantic knowledge. This deficit is better described as a category effect rather than a category-specific loss: that is, ADs are worse than normal elderly subjects on all categories of objects and when items are well matched for other relevant factors (familiarity in particular), differences in scores between categories are usually less than 25%. The degree of category specificity seen in subjects with focal lesions is rarely encountered, although such dissociations do occasionally occur (Mauri et al., 1994). Furthermore, within a large group of ADs (more than twenty) individuals can be identified who perform significantly worse on artefacts than on biological objets (Garrard et al., 1998; Laiacona et al., 1998). Some studies failed to find category effects (Gonnerman et al., 1997; Montanes et al., 1995; Tippett et al., 1996) particularly in certain semantic tasks such as category membership (Cronin-Golomb et al., 1992; Hodges et al., 1992; Montanes et al., 1996), and some researchers have only found a category effect within restricted groups, such as men (Laiacona et al., 1998), subjects with mainly verbal deficits (Montanes et al., 1995, 1996) or when analysis was carried out using a single-case approach (Laiacona et al., 1998). This detailed review thus underlines the variability in study results. At first sight, this variability appears rather baffling and discouraging. In the next section we will address some of the main elements that explain it.

FACTORS EXPLAINING VARIABLE RESULTS

Stimulus variables

Frequency.   As has already been discussed, some researchers have questioned the findings of category-specific deficits in AD on the basis that pertinent variables (such as colour or familiarity) of the stimuli were not adequately controlled for. Even if researchers have been able to respond to most of these objections, the dispute highlights the fact that the category of an object is not the only or even the principal determinant of semantic loss in AD. Rather, the factor that appears overwhelmingly to influence loss of knowledge is something related to the frequency with which an object is encountered, in that rarer objects are invariably "lost" before more commonly encountered objects. In experimental situations researchers have tried to take this factor into account by equating stimuli on available measures, such as printed word frequency, subjective familiarity ratings, prototypicality, and age of acquisition. Although these measures are highly correlated, each of these measures has its own merits and weaknesses depending on the experiment being carried out. For instance, prototypicality is an important factor to control for in an object classification task but it is problematic to equate stimuli on this basis in naming tasks because common objects can have two values of prototypicality. An example of an object with two values is the knife that has a high typicality value as a weapon and a low value as a tool. Furthermore, whole classes of objects might be more familiar than others, so that prototypicality has little meaning. For example, "apple" and "gun" are both equally typical for their categories (fruit and weapon) and yet "apple" is rated as much more familiar than "gun" (Snodgrass & Vanderwort, 1980). Word frequency would need to be taken into account as a factor in tasks using printed words because it can influence the ease with which a word can be read, although Snodgrass and Yuditsky (1996) found that it did not correlate with picture naming accuracy on the Snodgrass and Vanderwart set of pictures, and that it correlated only minimally with RT.

In picture naming tasks, familiarity ratings correlate highly with ADs' naming accuracy and, to affirm the presence of category effects, it is necessary to be sure that sets of stimuli are matched on this variable. In more recent years it has been found that an even better predictor of naming performance in normal subjects is the age of acquisition, with subjective ratings of age of acquisition concurring well with the order in which objects are "acquired" (Snodgrass & Yuditsky, 1996). Age of acquisition, however, is undoubtedly a multidimensional factor and hence more difficult to work with theoretically than familiarity. This is because we do not know why certain items surrounding a child might be acquired before others. It may be that children acquire knowledge about objects and concepts in the order in which they are repeatedly exposed to them. If this were the case then we could say that order of encounter inversely determines the order of loss in dementia. However, there is also the distinct possibility that the mind of the child is disposed to acquiring concepts by factors other than order and rate of encounter. Factors such as basic simplicity, personal relevance, and animacy need to be investigated. By factoring out "mind disposing" factors included in age of acquisition, we may be removing factors which interest us most, which are those which make an object more or less resilient to the effects of AD above and beyond the frequency with which an object is encountered.

Visual complexity and structural similarity. In tasks that involve pictures, visual complexity is another factor for which an attempt is frequently made to equate across categories. Here again, we wonder if removing the effects of "visual complexity" in an overly zealous manner is counterproductive, as it is difficult to know what is at the basis of visual complexity ratings. In Figure 7.1 we reproduce six drawings of birds taken from a larger battery of 328 pictures that 40 elderly normal subjects were asked to name and then rate according to visual complexity and familiarity. Below each picture are the visual complexity and familiarity ratings for each bird. In the complete battery, these measures are highly correlated (r = −.59), as they are (r = −.47) in the Snodgrass and Vanderwart (1980) study. As can be seen, other than the

Chicken 1.9 (4.9)   Owl 2.1 (4.6)   Rooster 2.3 (4.5)

Flamingo 2.7 (3.6)   Eagle 2.9 (3.8)   Peacock 3 (4.1)

Figure 7.1. Mean visual complexity (and familiarity) ratings for six line drawings of birds from a norming study of 328 pictures carried out with 40 normal elderly subjects.

number of lines that composed the illustration (consider the peacock, which has many lines and is rated very complex), subjects found less familiar birds with the same number of lines to be more complex than more familiar birds (compare the eagle and the owl). If visual complexity were only a second measure of familiarity and the number of lines, then equating semantic categories on this basis would pose no great problems. However, it is possible that included in the measure of visual complexity are measures of the "informativeness" or distinctiveness of traits. Snodgrass and Vanderwart (1980) suggested that the correlation between familiarity and visual complexity stems from conventions developed for the concept's representation. Highly familiar objects would develop efficient and simplified verbal and visual codes. If explanations of what the term "visual complexity" means are not taken into account, our understanding of category effects will be impoverished. Experiments that equate categories on terms or factors that are not clearly understood could either remove effects that point to the basis of category effects or produce results that imply a superficial perceptual basis for category effects when a deeper level of explanation should be considered.

Dixon, Bub, Chertkow, and Arguin (1999) raised the possibility that the apparent category deficits of ADs could be explained by the Humphreys, Riddoch, and Quinlan (1988) proposal that identification problems can arise from a failure to distinguish a given exemplar from visual and semantic neighbours within the same category. Dixon et al. (1999) contended that a major problem in identification studies was the inability to specify how visually similar or different objects were from other objects. They sought to address the problem of equating visual features in a quantifiable way. In a learning experiment, ADs and elderly normal controls were required to associate words to sets of meaningless synthetic shapes (blobs). Three of the blobs were visually distinct in that each blob varied on two dimensions from the other two; the other three blobs were visually similar in that they differed along only one dimension. At each session, eight ADs learned to associate the blob triads to one of four different word triads. The word triads varied along two dimensions: two categories (biological versus non-biological) and two levels of semantic closeness for each category (e.g. banjo, violin, guitar [close] versus wrench, carriage, kite [disparate]). The results show that both semantic closeness and visual similarity adversely affected the error rates of ADs and elderly normal controls, more so those of the ADs. On the other hand, when biological versus artefact word triads were equally close (or disparate) semantically, there was no effect of semantic category (e.g. banjo, violin, guitar versus lion, tiger, leopard).

Special categories.   There have been indications from behavioural results that specific semantic categories do not conform to the biological–non-biological division of semantics. In reviewing several studies that tested for category specificity in AD, Dixon et al. (1999) noted that it was generally the studies that avoided body parts in their biological stimuli or musical instruments in their non-biological stimuli that obtained a category effect. They found that the lack of a category effect when musical instruments were tested was revealing in that musical instruments, like biological objects such as animals, have many intraclass similarities both semantically and structurally. Such intraclass similarity could be the basis for category effects in AD, although it is worth noting that the presence of musical instruments is not quite predictive of finding a category effect; Fung et al. (2001) have since obtained category effects on a task of picture naming that included musical instruments as non-biological items. Nevertheless, Dixon et al.'s (1999) argument that what is crucial is the degree of intraclass similarity remains a valid consideration because there might be musical instruments, such as a drum, that are more distinctive than other instrument groupings (such as the many string instruments). As to the point that the identification of body parts is not differentially impaired, there are a few reasons why their inclusion within the category of "biological items" could muddy the conclusions that can be drawn. First, body parts might be represented differently, than say, animals, because they are an intrinsic part of our body image. Second, they are extremely familiar stimuli and, as is discussed later, the category effect is difficult to establish with very familiar stimuli. Besides the peculiarities of musical instruments and body parts, Montanes et al. (1995) have found that a category effect can be eliminated in a naming task if the pictures are in colour. The category that most benefitted from the colour cue was fruits and vegetables. Clearly, colour provides important information to aid in picture naming for all subjects. However, the presence of colour in the stimuli does not appear to be the crucial determinant of category effects; both Silveri et al. (1991) and Tippett et al. (1996) found category effects in AD using coloured stimuli.

Range of item difficulty.   Because it has been so important to control for factors such as familiarity and visual complexity, and because the number of stimuli for which these ratings are available is limited to more familiar objects, the control groups' accuracy was frequently at ceiling. This represents a major shortcoming of most reported studies—the pictures were simply too easy for normal subjects. There are important problems associated with using picture stimuli that are too easy to name. First, when control subjects are at ceiling one can reasonably ask whether the stimuli are accurately matched for difficulty. Second, there might be something that is atypical about the very familiar 50 or so objects that are used repeatedly across many studies. For instance, there have been suggestions that the right hemisphere is able to respond to highly frequent words in a way that it does not to less frequent words, whereas the left hemisphere processes the full range of word frequencies (Zaidel, 1990). In contrast, using very unfamiliar or difficult picture stimuli in ADs presents a very practical problem—their naming accuracy quickly falls to zero, and hence no category effect can emerge.

The use of very familiar stimuli can explain the lack of category effect in the Tippett (1996) study, in which they included seven very familiar body parts (e.g. ear, eye, foot) in the biological category. One way to determine whether category effects exist in normal subjects is to analyse RTs as well as accuracy data. Humphreys et al. (1988), and Snodgrass and Yuditsky (1996) have shown that normal subjects whose naming performance is nearly perfect demonstrate a category effect in their naming RTs. Here, the category effect is not one of biological versus non-biological but rather of structurally distinct categories (e.g. body parts, clothing, furniture) and structurally similar categories (e.g. animals, birds, fruit). Collecting accurate verbal RTs from ADs, however, is difficult as there are frequent mis-starts on words, which result in the removal of much data. None of the studies that we considered earlier used RT measures on a picture naming task.

An experimental method that can give a rough estimate of the effect of category on RTs in both elderly normal controls and ADs is the deadline procedure, in which stimuli are presented at a fixed rate and response accuracy is measured. If the subject is very slow in identifying objects, this becomes evident in the accuracy score. We have used this deadline method with the same stimuli in two positron emission tomography (PET) picture naming studies carried out, one with fifteen elderly normal controls (Whatmough et al., 2002) and one with fifteen ADs (Chertkow, Whatmough, Murtha, Bub, Fung & Gold 2000). The goal of the experiments was to examine how the effects of familiarity and semantic category interacted in the brain in each population. With this in view, four sets of pictures were selected, a set of highly familiar animals (Easy Animals), a set of less familiar animals (Hard Animals) and similarly two sets of manipulable artefacts (Easy Tools and Hard Tools). The sets were selected to produce equal performance across categories at each level of familiarity, with a mean accuracy of 70% for both Hard sets. Stimulus selection was based on naming accuracy and familiarity ratings collected from a norming study carried out on twenty men and twenty women of similar age and education as our test populations. In the norming study subjects were allowed unlimited time to name each picture. Under the deadline conditions of the PET experiment with a stimulus presentation rate of one per 2 seconds and a display time of 1 second, the elderly normal controls accuracy dropped for the Hard Animals resulting in a significant category effect at the Hard level (Figure 7.2) The ADs also demonstrated a category effect that was the same size at both familiarity levels. Further, the size of the category effect displayed by the elderly normal controls on the Hard sets was the same as for the ADs on both levels of familiarity (Hard and Easy).

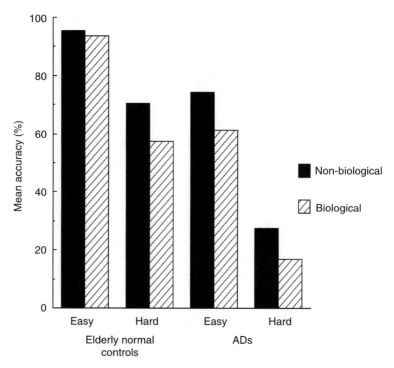

Figure 7.2. Mean accuracy of fifteen elderly normal control subjects and fifteen patients with probable Alzheimer's disease (ADs) on four picture naming blocks. Blocks of highly familiar and less familiar objects are designated, respectively, "Easy" and "Hard". (Adapted from Whatmough et al. [1999] and Chertkow et al. [2000].)

From the behavioural results of the PET experiments, then, we see that equating stimuli based on accuracy data alone might not be sufficient to remove subtle category effects present in normal populations. Fung et al. (2001), however, have been able to demonstrate that category effects are present even when both the accuracy and the RT of normal subjects is taken into account. They carried out a semantic association task similar to the Palms and Pyramids task (Howard & Patterson, 1992). In this experiment, subjects were asked to indicate by a button response which of two words was more closely related to a target word (e.g. lamb: sheep or goat?). The categories tested were animals, fruit and vegetables, clothing and furniture, tools, action verbs and abstract nouns. Stimuli for categories were equated for both accuracy and mean RT in elderly normal controls. The elderly normal controls performed at 90% accuracy across categories. Analysis of the accuracy data by category revealed that the ADs ($n = 17$) performed equally poorly on the biological and the abstract word categories (accuracy of approximately 67%)

and significantly better on the non-biological and action word categories (accuracy of approximately 79%).

Fung et al. (2001) also carried out a picture naming experiment with the same subjects. One of their principal concerns was that the stimuli from each category be matched based on familiarity norms from taken from a population of the same education and generation as the test population. A second concern was that the stimuli include less familiar stimuli so that normal subjects were not performing at ceiling, which could mask category effects in accuracy measures. There were 45 stimuli for each category from a range of familiarity, which included less well recognised objects. Biological stimuli included birds, insects, land animals, marine life, and fruit and vegetables. The non-biological stimuli included household utensils, carpenter tools, musical instruments, playthings, and means of transportation. They found that the elderly normal subjects' accuracy was the same for both major categories (80%), but that the ADs were significantly worse overall on the biological (31%) than on the non-biological (41%). Of the eighteen subjects (eight men and ten women), fifteen had greater error scores on the biological than on the non-biological with no indication that the effect was stronger for men than for women. We would argue on the basis of this study that the category effect in AD is real, although mild in strength.

Subject variables. A number of studies have emphasised the heterogeneity of the AD population with regards to the category effects encountered (Garrard et al., 1998; Gonnerman et al., 1997; Laiacona et al., 1998; Montanes et al., 1995, 1996). Subsets of the test population can differ in the relative strength of the semantic, verbal, and visuospatial deficits that they manifest. In addition to these qualitative differences in the population, as the disease advances, semantic memory loss increases. There can also be differences in the cognitive profile of elderly normal subjects (Valdois et al., 1990). Because of this heterogeneity, small groups of subjects and control subjects are perhaps not be sufficient to detect category effects that are not very large to begin with. This is particularly a problem in the Gonnerman study, in which the researchers wished to characterise the end of a spectrum of subjects that contained fifteen subjects in all.

To better answer the question of what is the nature of the category effect over a full range of naming performance, we (Whatmough et al., in press) carried out a naming experiment on a large cross-section of cognitively impaired elderly individuals (*n* = 72) who had been either diagnosed with Mild Cognitive Impairment (MCI, *n* = 16) or probable AD (*n* = 56). The MCI individuals were all clearly impaired in terms of explicit verbal memory but were within age-adjusted "normal limits" in terms of their picture naming on standardised tests, such as the Boston Naming Test (Kaplan, Goodglass, & Weintraub, 1983). About 15% of such individuals decline to a clear diagnoses of AD after 1 year, and close to 50% will be diagnosed as AD after 3 years follow-up (Grundman, Petersen, & Morris, 1996; Petersen et al., 1993). Subjects were asked to name fourteen line drawings from each of four categories: animals, fruits and vegetables, household tools, and clothing and furniture. The stimuli were selected according to pretest data we had collected from similarly aged and educated elderly normal men ($n = 20$) and women ($n = 20$) so that the biological stimuli and the artefact stimuli produced equal accuracy in naming performance and were judged to be of the same mean familiarity. The subjects included in the analysis were from a complete range of naming capabilities. Analysis of the subjects' naming scores for biological and artefacts did not show any initial advantage for biological stimuli, in contrast to the predictions of Gonnerman et al. (1997). Rather, we showed that from an initially equivalent performance on the stimuli there was a modest linear increase in the advantage of artefacts over biological items with declining naming performance (Figure 7.3). A small group of subjects ("other dementia" OD, $n = 14$), who were diagnosed with other forms of cognitive impairment, were also assessed. These included individuals diagnosed with focal frontotemporal dementia ($n = 5$), Mixed dementia (AD plus vascular elements, $n = 5$), Lewy body dementia ($n = 1$), and dementia due to normal pressure hydrocephalus ($n = 1$). Also included in the OD group were two individuals who were mildly impaired and deemed to have "vascular cognitive

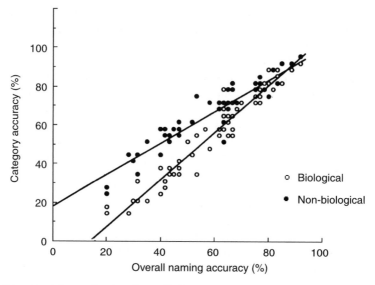

Figure 7.3.   Breakdown of patients' overall picture naming accuracy into their scores for biological and non-biological stimuli. Lines indicate the regression of each category onto overall accuracy. (Adapted from Whatmough et al., 1999.)

impairment" and one with MCI complicated by severe depression. When the naming scores by category of these other patients were entered individually into a regression model of the larger AD–MCI group, five (36%) had standard residual scores that deviated more than 2 SD, indicating either a greatly attenuated category effect, no effect, or an effect in the opposite direction (better biological naming than non-biological naming). As the mean MMSE scores of the OD group was similar to the AD group, this suggests that the category effect in AD is linked to the particular pattern of semantic decline seen in AD. Both OD subjects with dementias characterised by a strong semantic memory impairment (one subject suspected of having primary progressive aphasia, and another with a semantic dementia) had observed non-biological scores within the values predicted for the AD subjects. A fifteenth OD, a frontotemporal dementia subject with a primary progressive aphasia sydrome, had scores too low to enter into the model but demonstrated a category effect similar to the low scoring ADs. These results suggest that forms of dementia that are characterised by prominent semantic deficits show a similar category effect to AD.

Summary of category effects in Alzheimer's disease

(1) Group analyses of the performance of AD subjects on semantic memory tasks have revealed worse performance on biological objects than on non-biological objects. This category effect cannot be fully explained by stimulus related factors such as visual complexity, familiarity, prototypicality, or printed word frequency. The effect has been demonstrated on tasks such as picture naming, word to picture matching, object decision, semantic association, probe questioning, and naming to definition (Daum et al., 1996; Fung et al., 2001; Garrard et al., 1998; Laiacona et al., 1998; Mauri et al., 1994; Silveri et al., 1991; Whatmough et al., in press).

(2) The category effect is not always found when subjects are tested on very familiar items. One picture naming study (Chertkow et al., 2000), however, which used a deadline procedure, found a category effect for both familiar and less familiar objects. In that study, although accuracy was lower for the less familiar objects, the size of the category effect was the same at both levels of familiarity.

(3) Group analyses of the mean differences in performance for biological and non-biological concepts are usually not very large (approximately 20%) in comparison with focal lesion subjects, where an almost total loss for certain categories of concepts can sometimes be demonstrated. Some single-case studies of ADs, on the other hand, have reported category effects as great as those found in focal lesion subjects

(Gonnerman et al., 1997; Laiacona et al., 1998; Mauri et al., 1994). One study found the effect to be present only within a subgroup of ADs who had predominately verbal deficits (Montanes et al., 1995). Another study found that the effect of category on picture naming increased with worsening anomia (Whatmough et al., in press).

(4) One group study (Laiacona et al., 1998) found a gender bias in category effects, with men displaying preserved artefact naming more often than women. So far, no replications of this gender effect have been reported.

(5) In some tasks, such as category fluency, member dominance (judgement of best category membership), and ranking tasks, no effect of semantic category has been found (Cronin-Golomb et al., 1992; Hodges et al., 1992). One study (Montanes et al., 1996) found that ADs were better on sorting biological objects into categories (animals versus birds) than on sorting non-biological objects (tools versus vehicles).

(6) Within a group of ADs, multiple single-case analyses sometimes reveal a small number of subjects who are less accurate for artefacts than for biological items (Gonnerman et al., 1997; Laiacona et al., 1998; Whatmough et al., in press), but these subjects are not distinguishable as a group from other ADs either by MMSE or anomia scores. Superior knowledge for biological objects is not a general characteristic of either early or late loss.

(7) The category effect appears, for the moment, not to be a characteristic of other dementia such as Lewy body disease, frontotemporal dementia or vascular mixed dementia, where semantic memory loss is a less prominent feature (Whatmough et al., in press).

OBJECT VERSUS ACTION KNOWLEDGE; ABSTRACT VERSUS CONCRETE KNOWLEDGE

Before considering the explanations that have been put forward to explain the biological–non-biological effect, we will consider two other imbalances that have been reported with regards to concept knowledge. The hope is that what can be gleaned from these other findings would be, if not informative to the question at hand, at least harmonious with explanations put forward addressing the biological–non-biological deficit. The two other areas of investigation that have been examined are object versus action knowledge (or nouns versus verbs) and concrete versus abstract concepts.

Studies that have contrasted object and verb knowledge have produced contradictory results with some reporting better action naming and some superior object naming. Cappa et al. (1998) compared ten frontal–temporal dementia (FTD) subjects with nineteen ADs on a task of naming pictures for objects (both biological and non-biological) and pictures depicting actions such as washing or pulling. They found both groups to be worse on naming the actions than the objects but that the FTD subjects showed a greater category difference. Robinson, Grossman, White-Devine, and D'Esposito (1996) also found that seventeen out of twenty ADs were worse at naming pictures of actions than pictures of objects. They were also worse at matching a verb in print to its appropriate illustration out of a slate of four than performing the same task with nouns. Verbs and nouns were of the same frequency. Bushell and Martin (1997) also found abnormal effects for verbs but not for nouns in ADs. They found that semantic priming facilitated elderly normal controls in reading concrete nouns and motion verbs but that ADs were facilitated by semantic priming only in reading concrete nouns. Neither group of subjects was primed by semantic associates for either abstract words or non-motion verbs. The prime–target relationship, however, appears to have been different for the four types of words. Primes for abstract and non-motion verbs were predominately synonyms of the target (e.g. freedom–liberty; instruct–educate) whereas for the concrete nouns they often were not (e.g. gold–silver; tiger–lion). Perhaps synonyms are poorer semantic primers and this would partly explain the results.

In contrast with the above research, two studies have found better action naming than object naming. Williamson, Adair, Raymer, and Heilman (1998) administered the Boston Naming Test (Kaplan et al., 1983) and the Action Naming Test (Nicholas, Obler, Albert, & Goodglass, 1985) to ten ADs and ten elderly controls and selected for analysis the tests items for which word frequency values were available. When word frequency was entered into the analysis of accuracy rates as a covariate, only the ADs showed a word class effect, demonstrating better action naming than object naming. In an analysis of error type they found that both groups made proportionately more "no response" errors in object naming than in action naming.

In our laboratory, Fung et al. (2001) also examined naming of nouns and action verbs. Fung et al. contended that it was problematic to compare naming an action depicted by a static picture with naming the picture of an object. Whereas the object is fully represented in its static visual representation, identifying and naming an action requires a further level of abstraction across time. Moreover, they argued that in some cases recognition of the action could be facilitated by first recognising objects from the scene (e.g. we know the man is skating because he is wearing skates), which would be to the advantage of normal subjects but not necessarily the ADs. Fung et al. carried out experimental evaluations to see whether ADs would demonstrate performance differences on object and action naming when animated actions were used. In the animated versions, subjects viewed animated line drawings of people performing actions without any object present. Stimuli were selected such that elderly normal controls performed this naming task at a level of 80% accuracy for all classes of stimuli (static actions, animated actions, biological and non-biological objects). ADs were impaired at naming all categories of items, compared to the elderly controls. As Fung et al. had anticipated, the ADs were better at naming the animated actions (mean accuracy = 59%) than at naming the static line drawings of actions (mean accuracy = 36%). More important, the ADs' mean score for static action pictures was not significantly different from the combined scores for biological and non-biological object naming.

In a second task, subjects were asked to indicate which of two words was associated with a target word (e.g. lamb: goat, sheep). Target words were drawn from six semantic categories: two biological (animals, and fruit and vegetables), two non-biological (tools, and clothing and furniture), action verbs and abstract nouns. The mean accuracy rate of the elderly controls in this task was 88% and neither their accuracy nor their mean RTs varied significantly from category to category. The ADs were significantly less accurate (mean accuracy = 73%) than the normals. Further within-group comparisons showed that the AD subjects performed better on the non-biological categories than on the biological categories, and better on the action verbs than on the abstract nouns or the biological categories. Accuracy for abstract nouns was not significantly different from biological nouns. The results from both tasks indicated, first, that knowledge of action-verbs was not more impaired than knowledge of objects in AD. Second, the convergence of results from tasks using different stimuli types (i.e. pictures and words) and different response type (i.e. naming versus forced choice judgements) calls into question explanations of category effects that are based primarily on visuopeceptual or lexical–phonological deficits. Amodal semantic memory loss appears to be the major determinent of these category effects.

WHAT IS THE CAUSE OF CATEGORY EFFECTS IN ALZHEIMER'S DISEASE?

Three types of explanations for category effects in AD have been put forward. The first explanation is essentially the null hypothesis, according to which apparent category effects result from stimulus variables not specific to the categories. The second type of explanation is functional–anatomical, in that attributes deemed more important to the recognition of biological objects than non-biological are thought to be processed in a brain region preferentially compromised in AD. The third type of explanation attributes the pattern of category loss to an emergent property of non-focal deterioration within a semantic system, reflecting general features of the manner in which concepts are represented, organised, or processed.

Explanation 1: it is an epiphenomenon

The argument that apparent category effects result from poor matching of categories on important stimulus variables such as visual complexity and word frequency was put forth most strongly by Tippett et al. (1996) and Montanes et al. (1995). Having tallied the different characteristics of the category effect in AD, such as its modest effect size and its presence primarily in ADs with strong semantic (called by some "verbal") deficits, it is not surprising that some researchers have failed to obtain category effects. We would argue, however, that their objections have mostly been answered by the number and variety of other studies that have been carried out and have found that there is a category effect present in AD subjects that is not discernible in normal populations.

Three factors seem to be key elements in revealing a category effect. First, subjects must be quite anomic (which, we maintain, is an indication of severe semantic memory deficits in the case of the ADs). Second, stimuli must be sufficiently difficult so that normal subjects cannot perform the task at ceiling level. Finally, the category effect arises in tasks that demand unique identification or specification but not in tasks that require superordinate knowledge.

Explanation 2: location is everything

Most studies have provided a functional–anatomical explanation for the increased deficit in biological knowledge. This explanation, however, takes a number of forms. Silveri et al. (1991) note that HSE subjects, who are the main group of brain-damaged individuals who demonstrate a category-specific deficit for objects from the biological category, have lesions principally in the temporolimbic area, a cortical area also subject to early loss in AD. Silveri et al. suggested that living things might have a greater biological significance for humans than artefacts, and hence rely more on the amygdala and hippocampus. Daum et al. (1996) and Garrard et al. (1998) supported Warrington and Shallice's (1984) explanation that it is the visual features or structural representation of stimuli that are vulnerable to temporal lobe loss, and that the living categories such as animals and plant life are essentially distinguished, experienced, or encoded by visual–perceptual processes, whereas artefacts are encoded based on their functionality. Laiacona et al. (1998), who had found that gender interacted with the effect of category, also support the idea of a different weighting of information from the sensory and motor channels for the identification of living and non-living objects (Farah & McClelland, 1991; Warrington & McCarthy, 1987; Warrington & Shallice, 1984). To explain the additional gender effect, Laiocona et al. proposed that individual experience might further increase the imbalance in weighting and suggested that men have greater sensorimotor familiarity with the non-living category than women, and that this protects them from the effects of perceptual information loss for this category. They thus propose that naming of items from the living category requires greater perceptual processing, and that this takes place in the temporal lobes. However, given the fact that their finding of gender differences has not been replicated, the status of their arguments remains uncertain.

Similar functional–anatomical explanations have also been put forth to explain noun–verb or object–action effects. The problem with any such discussion at this point lies in the uncertainty regarding the basic phenomenology to be explained. Both Cappa (Cappa et al., 1998) and Robinson (Robinson et al., 1996) found verbs–actions to be more impaired than naming of nouns in AD, whereas Williamson and our group (Fung et al., 2001) found the opposite pattern using (we would argue) better stimuli.

Williamson et al. (1998), who found better action naming than object naming, also espouse a locationalist approach. The general impairment in naming due to semantic impairment would be due to pathology of left temporooccipito–parietal junction. Williamson et al. suggest that lexical retrieval is an important functional impairment in AD. The pattern of loss for action naming versus object naming might well reflect the different neural substrates for such lexical retrieval for nouns versus actions. Impaired lexical retrieval for objects would be due to lateral and inferior temporal pathology. Lexical retrieval for actions would involve, in contrast, premotor or prefrontal cortical areas or both which are relatively spared in AD. The category effect with specific impairment of object naming would therefore be at the level of lexical retrieval and not linguistic semantics.

To what extent is the functional–anatomic explanation tenable as a coherent explanation for the category effect seen in AD? Certainly there has been a growing body of evidence from functional imaging studies pointing to differences in the cortical representation for different concept categories (Martin, 1998; Martin et al., 1995). On the other hand, AD as a disease is distinguished by its anatomic variability and yet the category effect appears present (and in the same direction) in the large majority of individual cases as well in cases of frontotemporal dementia (see also Chapter 6). This would seem to call into question any explanation predicated on the anatomic distribution of lesions in AD. Critical tests of functional–anatomic hypothesis, however, will probably not originate in studies of brain-damaged individuals (where the lesions are too large and inexact), but will require future use of other methodologies.

Explanation 3: category effects reflect the organisation of semantic memory

In contrast with the preceding explanations, others have proposed that category effects in AD are an emergent property of the way concepts are represented within the semantic memory store. Gonnerman et al. (1997) do not deny that the location of lesions might be part of the explanation but they provide the following additional explanation of the pattern of loss they anticipate longitudinally in AD subjects. They propose that concepts are represented by a pattern of activation across a distribution of features. Some features ("intercorrelated features") are frequently activated together and so develop strong bonds among themselves, providing collateral support if one feature is weakened. Wings, for instance, are frequently associated with flight and beaks. Other features (distinguishing features) are more linked to specific concepts, such as black stripes in the case of "zebras" or serrated metal edges in the case of "saws". These distinguishing features are less affected by the coactivation of other features. The critical difference between biological and non-biological items is that biological items possess many more intercorrelated features than are encountered in non-biological items. Semantic degradation, according to Gonnerman et al. (1997) involves the random loss of features, both correlated and distinguishing. The early random loss of distinguishing features that are critical to the recognition of an object should be more likely to impair artefact identification than living object recognition because they receive little collateral support from other coactivated or correlated features. As the weight of loss accumulates, however, correlated activity will fail to support concepts and whole categories of biological items that are mutually dependent on each other will fall. The prediction of the model was therefore that there would initially be a living objects advantage followed by a non-living objects advantage, and this was partly supported by two case studies.

We see the problem with Gonnerman et al.'s model as two-fold. First, the model is strictly computational in nature, and relatively minor alterations to the computational weightings in a similar model have been found to produce opposite predictions (Moss & Tyler, 2000). Second, while the notion of models that attempt to capture the essential features of semantic memory is intriguing and often exciting, there are few guidelines as to the best way to adjudicate between the choice of weightings in any particular case (Farah & McClelland, 1991; McClelland & Rumelhart, 1985; Seidenberg & McClelland, 1989).

Given this inherent problem with computational models, we must fall back on the presence of empirical data to support the model's predictions. The support data offered by Gonnerman et al. were rather meagre, and our own investigations have reached very different conclusions. Having tested a large cohort of ADs with variable degrees of memory loss we (Whatmough et al., in press) fail to find evidence, at any level of severity, for a crossover from greater impairment on biological to greater impairment on biological items. Other studies (Garrard et al., 1998) have also failed to support the crossover notion.

Other models of semantic representations are consistent with the phenomenology encountered in AD. Dixon and colleagues investigated category specificity in a subject with visual agnosia (see Chapter 4; Dixon, Bub, & Arguin, 1997; Dixon, Mill, Chertkow, Bub, & Arguin, 1997), as well as AD subjects (Dixon et al., 1999). According to these researchers, category deficits, at least in certain cases, would be due to the greater structural and conceptual similarity between items within the biological category. This similarity within a class would make items harder to distinguish and uniquely identify. Dixon et al. (1999) similarly propose that in psychological space there will be an intersection of the influences of both the semantic and the visual dimensions that determine an object. The closer two objects are in this space, the more difficult they will be to distinguish. According to this formulation, the fact that an AD subject will be more frequently impaired in recognising a lion than a hammer is not due to a semantic category dichotomy between biological and non-biological objects. Rather, it results from the fact that a lion closely resembles other animals, both physically and semantically, whereas a hammer is more distinct in its structure and in its use. The greater distinctiveness of artefacts relative to biological items, both semantically and structurally, results in their greater resistance to the gradual erosion of semantic knowledge in AD and gives artefacts a small but significant advantage in tests of object identification.

Other computational models of semantic memory have been designed, built, and tested (Farah & McClelland, 1991; Small, Hart, Nguyen, & Gordon, 1995). These might well capture meaningful aspects of the semantic memory loss seen in AD subjects. Such models are most useful when they are robust enough to lead to the possibility of experimental falsifiability. The model of Gonnerman et al. allows for such experimental testing but, unfortunately, does not seem to be achieving empirical support. It is possible that other computational models of semantic memory might prove better able to both explain the semantic impairment seen in AD, and predict new phenomena derivable from clinical studies.

CONCLUSION

We began by describing the semantic memory loss in AD as a gradual erosion of knowledge for concepts and objects. As the distinctive aspects that help to identify objects erode, so does the AD subject's capacity to recognise them. The individual is left with only core elements that are similar to many other exemplars from the same category, leading to misidentification. The semantic category effect seen in AD appears to be robust in its replicability, but quantitatively modest. We have reviewed the large set of variables that can impact on the effect, and a range of theories brought to bear to explain it. We would argue that the "epiphenomenon" explanation has become increasingly untenable, and that the functional–anatomical explanation is probably overly simplistic and simply untestable at present. Category effects in AD might well be an emergent property of the organisation of semantic memory itself.

Models of semantic memory are, as often as not, simply reformulations of the underlying phenomena rather than true models with explanatory coherence. Of those models sufficiently robust to be deemed testable, we would argue that the model of Gonnerman et al. (1997) appears false in some important manner, as it is incompatible with our empirical results. In contrast, the formulation of Dixon et al. (1999) views category effects as an emergent property of the differing semantic densities of most living and nonliving categories. It is the greater distinctiveness of artefacts (relative to biological items) that explains the category effects encountered in a visual agnosic patient, ELM. Moreover, when AD subjects were studied with the same demanding experimental paradigm, very similar results emerged. This suggests strongly that the formulation of Dixon et al. (1999) can best explain the category effects seen in AD.

ACKNOWLEDGEMENTS

This work was supported by a postdoctoral fellowship grant to CW from the Medical Research Council of Canada (MRC), and grants to HC from the MRC, the FCAR (Quebec), and the Alzheimer's Society of Canada.

REFERENCES

Bayles, K.A., & Tomoeda, C.K. (1990). Naming and categorical knowledge in Alzheimer's disease: The process of semantic memory deterioration. *Brain and Language, 39(4)*, 498–510.

Bayles, K.A., Tomoeda, C.K., & Trosset, M.W. (1991). Alzheimer's disease effects on semantic memory: Loss of structure or impaired processing? *Journal of Cognitive Neuroscience, 3(2)*, 166–182.

Bushell, C.M., & Martin, A. (1997). Automatic semantic priming of nouns and verbs in patients with Alzheimer's disease. *Neuropsychologia, 35(8)*, 1059–1067.

Cappa, S.F., Binetti, G., Pezzini, A., Padovani, A., Rozzini, L., & Trabucchi, M. (1998). Object and action naming in Alzheimer's disease and frontotemporal dementia [see comment]. *Neurology, 50(2)*, 351–355.

Chertkow, H., & Bub, D. (1990a). Semantic memory loss in dementia of Alzheimer's type: What do various measures measure? *Brain, 113(2)*, 397–417.

Chertkow, H., & Bub, D. (1990b). Semantic memory loss in Alzheimer-type dementia. In M.F. Schwartz (Ed.), *Modular deficits in Alzheimer-type dementia. Issues in the biology of language and cognition* (pp. 207–244). Cambridge, MA: MIT Press.

Chertkow, H., Bub, D., Bergman, H., Bruemmer, A., Merling, A., & Rothfleisch, J. (1994). Increased semantic priming in patients with dementia of the Alzheimer's type. *Journal of Clinical & Experimental Neuropsychology, 16(4)*, 608–622.

Chertkow, H., Bub, D., & Caplan, D. (1992). Constraining theories of semantic memory processing: Evidence from dementia. *Cognitive Neuropsychology, 9(4)*, 327–365.

Chertkow, H., Whatmough, C., Murtha, S., Bub, D., Fung, D., & Gold, D. (2000). PET activation during picture naming in AD. *Brain and Language, 74(3)*, 345–347.

Cronin-Golomb, A., Keane, M.M., Kokodis, A., Corkin, S., & Growdon, J. H. (1992). Category knowledge in Alzheimer's disease: Normal organization and a general retrieval deficit. *Psychology and Aging, 7(3)*, 359–366.

Crowe, S.F., Dingjan, P., & Helme, R.D. (1997). The neurocognitive basis of word-finding difficulty in Alzheimer's disease. *Australian Psychologist, 32(2)*, 114–119.

Daum, I., Riesch, G., Sartori, G., & Birbaumer, N. (1996). Semantic memory impairment in Alzheimer's disease. *Journal of Clinical & Experimental Neuropsychology, 18(5)*, 648–665.

Dixon, M., Bub, D.N., & Arguin, M. (1997). The interaction of object form and object meaning in the identification performance of a patient with category-specific visual agnosia. *Cognitive Neuropsychology, 14*, 1085–1130.

Dixon, M.J., Bub, D.N., Chertkow, H., & Arguin, M. (1999). Object identification deficits in dementia of the Alzheimer type: Combined effects of semantic and visual proximity. *Journal of the International Neuropsychological Society, 5(4)*, 330–345.

Dixon, M., Mill, D., Chertkow, H., Bub, D., & Arguin, M. (1997). Visual and semantic determinants of object recognition deficits in early Alzheimer's disease. *Brain and Cognition, 35(3)*, 361–364.

Farah, M.J., & McClelland, J.L. (1991). A computational model of semantic memory impairment: modality specificity and emergent category specificity. *Journal of Experimental Psychology: General, 120*, 339–357.

Fung, T.D., Chertkow, H., Murtha, S., Whatmough, C., Péloquin, L., Whitehead, V., & Templeman, F.D. (2001). The spectrum of category effects in object and action knowledge in dementia of the Alzheimer's type. *Neuropsychology, 15(3)*, 371–379.

Garrard, P., Patterson, K., Watson, P.C., & Hodges, J.R. (1998). Category specific semantic loss in dementia of Alzheimer's type. *Brain, 121(4)*, 633–646.

Gonnerman, L., Andersen, E., Devlin, J., Kempler, D., & Seidenberg, M. (1997). Double dissociation of semantic categories in Alzheimer's disease. *Brain and Language, 57(2)*, 254–279.

Gordon, B. (1997). Models of naming. In H. Goodglass (Ed.), *Anomia: Neuroanatomical and cognitive correlates. Foundations of neuropsychology* (pp. 31–64). San Diego, CA: Academic Press, Inc.

Grundman, M., Petersen, R.C., Morris, J.C., Ferris, S., Sano, M., Farlow, M., Doody, R., Galasko, D., Ernesto, C., Thomas, R., & Thal, L. (1996). ADSC Cooperative Study. Rate of dementia of the Alzheimer type (DAT) in subjects with mild cognitive impairment. *Neurology, 46*, A403.

Henderson, V.W. (1996). The investigation of lexical semantic representation in Alzheimer's disease. *Brain and Language, 54(2)*, 179–183.

Hodges, J.R., & Patterson, K. (1995). Is semantic memory consistently impaired early in the course of Alzheimer's disease? Neuroanatomical and diagnostic implications. *Neuropsychologia, 33(4)*, 441–459.

Hodges, J.R., Patterson, K., Ward, R., Garrard, P., Bak, T., Perry, R., & Gregory, C. (1999). The differentiation of semantic dementia and frontal lobe dementia (temporal and frontal variants of frontotemporal dementia) from early Alzheimer's disease: A comparative neuropsychological study. *Neuropsychology, 13(1)*, 31–40.

Hodges, J.R., Salmon, D.P., & Butters, N. (1992). Semantic memory impairment in Alzheimer's disease: Failure of access or degraded knowledge? *Neuropsychologia, 30(4)*, 301–314.

Howard, D., & Patterson, K. (1992). *The Pyramids and Palm Trees Test: A test of semantic access from words and pictures.* Bury St. Edmunds: Thames Valley Test Company.

Huff, F.J., Corkin, S., & Growdon, J.H. (1986). Semantic impairment and anomia in Alzheimer's disease. *Brain and Language, 28(2)*, 235–249.

Humphreys, G.W., Riddoch, M.J., & Quinlan, P.T. (1988). Cascade processes in picture identification. *Cognitive neuropsychology, 5*, 67–103.

Kaplan, E., Goodglass, H., & Weintraub, S. (1983). *The Boston Naming Test*. Philadelphia: Lea & Febiger.

Knotek, P.C., Bayles, K.A., & Kaszniak, A.W. (1990). Response consistency on a semantic memory task in persons with dementia of the Alzheimer type. *Brain and Language, 38(4)*, 465–475.

Laiacona, M., Barbarotto, R., & Capitani, E. (1998). Semantic category dissociations in naming: Is there a gender effect in Alzheimer's disease? *Neuropsychologia, 36(5)*, 407–419.

McClelland, J.L., & Rumelhart, D.E. (1985). Distributed memory and the representation of general and specific information. *Journal of Experimental Psychology: General, 114(2)*, 159–188.

Martin, A. (1992a). Degraded semantic representations of objects in patients with Alzheimer's disease. *Paper presented at the International Neuropsychological Society Meeting*.

Martin, A. (1992b). Degraded knowledge representations in patients with Alzheimer's disease: Implications for models of semantic and repetition priming. In L.R. Squire & N. Butters (Eds.), *Neuropsychology of Memory* (2nd ed.). New York, NY: Guilford Press.

Martin, A. (1998). Organization of semantic knowledge and the origin of words in the brain. In N.G. Jablonski & L.C. Aiello (Eds.), *The Origin and Diversification of Language* (pp. 69–87). San Francisco, CA: Memoirs of the California Academy of Sciences.

Martin, A., Brouwers, B., & Cox, F.P. (1985). On the nature of the verbal memory deficit in Alzheimer's disease. *Brain and Language, 25(2)*, 323–341.

Martin, A., Haxby, J.V., Lalonde, F.M., Wiggs, C.L., & Ungerleider, L.G. (1995). Discrete cortical regions associated with knowledge of color and knowledge of action. *Science, 270(5233)*, 102–105.

Mauri, A., Daum, I., Sartori, G., & Riesch, G., (1994). Category-specific semantic impairment in Alzheimer's disease and temporal lobe dysfunction: A comparative study. *Journal of Clinical & Experimental Neuropsychology, 16(5)*, 689–701.

Miller, G.A., & Johnson-Laird, P.N. (1976). *Language and Perception*. Cambridge, MA: Harvard University Press.

Montanes, P., Goldblum, M.C., & Boller, F. (1995). The naming impairment of living and non-living items in Alzheimer's disease. *Journal of the International Neuropsychological Society, 1(1)*, 39–48.

Montanes, P., Goldblum, M.C., & Boller, F. (1996). Classification deficits in Alzheimer's disease with special reference to living and non-living things. *Brain and Language, 54(2)*, 335–358.

Moss, H.E., & Tyler, L.K. (2000). A Progressive category-specific deficit for non-living things. *Neuropsychologia, 38(1)*, 60–82.

Nebes, R.D. (1989). Semantic memory in Alzheimer's disease. *Psychological Bulletin, 106(3)*, 377–394.

Nebes, R.D., & Brady, C.B. (1988). Integrity of semantic fields in Alzheimer's disease. *Cortex, 24(2)*, 291–299.

Nebes, R.D., & Brady, C.B. (1992). Generalized cognitive slowing and severity of dementia in Alzheimer's disease: Implications for the interpretation of response-time data. *Journal of Clinical and Experimental Neuropsychology, 14(2)*, 317–326.

Nebes, R.D., Brady, C.B., & Huff, F.J. (1989). Automatic and attentional mechanisms of semantic priming in Alzheimer's disease. *Journal of Clinical and Experimental Neuropsychology, 11(2)*, 219–230.

Nebes, R.D., Brady, C.B., & Reynolds, C.F.D. (1992). Cognitive slowing in Alzheimer's disease and geriatric depression. *Journal of Gerontology, 47(5)*, 331–336.

Nebes, R.D., & Halligan, E.M. (1995). Contextual constraint facilitates semantic decisions about object pictures by Alzheimer Patients. *Psychology & Aging, 10(4)*, 590–596.

Nebes, R.D., & Halligan, E.M. (1996). Sentence context influences the interpretation of word meaning by Alzheimer patients. *Brain & Language, 54(2)*, 233–245.

Nebes, R.D., Martin, D.C., & Horn, L.C. (1984). Sparing of semantic memory in Alzheimer's disease. *Journal of Abnormal Psychology, 93*, 321–330.

Nicholas, M., Obler, L., Albert, M., & Goodglass, H. (1985). Lexical retrieval in healthy aging. *Cortex, 21(4)*, 595–606.

Ober, B.A., Dronkers, N.F., Koss, E., Delis, D.C., & Friedland, R.P. (1986). Retrieval from semantic memory in Alzheimer-type dementia. *Journal of Clinical & Experimental Neuropsychology, 8(1)*, 75–92.

Petersen, R.C., Smith, G.E., Tangalos, E.G., Kokmen, E., & Ivnik, R.J. (1993). Longitudinal outcome of patients with a mild cognitive impairment. *Annals of Neurology, 34*, 294–295

Riddoch, M.J., & Humphreys, G.W. (1987). Visual object processing in optic aphasia: A case of semantic access agnosia. *Cognitive Neuropsychology, 4*, 131–185.

Robinson, K., Grossman, M., White-Devine, T., & D'Esposito, M. (1996). Category-specific difficulty naming with verbs in Alzheimer's disease. *Neurology, 47(1)*, 178–182.

Sartori, G., & Job, R. (1988). The oyster with four legs: A neuropsychological study on the interaction of visual and semantic information. *Cognitive Neuropsychology, 5(1)*, 105–132.

Seidenberg, M., & McClelland, J. (1989). A distributed, developmental model of word recognition and naming. *Psychological Review, 96*, 523–568.

Silveri, M.C., Daniele, A., Giustolisi, L., & Gainotti, G., (1991). Dissociation between knowledge of living and non-living things in dementia of the Alzheimer type. *Neurology, 41(4)*, 545–546.

Silveri, M.C., & Gainotti, G. (1988). Interaction between vision and language in category-specific semantic impairment. *Cognitive Neuropsychology, 5(6)*, 677–709.

Small, S., Hart, J., Nguyen, T., & Gordon, B. (1995). Distributed representation of semantic knowledge in the brain. *Brain, 118*, 441–453.

Smith, S.R., Murdoch, B.E., & Chenery, H.J. (1989). Semantic abilities in dementia of the Alzheimer type. 1. Lexical semantics. *Brain & Language, 36(2)*, 314–324.

Snodgrass, J.G., & Vanderwort, M. (1980). A standardized set of 260 pictures: Norms for name agreement, image agreement, familiarity, and visual complexity. *Journal of Experimental Psychology: Human Learning and Memory, 6*, 174–215.

Snodgrass, J.G., & Yuditsky, T. (1996). Naming times for the Snodgrass and Vanderwart pictures. *Behavior Research Methods, Instruments, & Computers, 28(4)*, 516–536.

Tippett, L.J., Grossman, M., & Farah, M.J. (1996). The semantic memory impairment of Alzheimer's disease: Category-specific? *Cortex, 32(1)*, 143–153.

Valdois, S., Joanette, Y., Poissant, A., Ska, B., & Dehaut, F. (1990). Heterogeneity in the cognitive profile of normal elderly. *Journal of Clinical and Experimental Neuropsychology, 12(4)*, 587–596.

Warrington, E.K., & McCarthy, R.A. (1987). Categories of knowledge: Further fractionations and an attempted integration. *Brain, 110*, 1273–1296.

Warrington, E. K., & Shallice, T. (1984). Category specific semantic impairments. *Brain, 107*, 829–854 .

Whatmough, C. Chertkow, H., Murtha, S., & Hanratty, K. (2002). Dissociable brain regions process object meaning annd object structure during picture naming. *Neuropsychologia, 40*, 174–186.

Whatmough, C., Chertkow, H., Murtha, S., Templeman, D., Babins, L., & Kelner, N. (in press). The semantic category effect increases with worsening anomia in Alzheimer's type dementia. *Brain & Language*.

Williamson, D.J., Adair, J.C., Raymer, A.M., & Heilman, K.M. (1998). Object and action naming in Alzheimer's disease. *Cortex, 34(4)*, 601–610.

Zaidel, E. (1990). Language functions in the following complete cerebral commissurotomy and hemispherectomy. In R.D. Nebes & S. Corkin (Eds.), *Handbook of Neuropsychology, Volume 4* (pp. 115–150). New York, NY: Elsevier Science.

CHAPTER EIGHT

Factors underlying category-specific semantic deficits

Ken McRae and George S. Cree
University of Western Ontario, London, Canada

INTRODUCTION

For many years, psychologists have been fascinated by people whose behaviour deviates from the norm following brain injury. Over the past 20 years or so, patients' performance on various tasks has served as constraints on theories of cognition and perception. As part of this research, there has been a great deal of interest in category-specific semantic deficits, whereby patients show differentially impaired knowledge of living things, such as zebras and carrots, versus non-living things, such as helicopters and pliers. The main reason for the intense interest in category-specific deficits has been their promise for providing insights into the organisation of semantic memory. To date, a number of theories have been proposed regarding the factors that underlie category-specific deficits, but there are currently unresolved debates concerning each of them. A major barrier to resolving these debates has been the lack of empirically derived quantitative estimates of these factors for large sets of living and non-living things. Therefore, the purpose of the research reported herein is to use a set of semantic feature production norms that includes 206 living and 343 non-living things to shed light on the factors that underlie category-specific deficits, both at the level of the broad living–non-living distinction, and for the categories within those domains.

Category-specific deficits have been documented in patients with various forms of brain impairment, including focal brain injury (Warrington & McCarthy, 1983, 1987), herpes simplex encephalitis (Sartori & Job, 1988;

Silveri & Gainotti, 1988; Warrington & Shallice, 1984), and Alzheimer's disease (Gonnerman et al., 1997). Although the existence of such deficits has been challenged on the grounds that the stimuli used in many experiments were not adequately equated on factors such as visual complexity and concept familiarity (Funnell & Sheridan, 1992; Gaffan & Heywood, 1993; Stewart, Parkin, & Hunkin, 1992), recent research has provided ample evidence that category-specific deficits remain when these variables are controlled (Caramazza & Shelton, 1998; Farah, Meyer, & McMullen, 1996; Forde et al., 1997; Gainotti & Silveri, 1996). In addition, Hillis and Caramazza (1991) found a double dissociation between living and non-living things using identical stimuli, suggesting that although complexity and familiarity play a role in a concept's accessibility, an appeal to these variables is insufficient to explain all deficits. Therefore, we assume that the phenomena exist, and that it is possible to explain them in terms of damage to a normal semantic memory system.

The most straightforward hypothesis regarding category-specific deficits is that they provide a transparent view into the organisation of semantic memory in the mind and brain. For example, because some patients with focal lesions exhibit more severely impaired knowledge of living than non-living things, and others the opposite pattern, it could be concluded that semantic memory is organised by domain (and/or category),[1] and focal damage to a specific area of the brain disrupts knowledge about the concepts represented therein. A number of researchers have proposed models of semantic processing in which one or more components of the system are organised by taxonomic category (Collins & Quillian, 1969; Sartori & Job, 1988; see also Chapter 11 for arguments based on developmental data that semantic memory might be organised by category in the mind, but not necessarily in the brain). However, many cognitive neuropsychologists believe that this idea should be rejected for two reasons (Farah, Meyer, & McMullen, 1996). First, it violates existing knowledge about brain organisation, in that there is strong evidence that brain systems are organised by function and/or modality (Martin et al., 1995; Thompson-Schill, Aguirre, D'Esposito, & Farah, 1999). Second, a number of patients have presented with deficits that violate the strict living–non-living distinction. For example, some patients have demonstrated impaired knowledge of fruit and vegetables, but not animals (Hillis & Caramazza, 1991). Other patients who show living thing deficits have also shown deficits in their knowledge of musical instruments, foods, or

---

[1] Throughout this chapter we use "domain" to refer to living versus non-living things, "category" when referring to mid-level categories such as vehicle and insect, and "concept" when referring to the concepts that we have normed, such as *truck* and *grasshopper*, the vast majority of which would be considered at the basic level by most researchers. Note, however, that we use "category-specific deficits" generically.

gemstones (Silveri & Gainotti, 1988; Warrington & Shallice, 1984). A theory in which semantic memory is organised by taxonomic category offers no *a priori* explanation of how these patterns could occur.

If we reject the notion that semantic memory is organised by category, then how can these patterns of semantic deficits be explained? The strategy that many researchers have taken is to identify variables that might be relevant to the organisation of semantic memory, and that might pattern quantitatively differently in various parts of semantic space. Research to this point has focused on three such factors: (i) feature types (Farah & McClelland, 1991; Shelton & Caramazza, 1999; Tranel, Logan, Frank, & Damasio, 1997); (ii) feature correlations (Devlin, Gonnerman, Anderson, & Seidenberg, 1998); and (iii) distinguishing features (Garrard, Lambon Ralph, Hodges, & Patterson, 2001; Warrington & Shallice, 1984). Implementing this strategy requires having reasonable quantitative estimates of how these factors pattern in various domains and categories. In many cases, estimation has been conducted on an intuitive basis, which is certainly an insufficient method. In other cases, quantitative estimates have been derived using semantic feature production norms (Devlin et al., 1998; Garrard et al., 2001) or tasks in which subjects underline features from dictionary definitions (Farah & McClelland, 1991; Shelton & Caramazza, 1998). However, these studies have used small numbers of living and non-living thing concepts, ranging from 30 living and 30 non-living things (Devlin et al., 1998) to 48 living and 48 non-living things (Farah & McClelland, 1991; Shelton & Caramazza, 1998). Furthermore, although the limited number of concepts in these studies enabled testing hypotheses regarding the living–non-living distinction, it did not allow for testing hypotheses regarding complex patterns of impairments at the level of categories within those domains. In contrast, as part of an ongoing project that aims to understand semantic representations and computations, we have collected a set of feature norms that currently includes 206 living and 343 non-living things, and has enabled us to derive the categories to which people believe these concepts belong. We believe that these norms provide valid quantitative estimates that can serve as sufficient tests of whether the factors mentioned above account for category-specific deficits, and thus whether they are relevant to the organisation of semantic memory.

THE FEATURE NORMS

The feature norms have been collected over a number of years as part of an ongoing investigation of semantic memory. The concepts were chosen to include the stimuli most often used in studies of concepts and categorisation, semantic memory, and impairments of semantic memory. As such, they span a wide range of living and non-living things, and vary in terms of familiarity and typicality.

In the norming task, subjects, primarily undergraduate students, were given twenty to twenty-four concept names, such as *cat* and *chair*, with ten blank lines beneath each name. Subjects were asked to list features of the things to which the word refers. Subjects normed no more than two concepts that might be considered reasonably similar and, if two reasonably similar concepts were included in the same form, they were presented on separate pages. Thirty subjects listed features for each concept. After recording the features (which is described in detail for a subset of the concepts in McRae, de Sa, & Seidenberg, 1997), a representation was derived for each concept by retaining all features that were listed by at least five of thirty subjects. Thus, the norms provide empirically-based featural representations for 549 living and non-living things. The resulting representations for two example concepts are presented in Appendix A.

To conduct the analyses presented below, we needed to categorise the living and non-living things within these broad domains. One issue that must be addressed concerns how to decide which categories are psychologically real and which exemplars people regard as belonging to those categories. Typically, researchers have decided on the relevant categories and exemplars *a priori*. In contrast, we took an empirical approach. In the norming task, subjects often indicate the category or categories to which they believe the concept belongs. In fact, the instructions state that this is a reasonable piece of information to provide. To determine the category memberships of the 549 concepts, we selected from the norms all concepts for which a superordinate category was produced. A superordinate category was included in our analyses if there were at least five concepts for which it was produced by at least one subject, and there were at least two concepts for which it was listed by more than four subjects. All concepts listed by at least one subject for a category were included as exemplars, with a few exceptions. First, the category of food has been tested in the category-specific deficits literature using only non-living things such as *cake* and *pie*. Therefore, we removed all fruits, vegetables, and fish, plus *rice* and *walnut*, from the food category. Second, jewellery was included because of its close relationship to gemstones, even though the norms included only four exemplars. Furthermore, the following categories were not used: bug was excluded because it is synonymous with insect, which was included; toy was excluded because although some subjects categorised concepts such as *car* as a toy, the features they listed pertained to real cars, rather than toy ones; and *car*, *chair*, and *gun* were excluded because they appeared as concepts in other categories. These selection criteria resulted in 37 categories, ranging in size from 132 exemplars (animal) to 4 exemplars (jewellery). One consequence of devising categories in this manner is that some concepts are included in multiple categories. An extreme example is *alligator*, which was included in the animal, reptile, carnivore, and predator categories. Furthermore, 119 non-living things were not included in any category. Note that when we present analyses that investigate the living–non-living distinction without regard to specific categories, all 549 concepts were included. The list of concepts by category is presented in Appendix B.

The fact that our set of norms includes a large number of concepts is an important aspect of this research because it enables the computation of more stable, reliable estimates of various factors than in previous research. Perhaps even more importantly however, the 37 categories that are a product of the breadth of coverage of the norms include most of those used in published studies of category-specific deficits. This allowed us to investigate whether feature correlations, feature types, and distinguishing features can account for behavioural phenomena at a more detailed level than the living–non-living distinction.

CATEGORY-LEVEL TRENDS IN IMPAIRMENTS

Although few studies have conducted systematic explorations of category-specific deficits on a category-by-category basis, there are sufficient results in the literature to establish some general trends in the patient data. We found ten articles that have investigated deficits by category (Caramazza & Shelton, 1998; Farah & Wallace, 1992; Hart, Berndt, & Caramazza, 1985; Hart & Gordon, 1992; Hillis & Caramazza, 1991; Hillis, Rapp, Romani, & Caramazza, 1990; Saachet & Humphreys, 1992; Silveri & Gainotti, 1988; Warrington & McCarthy, 1983; Warrington & Shallice, 1984). From these articles, we identified seven trends in the patterns of category-level deficits found in the patient data, that is, which categories tend to be impaired and preserved together.

(1) Creatures serve as one cluster of concepts (note that we use the term "creatures" to avoid ambiguity with "animals", which is one of the 37 categories).
(2) Non-living things (excepting musical instruments, foods, and gemstones) serve as a cluster.
(3) Fruit and vegetables cluster together.
(4) Fruit and vegetables sometimes pattern with creatures and sometimes with non-living things in terms of impairment.
(5) Foods can be impaired along with living things.
(6) Musical instruments can be impaired along with living things.
(7) Gemstones can be impaired along with living things.

We chose to address these trends because our norms include creatures, fruit, vegetables, a number of non-living thing categories, musical instruments, and foods. Although the norms do not contain gemstones *per se*, they do include four exemplars of jewellery, which we hoped would be sufficiently similar to gemstones that they might provide some insight. We were unable to comment on an additional trend, namely that body parts can be impaired along with non-living things, because the norms do not currently include body parts.

In the remainder of the chapter, we investigate whether feature correlations, feature types, and/or distinguishing features can account for the basic living–non-living distinction, and for the seven category-level trends. To foreshadow our results, we find that: (i) feature correlations may be part of the story, but certainly are not all of it; (ii) analyses based on 28 feature types account both for the living–non-living distinction and the category-level trends; and (iii) distinguishing features provide further insight into the living–non-living distinction and the category-level patient data, particularly with respect to the prevalence of various patterns of deficits.

FEATURE CORRELATIONS

Since the 1970s, feature correlations have been central to theories of concepts and categories. For example, Rosch (1978) claimed that correlations among features form the basis of concepts, and Rosch et al. (1976) claimed that the basic level of conceptual representation is special because it corresponds to the level at which feature correlations best cohere within categories and distinguish among them. For these reasons, Malt and Smith (1984) stated that understanding feature correlations is key to understanding concepts and categorisation. In the remainder of this article, the term "feature correlation" refers to the fact that a pair of features are correlated if they tend to appear in the same basic-level concepts. For example, < flies > and < has feathers > are correlated because they occur together in things like robins, sparrows, and eagles.[2]

We have approached the question of how feature correlations could influence the computation of word meaning from the perspective provided by a distributed attractor network metaphor. Attractor networks are interactive, parallel processing models in which distributed representations form the basis for constructing stable states in a multidimensional state space. In such models, a word's meaning can be represented as a pattern of activation across a set of semantic features, and concepts are computed online as unique patterns of activation. During training, if the units representing two features are connected, the weight between those features is strengthened each time that

---

[2] The term "feature correlations" has also been used in the literature (Tyler & Moss, 1997) to refer to the form–functional correlations predominantly found in artefacts (< is sharp > < used for cutting >) and the correlations between perceptual and what Tyler and colleagues have termed biological functional features predominantly found in living things (< has eyes > < sees >). Garrard et al. (1999) referred to these as inter- and intra-correlations, respectively. These are discussed in the General Discussion on page 237.

the model is trained on a concept that includes both of those features. These weights directly influence the trajectory that the model follows through state space as it settles to an attractor state corresponding to the meaning of a word (McRae et al., 1997). Note that feature correlations also influence the computation of word meaning in attractor networks that do not include direct feature–feature weights, such as recurrent backpropagation (Cree, McRae, & McNorgan, 1999). Thus, attractor networks are a type of learning model that takes advantage of the statistical structure in the environment, of which feature correlations are an excellent example.

The attractor network approach led to the claim that feature correlations play a critical role in computing word meaning because they provide structure within semantics. This was in direct opposition to Forster's (1994) claim that distributed networks are not suitable candidate models of word meaning because they tend to function poorly with relatively arbitrary mappings, such as the mapping between word form (orthography or phonology) and word meaning in English and many other languages (particularly for monomorphemic words). However, Forster failed to take into account the structure/regularities present within the domains of orthography (certain letters tend to appear together), phonology (certain sounds tend to appear together), and semantics (certain features tend to appear together), each of which are a key source of regularity for lexical computations.

The claim that feature correlations are important for semantic computations is a major deviation from most theories of conceptual representation and word meaning (but see Billman & Heit [1988] and Billman & Knutson [1996] for incidental concept learning models that focus on feature correlations). In fact, feature correlations play no role in any current account based on spreading activation networks. In a semantic network model, encoding feature correlations requires linking every feature with every other feature, weighted by the degree of correlation (Smith & Medin, 1981). Crucially, researchers from this view contend that linking two features requires explicitly noticing that they are related. Therefore, this operation is deemed computationally intractable because the environment includes a huge number of possible feature pairs (Murphy & Wisniewski, 1989). In contrast, using an attractor network as the computational metaphor necessarily leads to learning statistical relationships between features.

McRae et al. (1997) began their investigation of feature correlations by collecting and analysing a set of feature norms that included 76 living thing and 114 non-living thing concepts (which is a proper subset of the current set). Using representations derived from those norms, the Pearson product moment correlation was calculated between feature pairs as expressed across the 190 basic-level concepts. (To avoid spurious correlations, this was restricted to features occurring in at least three concepts.) A large number of significant pairwise correlations were found (e.g. < flies > and < has feathers >

shared 43% of their variance), demonstrating that this form of semantic structure exists.

To test for the role of feature correlations in online computations, McRae et al. (1997) used a speeded feature verification task in which a concept name such as *deer* was presented for a short duration, followed by a feature name such as <hunted by people>. The subject's task was to indicate whether the feature was reasonably true of the concept. The variable of interest was the strength with which the target feature <hunted by people> was correlated with the remaining features of a concept, *deer* in this case. This variable, termed intercorrelational strength, was calculated by summing the proportion of shared variance between <hunted by people> and each of the other features of *deer* with which it was significantly correlated. Regression analyses using nine independent variables that were most likely to influence feature verification latency showed that intercorrelational strength was the best predictor, and that it predicted a significant proportion of the residual variance even after the other eight variables were forced into the regression equation. Combining this with the finding that intercorrelational strength did not predict off-line feature typicality ratings ("How typical is feature X for concept Y, on a scale of 1 to 9?"), McRae et al. (1997) concluded that feature correlations play a key role in the mechanism that computes word meaning.

McRae, Cree, Westmacott, and de Sa (1999) furthered this research using a group-wise ANOVA design. In their Experiment 1, they paired two concepts with a target feature that was strongly intercorrelated with the features of one of the concepts (<hunted by people> *deer*), but weakly intercorrelated with the features of the other (<hunted by people> *duck*). Nine variables that might influence verification latency were equated. Subjects verified the target feature more quickly when it was strongly intercorrelated with the other features of a concept, and the effect was larger when the concept name was presented for 300 ms prior to the feature name than when it was presented 2000 ms prior. McRae et al.'s (1999) Experiment 2 was identical except that two features were paired with a single concept (<is sharp> versus <is pointed> for *dagger*) and the feature name was presented prior to the concept name. In this case, the effect of feature correlations was larger for a long than for a short stimulus onset asynchrony (SOA: the time between the onset of the first stimulus, the feature name in Experiment 2, and the onset of the second stimulus, the concept name). The results were predicted by a connectionist attractor network in which correlated features play a key role in computing word meaning. Perhaps the most compelling aspect of the simulations was that the model predicted the contrasting interactions between intercorrelational strength and SOA.

Feature correlations in living versus non-living things

When McRae et al. (1997) analysed their feature norms, they found support for the claims of Gelman (1988) and Keil (1989) that living things tend to cohere around clusters of intercorrelated features whereas non-living things are less likely to do so. In other words, feature correlations were, overall, more plentiful and strong within living things. McRae et al. (1997) illustrated the role of feature correlations in living versus non-living things by conducting a short SOA semantic priming experiment using 36 living (*eagle–hawk*) and 54 non-living (*couch–sofa*) thing pairs. Priming effects for non-living things were predicted by similarity calculated in term of individual features, whereas similarity in terms of correlated feature pairs did not predict a significant proportion of the residual variance. In contrast, living thing priming effects were not predicted by similarity in terms of individual features, but were predicted by correlated features. Thus, because features are more densely intercorrelated for living than for non-living things, feature correlations have a stronger influence on the computation of living thing concepts. This experiment was also simulated using a connectionist attractor network.

Given that correlated features play a key role in semantic processing, and that their role differs quantitatively for living versus non-living things, it has been hypothesised that they are important for explaining category-specific deficits. For example, they were a key part of Devlin et al.'s (1998) account of category-specific deficits in patients with Alzheimer's disease (AD). Category-specific deficits are most often explained in terms of differential damage to a specific type of feature: perceptual in the case of living things, functional in the case of non-living things (Farah & McClelland, 1991). Because perceptual and functional features are assumed to be stored in separate areas of the brain (temporolimbic and frontoparietal, respectively), lesions localised to either region may preferentially damage one type of information, resulting in a category-specific impairment. Localised damage is compatible with some forms of neuropathology, such as herpes encephalitis. However, category-specific deficits have also been observed in patients with AD, a disease that causes more widespread, patchy damage in areas that typically include both temporolimbic and frontoparietal regions (Garrard, Patterson, Watson, & Hodges, 1998; Gonnerman et al., 1997; Silveri & Gainotti, 1988). Therefore, it is difficult to imagine how widespread damage could result in category-specific deficits without implicating other factors. Devlin et al. (1998) provided an account of category-specific impairments in AD using a model similar to that of McRae et al. (1997). To explain the simulation results, Devlin et al. appealed to differences in the density of correlated features for living versus non-living things, and the patterns of distinguishing features in the two domains.

Given the role that feature correlations have played in some accounts of category-specific deficits, we began our analyses by using the expanded set of norms to test whether they discriminate between living and non-living things. Table 8.1 presents a number of relevant statistics for the 206 living thing and 343 non-living thing concepts. Although in McRae et al.'s (1997) norms living things possessed a non-significantly greater number of features than did non-living things, this difference is robust in the larger set of norms. Furthermore, a greater percentage (and raw number) of the features of living than non-living things occur in three or more concepts (recall that this was the criterion for inclusion in the correlational analyses). The remainder of Table 8.1 presents three measures showing that the features of living things tend to be more correlated than those of non-living things. First, there are a greater number of significantly correlated feature pairs per living thing. Second, even if the number of features possessed by at least three concepts was equated, there would still be a greater number of correlated feature pairs for living things because the percentage of correlated pairs expressed in terms of the number of possible pairs is greater for living things. (Note that Garrard et al., 2001, reported significantly lower percentages of correlated feature pairs. However, their results presumably occurred because their small set of norms did not include sufficient numbers of concepts that overlapped in features in the manner necessary to discover the correlations.) Finally, mean intercorrelational density of a concept was calculated by summing the proportion of shared variance for all of its significantly correlated feature pairs. This provides a measure of how strongly a concept's features cluster, and is greater on average for living things. For example, *trout* contains 30 correlated feature pairs and has an intercorrelational density of 926, whereas *clock* contains only 1 correlated pair, and its intercorrelational density is only 13. In summary, these analyses replicate those of McRae et al. (1997) by showing that

TABLE 8.1
Feature correlation statistics for living versus non-living things

Dependent variable	Living		Non-living		$t(547)$
	M	SE	M	SE	
Features	14.1	0.3	12.3	0.2	5.6
Features in ≥ 3 concepts	10.9	0.2	7.1	0.2	14.2
% features in ≥ 3 concepts	78	1	58	1	13.1
Correlated feature pairs	18.2	0.9	6.4	0.4	13.1
% possible correlated pairs	31	1	22	1	6.1
Intercorrelational density	427	23	135	11	13.2

All t's are 2-tailed and significant at the .0001 level.

the features of living things are more densely intercorrelated than those of non-living things.

Feature correlations and the seven trends

To investigate whether feature correlations can account for the seven category-level trends described above, the 37 categories were sorted in descending order in terms of the mean percentage of correlated feature pairs per concept for each category (Table 8.2). To assist in understanding this analysis, the categories are labelled by seven sets: creatures, non-living things, fruit/vegetables, musical instruments, jewellery, food, and trees (the importance of which will become apparent). The most noticeable aspect of Table 8.2 is that there exists a great deal of variance within each domain, so that the sets do not group cleanly. For example, the creatures and non-living things are separated for the most part, but insects, amphibians, and reptiles have a low percentage of correlated feature pairs, whereas fashion accessories, clothing, and buildings have a high percentage. Furthermore, three of the fruit/vegetable categories are dense in terms of correlated feature pairs (as are trees and food), whereas plant is ranked 20th of 37. Finally, Table 8.2 might provide some insight into two counterintuitive results. Both musical instruments and jewellery are firmly embedded within the creatures and fruit/vegetables in terms of percentage of correlated feature pairs. Therefore, this might be one reason why these categories have been found to pattern with living things in terms of patients' deficits. In summary, although ranking categories in terms of feature correlations mirrors some of the key phenomena in the category-specific deficits literature, it fails to mirror others.

Our experiments and accompanying simulations with normal adults demonstrate that feature correlations play an important role in computing word meaning. Furthermore, because this variable quantitatively distinguishes between living and non-living things, it might be a factor underlying category-specific deficits, as suggested by Devlin et al.'s (1998) simulations. In addition, the manner in which feature correlation statistics vary by category suggests that it might be useful for understanding how impairments pattern on a category-level basis. One particularly interesting aspect of feature correlations is that they can be implicated without invoking arguments based on differential brain regions, and so are equally applicable to patients with focal or diffuse lesions. However, we agree with Shelton and Caramazza (1999) that although feature correlations might be part of an explanation of category-specific deficits, they are not sufficient to account for all relevant behavioural phenomena. Finally, it could be the case that these analyses fail to address potential influences of feature correlations, a point to which we return in the General Discussion (see p. 237).

TABLE 8.2
Categories sorted by percentage correlated feature pairs

Set	Category	Correlated feature pairs (%)
Tree	Tree	46.8
Creature	Fish	44.9
Non-living	Fashion accessory	41.0
Fruit/vegetable	Fruit	39.8
Creature	Bird	37.8
Non-living	Clothing	37.0
Non-living	Building	36.3
Fruit/vegetable	Root/tuber	32.1
Fruit/vegetable	Vegetable	30.8
Creature	Herbivore	30.6
Musical instrument	Musical instrument	29.9
Creature	Animal	29.8
Non-living	Appliance	29.6
Jewellery	Jewellery	29.0
Creature	Mammal	28.8
Creature	Pet	28.6
Creature	Scavenger	28.2
Creature	Predator	28.2
Fruit/vegetable	Plant	28.0
Creature	Carnivore	27.1
Creature	Seafood	25.0
Food	Food	25.0
Non-living	Furniture	24.2
Non-living	Weapon	23.8
Non-living	Vehicle	22.8
Creature	Rodent	21.4
Non-living	Container	19.9
Non-living	House	19.4
Non-living	Instrument	18.6
Non-living	Tool	17.8
Creature	Reptile	16.8
Non-living	Utensil	16.4
Creature	Amphibian	16.2
Non-living	Boat	16.0
Non-living	Shelter	15.0
Non-living	Machine	14.6
Creature	Insect	9.6

FEATURE TYPES

In this section, a number of analyses are presented to shed light on the relationship between type of knowledge (e.g. visual, functional) and category-specific deficits. Numerous researchers have claimed that feature type is key to explaining these deficits, and thus are an important determinant of the organisation of semantic memory. A number of researchers have argued that category-specific deficits can be explained in terms of damage to a semantic memory system that is organised by modality (Farah & McClelland, 1991; Warrington & McCarthy, 1987; Warrington & Shallice, 1984). Deficits can reflect differential weighting of information from various sensorimotor channels in the representations of living and non-living things. Therefore, deficits might not be living–non-living in their nature, but rather, sensory/functional, a viewpoint that Shelton and Caramazza (1999) claim is the currently received view of category-specific deficits. This theory has developed from Warrington and colleagues' proposal that there might be dissociable meaning systems corresponding to various sensory modalities. This notion seems plausible on the basis of current knowledge that distinct, yet interactive, brain areas are allotted to different modalities (Thompson-Schill et al., 1999). A key part of this proposal is the assumption that visual information is more important for the representations of living things, whereas functional information is more important for artefacts. Thus, a living thing deficit occurs if visual knowledge is disproportionately damaged, whereas a non-living thing deficit occurs if functional knowledge is disproportionately damaged.

Although this argument is intuitively appealing, little empirical evidence has been provided to support it. Perhaps the strongest evidence comes from Farah and McClelland (1991), who had subjects read dictionary definitions of 48 living and 48 non-living things and underline each occurrence of visual or functional descriptors, where functional was defined as "what the item does or what it is for". They found that the ratio of visual to functional features was substantially greater for living than for non-living things, thus discriminating between domains. Furthermore, these ratios were used as the basis for representations in a connectionist model that, when damaged, simulated a number of primary behavioral phenomena associated with category-specific deficits.

However, this research has been a point of controversy, primarily due to issues concerning how to partition among types of knowledge. For example, it is unclear whether the relevant classification should include visual features only (Farah & McClelland, 1991), or all sensory features (e.g. texture, smell, taste; Devlin et al., 1998; Shelton & Caramazza, 1999; Warrington & McCarthy, 1983). In an analogous fashion, functional features could be defined in terms of a narrow view (what it is used for), a slightly wider view such as that of Farah and McClelland (what it does and what it is used for), or an even wider view (what it is used for, how it is used, who typically uses it, where it is typically used, when it is typically used, and what it does). Perhaps all non-sensory aspects of people's knowledge should be taken into account, including what many researchers have termed encyclopedic knowledge (Shelton & Caramazza, 1999). Due to these uncertainties, feature types have been defined in a number of ways: Warrington and McCarthy discriminated between sensory and a relatively narrow view of functional features, Shelton and Caramazza between sensory and non-sensory features, and Laws, Evans, Hodges, and McCarthy (1995) between visual and associative features, to cite a few.

Because of this uncertainty, Caramazza and Shelton (1998) replicated Farah and McClelland's (1991) dictionary definition experiment with one important change; they asked subjects to underline either sensory or non-sensory descriptors. The resulting ratio of sensory to non-sensory descriptors was similar for the two domains, leading them to conclude that there was insufficient evidence for the sensory/functional hypothesis. In addition, Shelton and Caramazza (1999) presented further arguments that feature type is insufficient to account for the patterns of impairments found in category-specific deficits, including its inability to account for category-level behavioural phenomena.

Feature types in living versus non-living things

Given this controversy and the importance of feature types in theories of category-specific deficits, we replicated and extended previous results using our norms. Having subjects produce features in a norming task is less constrained than having them underline features in dictionary definitions, in that it is independent of lexicographers' intuitions regarding the information that is important to defining a concept. Due in part to this concern, Devlin et al. (1998) calculated feature type statistics from feature production norms that included 30 living and 30 non-living things. They used the same definition of functional features as did Farah and McClelland (1991), but counted sensory rather than visual features. They found a muted, but present, living–non-living difference. Although Devlin et al.'s ratios were based on feature norms collected in an identical fashion to our own, it is interesting to replicate the results with our much larger set.

Given that feature types have been defined in various ways, we calculated feature type ratios based on multiple definitions: visual features only; sensory features; a narrow view of functional features (what it is used for); a view of functional features that matches Devlin et al. (1998) and Farah and McClelland (1991; what it is used for, plus what it does); a wider view of functional features (what it is used for, what it does, how it is used, who uses it, and when it is used); and all non-sensory features (all features except sensory features). The resulting ratios can be found in Table 8.3, along with those of Caramazza and Shelton (1998), Devlin et al. (1998) and Farah and McClelland (1991). The crucial result is that feature type discriminates between living and non-living things only if the definition of functional features is narrow, more narrow even than that of Farah and McClelland. If

TABLE 8.3
Feature type ratios for living versus non-living things

Ratio	Living	Non-living
Farah and McClelland (1991)	7.7:1	1.4:1
Devlin et al. (1998)	3.0:1	1.4:1
Caramazza and Shelton (1998)	1.2:1	1.0:1
Visual: functional–narrow	5.6:1	1.5:1
Sensory: functional–narrow	6.4:1	2.2:1
Visual: functional–FM	1.9:1	1.2:1
Sensory: functional–FM	2.1:1	1.9:1
Visual: functional–wide	1.6:1	0.9:1
Sensory: functional–wide	1.8:1	1.4:1
Visual: non-sensory	0.7:1	0.5:1
Sensory: non-sensory	0.8:1	0.8:1

Functional–narrow, what it is used for; functional–FM, Farah and McClelland's (1991) definition; Functional–wide, what it is used for, how it is used, who uses it, when it is used, and what it does

the functional or non-sensory features include an entity's characteristic behaviours (what it does) or other non-sensory features, the ratios no longer discriminate. Therefore, these analyses support Shelton and Caramazza's (1999) claims that a dichotomous distinction along these lines does not illuminate our understanding of category-specific deficits.

On the other hand, it might be argued that the analyses presented in Table 8.3 should be considered in a positive light because the ratios calculated in terms of the narrow definition of functional features do differentiate between domains. Thus, these analyses could be viewed as successful because the narrow definition of functional features perhaps best matches the notion of what might be encoded within representations tied to the motor modality. Therefore, rather than dismissing feature type, we investigated it further by sorting the 37 categories on the basis of their visual:functional–narrow and sensory:functional–narrow ratios. The results of the sensory:functional–narrow sort are presented in Table 8.4. The visual:functional–narrow sort is not presented because it was virtually identical.

The first thing to note from Table 8.4 is that the top 12 categories are all creatures, with seafood (14th) and fish (18th) slightly separated from the others; thus, creatures are grouped together. The non-living things are also reasonably well grouped, with a tendency for low rankings. There is a substantial middle section, however, in which the fruit/vegetables are mixed with the non-living things. This is a positive result because fruit/vegetables are distinguished from creatures, but a negative result in that they are not distinguished from non-living things, and thus are not well grouped. A further

TABLE 8.4
Categories sorted by sensory : functional–narrow

Set	Category	Sensory:functional–narrow
Creature	Carnivore	115.0
Creature	Insect	66.0
Creature	Scavenger	55.0
Creature	Predator	47.5
Creature	Reptile	35.5
Creature	Amphibian	35.0
Creature	Rodent	23.0
Creature	Bird	22.7
Creature	Pet	22.0
Creature	Herbivore	18.8
Creature	Animal	11.7
Creature	Mammal	9.9
Jewellery	Jewellery	8.3
Creature	Seafood	5.0
Non-living	House	4.8
Fruit/vegetable	Fruit	4.7
Non-living	Shelter	4.3
Creature	Fish	4.1
Musical instrument	Musical instrument	3.9
Non-living	Clothing	3.7
Fruit/vegetable	Plant	3.6
Tree	Tree	3.6
Non-living	Fashion accessory	3.6
Food	Food	3.5
Non-living	Vehicle	3.0
Fruit/vegetable	Vegetable	2.5
Fruit/vegetable	Root/tuber	2.2
Non-living	Furniture	2.2
Non-living	Machine	2.2
Non-living	Boat	1.9
Non-living	Weapon	1.9
Non-living	Utensil	1.7
Non-living	Building	1.6
Non-living	Container	1.6
Non-living	Appliance	1.5
Non-living	Tool	1.5
Non-living	Instrument	1.5

positive result is that musical instruments and jewellery are highly ranked, in line with the fact that they sometimes pattern with the living things in the patient data. However, a number of other non-living thing categories are also intermingled (house, shelter, clothing, fashion accessory, and vehicle). Finally, note the variation within sets. The sensory: functional–narrow ratios of the creatures vary from 115:1 (carnivore) to 3:1 (fish). The non-living thing categories vary to a lesser degree because the maximum was 3.6:1 (house), with the minimum being 1.47:1 (instrument).

These analyses show that feature type can, to some extent, discriminate between domains and among categories in the appropriate ways. However, many feature types were omitted, so the exclusion of a great deal of people's knowledge about living and non-living things might be viewed as unnecessary and ill-advised. In fact, because so much information is excluded, it could be argued that the narrow definition of function needed to obtain these results compromises the theory in that it fails to shed maximal light on the organisation of semantic memory. Therefore, the questions of whether feature type provides insight into category-specific deficits, and whether it is one dimension along which semantic memory is organised, remain open.

A detailed classification by feature type

To further investigate these issues, more detailed feature-type analyses were conducted by dividing features into finer-grained classes and investigating whether they provide the information relevant to accounting for category-specific deficits. We classified each feature in the norms in terms of Wu and Barsalou's (2002, henceforth referred to as WB) taxonomy. This taxonomy is valuable for two main reasons. First, it is the most detailed and sophisticated method available for classifying features. Second, it offers an independent means of classifying features in that it was not developed with category-specific deficits in mind. Instead, it was developed to understand the role of what Wu and Barsalou call "perceptual simulations", whereby, as a natural consequence of thinking about entities and objects, people construct images of them and the situations within which they typically occur. In developing this feature set, Wu and Barsalou took the following factors into consideration (Barsalou, personal communication, December 1999):

(1) The set of feature types is designed to cover the tremendous variety of features that subjects generate when describing conceptual content.

(2) It is designed to capture the wide variety of information found in ontological kinds (Keil, 1989), and in event frames and verb arguments (Barsalou, 1992; Fillmore, 1968; Schank & Abelson, 1977).

(3) It is designed to correspond systematically to the modality-specific regions of the brain (e.g. motor, somatosensory, and visual cortices).

(4) The feature types for entities reflect well-established channels of sensory information in perception (e.g. shape, surface, occlusion, movement).

(5) The feature types reflect aspects of introspective experience, as well as aspects of sensorimotor experience.

In addition to this taxonomy being developed independently of issues regarding category-specific deficits, we classified our features 3 years ago on the basis of this taxonomy to better understand our norms, and then only later decided to apply it to category-specific deficits (we applied an earlier, slightly different version of the taxonomy to a subset of the current set of normed concepts).

The WB taxonomy partitions features into four major types (entity, situation, taxonomic, and introspective features), and then subdivides these. The list of feature types is presented in Appendix C, with a short explanation of each and examples taken from our norms. For our set of concepts, a few minor modifications were necessary. First, we added the feature type "made-of" because it was a frequently listed type of feature and did not fit into any existing WB feature type. Second, the ontological features were combined with the superordinate features to avoid introducing a living–non-living distinction. Third, abstract features were coded as systemic features (*bread* <is nutritious>) due to their close relationship. Finally, no spatial relations, situation quantities, situation events, situation states of the world, representational states, introspective quantities, repetitions, or meta-comments occurred in our norms, so these knowledge types were omitted.

The first question concerns whether the 28 WB feature types provide bases for discriminating between living and non-living things. The total number of each type for the living and non-living things is presented in Table 8.5, along with the mean number per concept and the ratio of those means. The living:non-living ratios are at least 2:1 for entity behaviours, internal surface features, quantities, manners, origins, cognitive operations, and superordinates. Conversely, the non-living:living ratios are at least 2:1 for the feature types made-of, function, action, participant, associated entity, time, contingency, and subordinate. Thus, there are a number of bases on which the domains are discriminated. Also note the differences in total numbers of features of each type. For example, there were numerous external surface features and functional features listed in the norms, whereas there were few origin and subordinate features.

Feature types and the seven trends

Given that a detailed analysis of feature type uncovered a number of bases for the living–non-living distinction, we conducted cluster analyses to investigate whether it might account for the seven category-level phenomena in the patient data. We constructed a matrix in which the 37 categories were represented in terms of salience of each of the 28 WB feature types. In this matrix, each element corresponds to the total number of features of that type possessed by the category's exemplars. For example, 133 function features were listed for the tools, so the tool–function element had a value of 133. Thus, the

TABLE 8.5
Total, mean per concept, and living:non-living ratio of features for WB feature types

Code	Feature type	Living		Non-living		Ratio of means (LT:NLT)
		Sum	*Mean*	*Sum*	*Mean*	
eae	Associated abstract entity	0	0.00	14	0.04	–
eb	Entity behaviour	392	1.90	147	0.43	4.4:1
ece	External component	463	2.25	433	1.26	1.8:1
ese	External surface feature	501	2.43	654	1.91	1.3:1
esi	Internal surface feature	115	0.56	85	0.25	2.2:1
eci	Internal component	75	0.36	118	0.34	1.1:1
em	Made-of	2	0.01	460	1.34	1:134.0
eq	Quantity	105	0.51	84	0.24	2.1:1
esys	Systemic feature	102	0.50	131	0.38	1.3:1
ew	Larger whole	6	0.03	9	0.03	1:1
sf	Function	197	0.96	830	2.42	1:2.5
sl	Location	249	1.21	231	0.67	1.8:1
sm	Manner	28	0.14	3	0.01	14.0:1
sor	Origin	36	0.17	22	0.06	2.8:1
sp	Participant	43	0.21	146	0.43	1:2.1
sa	Action	26	0.13	156	0.45	1:3.5
se	Associated entity	28	0.14	118	0.34	1:2.4
st	Time	18	0.09	65	0.19	1:2.1
ch	Superordinate	394	1.91	221	0.64	3.0:1
cc	Coordinate	12	0.06	37	0.11	1:1.8
ci	Individual	2	0.01	1	0.00	–
cl	Subordinate	9	0.04	29	0.08	1:2.0
cs	Synonym	8	0.04	24	0.07	1:1.8
ic	Contingency	12	0.06	94	0.27	1:4.5
ie	Evaluation	40	0.19	61	0.18	1.1:1
in	Negation	11	0.05	10	0.03	1.7:1
io	Cognitive operation	16	0.08	11	0.03	2.7:1
ia	Affect emotion	6	0.03	9	0.03	1:1

LT:NLT, living thing:non-living thing

37 categories were represented in terms of the salience of each feature type. An important consequence of coding vectors by feature type is that the resulting representation carries information about feature similarity. In representations based on individual features, such as those used in extant distributed models of semantic memory, the degree to which features are similar is not represented in any direct manner (although it may be represented to some extent in terms of feature correlations). For example, if each feature is represented by a separate node, <made of cotton> is as similar to <has wings> as it is to <made of wool>. In contrast, coding by feature type registers feature similarity at this level.

The WB category representations were entered into an average-linkage between-groups hierarchical cluster analysis using SPSS. This method of forming clusters begins by treating each of the 37 categories as a separate cluster, and then agglomerating categories, based on the average distances of all members in each cluster. Thus, categories and the resulting clusters are grouped together based on overall similarity of entire clusters, and not just the nearest or farthest neighbours of clusters, as some other methods do. Cosine, a measure of the angle between the category vector representations (the inner product of two vectors divided by the product of the vector lengths), was used as the measure of similarity. Comparable results were found using other clustering algorithms and measures of similarity. The resultant dendogram is presented in Figure 8.1. A dendogram such as this represents similarity in two basic ways. The distance between the terminal symbols (category names in this case) generally reflects the similarity between them. For example, clothing is directly above fashion accessory, and amphibian is directly above reptile. However, the more reliable indicator of similarity is the distance at which categories or clusters of categories are joined. The closer that the line joining two clusters is to 0 on the scale at the top of Figure 8.1, the more similar are the clusters. Note that this scale can be treated as arbitrary, except that 0 indicates identical clusters whereas 25 indicates minimal cluster similarity for this data set. The first thing to note is the existence of definable clusters corresponding to creatures, fruit/vegetables, and non-living things, respecting the tripartite division often found in category-specific deficits (Shelton & Caramazza, 1999). In addition, the cluster analysis closely mirrors the seven category-level trends.

To gain insight into how the WB feature type analysis accounts for category-specific deficits, we began by normalising the representations for the 37 categories, which corrects for differences in the raw number of concepts and features in the categories and is part of the cosine measure used in the cluster analysis. The variance of each feature type was then calculated across the 37 categories. A feature type's variance is related directly to its influence on the cluster results; if the cases (categories) do not vary on a variable (feature type), then there is no basis on which to differentiate among the cases and thus cluster them. Variance was greatest for functions, entity behaviours, made-of features, external components, internal components, superordinates, locations, external surface features, and internal surface features. The variance decreased by half from the internal surface features, which we included when investigating why the cluster analysis was successful, to the first excluded feature type—systemic features. Furthermore, when a principal components analysis was conducted on the same category by feature type representations, eight of these nine feature types loaded on the first three components, with locations being the exception (it dominated the fifth component). Therefore, those eight feature types were used to provide insight into the results of the cluster analysis (as suggested by the principal components

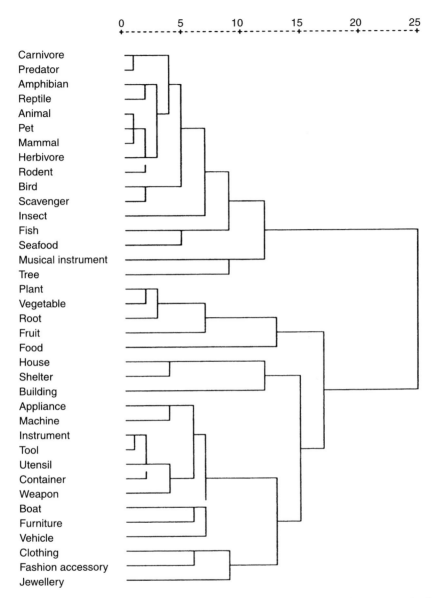

Figure 8.1. Cluster analysis based on the number of each of the 28 WB feature types in the 37 categories.

analysis, locations did not discriminate among categories in a coherent manner). These feature types comprised 74% of the total number of features relevant to the cluster analysis.

Creatures

The 14 creature categories cluster at the top of Figure 8.1. The creatures possess few functions (the 14 creature categories were among the 15 lowest ranked categories; creatures serve few functions for people), many entity behaviours (they were among the 16 highest; creatures do many things on their own), no made-of features at all (we do not think of a creature as "made of something"), a large number of superordinates (13 of the creature categories were among the 17 highest ranked categories; the categories in which creatures belong are relatively obvious and salient), and few internal surface features (no internal surface features were listed in the norms for 10 of the 14 categories because this information is not salient). Finally, 11 of the 14 highest ranked categories in terms of external components were living things (creatures possess many salient external parts). However, the creatures were not distinguished from non-living things on the basis of external surface features or internal components. That external surface features played little role in discriminating the sets of categories is somewhat surprising given the role that sensory features have played in theories of category-specific deficits.

Non-living things

The 15 non-living thing categories cluster at the bottom of Figure 8.1. The non-living things are, of course, high on functions; the top ten categories are all non-living things, with the remaining five categories intermingled with the fruit/vegetables. The made-of feature type perfectly distinguishes the non-living things from the other categories (what a non-living thing is made of is a salient aspect of them, but does not really apply to creatures or fruits and vegetables). The non-living things had few superordinate features; they comprised the lowest eleven categories on this feature type (the category that a non-living thing is a member of is typically less obvious). They are also separated from the creatures in terms of entity behaviours (non-living things tend to do little on their own), but again are mixed among the fruit/vegetables. They tend to possess fewer external components than do creatures, but they are not as well discriminated on the basis of this feature type. Finally, the non-living things were not distinguished from the other categories in terms of external surface features, internal components, or internal surface features.

Fruit/vegetables

There are two main results concerning the four fruit/vegetable categories; they cluster tightly, and they cluster at a late stage with the non-living rather than the living things. The fruit/vegetables are distinguished from the creatures and non-living things on the basis of internal surface features, with the four categories ranked second to fifth on this feature type (food being the top ranked). Furthermore, they are ranked fourth, seventh, eighth, and ninth in terms of internal components. These results reflect the fact that the insides of fruit and vegetables are salient because people open them up and eat them. The fruit and vegetables cluster with the non-living rather than the living things because they are sprinkled throughout them on the basis of function (people cook, bake, and eat them), entity behaviours (they do very little on their own), and external components (they tend to have few external parts, other than, for example, a peel and a stem). Finally, the fruit/vegetables were distributed among the thirteen highest ranked categories in terms of external surface features, and were not distinguished from creatures and non-living things in terms of superordinates.

Food

Although food contained only non-living things such as *cake* and *pie*, it clusters with the fruit/vegetables. It groups with them in terms of function (people eat them), entity behaviours (they do very little on their own), and internal surface features (their inside is salient because it is a major factor determining whether or not they are good to eat). Food clusters somewhat later with the fruit/vegetables because it deviates from them in terms of having a greater number of made-of features (an apple is not made of something, but a cake is), and fewer internal components (cakes and pies have few internal parts). Thus, the cluster analysis indicates that food may be impaired with living things because of its close relationship to fruit and vegetables in terms of salient feature types.

Musical instruments

This category serves as a valuable test case because it has often been found, counterintuitively, to pattern with living things. As in the patient data, musical instruments cluster with the creatures in the WB cluster analysis. This occurs because musical instruments are relatively low in functional features, where they are ranked between the living and non-living things (they are used for basically one reason, to play music). They are high in entity behaviours, ranking with the creatures, primarily due to the sounds that they make. It is interesting to note that when Tranel et al. (1997) conducted principal component analyses based on subjects' ratings of a number of dimensions of living and non-living things, they found that sounds are important for discriminating between categories. Musical instruments are ranked higher than all but one non-living thing category in terms of external surface features, and all but two in terms of superordinates. Finally, they are in the middle of the non-living things on made-of features, external components, and internal surface features.

Jewellery

We had hoped that jewellery might be an interesting test case because of its close relationship to gemstones, which have been found to pattern with living things in some patients. However, possibly because it is not a satisfactory proxy for gemstones, or because there were only four exemplars, jewellery clusters with the non-living things. Although it groups with creatures in terms of functions, it groups with non-living things on a number of other feature types, including entity behaviours, internal surface features, and made-of features.

A prediction: trees, bushes, flowers, and grass

The tree category is an interesting case because it clusters with the musical instruments, and hence with the creatures. Intuitively, one would think that trees, being a type of plant, should cluster with the fruit/vegetables; trees group with fruit/vegetables on the basis of external surface features, on which it is ranked third. However, it deviates sharply from the fruit/vegetables in terms of internal components and internal surface features, because people do not open up trees to eat them. Trees group with the creatures in terms of made-of features, superordinates, internal components, and functions, and with the non-living things in terms of entity behaviours (they are perceived to do little on their own). Therefore, an interesting prediction from this analysis is that plants that people do not eat, and thus serve few functions and do not possess salient internal characteristics, might pattern with creatures rather than fruit and vegetables in terms of impairments.

In summary, as Shelton and Caramazza (1999) have claimed, theories based on the notion of a binary classification of feature types do not appear to account for category-specific deficits in a manner that provides a great deal of insight into the organisation of semantic memory. In contrast, a detailed analysis of feature types using an independently motivated taxonomy shows that this variable can account for the broad living–non-living distinction, and provide insight into the seven category-level trends in the category-specific deficits literature that we were able to address with our present set of feature norms. Thus, these analyses can be taken as evidence that semantic memory is organised by type of knowledge both in the mind and brain.

DISTINGUISHING FEATURES

Distinguishing features (and their complement, shared features) have played a role in accounting for a number of primary empirical phenomena regarding normal subjects' performance in semantic tasks, such as typicality judgements (Rosch & Mervis, 1975), similarity judgements (Tversky's contrast rule, 1977), and semantic verification (Smith, Shoben, & Rips, 1974). Distinguishing features correspond to the aspects of people's knowledge that discriminate among or between similar concepts. For example, a feature such as <moos> is highly distinguishing, whereas <eats> is not. Distinguishing features may be crucial to understanding category-specific deficits because most tasks used to establish the existence of these deficits, such as picture naming, word to picture matching, and definitions to words, require distinguishing a specific concept from among similar ones. That is, to properly identify something as a zebra rather than a horse requires preserved knowledge of the features that distinguish them. Therefore, given the probabilistic nature of brain damage, the likelihood that a patient can discriminate a concept from among similar ones is related to the number or proportion of a concept's features that are distinguishing.

An important aspect of analyses of distinguishing features is that they provide information that is lacking in analyses of feature types. Unless a theory concerning how feature types map onto brain regions is coupled with a theory of why brain regions containing certain types of knowledge are more or less vulnerable to damage, feature type provides no information regarding what patterns of impairment are more or less likely to occur. Therefore, we investigated whether distinguishing features can account for an additional trend in the patient data, namely, that patients exhibiting living thing impairments are more frequent than those who show a greater impairment in their knowledge of non-living things.

Distinguishing features in living versus non-living things

To investigate whether distinguishing features make appropriate predictions for the living–non-living distinction, we calculated the percentage of a concept's features that are distinguishing. A distinguishing feature was defined as one that occurs in only one or two concepts in the norms (note that this is the complement to the 'greater than or equal to three concepts' criterion that was used for a feature to be included in the correlated features analysis). In concert with similar analyses conducted by Devlin et al. (1998) and Garrard et al. (2001) on smaller data sets, non-living things (42% of their features; 5.2 features per concept) possess a far greater percentage of distinguishing features than do living things (22% of their features; 3.2 features per concept).

TABLE 8.6
Categories sorted by percentage distinguishing features

Set	Category	Distinguishing features (%)
Creature	Herbivore	10.7
Creature	Fish	13.4
Creature	Bird	14.4
Creature	Seafood	16.2
Creature	Scavenger	16.4
Creature	Amphibian	17.6
Creature	Carnivore	17.7
Creature	Predator	18.1
Creature	Animal	19.6
Creature	Reptile	19.6
Creature	Rodent	19.8
Creature	Pet	20.1
Fruit/vegetable	Fruit	21.1
Creature	Mammal	23.6
Musical instrument	Musical instrument	24.7
Creature	Insect	25.2
Fruit/vegetable	Root/tuber	26.7
Fruit/vegetable	Vegetable	28.8
Fruit/vegetable	Plant	29.4
Tree	Tree	30.8
Non-living	Weapon	31.2
Non-living	Utensil	32.3
Non-living	Container	32.5
Non-living	Furniture	34.9
Non-living	Vehicle	35.7
Non-living	Clothing	37.7
Jewellery	Jewellery	41.2
Non-living	Tool	42.3
Non-living	Fashion accessory	42.8
Non-living	Machine	44.7
Non-living	House	44.8
Non-living	Boat	46.0
Food	Food	47.3
Non-living	Appliance	49.1
Non-living	Shelter	52.2
Non-living	Instrument	54.0
Non-living	Building	56.4

This difference provides insight into why numerous patients exhibit a greater impairment in their knowledge of living things, whereas few exhibit the opposite pattern.

Distinguishing features and the seven trends

As shown in Table 8.6, the 37 categories were sorted on the basis of the mean percentage of the exemplars' features that are distinguishing. This analysis groups the categories in a manner that corresponds well to the category-level trends in the patient data. Creatures possess a low percentage of distinguishing features; 12 of the 14 creature categories are the lowest ranked on this variable. The non-living thing categories are grouped perfectly in that each possesses a greater percentage of distinguishing features than any of the creature or fruit/vegetables categories. In addition, the fruit/vegetables group together, and are ranked between the creatures and non-living things.

The results for the food category are also interesting. In the WB cluster analysis, food clusters with the fruit/vegetables. Thus, on the basis of feature type, it seems unlikely that food would deviate from the fruit/vegetables in terms of impairment. However, if it did, the distinguishing features analysis suggests that food would be relatively preserved because its exemplars tend to possess a greater percentage of distinguishing features. In fact, Hart et al. (1985) reported data suggesting that foods can be spared when fruit and vegetables are relatively impaired.

A further positive result is that the distinguishing features analysis provides another reason why musical instruments might be impaired along with living things; they possess relatively few distinguishing features. This result coheres nicely with the WB feature type and correlated features analyses.

Finally, jewellery again appears to provide little insight into the gemstones deficits in that it is basically in the middle of the non-living things. In addition, the tree category sits at the junction of the fruit/vegetables and non-living things on this factor.

In summary, distinguishing features, which have been implicated in accounts of performance on various semantic tasks in normal individuals, capture the living–non-living distinction in a manner that matches the data in the category-specific deficits literature. Furthermore, distinguishing features account nicely for the category-level trends in the patient data.

GENERAL DISCUSSION

Like many other researchers, we believe that studies of category-specific semantic deficits provide a rich source of data for constraining theories of semantic memory. Furthermore, current evidence suggests that the empirical phenomena are more complex than the basic living–non-living distinction. The research to date has provided several stable trends in the patient data that can be interpreted in terms of damage to the normal semantic system. The major contribution of the present research is that we used a large set of norms to derive reliable quantitative estimates of feature correlations, feature types, and distinguishing features, and used those estimates to account for several category-level trends in the patient data.

The analyses provided a number of key results and some novel predictions. First, the living–non-living distinction was accounted for by WB feature types, distinguishing features, and correlated features. Furthermore, the distinguishing features analyses provide insight into why patients who exhibit a living thing impairment are reported more frequently than those who exhibit a non-living thing impairment. Note that the distinguishing and correlated features results replicate those of Garrard et al. (2001) and McRae et al. (1997). The novel and most compelling results are those associated with the category-level trends in the patient data. These complex patterns of category-specific deficits were accounted for by analyses based on WB feature types and distinguishing features, but not correlated features. In addition, the distinguishing features analysis demonstrated that certain categories, or sets of them, might be more or less vulnerable to damage, and that this pattern matches well with the patient data. It also showed why knowledge of food may be spared when knowledge of fruit/vegetables is relatively impaired. Finally, it is significant that the WB feature type and distinguishing features analyses provide mutually reinforcing results because, with respect to category-specific deficits, both the physical damage and the resulting behavioral phenomena are probabilistic in nature. For example, the creatures and non-living things were clearly discriminated in both analyses. The fruit/vegetables grouped well in both analyses, and did not group firmly with the creatures or non-living things in either. Furthermore, the musical instruments grouped with the creatures in both.

The analyses of the norms also provided two predictions. In the cluster analysis, trees grouped with creatures rather than fruit/vegetables. Therefore, we predict that knowledge of plants such as trees, bushes, flowers, and grass that serve few functions for humans, and thus do not possess salient internal components or internal surface features, might deviate from fruit/vegetables in terms of impairment. Note that no clear prediction regarding the relative frequency of patients that might have a trees impairment versus a fruit/vegetables impairment was provided by the distinguishing features analysis because the categories possessed a similar percentage of distinguishing features. A second prediction concerns the insect category. The insects clustered late with the creatures in the feature type analysis, possessed the highest percentage of distinguishing features of the creature categories, and possessed the lowest percentage of correlated feature pairs of any category. Therefore, it appears that patients might be found for which insects pattern differently from other creatures in terms of impairment.

WB types versus the visual (sensory)/ functional taxonomies

The WB feature type analyses suggest that semantic memory is organised by type of knowledge. This view coheres with recent evidence from neuroimaging studies suggesting that the semantic attributes of objects are stored close to the regions of the cortex that mediate their perception (Martin et al., 1995; Mummery, Patterson, Hodges, & Price, 1998; Thompson-Schill et al., 1999). Note that we are not arguing that each of the 28 WB feature types is represented in a different brain region. Rather, the taxonomy developed by Wu and Barsalou (2002) captures important facts regarding the organisation of semantic memory in the mind and brain.

Given the success of the WB taxonomy, it is important to note the key ways in which it differs from the sensory/functional taxonomies, both in terms of what feature types are included and what types are grouped together. One key difference is that in the WB analyses, entity behaviour discriminates creatures from non-living things, and is part of the explanation of why musical instruments can be impaired along with living things. In contrast, in a sensory/functional taxonomy, entity behaviour ("what it does") is included as functional knowledge, which obscures its role in accounting for the patient data (Farah & McClelland, 1991). A second important difference concerns the internal components and internal surface features, which are not treated as distinct feature types in a binary taxonomy. (It is unclear whether, in Farah and McClelland's analyses, for example, these types of features were excluded or formed a subset of the visual features.) These two feature types play a key role in grouping the fruit/vegetable categories, and in discriminating them from the creatures and non-living things. They were also a key reason why food clustered with the fruit/vegetables, and why trees clustered separately. Third, it is unclear whether the feature type made-of is included in various researchers' definitions of visual or sensory features. The cluster analysis shows that this type of feature reflects knowledge that discriminates among categories in key ways. Finally, one surprising aspect of the WB cluster analysis is that external surface features, which are presumably strongly related to the notions of visual and sensory features, played only a minor role in accounting for the category-level trends in the patient data. In summary, detailed analyses of feature types accounted for complex patterns of patient data that cannot be explained by binary taxonomies that exclude certain types of knowledge, or obscure differences among them.

Integrating the factors

Due to the complexity of the issues regarding the roles of feature correlations, feature types, and distinguishing features in accounts of semantic computations and category-specific deficits, we analysed the three factors separately, and our presentation mirrored this approach. However, these factors are interrelated in semantic memory, and one goal of further research should be to understand how and why they are related, and to clarify the representational and computational implications.

Although feature correlations play a role in the semantic computations of normal individuals, the present set of analyses suggests that they play a limited role in explanations of category-specific deficits. However, the role of feature correlations in understanding category-specific deficits may involve their interdependence with distinguishing features and feature types. For example, as suggested by Devlin et al. (1998) and Garrard et al. (2001), the notions of distinguishing and correlated features might best be considered as defining a continuum, rather than being separate variables. That is, it might be beneficial to consider a continuum that has the features that occur in only one concept at one end, those that appear in multiple concepts but are not part of clusters of co-occurring features in the middle of the continuum, and those that appear in multiple concepts in regular ways at the other end. Devlin et al. suggest that this continuum plays a role in understanding the aspects of people's knowledge that are relatively preserved or impaired across the time-course of a degenerative disease such as AD or semantic dementia.

We also expect interactions between feature correlations and feature types to play a role in explanations of category-specific semantic deficits. For example, the patterns of correlations within and between feature types such as external components, external surface features, internal components, internal surface features, entity behaviours, and functions might be important for understanding the structure of semantic memory. In a set of studies relevant to this issue, Moss, Tyler, and Jennings (1997) and Tyler and Moss (1997) have reported patient data suggesting that what they call "biological functional" information (e.g. that an animal <eats> and <breathes>; note that these are entity behaviours in the WB taxonomy) can be better preserved following neurological impairment than other associative functional information (e.g., where the animal is found or what it eats). They explained this in terms of differences in form–function intercorrelations both within and across domains. Essentially, they make two claims. First, they claim that the distinguishing features of artefacts are more strongly correlated with their functions than are the non-distinguishing features (e.g. sharp things are often used for cutting), whereas for living things, the distinguishing features are usually perceptual, and are not correlated strongly with function (e.g. cow <moos> and cow <produces milk>). Second, they claim that although individual artefacts usually have few functions, living things often have a number of biological functions (e.g. seeing and eating), and these features are highly correlated with specific perceptual features (e.g. eyes and mouths). The differences in these two types of correlations lead to the prediction that functional information should be relatively preserved for artefacts and living things: form–functional for artefacts, and perceptual–functional for living things. In addition, distinctive perceptual features for artefacts should be relatively more preserved than distinctive perceptual features for biological kinds. Moss et al. (1997) and Tyler and Moss (1997) have reported patient data consistent with these claims (but see Laws, 1998, for an alternative view). Finally, Durrant-Peatfield, Tyler, Moss, and Levy (1997) implemented these types of relationships in a feedforward connectionist model, demonstrating that a network using distributed representations produces results consistent with these predictions if it encodes form–function correlations and is sensitive to the degree to which a feature is distinguishing. Although we do not agree with all of the details of their account, we believe that an account that integrates feature type, correlated features, and distinguishing features is necessary to capture all of the relevant behavioural phenomena.

CONCLUSION

One issue that became apparent while conducting numerous analyses of the norms is that there exists a great deal of variation within domains, and sometimes even within categories, that must be considered when conducting experiments that purport to test various factors underlying category-specific deficits. Tables 8.2 and 8.4, for example, illustrate that substantial variance exists within both the creatures and non-living things on factors such as feature correlations and distinguishing features. The major concern regarding this variance is that researchers often test a theory of category-specific deficits by choosing a small sample of concepts from a large domain such as non-living things, with the implicit assumption being that a measure such as the percentage of distinguishing features has a uniform distribution within the domain. This is obviously false. Conducting experiments in a more rigorous fashion by obtaining reliable estimates of manipulated variables for experimental stimuli will enable conclusions to be drawn more confidently, and should lead to fewer contradictory results. In this vein, our large set of norms enabled testing hypotheses in a more empirically based, rigorous, and detailed manner, thus leading to insights regarding the factors underlying category-specific semantic deficits.

ACKNOWLEDGEMENTS

This work was supported by NSERC grant RGPIN155704 to the first author and an NSERC Postgraduate Fellowship to the second author. The authors thank Jeff Elman and Larry Barsalou for valuable suggestions regarding this research. Correspondence concerning this article should be addressed to Ken McRae, Department of Psychology, Social Science Centre, University of Western Ontario, London, Ontario, N6A 5C2. e-mail: mcrae@uwo.ca

REFERENCES

Barsalou, L.W. (1992). Frames, concepts, and conceptual fields. In E. Kittay & A. Lehrer (Eds.), *Frames, fields, and contrasts: New essays in semantic and lexical organisation* (pp. 21–74). Hillsdale, NJ: Lawrence Erlbaum Associates, Inc.

Billman, D., & Heit, E. (1988). Observational learning from internal feedback: A simulation of an adaptive learning method. *Cognitive Science, 12*, 587–625.

Billman, D., & Knutson, J. (1996). Unsupervised concept learning and value systematicity: A complex whole aids learning the parts. *Journal of Experimental Psychology: Learning, Memory, and Cognition, 22*, 458–475.

Caramazza, A., & Shelton, J.R. (1998). Domain-specific knowledge systems in the brain: The animate–inanimate distinction. *Journal of Cognitive Neuroscience, 10*, 1–34.

Collins, A.M. & Quillian, M.R. (1969). Retrieval time from semantic memory. *Journal of Verbal Learning and Verbal Behavior, 8*, 240–247.

Cree, G.S., McRae, K., & McNorgan, C. (1999). An attractor model of lexical conceptual processing: Simulating semantic priming. *Cognitive Science, 23*, 371–414.

Devlin, J.T., Gonnerman, L.M., Anderson, E.S., & Seidenberg, M.S. (1998). Category specific semantic deficits in focal and widespread brain damage: A computational account. *Journal of Cognitive Neuroscience, 10*, 77–94.

Durrant-Peatfield, M.R., Tyler, L.K., Moss, H.E., & Levy, J.P (1997). The distinctiveness of form and function in category structure: A connectionist model. In *Proceedings of the Nineteenth Annual Conference of the Cognitive Science Society* (pp. 193–198). Mahwah, NJ: Lawrence Erlbaum Associates, Inc.

Farah, M.J., & McClelland, J.L. (1991). A computational model of semantic memory impairment: Modality specificity and emergent category specificity. *Journal of Experimental Psychology: General, 120*, 339–357.

Farah, M.J., Meyer, M.M., & McMullen, P.A. (1996). The living/non-living dissociation is not an artifact: Giving an a priori implausible hypothesis a strong test. *Cognitive Neuropsychology, 13*, 137–154.

Farah, M.J., & Wallace, M.A. (1992). Semantically-bounded anomia: Implications for the neural implementation of naming. *Neuropsychologia, 30*, 609–621.

Fillmore, C.J. (1968). The case for case. In E. Bach & R. Harms (Eds.), *Universals in linguistic theory* (pp. 1–88). New York: Holt, Rinehart, & Winston.

Forde, E.M.E., Francis, D., Riddoch, M.J., Rumiati, R.I., & Humphreys, G.W. (1997). On the links between visual knowledge and naming: A single case study of a patient with a category-specific impairment for living things. *Cognitive Neuropsychology, 14*, 403–458.

Forster, K.I. (1994). Computational modeling and elementary process analysis in visual word recognition. *Journal of Experiment Psychology: Human Perception and Performance, 20*, 1292–1310.

Funnell, E., & Sheridan, J.S. (1992). Categories of knowledge? Unfamiliar aspects of living and non-living things. *Cognitive Neuropsychology, 9*, 135–153.

Gaffan, D., & Heywood, C.A. (1993). A spurious category-specific visual agnosia for living things in normal humans and nonhuman primates. *Journal of Cognitive Neuroscience, 5*, 118–128.

Gainotti, G., & Silveri, M.C. (1996). Cognitive and anatomical locus of lesion in a patient with a category-specific semantic impairment for living beings. *Cognitive Neuropsychology, 13*, 357–389.

Garrard, P., Lambon Ralph, M.A., Hodges, J.R., & Patterson, K. (2001). Prototypicality, distinctiveness and intercorrelation: Analyses of the semantic attributes of living and non-living concepts. *Cognitive Neuropsychology, 18*, 125–174.

Garrard, P., Patterson, K., Watson, P.C., & Hodges, J.R. (1998). Category-specific loss in dementia of the Alzheimer's type: Functional–anatomical correlations from cross-sectional analyses. *Brain, 121*, 633–646.

Gelman, S.A. (1988). The development of induction within natural kind and artifact categories. *Cognitive Psychology, 20*, 65–95.

Gonnerman, L.M., Anderson, E.S., Devlin, J.T., Kempler, D., & Seidenberg, M.S. (1997). Double dissociation of semantic categories in Alzheimer's disease. *Brain and Language, 57*, 254–279.

Hart, J., Berndt, R.S., & Caramazza, A. (1985). Category-specific naming deficit following cerebral infarction. *Nature, 316*, 439–440.

Hart, J., & Gordon, B. (1992). Neural subsystems for object knowledge. *Nature, 359*, 60–64.

Hillis, A., & Caramazza, A. (1991). Category specific naming and comprehension impairment: A double dissociation. *Brain, 114*, 2081–2094.

Hillis, A., Rapp, B., Romani, C., & Caramazza, A. (1990). Selective impairments of semantics in lexical processing. *Cognitive Neuropsychology, 7*, 191–243.

Keil, F.C. (1989). *Concepts, kinds, and cognitive development*. Cambridge, MA: MIT Press.

Laws, K.R. (1998). Why leopards never change their spots: A reply to Moss, Tyler and Jennings. *Cognitive Neuropsychology, 15*, 467–479.

Laws. K.R., Evans, J.J., Hodges, J.R., & McCarthy, R. (1995). Naming without knowing and appearance without associations: Evidence for constructive processes in semantic memory? *Memory, 3*, 409–433.

McRae, K., Cree, G.S., Westmacott, R., & de Sa, V.R. (1999). Further evidence for feature correlations in semantic memory. *Canadian Journal of Experimental Psychology: Special Issue on Models of Word Recognition, 53*, 360–373.

McRae, K., de Sa, V.R., & Seidenberg, M.S. (1997). On the nature and scope of featural representations of word meaning. *Journal of Experimental Psychology: General, 126*, 99–130.

Malt, B.C., & Smith, E.E. (1984). Correlated features in natural categories. *Journal of Verbal Learning and Verbal Behavior, 23*, 250–269.

Martin, A., Haxby, J.V., Lalonde, F.M., Wiggs, C.L., & Ungerleider, L.G. (1995). Discrete cortical regions associated with knowledge of color and knowledge of action. *Science, 270*, 102–105.

Moss, H.E., Tyler, L.K., & Jennings, F. (1997). When leopards lose their spots: Knowledge of visual properties in category-specific deficits for living things. *Cognitive Neuropsychology, 14*, 901–950.

Mummery, C.J., Patterson, K., Hodges, J.R., & Price, C.J. (1998). Functional neuroanatomy of the semantic system: Divisible by what? *Journal of Cognitive Neuroscience, 10*, 766–777.

Murphy, G.L., & Wisniewski, E.J. (1989). Feature correlations in conceptual representations. In G. Tiberghien (Ed.), *Advances in cognitive science, Vol. 2: Theory and applications* (pp. 23–45). Chichester, UK: Ellis Horwood.

Rosch, E. (1978). Principles of categorization. In E. Rosch & B.B. Lloyd (Eds.), *Cognition and categorization* (pp. 27–48). Hillsdale, NJ: Lawrence Erlbaum Associates, Inc.

Rosch, E., & Mervis, C.B. (1975). Family resemblances: Studies in the internal structure of categories. *Cognitive Psychology, 7*, 573–605.

Rosch, E., Mervis, C.B., Gray, W.D., Johnson, D.M., & Boyes-Braem, P. (1976). Basic objects in natural categories. *Cognitive Psychology, 8*, 382–439.

Sacchett, C., & Humphreys, G.W. (1992). Calling a squirrel a squirrel but a canoe a wigwam: A category-specific deficit for artefactual objects and body parts. *Cognitive Neuropsychology, 9*, 73–86.

Sartori, S., & Job, R. (1988). The oyster with four legs: A neuropsychological study on the interaction of visual and semantic information. *Cognitive Neuropsychology, 5*, 105–132.

Schank, R.C., & Abelson, R.P. (1977). *Scripts, plans, goals and understanding*. Hillsdale, NJ: Lawrence Erlbaum Associates, Inc.

Shelton, J.R., & Caramazza, A. (1999). Deficits in lexical and semantic processing: Implications for models of normal language. *Psychonomic Bulletin and Review, 6,* 5–27.

Silveri, M.C., & Gainotti, G. (1988). Interaction between vision and language in category-specific impairment. *Cognitive Neuropsychology, 5,* 677–709.

Smith, E.E., & Medin, D.L. (1981). *Categories and Concepts.* Cambridge, MA: Harvard University Press.

Smith, E.E., Shoben, E.J., & Rips, L.J. (1974). Structure and process in semantic memory: A feature model for semantic decisions. *Psychological Review, 81,* 214–241.

Stewart, E., Parkin, A.J., & Hunkin, N.M. (1992). Naming impairments following recovery from herpes simplex encephalitis: Category specific? *Quarterly Journal of Experimental Psychology, 44A,* 261–284.

Thompson-Schill, S.L., Aguirre, G.K., D'Esposito, M., & Farah, M.J. (1999). A neural basis for category and modality specificity of semantic knowledge. *Neuropsychologia, 37,* 671–676.

Tranel, D., Logan, C.G., Frank, R.J., & Damasio, A.R. (1997). Explaining category-related effects in the retrieval of conceptual and lexical knowledge for concrete entities: Operationalization and analysis of factors. *Neuropsychologia, 35,* 1329–1339.

Tversky, A. (1997). Features of similarity. *Psychological Review, 84,* 327–352.

Tyler, L.K., & Moss, H.E. (1997). Functional properties of concepts: Studies of normal and brain-damaged patients. *Cognitive Neuropsychology, 14,* 511–545.

Warrington, E.K., & McCarthy, R. (1983). Category specific access dysphasia. *Brain, 106,* 859–878.

Warrington, E.K., & McCarthy, R. (1987). Categories of knowledge: Further fractionation and an attempted integration. *Brain, 110,* 1273–1296.

Warrington, E.K., & Shallice, T. (1984). Category specific semantic impairments. *Brain, 107,* 829–854.

Wu, L.L., & Barsalou, L.W. (2002). *Perceptual simulation in property generation.* Manuscript under review.

APPENDIX A: EXAMPLES OF LIVING AND NON-LIVING THING CONCEPTS FROM FEATURE NORMS

Feature	Production frequency	WB classification
Moose		
a herbivore	8	superordinate
a mammal	9	superordinate
an animal	17	superordinate
eaten as meat	5	function
has four legs	12	quantity
has antlers	23	external component
has fur	7	external component
has hair	5	external component
has hooves	5	external component
has legs	14	external component
hunted by people	17	participant
is brown	10	external surface feature
is large	27	external surface feature
lives in wilderness	8	location
lives in woods	14	location
Knife		
a utensil	19	superordinate
a weapon	11	superordinate
cutlery	5	superordinate
found in kitchens	8	location
has a blade	11	external component
has a handle	14	external component
is dangerous	14	systemic feature
is serrated	8	external surface feature
is sharp	29	external surface feature
is shiny	5	external surface feature
made of metal	7	made of
made of stainless steel	5	made of
made of steel	8	made of
used by butchers	5	participant
used for cutting	25	function
used for killing	7	function
used with forks	6	associated entity

APPENDIX B: THE CONCEPTS FROM THE NORMS, ORGANISED BY CATEGORY

Living things: creatures

Animal	alligator, bat (animal), bear, beaver, beetle, bison, blackbird, bluejay, budgie, buffalo, bull, butterfly, buzzard, calf, camel, canary, caribou, cat, caterpillar, catfish, cheetah, chickadee, chicken, chimp, chipmunk, clam, cockroach, cougar, cow, coyote, crab, crocodile, crow, deer, dog, dolphin, donkey, dove, duck, eagle, eel, elephant, elk, emu, falcon, fawn, finch, flamingo, fox, frog, giraffe, goat, goldfish, goose, gopher, gorilla, groundhog, guppy, hamster, hare, hawk, herring, hornet, horse, hyena, iguana, lamb, leopard, lion, lobster, mackerel, mink, minnow, mole (animal), moose, moth, mouse, nightingale, octopus, oriole, ostrich, otter, owl, ox, panther, parakeet, partridge, peacock, pelican, penguin, perch, pheasant, pig, pigeon, platypus, pony, porcupine, python, rabbit, raccoon, rat, rattlesnake, raven, robin, rooster, salamander, salmon, seal, sheep, shrimp, skunk, snail, sparrow, spider, sponge, squid, squirrel, starling, stork, swan, tiger, toad, tortoise, trout, tuna, turkey, turtle, vulture, walrus, whale, woodpecker, worm, zebra
Mammal	bat (animal), bear, beaver, bison, buffalo, bull, calf, camel, caribou, cat, cheetah, chimp, chipmunk, cougar, cow, coyote, deer, dog, dolphin, donkey, elephant, elk, fawn, fox, giraffe, goat, gopher, gorilla, groundhog, hamster, hare, horse, hyena, lamb, leopard, lion, mink, moose, mouse, otter, ox, pig, platypus, pony, porcupine, rabbit, raccoon, rat, seal, sheep, skunk, squirrel, tiger, walrus, whale, zebra
Rodent	chipmunk, gopher, groundhog, hamster, mole (animal), mouse, rabbit, raccoon, rat, squirrel
Bird	blackbird, bluejay, budgie, buzzard, canary, chickadee, chicken, crane, crow, dove, duck, eagle, emu, falcon, finch, flamingo, goose, hawk, nightingale, oriole, ostrich, owl, parakeet, partridge, peacock, pelican, penguin, pheasant, pigeon, raven, robin, rooster, seagull, sparrow, starling, stork, swan, turkey, vulture, woodpecker
Fish	catfish, cod, goldfish, guppy, herring, mackerel, minnow, perch, salmon, sardine, trout, tuna
Reptile	alligator, crocodile, eel, iguana, python, rattlesnake, salamander, toad, tortoise, turtle
Amphibian	crocodile, frog, salamander, toad, turtle
Seafood	clam, crab, lobster, shrimp, squid
Insect	ant, beetle, butterfly, caterpillar, cockroach, flea, grasshopper, hornet, housefly, moth, spider, wasp
Carnivore	alligator, bear, buzzard, cheetah, cougar, coyote, crocodile, dog, eagle, falcon, fox, hawk, hyena, leopard, lion, panther, porcupine, tiger, vulture
Predator	alligator, cat, cheetah, cougar, coyote, eagle, falcon, fox, hawk, hyena, leopard, lion, mink, panther, tiger, vulture
Scavenger	buzzard, crow, hawk, hyena, raccoon, rat, raven, vulture
Herbivore	buffalo, caribou, deer, elk, gopher, grasshopper, hare, moose, otter, ox, porcupine, skunk, squirrel, turtle
Pet	bat, budgie, canary, cat, chickadee, dog, finch, goldfish, guppy, hamster, hare, iguana, mink, mouse, parakeet, pigeon, pony, python, rabbit, rat, salamander, turtle

Living things: fruit/vegetables (and some plants)

Fruit	apple, avocado, banana, blueberry, cantaloupe, cherry, coconut, cranberry, grape, grapefruit, honeydew, lemon, lime, mandarin, nectarine, orange, peach, pear, pineapple, plum, prune, pumpkin, raisin, raspberry, rhubarb, squash, strawberry, tangerine, tomato
Vegetable	asparagus, avocado, beans, beets, broccoli, cabbage, carrot, cauliflower, celery, corn, cucumber, eggplant (aubergine), garlic, lettuce, mushroom, olive, onions, parsley, peas, pepper, pickle, potato, pumpkin, radish, rhubarb, rice, spinach, squash, tomato, turnip, yam, zucchini (courgette)
Root/tuber	beets, carrot, garlic, potato, radish, turnip, yam
Plant	asparagus, beans, beets, celery, corn, cucumber, dandelion, eggplant (aubergine), honeydew, oak, onions, parsley, pineapple, rhubarb, seaweed, squash, tomato, vine, willow

Non-living things

Clothing	belt, blouse, boots, bra, camisole, cap (hat), cape, cloak, coat, dress, earmuffs, girdle, gloves, gown, hose (leggings), jacket, jeans, leotards, mink (coat), mittens, nightgown, nylons, pajamas, pants, parka, robe, scarf, shawl, shirt, shoes, skirt, slippers, socks, sweater, swimsuit, tie, trousers, tunic, veil, vest
Fashion accessory	belt, bracelet, cane, gloves, necklace, tie, vest
Tool	axe, bolts, broom, brush, chain, chisel, clamp, comb, corkscrew, crowbar, drill, file, fork, hammer, hatchet, hoe, ladle, level, microscope, needle, paintbrush, pencil, pliers, rake, sandpaper, scissors, screwdriver, screws, shovel, sledgehammer, spade, spear, stick, tomahawk, vice, wheelbarrow, wrench
Utensil	bowl, broom, colander, corkscrew, cup, dish, fork, grater, hatchet, knife, ladle, mixer, mug, paintbrush, pan, pen, pencil, pot, racquet, spatula, spoon, strainer, tongs
Container	ashtray, bag, barrel, bin (waste), bottle, box, bucket, freezer, jar, mug, pot, sack, urn
Instrument	bayonet, club, crayon, drill, hammer, microscope, pencil, ruler, scissors, screwdriver, spoon
Appliance	blender, dishwasher, drill, fan (appliance), freezer, fridge, kettle, machine, microwave, mixer, oven, radio, stove, telephone, toaster
Machine	blender, catapult, crane (machine), helicopter, mouse (computer), projector, tank (army), tractor, typewriter
Weapon	armour, axe, bat (baseball), baton, bayonet, bazooka, belt, bomb, bow (weapon), cane, cannon, catapult, club, crossbow, crowbar, dagger, grenade, gun, hammer, harpoon, hatchet, hoe, knife, machete, missile, pistol, revolver, rifle, rock, rocket, shield, shotgun, shovel, sledgehammer, slingshot, spear, stick, stone, sword, tomahawk, whip
Furniture	bookcase, bureau, chair, couch, desk, dresser, lamp, rocker, shelves, sofa, table
Vehicle	airplane, ambulance, bike, bus, canoe, car, cart, dunebuggy, helicopter, jeep, motorcycle, sailboat, scooter, ship, skateboard, submarine, tank (army), tractor, trailer, tricycle, trolley, truck, van, wagon, yacht
Boat	canoe, raft, sailboat, ship, yacht
Shelter	apartment, cabin, cottage, house, nest, tent
House	apartment, bungalow, cottage, hut, kennel, shell
Building	barn, cathedral, chapel, church, inn, kennel, shed, skyscraper

Test cases

Food   biscuit, bread, cake, cheese, pickle, pie
Musical instrument   accordion, bagpipe, cello, clarinet, drum, flute, guitar, harmonica, harp,
                      harpsichord, keyboard (musical), piano, saxophone, trombone, trumpet,
                      tuba, violin
Jewellery   bracelet, chain, crown, necklace
Tree   birch, cedar, oak, pine, willow

APPENDIX C: SLIGHTLY MODIFIED VERSION OF THE WU AND BARSALOU (2002, WB) FEATURE TAXONOMY

Entity features (e)

External component (ece): A three-dimensional component of an entity that, at least to some extent, normally resides on its surface. *coconut* < has a shell >; *tricycle* < has pedals >

External surface feature (ese): An external feature of an entity that is not a component and that is perceived on or beyond the entity's surface, including shape, colour, pattern, texture, size, touch, smell, taste. *apple* < is red >; *blender* < is loud >

Internal component (eci): A three-dimensional component of an entity that normally resides completely inside the closed surface of the entity. *cherry* < has a pit >; *car* < has an engine >

Internal surface feature (esi): An internal feature of an entity that is not a component, that is not normally perceived on the entity's exterior surface, and that is perceived only when the entity's interior surface is exposed, including colour, pattern, texture, size, touch, smell, taste. *blueberry* < tastes sweet >; *fridge* < is cold >

Entity behaviour (eb): An intrinsic action that is characteristic of an entity's behaviour, and that is not an entity's normal function for an external agent. *dog* < barks >; *clock* < ticks >

Entity made-of (em): A specification of the materials of which the entity is made. *oak* < made of wood >; *sink* < made of enamel >

Quantity (eq): A numerosity, frequency, or intensity of an entity or its features. *giraffe* < has a long neck >; *slippers* < come in pairs >

Associated abstract entity (eae): An abstract entity associated with the target entity and external to it [no features appeared with any living thing] *harp* < associated with angels >

Systemic feature (esys): A global systemic feature of an entity or its parts, including states, conditions, abilities, traits. *dolphin* < is intelligent >; *car* < is fast >

Larger whole (ew): A whole to which an entity belongs. *ant* < lives in a colony >; *basement* < part of a house >

Situation features (s)

Function (sf): A typical role that an entity serves for an agent. *tomato* < eaten >; *bed* < used for sleeping >

Action (sa): An action that a participant performs in a situation. *strawberry* < is picked >; *screws* < used by turning >

Participant (sp): A person in a situation who typically uses an entity or performs an action on it and/or interacts with other participants. *carrot* < eaten by rabbits >; *wand* < used by magicians >

Location (sl): A place where an entity can be found, or where people engage in an event or activity. *zebra* < lives in Africa >; *cupboard* < found in kitchens >

Origin (sor): How or where an entity originated. *walnut* < grows on trees >; *gloves* < are knitted >

Time (st): A time period associated with a situation or with one of its features. *turkey* < eaten at Thanksgiving >; *cabin* < used for vacations >

Manner (sm): The manner in which action or behaviour is performed. *turnip* <eaten by cooking>; *pie* <eaten by baking>

Associated entity (se): An entity in a situation that contains the target concept. *lobster* <eaten with butter>; *saucer* <used with tea cups>

Taxonomic categories (c)

Superordinate (ch): *deer* <a mammal>; *hammer* <a tool>

Subordinate (cl): *lettuce* <romaine>; *pants* <bell bottoms>

Individual (ci): *deer* <Bambi>; *doll* <Barbie>

Synonym (cs): *calf* <baby cow>; *sink* <basin>

Coordinate (cc): *coyote* <dog>; *veil* <hat>

Introspective features (i)

Affect/emotion (ia): An affective or emotional state toward the situation or one of its components by either the subject or the participant. *wasp* <is annoying>; *bomb* <is frightening>

Evaluation (ie): A positive or negative evaluation of a situation or one of its components by either the subject or a participant. *fawn* <is cute>; *gown* <is fancy>

Contingency (ic): A contingency between two or more aspects of a situation, including if, enable, cause, because, depends, requires. *garlic* <causes bad breath>; *shirt* <requires ironing>

Cognitive operation (io): An operation on a cognitive state, including comparison, retrieval, learning. *buffalo* <like a cow>; *magazine* <like a book>

Negation (in): An explicit mention of the absence of something, with absence requiring a mental state that represents the opposite. *ostrich* <cannot fly>; *vest* <has no sleeves>

CHAPTER NINE

Connectionist perspectives on category-specific deficits

Timothy T. Rogers
Department of Psychology and the Center for the Neural Basis of Cognition, Carnegie Mellon University, Pittsburgh, USA

David C. Plaut
Departments of Psychology and Computer Science and the Center for the Neural Basis of Cognition, Carnegie Mellon University, Pittsburgh, USA

INTRODUCTION

Theories of semantic memory tend between two poles. At one extreme is a view often associated with the connectionist enterprise: that the semantic system is a unitary, homogeneous mass, without functional or neuroanatomic specialisation, that capitalises on statistical regularities in the environment in learning about and processing semantic information. On this account, double dissociations of semantic memory are explained in terms of the processing mechanisms characteristic of neural networks, the statistical structure of the environment, and various psycholinguistic factors such as familiarity, frequency, and visual complexity. At the other extreme is a view positing that semantic memory is parcelled functionally and neuroanatomically into a set of discrete processing modules, each tied to a particular modality and/or semantic domain. Under this hypothesis, double dissociations of semantic memory arise from damage to one or another of these modules, or the connections between them.

In this chapter, we will argue that neither extreme position is likely to prove satisfying. Theories that eschew any form of neuroanatomic specialisation are unlikely to capture the variety of dissociations reported in the literature, whereas extreme modular views lack explanatory power. Accordingly, most computational models of semantic memory place themselves somewhere in the middle by adopting at least some form of neuroanatomic specialisation.

A number of interesting questions arise from this stance. What kind of specialisation exists? How and why does it occur? How is it related to the structure of the environment and mechanisms of learning in the brain? Here we find a much greater degree of variability across theories and models. Some assume only the grossest forms of neuroanatomic specialisation, whereas others posit many fine-grained distinctions. Some theories suggest that hard boundaries exist between anatomical regions with specific functions; others adopt more graded forms of specialisation.

Although connectionist models are sometimes caricatured as homo-geneous blobs without form or specialised function, in practice they offer a useful means of exploring the space between these opposing views. All connectionist models incorporate some degree of built-in architectural specialisation, in their organisation into groups of units, their patterns of connectivity, their unit parameters, and their learning rules. Most also adapt to the statistical structure of their virtual environments, acquiring through experience the ability to perform model analogues of cognitive tasks. Thus the theorist is at liberty to build as much or as little "anatomical" structure into a model's architecture as necessary. Explorations of the computational properties of such systems can then clarify the extent to which such assump-tions are warranted by the data.

Throughout this chapter, we will focus on aspects of the connectionist approach that render these models well-suited to addressing neuro-psychological data. Unlike more traditional box-and-arrow-drawings, con-nectionist models allow the theorist to specify in explicit, computational terms the internal structure of representations in different areas of the system (Allport, 1985). Computer simulations have shown that representational structure has important consequences for the behaviour of neural systems under damage, in a variety of domains. In some cases, these effects can lead to apparent double dissociations even in a homogeneous network with no assumed neuroanatomic specialisation (Bullinaria & Chater, 1995; Devlin, Gonnerman, Andersen, & Seidenberg, 1998; Mayall & Humphreys, 1996; Moss, Tyler, Durrant-Peatfield, & Bunn, 1998). In others, double-dissociations might arise from damage to anatomically distinct areas that are in no way specialised to subserve the cognitive functions dissociated (Plaut & Shallice, 1993; Plaut, 1995).

Such findings call into question the conclusion frequently drawn from case studies forming double dissociations, that the dissociated functions must be subserved by modules that may be damaged indepen-dently. An investigation of the computational properties of connectionist networks in pathology can help the theorist to understand when these conclusions are justified, and under what conditions a double dissociation might be observed in a homogeneous system, or as a result of damage to anatomically distinct areas that nevertheless do not constitute independent neural modules specialised to subserve the dissociated cognitive faculties.

To illustrate how these properties of connectionist nets can help us to understand patterns of impairment in the domain of semantic cognition, we will begin by describing an influential model of category specific deficits put forward by Farah and McClelland (1991). The model is a simple implementation of the sensory–functional (SF) hypothesis: that semantic information about the perceptual and functional properties of objects is stored in anatomically distinct areas of cortex; and that apparent category-specific deficits arise because different semantic domains rely to a greater or lesser degree on sensory or functional information in their representation (Warrington & Shallice, 1984). The Farah–McClelland (FM) model builds in what is essentially an anatomical segregation between areas that represent sensory and functional semantic information. It also incorporates learning mechanisms that serve to associate these semantic features with one another, and with more peripheral visual and verbal representations. The marriage of given anatomical specialisation with domain–general learning mechanisms permits the model to account for a broad variety of data, and probably constitutes the best theoretical account of category-specific deficits to date.

Despite its considerable appeal, the FM model has recently come under criticism from some quarters, for a couple of reasons. First, developments in the case literature suggest that the model as formulated cannot capture the full range of patient data. Second, efforts to measure empirically the degree to which various categories rely on "sensory" and "functional" information in their definitions have lead some to question the validity of such a distinction. In the next section (p. 265), we will discuss some alternatives to the sensory–functional hypothesis that have been put forward recently, focusing in particular on two opposing hypotheses. The domain-specific knowledge hypothesis postulates that knowledge of different semantic domains is subserved by anatomically distinct cortical modules, dedicated at birth, that have developed over ontogeny under evolutionary pressures (Caramazza & Shelton, 1998). We argue that the domain-specific knowledge hypothesis raises far more questions than it answers, and in fact offers no leverage on the problems encountered by the FM model. In contrast, unitary–semantics hypotheses posit that some category-specific deficits can be explained without any reference to the anatomical organisation of cortex, but rather in terms of learned sensitivity of the system to the statistical properties of the environment (Devlin et al., 1998; Hillis, Rapp, & Caramazza, 1995; Hillis, Rapp, Romani, & Caramazza, 1990; McRae, de Sa, & Seidenberg, 1997; Moss et al., 1998; Tippett, McAuliffe, & Farah, 1995).

We will argue that each of these extreme positions has problems that undermine its adequacy. The thesis that semantic memory is subserved by multiple, anatomically distinct cortical modules offers no leverage on the empirical challenges faced by the sensory–functional hypothesis, and lacks explanatory power. However, the antithesis to this view, expressed in the unitary–semantics hypothesis, is unlikely to explain the full range of patient deficits reported in the literature.

Where, then, is an appropriate synthesis? In the final section (see p. 278, we consider an approach that has been successful in accounting for data in other domains of semantic cognition—namely, semantic dementia—and which we believe holds promise for understanding category-specific impairments as well (Rogers et al., 1999). Like the FM model, this theory builds on anatomical differences already known to exist in the brain. However, differential performance in living and non-living domains is understood with reference to the similarity structure of representations in different surface modalities. We will discuss how the same properties that lead to structured deterioration in semantic dementia might be extended to account for seeming category-specific deficits as well, in this framework.

THE FARAH-McCLELLAND MODEL

The origin of recent interest in category-specific semantic impairments is usually attributed to two papers published by Warrington and her collaborators in the mid-1980s (Warrington & McCarthy, 1983; Warrington & Shallice, 1984). The first of these was a case study of VER, a patient with extensive left hemisphere damage due to stroke, who presented with a severe global dysphasia. Although VER was unable to produce even simple propositional statements, Warrington and McCarthy were able to show that she had some spared verbal comprehension, through the use of a word-to-picture matching task. This sparing appeared to strongly favour particular semantic categories: VER's performance was much better for flowers, animals, and foods than for man-made objects. Because man-made objects are generally much more familiar than, for example, flowers and animals (Warrington & McCarthy, 1983), the dissociation could not be explained on the basis of familiarity alone. Thus Warrington and McCarthy speculated that VER showed an impairment of semantic knowledge about non-living things.

This conclusion was reinforced by a second study of four patients recovering from herpes encephalitis, who appeared to have the reverse dissociation: greater difficulty identifying living relative to non-living things (Warrington & Shallice, 1984). All four exhibited worse performance for living relative to non-living things in a match-to-sample task like the one used with VER. For the two patients with sufficiently spared expressive speech (JBR and SBY), the asymmetry was also apparent for picture naming, description, definition, and word-to-picture matching tasks. In these two cases, the difference was quite dramatic. For example, patient JBR correctly identified only 6% of the living things on which he was tested, but was able to identify 90% of the non-living objects. The difference between living and non-living objects persisted strongly when stimuli were controlled for familiarity and word frequency.

Warrington and Shallice (1984) further tested JBR on his ability to identify 12 items from each of 26 categories selected from the Battig and Montague category norms (Battig & Montague, 1969). JBR identified significantly fewer items than expected on the basis of item frequency alone for 12 of the 26 categories; of these, 7 were either living things or foods. By contrast, of the 14 categories for which JBR was at or above expected performance, only 2 could be considered categories of living things (animals and body parts).

Together, these early papers formed the two sides of a double dissociation of semantic knowledge for living and non-living things. Since their publication, many reports of selective deficits for knowledge of living things have appeared in the literature (De Renzi & Lucchelli, 1994; Farah, McMullen, & Meyer, 1991; Hart & Gordon, 1992; Saffran & Schwartz, 1994; Silveri & Gainotti, 1988). A smaller but still considerable number of reports of selective impairment for non-living things have also been published (Behrmann & Lieberthal, 1989; Hillis et al., 1990; Sacchett & Humphreys, 1992). There have been some efforts to explain such findings with an appeal to uncontrolled stimulus factors such as visual complexity, word frequency, and familiarity. For example, Funnell and Sheridan (1992) showed that performance on naming tasks can vary dramatically with such factors as familiarity and frequency; and Stewart, Parkin, and Hunkin (1992) reported a patient with an impairment for naming living relative to non-living objects, which disappeared when nuisance factors were controlled. However, several cases are now on record describing patients who continue to show unequal performance for living and non-living things, even when stimuli have been carefully controlled or when the effects of confounding variables have been regressed out (Farah et al., 1991; Hillis & Caramazza, 1991; Kurbat, 1997; Kurbat & Farah, 1998).

For both empirical and theoretical reasons, Warrington and Shallice (1984) did not interpret their results as implying that different cortical areas are responsible for representing knowledge about semantically distinct domains. First, the pattern of spared and impaired categories across their patients did not respect rigid semantic boundaries. Although JBR was generally worse at naming living things, he also showed impaired performance for several categories of non-living objects: metals, types of cloth, musical instruments, and precious stones. Also, his ability to name body parts (arguably living things) was relatively intact. The mirror-image of this pattern impaired knowledge of non-living things in general, with the conjoint sparing of metals, cloth, musical instruments, and precious stones was later reported by Warrington and McCarthy (1987) in patient YOT. Thus, the data were not consistent with the hypothesis that knowledge of living things is subserved by one cortical region, and knowledge of non-living things is subserved by another.

Instead, Warrington and Shallice (1984) proposed an anatomical division of labour along an independently motivated anatomical division: perception and action. They suggested that living things are primarily differentiated on the basis of their perceptual properties, whereas artefacts are more often differentiated on the basis of their function. If knowledge of functional and perceptual attributes are stored in anatomically distinct areas, damage to one region might result in differential impairments for knowledge of living relative to non-living things, or vice versa. This theory provided an elegant explanation for the conjoint disturbance of (for example) musical instruments and living things, under the assumption that musical instruments, like living things, are differentiated primarily on the basis of perceptual properties. Similarly, one might expect that body parts are distinguished not on the basis of what they look like, but by their functional properties; hence the reason body-part and artefact knowledge were spared together in JBR, and impaired together in YOT. Caramazza and Shelton (1998) have recently termed Warrington and Shallice's theory the sensory–functional hypothesis.

Overview of the model

An influential computational implementation of the sensory–functional hypothesis was put forward by Farah and McClelland (1991). In addition to demonstrating that the theory was indeed tractable, computer simulations with the model showed that it also had some counterintuitive implications. The model is illustrated in Figure 9.1. Each layer consists of an assembly of simple neuron-like processing units, connected as shown, whose activity may range between −1 and 1. The units are linked to one another by means of

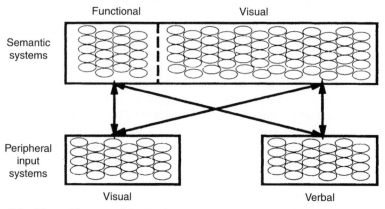

Figure 9.1. The architecture of the Farah and McClelland model. (Redrawn, with alterations, from Farah and McClelland, 1991, Figure 1, p. 343).

weighted connections, which can take any positive or negative value, and which determine the extent to which one unit's activity can influence the activity of anothers. Associated with each pair of connected units are two such connections: one that permits activation to flow from the first unit to the second, and one that permits activation to flow in the other direction. Because activation can propagate in either direction between any pair of connected units, the network is said to be recurrent.

Representations of objects in the model take the form of distributed patterns of activity across groups of units. The units themselves can be thought of as each responding to some aspect of the entity represented by the whole pattern, although these aspects need not be nameable features or correspond in any simple way to intuitions about the featural decomposition of the concept. In the semantic layers, some units may respond to objects with some particular visual property, while others may respond to aspects of the object's functional role. In the visual layer, patterns of activity correspond to more peripheral visual representations, whereas patterns of activity in the verbal layer form representations of words.

The presentation of a stimulus to the model causes an initial pattern of activity across units in one of the peripheral layers, with some of the units activated and some not. During processing, the state of each unit is determined by calculating the sum of its inputs weighted by the strength of the connection between units. This sum is passed through a non-linear squashing function bounded at -1 and 1, and the activation state of the unit is then updated. Thus, the activation of a unit at any point in time is determined jointly by the activation states of the other units in the network to which it is connected, and the magnitude of the weights between them.

The initial stimulus pattern presented to the network begins to change as each unit receives input from the other connected units. This dynamic flow of activation proceeds until the unit states stop changing, at which point the network is said to have settled into a steady state or attractor. The location of such stable configurations depends upon the connection weight matrix. The role of learning in this model is to configure the weights in such a way that, when the network is presented with a particular word or picture as input, it will settle into a stable state in which the correct pattern of activity is observed across units in the visual, verbal, and semantic layers.

Farah and McClelland created representations for ten "living" and ten "non-living" objects, by generating random patterns of -1 and $+1$ across all three layers of units in the model. Each unique pattern corresponded to a representation of an individual item. Representations of living and non-living things differed only in the proportion of active semantic units in the functional and perceptual pools. These were set to match the observed ratio of perceptual to functional features of objects in dictionary definitions (as discussed later). Living things in the model were represented with an average of 16.1 visual and 2.1 functional units active; whereas non-living things were represented with an average of 9.4 visual and 6.7 functional units active. All patterns had some units active in both semantic pools. The verbal and visual representations were random patterns generated in the same way for living and non-living items.

To find a configuration of weights that would allow the network to perform correctly, the authors used an error-correcting learning algorithm called the delta rule (McClelland & Rumelhart, 1985; Rumelhart, Hinton, & McClelland, 1986). On each trial, an item was selected at random and either its verbal or its visual representation was presented to the model. The network was allowed to settle for a fixed period of time, at which point the actual unit states were compared to the desired states. This discrepancy is referred to as the model's error: under the delta rule, error is calculated for all units in the model. The weights received by each unit in turn are adjusted by a small amount to reduce the error of that unit. After several iterations, the discrepancy between observed and desired states across all units is virtually eliminated and the trained model generates the correct semantic, verbal, and visual patterns when presented with either a word or a picture as input.

Of interest was the behaviour of the model when its semantic units were damaged. Under the sensory–functional hypothesis, units representing the functional–semantic aspects of an item can be damaged independently of the units representing the perceptual–semantic properties of that item. How does the performance of the model deteriorate with increasing damage to each of these pools of units?

To simulate neural trauma in the network, Farah and McClelland (1991) simply deleted some proportion of the units in either the perceptual semantic pool or the functional semantic pool. They then tested the ability of the network to perform model analogues of picture naming and match-to-sample tasks. In the former, the model was presented with the picture of an object (by applying a pattern of activity to the visual units), and allowed to settle to a steady state. The resulting pattern of activity across the word units could then be read off and compared to all the patterns in the training corpus. The model's response was considered correct if the pattern of activity across word units was more similar to the correct pattern than to any other pattern. The same procedure was employed in the match-to-sample task, using a word as input and examining patterns of activity across visual units to determine the response.

Two aspects of their results are of interest. First, the model showed a clear double dissociation in its ability to name living and non-living things. When visual semantic units were destroyed, the model exhibited a greater naming impairment for living relative to non-living objects. The opposite was true when functional units were destroyed. Second, and more interesting, in neither case was the model completely unimpaired in the "spared" domain.

Although the model was worse at naming living things when perceptual semantic features were destroyed, it was also impaired at naming non-living things. Living things rely more heavily on perceptual semantic features in the model but such features inform the representation of both living and non-living objects to some degree. As this knowledge deteriorates in the model, it tends to affect naming performance for both domains, albeit to differing degrees. The same graded impairments are also witnessed in the patient data—profound impairments in one domain are, almost without exception, accompanied by mild impairments in the relatively spared domain.

Farah and McClelland (1991) also examined the ability of the network to retrieve functional and perceptual semantic information when given a picture or a word as input. Considering only the perceptual or the functional unit pools, they compared the pattern of activity in the damaged network when it had settled to the correct pattern, for each object. The network was considered to have spared knowledge of the perceptual properties of an item if the observed pattern of activity across perceptual semantic units was closest to the correct pattern; and spared knowledge of functional properties if the observed pattern across functional semantic units was closest to the correct pattern.

The simulations showed that the loss of semantic features in one modality had important consequences for the ability of the model to retrieve properties in the spared modality. When perceptual semantic features were lost, the model had a tendency to generate an incorrect pattern of activity across functional semantic units, especially for living things. The reason is that the reciprocal connections among semantic features lead the network to rely on activity in perceptual semantic units to help produce the appropriate patterns across functional units. When this activation is reduced or disrupted as a result of damage, these lateral connections can interfere with the ability of the model to find the correct states even in the spared units. Thus, the loss of perceptual semantic knowledge that occurs with trauma to the cortical areas subserving such knowledge can precipitate a disruption of semantic knowledge in the functional modality, especially for categories that rely to a large extent on perceptual information in their representation. Of course, the reverse is true when functional semantic features are damaged.

The FM model also accounts for a variety of related neuropsychological findings. For example, McCarthy and Warrington (1988) described a patient with a seeming category-specific deficit for living things, but only when tested verbally. Farah and McClelland (1991) explained this pattern of performance by positing a lesioning of the connections between verbal representations and visual semantic units. When the model was lesioned in a similar fashion, it was impaired at generating the correct semantic representations from a verbal input, especially for living things; but unimpaired at finding the correct semantic pattern from visual input. The opposite pattern—good performance when tested verbally, but poor performance on visual tests of category knowledge—has been observed in visual agnosics, who often show poorer performance when tested with pictures of living things (Carbonnel, Charnallet, David, & Pellat, 1997; Dixon, 1999). Riddoch and Humphreys (1987) and others (Arguin, Bub, & Dudek, 1996; Dixon, Bub, & Arguin, 1997; Lecours et al., 1999) have suggested that the data across such patients are best explained by supposing that the connections between visual and semantic representations have been disrupted. Although to our knowledge it has not been explicitly demonstrated, such a lesion in the FM model would be expected lead to greater impairment of living relative to non-living things, for the reasons we have discussed.

Additional empirical issues

A number of other studies, many involving functional neuroimaging, have supported the general thesis that knowledge of functional and perceptual attributes are mediated by distinct brain regions. For example, Martin et al., (1995) used PET to show that discrete cortical regions were differentially active when subjects were shown a black-and-white drawing of an object, and required to name either its colour or a characteristic action associated with it. The colour-naming condition produced increased activation in the ventral temporal lobes, whereas the action-naming condition produced enhanced activation of the left, posterior middle temporal gyrus. Mummery, Patterson, Hodges, and Price (1998) reported similar findings in a match-to-sample task in which subjects were required to select the object that matched the sample either in its colour or in its typical location. Matching on the basis of locale lead to increased activation of the posterior temporal–occipital–parietal junction, superior to the "action-naming" area identified by Martin et al. (1995). Matching on the basis of colour activated left ventral temporal cortex, just as did colour naming in the Martin et al. (1995) study.

These findings correspond well with converging evidence that the middle temporal gyrus is more strongly activated in semantic tasks involving tools, relative to those involving animals; and that the reverse is true for the posterior ventral temporal cortex (Chao, Haxby, & Martin, 1999; Damasio, Grabowski, Tranel, & Hichwa, 1996; Moore & Price, 1999; Perani, Cappa, Bettinardi, & Bressi, 1995; Perani et al., 1999). Chao et al. (1999) point out that the middle temporal gyrus is proximal to areas of cortex that process information about non-biological motion (Zeki et al., 1991). Hence, they suggest that this area might code information about object use-associated motion, and consequently could be more important in representing artefacts than animals.

Outside the temporal cortex, a few studies have reported that prefrontal motor areas may be engaged in semantic tasks involving tools, relative to those involving animals (Martin et al., 1996; Perani et al., 1995; Spitzer, Kwong, Kennedy, & Rosen, 1995; Spitzer et al., 1998). Other studies have failed to find such a relationship (Moore & Price, 1999; Mummery et al., 1998); however, these imaging results are consistent with findings reported by Gainotti, Silveri, Daniele, and Giustolisi (1995), who surveyed the reported anatomical locus of damage in several patients with category specific deficits. These authors found that patients with impaired knowledge of living things were more likely to have damage to the medial temporal cortex, proximal to areas that process colour information; whereas those with impaired knowledge of artefacts were more likely to have frontoparietal lesions, proximal to motor planning areas. Thus, although there are a variety of studies that are generally consistent with the sensory–functional hypothesis, much work remains to be done in this area.

Data from the domain of neuropsychology have provided mixed support for the sensory–functional hypothesis. The hypothesis would seem to predict that patients with impaired knowledge of living things should also show worse performance on tasks tapping their knowledge of the perceptual (relative to functional) attributes of living things. In the FM model, this prediction is borne out: when perceptual semantic units are damaged, the model has a harder time finding the correct pattern of activity across these units than across the functional semantic units, especially for the domain of living things. And, indeed, several studies have found similar results in patients (Basso, Capitani, & Laiacona., 1988; Bunn, Tyler, & Moss, 1998; De Renzi & Lucchelli, 1994; Forde et al., 1997; Gainotti & Silveri, 1996; Powell & Davidoff, 1995; Sartori & Job, 1988; Silveri & Gainotti, 1988).

The interpretation of these results, however, is not straightforward. Caramazza and Shelton (1998) have argued that none of the studies described above employed adequate stimulus controls. In some cases, the items measuring functional knowledge were easier than the items assessing perceptual knowledge. In other studies, stimulus items were not controlled for familiarity, frequency, visual complexity, age of acquisition, and other psycholinguistic factors. These shortcomings have led Caramazza and Shelton (1998) to make the strong claim that, in fact, there is no compelling evidence that perceptual knowledge and knowledge of living things are conjointly impaired in pathology. There are now several cases on record using strictly controlled stimulus materials, showing patients with apparent category-specific deficits whose knowledge of the perceptual and functional attributes of objects in the impaired domain is equally poor (Caramazza & Shelton, 1998; Laiacona, Barbarotto, & Capitani, 1993; Lambon Ralph, Howard, Nightingale, & Ellis, 1998; Samson, Pillon, & De Wilde, 1998).

Moreover, Lambon Ralph et al. (1998) have reported a semantic dementia patient (IW) with impaired knowledge of the perceptual properties of objects, but without a corresponding category-specific impairment. On tests of naming from definition, IW was fairly accurate for both living and non-living things when the definitions included functional/associative properties, but was near chance for both domains when the definitions included only perceptual properties.

The sensory–functional hypothesis has attracted further criticism on the grounds that some of the patterns identified early on by Warrington and Shallice (1984) have not held up as the case literature has expanded. For example, although many studies have found inanimate but "sensory" categories, such as fabrics and musical instruments, to be spared or impaired along with categories of living things (Basso et al., 1988; De Renzi & Lucchelli, 1994; Sheridan & Humphreys, 1993; Silveri & Gainotti, 1988), it is no longer clear that such patterns are consistent. Other researchers claim to have found patients with semantic deficits restricted to more specific semantic categories, such as animals (Hillis & Caramazza, 1991), body parts (Shelton, Fouch, & Caramazza, 1998), and fruit and vegetables (Farah & Wallace, 1992; Hart, Berndt, & Caramazza, 1985). Again, most of this work is difficult to interpret because appropriate controls have rarely been performed; and, too often, conclusions about a patient's "semantic" impairments are drawn solely from picture-naming data, with no attempt to determine whether the observed deficits are specific to language (Caramazza & Shelton, 1998). Even so, at the very least, it seems safe to conclude that there is considerable variability across patients in the particular categories of knowledge they retain.

Simplifications adopted by the FM model

These developments have generally been interpreted as problematic for the sensory–functional hypothesis. Although they do appear to violate some predictions made by the FM model, it is not clear to us whether the model's shortcomings in this respect are due to theoretically interesting flaws or to uninteresting simplifying assumptions made by Farah and McClelland (1991) in their implementation. There are three respects in which the FM model is too underspecified to yield clear predictions about the conjoint disruption of particular semantic categories on the one hand, and modalities of semantic information on the other.

First, Farah and McClelland used random patterns of activity to represent items in the visual, verbal, and semantic layers of the network. This is certainly an oversimplification of affairs and the contribution of this choice to the behaviour of the network should not be underestimated. It is now well known that the similarity structure of representations has a strong impact on the pattern of errors made by connectionist networks following damage (see Plaut, McClelland, Seidenberg, & Patterson, 1996; Plaut & Shallice, 1993). Items that have similar internal representations are more likely to be confused with one another when the network is damaged. Structured representations can also cause the behaviour of the network to be more robust under damage and can result in non-linear decrements in performance, depending on the extent to which categories of objects are comprised of bundles of mutually reinforcing features (McRae et al., 1997; Moss et al., 1998; Plaut, 1995). Such effects form the basis for several quite different accounts of category-specific deficits, which we will discuss in the next section. It is not clear how the patterns of deterioration observed in the FM model would change if such structure were incorporated into the representations of the network.

Second, Farah and McClelland used a closest-match paradigm to decide whether internal representation states were correct under damage. A more strict criterion for correct performance would presumably result in a greater number of errors and it is possible that under these conditions, damage to perceptual units (for example) could result in the network being equally impaired at retrieving visual and functional semantic information, primarily for categories of living things.

Finally, the model does not make explicit the relationship between patterns of activity across sensory and functional units, and the ability of the system to make judgements about the presence or absence of particular semantic features in an attribute listing or verification task. The semantic units in the FM model are not meant to stand for explicit knowledge about the presence or absence of particular object attributes. Thus, there is no way to know, from the disturbed pattern of activity across semantic units, just what the model "knows" and what it doesn't know.

There might be some confusion about this last point. Farah and McClelland did indeed consider explicit object properties, as they appear in dictionary definitions, in order to provide an empirical basis for selecting the ratio of sensory to functional features when constructing semantic representations of living and non-living objects in the model. They had subjects read dictionary definitions of objects in various categories and underline all the words describing either the sensory properties of the object or its functional properties. From these data, they calculated the average ratio of sensory to functional features for definitions of living and non-living things, and employed these ratios in generating the random strings comprising the semantic representations used in the network. However, they state that the sensory and functional semantic units in the network are not meant to correspond to general intuitions about the featural decomposition of objects; that is, these units are not meant to stand for explicit object attributes. Instead, the authors assume that this measure provides a valid indication of the extent to which various objects rely on sensory and functional information in their definitions.

Whether or not this assumption is warranted is another point of contention. Caramazza and Shelton (1998) take issue with the general claim that sensory information is more important for representations of living things, while functional information is more important for representations of non-living things. To support their point, they replicated Farah and McClelland's dictionary study with a slight variation in the instructions. Instead of under-lining either sensory or functional properties of objects, subjects were told to underline words describing either sensory or non-sensory properties of objects. Under these conditions, the ratio of sensory to non-sensory proper-ties did not differ significantly between categories of living and non-living things.

Nevertheless, other studies designed to assess the attribute structure of objects in different categories have also found differences between categories of living and non-living things, in their reliance on sensory or functional properties (McRae et al., 1997; Rosch et al., 1976). Recently, Garrard, Lam-bon Ralph, Hodges, and Patterson (2001) had subjects list the properties of 64 items in living and non-living domains, in response to prompting ques-tions designed to extract both sensory and functional information. They clas-sified each feature according to the following criteria: as sensory if they could be appreciated in some sensory modality (e.g. "an eagle is large" or "a saw is sharp"); as functional if they described an action, activity, or use of an item (e.g. "a cat can catch mice," or "an owl can fly,"); as encyclopaedic if they described some other associative relationship (e.g. "a tiger is found in India", "a toaster is kept in the kitchen"); and as categorical if they named a category to which the object belonged (e.g. "a dog is an animal"). Their findings confirmed the conclusions from both Farah and McClelland (1991) and Caramazza and Shelton (1998). Considering only the sensory and functional features, living things had a greater proportion of sensory features listed per item than non-living things. Pooling functional and encyclopaedic features together, this difference between domains disappeared, because subjects tended to list a greater number of encyclopaedic features per item in the domain of living things.

More relevant to the sensory–functional hypothesis, Garrard et al. (2001) found that living things tended to be differentiated primarily on the basis of their perceptual features, whereas artefacts were differentiated from one another primarily on the basis of their function. This result speaks more directly to Warrington and Shallice's initial proposal, that living things are differentiated on the basis of their appearance, whereas artefacts are distinguished primarily according to their use (Warrington & Shallice, 1984).

As yet there is little consensus regarding the best way to measure the attribute structure of categories, and their reliance on sensory or functional information. Clearly, though, the FM model is underspecified in this respect. The model assumes anatomic segregation between areas representing the functional and perceptual properties of objects but does not make explicit how these representations support the recollection of particular sensory or functional properties, or indeed how and why such structure arises in the first place.

Summary of the FM model

Despite its shortcomings, the sensory–functional hypothesis and its incarnation in the FM model make sense of a broad variety of phenomena in neuropsychology. Whether or not a more detailed implementation of the sensory–functional hypothesis will be able to accommodate the anomalies in the patient data described earlier is an empirical question. In a later section we will discuss one approach that appears promising. First, though, we turn to two alternatives to the sensory–functional hypothesis that have recently been put forward, exemplifying polarised reactions to these developments.

ALTERNATIVE THEORIES OF CATEGORY-SPECIFIC DEFICITS

In the years since the publication of the FM model there have been two major influences on theories of semantic memory and category-specific deficits. The first is the remarkable expansion of the relevant case literature. Since Warrington and McCarthy's (1983) work in the mid-1980s there have been at least 97 case studies of patients with purported category-specific deficits (Lambon Ralph, personal communication). As we have already intimated, this wealth of data has been both a help and a hindrance. Certainly, the accumulation of information has reduced the need for theoretical speculation, but the considerable variability in the test items, methods, and controls adopted have made it nearly impossible to compare results across studies. The field awaits a critical review and synthesis of this material but, in the mean time, there has been a preponderance of new ideas about how best to capture central tendencies in the group data on the one hand, and the range of effects across all patients on the other.

The second important development in the past decade has been an increasing appreciation of the counterintuitive ways that complex systems, as embodied in connectionist networks, behave under pathology. Computer simulations are playing an increasingly important role in the explanation of a variety of cognitive phenomena and these ideas have had a strong impact in the domain of semantic cognition—in some cases, leading theorists to dispense with traditional cognitive constructs all together.

In this section, we will consider two reactions to these opposing pressures. First, we discuss Caramazza and Shelton's (1998) thesis that semantic categories constrain the functional neuroanatomy of the brain. Second, we address the antithesis, put forward in different forms by a variety of theorists, that semantic knowledge is subserved by a unitary and anatomically homogeneous neural system.

Thesis: the domain-specific knowledge hypothesis

One natural reaction to the literature on category-specific deficits is to suggest that knowledge of different semantic domains is mediated by different cortical systems, which might be damaged independently from one another. This is the stance taken recently by Caramazza and Shelton (1998), in response to the perceived incapacity of the sensory–functional hypothesis to account for variability in the case literature. They write (Caramazza & Shelton, 1998, p. 9):

> The hypothesis we wish to entertain is that evolutionary pressures have resulted in specialised mechanisms for perceptually *and* conceptually distinguishing animate and inanimate kinds, leading to a *categorical* organisation of this knowledge in the brain.

We will call this hypothesis the domain-specific knowledge hypothesis. The arguments these authors marshal to support their thesis rest primarily on a critical analysis of the sensory–functional hypothesis, much of which we have already discussed. In their view, the empirical phenomena described earlier are grounds for rejecting the sensory–functional framework all together. According to Caramazza and Shelton:

(1) The SF hypothesis does not predict the occurrence of category-specific deficits with equal impairment of sensory and functional features, although there is good evidence that such patients exist.
(2) The SF hypothesis predicts that impaired knowledge of the sensory or functional properties of objects should always be accompanied by a category-specific deficits, but there are counterexamples to this prediction.
(3) The SF hypothesis suggests that patients with deficits for living things should have greater difficulty retrieving the sensory (relative to the functional) properties of objects, and that the reverse should be true of patients with deficits for non-living things. There is no adequately controlled study documenting a patient with a category-specific impairment and the conjoint impairment of knowledge for the corresponding (sensory or functional) modality. Studies that claim to have shown such an association either did not control for the difficulty of the judgement, or for other confounding factors.
(4) Under the SF hypothesis, patterns of spared and impaired categories across patients should be consistent. The patient record shows instead that this is not the case. There is no good evidence that "perceptually"

defined categories such as cloth, minerals, and musical instruments, are jointly spared or impaired with knowledge of living things.

(5) The SF hypothesis leaves no room for the impairment of categories more specific than the global categories living and non-living, although such patients have now been reported. There is good evidence that the categories foods/plants, animals, and other things can be selectively and independently impaired in neuropathology.

Of course, these conclusions depend upon one's reading of a complicated literature. But accepting for the moment this interpretation of the data, it behooves us to consider the ability of the domain-specific knowledge hypothesis to address the shortcomings of the FM model. It is not clear that we gain any leverage on these problems by invoking domain-specific semantic modules. According to Caramazza and Shelton (1998, p. 9), "[one] expectation derived from this hypothesis is that (everything else being equal) category-specific deficits should result in comparable impairments for the visual and functional attributes of a concept". As we have noted, a handful of patients have indeed presented with apparent category-specific deficits and equal impairment of sensory and functional attributes. However, it is not clear how the domain-specific knowledge hypothesis might account for dissociations that do fall along sensory/functional lines, for example, patients with impaired knowledge for the sensory or functional attributes of objects, regardless of category, or patients who appear to have conjoint modality- and category-specific deficits. Caramazza and Shelton do not deny that such cases exist—indeed, their rejection of the SF hypothesis rests in part on the existence of these patients. But the theory offers no means of anticipating or interpreting these findings.

Also unspecified under the domain-specific knowledge hypothesis is an explanation of why category-specific deficits so rarely confine themselves to even very broad semantic domains. As we have noted, patients with so-called category-specific deficits are almost never completely unimpaired in the relatively spared domain. Warrington and Shallice's (1984) conclusion that "perceptually" defined categories, such as minerals and musical instruments, are consistently spared or impaired along with categories of living things might have been premature; however, there is little doubt that patients with deficits for living things in general can also have great difficulty with particular categories of non-living things. One of the strong points of the FM model is that it makes explicit how such graded impairments might arise.

These limitations are arguably to be expected from any immature theory. However, it is difficult to imagine how the theory might be developed without running into major difficulties. Consider Hart and Gordon's (1992) study of KR, a patient who presented with a severe anomia specific to animals. KR showed perfect performance verifying the functional and perceptual properties of artefacts, as well as the functional properties of animals, but had difficulty verifying the perceptual properties of animals. Furthermore, KR's impairment was only apparent when tested verbally. For example, she was able to discriminate appropriately from inappropriately coloured pictures of animals, but performed poorly on the same test when the colours were given verbally. Caramazza and Shelton conclude that KR shows an impairment for the sensory properties of animals specific to the verbal modality. It is not obvious how such a pattern would occur under the domain-specific knowledge hypothesis. It would not do to suggest that KR had an impairment specific to the "animal" area of the semantic system, because such an impairment would affect both the sensory and functional properties of animals in all testing modalities. Nor would it do to posit a lesion specific to language areas, because such damage should affect knowledge of the sensory and functional properties of both living and non-living categories. Indeed, it seems the only way to explain this data in a manner consistent with the domain-specific knowledge hypothesis is to posit the existence of dedicated neural circuits, not only for the representation of animals but also for the representation of the perceptual properties of animals as expressed verbally.

This train of thought leads us toward a model in which semantic knowledge is subserved by a large number of independent, highly specialised neural modules, each tied to a particular semantic domain, type of information, and modality (see Coltheart et al., 1998). The problems with such a model are obvious. As the number of supposed innately specified modules increases, it becomes increasingly difficult to understand why some combinations of deficit are observed frequently (such as the conjoint impairment of animals and foods) and others are observed rarely or not at all (e.g. the conjoint impairment of artefacts and foods). It also becomes more difficult to accept that such modules have developed in response to evolutionary pressures—or at least, more difficult to construct, after the fact, an evolutionary rationale for the existence of such highly specialised modules.

Furthermore, the theory does not help us to understand other disturbances of semantic cognition. Another strength of the FM model is that it ties together data from patients with category-specific dysphasias and visual agnosias. The domain-specific knowledge hypothesis does not explain why visual agnosics are often worse at identifying living things, even when the stimulus items are controlled for confounding visual and psycholinguistic factors (Arguin, Bub, & Dudek, 1996; Dixon, 1999). Nor does it explain the occurrence of generalised semantic deficits that do not favour some categories over others, such as are observed in semantic dementia (Snowden, Goulding, & Neary, 1989; Hodges, Patterson, Oxbury, & Funnell, 1992; Hodges, Graham, & Patterson, 1995).

In addition to these empirical challenges, the theory seems to us to lack any real explanatory power. If, as Caramazza and Shelton (1998) claim, the data support the conclusion that categories of living things, foods, and artefacts are the only ones that may be selectively impaired, what does it add to propose that the brain must have evolved special modules for processing information about each of these domains? To their credit, they acknowledge that, "... unless we can independently motivate the assumption of categorical organisation of conceptual knowledge, we would have merely assumed what we are trying to explain—an infelicitous circularity" (Caramazza & Shelton, 1998, p. 18).

We, of course, agree. In search of the desired motivation, the authors adopt an evolutionary perspective, arguing that there is a high fitness value to the evolutionary adaptations that would allow an organism to discriminate between predators and prey, and to identify food sources. Under this view, it makes sense that the only three innately specified semantic domains are those of foods, animals, and "other things". Tellingly, Shelton and Caramazza have already amended this claim to admit category-specific deficits for finer-grained but "evolutionarily motivated" categories such as body parts (Shelton et al., 1998); and have even suggested that impairments specific to "non-evolutionary" categories might be observed as a consequence of mechanisms similar to those adopted by the SF hypothesis (Shelton & Caramazza, 1999).

However, taking the domain-specific knowledge hypothesis at face value, speculation about which semantic domains are innate is necessarily *post-hoc*; and it is difficult to seriously conclude that such activity provides independent motivation for the theory. *Post-hoc* evolutionary arguments have been made, with varying degrees of success, to support a host of differing claims about which semantic distinctions are given innately and which are learned (Carey & Spelke, 1994; Pinker, 1994, 1997; Springer & Keil, 1991; Wellman & Gelman, 1997). In the absence of converging empirical evidence to support them, such claims amount to little more than restatements of the data.

Furthermore, there are good reasons why the categories of foods, animals, and artefacts might be special, quite apart from their fitness value. Statistical analyses of attribute-listing studies have shown that, simply on the basis of their propensity to share properties, objects cluster naturally into these global categories. Garrard et al. (2001) entered 64 items from an attribute-listing study into a hierarchical clustering algorithm, based on the vector of properties attributed to each object by subjects in the study. The algorithm divided the various objects into three broad clusters, corresponding to the categories of animals, foods, and artefacts. It is at least possible, then, that the statistical structure of the environment contributes to the differentiation of objects into global categories. We will return to this idea later.

In summary, the expansion of the case literature in recent years, and the accompanying increase in the variability of deficits reported across patients, have led some theorists to reject the sensory–functional framework outright. As an alternative, Caramazza and Shelton (1998) propose that evolutionary pressures have led to the development (across phylogeny) of separate neural modules dedicated to storing semantic information (both sensory and functional) about the categories of animals, foods, and artefacts. We have argued that such an account is likely to fail for several reasons. First, it appears equally vulnerable to the empirical criticisms levelled against the sensory–functional hypothesis. To explain the range of deficits reported in the literature, one must posit multiple independent neural modules, each restricted to storing a particular kind of information about a single semantic domain, in a single modality. However, if this view is correct, it is not clear why some combinations of deficit occur frequently and that others are observed rarely or not at all. Second, the theory does not account well for other disorders of semantic cognition, such as visual agnosia and semantic dementia. Third, it provides no explanation of the graded nature of category-specific deficits or the sloppy boundaries between impaired and spared domains. Finally, the theory has little explanatory power and seems to us to be little more than a redescription of the data.

Antithesis: unitary semantics hypotheses

As the patient record has expanded, so has our understanding of the counter-intuitive ways that complex neural systems can behave under damage. Connectionist models have demonstrated that the behaviour of such systems can vary dramatically depending upon the theorist's assumptions about how internal representations are structured. Traditional neuropsychological approaches often do not take into account representational structure (Allport, 1985), attributing cognitive deficits in neuropathology to the all-or-none impairment of broad areas of cortex, whose finer details remain unspecified. Connectionist models have allowed the theorist to explore the inner workings of such black boxes and, as a consequence, there has been an increasing appreciation of the extent to which representational structure can contribute to the ordered breakdown of cognitive function, even in anatomically homogeneous systems. This progress has led other researchers to explore the possibility that category-specific deficits might be explained without reference to the functional and anatomical specialisation of the cortex. Following Caramazza, Hillis, Rapp, and Romani (1990), we will refer to such approaches as unitary semantics hypotheses.

The central challenge of a unitary semantics hypothesis is to explain how double dissociations of semantic memory can occur without invoking any neuroanatomical specialisation in the semantic system. In other domains of cognition, such as word reading, it has been demonstrated that the ability of a network to perform correctly under damage can differ for various stimuli, depending upon their propensity to participate in regular or systematic mappings. Items that conform to systematic input–output mappings, such as the "regular" items in an orthography-to-phonology translation, are often easier for a network to learn and might be more robust to small perturbations in the weights. Items that do not adopt such regularities, such as "irregular" words, can be more difficult to learn and more vulnerable to damage. Several researchers (Devlin et al., 1998; McRae et al., 1997; Moss et al., 1998; Tippett et al., 1995) have suggested that these properties of neural networks might give rise to category-specific deficits, under the assumption that the domains of living and non-living things share differing degrees of structure.

To understand how such an account might work, consider a model of naming put forward by Devlin et al. (1998), illustrated in Figure 9.2. In this network, word sounds are represented by random patterns of activity across the layer labelled phonology, whereas semantic representations are reflected by patterns of activity across the semantic units. Each layer is recurrently connected to a hidden set of clean-up units: additional units that permit the network to form attractors corresponding to representations of an object's name and identity (Hinton & Shallice, 1991). The layers are also fully interconnected.

Devlin et al. (1998) constructed semantic and phonological representations for each of 60 objects, from various living and non-living categories. Phonological patterns were simply random binary vectors across the 40 phonological units. Like the FM model, semantic representations were composed of units encoding either sensory or functional properties of objects. Unlike the FM model, however, Devlin et al. built varying degrees of

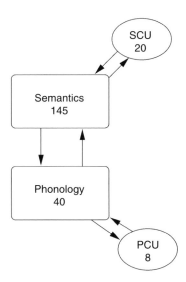

Figure 9.2.   Devlin et al.'s model of category-specific deficits in DAT. (Redrawn from Devlin et al., 1998, Figure 2, p. 82.)

similarity into their semantic representations, depending on each object's category. Exemplars of categories in the domain of living things were more likely to share features with one another, whereas non-living things were more likely to be composed of idiosyncratic features. Also, living things had a higher proportion of correlated features (across items) in their representations than did non-living things. Thus, the semantic representations for two kinds of bird were more similar to one another than to the representation of, for example, car; and, across living things, there was a higher incidence of features that consistently occurred together (such as wings, feathers, beak).[1]

The network was trained using the delta rule, just as described for the FM model. In its trained state, the presentation of a semantic representation would lead the network to generate the appropriate pattern of activity across the phonology units; whereas the presentation of an item's name would lead the network to generate the correct identity representation across the semantic units. Of particular interest was the network's behaviour when connections to the semantic units (both sensory and functional) were damaged indiscriminately. Would the incorporation of structure into the semantic representations cause the network to show doubly dissociated category-specific deficits in naming with increasing amounts of damage?

Devlin et al. (1998) ran several simulations of damage, each time removing some proportion of weights in the network and stepping through the set of training stimuli to assess performance. The results of one such run are illustrated in Figure 9.3. With small amounts of damage, the network frequently had greater difficulty naming non-living objects. However, as damage accumulated, the network showed a "critical mass" effect in the domain of living things. Its ability to name these objects declined sharply, so that with greater amounts of damage, the network showed the reverse dissociation: greater difficulty naming living relative to non-living things. Devlin et al. attributed this result to the structural differences between semantic representations of living and non-living things in their model. Groups of objects that share structure, in the form of overlapping, intercorrelated features, are robust to small amounts of damage, because the network can "fill in" missing features on the basis of its knowledge about how properties co-occur with one another, as encoded by the interconnecting weights. Because such bundles of mutually reinforcing features are assumed to occur more frequently for categories of living things, this property is reflected in a category-specific deficit favouring living things under small amounts of damage. However, as damage increases, shared structure becomes a liability. Once whole groups of

---

[1] These statistical properties of the training set were based on the results of an attribute listing task showing that there were a greater number of shared features among the domain of living relative to non-living things, and more correlations among features for categories of living relative to non-living things.

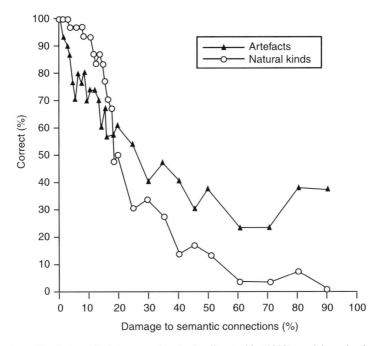

Figure 9.3. Simulation of picture naming in Devlin et al.'s (1998) model, under increasing amounts of damage. With small amounts of damage, the greater degree of structure among living things benefits the performance of the network for these items, resulting in a modest category-specific deficit favouring living things. With greater amounts of damage, the network shows a "critical mass" effect for living things: its ability to name them degrades increasingly rapidly, so that in later stages the network shows a category-specific deficit favouring non-living things. (Reprinted from Devlin et al., 1998, Figure 6, p. 88.)

mutually reinforcing features are lost, the network is unable to fill in the gaps correctly. In fact, it might make incorrect inferences on the basis of its remaining weights and, as a consequence, its ability to name degrades rapidly. By contrast, objects represented primarily by idiosyncratic properties, which tend to be non-living things, are relatively immune to these forces. Hence, the ability to name such objects degrades more linearly with increasing damage.

Closely related accounts have been put forward by a number of other theorists (McRae et al., 1997; Moss et al., 1998; Tyler & Moss, 1998). Although these hypotheses share the same general form, they vary in the degree and kind of structure assumed to exist across categories. For example, Tyler and Moss (1997) suggest that there are differences between animals and artefacts in their form–function correlations. Perceptual properties that are shared in the animal domain (e.g. eyes, legs) also tend to be correlated with functional attributes (e.g. seeing, walking). In the artefact domain, the idio-syncratic visual features tend to be correlated with functional attributes (e.g.

has a blade co-occurs with *can cut*). As a consequence, their model makes exactly the opposite prediction about how semantic knowledge should degrade with generalised damage: under small amounts of deterioration, living things ought to be impaired relative to artefacts, while the reverse should be true for extensive lesions (Moss et al., 1998).

We have focused on the Devlin et al. (1998) model because it offers the opportunity to discuss the limitations as well as the strengths of this approach. We have two principal reservations regarding Devlin and colleagues' work. The first stems from the manner in which the behaviour of the network under damage was assessed, and calls into question the authors' interpretation of their model's impaired performance. The second applies more generally to the capacity of unitary–semantics hypotheses to account for the range of patient data.

In Figure 9.3, we showed the results from one of 50 simulations of damage in Devlin et al.'s study. On this particular trial, the network showed the desired pattern of performance. On 12 of the 50 trials, however, the network did not show this behaviour. In 11 trials, it exhibited worse performance for living things throughout the progression of deterioration and in 1 trial it actually showed the reverse pattern from that expected: better performance on non-living things with small amounts of damage and better performance on living things with large amounts of damage. Thus, under damage, the network displayed a range of behaviours, only some of which support the conclusions drawn by the authors. Put another way, had Devlin and colleagues elected to focus on a different set of damage trials, they might have drawn quite different conclusions. Because the network's pattern of performance varies from trial to trial, the interpretation of its behaviour is subject to confirmation bias: it is easy to draw attention only to those trials that support one's hypothesis and to explain away those that do not. The problem is exacerbated by the fact that the propensity of the model to show a particular distribution of behaviours under damage can vary depending upon parameter choices not constrained by the theory, such as the number of training patterns, the number of hidden units, and the number of features per item in the training corpus (Perry, 1999). Thus, although the model showed the predicted pattern of behaviour on the majority of the damage trials reported by Devlin et al., it might not have done so under a different choice of model parameters.

Of course, this dilemma is not specific to the Devlin et al. (1998) model but is endemic to any connectionist model of a neuropsychological syndrome wherein damage is administered to the network at random. Under this circumstance, the behaviour of the model will always vary from one instance of damage to the next. If the model only occasionally shows the effect of interest, to what extent does it provide an adequate explanation of the phenomenon?

One response to the situation is to point out that, if the behaviour of the model varies as a function of damage, so does that of the patients. Although difficult to prove empirically, it is conceivable that two patients with lesions of comparable magnitude to the same cortical areas can nevertheless exhibit markedly different cognitive deficits. Perhaps, then, the variability of the behaviour of the model across different instances of damage is more of an asset than a liability, because it allows one to model the distribution of possible deficits across a set of patients with qualitatively similar lesions. Under this view, a single instance of damage to the model is analogous to a single case study in the literature. Thus, to explain a particular patient's data, one need simply demonstrate that the model is occasionally capable of showing the predicted pattern of breakdown, that is, that the case to be explained falls somewhere within the range of behaviours produced by the network across different instances of damage. This is the strategy adopted by Devlin et al. (1998) who, in writing about patients with Alzheimer's disease (AD), stated that "the variability in the effects of damage on performance in the modelling results is consistent with the variability observed among AD subjects, and helps to explain some seeming inconsistencies in the behavioural literature" (Devlin et al, 1998, p. 87; also see Mayall & Humphreys, 1996, and Joanisse & Seidenberg, 1999).

However, this approach is problematic. Connectionist networks are, of necessity, orders of magnitude smaller than the actual systems they are intended to model. Consequently, random damage to a given anatomical region is likely to yield much more variable behaviour from trial to trial in the model than in the actual system. If the model's behaviour under damage is more variable than the actual system's, it is more likely to occasionally exhibit patterns of deficit under pathology that do not arise from general properties of the network, but from a kind of sampling error. Given the small scale of the network, there is always the possibility on a given trial that, just by chance, the weights will be altered in such a way that the network displays a pattern of behaviour supporting almost any hypothesis. Thus, for any single instance of damage, it is not clear to what extent the behaviour of the network results from theoretically interesting properties or from the whims of chance on the given trial (see Plaut, 1995, for further discussion).

A better strategy, on our view, is to examine the behaviour of the network averaged across many different instances of damage. Under this approach, a single case is modelled not by a single administration of damage to the network but by damaging the network several times and assessing its average behaviour. This method has several advantages. First, it eliminates the influence of confirmation biases on the interpretation of network performance by providing an objective measure of performance that does not allow the theorist to pick and choose which trials to include. Second, it greatly reduces the likelihood that the observed patterns of deficit result from sampling error in selecting the weights or units to be lesioned. Third, it requires the theorist to provide an actual explanation of why patients differ, instead of simply attributing patient variability to chance. That is, to account for data across a variety of patients, the theorist must identify those parameters of the model that lead it, on average, to behave like patient X under one choice of values, and like patient Y under a different choice. When the effects of such parameters are understood in the model, the theorist is a step closer to understanding how they might operate in the actual system. Although Devlin et al. (1998) demonstrate that their model is capable of showing the predicted behaviour, and they provide a good explanation for why this might be, they leave us wondering why, if their theory is correct, the model does not show the predicted behaviour on 22% of the trials, and why the model does not show the effect at all when its performance is averaged across all 50 damage trials. A more satisfactory account would shed light on the factors that lead the network to behave sometimes in one way, sometimes in another, and would relate these back to assumed properties of the actual system.

Although our strategy has the benefit of providing a clear criterion for interpreting the network's impaired performance, it also has the consequence of reducing the range of behaviours that a network can "explain." In examining only the central tendencies in the model's behaviour for a given type of lesion, it becomes more difficult to account for extreme cases in the literature. It might be fairly easy to show that such cases fall within the range of behaviours produced by a network under damage; but considerably more difficult to construct a network that, on average, behaves as a single extreme case.

For this reason, it seems unlikely to us that unitary–semantics hypotheses of the kind we have discussed will be capable of explaining the full range of reported category-specific patients. All of the unitary–semantics theories to which we have made reference predict that performance on semantic tasks should, on average, decline, as illustrated in Figure 9.3. Each of these models might, by chance, show almost any pattern of breakdown on a single trial of damage. However, barring the consideration of individual damage trials, they all make clear predictions about the range of deficits that ought to be observed in the literature. Patients with dissociations of knowledge favouring items in the unstructured domain (whichever it may be under a given theory) should never be at ceiling for such items, but must always show at least a mild impairment. Similarly, patients with preserved knowledge of the "structured" domain must never show chance performance in the unstructured domain, but should always have some spared knowledge for such items. However, the existence of extreme cases in the literature (for example, JBR and SBY; see Warrington & Shallice, 1984) contradict these predictions. Simply attributing these cases to chance hardly constitutes a satisfactory explanation, but we see no other way for unitary semantics theories to accommodate them.

There are also empirical findings that, *prima facie*, seem incompatible with a unitary–semantics hypothesis. As we have already noted, functional neuroimaging studies suggest that different cortical areas might be differentially involved in processing information about different kinds of objects (Martin et al., 1995), or in processing different kinds of semantic information about objects (Mummery et al., 1998), and these results are consistent with differences in the neuropathology that accompanies impaired knowledge of living or non-living things (e.g. Gainotti et al., 1995; Damasio et al., 1996). Although these studies are by no means conclusive, they do not fit well into the unitary–semantics framework.

Of course, there is no reason why the principles illustrated in unitary–semantics models do not act in concert with principles of anatomical specialisation to provide a full account of the data. In fact, Devlin et al. (1998) replicate Farah and McClelland's results in their own model, by administering focal damage to either the functional– or sensory–semantic units in their architecture. They suggest that some severe cases of category-specific deficits could result from such anatomically localised lesions to sensory or motor areas as indicated by the sensory–functional hypothesis, whereas other more graded impairments could arise from general damage to the entire system, under the assumption that semantic representations share structure. Aside from our concerns about how the model was tested, it seems possible that some variation on this approach might ultimately prove fruitful, as we suggest in the next section.

Even from this stance, however, there remain many important questions to be answered. There is still little consensus regarding the extent to which representations of various kinds of objects share structure, or which kinds of structure contribute to the preservation of semantic knowledge in the face of damage (Garrard et al., 2001; Moss et al., 1998). As we have seen, different positions on this issue can lead to radically different predictions about the patterns of deficits that should be observed in the patient data, even if one ignores extreme cases.

There is as yet little empirical data available to illuminate any potential relationship between the overall extent of cortical damage, and the relative preservation of knowledge for animal and artefact categories. Gonnerman et al. (1997) reported cross-sectional data from 15 patients with dementia of the Alzheimer's type (DAT) with impaired semantic memory, supporting Devlin et al.'s (1998) theory. Patients with mild cognitive impairment, as assessed by overall naming performance, showed a slight preservation of knowledge for the names of living relative to non-living things, whereas patients with a greater degree of dysfunction showed quite pronounced category-specific deficits favouring artefacts. However, Garrard, Patterson, and Hodges (1998) failed to replicate these results in another cross-sectional study of DAT, using a different measure of overall cognitive impairment. Moreover, cases of semantic dementia—a progressive syndrome in which semantic knowledge undergoes a profound degradation—typically do not show the consistent preservation of one semantic domain relative to another (Hodges et al., 1995; Lambon Ralph, Graham, Patterson, & Hodges, 1999).

In summary, connectionist instantiations of unitary–semantics hypotheses have demonstrated that representational structure can have profound consequences for the pattern of decline witnessed in different semantic domains. In some cases, such structure can lead to mild double-dissociations in a network under increasing amounts of damage applied to the same locus. However, the range of effects such networks can show has probably been overestimated. Barring the consideration of individual, idiosyncratic instances of damage, it is unlikely that a unitary–semantics theory can produce the degree and variety of category-specific deficits that have been observed in patients.

SYNTHESIS: A PROMISING APPROACH

On the one hand, models that invoke independent and innate neural processing modules to explain category-specific deficits are too fragmented and underspecified to provide a satisfying explanation of the data. On the other hand, the limited ability of homogeneous connectionist models to explain extreme double dissociations suggest that some anatomical differentiation must be invoked to accommodate the range of patient data. A fruitful middle ground can be found in models that incorporate principles of anatomical specialisation and representational structure to explain the data. It is too early to determine whether the principles that emerge from further investigation in this direction will provide a full account of category-specific deficits. However, recent work in other domains of semantic cognition has been successful in explaining a variety of related phenomena. In the last section of this chapter, we consider a model of semantic dementia put forward by Rogers et al. (1999), which suggests a promising direction for future research.

Semantic dementia refers to the progressive deterioration of semantic memory that is often observed as a consequence of the cortical atrophy that accompanies Pick's disease (Snowden et al., 1989). Patients suffering from the disorder exhibit a marked anomia and a profound difficulty with semantic tasks such as word-to-picture matching, word and picture sorting, attribute listing, definition, and the Pyramids and Palm Trees Test (Hodges et al., 1995; Howard & Patterson, 1992); other cognitive faculties, however, seem remarkably spared. Patients with semantic dementia make an interesting contrast to those with herpes encephalitis (the vast majority of category-specific cases) because they do not show relative sparing of some semantic domains over others. For example, although patient IW (described earlier) was apparently worse at retrieving the sensory relative to the functional properties of objects, her ability to name, draw, and define living and non-living objects was equally impaired (Lambon Ralph et al., 1998); this appears to be true of semantic dementia patients generally (Hodges et al., 1995).

Although they do not show category-specific deficits in their overall correct performance, semantic dementia patients do show different patterns of incorrect responding when naming animals compared to artefacts. Rogers et al. (1999) interpreted these differences in the context of a connectionist model similar in many respects to those discussed above. The model was proposed to explain the generalised deterioration of semantic memory without preferential sparing of one domain over another but, like semantic dementia patients, it showed different patterns of errors for living and non-living things. The principles that lead to these differences in the model might help us understand how category-specific deficits can arise from neuroanatomic differences already known to exist in the brain.

The Rogers et al. (1999) model is illustrated in Figure 9.4. Like the FM model, it uses semantics to map between verbal and visual representations, whose structures are determined by the physical properties of the environment. In learning to do so, the network acquires internal representations of objects that reflect their semantic relations (Hinton, 1986; Rumelhart & Todd, 1993).

Each unit in the visual layer responds to some aspect of an object's appearance, such as its shape, texture, colour, or shading. Each unit in the verbal layer represents a propositional statement describing the object, for example, its name, or other explicit attributes that can be expressed verbally. When a picture is presented to the network, units in the visual layer are clamped to the corresponding pattern and the job of the network is to activate the propositional features that apply to the item depicted. Conversely, when the network is presented with a name or a verbal description of an object, the corresponding propositional features in the *verbal* layer are clamped and the network must correctly activate the appropriate visual units, as well as any propositional units not specified in the input.

Like Devlin et al. (1998), the authors assumed that objects in the world share different degrees of visual and propositional structure, depending upon their category membership. On the basis of similarity measures derived from the featural decomposition of drawings, they constructed visual representations for 32 items drawn from two living (birds and land animals) and two non-living (vehicles and household objects) categories. Following the results of Garrard et al.'s (2001) attribute-listing study, they also constructed propositional representations, intended to capture regularities in the verbal descriptions that people apply to various objects. Items with similar verbal descriptions were represented by similar patterns of activity across the

280

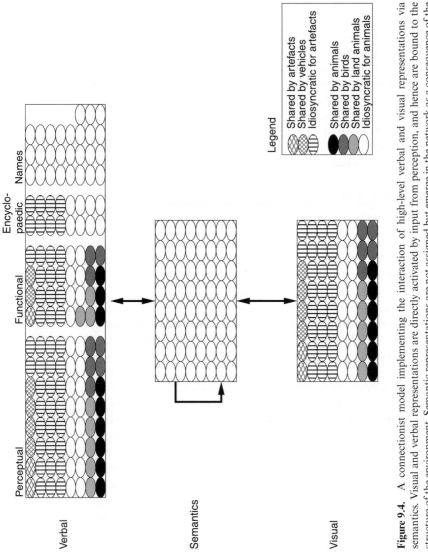

Figure 9.4. A connectionist model implementing the interaction of high-level verbal and visual representations via semantics. Visual and verbal representations are directly activated by input from perception, and hence are bound to the structure of the environment. Semantic representations are not assigned but emerge in the network as a consequence of the learning algorithm and the structure of the surface representations. The illustration shows the number of distinctive features, and the number of features shared across domain (living thing/artefact) and superordinate category. The top units are local representations of propositional features, such as "can fly" and "has a long neck".

verbal units. These propositions might describe any of the sensory, functional, or encyclopaedic properties of an object. Note, though, that a propositional feature describing a visual property is quite distinct from the visual property itself in this model. Instances of living things had a greater tendency to share both visual and propositional features than did instances of non-living things.

Unlike either Devlin et al. (1998) or Farah and McClelland (1991), Rogers et al. (1999) did not construct semantic representations for the objects in their corpus. Instead, they trained the network with a variant of the backpropagation learning algorithm suited to recurrent networks. Like the delta rule described earlier, backpropagation uses the discrepancy between observed and desired activations to adjust weights in the network so that its performance improves. However, backpropagation also allows error derivatives to be passed backward through intermediate units whose representations are unspecified. For example, the error signal from verbal units in the Rogers et al. (1999) model could be used to adjust the weights connecting visual and semantic units, without having to specify a particular mediating pattern of activity in the semantic layer. Thus, the network was able to acquire the mappings between verbal and visual patterns without having assigned intermediate representations (Rumelhart & Todd, 1993). In so doing, it came to represent each object in its environment with a stable pattern of activity across its hidden unit. Because these patterns were discovered by the learning algorithm, they can be considered learned internal representations (Rumelhart, McClelland, & PDP Research Group, 1986).

An interesting property of the internal representations that evolve in backpropagation nets is that they capture the similarity structure across their inputs and outputs (Hinton, 1986). In the Rogers et al. (1999) model, semantically related items come to be represented by similar patterns of activity across the hidden units by virtue of the tendency for objects in the same category to share visual and propositional features. Because this tendency is much stronger among animals than among artefacts, the network's representations of animals are much more rigidly structured. The steady states that represent individual birds, for example, are very similar to one another, whereas the attractors that correspond to individual vehicles are much more widely dispersed in representation space. Furthermore, representations of birds and land animals, although fairly distinct, are still more similar to one another than to the various vehicles and household objects. Thus, the network comes to acquire representations that capture the degree of semantic relatedness among objects, by virtue of the backpropagation learning algorithm operating on patterns that share structure.

To understand how the behaviour of the model deteriorates in pathology, Rogers et al. (1999) lesioned the network by removing an increasing proportion of all its weights. They then assessed its performance on a model

analogue of a picture naming task, in which the damaged network was presented with a visual representation as input and was allowed to settle to a
steady state. To determine the model's response, they simply selected the
name unit most strongly activated above its midpoint (0.5). The authors
damaged the network several times, and tested its ability to name all 32 items
in its vocabulary. The responses were coded as "correct" if the damaged
network gave the same response as the undamaged network; as "superordinate errors" when the damaged network gave a correct but more general
response than the undamaged network; as "semantic errors" when the
damaged network gave an incorrect response from the same superordinate
category as the correct response; and as "no response" when the network
was unable to activate any name unit above 0.5.

The most interesting result for our purposes is that the network showed a
different pattern of responses for animals and artefacts. It made a greater
proportion of "no responses" at all levels of impairment in response to artefacts, but a greater proportion of "superordinate" and "semantic" errors
when naming animals. This is just the pattern of errors found in picture
naming with semantic dementia patients (Rogers et al., 1999). That is, both
the model and the patients are more likely to give an incorrect response for
living things, but less likely to give a response at all for non-living things.

We can understand this behaviour by considering the similarity structure
of the internal representations of the network. Recall that the attractors
corresponding to individual land animals are quite similar to one another,
whereas the attractors corresponding to various vehicles are more widely
distributed in representation space. As connections in the network are
lesioned, this attractor structure degrades and the steady states in the space
might drift or disappear. Because the representations for various land animals are all similar to one another, such drift is likely to land the network in
the incorrect attractor. For example, with damage, the attractor state for *pig*
might become unstable. If this happens, "pig" stimuli can be drawn into
nearby attractors that have not yet degraded, or into spurious attractors that
have formed as a result of damage. Because of the learned similarities
between land-animals, such proximal attractors are likely to correspond to
the representations of semantically related items, such as *dog*. Accordingly,
the network will attribute to the pig the properties it knows to be true of dogs.
In some cases—namely, for those properties common to dogs and pigs—the
network can still make correct inferences about the object. For example,
because the name "animal" applies both to pigs and to dogs, the network will
correctly verify that the pig is an animal, even if it falls into the attractor for
dog. However, properties that serve to differentiate dogs from pigs might be
lost or misattributed when the network's weights are perturbed; for example,
the network might attribute the property *is furry* to the pig when it falls into
the *dog* attractor. Under this view, errors of commission (such as calling the

pig a "dog") occur more frequently in highly structured domains, because there is a greater likelihood that the network will fall into a neighbouring attractor when damaged.

By contrast, in the domain of non-living things, there are few proximal attractors into which a given item can fall when its own representation becomes unstable. For example, the model's representation of *spinning wheel* can drift quite far before being captured by another non-living object representation. As it wanders into uninformative areas of the space, the network will become increasingly unable to make any inference about the properties of the spinning wheel. As long as it avoids falling to the wrong attractor state, however, the network will not attribute inappropriate properties to the item. Thus, in unstructured domains, the model will increasingly omit properties, but will relatively rarely make errors of commission.

Although intended to explain the generalised impairments observed in semantic dementia, this work also has implications for a theory of category-specific deficits. The Rogers et al. (1999) framework builds in anatomical distinctions between semantic association cortex and the areas that subserve sensorimotor representations in various modalities. The model implements visual and verbal surface modalities, but these are not the only kinds of information available from the environment. Other surface properties of objects, such as their feel, their taste, and the motor actions they afford, might also reasonably be expected to inform deep semantic representations. In particular, the various ways in which we engage an object in behaviour likely play an important role in our understanding of the object's identity—especially for artefacts.

The representations that subserve our ability to act on objects, which we assume to reside in an area of cortex separate from semantic, visual, and verbal areas, could share a degree of structure not mirrored in visual or verbal representations. Objects that afford similar actions, such as a typewriter and a piano, could induce similar representations across areas of cortex that subserve action. This structure might serve to inform the semantic similarities between objects just as visual and verbal representations are assumed to do in the Rogers et al. model. Furthermore, we might expect artefacts and living things to differ in the amount of structure they share across the actions with which they are associated (Moss et al., 1998). Just as living things share a high degree of visual structure, whereas artefacts do not, artefacts might share a higher degree of structure across action representations than do living things (Plaut, 1998).

This speculation leads us to a general framework in which semantic representations mediate activity among surface visual, verbal, and action representations. Under this view, lesions to the connections between semantics and either of visual or action areas could result in different category-specific deficits. Damage to the connections between semantics and action representations might lead the network to confuse various artefacts with one another, because such objects share structure in the "action" modality. By contrast, damage to the connections between vision and semantics could lead the network to confuse living things with one another, because of the high degree of visual structure shared in that domain. Deficits specific to language might manifest when the links between verbal and semantic areas are damaged, while the deficits apparent in semantic dementia could arise from generalised deterioration of the semantic units themselves. Thus, like the FM model, the theory has the potential to draw together phenomena from various neuropsychological syndromes. It is also consistent with the data from neuroimaging and neuropathology findings we have discussed.

CONCLUSION

Although these ideas are speculative at best, they illustrate how known properties of recurrent connectionist networks might be extended to account for category-specific deficits in a manner consistent with the sensory–functional hypothesis, without introducing anatomical distinctions that have not been shown to exist in the brain. Whether or not these principles can accommodate the entire range of patient behaviour is an empirical question. Nevertheless, it seems likely that no story will be complete without appealing both to the structure of representations in the semantic system and the neuroanatomical architecture of cortex.

ACKNOWLEDGEMENTS

The research was supported by an NIMH FIRST award (MH55628) to the second author and by NIMH Program Project Grant MH47566 (J. McClelland, PI). Correspondence regarding this article may be sent either to Tim Rogers (trogers@ cnbc.cmu.edu) or to David Plaut (plaut@cmu.edu), Mellon Institute 115-CNBC, Carnegie Mellon University, 4400 Fifth Avenue, Pittsburgh PA 15213-2683, USA.

REFERENCES

Allport, D.A. (1985). Distributed memory, modular systems and dysphasia. In S.K. Newman & R. Epstein (Eds.), *Current perspectives in dysphasia*. Edinburgh: Churchill Livingstone.

Arguin, M., Bub, D., & Dudek, G. (1996). Shape integration for visual object recognition and its implication in category-specific visual agnosia. *Visual Cognition, 3(3)*, 221–275.

Basso, A., Capitani, E., & Laiacona, M. (1988). Progressive language impairment without dementia: A case with isolated category specific semantic impairment. *Journal of Neurology, Neurosurgery and Psychiatry, 51*, 1201–1207.

Battig, W.F., & Montague, W.E. (1969). Category norms for verbal items in 56 categories: A replication and extension of the connecticut category norms. *Journal of Experimental Psychology, 80, Monograph Supplement 3, Part 2.*

Behrmann, M., & Lieberthal, T. (1989). Category-specific treatment of a lexical semantic deficit: A single case study of global aphasia. *British Journal of Communication Disorders, 24*, 281–299.

Bullinaria, J.A., & Chater, N. (1995). Connectionist modelling: Implications for cognitive neuropsychology. *Language and Cognitive Processes, 10*, 227–264.

Bunn, E.M., Tyler, L.K., & Moss, H.E. (1998). Category-specific and semantic deficits: The role of familiarity and property type re-examined. *Neuropsychology, 12*, 367–379.

Caramazza, A., Hillis, A.E., Rapp, B.C., & Romani, C. (1990). The multiple semantics hypothesis: Multiple confusions? *Cognitive Neuropsychology, 7*, 161–189.

Caramazza, A., & Shelton, J.R. (1998). Domain-specific knowledge systems in the brain: The animate–inanimate distinction. *Journal of Cognitive Neuroscience, 10(1)*, 1–34.

Carbonnel, S., Charnallet, A., David, D., & Pellat, J. (1997). One or several semantic system(s)? maybe none: Evidence from a case study of modality and category-specific 'semantic' impairment. *Cortex, 33(3)*, 391–417.

Carey, S., & Spelke, E. (1994). Mapping the mind: Domain specificity in cognition and culture. In L.A. Hirschfeld (Ed.), *Mapping the Mind: Domain Specificity in Cognition and Culture* (pp. 169–200). New York: Cambridge University Press.

Chao, L.L., Haxby, J.V., & Martin, A. (1999). Attribute-based neural substrates in temporal cortex for perceiving and knowing about objects. *Nature Neuroscience, 2(10)*, 913–919.

Coltheart, M., Inglis, L., Michie, P., Bates, A., & Budd, B. (1998). A semantic subsystem of visual attributes. *Neurocase, 4*, 353–370.

Damasio, H., Grabowski, T.J., Tranel, D., & Hichwa, R.D. (1996). A neural basis for lexical retrieval. *Nature, 380(6574)*, 499–505.

De Renzi, E., & Lucchelli, F. (1994). Are semantic systems separately represented in the brain? The case of living category impairment. *Cortex, 30(1)*, 3–25.

Devlin, J.T., Gonnerman, L.M., Andersen, E.S., & Seidenberg, M.S. (1998). Category-specific semantic deficits in focal and widespread brain damage: A computational account. *Journal of Cognitive Neuroscience, 10(1)*, 77–94.

Dixon, M. (1999). Tool and bird exemplar identification in a patient with category-specific visual agnosia. *Brain and Cognition, 40(1)*, 97–100.

Dixon, M., Bub, D., & Arguin, M. (1997). The interaction of object form and object meaning in the identification performance of a patient with category-specific visual agnosia. *Cognitive Neuropsychology, 14(8)*, 1085–1130.

Farah, M.J., & McClelland, J.L. (1991). A computational model of semantic memory impairment: Modality-specificity and emergent category-specificity. *Journal of Experimental Psychology: General, 120(4)*, 339–357.

Farah, M.J., McMullen, P.A., & Meyer, M.M. (1991). Can recognition of living things be selectively impaired? *Neuropsychologia, 29(2)*, 185–193.

Farah, M.J., & Wallace, M.A. (1992). Semantically-bounded anomia: Implications for the neural implementation of naming. *Neuropsychologia, 30*, 609–621.

Forde, E.M.E., Francis, D., Riddoch, M.J., Rumiati, R.I., & Humphreys, G.W. (1997). On the links between visual knowledge and naming: A single case study of a patient with a category-specific impairment for living things. *Cognitive Neuropsychology, 14(3)*, 403–458.

Funnell, E., & Sheridan, J. (1992). Categories of knowledge? Unfamiliar aspects of living and non-living things. *Cognitive Neuropsychology, 9(2)*, 135–153.

Gainotti, G., & Silveri, M.C. (1996). Cognitive and anatomical locus of lesion in a patient with with a category-specific semantic impairment for living beings. *Cognitive Neuropsychology, 13*, 357–389.

Gainotti, G., Silveri, M.C., Daniele, A., & Giustolisi, L. (1995). Neuroanatomical correlates of category-specific semantic disorders: A critical survey. *Memory, 3*, 247–265.

Garrard, P., Lambon Ralph, M.A., Hodges, J.R., & Patterson, K. (2001). Prototypicality, distinctiveness and intercorrelation: Analyses of the semantic attributes of living and non-living concepts. *Cognitive Neuroscience, 18*, 125–174.

Garrard, P., Patterson, K., & Hodges, J.R. (1998). Category-specific semantic loss in dementia of Alzheimer's type: functional–anatomical correlations from cross-sectional analyses. *Brain*, *121*, 633–646.

Gonnerman, L.M., Andersen, E.S., Devlin, J.T., Kempler, D., & Seidenberg, M.S. (1997). Double dissociation of semantic categories in Alzheimer's disease. *Brain and Language*, *57*, 254–279.

Hart, J., Berndt, R.S., & Caramazza, A. (1985). Category-specific naming deficit following cerebral infarction. *Nature*, *316*, 439–440.

Hart, J., & Gordon, B. (1992). Neural subsystems for object knowledge. *Nature*, *359*, 60–64.

Hillis, A.E., & Caramazza, A. (1991). Category-specific naming and comprehension impairment: A double dissociation. *Brain*, *114*, 2081–2094.

Hillis, A.E., Rapp, B., & Caramazza, A. (1995). Constraining claims about theories of semantic memory: More on unitary versus multiple semantics. *Cognitive Neuropsychology*, *12(2)*, 175–186.

Hillis, A.E., Rapp, B., Romani, C., & Caramazza, A. (1990). Selective impairments of semantics in lexical processing. *Cognitive Neuropsychology*, *7*, 191–243.

Hinton, G.E. (1986). Learning distributed representations of concepts. In *Proceedings of the 8th Annual Conference of the Cognitive Science Society* (pp. 1–12). Hillsdale, NJ: Lawrence Erlbaum Associates, Inc.

Hinton, G.E., & Shallice, T. (1991). Lesioning an attractor network: Investigations of acquired dyslexia. *Psychological Review*, *98(1)*, 74–95.

Hodges, J.R., Graham, N., & Patterson, K. (1995). Charting the progression in semantic dementia: Implications for the organisation of semantic memory. *Memory*, *3*, 463–495.

Hodges, J.R., Patterson, K., Oxbury, S., & Funnell, E. (1992). Semantic dementia: Progressive fluent aphasia with temporal lobe atrophy. *Brain*, *115*, 1783–1806.

Howard, D., & Patterson, K. (1992). *Pyramids and palm trees: A test of semantic access from pictures and words*. Bury St. Edmunds, UK: Thames Valley.

Joanisse, M.F., & Seidenberg, M.S. (1999). Impairments in verb morphology after brain injury: A connectionist model. *Proceedings of the National Academy of Science, USA*, *96*, 7592–7597.

Kurbat, M.A. (1997). Can the recognition of living things really be selectively impaired? *Neuropsychologia*, *35(6)*, 813–827.

Kurbat, M.A., & Farah, M.J. (1998). Is the category-specific deficit for living things spurious? *Journal of Cognitive Neuroscience*, *10(3)*, 0898–929.

Laiacona, M., Barbarotto, R., & Capitani, E. (1993). Perceptual and associative knowledge in category specific impairment of semantic memory: a study of two cases. *Cortex*, *29*, 727–740.

Lambon Ralph, M.A., Graham, K., Patterson, K., & Hodges, J.R. (1999). Is a picture worth a thousand words? Evidence from concept definitions by patients with semantic dementia. *Brain and Language*, *70(3)*, 309–335.

Lambon Ralph, M.A., Howard, D., Nightingale, G., & Ellis, A.W. (1998). Are living and non-living category-specific deficits causally linked to impaired perceptual or associative knowledge? Evidence from a category-specific double dissociation. *Neurocase*, *4*, 311–338.

Lecours, S., Arguin, M., Bub, D., Caille, S., & Fontaine, S. (1999). Semantic proximity and shape feature integration effects in visual agnosia for biological kinds. *Brain and Cognition*, *40(1)*, 171–174.

McCarthy, R., & Warrington, E.K. (1988). Evidence for modality-specific meaning systems in the brain. *Nature*, *334*, 428–430.

McClelland, J.L., & Rumelhart, D.E. (1985). Distributed memory and the representation of general and specific information. *Journal of Experimental Psychology: General*, *114(2)*, 159–188.

McRae, K., Sa, V.R. de, & Seidenberg, M.S. (1997). On the nature and scope of featural representations of word meaning. *Journal of Experimental Psychology: General*, *126(2)*, 99–130.

Martin, A., Haxby, J.V., Lalonde, F.M., Wiggs, C.L., & Ungerleider, L.G. (1995). Discrete cortical regions associated with knowledge of color and knowledge of action. *Science*, *270*, 102–105.

Martin, N., Gagnon, D.A., Schwartz, M.F., Dell, G.S., & Saffran, E.M. (1996). Phonological facilitation of semantic errors in normal and aphasic speakers. *Language and Cognitive Processes*, *11(3)*, 257–282.

Mayall, K., & Humphreys, G. (1996). A connectionist model of alexia: Covert recognition and case mixing effects. *British Journal of Psychology*, *87(3)*, 355–402.

Moore, C.J., & Price, C.J. (1999). A functional neuroimaging study of the variables that generate category-specific object processing differences. *Brain*, *122*, 943–962.

Moss, H.E., Tyler, L.K., Durrant-Peatfield, M., & Bunn, E.M. (1998). Two eyes of a see-through: Impaired and intact semantic knowledge in a case of selective deficit for living things. *Neurocase*, *4*, 291–310.

Mummery, C.J., Patterson, K., Hodges, J.R., & Price, C.J. (1998). Functional neuroanatomy of the semantic system: Divisible by what? *Journal of Cognitive Neuroscience*, *10(6)*, 766–777.

Perani, D., Cappa, S.F., Bettinardi, V., & Bressi, S. (1995). Different neural systems for the recognition of animals and man-made tools. *Neuroreport*, *6(12)*, 1637–1641.

Perani, D., Schnur, T., Tettamanti, M., Gorno-Tempini, M., Cappa, S.F., & Fazio, F. (1999). Word and picture matching: A PET study of semantic category effects. *Neuropsychologia*, *37(3)*, 293–306.

Perry, C. (1999). Testing a computational account of category-specific deficits. *Journal of Cognitive Neuroscience*, *11(3)*, 312–320.

Pinker, S. (1994). *The language instinct*. New York: Morrow.

Pinker, S. (1997). Words and rules in the human brain. *Nature*, *387(6633)*, 547–548.

Plaut, D.C. (1995). Double dissociation without modularity: Evidence from connectionist neuropsychology. *Journal of Clinical and Experimental Neuropsychology*, *17(2)*, 291–321.

Plaut, D.C. (1998). Systematicity and specialization in semantics. In D. Heinke, G. W. Humphreys, & A. Olson (Eds.), *Connectionist models in cognitive neuroscience: Proceedings of the fifth annual neural computation and psychology workshop*. New York: Springer.

Plaut, D.C., McClelland, J.L., Seidenberg, M.S., & Patterson, K. (1996). Understanding normal and impaired word reading: Computational principles in quasi-regular domains. *Psychological Review*, *103*, 56–115.

Plaut, D.C., & Shallice, T. (1993). Deep dyslexia: A case study of connectionist neuropsychology. *Cognitive Neuropsychology*, *10(5)*, 377–500.

Powell, J., & Davidoff, J. (1995). Selective impairments of object knowledge in a case of acquired cortical blindness. *Memory*, *3*, 435–461.

Riddoch, M.J., & Humphreys, G.W. (1987). A case of integrative visual agnosia. *Brain*, *110*, 1431–1462.

Rogers, T.T., Lambon Ralph, M., Patterson, K., McClelland, J.L., & Hodges, J.R. (1999). A recurrent connectionist model of semantic dementia. In *Proceedings of the Cognitive Neuroscience Society*, Washington DC, A Supplement to the *Journal of Cognitive Neuroscience*, *48*.

Rosch, E., Mervis, C.B., Gray, W., Johnson, D., & Boyes-Braem, P. (1976). Basic objects in natural categories. *Cognitive Psychology*, *8*, 382–439.

Rumelhart, D.E., Hinton, G.E., & McClelland, J.L. (1986). A general framework for parallel distributed processing. In D.E. Rumelhart, J.L. McClelland, & the PDP Research Group (Eds.), *Parallel distributed processing: Explorations in the microstructure of cognition*. (Vol. 1, pp. 45–76). Cambridge, MA: MIT Press.

Rumelhart, D.E., McClelland, J.L., & PDP Research Group, the. (1986). *Parallel distributed processing: Explorations in the microstructure of cognition*. (Vol. 1). Cambridge, MA: MIT Press.

Rumelhart, D.E., & Todd, P.M. (1993). Learning and connectionist representations. In D.E.

Meyer & S. Kornblum (Eds.), *Attention and Performance XIV: Synergies in experimental psychology, artifical intelligence, and cognitive neuroscience* (pp. 3–30). Cambridge, MA: MIT Press.

Sacchett, C., & Humphreys, G.W. (1992). Calling a squirrel a squirrel but a canoe a wigwam: A category-specific deficit for artefactual objects and body parts. *Cognitive Neuropsychology, 9(1)*, 73–86.

Saffran, E.M., & Schwartz, M.F. (1994). Of cabbages and things: Semantic memory from a neuropsychological perspective: A tutorial review. In C. Umilta & M. Moscovitch (Eds.), *Attention and Performance XV: Conscious and non-conscious aspects of cognitived processing* (pp. 507–536). Hillsdale, NJ: Lawrence Erlbaum Associates, Inc.

Samson, D., Pillon, A., & De Wilde, V. (1998). Impaired knowledge of visual and non-visual attributes in a patient with a semantic impairment for living entities: A case of a true category-specific deficit. *Neurocase, 4(4/5)*, 273–290.

Sartori, G., & Job, R. (1988). The oyster with 4 legs: A neuropsychological study on the interaction of visual and semantic information. *Cognitive Neuropsychology, 5*, 105–132.

Shelton, J.R., & Caramazza, A. (1999). Deficits in lexical and semantic processing: Implications for models of normal language. *Psychonomic Bulletin & Review, 6*, 5–27.

Shelton, J.R., Fouch, E., & Caramazza, A. (1998). The selective sparing of body part knowledge: A case study. *Neurocase, 4*, 319–351.

Sheridan, J., & Humphreys, G.W. (1993). A verbal-semantic category-specific recognition impairment. *Cognitive Neuropsychology, 10*, 185–200.

Silveri, M.C., & Gainotti, G. (1988). Interaction between vision and language in category-specific semantic impairment. *Cognitive Neuropsychology, 5*, 677–709.

Snowden, J.S., Goulding, P.J., & Neary, D. (1989). Semantic dementia: A form of circumscribed cerebral atrophy. *Behavioral Neurology, 2*, 167–182.

Spitzer, M., Kischka, U., Gueckel, M.E., Bellemann, M.E., Kammer, T., Seyyedi, S., Weisbrod, M., Schwartz, A., & Brix, G. (1998). Functional magnetic resonance imaging of category-specific cortical activation: Evidence for semantic maps. *Cognitive Brain Research, 6(4)*, 309–319.

Spitzer, M., Kwong, K.K., Kennedy, W., & Rosen, B.R. (1995). Category-specific brain activation in fMRI during picture naming. *Neuroreport, 6(16)*, 2109–2112.

Springer, K., & Keil, F. (1991). Early differentiation of causal mechanisms appropriate to biological and nonbiological kinds. *Child Development, 62*, 767–781.

Stewart, F., Parkin, A.J., & Hunkin, N.M. (1992). Naming impairments following recovery from herpes simplex encephalitis: Category specific? *Quarterly Journal of Experimental Psychology, 44A*, 261–284.

Tippett, L.J., McAuliffe, S., & Farah, M.J. (1995). Preservation of categorical knowledge in Alzheimer's disease: A computational account. *Memory, 3*, 519–553.

Tyler, L.K., & Moss, H.E. (1997). Functional properties of concepts: Studies of normal and brain-damaged patients. *Cognitive Neuropsychology, 14(4)*, 511–545.

Tyler, L.K., & Moss, H.E. (1998). Going, going, gone . . . ? Implicit and explicit tests of conceptual knowledge in a longitudinal study of semantic dementia. *Neuropsychologia, 36(12)*, 1313–1323.

Warrington, E.K., & McCarthy, R. (1983). Category-specific access dysphasia. *Brain, 106*, 859–878.

Warrington, E.K., & McCarthy, R. (1987). Categories of knowledge: Further fractionation and an attempted integration. *Brain, 110*, 1273–1296.

Warrington, E.K., & Shallice, T. (1984). Category specific semantic impairments. *Brain, 107*, 829–853.

Wellman, H.M., & Gelman, S.A. (1997). Knowledge acquisition in foundational domains. In D. Kuhn & R. Siegler (Eds.), *Handbook of Child Psychology, Volume 2: Cognition, perception and development* (pp. 523–573). New York: John Wiley and Sons.

Zeki, S. (1991). A direct demonstration of functional specialization in human visual cortex. *Journal of Neuroscience, 11*, 641–649.

Zeki, S. Watson, J.D., Lueck, C.J., Friston, K.J., Kennard, C., & Frackowiak, R.S. (1991). A direct demonstration of functional specialization in human visual cortex. *Journal of Neuroscience, 11*, 641–649.

CHAPTER TEN

Exemplar models and category-specific deficits

Koen Lamberts
University of Warwick, UK

Laura Shapiro
University of Birmingham, UK

INTRODUCTION

In recent years, there have been numerous reports of patients with brain damage who show selective identification or recognition deficits for objects from specific categories (see Forde [1999] and Humphreys & Forde [2001] for reviews). The most common deficit appears to be a selective impairment in the identification of living things, accompanied by relatively unimpaired recognition or identification of artificial or non-living objects. However, despite the large number of reported cases with category-specific processing deficits, there is still no agreement on the mechanisms that produce these deficits. It is not even clear whether all such cases can be understood in terms of a single process or mechanism, or whether category-specific deficits can be caused by a variety of different factors. In this chapter, we explore category-specific deficits from a theoretical viewpoint that evolved from recent research on perceptual categorisation and identification. Although some efforts have been made to model category-specific deficits with connectionist models (e.g. Farah & McClelland, 1991; Humphreys, Lamote, & Lloyd-Jones, 1995), we are not aware of any attempts to apply classical models of categorisation and identification[1] to the neuropsychological data on category-specificity (with

---

[1] In this chapter, we use the terms "categorisation", "identification", and "recognition" in the following way. "Categorisation" refers to a decision situation, in which objects have to be assigned to categories. The number of categories (i.e. the number of response alternatives) is smaller than the number of different objects that can occur, which implies that several objects

the exception of a study by Dixon, Bub, & Arguin [1997] which will be discussed in detail later).

Current theories of categorisation (and identification, which is a special case in which each object forms its own category) can be divided into five groups. The first group is that of exemplar models, which assume that categorisation of an object depends on the similarity of that object to instances in memory (Estes, 1994; Kruschke, 1992; Medin & Schaffer, 1978; Nosofsky, 1986). Second, there are decision-bound models, which are based on the multidimensional generalisation of classical signal detection theory (Ashby & Lee, 1991; Ashby & Maddox, 1993). According to these models, stimuli correspond to points in a multidimensional space. The perceptual representations of stimuli are assumed to be variable from trial to trial, due to intrinsic noise in the perceptual system. For categorisation, people are assumed to establish linear or non-linear category decision bounds in the multidimensional stimulus space. Categorisation depends on the position of the stimulus representation on a given trial relative to the decision bounds. Third are the models that explain category decisions based on the application of formal rules (Nosofsky, Palmeri, & McKinley, 1994). The fourth group contains various connectionist models of categorisation (Gluck & Bower, 1988), which attempt to explain categorisation in terms of associative links between input information and response alternatives. Finally, there have been recent proposals for combined models of categorisation, which integrate elements from two or more of the theories listed above (Ashby, Alfonso-Reese, Turken, & Waldron, 1998; Erickson & Kruschke, 1998).

In this chapter, we focus exclusively on exemplar models of categorisation and identification. There are several reasons for this choice. Exemplar models have an impressive empirical track record. They can explain categorisation and identification of a wide range of different stimuli in a wide range of situations (Lamberts, 1994, 1995, 1998, 2000; Lamberts & Freeman, 1999; Medin & Schaffer, 1978; Nosofsky, 1984, 1986, 1987, 1991a, 1992; Nosofsky & Palmeri, 1997). Conceptually, exemplar models are well developed and understood, and their relations with other classes of models have been explored in great detail (Alfonso-Reese & Ashby, 1995; Ashby & Maddox, 1993; Nosofsky, 1991b). Finally, exemplar models provide a unifying framework for a broad range of seemingly disparate cognitive tasks (Brockdorff & Lamberts, 2000; Estes, 1994; Lamberts, 2002; Nosofsky, 1991a; Nosofsky & Zaki, 1998; Palmeri, 1997).

---

require the same response. "Identification" is a special case of categorisation, in which each object forms its own category. In an identification task, the number of response alternatives is the same as the number of possible objects. Finally, "recognition" refers specifically to old–new recognition, in which a decision is made as to whether an object has been encountered before, regardless of its category membership or identity.

EXEMPLAR MODELS OF CATEGORISATION
AND IDENTIFICATION

According to exemplar models, learning involves the storage of instances in memory. Exemplar models do not assume that learning involves the computation of summary representations for categories or other groups of stimuli (as presumed in prototype models or rule-based models). Instead, it is assumed that each encounter with a stimulus leaves a separate trace in memory, and that subsequent categorisation, identification, or recognition depends on the retrieval of these specific memory traces. There are usually no constraints on the kind of information that can be contained in a memory trace. Exemplar information can be perceptual (referring to structural or surface properties of the object; Humphreys, Riddoch, & Quinlan, 1988) or semantic (referring to aspects of its meaning).

Probably the most successful exemplar model to date is Nosofsky's (1986) Generalised Context Model (GCM). The GCM assumes that stimuli can be defined as points in a multidimensional psychological space. Each dimension of the space corresponds to a particular aspect of the stimulus (such as colour, size, etc.). Although the GCM is intended primarily as a model of perceptual categorisation, dimensions can also refer to abstract or semantic stimulus attributes. Similarity between stimuli is defined as a decreasing function of the distance between the stimuli in the psychological space. We will use the following definition of similarity (which is a special case of the similarity notion of the GCM; see Nosofsky, 1986):

$$\eta_{ij} = \exp[-c(\sum_{p=1}^{P} w_p |x_{ip} - x_{jp}|)] \tag{10.1}$$

In this equation, the similarity between the representations of two stimuli (i and j) is a decreasing exponential function of the weighted sum of differences between the stimuli along the stimulus dimensions. w_p is the weight of dimension p, and x_{ip} and x_{jp} are the values of stimulus i and stimulus j on dimension p. If a dimension is more heavily weighted, a difference along that dimension will affect the similarity value more than a difference along a dimension with less weight. The parameter c is an index of discriminability. This index determines how quickly similarity decreases as a function of the distance between the stimulus representations (see Lamberts [1994] for an extensive discussion of the role of this parameter). If c is high, stimuli are highly discriminable, meaning that even a small difference between them will result in a relatively low similarity value. Unless we explicitly note otherwise, we will simply omit dimension weights from this equation in our applications of the GCM (thus assuming that all dimensions have the same weight).

If there are two alternative categories, the GCM assumes that the probability that a stimulus is classified in a given category depends on the summed similarity of that stimulus to the exemplars of the category on the one hand, and the total similarity of the stimulus to all exemplars in both categories on the other hand. The version of the GCM that we will use states that the probability that a stimulus i is classified into category C is given by:

$$P(R_C|S_i) = \frac{\sum_{j \in C} \eta_{ij}}{\sum_k \eta_{ik}} \qquad (10.2)$$

The GCM also applies to identification tasks, in which there are as many response alternatives as stimuli (in other words, each stimulus requires a unique response). The only difference with the categorisation model is in the choice rule, which becomes:

$$P(R_j|S_i) = \frac{\eta_{ij}}{\sum_k \eta_{ik}} \qquad (10.3)$$

This rule states that the probability of a response j to stimulus i is a function of the similarity between stimulus i and exemplar j (which has associated response j) on the one hand, and the total similarity of stimulus i to all exemplars in memory on the other hand. Because self-similarity is 1 in the GCM, the probability of correct identification thus becomes:

$$P(Correct|S_i) = \frac{1}{\sum_k \eta_{ik}} \qquad (10.4)$$

Although exemplar models have been used primarily to account for categorisation, identification and recognition in normal individuals, there have been a few attempts to apply exemplar models to neuropsychological data. An important application by Dixon, Bub, and Arguin (1997) will be discussed later in this chapter. Nosofsky and Zaki (1998) have recently shown that an exemplar model can provide insight into complex patterns of performance in patients with amnesia. The starting point of their work was a series of experiments by Knowlton and Squire (1993), in which groups of normal and amnesic patients categorised or made old/new judgements for sets of visual patterns. The results showed that the normal controls performed much better than the patients on old/new recognition, whereas both groups performed at a similar level in categorisation. Knowlton and Squire (1993) interpreted this result in terms of multiple memory systems, with an implicit system responsible for the acquisition of categorical knowledge, and a declarative system responsible for old/new recognition. In amnesics, the declarative system was supposed to be damaged (causing poor recognition performance), but an intact implicit system would still allow normal categorisation performance. Nosofsky and Zaki (1998) showed that it was not necessary to assume that the dissociation in task performance reflected an underlying dissociation in processing systems. Specifically, Nosofsky and Zaki (1998) demonstrated that a single exemplar model explained Knowlton and Squire's (1993) data, if it was assumed that brain damage led to a parameter change. A model in which the discriminability parameter c (see equation 10.1) had a smaller value for amnesic patients than for normal controls produced the dissociation between categorisation and recognition observed by Knowlton and Squire (1993), without having to assume separate subsystems for these tasks. Moreover, the model also explained the results from two other studies (Knowlton, Mangels, & Squire, 1996; Knowlton, Squire, & Gluck, 1994), on exactly the same assumptions. The discriminability parameter (c in equation 10.1) determines how steeply similarity decreases with increasing distance between stimulus representations. If c is high, processing is very selective, and perfect matches between representations are weighted far more in decision making than imperfect matches. If c is low, even poor matches produce relatively high similarity values. The value of c can have a great impact on the behaviour of exemplar models. For instance, Lamberts (1994) showed that changes in discriminability can produce model behaviour that ranges from a nearest-neighbour model (in which only the most similar exemplar determines categorisation) to a nearly linear prototype model (in which similarity to the "average" or prototype of the category determines choice). Nosofsky and Zaki's (1998) results show the potential of exemplar models to provide a single-systems explanation for dissociations that seem to invite a multiple-systems interpretation. The importance of this work for the interpretation of category-specific deficits is obvious. In the past, these deficits too have been explained in terms of multiple semantic or memory systems (Caramazza & Shelton, 1998; Sartori & Job, 1988; Silveri & Gainotti, 1988; Silveri, Daniele, Giustolisi, & Gainotti, 1991), and we will attempt to show that an exemplar account produces category specificity, without having to assume multiple storage or retrieval systems.

EXEMPLAR STORAGE AND CATEGORY-SPECIFIC DEFICITS

Now that we have defined the principles of exemplar models, we can explore the implications of such models for understanding the category-specific deficits reported in the literature. Although most deficit studies have used identification as the main task, we will discuss both identification and categorisation.

An important aspect of any model of neuropsychological deficits is the implementation of brain damage in terms of the model's components and processes. Because we do not know the physiological mechanisms that might support processes such as those defined in exemplar models, we can only postulate plausible ways in which neurological damage could alter the characteristics of the psychological model. In this chapter, we will investigate two possible effects of neurological damage. Following Nosofsky and Zaki (1998), we will explore the effects of decreased stimulus discriminability. We will also investigate the non-selective loss of features of stored exemplars. Not only are these two plausible consequences of brain damage, their effects are also quite similar to those resulting from other possible damage processes (such as loss of the ability to process particular dimensions). Of course, it is possible that neurological damage has other, unanticipated effects. It is conceivable, for instance, that a loss of exemplar information would be accompanied by noise in decision making. For the purpose of clarifying and exploring the predictions of exemplar theories for category-specific deficits, assuming that brain damage results in random loss of features or decreased discriminability is quite sufficient.

Before we could start the modelling work with the GCM, we had to explore the structure of the objects within the categories that we were going to study. The stimulus dimensions that may underlie the representations of living and non-living objects are unknown, so we had to make *a priori* assumptions about the structure of the living and non-living categories. These assumptions are crucial for the modelling work. Even without formal demonstration, it is obvious that category-specific deficits are unlikely to emerge through feature loss (or any other mechanism) if the damage is non-selective and the categories have the same underlying structure. On these conditions, category-specific deficits would only occur if the damage somehow affected exemplars from one category much more than exemplars from the other category. If damage is non-selective (as we will assume in all the modelling), one would expect both categories to suffer to the same extent. Category-specific deficits could only emerge exceptionally, as a result of random variation in the damage effects. However, for categories that are fairly large and that contain objects with a large number of features (such as the living and non-living categories), category-specific deficits would be extremely rare. Moreover, both categories would have the same likelihood of being selectively affected, and this is contradicted by the far higher incidence of category-specific deficits for living things in patients with brain damage. From these considerations, it is quite clear that exemplar models will predict systematic category-specific deficits only as a consequence of non-selective damage if the categories involved are somehow different from each other. In the following section, we explore the differences between living and non-living objects that may be relevant for understanding category-specific deficits.

DIFFERENCES BETWEEN LIVING AND
NON-LIVING OBJECT CATEGORIES

In many studies in which category-specific deficits were reported, the stimuli were taken from Snodgrass and Vanderwart's (1980) collection of object drawings. Snodgrass and Vanderwart (1980) have supplied norms for name agreement, image agreement, familiarity, and visual complexity for their picture set, so it is relatively straightforward to determine whether the living and non-living objects used in studies that report category-specific deficits differed on these variables, or to design studies in which these variables are controlled. Interestingly, when familiarity, word frequency and name agreement were matched for living and non-living stimuli, Funnell and Sheridan (1992) found that a disproportionate impairment for living things disappeared in one patient. Gaffan and Heywood (1993) and Stewart, Parkin, and Hunkin (1992) also found that the poorer performance for living things compared to non-living things observed in their patient disappeared once word frequency, familiarity and visual complexity were matched for the two categories. However, Farah, Meyer, and McMullen (1996) found that when two of their patients were tested on exactly the same set of pictures but with further replications, their selective deficits for living things remained. Gainotti and Silveri (1996) and Kurbat (1997) also found that category-specific effects occurred in their patients when the normed variables were controlled. Together, these results indicate that category-specific effects are not purely due to any differences in familiarity, word frequency, and name agreement that might exist between the categories of living and non-living things.

A potentially far more relevant difference between living and non-living object categories concerns the similarity relations that exist between the category members. Various studies have suggested that the similarity structures of the living and non-living categories in the Snodgrass and Vanderwart (1980) set are not equivalent (Humphreys et al., 1988; Gaffan and Heywood, 1993; Humphreys et al., 1995). By similarity, we mean similarity in the purely perceptual sense; for instance, pictures of a horse and a dog are perceptually similar because they both contain the same components (such as head, neck, body, and legs). When Humphreys et al. (1988) asked normal participants to list the parts of living and non-living things, living things showed up as having more shared parts than non-living things. The authors also compared the outline contours of standardised drawings from different categories by normalising all the Snodgrass and Vanderwart pictures for size and orientation, and then overlaying each picture with every other picture from the same category on a grid and calculating the overlap. The living things tended to have higher degrees of contour overlap than the non-living things.

Further evidence that perceptual similarity is higher within living categories than within non-living categories was provided by Gaffan and Heywood

(1993), using the Snodgrass and Vanderwart (1980) picture set. Normal subjects made more errors naming living than non-living things when stimulus quality was degraded, indicating that living things are less visually discriminable (i.e. more perceptually similar) than non-living things. The authors also trained monkeys to make discriminative responses to pictures of living and non-living things and found that the monkeys took longer to learn the living responses than non-living responses. Specifically, their difficulty in distinguishing among living things increased steeply as the number of living things to be discriminated increased. The authors concluded that the high levels of perceptual overlap in living categories caused the difficulties in discrimination between these items.

We have replicated these findings ourselves. Ten subjects (undergraduate students) gave pairwise ratings of perceptual similarity for a randomly chosen set of 15 living and 15 non-living pictures from the Snodgrass and Vanderwart set. The subjects were asked to ignore what the pictures actually represented and to concentrate entirely on the perceptual characteristics of the drawings on the screen. They were asked to give each pair a rating between 0 and 9, where 0 was for a pair that look nothing like each other and 9 was for a pair that was almost identical. The living pairs were rated as being more similar to each other than the non-living pairs; the mean rating for living pairs was 3.69, compared to 2.49 for the non-living pairs. This effect was significant ($t(9) = 10.39$, $p < .001$).

We have also achieved the same result by using the reaction time to decide that two pictures were different as a measure of similarity. It was assumed that, for two very dissimilar pictures, participants would be able to decide very quickly that they were different. However, for two very similar pictures, more features would have to be processed before the differences became apparent and reaction times would be much slower (see Lamberts, Brockdorff & Heit, in press). In this experiment we used 48 of the pictures selected by Funnell and Sheridan (1992), where norm values for word frequency, familiarity and visual complexity were equivalent for the living and non-living pictures. This particular set is useful to judge whether the living and non-living categories differ in their similarity profile, even when these other factors are controlled. The 24 living pictures and 24 non-living pictures were grouped into pairs of identical and different pictures within the living and non-living categories. The mean time taken to correctly decide that two pictures were different was significantly longer for the living pairs (531 ms) than for the non-living pairs (518 ms) ($F(1, 19) = 21.79$, $p < .001$), indicating that the living pictures are more similar to each other than the non-living pictures.

We have outlined good evidence that perceptual similarity is not equivalent within living and non-living categories. All the above findings indicate that for the Snodgrass and Vanderwart (1980) set, the living pictures are perceptually more similar to each other than the non-living pictures. The

Snodgrass and Vanderwart set is used to test most patients with category-specific deficits. Therefore, we decided to design the categories used in the simulation work with the GCM in such a way that one category contained elements that were more similar to each other than the other category.

SIMULATING CATEGORY-SPECIFIC DEFICITS

In all the modelling work that we report in this chapter, two categories of simulated objects were used. Each category contained 20 exemplars, and each exemplar consisted of 15 continuous dimensions. The categories were constructed in the following way. First, we defined a prototype for each category. The prototype of the first category had a value of 0 on all 15 dimensions, whereas the prototype of the second category had a value of 1 on all dimensions. Next, the prototypes were used to generate the exemplars within each category (the prototypes themselves were not part of the categories). Exemplars were generated by random distortion of the category prototypes. Each exemplar from the first category was obtained by adding a random number to the prototype value for each dimension. The random numbers for this category were drawn from a rectangular distribution with a mean of 0 and range from −0.3 to +0.3. The exemplars from the second category were generated in a similar fashion, except that the range of the random numbers was from −1 to +1. As a result, there was more variability in the second category, and the exemplars from this category were less similar to each other than the exemplars from the other category. We will call the first category the "homogeneous" category, and the second the "heterogeneous" category. Within each category, a total of 20 exemplars were generated.

The effects of brain damage were first simulated by randomly removing features from the 40 exemplars that made up the memory set. The expected proportion of deleted features varied between 0 (intact memory) and 0.9 (severe loss of feature information). At each level of damage, we simulated 1000 cases. In the simulation, the dimension(s) that corresponded to a missing exemplar feature were simply omitted from the similarity calculations. For each case, the GCM was applied to generate a predicted proportion of correct identification responses across all the exemplars within each category. The model was also used to predict proportions of correct categorisation responses across all exemplars within each category. The only model parameter that needed clamping was c, the discriminability index (see equation 10.1). To obtain a better overview of the model's range of predictions, we repeated the entire simulation experiment with different values of c.

Figure 10.1 shows the simulation results, separately for identification and categorisation within the two categories, and for two different values of c (3.0 and 5.0, respectively).

The simulated results for the identification task showed a strong contrast

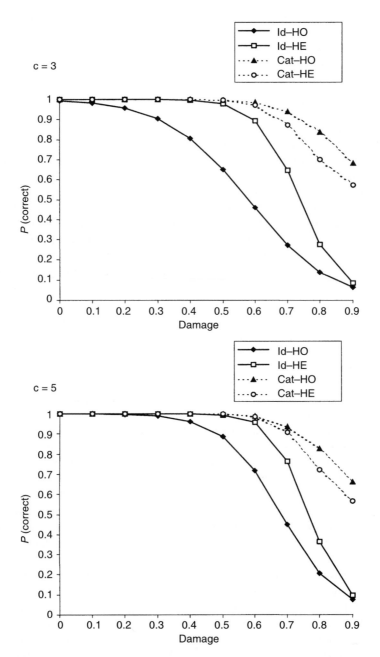

Figure 10.1. Simulation results (proportion correct responses) for identification (Id) and categorisation (Cat) of stimuli in homogeneous (HO) and heterogeneous (HE) categories as a function of discriminability (c) and exemplar damage.

between the two categories. Loss of features had a stronger detrimental effect on the identification of the objects in the homogeneous category than on identification of the objects in the heterogeneous category. For the categorisation task, however, the opposite pattern occurred. Categorisation of the heterogeneous objects declined more rapidly than categorisation of the homogeneous objects. (Note that the absolute difference in performance between the identification and categorisation tasks is partly due to the different levels of expected chance performance in the two tasks). This pattern occurred for both values of c in this simulation, and further modelling work showed that it occurred across a wide range of category structures and parameter settings. Whenever one category contained exemplars that were more similar to each other than the exemplars in the other category, feature loss affected identification performance more in the category with similar exemplars, whereas it affected categorisation more in the category with relatively dissimilar exemplars. Intuitively, it is easy to understand why this pattern emerges. Identification, in which each stimulus requires a unique response, is more difficult if a stimulus has close neighbours. If features are lost, a stimulus might become less distinguishable from one or more other stimuli, and performance will drop. For categorisation, however, close neighbours help, because the probability of a correct response depends on the total similarity of a stimulus to all exemplars within a category. If a stimulus has many close neighbours, even a large proportion of features can be lost before performance drops significantly.

Figure 10.2 summarises the model's predictions for identification and categorisation of homogeneous and heterogeneous objects, on the assumption that feature memory is intact, but for different levels of stimulus–exemplar discriminability (c). It is immediately clear that the effects of variation in c are almost identical to the effects of random feature loss. This is not surprising, given that random feature loss will reduce the average distance between stimuli, just as lower discriminability does.

The simulation results show that a difference in internal similarity structure is sufficient to explain category-specific identification deficits as a consequence of non-selective damage. At the same time, the model also shows that an identification deficit for a homogeneous category should be accompanied by a categorisation deficit for a heterogeneous category, if the similarity structure of these two categories is the main factor responsible for selective deficits. In the following sections, we explore whether reported patient data are compatible with these predictions.

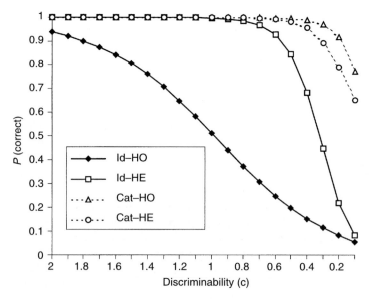

Figure 10.2. Simulation results (proportion correct responses) for identification (Id) and categorisation (Cat) of stimuli in homogeneous (HO) and heterogeneous (HE) categories as a function of discriminability (c).

IDENTIFICATION OF LIVING AND NON-LIVING OBJECTS

Case studies of category-specific deficits have concentrated mainly on identification performance. In almost all reported cases, identification is disproportionately poor for stimuli from living categories (Basso, Capitani, & Laiacona, 1988; Caramazza & Shelton,1998; De Renzi & Lucchelli, 1994; Farah & Wallace, 1992; Forde et al., 1997; Sartori & Job, 1984; Sheridan & Humphreys, 1993; Silveri & Gainotti, 1988; Warrington & Shallice, 1984). For example, Warrington and Shallice (1984) reported four patients with difficulties in visual identification. The comprehension capacities of two patients (JBR and SBY) were examined in detail and a dissociation between living and non-living things was observed. JBR correctly identified 6% of living pictures compared to 90% of non-living pictures. A similar pattern of performance was observed for SBY, who correctly identified none of the living pictures and 75% of the non-living pictures. Similarly, Farah and Wallace (1992) reported a patient, TU, whose naming was disproportionately poor for fruit and vegetables, even when familiarity and name frequency were taken into account. In naming the Snodgrass and Vanderwart line drawings, he correctly named 54% of fruit and vegetables compared with 87% of other categories. His naming latencies were also much slower for fruit and vegetables than for other categories. Caramazza and Shelton (1998) also reported a patient, EW, with a disproportionate impairment in naming living things. For a subset of the Snodgrass and Vanderwart pictures, matched for familiarity and name frequency, EW correctly named 55% of animals and 82% of non-animals.

In addition to recording absolute identification performance for different categories of objects, it is also informative to look at the different types of errors that are reported for living and non-living things. Arguin, Bub, and Dudek (1996; see also Dixon et al., 1997) reported the case of a patient, ELM, who showed a selective impairment for naming living objects (39% correct responses to 66 pictures of animals, birds, insects, fruit, and vegetables), with relatively intact naming of non-living objects (88% correct responses to 79 pictures of tools, clothing, instruments, etc.). Interestingly, Arguin et al. reported a confusion matrix from a word–picture matching task, which showed that ELM tended to confuse the identities of living objects with similar shapes (e.g. banana, carrot, and cucumber were often confused with each other, and also apple, onion, orange, and tomato). This response pattern is entirely in agreement with the predictions of the GCM. According to the model, the probability that two individual items are confused depends directly on their similarity, and the model therefore predicts clusters of confusion between similar items.

Several other reports have shown that patients with category-specific deficits for living things are more likely to confuse living things with other living things than non-living things with other non-living things (Moss, Tyler, Durrant-Peatfield, & Bunn, 1998; Stewart et al., 1992; Warrington & Shallice, 1984). For instance, Stewart et al.'s (1992) patient, HO, gave the name of another object in the same category for 31.6% of the living things that were shown to him, whereas only 9.1% of his errors for non-living things were in the same category. Moss et al. (1998) tested their patient, RC, in a word–picture matching task, in which a spoken word was presented and the patient had to select the corresponding picture from an array of four. In addition to the target, there was always one distracter from the same category, and two distracters from other categories. RC was significantly more accurate in identifying non-living targets than living targets. On living targets, the vast majority of his errors (86%) were within-category errors, in which he chose an alternative from the same category as the target.

According to the GCM, the probability that an incorrect response will be given that corresponds to a stimulus from the same category as the target (which we will call a within-category identification error) is given by:

$$P(Error\ within\ category|S_i = \frac{(\sum_{j \in C} \eta_{ij}) - 1}{\sum_k \eta_{ik}}$$ (10.5)

if the target stimulus belongs to category C and all symbols have the same meaning as before. This probability is exactly the same as the probability of categorisation of the stimulus into the correct category, minus the probability of identifying the stimulus correctly. The probability of an error outside category for a stimulus i from category 1 is:

$$P(\textit{Error outside category}|S_i) = \frac{\sum_{j \in C_{ali}} \eta_{ij}}{\sum_{k} \eta_{ik}} \qquad (10.6)$$

which is identical to the probability that the stimulus would be categorised into the wrong category. Figure 10.3 shows the probabilities of identification errors within and outside category across the homogeneous and heterogeneous stimuli used in the simulation, for different proportions of feature loss.

Within-category identification errors are much more likely than outside-category errors for the homogeneous stimuli. For the heterogeneous stimuli, within-category identification errors are still more likely than outside-category errors, but the difference is much smaller than for the homogeneous stimuli. These predictions are in agreement with the confusion data that have been discussed.

Arguin et al. (1996) and Dixon et al. (1997) have reported another series of

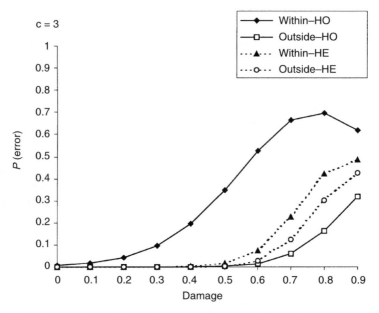

Figure 10.3. Simulated probability of identification errors within and outside category across homogeneous (HO) and heterogeneous (HE) stimuli, for different proportions of feature loss.

identification experiments with their patient ELM, which are very relevant to our account of category-specific deficits (see also Chapter 4). As we noted before, an important problem for any similarity-based account of category-specific deficits is that the dimensions that are used to encode real objects are unknown. In mainstream categorisation research, this problem is overcome by using artificial stimuli that vary along well-defined dimensions (Lamberts, 1995, 1998; Lamberts & Freeman, 1999; Medin & Schaffer, 1978), or by using techniques such as multidimensional scaling to infer the locations of stimuli with continuous dimensions in psychological space (Nosofsky, 1992; Nosofsky & Palmeri, 1997). Arguin et al. (1996) chose the first solution, and overcame the problem of unknown stimulus dimensions by using a set of artificial stimuli that varied on three dimensions. The stimuli were computer-generated blobs that varied in bending, elongation, and tapering. Four different blobs were presented simultaneously in the four corners of the screen, for a short time. One of these blobs was then presented centrally, and ELM was asked to point to that blob's former location. The most important manipulation in this experiment was the structure of the set of four blobs presented in a single trial. In single-dimension sets, the four blobs differed on one dimension only, and all had the same values on the other two dimensions. In conjunction sets, the blobs varied on two dimensions and the third dimension was held constant. The conjunction sets were designed such that both variable dimensions needed to be processed in order to identify the stimulus. ELM performed consistently better on the single-dimension sets (29% errors) than on the conjunction sets (57% errors). Arguin et al. further showed that ELM did not have a perceptual problem with processing multiple dimensions, from which they inferred that his problems with conjunctive sets were based in memory.

Dixon et al. (1997) argued that ELM's performance in the Arguin et al. (1996) study was incompatible with any of the existing neuropsychological theories of category-specific deficits. However, they did show that an exemplar model of identification (Kruschke's [1992] ALCOVE model) could explain the results. ALCOVE is based directly on the GCM. It is presented as a connectionist model, in which backpropagation is used to learn dimension weights and exemplar strengths. Because Dixon et al. (1997) did not attempt to fit learning curves, there is no real need to apply ALCOVE to their data, and we will therefore present their arguments in terms of the GCM. Dixon et al. (1997) point out that optimal performance in the single-dimension task would be achieved by selectively weighting the relevant dimension more than the two irrelevant dimensions. This is predicted by the attention–optimisation hypothesis (see Lamberts, 1999; Nosofsky, 1986), which states that subjects will tend to use dimension weights that maximise performance in a given task. ALCOVE is designed explicitly to implement this selective weighing process. In the conjunctive conditions, the same weighting mechanism should emphasise the two relevant dimensions. Dixon et al. (1997) show that the exemplar model predicts ELM's performance, if it is assumed that dimension weights are close to optimal and stimulus discriminability is low (which is the same assumption as that of Nosofsky & Zaki, 1998). Arguin et al.'s (1996) results are thus entirely compatible with our exemplar-based account. The exemplar model also explains other, potentially more puzzling, aspects of ELM's performance. In another series of experiments, Dixon et al. (1997) showed that the dimensionality effect of the earlier study was modulated by semantics. When the same shapes were paired with semantically close or disparate sounds or labels, ELM's error rates in the conjunctive task showed a strong correlation with the semantic proximity of these sounds or labels, whereas there was no such relation in the single-dimension task. An exemplar model predicts these effects, if it is assumed that discriminability is low, that optimal weighting occurs, and that the stimulus labels form an intrinsic part of the stimulus representation, such that similarity depends both on visual and semantic features (Dixon et al., 1997).

CATEGORISATION OF LIVING AND NON-LIVING OBJECTS

Although most studies of category-specific deficits have focused on naming or identification, it is important for an evaluation of our account to contrast identification performance with categorisation. Objects can be categorised at many different levels (see Murphy & Lassaline, 1997), and we are not aware of many systematic comparisons between categorisation performance at different levels in patients with category-specific identification deficits. However, there have been several studies that show preserved categorisation abilities in categories for which naming deficits occurred, as predicted by the GCM.

Forde et al. (1997) carried out a number of experiments with their patient SRB, and found that his naming ability (tested with the Snodgrass and Vanderwart pictures, photographs, and real objects) was impaired more for living objects than for non-living objects. Reaction times were slower and more errors were made for items from living categories, and this was not confounded by name-frequency, familiarity, or visual complexity. Forde et al. (1997, experiment 19) also examined SRB's ability to categorise living and non-living things. He was shown line drawings of fruit, vegetables, animals, and tools and asked to classify them into their respective categories. SRB scored very highly in this task. His only errors were classifying a watermelon as a vegetable and an artichoke as a fruit.

Caramazza and Shelton (1998) observed that their patient, EW, made many more errors when naming living pictures than non-living pictures. The authors commented that the nature of the errors EW made for living things were quite different to the kinds of errors made for non-living things. In particular, for 34/47 living pictures, EW either said "I have no idea what it is" or produced a semantically related response. For example, when shown a picture of a zebra, EW responded, "Gorilla, I think but I'm not sure". By contrast, she produced only 5/137 semantic or "don't know" responses to items in other semantic categories. Caramazza and Shelton (1998) also observed that EW could distinguish animals from artefacts so she had no selective impairment in categorising animals. EW was also shown to have no difficulty in answering questions concerning attributes shared by all members of a category. This indicates, again, that her problem lay in distinguishing amongst highly similar exemplars whereas she was unimpaired for tasks that require grouping.

Moss et al. (1998) have looked explicitly at categorisation versus identification performance for their patient, RC. Tested with the Snodgrass and Vanderwart picture set, RC was able to name 50% of the pictures of artefacts, compared to only 9% of pictures of living things. Similar results were obtained in a naming task with a different set of stimuli (photographs matched for familiarity). In many cases in which RC failed to name the item, he was still able to provide some information about it. For 63% of the naming errors made on the living things in the test set, this included the correct superordinate name (e.g. *animal* for *donkey*, or *fruit* for *peach*), which indicates that his categorisation abilities with these objects were relatively well preserved. Superordinate names were hardly ever produced for the non-living things. It is interesting to note that Stewart et al.'s (1992) patient HO produced a similar pattern of errors in a naming task. For 10.5% of the errors HO made to living pictures he gave the superordinate name, but he did this for only 4.5% of his errors for non-living pictures. This indicates that, for the living things, he was sometimes aware of the category the object was from even when he could not identify the object. Moss et al. (1998) also carried out a direct test of RC's ability to categorise colour photographs of living and non-living objects into their superordinate categories. RC was able to categorise the living things very accurately (93% correct), scoring within the normal range. However, his ability to categorise the non-living objects (83% correct) was below the range for controls.

To summarise, we have shown that, for patients, identification is most often worse for living things than for non-living things, whereas classification performance shows the opposite trend. Patients can often categorise living things even when the individual name is not known. They are often able to identify the superordinate for living things and often confuse the target with a member of the same category. This is less often the case for non-living things. In the cases where grouping of living and non-living things is compared, patients' selective deficit for living things disappears and in some cases, they perform better for living than non-living things for these tasks. The GCM predicts all these differences.

IS A SIMILARITY-BASED ACCOUNT SUFFICIENT
TO EXPLAIN CATEGORY-SPECIFIC DEFICITS?

Thus far, we have demonstrated that a classical exemplar model of categorisation and identification predicts significant aspects of category-specific deficits in patients with visual agnosia, if it is assumed that the categories of living and non-living objects have a different internal similarity structure. The question remains whether such a simple account is sufficient to explain all aspects of performance in patients with category-specific deficits.

The model that we proposed certainly fails to explain why some patients show identification deficits for non-living objects. Indeed, although the vast majority of studies have reported identification deficits for living things, there have been a few reports of patients with impaired identification of non-living objects (Hillis & Caramazza, 1991; Sacchett & Humphreys, 1992; Warrington & McCarthy, 1983, 1987, 1994). Without attempting to dismiss these findings, it is worthwhile to explore their implications for our account. In the three case studies by Warrington and McCarthy (1983, 1987, 1994), the stimuli were not matched for a number of potential confounds, including frequency, visual complexity, and familiarity (see Funnell & Sheridan, 1992). It is possible that one or more of these variables contributed to the unusual outcome of the case studies. However, the same argument does not apply to the results reported by Hillis and Caramazza (1991) and Sacchett and Humphreys (1992). Hillis and Caramazza (1991) used the same stimuli and test procedures with two patients, one of whom showed a selective deficit for living things, whereas the other was impaired on non-living things. Sacchett and Humphreys (1992) controlled for a number of confounding variables, and still observed a selective naming deficit for non-living things.

It is clear that the exemplar model that we used cannot explain these last two sets of data, without making additional assumptions about the structure of categories of living and non-living objects or about the effects of brain damage. In fact, the model can readily produce a double dissociation like the one reported by Hillis and Caramazza (1991) (or any other dissociation, for that matter) if it is assumed that damage is selective and somehow affects exemplars from one category more than exemplars from another category. Alternatively, one could assume that particular stimulus dimensions would have different weights in the identification of living and non-living objects. A commonly cited distinction is that between functional and perceptual features, where the former are assumed to be more important for the identification of non-living objects, and the latter have more weight in the identification of living things (see Farah & McClelland, 1991; Sacchett & Humphreys, 1992; Warrington & Shallice, 1984). On these assumptions, the model can produce a double dissociation between identification of living and non-living objects by selective damage to the representation or the processing of perceptual or functional stimulus dimensions. However, neither of these accounts are very satisfactory. Apart from being largely *ad hoc*, they fail to explain why selective deficits for non-living objects are so rare. Perhaps it is safest to reserve judgement about the importance of deficits for non-living objects until more cases have been documented and the crucial variables that underlie these deficits are better understood.

Other data that are potentially challenging for the model are those obtained in conditions where similarity within categories has been controlled or measured, and in which category-specific identification deficits appear unrelated to similarity differences between categories. For instance, Sartori, Miozzo, and Job (1993) claim that higher perceptual similarity between living things is not the cause of their patient's impairment. Sartori et al. (1993) tested their patient, Michelangelo, using drawings of animals and artefacts taken from the Snodgrass and Vanderwart set plus line drawings in a similar style. Seven subsets of animals and six subsets of artefacts were chosen with high within-set visual and semantic similarity. Undergraduates rated the global similarity of items in each subset and the ratings for animal and artefact subsets did not differ significantly. When Michelangelo was asked to name these pictures, his selective deficit for living things remained.

These results were not confirmed in a number of other studies, in which similarity-related effects have been observed directly. Livingstone (1988) studied a patient's ability to point to a named picture either amongst visually similar or visually dissimilar distracters, and found that the patient performed much better when in the visually dissimilar condition, even within living categories for which he was impaired.

Forde et al. (1997) provided direct evidence that similarity rather than the living/non-living distinction was the crucial variable in SRB's performance. The authors have taken into account the structural similarity of the pictures when testing SRB's naming ability. They used the 76 Snodgrass and Vanderwart pictures from Humphreys et al. (1988), who grouped these pictures into structurally similar categories (animals, fruit, vegetables) and structurally different categories (clothing, tools, furniture). Structural similarity was determined by the number of rated common parts per category and the average percentage of contour overlap relative to other objects from the same category. Forde et al. (1997) found that SRB was significantly more impaired at naming items from structurally similar categories (71% correct) compared to structurally dissimilar categories (95% correct). In fact, when a regression analysis was carried out on SRB's reaction time to name 59 Snodgrass and Vanderwart pictures, the authors found that the living–non-living distinction was not a significant predictor of performance when measures of structural similarity were taken into account. Instead, degree of contour overlap with other category members was the only significant predictor. Further evidence that structural similarity is behind SRB's deficit is that his subordinate naming of items from two categories of particular interest to him—dogs and cars—was very poor. He was worse for dogs (17%) than cars (57%) but this general problem at retrieving subordinate names is consistent with the hypothesis that high levels of structural similarity between category members make identification difficult.

Together with the results that we have reviewed in the previous sections, such findings suggest that similarity is often at the root of patients' problems in identifying living things. Studies in which a selective deficit remains after similarity is controlled run counter to the general trend. In the case of Sartori et al.'s (1993) study, it is doubtful as to whether their measure of similarity was adequate. They found that when ratings of overall similarity were obtained for subsets of pictures, no differences between living and non-living sets were found. This certainly does not stand up to findings from our own experiments, in which more rigorous measures of similarity were made for pictures from the Snodgrass and Vanderwart set. Humphreys et al.'s (1998) analyses of shared parts and contour overlap, Gaffan and Heywood's (1993) discriminability analyses, and our own pairwise ratings and reaction time experiments all showed the living pictures to be reliably more similar to each other than the non-living pictures. The stimuli used by Sartori et al. (1993) mainly included Snodgrass and Vanderwart pictures, so it is likely that the average perceptual similarity still differed between categories. Sartori et al.'s (1993) assessment of similarity was perhaps not sensitive enough to show relevant differences between the categories.

CONCLUSIONS

We have demonstrated in this chapter that a classical exemplar model of categorisation and identification explains many aspects of category-specific deficits in patients with brain damage, on the assumption that the categories involved have a different similarity structure. The most important prediction from the model concerns the apparent dissociation between identification and categorisation. The neuropsychological data that allow a comparison between these two tasks generally support the model's predictions.

The exemplar account does have some characteristics that make it an attractive alternative for existing models of category-specific deficits. The model has been developed outside the neuropsychological literature, and has become one of the best-tested and most productive theories of perceptual categorisation, identification, and recognition. The model's simplicity and formal rigour are further assets. Of course, we cannot claim that exemplar models readily explain all aspects of category-specificity, but the scope and implications of the model certainly merit further study.

Another important topic for further work would be to explore the relation between our proposal and other single-systems accounts of category-specific deficits. For instance, there is a complex relation between various connectionist models of category-specific deficits (Devlin, Gonnerman, Anderson, & Seidenberg, 1998; McRae, de Sa, & Seidenberg, 1997; see also Chapter 9) and our exemplar account. Several connectionist accounts rely heavily on the notion that patterns of correlations between features are important for understanding category-specific deficits, and there is independent empirical evidence to confirm the importance of these correlation patterns (see Chapter 8). Exemplar models preserve complete information about feature correlations, and they seem therefore excellently suited to explain the role of correlations in category-specific deficits.

ACKNOWLEDGEMENTS

The work in this chapter was supported by a BBSRC grant to K.L., and a BBSRC Research Studentship to L.S. We thank Andrew Olson, Evan Heit, Nick Chater, Noellie Brockdorff, and Robert Nosofsky for their helpful comments.

REFERENCES

Alfonso-Reese, L.A., & Ashby, F.G. (1995). Categorisation as probability–density estimation. *Journal of Mathematical Psychology, 39*, 216–233.

Arguin, M., Bub, D., & Dudek, G. (1996). Shape integration for visual object recognition and its implication in category specific visual agnosia. *Visual Cognition, 3(3)*, 221–275.

Ashby, F.G., Alfonso-Reese, L.A., Turken, A.U., & Waldron, E.M. (1998). A neuropsychological theory of multiple systems in category learning. *Psychological Review, 105*, 442–481.

Ashby, F.G., & Lee, W.W. (1991). Predicting similarity and categorisation from identification. *Journal of Experimental Psychology: General, 120*, 150–172.

Ashby, F.G., & Maddox, T.W. (1993). Relations between prototype, exemplar and decision bound models of categorisation. *Journal of Mathematical Psychology, 37*, 372–400.

Basso, A., Capitani, E., & Laiacona, M. (1988). Progressive language impairment without dementia: A case study with isolated category-specific semantic defect. *Journal of Neurology, Neurosurgery and Psychiatry, 51*, 1201–1207.

Brockdorff, N., & Lamberts, K. (2000). A feature-sampling account of the time course of old–new recognition judgments. *Journal of Experimental Psychology: Learning, Memory and Cognition, 26*, 77–102.

Caramazza, A., & Shelton, J.R. (1998). Domain specific knowledge systems in the brain: The animate–inanimate distinction. *Journal of Cognitive Neuroscience, 10(1)*, 1–34.

De Renzi, E., & Lucchelli, F. (1994). Are semantic systems separately represented in the brain? The case of living category impairment. *Cortex, 30*, 3–25.

Devlin, J., Gonnerman, L., Anderson, E., & Seidenberg, M. (1998). Category-specific deficits in focal and widespread damage: A computational account. *Journal of Cognitive Neuroscience, 10(1)*, 77–94.

Dixon, M.J., Bub, D.N., & Arguin, M. (1997). The interaction of object form and object meaning in the identification performance of a patient with category-specific visual agnosia. *Cognitive Neuropsychology, 14*, 1085–1130.

Erickson, M.A., & Kruschke, J.K. (1998). Rules and exemplars in category learning. *Journal of Experimental Psychology: General, 127*, 107–140.

Estes, W.K. (1994). *Classification and cognition*. New York: Oxford University Press.

Farah, M.J. & McClelland, J.L. (1991). A computational model of semantic memory impairment: Modality specificity and emergent category specificity. *Journal of Experimental Psychology: General, 120*, 339–357.

Farah, M.J., Meyer, M.M., & McMullen, P.A. (1996). The living/nonliving dissociation is not an artifact: Giving an *a priori* implausible hypothesis a strong test. *Cognitive Neuropsychology, 13*, 137–154.

Farah, M.J., & Wallace, M.A. (1992). Semantically bounded anomia: Implications for the neural implementation of naming. *Neuropsychologia, 30(7)*, 609–621.

Forde, E.M.E. (1999). Category-specific recognition impairments for living and nonliving things. In G.W. Humphreys (Ed.), *Case studies in the neuropsychology of vision.* (pp. 111–132). Hove, UK: Psychology Press.

Forde, E.M.E., Francis, D., Riddoch, M.J., Rumiati R., & Humphreys, G.W. (1997). On the links between visual knowledge and naming: A single case study of a patient with a category-specific impairment for living things. *Cognitive Neuropsychology, 14(3)*, 403–458.

Funnell, E., & Sheridan, J. (1992). Categories of knowledge? Unfamiliar aspects of living and nonliving things. *Cognitive Neuropsychology, 9*, 135–153.

Gaffan, D., & Heywood, C.A. (1993). A spurious category-specific visual agnosia for living things in normal human and nonhuman primates. *Journal of Cognitive Neuroscience 5*, 118–128.

Gainotti, G., & Silveri, M.C. (1996). Cognitive and anatomical locus of lesion in a patient with a category-specific semantic impairment for living beings. *Cognitive Neuropsychology, 13*, 357–389.

Gluck, M.A., & Bower, G.H. (1988). From conditioning to category learning: An adaptive network model. *Journal of Experimental Psychology: General, 117*, 225–244.

Hillis, A.E., & Caramazza, A. (1991). Category-specific naming and comprehension impairment: A double dissociation. *Brain, 114*, 2081–2094.

Humphreys, G.W., & Forde, E.M.E. (2001). Hierarchies, similarity, and interactivity in object recognition: category-specific neuropsychological deficits. *Behavioral and Brain Sciences, 24*, 453–465.

Humphreys, G.W., Lamote, C., & Lloyd-Jones, T. J. (1995). An interactive activation approach to object processing: Effects of structural similarity, name frequency and task in normality and pathology. *Memory, 3*, 535–586.

Humphreys, G.W., Riddoch, M.J. & Quinlan, P.T. (1988). Cascade processes in picture identification. *Cognitive Neuropsychology, 5*, 67–103.

Knowlton, B.J., Mangels, J.A., & Squire, L.R. (1996). A neostriatal habit learning system in humans. *Science, 273*, 1399–1402.

Knowlton, B.J., & Squire, L.R. (1993). The learning of categories: Parallel brain systems for item memory and category knowledge. *Science, 262*, 1747–1749.

Knowlton, B.J., Squire, L.R., & Gluck, M.A. (1994). Probabilistic classification learning in amnesia. *Learning and Memory, 1*, 106–120.

Kruschke, J.K. (1992). ALCOVE: An exemplar-based connectionist model of category learning. *Psychological Review, 99*, 22–44.

Kurbat, M.A. (1997). Can the recognition of living things really be selectively impaired? *Neuropsychologia, 35(6)*, 813–827.

Lamberts, K. (1994). Flexible tuning of similarity in exemplar-based categorisation. *Journal of Experimental Psychology: Learning, Memory and Cognition, 20*, 1003–1021.

Lamberts, K. (1995). Categorisation under time pressure. *Journal of Experimental Psychology: General, 124*, 161–180.

Lamberts, K. (1998). The time course of categorisation. *Journal of Experimental Psychology: Learning, Memory, and Cognition, 24*, 695–711.

Lamberts, K. (1999). Attention supports perceptual categorisation. *Visual Cognition, 6*, 93–99.

Lamberts, K. (2000). Information-accumulation theory of speeded categorisation. *Psychological Review, 107*, 227–260.

Lamberts, K. (2002). Feature sampling in categorisation and recognition of objects. *Quarterly Journal of Experimental Psychology, 55A*, 141–154.

Lamberts, K., and Brockdorff, N., & Heit (In press). Perceptual processes in matching and recognition of complex pictures. *Journal of Experimental Psychology: Human Perception and Performance*.

Lamberts, K., & Freeman, R. P. J. (1999). Building object representations from parts: Tests of a stochastic sampling model. *Journal of Experimental Psychology: Human Perception and Performance, 25*, 904–926.

Livingstone, M.S. (1988). Art, illusion and the visual system. *Scientific American, 258*, 78–86.

McRae K., de Sa, V.R., & Seidenberg M.S. (1997) On the nature and scope of featural representation of word meaning. *Journal of Experimental Psychology General, 126*, 99–130

Medin, D.L., & Schaffer, M.M. (1978). Context theory of classification learning. *Psychological Review, 85*, 207–238.

Moss, H.E., Tyler, L.K., Durrant-Peatfield, M.R., & Bunn, E.M. (1998). 'Two eyes of a see-through': Impaired and intact semantic knowledge in a case of a selective deficit for living things. *Neurocase, 4*, 291–310.

Murphy, G.L., & Lassaline, M.E. (1997). Hierarchical structure in concepts and the basic level of categorisation. In K. Lamberts & D. Shanks (Eds.), *Knowledge, concepts and categories* (pp. 93–131). Hove, UK: Psychology Press.

Nosofsky, R.M. (1984). Choice, similarity, and the context theory of classification. *Journal of Experimental Psychology: Learning, Memory and Cognition, 10*, 104–114.

Nosofsky, R.M. (1986). Attention, similarity, and the identification–categorisation relationship. *Journal of Experimental Psychology: General, 115*, 39–57.

Nosofsky, R.M. (1987). Attention and learning processes in the identification and categorisation of integral stimuli. *Journal of Experimental Psychology: Learning, Memory, and Cognition, 13*, 87–109.

Nosofsky, R.M. (1991a). Tests of an exemplar model for relating perceptual classification and recognition memory. *Journal of Experimental Psychology: Human Perception and Performance, 17*, 3–27.

Nosofsky, R.M. (1991b). Relation between the rational model and the context model of categorisation. *Psychological Science, 2*, 416–421.

Nosofsky, R.M. (1992). Similarity scaling and cognitive process models. *Annual Review of Psychology, 43*, 25–53.

Nosofsky, R.M., & Palmeri, T. J. (1997). An exemplar-based random walk model of speeded classification. *Psychological Review, 104*, 266–300.

Nosofsky, R.M., Palmeri, T.J., & McKinley, S.C. (1994). Rule-plus-exception model of classification learning. *Psychological Review, 101*, 53–79.

Nosofsky, R.M., & Zaki, S.R. (1998). Dissociations between categorisation and recognition in amnesic and normal individuals: An exemplar-based interpretation. *Psychological Science, 9*, 247–255.

Palmeri, T.J. (1997). Exemplar similarity and the development of automaticity. *Journal of Experimental Psychology: Learning, Memory, and Cognition, 23*, 324–354.

Sacchett, C., & Humphreys, G.W. (1992). Calling a squirrel a squirrel but a canoe a wigwam: A category-specific deficit for artefactual objects and body parts. *Cognitive Neuropsychology, 9*, 73–86.

Sartori, G., & Job, R. (1988). The oyster with four legs: A neuropsychological study on the interaction of visual and semantic information. *Cognitive Neuropsychology, 5(1)*, 105–132.

Sartori, G., Miozzo, M., & Job, R. (1993). Category-specific naming impairments? Yes. *Quarterly Journal of Experimental Psychology, 46(3)*, 489–504.

Sheridan, J., & Humphreys, G.W. (1993). A verbal-semantic category-specific recognition impairment. *Cognitive Neuropsychology, 10 (2)*, 143–184.

Silveri, M.C., & Gainotti, G. (1988). Interaction between vision and language in category-specific semantic impairment. *Cognitive Neuropsychology, 5(6)*, 677–709.

Silveri, M.C., Daniele, A., Giustolisi, L., & Gainotti, G. (1991). Dissociation between knowledge of living and nonliving things in dementia of the Alzheimer type. *Neurology, 41*, 545–546.

Snodgrass, J.G., & Vanderwart, M. (1980). A standardised set of 260 pictures: Norms for name agreement, image agreement, familiarity, and visual complexity. *Journal of Experimental Psychology: Human Learning and Memory, 6*, 174–215.

Stewart, F., Parkin, A.J., & Hunkin, N.M. (1992). Naming impairments following recovery from herpes simplex encephalitis. *Quarterly Journal of Experimental Psychology, 44*, 261–284.

Warrington, E.K., & McCarthy, R. (1983). Category-specific access dysphasia. *Brain, 106*, 859–878.

Warrington, E.K., & McCarthy, R. (1987). Categories of knowledge: Further fractionations and an attempted integration. *Brain, 110*, 1273–1296.

Warrington, E.K., & McCarthy, R. (1994). Multiple meaning systems in the brain: A case for visual semantics. *Neuropsychologia, 32*, 1465–1473.

Warrington, E.K., & Shallice, T. (1984). Category-specific semantic impairment. *Brain, 107*, 829–854.

CHAPTER ELEVEN

On the foundations of the semantic system

Jean M. Mandler
University of California, San Diego, USA and
University College London, UK

.

INTRODUCTION

The purpose of this chapter is to use what we know about concept formation in infancy to shed light on the organisation of the semantic system. In turn this work might be useful to those trying to characterise the nature of the breakdown of the semantic system under brain damage. I use the terms "conceptual" and "semantic" interchangeably here, because they are often treated as synonyms in the adult literature. However, it should be noted that the foundations of the conceptual system are laid down before language is learned and I do not mean to imply any linguistic knowledge by the use of the term "semantic".

The points I wish to make are the following: first, a distinction between animals and non-animals (or things) is one the earliest conceptual divisions that infants make. This distinction is not the same as the animate–inanimate distinction as that has been traditionally understood in the literature, a point I explicate below. Second, no special domain-specific mechanisms or evolutionary pressures are required for such a distinction to be formed. Third, some of the early subdivisions of the initial broad conceptualisations that infants make might be somewhat unprincipled, at least as far as scientific or ontological taxonomies are concerned. Fourth, in spite of the odd nature of some infant categories, overall they are formed hierarchically from the start. All the infant data indicate that the conceptual system is categorical from its inception, with global categories being formed first, followed by subdivisions of these broader categories. There could well be different amounts of visual and functional information associated with various categories, such as animals versus artefacts, but these are secondary characteristics, not the basis for conceptual organisation.

THE FIRST CONCEPTS

Only recently have the foundations of conceptualisation begun to be studied in a systematic fashion. Because of Piaget's writings (e.g. Piaget, 1952) it was long assumed that conceptualisation begins fairly late in ontogeny. Infants were said to be purely sensorimotor creatures. They were attributed with the ability to parse the world into objects, to recognise them,[1] and to learn how to interact with them. However, they were assumed not to form explicit concepts with which to think, to be able to recall the past or imagine the future, until sometime late in the second year of life. Piaget also assumed that when infants finally did begin to form concepts, these were often confused, changeable in their definitions, and poorly related to each other. Indeed he called the concepts of 2-year-olds "preconcepts" because of their putative lack of organisation and their mutability (Piaget, 1951). Along with these assumptions, Piaget also claimed that children's first concepts are imagistic and concrete, as opposed to schematic and abstract, a view that has been popular ever since.

Because infants were assumed not to be forming concepts, there seemed to be little point to studying concept formation during infancy. By default, then, investigation of the earliest concepts took place after children had begun to learn language, and indeed they were often equated with early words. This equation, however, left the way open for the conflation of learning concepts with learning word meanings. These are not the same processes. First, concept formation begins many months before language begins. Second, children can only learn the words that are spoken to them. Because the majority of object nouns addressed to children are at what is known as the "basic level", the first such nouns that children learn tend to be of that type.[2] However, the

---

[1] The difference between implicit processes such as perceptual identification (Jacoby, 1983) or primitive recognition (Mandler, 1984) and explicit recognition went unacknowledged in Piaget's formulation.

[2] There has never been an adequate definition of the basic level (see Mandler, 1997), but the notion, introduced by Rosch (Rosch & Mervis, 1975) was based originally on the level of the genus in common taxonomies of plants and animals (Berlin, Breedlove, & Raven, 1973). Thus "dog", "bass", and "maple" would be basic-level concepts. Because this level frequently did not match adult judgements or the language used to children, the term gradually became a synonym for the presumed intension of children's first words (e.g. fish and tree, rather than bass and maple). Intuition (unfortunately, often language-based) was used to determine a basic level for furniture (e.g. chair), musical instruments (e.g. piano), and other artefacts.

fact that children might learn the word "dog" before the word "animal", in itself that tells us little about their interpretation of the word's meaning (i.e. the concept they understand by it). This is shown clearly by the common phenomenon in early language of overextension, in which a word such as "dog" is used to refer to animals in general (Clark, 1983). About a third of the first nouns learned in English are overextended for at least some period of time (Rescorla, 1980). Because children use language to communicate, one might think that overextension can be accounted for by the necessity of making a very limited vocabulary serve multiple purposes. Although this might well account for some overextension in production, overextension occurs at about the same rate in comprehension (Behrend, 1988; McDonough, in press). Therefore, overextension must to some extent reflect the broader concepts that children are using to understand words such as "dog".

Although many developmental researchers were sensitive to the possible confounding of concept learning and word learning, a great deal of reliance was placed on word usage by Piaget and others when interpreting the concepts underlying the first words. The fact that early noun vocabulary is almost exclusively basic-level also fits well with Rosch's theory that basic-level concepts are the easiest to learn (e.g. Mervis & Rosch, 1981), and these merged into the strong conclusion that children's first object concepts are at the basic level. This view was widely accepted until quite recently, and is still the standard interpretation in many textbooks.

However, as I have discussed elsewhere (Mandler, 1997, 1998b), the notion that the first concepts are at the basic level rested on a slim and somewhat dubious database and, in any case, was derived for the most part by studying children aged 3 years and older. Clearly, one needs to look at concepts in their initial stages and, contrary to Piagetian theory, we now know that the first concepts are formed in infancy. These concepts, unaffected by language learning, are very different from the basic-level concepts that had been posited as the foundation on which the conceptual system is built up.

Before laying out the evidence, it is important to note one implication of the view that basic-level concepts are the first to be formed, with its corollary that understanding superordinate concepts is a later achievement (Mervis, 1987). If young children first learned a concept of a dog but did not see any relationship between it and a rabbit or a cow, or if they learned a concept of a chair but did not see any relationship between it and a table or a bed, then the organisation of the conceptual system would be wide open, without any principled basis for its development. I raise this issue because it is reminiscent of some discussion in the literature of whether there is a categorical basis for the semantic system. For example, although themselves supporting a categorical organisation of the semantic system, Caramazza and Shelton (1998) state that this notion "has never been entertained seriously". This remark is too

strong, because many researchers have emphasised the categorical organisation of the human knowledge system (Collins & Quillian, 1969; Mandler,
1967). The effects of that organisation are evident in free recall, in recognition
tests, and in the order in which items are generated from semantic memory
(Bower, Clark, Lesgold, & Winzenz, 1969; Graesser & Mandler, 1978; Mandler
& Rabinowitz, 1981; Reynolds & Goldstein, 1974). Caramazza and Shelton's
comment might be directed more towards brain organisation than conceptual
organisation but it does indicate that the point has seemed debateable to
some (Farah & McClelland, 1991; see also McRae and Cree, Chapter 8). In
contrast, the brunt of the argument being made here is that the way in which
the system is acquired entails a categorical organisation from the start.

Laraine McDonough and I have applied three techniques to the study of
infant concepts. All of them measure infants' interactions with realistic little
replicas of real-world objects. None of them require instruction but rely
solely on infants' spontaneous tendencies to categorise objects and to imitate
actions they observe. The first, the object manipulation task, is based on work
by Ruff (1976). It is suitable for use from around 6 to 12 months of age (it
tends to bore older infants) and we have used it beginning at 7 months. This is
about as early as infants can manipulate objects with enough skill to be able
to concentrate on the objects rather than what their hands are doing. The
infants are handed objects from a given category to manipulate one at a time,
and then are handed a new object, which is sometimes from another category.
If they find the new object different, they will examine it longer. We have
examined both global, domain-level categories such as animals and vehicles
and within-domain (so-called basic-level) categories such as dogs and
rabbits. (We use the terms global and/or domain-level because it does not
seem appropriate to use the term superordinate for categories that are undifferentiated into subclasses.)

This is the only conceptual categorisation task we have found that can be
used with such young infants. Unfortunately, the results can sometimes be
ambiguous in the sense that categorisation might take place either on the
basis of what the objects look like (i.e. a purely perceptual categorisation) or
what they represent (i.e. a conceptual or semantic categorisation). This ambiguity has caused several researchers to suggest that infants are responsive
only to perceptual features and do not need conceptual representations to
carry out the task; that is, when infants categorise animals and vehicles they
do so on perceptual grounds alone. However, enough research has now
been carried out to make it unlikely that infants rely only on perceptual
information when categorising objects in this task.

The main findings have been that from about 7 months of age infants are
sensitive to the global categories of animals, vehicles, and furniture, distinguishing each from the other (Mandler & McDonough, 1993, 1998a). At
the same time, between 7 and 11 months they are not differentially responsive

to the categories of dogs, cats, rabbits, and fish. They also do not differentiate tables from beds or chairs on this task. This pattern of results is not one that can easily be explained on perceptual grounds alone. It is known that with about the same amount of exposure infants as young as 3 months can discriminate realistic pictures of dogs from cats and tables from chairs (Behl-Chadha, 1996; Quinn, Eimas, & Rosenkrantz, 1993), so the failure to discriminate different animal and furniture kinds on the object examination task is difficult to explain without reference to infants' conceptualisations of what the objects represent. Especially convincing is the fact that infants categorise the birds and aeroplanes shown in Figure 11.1 as different on the object examination task, even though they are perceptually highly similar.[3] The difference in results on picture and object tasks appears to be due in part to young infants being conceptually more engaged when they are interacting with objects than when they are merely staring at pictures.

Infants do make some within-domain distinctions on the object examination test; they differentiate dogs from birds. This finding is genuinely ambiguous because it could easily be due to perceptual factors (the two

Figure 11.1.   The models of birds and aeroplanes categorised by 9-month-olds.

---

[3] We tested only 9- and 11-month-olds on this contrast because the lack of coordination of 7-month-olds made using objects with relatively sharp points possibly dangerous. There is a good reason for giving infants stuffed animals rather than plastic models!

categories are perceptually very different) rather than to any appreciation of differences in kind. Infants also distinguish between cars, motorcycles, and aeroplanes. We do not know why distinctions should be made earlier among vehicles than among most animals or furniture, but we have found this result in several experiments (although not all). We originally assumed it might be due to familiarity, because infants in southern California spend so much time travelling in cars, from which they observe a great variety of traffic. However, once we found they were insensitive to furniture kinds, a familiarity explanation became unlikely, because they have clearly had as much experience with common furniture types as with vehicles. Perhaps it is a combination of familiarity plus interest in moving things, but we do not yet know the reason for the finding.

We know the most about categorisation of animals, vehicles, and furniture, but we do have some information on two other domains. Eleven-month-old infants differentiate both animals and vehicles from plants. Because of our concern that younger infants might swallow parts of the plastic plants we used, 11 months was the youngest age we tested on this distinction; categorisation could well occur earlier. We also know that at 9 months infants do not categorise kitchen utensils when contrasted with furniture but are successful by 11 months. Overall, the pattern of results from this test is that global categories, with the possible exception of vehicles, are distinguished from other global categories earlier than basic-level categories are distinguished from other basic-level categories within the same domain.

The second test we have used is the sequential touching task. This task, invented by Ricciuti (1965), consists of putting eight objects from two categories in front of infants and encouraging them to play with them. It is suitable for infants from about 15 months of age. Although the task can be used with year-old infants, it is more difficult to handle, because at least eight objects are needed to reliably measure categorisation. Young infants tend to be overwhelmed when presented with many objects at once and some do not respond at all. One- to 2-year-olds rarely sort objects into piles but the order in which they touch them tells us if they are sensitive to their categorical relatedness. The measure used is number and length of sequential runs of touches to one category or the other. This test can be considered a developmental precursor to the sorting tests used to study classification in older children. Riciutti only studied categorisation of geometric forms, a perceptual task. Later, Nelson (1973) and Sugarman (1983) extended the work to include little models of real-world objects, but did not study these systematically. Mandler, Fivush, and Reznick (1987) explored the statistical properties of the technique, such as how often runs of touches to objects within a category occur by chance, thus making it a more useful tool for comparing different categories and ages.

In Mandler, Bauer, and McDonough (1991) we used this technique to study 18-, 24-, and 30-month-olds' categorisation of basic-level and super-ordinate categories in the animal and vehicle domains. For all three ages, we found categorisation at the domain level (animals versus vehicles) and at the life-form level of dogs versus fish and birds, as well as cars versus aeroplanes.[4] It appears that there might be a relatively early tripartite division among land-, air-, and sea-animals and vehicles. We found little basic-level categor-isation (dogs versus horses or rabbits, cars versus trucks or motorcycles) at 18 months, and even at 24 months only about half the children categorised at this level. It should be noted that on this task, which is a more stringent test of conceptual categorisation than the object examination task, vehicles were not subcategorised earlier than animals. Other tests using this technique showed that 2-year-olds differentiated animals from plants, and kitchen uten-sils from furniture, but did not distinguish between different kinds of plants (trees and cactuses), utensils (spoons and forks), or furniture (table and chairs).

Finally, we also used this task to study the associative categories of kitchen things and bathroom things (Mandler et al., 1987). We found that 14-month-olds distinguished between these perceptually highly diverse categories. These are not the usual taxonomic categories, of course, but are based on spatial and/or temporal associative factors. The fact that categories can be formed on such a basis is one of the reasons that infants create some "unprincipled" categories in addition to the "taxonomic" ones already discussed. Even taxo-nomic categories can be at least partially based on spatial factors such as location, for example the early division between land and air animals and vehicles.

In the last few years we have used a third task that has proven extremely useful in cataloguing the boundaries of infant concepts. We call it a general-ised imitation task (Mandler & McDonough, 1996). We model a simple event, such as giving a little replica of a dog a drink from a cup. Instead of giving the infants the same objects to use to imitate what they have observed, we vary the choices available to them. For example, along with the cup we might give an infant a bird and an aeroplane, or another dog and a cat. We record which object the infants choose to imitate the event, and sometimes their second choice as well (if any is made). We have used this task with 9- and 11-month-olds (McDonough & Mandler, 1998), obtaining results similar to those obtained with 14-month-olds, but 9 months is the lower limit of infants' ability to imitate events when objects are to be

---

[4] We did not contrast cars and boats because of developmental lore that young children do not consider boats to be vehicles. However, other data from this task suggest that infants do include boats in a vehicle category.

manipulated and we do not get a large proportion of infants doing so at this age.[5]

The generalised imitation task can be used in two ways. First, it can be used to assess inductive inferences, to see how far infants generalise the properties they have observed with specific objects. This in turn gives us information about the breadth of infant conceptual categories. In our first experiments using the technique (Mandler & McDonough, 1996) we modelled for 14-month-olds the animal properties of drinking and sleeping and the vehicle properties of turning an ignition key and giving rides. For example, after modelling giving a little person a ride on top of a car, we gave the infants the little person and a truck and a rabbit, or an aeroplane and a bird (with outstretched wings). The infants generalised the modelled behaviour across the entire appropriate domain and rarely used an item from the inappropriate domain. This was true whether the test exemplars were similar or dissimilar in appearance to the objects used for the modeling. We also tested infants on unusual exemplars, such as aardvarks and forklifts, with exactly the same result. Finally, we modelled the incorrect behaviour (for example, giving a car a drink or trying to turn an ignition key on a dog) and again gave the infants a choice between an animal and a vehicle. The results were virtually the same. Even when seeing both correct and incorrect behaviour modelled, only a few more infants imitated the behaviour with an incorrect exemplar than in the previous two experiments. This result is important, because it shows that the infants are using their existing conceptual knowledge about animals and vehicles and are not merely aping whatever the experimenter does.

Another example indicating the representational nature of the infants' responding is that when we model behaviour that is appropriate for both domains (going into a building and being washed), they imitate these actions with both animals and vehicles, regardless of which domain we use for the modeling (Mandler & McDonough, 1998b). This behaviour is quite different from the way they restrict their imitation of domain-specific properties such as drinking or turning an ignition key. Clearly, they are not just playing a game of "follow the experimenter" but are treating the little replicas as representations of the real world, to be treated accordingly.

I stress this point because some people are surprised that infants have any understanding of physical representations. In part because of Piaget's theory, as well as research by DeLoache (1989) showing that young children experience difficulty in using scale models, many researchers assume that understanding the symbolic function of objects is late to develop. However,

---

[5] In all the experiments reported here, each infant was tested on each of the events under study. Typically there were four of these per experiment, which is about the maximum number of times an infant will imitate in a single session.

DeLoache's scale models and the task she uses are complex; it is a very simple form of symbolic representation that we see at work in our generalised imitation tasks. The infants need only to recognise the objects and what is being done to them (more or less the same as recognising what is happening in a film) and then to imitate what they have observed.

The generalised imitation task is also useful in determining how infants construe events. Here, the issue is not how far they are willing to generalise observed behaviour, but rather just how specifically they conceptualise what they observe. In the experiments just described we saw that infants generalise to the limits of the domain for both animals and vehicles. But we can also ask what exactly infants understand when they see a dog being given a drink. Do they construe the event as a dog being given a drink (in which case they should choose another dog to use as a substitute in preference to a cat), or as a land animal being given a drink (in which case they might choose a cat or a rabbit for a substitute as often as another dog), or as an animal being given a drink (in which case they might choose a bird or a fish)?

We have carried out a series of such contrasts (Mandler & McDonough, 1998b). When we gave a dog a drink or put a dog to bed, and then gave 14-month-olds the prop along with another dog and any other land animal, the infants were just as likely to chose the other animal (cat or rabbit) as the dog. On the other hand, if we gave them another dog with a bird, they were more likely to choose the dog, although they then often went on and gave the bird a drink too. They were virtually telling us, "I saw you give a land animal a drink, but birds drink too". ("Land animal" is our adult construal, of course. We do not know at this point whether infants are mainly responsive to the location where these animals are found, or to their legs or texture, or to a combination of properties.)

The picture is different with vehicles. Here we found that there was a tendency to pick an exemplar from the same subcategory for their imitations. For example, when we turned a key against a car, they were more likely to choose another car than a motorcycle or an aeroplane to demonstrate keying. They also tended to use the other vehicle less often as a second choice for their imitations, especially the aeroplane. The infants seemed to be telling us, "I saw you use a key on a car".[6] Thus, congruent with the data from the object examination test (although not with the sequential touching test) greater differentiation was exhibited in the vehicle domain than in the animal domain.

---

[6] It is somewhat surprising that relatively few infants picked an aeroplane as a second choice, given that in our previous induction work (Mandler & McDonough, 1996) they were willing to key aeroplanes. Obviously, the contrasts used are important in determining acceptable objects for imitation. In the context of an animal, it seemed OK to the infants to use a key with an aeroplane, in the context of a car, much less so. This suggests that the technique might be used to study relative certainty of inductive generalisations, but that remains for future research.

Overall, the data from these tests tell us that at 14-month-old infants are still construing the various animals they see quite broadly. They seem not to be conceptually differentiating one kind of land animal from another. On the other hand, they have already made at least some divisions within land vehicles. This raises the issue of whether there is an important difference in the rate at which concepts about different kinds of animals (or natural kinds) are acquired in contrast to different kinds of artefacts. We have begun to study this issue, although a great deal remains to be done.

One way to approach this question is to assess the extent to which infants generalise properties that are appropriate for only one subcategory to other subcategories within the same domain. We asked, for example, when infants learn that dogs chew on bones but birds do not, or that cups are used for drinking but pans are not. This issue concerns the course of acquisition of the functional properties associated with specific kinds within a domain, rather than the acquisition of properties associated with all or most members of a domain. As the data will make evident, infants learn properties relevant to whole domains (such as that animals eat) before they learn properties specific to particular subcategories (such as that dogs eat bones).

Our assessment of knowledge about within-domain kinds, described here, might seem somewhat haphazard. That is because it is difficult to find functional properties associated with specific animals or artefacts that 14-month-olds both know and can act out. In each case, we modelled an association we deemed likely for an infant to know. For example, infants this age have ample experience of drinking from both cups and mugs, but they would not have seen (or only rarely) anyone drinking from a pan. Similarly, by 1 year of age infants are being taught that sniffing is an appropriate response to flowers of various sorts, but only rarely would they see someone sniff a tree. As discussed earlier, infants try to reproduce what they have seen within the limits of their understanding and the choices available to them. Because in each case the appropriate choice was more similar to the modelled object than was the inappropriate object, choice of the latter is evidence for a failure to conceptually differentiate the two choices from each other. This is the kind of behaviour an adult might carry out when imitating a model sitting down, for example. In carrying out the imitation, if there is more than one chair present, the adult might pick either one. A chair is a chair, even if each has a different physical appearance. Similarly, for an infant a small container is a small container, even though one is a cup and the other a pan.

In our first experiment on this issue we examined two natural-kind and two artefact properties (Mandler & McDonough, 1998b). For the animal properties, we modelled a dog chewing on a bone and tested generalisation with another dog and a goose. We also modelled sniffing a flower and tested generalisation with another flower and a tree. For the artefact properties we modelled drinking with a cup and tested generalisation with a mug and a

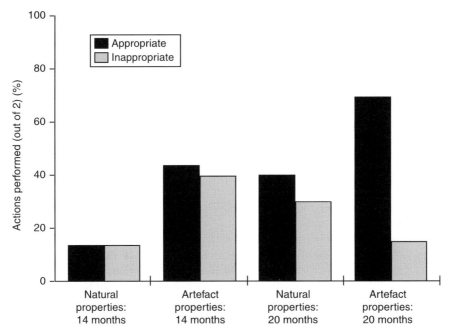

Figure 11.2. Generalisation of basic-level properties of natural kinds and artefacts by 14- and 20-month-olds.

frying pan. We also modelled sleeping in a crib and tested generalisation with a bed and a bathtub. As can be seen in Figure 11.2, at 14 months, the infants generalised these properties to both appropriate and inappropriate exemplars, and this happened for both the natural kinds and artefacts (although the infants were less likely to imitate the natural-kind properties, suggesting that they were less familiar with them). At 20 months, they still generalised the natural-kind properties equally often to appropriate and inappropriate objects, but had begun to narrow down their responses in the artefact domains. That is, they still made a goose chew on bones and a person sniff trees, but now they were more likely to restrict drinking to a cup not a pan and sleeping to a bed not a bathtub.

In our next set of studies (Mandler & McDonough, 2000) we replicated these findings in the artefact domain with new examples. We studied 14-, 19-, and 24-month-olds. We modelled four properties associated with specific household artefacts: washing a plate in a sink, sitting on a chair at a dining table, brushing hair, and pounding with a hammer. Washing was tested by giving the children another sink and a bathtub, sitting at table by giving the children another chair and a toilet, brushing hair by giving them another hairbrush and a toothbrush, and pounding by giving them another hammer and a wrench. Fourteen-month-olds were haphazard in their choices of objects to use for their imitations; by 19 months they were by and large correct.

Once again, it is not the case that 14-month-olds tend to pick randomly in this situation. Rather, they pick objects to use for their imitations in terms of the available choices and what they have understood. A control experiment demonstrated this. When the incorrect choices were more distantly related to the correct choices, 14-month-olds performed well. In this experiment a bed was used as the incorrect choice for washing a plate, a spoon was the incorrect choice for brushing hair, a little car was the incorrect choice for sitting at table, and a plastic cup was the incorrect choice for hammering. Relatively few infants made these incorrect choices. It seems clear that at this age infants are not depending merely upon simple physical descriptions (such as "largish container" or "hand-sized elongated object") or the affordances implied by these physical descriptions to determine the function of household objects. They might confuse a sink and a bathtub as appropriate for washing dishes, perhaps because they have seen both being filled with water or because washing of some sort takes place in both, but they do not confuse a sink and a bed, despite their overall container-like shapes. (An interesting asymmetry making a possible exception is that infants this age do treat both beds and bathtubs as possible places for sleeping, perhaps because they have been put down to nap in so many kinds of furniture; Mandler & McDonough, 1998b.) Similarly, even though they are not clear about the different uses of various brushes, they know that spoons are not used for grooming hair, despite their rough similarity in shape. Thus, by 14 months infants have developed some fairly broad but not yet detailed, conceptualisations of the functions of household artefacts.

We also tested properties associated with specific kinds of vehicles and compared children's response to them compared to specific kinds of animal properties. The vehicle properties were wearing a helmet when riding an all-terrain vehicle (a three-wheeled motorcycle), tested using another motorcycle and a car; and putting petrol into a car, tested by another car and a child's wagon. The animal properties were feeding a rabbit a carrot, tested with a different rabbit and a bird; and a bird sitting in a nest, tested with a different bird and a rabbit. The results fit the pattern of the previous experiments. The 14-month-olds did not do well on either animals or vehicles. By 19 months, they were highly successful on the vehicle tests and still poor on the animal tests. By 24 months they were successful even on animal properties. These data are important because they tell us that the improvement in performance with age is not merely due to better ability to match what the modeller does; the same 19-month-olds who imitated vehicle properties well did poorly with animal properties.

In summary, we can reach the following tentative conclusion about the order of acquisition of artefact and animal kinds (and plants as well, although the database is smaller). The characteristic behaviours associated with specific household artefacts and vehicles are learned earlier in ontogeny than those associated with specific animal kinds (or plants). The data we have collected form a coherent picture, but I stress that we have sampled only the relevant domains and studied a single population. It seems likely that infants in southern California, where these data were collected, have much more experience with a variety of artefacts than they do with animals, so we have no reason to think this order of acquisition is necessarily universal. We also don't yet know how much infants generalise from people to other animals. In addition, it should be emphasised that these data have to do with differentiation within the domains of animals, plants, vehicles, and household artefacts, and not with the acquisition of the domain-level concepts themselves. Those highest-level concepts probably all begin to be learned more or less contemporaneously and very early in life.

These data also highlight another point that is relevant to our understanding of the fundamentally categorical and hierarchical nature of the conceptual system. The data make clear that associative learning is dependent upon the interpretation of the meaning of objects, not upon their physical features. Infants have only seen people drink from cups and mugs, but nevertheless associate drinking with other containers, such as pans. They have been washed in bathtubs and observed washing dishes in sinks, but associate washing dishes in bathtubs as well. These examples, along with many others, such as associating sleeping with fish and using a key with aeroplanes (Mandler & McDonough, 1996), or chewing bones with birds, make plain that associative learning is not under the control of object features or appearance, but of object meaning.

One could, if thinking in a connectionist mode, describe these associations as due to domain-level categories acting as attractor basins (Plaut & Shallice, 1993), but this does not explain how meaning is used to form the attractors in the first place. Even within a feature analysis, features occur at different levels of generality (see Chapter 8) and one would need to explain why certain higher-level features form attractor basins and lower-level ones do not. The crucial point is that if a dog is interpreted as an animal, then observed behaviours of dogs, such as sleeping or chewing bones, become associated not just with dogs but with animals as a class, and hence are generalised to fish and birds. The higher-order concept is determining what will be learned about its exemplars. This is just one of the reasons why acquisition of concepts about objects involves a hierarchical form of categorisation at its heart. Other reasons are discussed in the next section.

THE MEANING OF THE FIRST CONCEPTS

I have discussed what some of the first concepts are, such as animal, furniture, vehicle, and plant, but have not yet considered what the content of these global concepts might be. I do so briefly in this section, but note that it is much easier to determine that infants have some concept of animal than to determine exactly what this consists of. We have the most data about the concept of animal, although the corpus is not systematic, having been collected for a variety of purposes. Nevertheless, I believe we can glean a general picture of what the earliest concept of animal might be like, and thus what the meaning is that controls the building-up of associations.

To start the process, infants are especially attracted by moving objects (Kellman, 1993). This interest might be built in, but it might also be determined at least in part by the initial limitations of infants' perceptual systems, such as poor acuity in the first few weeks of life (Banks & Salapatek, 1983). Indeed, given newborns' relatively slow processing, they might not at first retain much information out of many events except crude descriptions of the paths that objects take. I have suggested that analysis of these paths is crucial for creating a first concept of animal. Even if young infants do not take in many details about an object, from early on they are capable of observing at least three general characteristics of moving objects. First, some objects move in a biological way and others either do not move at all, or if they do move, do so in a more "mechanical" way. In terms of data, it has been shown that infants perceptually differentiate the motion of people from similar but biologically incorrect motion as young as 3 months of age (Bertenthal, 1993). This is a differentiation that does not have to be built in; it is a characteristic of the perceptual system to isolate the principal components of visual patterns early in learning. Second, some objects start motion on their own whereas others move only if contacted by another object. From as young as 4 months, infants have learned something about how hands interact with objects (Needham & Baillargeon, 1993) and also are sensitive to the difference between physically caused motion and self-starting motion (Leslie, 1982). By 5 months they are also interpreting activities in terms of goals (for example, whether a hand is reaching to pick up an object), not in terms of movement *per se* (Woodward, 1995). Third, by 3 months infants are sensitive to whether objects interact contingently with them (Frye, Rawling, Moore, & Myers, 1983; Watson, 1972), and a few months later whether they interact contingently with others (Molina, Spelke, & King, 1996).

I have suggested that infants redescribe these characteristics of moving objects, so that their parameters become reduced to highly simplified descriptions such as "irregular motion", "self-motion", or "interacts with other objects from a distance" (Mandler, 1992). These redescriptions characterise events, that is, they give a very abstract description of what animals do. They omit physical details and so these notions are independent of the actual appearance of the movement of any particular object or whether its motion is realised by legs, fins, or wings. Nevertheless, a combination of several such meanings is sufficient to establish a primitive concept of animal in the sense that they create a non-perceptual description (or very abstract perceptual description) of the sort of thing an animal is (see Mandler [1992] for discussion of the process by which perceptual information can be turned into conceptual meanings and the way in which these meanings might be represented). Thus, a likely first concept of animal is a thing that moves by itself and interacts with other objects from a distance. Note that this concept does not include information about physical features. Of course, various features, such as legs, wings, and fins, become associated with the concept, but need not be part of its core meaning. Santos and Caramazza (Chapter 1) make a similar point.

We have less information about what the earliest concepts of furniture, utensils, vehicles, and plants are like, but again, to start the process off, the same kind of redescription of events should be at work. Non-animals either don't move at all, or if they do, the paths they follow are very different from those of animals. Non-animals start motion only when something else comes in contact with them, the paths they follow are typically quite different from animal paths and they do not interact with other objects from a distance. This difference between the doers and "the done to" characterises all the events infants observe. Therefore, there is enough information in the perceptual data they have to work with to distinguish between animals and non-animals.

This first conceptual division is necessarily abstract because it is based on relations between things. These relations are often functional (Nelson, 1985) but early in infancy must be understood in an even more abstract way. For example, infants are apt to attend to the contingency between hands and objects beginning to move before they understand the function the hand is carrying out. This characteristic of early object concepts, incidentally, means that the traditional view that concepts develop from the concrete to the abstract is mistaken (see Keil [1988] for a similar observation). Early concepts are abstract because their content is relational and applicable to large domains and, as discussed in the last section, only gradually become narrowed down to specific details.

For example, infants appear to have a general concept of containment as early as 6 months. Baillargeon, Kotovsky, & Needham (1995) showed that they know that containers hold things and require bottoms to do so. About this time they also learn that larger objects cannot go into smaller containers (Aguiar & Baillargeon, 2000). However, many of the details are picked up rather slowly and perhaps somewhat haphazardly. Thus, at 14 months infants do not yet know that pans are not appropriate to drink from, or that dishes are not washed in bathtubs, even though they do understand that a bed (a container with sides, headboard, and footboard) is not an appropriate place for washing. These kinds of findings suggest that differentiation of the functions of various household objects might be learned in a piecemeal fashion, so that anomalous associations can exist along with correct associations. Acquiring true "basic-level" understanding appears to be a gradual process. Children might first learn that certain kinds of objects are containers, then that small containers, whether cups or pans, are used for drinking and large containers are used for washing and sleeping, then that some large containers are used for sleeping and others only for washing, and finally the specifics that differentiate bathtubs from sinks. This specific developmental progression is speculative, of course, because we have only collected some of the relevant data. More generally, amount of experience with the various subclasses of the global domains we have studied undoubtedly affects the rate at which they become differentiated. Overall, however, the general developmental trend of conceptualisation advancing downwards from a superordinate to a subordinate level has been found consistently for both animate and inanimate domains.

The abstract and general properties of global domains that young infants learn can be characterised as essential. This is not the same sense of "essence" as used by Keil, Kim, and Greif (Chapter 13). These authors discuss essence in more sophisticated terms than are appropriate for infancy, referring to the differing substances that make up each distinct kind, the needs of living things, and the functional uses of artefacts. Infants have not yet attained such knowledge; nevertheless they are firmly on the road to conceiving fundamental differences among things (even if at first only globally). Their behaviour when asked to imitate actions that violate their conceptions tells us that, young as they are, they do not accept category errors lightly! It seems not inappropriate to call their initial notions of animals and artefacts essential, in the sense that they form the core of what makes something an animal or an artefact. Indeed, it seems plausible that even as adults our most basic, fundamental, "Ur" view of what animals are is that they are things that can move themselves and that inanimate objects are things that cannot. We could tolerate the news that tiger DNA can transmute into leopard DNA more easily than that a stone could move by itself. So I would argue that in some sense substance is not the core of our essentialist beliefs, but instead something more primitive and less reflective. Indeed, I would claim that it is the notions formed early in infancy that form the skeletal structure of adult conceptions, such as those discussed by Keil et al. (Chapter 13).

IMPLICATIONS FOR THE ORGANISATION OF THE ADULT CONCEPTUAL SYSTEM

The most important message from this research is that the conceptual system is organised categorically from its inception. Furthermore, it does not appear necessary to start the process off by building in an initial division of animal versus artefact, as several researchers have suggested (Gelman, 1990; Spelke, 1994). The available data suggest that this distinction is easily learnable from the spatial and movement information presented by the visual system. A related issue is whether there are different rates of learning distinctions within these large domains. Caramazza and Shelton (1998) suggested an evolutionary basis for an animate–inanimate distinction because the domain-level categories of animals, plants, and artefacts can be damaged independently of each other. They suggested that this might be due to "specific adaptations for recognising and responding to animal and plant life". If there were dedicated mechanisms for processing animals and plants, one would expect learning different animal and plant kinds to be especially easy. Although Caramazza and Shelton (1998) do not put it in this way, I take this to be the implication of their hypothesis that there are "specialized mechanisms for the recognition and categorisation of the members of the categories for which specific adaptations have evolved". However, our data say that conceptualising animal and plant kinds is more difficult for infants than conceptualising kinds of artefacts. The type of learning infants do appears to be the same for animals, plants, and artefacts but, at least in our culture, it is slower for animals and plants. This difference is not what one would predict from an evolutionary hypothesis that emphasises special adaptations for learning in these domains. More seriously for an evolutionary argument, perhaps, even American adults are very poor at distinguishing different kinds of plants and animals, especially non-mammals. As Rosch et al. (1976) discovered, most American college students have little idea about the properties that distinguish one fish from another or one kind of deciduous tree from another, both in terms of what they look like and their other characteristic features. These properties are either taught by the culture or tend to remain unlearned.

The initial division between the domains of animals and artefacts might well have an evolutionary basis but it can also be explained by the mammalian tendency to attend to motion. As discussed in the last section, analysis of the way that objects move and the kinds of paths that they take seems to be one of the first conceptualising activities of the mind. Of course, the tendency to focus on motion is important from an evolutionary perspective but that is not the same as a propensity for special learning of animals and plants. Needless to say, I agree with Caramazza and Shelton's emphasis on the categorical organisation of the semantic system, but I believe there are sufficient grounds for this organisation to be learned rather than built in. A distinction between animals and artefacts can be based entirely on the perceptual input available to infants and their ability to categorise the different roles these two types of objects play in events (Mandler, 1992, 2000). If this is the case then one would expect more similarities than differences in learning in the different domains. Aside from faster differentiation of the artefact domains we have studied, overall the course of learning looks very similar.

Regardless of whether there is an innate basis for the initial distinction between animals and artefacts, its importance lies in the inevitable consequence for the organisation of the conceptual system. If it is the case that infants at first divide the world into animals and inanimate things, then every time a new category is learned within these global domains it is necessarily learned as a subdivision of this larger division. This procedure guarantees a hierarchically organised categorical system. This system might eventually become an extremely complex heterarchy, owing to the many cross-references and connections that arise with experience. However, the fundamental underlying structure of the conceptual system about objects is necessarily hierarchical. A corollary of this conclusion is that, virtually from the beginning, the features that describe categories come in more than one level of generality.

We see a hierarchy being formed especially clearly in the case of the division of animals into subtypes (although the data on vehicles are similar). Our data suggest that animals are first conceptually divided into land animals and birds, with fish being perhaps a slightly later division. (In the urban society of San Diego, even though the city is on an ocean, fish as living creatures do not usually figure in the daily lives of infants.) Over the first year or two children gradually begin to be exposed to a variety of mammals. With some, such as dogs and cats, they might have daily experience. They see the differences between these two animal kinds from an early age (Quinn et al., 1993). However, on the object examination test they do not categorise them as different until 11 months of age (Mandler & McDonough, 1998a) and, in terms of generalising from one to the other, they still treat them as equivalent at 14 months (Mandler & McDonough, 1998b). This means that for a very long period dogs and cats are treated as either the same or as minor variants on each other, which means that their animal (or land animal) status is firmly established throughout the period infants are learning to differentiate them conceptually.

I do not want to give the impression that this process of differentiation is systematic or that the resulting system is scientifically tidy. Among other difficulties, it seems unlikely that infants see any relationship between animals and plants. That is, the first division does not appear to be an animacy–inanimacy distinction, in so far as animacy is meant to include all living things. Rather it appears to be an animal–non-animal distinction. The animate–inanimate distinction is an adult theoretical construction rather than a species-characteristic way of viewing the world. If my characterisation of the basis for the first concept of animal is correct, self-starting movement, movement through the environment, and contingent interactions from a distance are crucial. These do not characterise plants. We do not have data comparing the two domains earlier than 11 months, but at that time infants clearly differentiate between them. So it seems likely that there is a more fundamental distinction than the animate–inanimate one, namely the distinction between animals and other things.

A similar untidiness can be seen in our data indicating that artefacts are divided at least into furniture and vehicles from an early age. Although this is a neat enough taxonomic distinction, it too could be an overly adult characterisation. It might be more accurate to say that infants divide artefacts into indoor and outdoor things. Some years ago when we were exploring the sequential touching task, Pat Bauer and I found a category of manipulable household items that our subjects differentiated from vehicles (unpublished data). We discovered this category when we tried to assess responding on the sequential touching test when there was only one taxonomic category available. We contrasted vehicles with what we considered to be an unrelated set of things. The items in the sets we used (a lamp, hairbrush, teacup, and wristwatch, or a chair, guitar, spoon, and shoe) seemed to us to come from different semantic categories. To our surprise, our 17- and 20-month-old subjects showed clear categorisation of these items when they were contrasted with vehicles. In retrospect, what we considered to be a non-categorised group could all be considered household items (or perhaps manipulable things typically found indoors). It wasn't until I read Warrington and McCarthy's (1987) case study of YOT, who seemed to have a category of indoor things, that it occurred to me we might have inadvertently provided the children with a normal "child's category". My hunch is that there will be lots of these—categories that do not fit neatly into our accustomed taxonomic systems but that make sense from the point of view of what matters to the 1- or 2-year-old. Other examples are the categories of kitchen things and bathroom things, which children as young as 14 months differentiate on the basis of the context in which different activities take place (Mandler et al., 1987).

Similar comments can be made about the category of food. It is highly unlikely that infants in our culture see any relationship between food and living things. Food is an early developing category. Unfortunately, it is difficult to study by the methods we have been using. It might be called an attractive nuisance, because even when made of plastic, infants dwell on representations of food to the exclusion of most other items presented to them. That very fact suggests that a food category is an early accomplishment, but we have few details. What little we do know about it, however, suggests that although infants differentiate food from animals and plants, they are slow to categorise different kinds of food, such as fruit, meat, and vegetables. Although there are few data in infancy, the overextension data on language understanding in the second year suggest haziness about different types of food (McDonough, in press). Indeed, it has been suggested that the initial organisation of this domain is by type of meal (breakfast, lunch, and dinner) rather than by taxonomic structure of the foods themselves (Lucariello & Nelson, 1985).[7] Certainly, infants do not understand fruit and vegetables as part of the plant domain.

One proposal for the first subdivisions of animals and non-animal things into more detailed categories is laid out in Table 11.1. In it animals, non-animal things, and food are considered foundational. I have put an asterisk by the category of buildings to indicate we have no data and this is merely a prediction. I would expect a category of buildings to be learned fairly early, although infants are on the whole uninterested in large immoveable objects. We do have some data at 14 months showing they understand that both animals and vehicles can go into buildings (Mandler & McDonough, 1998b), which is the kind of abstract relational characterisation one expects from the first conceptualisations of a domain. In addition, infants should have enough experience to differentiate between homes and supermarkets from a fairly early age. We also have relatively little data on food, but because of the special status food has in an infant's life I have assumed it is categorised separately from other non-animal things from an early age.

In this proposal, which is the same as that suggested by Santos and Caramazza (see Chapter 1), there is no overarching animate–inanimate, or living–non-living distinction, but only three divisions of the world, each separate from the others. Of course, this division is speculative. It is possible that food might be considered just another non-animal thing, in which case the initial division reduces to an animal–non-animal distinction. What we do know is that the categories of animals, furniture, and vehicles are differentiated from each other at least by 9 months of age and plants by 11 months. At 9 months, kitchen utensils are not yet differentiated from furniture, but they

TABLE 11.1
One possible early organisation of the conceptual system

Animals	Non-animal things		Food
	Indoor things	Outdoor things	
	Furniture Utensils	Vehicles Plants Buildings*	

---

[7] In reference to a query Santos and Caramazza pose in Chapter 1, the little data we have suggest that young children do not distinguish between artificial foods, such as cookies, and natural foods, such as apples.

are by 11 months, giving some support to the grouping of both of them under a category of indoor things that initially is undifferentiated but soon begins to be subdivided.

In so far as the breakdown of the semantic system under brain damage is concerned, the main message of the acquisition data is that for each of the seven categories mentioned in Table 11.1, one would expect a common pattern of lower level distinctions to be lost before higher level ones. Because of the nature of the learning process, in which each new distinction is learned as a subdivision of a superordinate category, the superordinate distinctions should be the most firmly established and therefore one would expect a pattern of "first in, last out" (Mandler, 1997, 1998a). The available literature suggests exactly that pattern (Patterson & Hodges, 1995; Warrington, 1975). For example, in their systematic study of the loss of knowledge in a patient with semantic dementia, Hodges, Graham, and Patterson (1995) found that at first low-level distinctions were lost, then higher levels such as the division of animals into land and air creatures, and only very late in the course of degeneration was the unique beginner level itself sometimes misattributed. The sequence itself is perhaps not surprising, only the systematicity of the findings. One can lose details about tigers (for example, whether they are African or Indian animals) while still retaining enough information to differentiate tigers from other animals, but if one no longer knows what an animal is, it would seem virtually impossible to retrieve the fact that tigers are Indian animals. Thus, the breakdown data are consistent with the acquisition data, and the latter are only consistent with a model in which the conceptual system is learned and organised hierarchically from the top down.

Although the way in which the conceptual system is first learned and organised predicts the order in which semantic information is lost, it is silent on the issue of which domains might be most vulnerable to brain damage. For example, the initial organisation of the conceptual system proposed in Table 11.1 does not predict the associations among damaged categories that have been observed in the neuropsychological literature, such as living versus nonliving things (Warrington & Shallice, 1984). On the hypothesis that animals and plants belong to a common category, if the category of animals, for example, was damaged it might be more likely that plants rather than artefacts would be damaged as well. This association is not a necessary one, however, because the category of animals can be damaged by itself (Caramazza & Shelton, 1998). Indeed, the acquisition data are more consistent with a separation of these two categories than with their being part of a larger "animate" distinction, as discussed earlier. Nor do the suggested initial organisations predict why animal kind differences are more apt to be disrupted under brain damage than are artefacts (see Saffran & Schwartz [1994] for a summary).

Santos and Caramazza (Chapter 1) suggest that this finding is due to our evolutionary history. It seems to me just as tempting to relate these common patterns of breakdown to the fact that individual animal and plant kinds are more difficult to learn in the first place. However, I suspect the answer will be more fundamental than that, perhaps involving a common factor that influences both acquisition and breakdown. In our society most of us have much less experience with animals or plants than with artefacts. This begins in infancy. This is not meant to imply that animals are unfamiliar or that familiarity is not an important factor in the breakdown of semantic knowledge (Funnell & Sheridan, 1992) But familiarity is not the same as the continuous interaction with objects that takes place, day in and day out, over the course of decades. It might be this kind of daily interaction that is crucial in maintaining the conceptual system. We might judge (as I do) that both dogs and spoons are highly familiar, but it is the latter that most of us deal with on a daily basis. In that sense, the knowledge of animals and plants in modern society is more fragile. This is an area that cries out for crosscultural neuropsychology studies. It seems possible that among people whose lives involve daily interaction with animals, the loss of the animal category would be less frequent.

At the same time, the suggestion originally made by Warrington and Shallice (1984), and more recently amended and modified by Borgo and Shallice (2001), that categories whose identity depends more on sensory qualities than on functional or associative ones might be most at risk, is of interest *vis à vis* the acquisition data. Perhaps the relatively slow acquisition of animal and plant kinds that our data indicate is not so much due to lack of interactive experience with them as to the fact that infants do not rely on perceptual appearance to determine conceptual kind. In our research, McDonough and I have found over and over again that what things look like does not particularly influence infants' conceptual choices in the tasks we have used. Because their attention is directed to what things do or what is done to them, perceptual differences among different kinds of animals or plants (or, for that matter, food) do not seem to play a major role in developing and consolidating these categories. As discussed earlier, even very young infants can see the perceptual differences between one animal and another, but it takes many months before they learn anything else that distinguishes them because their conceptual core (for example, "a self-moving interacter") is the same for all.

To join this point to the cultural one just mentioned, infants in our culture are for the most part not given much information about the difference in what one animal and another does (and virtually nothing about what one does with one plant versus another). Not surprisingly, then, even 18-month-olds act as if one mammal is equivalent to another. It might be, then, that if one does not have extensive interaction with different animals (or plants), the primary database one has about what distinguishes one from another is perceptual. This might not be a sufficient basis to create impervious categorical distinctions between one animal (or plant) kind and another.

Finally, I want to emphasise that this discussion has been about the organisation of the semantic system, not the organisation of the brain. These are not the same thing, although they appear to be equated in some neuropsychological discussions. The information I have provided is about the organisation of the mind, not the brain. The developmental data make clear that the semantic system is indeed organised categorically. It is to be hoped that this fact is useful to neuroscientists studying brain organisation but there are many possible reasons for selective damage to the conceptual system other than the way it is organised. As McRae and Cree (Chapter 8) have shown, the number of distinguishing features associated with different categories varies considerably and, as they suggest, this might account to some extent for the patterns of categorical loss found in various kinds of brain impairment. Two facts needs to be borne in mind, however. First, the deficits under discussion are still categorical in nature, even if they are partly due to a relative paucity of distinguishing features. Second, much of the relevant literature concerns the difficulties patients have in distinguishing one instance of a category from another, not in distinguishing animals, for example, from furniture or plants. It might be more difficult to discriminate a sheep from a goat than a hammer from a saw, but it is surely easier still to discriminate an animal from a tool. In searching for the details of the brain organisation associated with category-specific deficits, we must not lose sight of categorical organisation itself.

REFERENCES

Aguiar, A., & Baillargeon, R. (2000). Perseveration and problem solving in infancy. In H. Reese (Ed.), *Advances in child development and behaviour*, Vol. 27. San Diego: Academic Press.

Baillargeon, R., Kotovsky, L., & Needham, A. (1995). The acquisition of physical knowledge in infancy. In G. Lewis, D. Premack, & D. Sperber (Eds.), *Causal understandings in cognition and culture*. Oxford: Oxford University Press.

Banks, M. S., & Salapatek, P. (1983). Infant visual perception. In M.M. Haith & J.J. Campos (Eds.), *Infancy and developmental psychobiology*, Vol. 2 of P.H. Mussen (Series Ed.), *Handbook of child psychology*. New York: Wiley.

Behl-Chadha, G. (1996). Superordinate-like categorical representations in early infancy. *Cognition, 60*, 104–141.

Behrend, D.A. (1988). Overextensions in early language comprehension: Evidence from a signal detection approach. *Journal of Child Language, 15*, 63–75.

Berlin, B., Breedlove, D.E., & Raven, P.H. (1973). General principles of classification and nomenclature in folk biology. *American Anthropologist, 75*, 214–242.

Bertenthal, B. (1993). Infants perception of biomechanical motions: Intrinsic image and knowledge-based constraints. In C. Granrud (Ed.), *Visual perception and cognition in infancy*. Hillsdale, NJ: Erlbaum.

Borgo, F., & Shallice, T. (2001). When living things and other "sensory quality" categories go together: A novel category-specific effect. *Neurocase, 7*, 201–220.

Bower, G.H., Clark, M.C., Lesgold, A.M., & Winzenz, D. (1969). Hierarchical retrieval schemes in recall of categorised words lists. *Journal of Verbal Learning and Verbal Behaviour, 8*, 323–343.

Caramazza, A. & Shelton, J.R. (1998). Domain-specific knowledge systems in the brain: The animate–inanimate distinction. *Journal of Cognitive Neuroscience, 10*, 1–34.

Clark, E.V. (1983). Meanings and concepts. In J.H. Flavell & E.M. Markman (Eds.), *Cognitive development*, Vol. 3 of P.H. Mussen (Series Ed.), *Handbook of child psychology*. New York: Wiley.

Collins, A.M,. & Quillian, M.R. (1969). Retrieval time from semantic memory. *Journal of Verbal Learning and Verbal Behaviour, 8*, 240–247.

DeLoache, J.S. (1989). Young children's understanding of the correspondence between a scale model and a larger space. *Cognitive Development, 4*, 121–139.

Farah, M.J., & McClelland, J.L. (1991). A computational model of semantic memory impairment: Modality specificity and emergent category specificity. *Journal of Experimental Psychology: General, 120*, 339–357.

Frye, D., Rawling, P., Moore, C., & Myers, I. (1983). Object-person discrimination and communication at 3 and 10 months. *Developmental Psychology, 19*, 303–309.

Funnell, E., & Sheridan, J.S. (1992). Categories of knowledge? Unfamiliar aspects of living and nonliving things. *Cognitive Neuropsychology, 9*, 135–153.

Gelman, R. (1990). First principles organize attention to and learning about relevant data: Number and the animate-inanimate distinction as examples. *Cognitive Science, 14*, 79–106.

Graesser, A.C., & Mandler, G. (1978). Limited processing capacity constrains the storage of unrelated sets of words and retrieval from natural categories. *Journal of Experimental Psychology: Human Learning and Memory, 4*, 86–100.

Hodges, J.R., Graham, N. & Patterson, K. (1995). Charting the progression of semantic dementia: Implications for the organisation of semantic memory. *Memory, 3*, 463–495.

Jacoby, L.L. (1983). Perceptual enhancement: Persistent effects of an experience. *Journal of Experimental Psychology: Learning, Memory, and Cognition, 9*, 21–38.

Keil, F.C. (1988). Cognitive science and the origins of thought and knowledge. In R.M. Lerner (Ed.), *Theoretical models of human development*, Vol. 1 of W. Damon (Series Ed.), *Handbook of child psychology*. New York: Wiley.

Kellman, P.J. (1993). Kinematic foundations of infant visual perception. In C.E. Granrud (Ed.), *Visual perception and cognition in infancy*. Hillsdale, NJ: Erlbaum.

Leslie, A. (1982). The perception of causality in infants. *Perception, 11*, 173–186.

Lucariello, J., & Nelson, K. (1985). Slot-filler categories as memory organisers for young children. *Developmental Psychology, 21*, 272–282.

Mandler, G. (1967). The organisation of memory. In K.W. Spence & J.T. Spence (Eds.), *The psychology of learning and motivation: Advances in research and theory*. New York: Academic Press.

Mandler, G., & Rabinowitz, J.C. (1981). Appearance and reality: Does a recognition test really improve subsequent recall and recognition? *Journal of Experimental Psychology: Human Learning and Memory, 7*, 79–90.

Mandler, J.M. (1984). Representation and recall in infancy. In M. Moscovitch (Ed.), *Infant memory*. New York: Plenum.

Mandler, J.M. (1992). How to build a baby: II. Conceptual primitives. *Psychological Review, 99*, 587–604.

Mandler, J.M. (1997). Development of categorisation: Perceptual and conceptual categories. In G. Bremner, A. Slater, & G. Butterworth (Eds.), *Infant Development: Recent Advances*. Hove: Psychology Press.

Mandler, J.M. (1998a). The rise and fall of semantic memory. In M. Conway, S. Gathercole, & C. Cornoldi (Eds.), *Theories of memory II* (pp 147–169). Hove: Psychology Press.

Mandler, J.M. (1998b). Representation. In D. Kuhn & R. Siegler (Eds.), *Cognition, perception, and language*, Vol. 2 of W. Damon (Series Ed.), *Handbook of child psychology*. New York: Wiley.

Mandler, J.M. (2000). Perceptual and conceptual processes in infancy. *Journal of Cognitive Development, 1*, 3–36.

Mandler, J.M., Bauer, P.J., & McDonough, L. (1991), Separating the sheep from the goats: Differentiating global categories, *Cognitive Psychology, 23*, 263–298.

Mandler, J.M., Fivush, R., & Reznick, J.S. (1987). The development of contextual categories. *Cognitive Development, 2*, 339–354.

Mandler, J.M., & McDonough, L. (1993). Concept formation in infancy. *Cognitive Development, 8*, 291–318.

Mandler, J.M. & McDonough, L. (1996). Drinking and driving don't mix: Inductive generalisation in infancy. *Cognition, 59*, 307–335.

Mandler, J.M. & McDonough, L. (1998a). On developing a knowledge base in infancy. *Developmental Psychology, 34*, 1274–1288.

Mandler, J.M. & McDonough, L. (1998b). Studies in inductive inference in infancy. *Cognitive Psychology, 37*, 60–96.

McDonough, L. (in press). Basic-level nouns: First learned but misunderstood. *Journal of Child Language*.

McDonough, L. & Mandler, J.M. (1998). Inductive generalisation in 9- and 11-month olds. *Developmental Science, 1*, 227–232.

Mervis, C.B. (1987). Child-basic object categories and early lexical development. In U. Neisser (Ed.), *Concepts and conceptual development*. Cambridge: University of Cambridge Press.

Mervis, C.B., & Rosch, E. (1981). Categorization of natural objects. *Annual Review of Psychology, 32*, 89–115.

Molina, M., Spelke, E.S., & King, D. (1996). The animate-inanimate distinction in infancy: Sensitivity to distinctions between social interactions and object manipulations. Poster presented at the Tenth International Conference on Infant Studies, Providence, RI.

Needham, A. & Baillargeon, R. (1993). Intuitions about support in 4.5-month-old infants. *Cognition, 47*, 121–148.

Nelson, K. (1973). Some evidence for the cognitive primacy of categorization and its functional basis. *Merrill-Palmer Quarterly, 19*, 21–39.

Nelson, K. (1985). *Making sense: The acquisition of shared meaning*. San Diego: Academic Press.

Patterson, K. & Hodges, J.R. (1995). Disorders of semantic memory. In A.D. Baddeley, B.A. Wilson, & F.N. Watts (Eds.), *Handbook of Memory Disorders*. London: Wiley.

Piaget, J. (1951). *Play, dreams, and imitation in childhood*. New York: W. W. Norton.

Piaget, J. (1952). *The origins of intelligence in the child*. New York: International Universities Press.

Plaut, D.C., & Shallice, T. (1993). Deep dyslexia: A case study of connectionist neuropsychology. *Cognitive Neuropsychology, 10*, 377–500.

Quinn, P.C., Eimas, P.D., & Rosenkrantz, S.L. (1993). Evidence for representations of perceptual similar natural categories by 3-month-old and 4-month-old infants. *Perception, 22*, 463–475.

Rescorla, L.A. (1980). Overextension in early language development. *Journal of Child Language, 7*, 321–335.

Reynolds, J.H., & Goldstein, J.A. (1974). The effects of category membership on memory scanning for words. *American Journal of Psychology, 87*, 487–495.

Ricciuti, H.N. (1965). Object grouping and selective ordering behaviour in infants 12 to 24 months old. *Merrill-Palmer Quarterly, 11*, 129–148

Rosch, E., & Mervis, C.B. (1975). Family resemblances: Studies in the internal structure of categories. *Cognitive Psychology, 7*, 573–605.

Rosch, E., Mervis, C.B., Gray, W., Johnson, D., & Boyes-Braem, P. (1976). Basic objects in natural categories. *Cognitive Psychology, 3*, 382–439.

Ruff, H. (1976). Components of attention during infants' manipulative exploration. *Child Development, 57*, 105–114.

Saffron, E.M., & Schwartz, M.F. (1994). Of cabbages and things: Semantic memory from a neuropsychological perspective – A tutorial review. In C. Umiltá & M. Moscovitch (Eds.), *Attention and Performance XV: Conscious and unconscious information processing* (Vol. 3). Cambridge, MA: MIT Press.

Spelke, E.S. (1994). Initial knowledge: six suggestions. *Cognition, 50*, 431–445.

Sugarman, S. (1983). *Children's early thought*. Cambridge, England: Cambridge University Press.

Warrington, E.K. (1975). The selective impairment of semantic memory. *Quarterly Journal of Experimental Psychology, 27*, 635–657.

Warrington, E.K., & McCarthy, R.A. (1987). Categories of knowledge: Further fractionations and an attempted integration. *Brain, 110*, 1273–1296.

Warrington, E.K., & Shallice, T. (1984). Category specific semantic impairments. *Brain, 107*, 829–854.

Watson, J. (1972). Smiling, cooing, and "the game." *Merrill-Palmer Quarterly, 18*, 323–340.

Woodward, A.L. (1995). *Infant's reasoning about the goals of a human actor*. Paper presented at the Biennial Meetings of the Society for Research in Child Development, Indianapolis, IN.

CHAPTER TWELVE

Animates and other separably moveable objects

Kaveri Subrahmanyam
California State University, Los Angeles, USA

Rochel Gelman
*University of California, Los Angeles and Rutgers Center for Cognitive
Science, Piscataway, New Jersey, USA*

in collaboration with

Alyssa Lafosse
University of California, Los Angeles, USA

INTRODUCTION

We hold that the origin and development of the animate–inanimate distinction benefits from principled, domain-specific considerations about causality (Gelman, 1990; Gelman, Durgin, & Kaufman, 1995; Gelman & Spelke, 1981; Williams, 2000; Williams & Gelman, 1995). We share with Caramazza (Chapter 1 and Caramazza & Shelton, 1998) the view that the animate–inanimate distinction is domain-specific, universal, and at least as much conceptual as it is perceptual. Our position is consistent with Heider and Simmel's (1944) argument that the motion paths of objects and their interactions are interpreted with schemas (see also Goffman, 1974; Hochberg, 1978). It also dovetails with Keil's ideas about mental devices that resonate to domain-relevant inputs (Keil, 1995; Keil, Kim, & Greif, Chapter 13) and Leslie's (1995) assumptions that animate objects have agency and are goal-directed. Our perspective differs from ones that attribute the acquisition of the animate–inanimate distinction to either general information perceptual and semantic processes (Warrington & Shallice, 1984), the sensory and/or perceptual detection of different kinds of motion variables, and/or the subsequent abstraction of various kinds of motion schemes for animate and inanimate objects (Oakes & Cohen, 1995; Mandler, 1992 and Chapter 11; Premack, 1995).

To develop our position we start with a general point. There is no question that various perceptual characteristics of trajectories, photographs, and other replicas of animate and inanimate objects can influence decisions about their identity. Although perceptual characteristics of animate and inanimate objects are relevant, it is an open question as to what perceptual information an observer will use for a given item. Perceptual cues that might seem salient to us need not be so from the observer's perspective; conversely, observers might focus on what we consider irrelevant or neutral characteristics. Such problems of stimulus indeterminacy contribute significantly to our move to say that the issue of relevance is informed by conceptual as well as perceptual matters (Gelman & Williams, 1998).

ON THE PROBLEM OF SELECTIVE ATTENTION

Massey and Gelman (1988; Massey, 1988) showed 3- and 4-year-old children photographs of novel objects like those in Figure 12.1 and asked them whether each could move itself both up and down a hill. The children did rather well and even could justify many of their responses. On the one hand, they might claim the echidna could accomplish the actions because it had feet and "was walking"—even though no feet can be seen and it is still. On the other hand, they said the statue could not move up and down a hill because its feet were "not real", "pertend", "too shiny", or part of a "furniture–animal". Some children even pointed to the very thin antennae on the "bug" to justify their claim that a mainly shiny, hard-surfaced object could move itself. These kinds of answers are hardly what one expects from young children who often are described as "perception bound". Instead, they reveal an active tendency to attend selectively, sometimes to minute aspects, and even misinterpret aspects of photographs with respect to causal considerations. For us, this means that the children were attending to information that could indicate whether the photographed item had movement enabling parts that were intrinsic to animate objects. They also seemed interested in clues about whether an object was made out of the kind of stuff that goes along with the capacity for self-generated actions. Hence, in the words of some children, the material had to be "real" or "not pretend", or from our point of view, biological stuff.

These results are one kind of selective attention or interpretative focus that encourages us to assume that young children, as well as adults, use a domain-specific set of principles to learn about animate and inanimate objects. Data from experiments on how individuals use motion path information provide another major reason for us to favour our position, because it turns out that motion path information is neither necessary nor sufficient for the identification of animate and inanimate objects and events (Gelman et al., 1995; Williams, 2000). Such findings are problematic for those who assume that

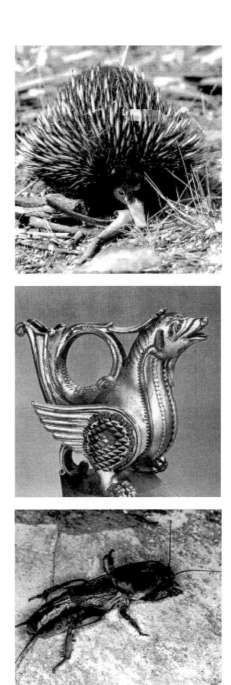

Figure 12.1. Scans of three photographs based on Massey and Gelman (1998). From top to bottom, these are an echidna, a statue, and a "bug".

animacy is grounded on perceptions of particular kinds of complex movement paths and that these, can, on their own, yield veridical animate or
inanimate attributions (Bassili, 1976; Mandler, 1992 and Chapter 11; Morris,
Nisbett, & Peng, 1995; Premack, 1995; Stewart, 1984).

Stewart (1982, 1984) proposes that we perceive a moving object as
inanimate when its motion path is consistent with Newtonian laws of
motion. If the motion path violates Newtonian principles, then we perceive
animacy and attributions like intentions desires, hunger, affection, etc. To
obtain evidence for her theory, Stewart showed college students a
computer-generated dot moving on the screen in ways that were either
consistent or were not consistent with Newtonian mechanics. Gelman et
al.'s (1995) additional analyses of Stewart's data, in combination with new
studies, yielded a number of results that represent departures from
Stewart's predictions. For example, the perception of a path curving upwards
on the screen lent itself to a wide range of perspectives and causal interpretations, including "... a bicyclist going around a corner"; "... a
balloon and the wind was blowing and it went like this, this, like a helium
balloon. It got caught up in the air"; "... a horse climbing a mountain";
"... some kind of magnetic ball that encountered a field that pushed it
away".

The above descriptions are revealing on another level. They embed within
them an account of how the "object" might have moved along the path in
question. The "hows" were all about unseen causal factors that could support
the way the object moved, including wind blowing, a horse climbing, and a
magnetic ball in a field. These kinds of answer provide especially compelling
evidence for our argument that the displays were fodder for causal
principles—ones that encouraged interpretation of the motion paths in terms
of the possible agents and conditions that generated the trajectories. What
was perceived was interpreted with reference to the conditions that can cause
the seen trajectory, even if this means inventing invisible forces, mountains, or
magnetic fields.

One might hold that the preceding argument is reasonable, but only for
adults who have had a chance to learn about different causal variables. Surely,
the argument would continue, young children will not have such knowledge at
their disposal to embellish their perceptions. If so, there is an interesting
developmental prediction. This is that young children will be more likely than
adults to rely on the surface information given in a motion path. It turns out
that, if anything, 3- and 4-year-olds are more likely to "import" unseen or
unheard information about energy sources when they decide whether a
motion of an unidentified object was that of an animate or inanimate object
moving in the dark, in a particular setting. Williams' (2000) dissertation
provides a lovely demonstration of this. He showed groups of adults, 3- and
4-year-olds a series of dots moving along various trajectories, having first

presented priming material that gave information about settings and the physical forces therein.

The setting information for each trajectory was comprised of a still (frozen) clip from a video of a scene, for example, a high cliff dropping into a moving stream that had some trees along its banks. On some trials, there also was the sound of running water or a wind. Williams ended the presentation of a given setting by rendering the screen completely dark. Next, a pinpoint of light appeared somewhere on the screen. Pretest training encouraged people to think that the light was attached to an object that was now moving in the darkened scene. This contributed to the impression of a particular object that was moving in the just-shown, but now pitch-black, environment. For example, the light on the body of an object seemed to move along the top of the cliff, drop straight down from the cliff, smoothly or not, in silence or not, in or just above the river, and so on. After viewing each event sequence, subjects were shown pairs of photographs, one each of an animate and an inanimate object (e.g. a duck and a leaf) and asked which one they had just watched move in the dark. Williams expected subjects to choose inanimate objects when the just-seen motion paths were force-consistent and animate objects with paths that were force-inconsistent. So, for example, he predicted that a dot that stopped and started, and even changed direction, as it moved along the silent river scene, would be paired with the duck.

Adults were especially likely to pair pictures of the animate and inanimate choices in response to whether the setting events were or were not force-consistent. Children's judgements were more variable, but this variability was not due to a failure of the children to use the trajectory information. Both children and adults were especially inclined to give motion explanations that were consistent with their judgements. The difference between the children and adults was due to the youngsters' tendencies to import force conditions that were not part of the setting display! For example, children who paired the leaf, and not the duck, with the trajectory that just moved in a force-inconsistent manner, "imported" a relevant force. They said that "the wind blowed it around", even though there was no sound of wind during the stimulus presentation. Thus, the use of motion path information was only part of the information they used to construct a coherent account of the event and related causal sources of energy. Once again, we see that the trajectories were an important, but not determining, source of relevant information for the assignment of animacy.

To repeat, we are not claiming that perceptual information is irrelevant to the animate–inanimate distinction. Rather, our point is that the definition of what is relevant is deeply related to the causal knowledge structures that individuals bring to the tasks of learning: (i) which separably moving objects are animate and which are not; and (ii) how to categorise exemplars of each class (Wilson & Sperber, 1986). Surface perceptual similarity regarding the parts and shape of objects surely provides some relevant information. Many animals do have parts in common (Carey, 1985; Tversky & Hemenway, 1984). However, such information is neither sufficient, nor necessary. The echidna in Figure 12.1 has almost no parts/features that overlap with those of commonly encountered animals. In contrast, the statue has a considerable number of animal-like parts. When children are encouraged to adopt a causal frame of reference, this influences what they take to be salient. Seemingly subtle cues for material kind become salient because they are relevant for deciding whether something is animate or not (see Massey [1988] for further details). Putting matters this way, it is less surprising that young children say that a statue cannot engage in self-motion because its feet are "not real", because it is not enough to have parts that look like those of a living animal—they have to be composed of the right kind of stuff and it is important to attend to clues that are relevant as regards material composition. In a similar way, it is not enough for an object to move on its own; again, it has to be composed of the right stuff. Why?

The fact that animate objects can cause themselves to move or change and that inanimate objects cannot goes hand in hand with the fact that inanimate and animate objects are composed of different kinds of matter. Animate objects are composed of biological matter; inanimate objects are not. Although all objects obey the laws of physics, animate objects also obey biochemical ones. In fact, the cause of animate motion and change comes from the channelled release of internally stored chemical energy that is characteristic of biological entities. Animate motions have a quality of function (purpose or goal-directedness). This is a direct consequence of their governance by biological control mechanisms. These enable adjustments of, and coordination of, component actions, both as a whole and as separate components. These adjustments can be to social as well as non-social environments. The effect is an ability to adapt to unforeseeable changes in circumstances and interact with social and non-social environments. The cause of inanimate motion is an external force, and there is always a transfer of energy from one object to another or a conversion of potential energy to kinetic energy. This is true even when a person serves as an agent.

Although most people do not have articulate scientific knowledge about the connection between biological matter and animate motion, even young children have relevant intuitions (see Williams [2000] for a recent review). They know that the source of animate action is intrinsic to the object. We think this is because of domain-specific causal principles that serve to encourage attention to, and separate categorisation of, objects as a joint function of whether they are capable of self-generated motion or not *and* made of biological stuff or not. Our thesis is that domain-specific casual principles organise attention to and learning about separably moveable things. Of course, we do not assume that young children are endowed with a rich, scientific understanding of the biological world. Indeed, the fact that plants do not move as a whole is one key reason we think individuals treat plants and animates differently. At a later point in the chapter we will add evidence to the growing view that young children do not know that plants and animals share deep biological characteristics (Carey, 1985; see also Chapter 11).

MORE ON THE NOTION OF SPECIFIC DOMAINS

Gelman defines a domain of knowledge by appealing to the notion of a set of interrelated principles (Gelman, 1990; Gelman & Williams, 1998). A given set of principles, the rules of their application, and the entities to which they apply together constitute a domain. Different structures are defined by different sets of principles. Therefore, we can say that a body of knowledge constitutes a domain of knowledge if we can show that a set of interrelated principles organises its rules of operation and entities. Sets of principles carve the psychological world at its joints, producing distinctions that guide and organise our differential reasoning about entities in one domain versus another. In this way, available domain-specific structures encourage attention to data that has the potential to nurture learning about that domain; they help learners find inputs that are relevant for knowledge acquisition and problem solving within that domain.

A specific domain of knowledge might or might not be part of our human endowment. Clearly, one mark of human intelligence is the ability of individuals to acquire new domains of knowledge, including ones about cognitive neuroscience, chess, computer programming, or even sushi making. It is necessary to distinguish between those specific domains whose skeletal structures outline and enable domain-relevant learning by all normal human beings and those that do not. The latter depend on learners' interests and take a great deal of time and effort to mount (Bransford, Brown, & Cocking, 1999). This is in no small part due to the fact that learners have to acquire both the new structure and the domain-relevant knowledge. Although the innate domain-specific principles that support learning in a given domain are exceedingly skeletal to start with, they nevertheless constitute a structure. Whenever a structure is available, learning is facilitated. This is why some acquisition moves rather quickly, and seemingly on the fly, in some domains, but not in others.

Gelman (1990, 1994) proposed that attention to, and learning about, relevant characteristics of separately moveable objects benefits from domain-relevant processing mechanisms that are informed by first causal principles. As already discussed, these correspond to deep and fundamental distinctions about the fact that animate and inanimate objects differ in terms of their material, structural composition, potential for interaction, and their energy sources of motion or transformations. Animate objects are made of biological matter, a kind of matter for which the cause of growth, self-initiated movement, and other transformations are intrinsic to the objects themselves. The cause of inanimate motion is an external force (the external agent principle), and there is always a transfer of energy from one object to another or a conversion of potential energy to kinetic energy. It is important to the causal–principle argument that these differences go hand in hand with the fact that animate objects are composed of biological matter and honour biological principles, whereas inanimate objects are composed of non-biological material and honour principles of inanimate causation. In addition, animate motions have a quality of directedness or purpose, and biological control mechanisms make it possible for animates to respond (or adjust) to environments—be these social or non-social—and adapt to unforeseeable changes in circumstances (Gallistel, 1990; Gelman et al., 1995).

These distinctions are captured in Gelman's animate causal principle, "the innards principle" and in her inanimate causal principle, "the external–agent principle". The argument is that higher-order causal principles direct attention to a combination of information, including kind of matter, source of energy, and trajectories. As regards objects obeying the innards principle, the energy source for movements, transformations, perceptions, and interactions is intrinsic to biological objects and thus is contained within the objects themselves. As regards objects obeying the external-agent principle, the movements, transformations, and interactions of non-biological objects are caused by agents and forces of nature that are external to the objects themselves. We do not assume that, early in development, one necessarily has an explanation system of intrinsic energy sources and exchange, or even of what it means to say the source of energy is embodied in the object (see also Williams, 2000). Similarly, we do not assume that there is a universal explanation system of external energy sources and exchange. But we do assume that high-level causal principles organise the uptake of data that contribute to the causal explanation system of a culture. This distinction between causal principles and explanatory systems is expanded in a further section.

Why do we postulate the innards and external–agent principles if we do not assume that one has a theoretical understanding of them? A key reason has to do with the need to achieve a solution to the problem of attention to, and coherent learning about, examples of animate versus inanimate objects. We have already presented several sets of results that illustrate the need to have an account of the constructivist aspects of attention. The innards principle offers one such account because it serves to draw attention to that constellation of perceptual information about those natural objects that move and interact on their own. Even infants are sensitive to cues for biomechanical motions and intentionality (Bertenthal, 1993; Gergely, Gergely, Szilvia, & Orsolya, 1999; Poulin-Dubois, 2000; Premack, 1995) and the differential role of contact in the movement of animate and inanimate objects (Spelke, Phillips, & Woodward, 1995). A second reason is that, given that the innards principle serves as a domain-relevant organising device, it provides young children with a way to sort and then correctly assimilate mental-state predicates such as think, want, and so on. To be sure, it is one thing to assimilate such inputs and quite another thing to understand them. But it does help to accumulate relevant data in some coherent way. Otherwise, it is extremely hard to acquire understanding. Similarly, the external–agent principle supports the processing and interpretation of data about objects that move as a function of external energy sources (e.g. from collisions, wind, moving water) as well as details about its size, smoothness or roughness, rigidity, etc. (Baillargeon, 1998; Williams, 2000).

If we are right, then even very young children will not confuse machines with animate objects. A major aim of this chapter is to update and relate our "first-principles" position to other worldly things, especially different kinds of machine (e.g. computers, televisions). After we expand on our general prediction about machines, we present data that we have collected about children's and adults' ideas about a wide variety of things, including animates, simple artefacts (e.g. chairs, spoons), machines and even a plant.

THE CASE OF MACHINES

Machines are made of the wrong stuff to meet the domain-specific criteria that outline the equivalence class of separably moveable animate things. True, a machine can seem to move on its own but, in the absence of some animate agent, it does not anticipate and intentionally adjust to unexpected environments. Further and critically, from a novice's point of view, it is made out of non-biological stuff, stuff that is rigid, hard, and so on. Thus, the information as to whether a novel object is animate or inanimate either is indeterminate, inconsistent, or even internally contradictory. Which of these characterisations apply to a given example depends on the kind of machine in question.

Whereas some machines, like cars, appear to move on their own, others, like computers, appear to think and communicate, do not exhibit bio-mechanical motions, and do not adjust especially well to local environmental problems (Gelman et al., 1995). For example, robots are not especially good at adjusting their motions to local perturbations in the environment and are at risk of falling into holes or toppling over protuberances. In contrast, so predictable is the animate world's ability to deal with unanticipated holes, bodies of water, oil-slicks, branches that come below the head, sun in one's eyes, weather changes, and so on, that we almost forget how remarkable are the action abilities of the animate world. Aside from these fundamental differences regarding sources of energy, movement patterns, and reactions to environments, machines are made of the wrong stuff. Because we assume that causal principles yoke information about objects' composition to their motion trajectories, we predict that children and adults will assume that machines lack the animate, domain-specific capacities of growth, nutrient consumption, reproduction, respiration, and perception. Therefore, machines will not be classified as either clear cases of animates or clear cases of inanimates. Instead, they will be assigned to a separate category.

As machines are man-made artefacts, knowledge of particular kinds of machines depends on opportunities to encounter and learn about them (see Chapter 13). Still, if causal principles direct attention to concerns about the source of motion of an object, children should be inclined to ask about or make up external–agent accounts. Further, there should be little, if any, tendency for young children to endow machines with animate properties. These predictions might surprise those familiar with the Piagetian tradition, within which there has been a longstanding tendency to assume that young children will confuse machines with animate objects and therefore imbue them with animistic attributes. Piaget's (1929) claim that children were animistic was based on his finding that young children sometimes said that inanimate objects such as the sun, the wind, cars, bicycles, clocks, watches, ovens, and fires are alive. According to him, children progress from attributing life to any moving, active object to eventually attributing life only to animals and plants.

There are several problems with Piaget's conclusions. First, young children do not have a clear understanding of the word "alive", even for animals and plants (Carey, 1985). Second, children were classified as animists if they gave only one such explanation during a long interview, hardly the kind of criterion that merits the attribution of a worldview. Third, even adults have murky notions about the nature of the sun, fire, and wind, items that were used frequently by Piaget. Finally, several lines of research show that preschool children are not universal animists, and there now is some research that focuses on the question of whether young children classify machines together with animates. The indications are that they do not.

Simons and Keil (1995) report that, by about 4 years, children consistently choose natural-kind objects (animal insides or rocks) as potential insides for animals, and artefacts (machine insides or blocks) as potential insides for machines. They conclude that children expect the insides of animals and machines to differ, although they lack knowledge about the specific physical appearance of those insides. Rosengren, Gelman, Kalish, and McCormick (1991) report that children believe that animals, but not artefacts (such as a light bulb or telephone), get larger over time. Finally, Backesheider, Shatz, and Gelman (1993) found that 3- and 4-year-old children believe that objects such as a television or a car cannot regrow if damaged, but must be fixed by human intervention.

These findings begin to show that children do not confuse animates and machines. Still, important questions about how they conceptualise these hybrid objects remain unanswered. First, machines are not a homogeneous category. There are some machines that move, such as cars and aeroplanes. There are other machines that have sentient and "intelligent" properties but were not designed to move, for example, computers and robots. Still other machines mimic communicative functions, for example, televisions and radios. Our informal observations of adults' interactions with these various kinds of machines led us to conjecture that it is the adult, not the young child, who adopts an animistic stance when using or interacting with certain machines. We might say "My car's engine just died" or "How dare you behave so badly when you're supposed to be printing my important manuscript?". These particular animistic statements are surely dependent on our knowledge and experience with objects that "mimic" some aspect of animate objects. One has to learn about both the machine and the relevant animate properties of humans or animals.

FURTHER THEORETICAL ISSUES

Although we might attribute knowledge to computers, it is unlikely that we would do the same with vacuum cleaners. The attributions are selective and depend on the kind of machine in question. Given the preceding discussion, we expected that adults would be more likely than young children to attribute some animate properties to machines. Scaife and Van Duuren (1995) present evidence that is consistent with this conjecture. They reported that, although 5-year-olds attributed a brain to a person, they were not willing to do so for a computer or robot. By about 11 years of age, not only were children more inclined to grant a computer and robot a brain, they knew a great deal more about the relevant variables. They could assign the CPU box correctly and identify the composition of real brains (nerve cells and neurons versus blood, bones, and meat).

Our argument that many animistic answers depend on knowledge of both the animate and inanimate objects in question serves to highlight a theme of our work on domain-specific principles. Although innate principles in a domain facilitate some kinds of domain-relevant learning, they do not guarantee mastery of advanced levels of understanding in that domain. For example, although principles of counting and arithmetic support some early learning about adding and subtracting with the count numbers, they do not do the same for subsequent learning about rational numbers and their relevant operations (Gelman & Hartnett, 1998). Similarly, the way young children make use of abstract causal principles to assign objects to either the animate or inanimate category need not be sophisticated. Given these principles, one can know machines are not animate because they are made of the wrong stuff—even though they might move on their own. However, it is one thing to be able to place a given object in the right memory-filedrawer and quite another to know great deal about it. First principles about causality can help learners move onto and stay on relevant learning paths. They can serve to encourage attention to those aspects in the environment that are relevant to learning about the in's and out's of animate and inanimate objects. They do not, however, determine the particular explanations that learners achieve. Indeed, they do not guarantee that ideas about mechanisms will be congruent with those held by experts. As Keil et al. (Chapter 13) show, many adults fail to achieve a correct understanding of scientific accounts of mechanisms.

In the following section we present results from new studies we have done. These bear on our ideas about clear cases of animates and inanimates, as well as machines. As we also ask about simple artefacts and a plant, the findings offer an opportunity to consider a number of different accounts of the animate and inanimate distinction. These include accounts that grant preschool children biological theories (Hatano & Inagaki, 1994; Keil, 1994; Wellman, 1990) and ones that favour domain-general perceptual and semantic processes (Warrington & Shallice, 1984). For the reasons covered earlier, we expected that young children would falter on questions about mental phenomena, such as thinking and remembering.

Although we contend that young children know that animate actions are due to energy sources within the actor, we have no reason to assume that young children are prone to develop explanation systems that parallel modern, Western philosophical theories of mind. We share Carey's (1985) view that early knowledge about biological entities is naive and limited. Indeed, we anticipated that children would treat plants as belonging to yet another separate category. Plants are in the biological world, insofar as they are composed of biological matter, and share some quintessential animate properties, such as breathing, growing, and food consumption. Yet, they do not move as a whole, do not interact, and do not have a capacity for communication. Therefore, young children should place plants in a category that is separate from animals and artefacts.

These various considerations motivated our studies with young children and adults, where we questioned them about a variety of attributes in different categories. In the first study (The Picture Sorting Study), we used a picture sorting task in which we asked children and adults to sort through photographs of different kinds of items based on whether or not they showed a range of animate attributes. For example, they had to sort pictures of worldly objects into two piles—one pile consisting of objects that can talk and one consisting of objects that cannot talk. In the second study (The Interview Study), we did not use photographs but rather asked target questions about different animals, simple artefacts, machines, and plants. Our questions centered on different animate attributes, such as moving, breathing, and remembering; we also asked the subjects to provide justifications for their answers.

Our studies bear on the Warrington and Shallice (1984) hypothesis that the animate-inanimate distinction is grounded in a semantic system, such that visual information is relevant to animates but functional information is relevant to inanimates. If we assume that the visual processing system is active when visual stimuli are present (as in the picture sorting task) then, on the Warrington and Shallice hypothesis, children should do better on the animate items in the picture sorting task than on the interview task. If visual information is not relevant to the inanimate items, the visual–verbal variable should have little effect for inanimate items and machines.

THE STUDIES

We begin by describing the materials and procedures of the studies. We organise the findings with reference to different kinds of questions one might ask about children's understanding of animates, inanimates, and other worldly things.

The picture sorting study

Three- and 4-year-old children (mean age = 3.6 years and 4.4 years for the 3- and 4-year-olds, respectively) and adults participated in this study. There were twelve individuals in each age group. They were shown twenty black and white photographs of 3-dimensional objects and were asked to sort them into two piles, with one pile made up of items that displayed a particular animate property and the other pile made up of items that did not display that property. This sorting was done several times, once each for the animate properties of "can move by itself", "needs to eat", "can talk", "can think and remember", and "can feel happy and sad" (Table 12.1). The pictured items included animates (person, dog, cat, elephant, and bug), simple artefacts (chair/stool,

TABLE 12.1
Questions and *post-hoc* comparisons for the picture sorting study

What X does/does not do	Significant interactions*
Eat	Adults more likely than children to attribute to bug and plant
Move	3- and 4-year olds said "yes" to self-motion for aeroplanes and cars (these are not examples of childhood animism; see text)
Talk	Adults and 4-year-olds more likely to attribute to robots
Be happy and sad	4-year-olds and adults more likely to attribute happy and sad to a cat, dog, and elephant
Think and remember	Adults more likely to attribute remember to an elephant

* All main effects and interactions were assessed by ANOVA and Tukey *post-hoc* comparisons (HSD = .43, p < .01).

spoon, keys, and lamp), machines (vacuum cleaner, radio, television, aeroplane, car, computer, and robot), a plant, and filler items (apple, rock, and doll).

For the children, we used a cover story involving the penguin puppet, "Pokey",[1] who was visiting Los Angeles from the North Pole. A child was told that Pokey was confused about things found here in Los Angeles because it was so different from the North Pole. Pokey thus had questions about things found in Los Angeles, and wanted the child to answer them. For each question, the child was told that some things exhibited a particular animate attribute, whereas others did not. For example, for the Move question, the tester told the child, "Some things move by themselves, whereas some things do not". The child was then shown the photographs and told that Pokey wanted to find all the things that could move by themselves.

The tester then presented the photographs, one at a time, said the name of the object in the picture, and asked the child whether or not the item possessed the attribute in question. For example, the tester would say "Can a person move by itself? Yes it can? or No it cannot?". If the child said "Yes", the tester placed the card in the "can move by itself" pile close to Pokey; if the child said "No", the tester placed the card in the "cannot move by itself" pile further away from Pokey. After all twenty photographs had been shown for each target question,[2] the experimenter noted the items that had been placed in the "yes" pile. The procedure was identical for the adults, except that they were informed that the task was originally designed for children.

The interview study

In this study, we talked to 4- and 5-year-old children (mean age = 4.5 years and 5.2 years, respectively) and adults. There were twelve individuals in each age group. We asked them eight questions about each of nineteen items. Six questions dealt with various animate properties, including action properties (move and talk), anatomical/physiological properties (brain and breathe), and mental/sentient properties (think and remember). These questions were

---

[1] Past research has found that use of a puppet greatly enhances preschool children's performance on experimental tasks, where the experimenter is often in the pragmatically odd situation of asking the child for information that he/she would clearly know as an adult. By getting the puppet to ask the question instead, the task becomes more realistic and can elicit a higher and more accurate rate of responding.

[2] All twenty photographs were shown for a property before proceeding to the next one. Two random orders were used to present the properties, with Move being the first in one order, and Eat being the first in the other. For each property, the photograph of the person was always shown first, followed by the other pictures in random order, with different random orders being used for the different properties.

similar in format. For example, "Does a plant move? If yes, how does it move? If not, why not?". The other two questions dealt with the inside and outside and origin of each item. For example, "What is on the inside of a dog? What is on the outside of a dog?" and "Where does a car come from? Does it come from a mommy or does some one make it?".

For a given question, we asked them about the nineteen items in successive order. Table 12.2 presents the format of the questions. The items were similar to those used in the Picture Sorting Study, and included animates (person, dog, elephant, and bug), simple artefacts (chair/stool, spoon, and clock), machines (vacuum cleaner, radio, television, aeroplane, car, computer, and

TABLE 12.2
Questions and resulting reliable *post-hoc* comparisons for the Interview Study

1st question	*2nd question*	*Kind of results*
Does X move?	If yes, how does it move? If not, why not?	Adults more likely to attribute move to a plant compared to 4- and 5-year-olds; Adults more likely to attribute move to clock compared to 4-year-olds
Does X talk?	If yes, how does it talk? If not, why not?	All subjects attributed talk to person; Only adults attributed talk to a bug, dog, and a radio
Does X breathe?	If yes, how does it breathe? If not, why not?	Adults attribute breathe more often to a bug and a plant compared to the 4- and 5-year-olds; Adults and 5-year-olds attribute breathe more often to an elephant compared to the 4-year-olds
Does X have a brain?	If yes, why does it have a brain? If not, why not?	Adults more likely to attribute a brain to a bug and an elephant compared to the 4- and 5-year-olds
Does X remember?	If yes, how does it remember? If not, why not?	Adults more likely to attribute remember to a bug, elephant, and a computer
Does X think?	If yes, how does it think? If not, why not?	Adults more likely to attribute think to a bug compared to the 4- and 5-year-olds; Adults more likely to attribute think to an elephant compared to the 5-year-olds
Where does a X come from?	Does it come from a mommy, or does some one make it?	
What is on the inside of X?	What is on the outside?	

Post-hoc comparisons (Tukey's HSD = 0.43, p < .05)*.

robot), a plant, and filler items (apple, rock, sun, and doll).[3] As there were eight questions about nineteen items, the entire interview took between 30 and 45 minutes; whereas most children finished the interview in one session, we administered the interview over two sessions for a few of the younger children.

QUESTIONS ADDRESSED BY THE STUDIES

1. Do children and adults distinguish between animates and machines?

Across both studies, we found evidence that the children[4] consistently and clearly distinguished between animate and other kinds of things, notably machines (we deal with their categorisation of simple artefacts and plants in questions 4 and 5). There are several lines of evidence for this conclusion.

First, analysis of the number of "yes" responses to the categories of different items (Table 12.3) revealed that the children were more likely to attribute the animate properties to the animates than to the simple artefacts or machines.[5] As can be seen, they sometimes granted an animate property to a machine; this usually happened for the question about moving for a car, aeroplane, and robot. The ability to talk also was attributed to a robot. This attribution of the action properties to the machines was decidedly selective. For example, they allowed that a radio could talk but not move, and that a car could move but not talk. Only occasionally did they attribute the anatomical/physiological properties (brain and breathe) or the sentient properties (think

---

[3] The items were presented in one of two quasi-random orders. For both orders we started with the following items: person, dog, plant, apple, and rock; the rest of the items were then presented in one of two random orders.

[4] As there were no reliable age effects for the children, we collapsed the data from the 3- and 4-year-olds in study 1 and the 4- and 5-year-olds in study 2.

[5] For study 1, "Yes" and "No" responses to each item were analysed by an overall repeated measures analysis of variance with item (20) and property (5) as the within-subjects factors, and age (3) as the between-subjects factor. The overall analysis yielded an interaction of age and item $F(38, 627) = 5.34, p < .01$ as well as an interaction of age, item, and property $F(152, 2508) = 1.98$, $p < .01$. The three-way interaction of age, item, and property was analysed by separate mixed ANOVAs for each of the five properties. Each of these analyses had item (20) as the within-subjects factor and age (3) as a between-subjects factor. For study 2, a preliminary omnibus mixed analysis of variance was done with item (19) and property (6) as the within-subjects factors, and age (3) as the between-subjects factor. There were no main effects, but we obtained a reliable interaction of age and item $F(36, 576) = 5.06, p < .01$ which was modulated by a three-way-interaction of age, item, and property $F(180, 2880) = 1.45, p < .01$. The three-way interaction was analysed by separate mixed ANOVAs for each of the six properties; each of these analyses was done with item (19) as a within-subjects factor and age (3) as a between-subjects factor. Results of the *post-hoc* comparisons are reported in Table 12.1 for the Picture Sorting Study and Table 12.2 for the Interview Study.

TABLE 12.3
Percent "yes" answers given by children and adults for each predicate

	Predicate					
*Age/item**	*Move*	*Talk*	*Breathe*	*Brain*	*Think*	*Remember*
Child						
Person	100	100	100	95	95	86
Dog	95	28	92	68	59	45
Elephant	95	32	67	55	41	41
Bug	95	9	50	45	27	41
Plant	9	0	33	0	14	5
Rock	9	0	0	5	9	5
Spoon	9	0	0	9	5	0
Clock	50	0	0	9	5	14
Vacuum	50	5	8	14	5	9
Car	72	5	0	0	5	9
Aeroplane	72	0	0	9	0	5
Robot	90	59	17	23	36	36
TV	0	14	8	5	14	14
Computer	0	9	8	14	9	18
Doll	36	5	17	18	23	36
Adult						
Person	100	100	100	100	100	100
Dog	100	67	100	100	92	92
Elephant	100	58	100	100	83	92
Bug	100	42	100	92	83	92
Plant	58	0	83	8	0	0
Rock	17	0	8	0	0	0
Spoon	25	0	0	0	0	0
Clock	100	8	0	0	0	0
Vacuum	83	8	0	0	0	0
Car	75	8	17	0	0	0
Aeroplane	92	17	0	0	0	8
Robot	92	75	0	0	25	50
TV	33	42	0	0	0	0
Computer	33	42	0	8	0	67
Doll	50	42	0	0	0	0

* The item doll is shown at the end of the machine cluster of items. Adults were more inclined to say dolls move and talk, justifying their "yes" by appealing to the mechanisms of talking and walking dolls. Data for apple, chair, and radio are not shown because they do not change any patterns. Radios were treated like TVs.

and remember) to an inanimate object. The only machine that was given the capacity to think and remember was a robot, presumably because of subjects' knowledge about this category.

Thus, the attribution of potential animate properties to machines was selective in a way that we expected. It was consistent with the proposal that animates and machines are treated as different kinds of things. The same conclusion holds when we look at the explanations accompanying the "yes" or "no" attributions. An explanation was coded as correct if it was appropriate for a given item. For example, the response "a computer moves" was scored as correct if the participant explained that the motion was caused by an agent outside the computer; in contrast, it was scored as incorrect if the participant said the computer moved by itself. Table 12.4 shows sample protocols of correct and incorrect responses for selected items. The responses

TABLE 12.4
Examples of children's and adults' answers in the interview study

Property/capability and item	Age group	Answer
Correct answers		
Move – Elephant	Child	Yes, it walks
Move – Car	Child	Yes, when driven
Move – Plant	Adult	No, no legs
Talk – Vacuum	Child	No, no mouth
Talk – Plant	Child	No, no lips
Talk – Radio	Adult	No, inanimate object
Talk – Bug	Adult	No, no language
Breathe – Dog	Child	Yes, has lungs
Breathe – Plant	Child	Yes, with its leaves
Breathe – Radio	Adult	No, it's a machine
Breathe – Car	Adult	No, no lungs
Think – Person	Child	Yes, it has a brain
Think – Vacuum	Child	No, not alive
Think – Computer	Adult	No, it's man-made
Think – Plant	Adult	No, doesn't have a mind
Remember – Person	Child	Yes, coz he has a mind
Remember – Car	Child	No, coz it doesn't have a brain
Remember – Robot	Adult	No, not living, unknown
Remember –Plant	Adult	No, doesn't have a brain
Brain –Person	Child	Yes, to think
Brain –Computer	Adult	No, it's not living.
Brain – Plant	Adult	No, it doesn't think
Incorrect answers		
Move – Dog	Child	No, animals don't move
Move – Chair	Adult	Yes, can change states like rot
Talk – Doll	Child	Yes, with mouth
Talk – Radio	Adult	Yes, with speakers
Breathe –Bug	Child	No, because it stings people
Breathe – Car	Adult	Yes, turn fan on
Think – Dog	Child	No, no brain
Remember – Elephant	Child	No, no brain
Remember – Elephant	Adult	No, not by self, usually train
Brain – Robot	Adult	No, no control centre

TABLE 12.5
Percentage of correct answers

Property and age	Correct(%)
Move	
Children	92.3
Adults	95.6
Talk	
Children	90.2
Adults	94.3
Breathe	
Children	75.4
Adults	96.9
Think	
Children	73.7
Adults	94.7
Remember	
Children	72.0
Adults	95.6
Brain	
Children	66.0
Adults	98.7

were coded jointly by the authors and checked by the collaborator. Table 12.5 shows the percentage of correct answers offered by the children and adults for the different properties summed across different item kinds. Overall, children offered 92.3% of correct answers for move, 90.2% for talk, 75.4% for breathe, 73.7% for think, 72% for remember, and 66.0% for brain.[6] Chi-square goodness-of-fit tests confirmed that the number of correct answers (versus incorrect, don't know, and other responses collapsed together) was above chance for all properties for both the children and adult samples (all $p < .01$). Not only did children offer correct justifications, they were just as likely to do so as the adults (all $p < .01$).

Further evidence that children, like adults, distinguish between animates and machines comes from a qualitative code of children's explanations (Table 12.6). As shown in Figure 12.2, the children consistently used different explanations to justify their responses for the different item kinds. For animates, they appealed to the presence of animate parts (e.g. bones, muscles, blood), causes (e.g. wants to move), and notions (e.g. alive, living) to justify their attributions. For the machines, they invoked the absence of animate

---

[6] We discuss the fact that children were more accurate on some as against other properties in a subsequent section.

TABLE 12.6
Qualitative code of explanations

Category code and description	Examples
I Presence/absence of animate (+ /–A) **including:**	
1. Animate parts (innards/external)	1. Bones, muscle, blood, legs, mouth
2. Animate motion	2. Flies, walks, takes in air
3. Animate causes	3. Wants to move
4. Life terms	4. Alive, living
5. Other animate features	5. Ability, perception
II. Presence/absence of inanimate (+ /–I)	
1. Inanimate parts and mechanisms	1. Batteries, wheels, engines
2. Inanimate materials	2. Plastic, metal
3. Inanimate motion	3. Flies, when an aeroplane
III. External causes (E)	
1. Action of a person (EM)	1. Someone drives it, flies it, programmes it
2. Forces of nature (EN)	2. Wind, earthquake, gravity
IV. Plant properties (+ P)	
1. Plant parts, plant features	1. Leaves, stem
2. Plant mechanisms	2. Stationary, leaves move toward sun, photosynthesis
V. Tautology (TA)	
1. Re-statement as to whether item displays property	1. Doesn't, doesn't talk, just does,
2. Statement of the item's category, etc.	2. Just an apple
VI. Causal essence/origin (C)	Comes with it, built with it, not meant to, DNA, genetics, needs one, supposed to, instinct
VII. Function (F)	
1. Function or use of the item	1. For eating, for sitting on, we watch TV
VIII. Attributes (T)	
1. Perceptual and other properties and attributes (surface similarity)	1. Stays in kitchen, makes noise
IX. Other + Bizarre (O)	He is my friend
X. Don't know (DK)	I don't know; because

features and/or the presence of inanimate parts (wheels), inanimate mechanisms (batteries, engines), inanimate materials (plastic, metal), and external sources of energy to explain their attributions.

Children's answers to the inside/outside question provide additional support that they distinguished between the insides and outsides of animates and machines. Both children and adults appealed to animate 'innards' (blood, bones) and animate externals (wings, eyes) for the animates, but appealed to inanimate materials (plastic, glass), constituent parts (buttons, knobs), and inanimate mechanisms (electricity) for the machines. Children, like adults, think that animate objects can have blood and bones on their insides, but not wires and batteries. Again, we see that the children used different explanations when responding to the different kind of objects.

In sum, young children know that when machines mimic an animate property, they do so because they obey the external–agent principle. Thus, they know that moving machines move because of energy extrinsic to the object, such as the energy from a battery or an agent, whereas animates move as a result of intrinsic variables. Even though children attributed an potentially animate property, such as move, to a machine, they did not behave as general animists. Their projection of animate attributes was suitable and selective. Children flexibly switched their item attribution of a property and their accompanying explanation for their attribution based upon the question. It is clear that children place animates and machines in separate categories. So, what do young children think about animate objects?

2. What are children's concepts about animates like?

Some hold that young children's ideas about animate objects are organised by a content-rich theory of biology (Hatanao & Inagaki, 1994; Keil, 1994; Wellman & Gelman, 1998; Williams, 2000). Our findings encourage us to favour the conclusion that early knowledge is embedded in a more skeletal set of causal principles and beliefs about the actions and reactions of animates and other worldly things (Gelman, 1990). Indeed, our findings converge on ones Carey (1985) presented when she concluded young children do not have a biological theory.

Recall the results from the ANOVAs on the "yes" attributions reported earlier in question 1. As reported in Tables 12.1 and 12.2, children did not treat all animate objects alike. Like the adults, they consistently attributed the animate properties to a person. But unlike the adults, they were reluctant to attribute particular animate properties to other animates, such as bug, dog, or elephant. To give some examples, in study 1 they were less likely than the adults to attribute "eat" to a bug and plant, and "feels happy" to a cat, dog, and elephant. Similarly, in study 2, they were again less likely to attribute "breathe" to a bug and a plant, and "think" and "remember" to a bug. The only exception was "move," which children generally attributed to all animate items in both studies. Following Carey (1985), on a theory-rich biological account of animate concepts, children should generalize all properties relevant to one animate kind (here, a person) to other objects belonging to the same ontological category (e.g. an elephant and a bug). But they did not consistently generalise animate properties. This was so even for the property

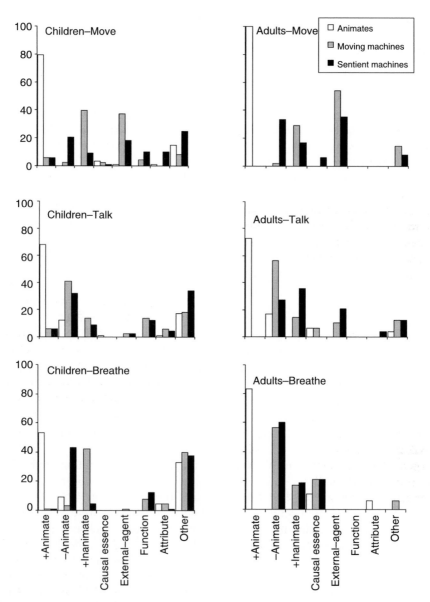

Figure 12.2. Percentage of subjects who offered different kinds of explanations for animates versus machines for the six animate properties.

"breathe". Our results are similar to those of Carey (1985), who holds that young children do not have a biological theory.

Converging evidence for the Carey position comes from data on the

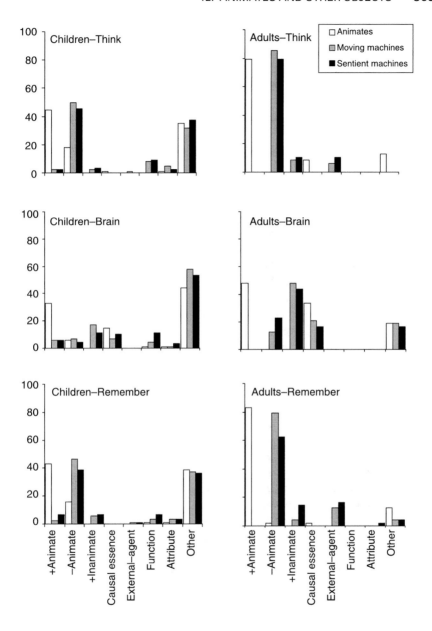

accuracy of children's attributions and explanations/justifications. Table 12.7 presents the mean number of correct answers offered by the children for the animates (person, elephant, dog, and bug), moving machines (car, aeroplane, robot, and vacuum cleaner), and sentient machines (computer, robot, radio,

TABLE 12.7

Mean number of correct answers offered by the children and adults for the animates, moving machines, and sentient machines*

Property	Age	Animates	Moving machines	Sentient machines
Move	Children	**3.59**	**3.64**	**3.50**
	Adults	**3.83**	**4.00**	**3.92**
Talk	Children	2.96	**3.55**	**3.27**
	Adults	**3.33**	**3.67**	**3.58**
Breathe	Children	2.27	**3.00**	**3.23**
	Adults	**3.83**	**3.75**	**4.00**
Think	Children	2.00	**3.18**	**3.05**
	Adults	**3.50**	**4.00**	**4.00**
Remember	Children	1.82	**3.05**	2.91
	Adults	**3.33**	**3.83**	**4.00**
Brain	Children	2.32	2.55	2.73
	Adults	**3.92**	**3.75**	**3.67**

*As there are 4 items in each group the maximum possible in each cell is 4. Mean values greater than 3 are shown in bold.

and television) collapsed together. The children were equally accurate for the animates and machines when explaining responses for "move". However, for the other animate properties they were considerably more accurate on the machines than on the animates. Children had much more difficulty providing correct explanations when asked about animates than when asked about machines. They could articulate why machines lack animate properties but not why animates possess what are fundamental animate, biological, properties.

We also examined whether the children offered sophisticated explanations when invoking animate causes for their attribution (or lack of attribution) of a property. Responses such as "alive", "not alive", "living", "not living", "having the ability", and "no ability", were coded as ones that reflected a biological interpretation of the animate category. Answers that simply alluded to animate parts (e.g. an elephant breathes with its trunk) or animate mechanisms were treated as simple explanations that did not originate in a theory-rich notion of animates as biological/physiological entities. Among the children, all 85 of the sophisticated explanations (total possible = 2508) came from just 3 out of 24 children, with 83.5% coming from one 5-year old! In contrast, all the adults offered some sophisticated responses. Still, even their tendency to provide theoretical-type explanations was not overwhelming. There were only 254 such explanations out of a possible number of 1368. The percentage of such explanations from individual subjects ranged from 0.4% to 18.5%, and many of these "sophisticated explanations" sounded like bits of information that students had memorised in a high school or introductory level college biology course. These included "because it is a living thing", "to perform motor and sensory functions", and "born with it—part of biological processes".

Finally, the data from the "origin" question are relevant here. The "Where does X come from?" question was a forced-choice question, with one option referring to biological origin (does it come from a mommy and daddy?) and the other option referring to non-biological origin (does someone make it?). Children responded at chance, and only about 50% of their responses were correct. When asked for an explanation, they mostly appealed to agents (e.g. parents, mommy) and not to core biological mechanisms such as sex and eggs. A few even appealed to environmental niches (both natural ones, such as forest and ocean, and man-made ones, such as store and zoo), God, and man-made production processes (e.g. someone made it).

To sum up, although the children attributed all the animate properties to a person, their attribution of these to other animals was selective. Further, their explanations, although reasonable, rarely alluded to complex, theory-driven notions of being animate or alive. Thus, it is hard to maintain that the young children in our studies were calling on a biological organisation of the animate category. This conclusion places us closer to Carey (1985) than researchers who grant young children intuitive biological theories. Nevertheless, there are some key ways in which we differ from Carey.

Carey favours a "person-first" account or young children's knowledge and development of the nature of items in the animate category. That is, she argues that young children's generalisations of animate predicates are a function of the extent to which other objects are similar to people. Accordingly, items that share person-like characteristics are more likely to be treated as animate. This is true whether or not they are animate. Thus, a robot or walking doll is about as good a candidate for inclusion in the animate category as a dog. In contrast, an invertebrate should be an especially poor case of animate, given how little it looks like a person or even a vertebrate. But, as we have seen, these predictions about the conceptual similarity space are not supported. First, Massey and Gelman (1998) found that preschoolers say that invertebrates can move themselves up and down a hill by themselves but statues cannot. Second, young children are less inclined than adults to attribute animate predicates to robots. That is, they are not especially animistic about machines, at least when they think about them in the context of clear cases of animates and non-machine inanimates.

3. Who are the animists?

The percentage of adult "yes" responses to whether machines possess animate properties suggests that, if anyone, it is the adults who are the animists.

Most adults told us that machines move and talk.[7] Furthermore, many adults indicated that a robot thinks and that a robot and computer can remember. Very rarely did they say that artefacts and machines breathe and have a brain. This trend of selective animistic attributions, particularly of the action properties, supports our prediction that it is knowledge of, and experience with, machines that encourages animism in adults. It is not uncommon for us to talk to our computer while working on it and say something like "Why are you doing this to me today?". Similarly, most of us would say that computers have a memory and thus can remember; however, few of us would say that they think in the sense that humans do.

The nature of adults' explanations make it clear that they are not really animists. It is not as if we have reason to believe that they think machines have real brains and intentionally move or talk. Instead, their accounts are metaphorical and dependent on the result of their past experience with such objects. When we consider the kind of explanations they gave for "move" and "talk" (see Figure 12.2), we see that they appealed to animate parts (e.g. bones, muscles, blood), animate causes (e.g. wants to move), and animate predicates (e.g. alive, living) for the "real" animates. In contrast, for the machines, they noted the absence of animate parts and causes and went on to talk about, inanimate parts (wings, wheels), mechanisms (batteries, engines), materials (plastic, metal), and external energy sources (e.g. the actions of a person). So, although the adults attributed "move" and "talk" to the machines, they made it clear that they did not think of these as actions that are due to an intrinsic capacity for self-generated motion. Most importantly, they appealed to external causal sources of energy when asked to justify their answers. For us, this kind of selective attribution of animate properties is cultivated. It requires understanding about both the animate properties and the nature of the machine. Hence, we say that it is metaphorical animism.

4.   Do children distinguish between different kinds of inanimate artefacts?

We asked about only two simple artefacts, chair and spoon. Nevertheless, the children's responses for these inanimate objects are revealing. Analyses of the number of "yes" responses (see Tables 12.1, 12.2 and 12.3) revealed that children not only distinguished between simple artefacts and animates, but also between simple artefacts and machines. No child thought that a chair could move, and less than 10% replied that a spoon could move. Furthermore, the same children said that machines, particularly the ones designed by people to do so, were the ones that could move. Not only do

---

[7] Note that their attribution of "move" was weaker for the sentient machines and their attribution of "talk" was weaker for the moving machines.

young children distinguish between animates and inanimates, they also discriminate between different kinds of inanimates.

5. Do adults and children treat plants as a separate category?

There is no doubt that adults treat plants as a biological category that is both like and different from animals. About 83% of the adults said that plants breathe (or show respiration, as many referred to it); 58% said that plants move; and a few even said plants possess other animate properties (Table 12.3). Although many of the adults said that plants move, it would be a mistake to conclude that they used this predicate in the same way that they do with animals. When they were asked to explain their attributions, they talked about parts (i.e. leaves) moving in response to the wind, the sun, or a person moving a potted plant. For them, a plant is not self-moveable, as a whole, and therefore not animate. Additionally, when asked about the origin of a plant, they appealed to seeds and the ground; in contrast, they appealed to man-made processes (e.g., someone made it, made in a factory) for the machines but to biological agents (e.g., mother, parents) for the animates.[8]

The children showed a similar, albeit less strong, pattern of responses. About 33% said that a plant can breathe, compared to 14% for think, 9% for move, 5% for remember, and 0% for talk and has a brain. While they attributed the property of breathe to a plant, they did not attribute a brain to it. Neither did they attribute the sentient animate properties of think and remember nor the action/communication property of talk to plants. Again, there was a selective uptake of our test list of " animate" properties. This restricted pattern of attribution went along with different answers about the insides and outsides of a plant. When asked about the insides of a plant, children talked about seeds and "plant stuff". When asked about the outsides, they talked about leaves, petals, and even dirt.

Perhaps the best evidence that plants were considered members of separate categories from animates and machines is the fact that we had to create a separate code to score explanations about a plant. Plant-specific responses were never given in connection with animates or machines. Thus, for the six questions dealing with move, talk, breathe, think, remember, and brain, we developed the category of "plant properties" (e.g. moving towards the sun, growing, photosynthesis). For the question on insides and outsides, we developed the categories of "plant internals" (e.g. seed, xylem) and "plant externals" (leaves, petals). Finally, for the origin question, we developed the category of "gardening activities" to include answers appealing to planting

---

[8] Adults occasionally referred to the animate mechanism of sex when talking about the origin of animates.

and watering. Thus, we were forced to recognise that questions about plants tapped a different categorical system compared to ones about animates and machines. In other words, terms such as breathe or move are better thought of as homonyms with different meanings, depending on whether they refer to an example of an animal or a plant (Keil, 1979).

6. Do children have a rich theory of mind?

Children's responses to questions about think, remember, and brain are relevant to discussions about a theory of mind. First, as seen in Table 12.3, children did not do very well on these questions compared to questions on move, talk, and breathe. This is especially true of the non-human animates—many of the children said that bugs and elephants might have a brain but could not remember or think.

Second, children had difficulty talking about mental phenomena (see Table 12.5, which shows the percentage of correct answers). Overall, children were much better at explaining why an object can move, talk, and breathe. In contrast, they were less accurate when responding about remember, think, and brain and had considerable difficulty explaining why animates can think, remember, and have a brain (see Table 12.7, which shows the mean number of correct and appropriate answers for the animates, moving machines, and sentient machines). Perhaps this stems from a reluctance to attribute such mental phenomena to non-human animates. It therefore is possible that young children's theory of mind is restricted to humans.

ON HOW THE ANIMATE–INANIMATE DISTINCTION IS ORGANISED

Overall, our results are consistent with the Caramazza and Shelton (1998) hypothesis that the general distinction between animate and inanimate is domain-specific. Children and adults answer questions about animals and inanimates in qualitatively different ways. Their explanations about the motion of separably moveable objects, be they animate or inanimate, were conceptually based. Motion by separably moveable animate objects was generally attributed to intrinsic causes, such as the presence of animal parts (legs, muscles), animate causes (e.g. wants to move), and animate notions of living and life. The potential for the movement of inanimates was attributed to extrinsic causes such as transport by an agent, wind, gravity, and collision with barriers. Children clearly knew that a plant as a whole does not move on its own; only parts move, and then in response to external forces. When talking about motion they did not confuse either plants or machines with animals, even though these latter objects can appear to "move" on their own. Children, like adults, seem to interpret the predicate "move" with respect to the kind of category they are asked about and then the energy sources that pertain to that category.

Such explanatory coherence about the motion of a kind (self-induced versus other-induced) supports our view that the animate–inanimate distinctions has its origins in both principled conceptual and perceptual processes. There is no question that perceptions about motion are relevant to the build-up of knowledge about particular animate and inanimate objects. However, motion paths by themselves can be ambiguous (see the earlier discussion). That is, a similarity function that is based on kinds of motion paths does not lead to the assignment of all and only one class of motion paths to the abstraction "animate", and all and only a different class of motion paths to the abstraction "inanimate". This is our main difficulty with the Mandler hypothesis (1992 and Chapter 11) that infants first develop image schemas of self-motion and caused motion through domain-general processes of perceptual analysis of spatiotemporal differences between different kinds of motion events, because we do not see what motivates the modification of these schemas to form "self-moving animate" and "caused-to-move inanimate" schemas, which then provide a foundation for conceptualisation about animate and inanimate things—there is no account of why cause becomes a relevant conceptual framework. These kinds of consideration link conceptual principles about causality to problem of classification. A major function of the principles is to draw attention to those perceptual inputs that are relevant to learning about the animate–inanimate distinction and ones within these.

Support for our domain-specific account of the animate–inanimate distinction is provided by children's and adults' abilities to pair their answers about an object's possible motion with relevant comments about their material composition and the inside of these objects. Children's answers about the insides and outsides of objects were again conceptually driven. Animate objects were said to have animate "innards" (blood and bones) and animate externals (wings and eyes), whereas inanimate objects were said to have inanimate parts and materials (plastic and glass) for their insides and outsides. Children switched their category of answers depending on which conceptual category the item belonged to.

A "THEORY" OF ACTION

Overall, children were good at questions about motion and communication (talk), leading us to believe that knowledge about the difference between animate and inanimate objects reflects the acquisition of a theory about actions, interactions, and reactions of objects. This line of explanation also helps explain why even young children quickly learn about environmental conditions that are relevant to the different ways that animates and inanimates move and do not treat machines as if they were new examples of animate objects. For example, they know that a leaf can move if there is a wind (Williams, 2000), that a young animal might need help from an adult to move up a large hill (Massey & Gelman, 1988), and that dolls can walk if they have a battery (Gelman, Spelke, & Meck, 1983). In contrast, children were not very knowledgeable about mental phenomena and had difficulty talking about mental phenomena, such as thinking and remembering.

Our results bear on the Warrington and Shallice (1984) position that the animate–inanimate distinction is grounded in domain-general sensory and functional processes. First, the theory of action was not more or less import-ant for animate as opposed to inanimate objects. Even when children seemed to be appealing to visible parts to justify their attribution of a property to an item (e.g. a dog walks with its legs), they tended to focus on the parts most functionally relevant, such as legs for movement or mouths for breathing. Hence, it is hard to argue that visual information is more relevant to the animate category or that functional information is not relevant to the ani-mate category. This would seem to be a problem for the Warrington and Shallice (1984) position. So too is the fact that the young children in our studies did as well on the task without pictures as the one with pictures.

Children in our studies were not significantly different from the adults in terms of their ability to distinguish between animates and inanimates. Although they gave fewer sophisticated explanations than the adults for the presence of animate properties, even the adults did not offer them consist-ently. The finding that the adults did not respond very differently from the children is consistent with our position that first principles encourage learners to attend to relevant information (in this case, about animates and inani-mates). Ours is a theory about everyday knowledge that is learned on the fly. It is not about the problem of how people come to share ideas about mechan-isms that are held by experts. Clearly, for the adults in our study, like those in other studies (see Chapter 13), the animate–inanimate distinction was not grounded in modern-day scientific theory. This would require conceptual change of the kind proposed by Carey and Spelke (1994), one that presumably occurs as a result of formal scientific training.

If young children do benefit from the availability of causal principles that focus on the causal conditions of the motions and interactions of objects in the world, this helps explain why they classify plants and animals differently. It also offers an account of children's selective uptake of the predicate "talk" for animates and machines that mimic communication, and thus their very limited tendency towards animism. Whether this conceptual foundation develops into richer theories or metaphorical interpretations of worldly objects is then very much a matter of experience and education. How domain-specific or domain-general these kinds of learning are remains an open question.

ACKNOWLEDGEMENTS

This work was begun when KS was a postdoctoral research associate in the Gelman Cognitive Development Laboratory at UCLA. The authors acknowledge the assistance of Girlie Delacruz, Heather Jones, and Stephanie Reich in all aspects of this research. Partial support for this work came from NSF grant #SBR-9209741 to RG and a creative award from California State University, Los Angeles, to KS. Portions of this research were presented at the Biennial Meeting of the Society for Research in Child Development, April 1997, in Washington, DC.

Send correspondence to Rochel Gelman, *rgelman@ruccs.rutgers.edu*, Rutgers Center for Cognitive Science, 172 Freylinghuysen Rd, Piscataway, NJ 08854-8020, USA.

REFERENCES

Backscheider, A.G., Shatz, M., & Gelman, S.A. (1993). Preschoolers' ability to distinguish living kinds as a function of regrowth. *Child Development, 64*, 1242–1257.

Baillargeon, R. (1998). Infants' understanding of the physical world. In E. M. Sabourin & E.F. Craik (Eds.), *Advances in psychological science, Vol. 2: Biological and cognitive aspects* (pp. 503–529). Hove: Psychology Press.

Bassili, J.N. (1976). Temporal and spatial contingencies in the perception of social events. *Journal of Personality and Social Psychology, 33*, 680–685.

Bransford, J.D., Brown, A.L., & Cocking, R.R. (1999) *How people learn: Brain, mind, experience, and school*. Washington, DC: National Academy Press.

Bertenthal, B.I. (1993). Infants' perception of biomechanical motions: Intrinsic image and knowledge-based constraints. In C. Ganrud (Ed.), *Visual perception and cognition in infancy: Carnegie-Mellon symposia on cognition* (pp. 175–214). Hillsdale, NJ: Lawrence Erlbaum Associates, Inc.

Caramazza, A., & Shelton, J.R. (1998). Domain-specific knowledge systems in the brain: The animate–inanimate distinction. *Journal of Cognitive Neuroscience, 10*, 1–34.

Carey, S. (1985). *Conceptual change in childhood*. Cambridge, MA: MIT Press.

Gallistel, C.R. (1990). *The organization of learning*. Cambridge, MA: MIT Press.

Gelman, R. (1990.). First principles organize attention to and learning about relevant data: Number and animate–inanimate distinction as examples. *Cognitive Science, 14*, 79–106.

Gelman, R. (1994). Constructivism and supporting environments. In D. Tirosh (Ed.), *Implicit and explicit knowledge: An educational approach* (Vol. 6). New York: Ablex.

Gelman, R., Durgin, F., & Kaufman, L. (1995). Distinguishing between animates and inanimates: Not by motion alone. In D. Sperber, D. Premack, & A.J. Premack (Eds.), *Causal cognition: A multidisciplinary debate (pp. 150–184)*. Oxford: Clarendon Press.

Gelman, R., & Hartnett, P. (1998). Early understandings of numbers: Paths or barriers to the construction of new understandings? *Learning and Instruction, 8*, 341–374.

Gelman, R., & Spelke, E.S. (1981). The development of thoughts about animate and inanimate objects: Implications for research on social cognition. In J.H. Flavell & L. Ross (Eds), *Social cognitive development: Frontiers and possible futures* (pp. 43–66). Cambridge: Cambridge University Press.

Gelman, R., Spelke, E., & Meck, E. (1983). What preschoolers know about animate and inanimate objects. In D. Rogers & J.A. Sloboda (Eds.), *The acquisition of symbolic skills*. London: Plenum.

Gelman, R., & Williams, E.M. (1998). Enabling constraints for cognitive development and learning: Domain specificity and epigenesis. In D. Kuhn & R.S. Siegler (Eds.), *Handbook of child psychology, Vol. 2: Cognition, perception, and language* (5th ed., pp. 575–630). New York: Wiley.

Gergely, C., Gergely, G., Szilvia, B., & Orsolya, K. (1999). Goal attribution without agency cues: The perception of "pure reason" in infancy. *Cognition, 72,* 237–267.

Goffman, E. (1974). *Frame analysis.* Cambridge, MA: Harvard University Press.

Hatano, G., & Inagaki, K. (1994). Young children's naive theory of biology. *Cognition, 50,* 171–188.

Heider, F., & Simmel, M. (1944). An experimental study of apparent behavior. *American Journal of Psychology, 57,* 243–259.

Hillis, A.E., & Caramazza, A. (1991). Category-specific naming and comprehension impairment: A double dissociation. *Brain, 114,* 2081–2094.

Hochberg, J. (1978). *Perception* (3rd ed.). Englewood Cliffs, NJ: Prentice-Hall.

Keil, F.C. (1979). *Semantic and conceptual development: An ontological perspective.* Cambridge, MA: Harvard University Press.

Keil, F.C. (1994). The birth and nurturance of concepts by domains: The origins of concepts of living things. In L.A. Hirschfeld & S.A. Gelman (Eds.), *Mapping the mind: Domain specificity in cognition and culture,* (pp. 234–254). New York: Cambridge University Press.

Keil, F.C. (1995). The growth of causal understanding of natural kinds. In D. Sperber, D. Premack, & A.J. Premack (Eds.), *Causal cognition: A multidisciplinary debate* (pp. 234–267). Oxford: Clarendon Press.

Leslie, A.M. (1995). A theory of agency. In D. Sperber, D. Premack, & A.J. Premack (Eds.), *Causal cognition: A multidisciplinary debate* (pp. 121–149). Oxford: Clarendon Press.

Mandler, J.M. (1992). How to build a bay: II. Conceptual primitives. *Psychological Review, 99,* 587–604.

Massey, C.M. (1988). *The development of the animate–inanimate distinction in preschoolers.* Unpublished dissertation, University of Pennsylvania, Philadelphia, USA.

Massey, C.M., & Gelman, R. (1988). Preschooler's ability to decide whether a photographed unfamiliar object can move itself. *Developmental Psychology, 24,* 307–317.

Morris, M.W., Nisbett, R.E., & Peng, K. (1995). Causal attribution across domains and cultures. In D. Sperber, D. Premack, & A.J. Premack (Eds.), *Causal cognition: A multidisciplinary debate* (pp. 577–614). Oxford: Clarendon Press.

Oakes, L.M., & Cohen, L.B. (1995). Infant causal perception. In C. Rovee-Collier & L.P. Lipsitt (Eds.), *Advances in infancy research* (vol. 9, pp. 1–54). Norwood, NJ: Ablex Publishing Corporation.

Piaget, J. (1929). *The child's conception of the world.* London: Routledge & Kegan Paul.

Poulin-Dubois, D. (2000). Infants' distinction between animate and inanimate objects: The origins of naive psychology (pp. 257–280). In P. Rochat (Ed.), *Early social cognition.* Hillsdale, NJ: Lawrence Erlbaum Associates, Inc.

Premack, D. (1995). Cause/induced motion: Intention/spontaneous motion. In J.-P. Changeux & J. Chavaillon, (Eds.), *Origins of the human brain.* (pp. 286–309). Oxford: Clarendon Press/ Oxford University Press.

Rosengren, K.S., Gelman, S.A., Kalish, C.W., & McCormick, M. (1991). As time goes by: Children's early understanding of growth in animals. *Child Development, 62,* 1302–1320.

Scaife, M., & van Duuren, M. (1995). Do computers have brains? What children believe about intelligent artifacts. *British Journal of Developmental Psychology, 13,* 367–377.

Simons, D.J., & Keil, F.C. (1995). An abstract to concrete shift in the development of biological thought: The 'insides' story. *Cognition, 56,* 129–163.

Spelke, E.S., Phillips, A., & Woodward, A.L. (1995). Infants' knowledge of object motion and human action. In D. Sperber, D. Premack, & A.J. Premack (Eds.), *Causal cognition: A multidisciplinary debate* (pp. 44–77). Oxford: Clarendon Press.

Stewart, J.A. (1982). *Perception of animacy.* Unpublished Doctoral Dissertation, University of Pennsylvania, Philadelphia, USA.

Stewart, J.A. (1984, November). *Object motion and the perception of animacy*. Paper presented at the meetings of the Psychonomic Society, San Antonio, TX.

Tversky, B., & Hemenway, K. (1984). Objects, parts, and categories. *Journal of Experimental Psychology: General, 113*, 169–193.

Warrington, E.K., & Shallice, T. (1984). Category specific semantic impairments. *Brain, 107*, 829–854.

Wellman, H.M. (1990). *The child's theory of mind*. Cambridge, MA: MIT Press.

Wellman, H.M., & Gelman, S.A. (1998). Knowledge acquisition in foundational domains. In D. Kuhn & R.S. Siegler (Eds.), *Handbook of child psychology, Vol. 2: Cognition, perception, and language* (5th ed., pp. 523–574). New York: Wiley.

Williams, E.M., & Gelman, R. (1995, March). *Preschoolers' theory of action: Causal accounts of why familiar animate and inanimate objects start and stop*. Paper presented at the bi-annual meeting of the Society for Research in Child Development, Indianapolis, IN.

Williams, E.M. (2000). *Causal reasoning by children and adults about the trajectory, context, and animacy of a moving object*. Unpublished Doctoral Dissertation, University of California, Los Angeles.

Wilson, D., & Sperber, D. (1986). *Relevance*. Oxford: Blackwell.

CHAPTER 13

Categories and levels of information

Frank Keil, Nancy S. Kim, and Marissa L. Greif
Department of Psychology, Yale University, USA

INTRODUCTION

It is a truism that we all must lump entities into equivalence classes if we are to make any sense of the world around us. It has also generally been acknowledged that there is a potentially infinite number of ways in which we could treat a class of things as equivalent. However, an important issue that has not yet received ample attention is a systematic consideration of the levels at which our conceptual representations might originate. By the time we become adults, we routinely think about classes of things that seem to encompass far more complex relations than any kind of perceptual similarity alone. Tools, vehicles, and living kinds are universal examples, as are classes of intangible things such as odd numbers, puns, or riddles. No one doubts that we are readily able to think about these classes of things, or that we use them in many kinds of everyday reasoning. However, there remains an enormous debate over how our knowledge of such classes emerges in development, and how this knowledge is neurally instantiated.

In this chapter, we will consider an integrative approach to these questions. The traditional approach has been to assume that perceptual features are more basic to categorisation than conceptual ones. In contrast, here we will argue for a framework in which the default assumption is that multiple levels of information are used to distinguish categories in the world, and that no one kind of feature, perceptual or conceptual, is privileged developmentally.[1] We will suggest that taking a more synthesised perspective that links research from developmental, neuropsychological, individual difference, and comparative viewpoints can clarify how we use these different levels and how we might distinguish them empirically.

A HETEROGENOUS WORLD AND THE PLURALITY OF SCIENCE

Surely the most intense and systematic efforts to make sense of the world arise from the actions of a formal scientific discipline and its practitioners. Although it is possible that the ways in which the formal sciences proceed and carve up the world might be quite different from how individuals make sense of their world at a more intuitive and informal level, recent discussions suggest that the similarities could be more striking than the differences. It appears that everyday science is not nearly as formal and logically structured as was traditionally thought. In fact, science is characterised by hunches, gaps, and serendipity (Dunbar, 1994), making the distance to intuitive theories seem quite small. Thus, thinking about how scientific theories and thought are structured might give us useful clues regarding how people's naive theories and conceptual thought are accrued.

Given the putative similarity between naive theories and scientific enterprise, recent radical shifts in the philosophy of science have significant ramifications for how all of us might make sense of the world. First, there has been general acquiescence that reductionism is unlikely to succeed as a way of doing science. Even when it might be possible to state the laws of one science, such as cellular biology, in the terms of a more molecular level, such as organic chemistry, it is clear that the ability to execute the science of biology solely in terms of the language of organic chemistry is likely to be such a cumbersome and unwieldy exercise as to be cognitively and computationally impossible (Salmon, 1989). Moreover, this example of cellular biology versus chemistry takes near neighbours with an intuitively plausible theoretical connection; the matter becomes much more complicated in trying to explain, say, cognition in terms of physics (Fodor, 1975).

The failure of reductionism has naturally led to the question of whether the nature of explanation is the same in all the different levels of science. That is, do explanations at these different levels seem to have the same kinds of structural principles, and do they incorporate the same kinds of causal relations? This is a surprisingly recent area of inquiry but the repeated conclusion

---

[1] It might be argued that it is difficult or impossible to distinguish the perceptual from the conceptual at some level of analysis. However, for the purposes of our arguments, they are readily distinguishable within the broad range of features we refer to: low-level perceptual to high-level conceptual (i.e. theory of mind).

seems to be that the different levels of science do indeed vary in their structural and relational properties because they track different kinds of entities in the world. Thus, the current shift to more realist approaches in science (Boyd, 1999) embraces the idea that different patterns of regularities in the world might require different kinds of theoretical structures to best understand them. From this standpoint, it is clear that the differences among the theories are highly abstract and cannot be sufficiently stated solely in terms of perceptual features. Biological theories might be contrasted with those of physical mechanics because they usefully employ teleological arguments. Cognitive theories may be distinguished from both biology and mechanics because of their reference to beliefs, desires, and computational states. If the theories of various disciplines constitute different domains of thought, and if the concepts and designated categories within these theories inherit many of the distinctive properties of the theory in which they are embedded, then important differences among such classes of concepts will include highly abstract cognitive, not just perceptual, differences. In this way, underlying explanatory structures may manifest themselves in intuitive scientific theories that both lay people and the scientific establishment use to successfully understand concepts within domains like mechanics and biology.

Thus, it seems reasonable that, as adults at least, we have many intuitive theories that are organised in ways that resonate best with only some patterns in a heterogeneously structured world. Moreover, these theories are important to understanding how we cluster things into the same classes. The theories tell us which features to weigh as relevant and how much to weigh them in categorisation (Ahn, Kim, Lassaline, & Dennis, in press). We assess similarity with respect to our theories of what properties matter and why (Medin & Shoben, 1988). Some have argued that the need for theories of a heterogeneous world has lead to the need for an "adapted mind", such that the cores of naive theories were naturally selected for over a period of evolution (Cosmides & Tooby, 1994). A critical research question stemming from this argument centres around the extent to which our minds do need to be biologically adapted in this way, and at what level of processing. The debate has been sharpened in recent years by a surge of research on category-specific impairments, those patterns of brain damage that lead to difficulties in thinking and talking about broad categories such as animals or tools. The implication of such research, of course, is that there exists some sort of specialisation in the brain for domain-specific categories. The debate concerns the nature of that specialisation. In a recent review, for instance, Humphreys and Forde (in press) argued that the underlying neural substrate cannot be understood as arising from only one level in the cognitive system. In this way, the distinction in deficits cannot be captured simply by a sensory versus non-sensory description. Instead, they proposed that such difficulties could involve possible deficits at several different levels that are hierarchically organised and highly interactive. Importantly, they argue that there is a large role for "re-entrant processing". Here, objects initially activate structural descriptions and associative/functional knowledge in memory. Then top-down processing proceeds to the perceptual level which allows the object to be discriminated from other entities. This allows name retrieval to occur. Damage at any point in the pathway can lead to differential deficits in categorical knowledge about living and non-living things depending on the reliance of those categories on perceptual versus functional features.

Indeed, there is a broad continuum of processing levels at which category-specific impairments might occur, ranging from low-level percepts to high level cognition. The immediate question, then, is at what level or levels we have these domain specific specialisations. Obviously, this is an extremely complicated question and, for the sake of clarity, we will first approach it by considering two examples of category-specific impairments: artefacts and animals.

LEVELS OF DOMAIN SPECIFICITY

Generally speaking, some individuals with particular areas of brain damage appear to have deficits in the ability to think about artefacts such as tools. Conversely, others, with different lesions, have difficulties thinking about animals (whether these labels encompass the precise range of these categories will be discussed later on). To begin thinking about how our conceptual representations of tools and animals might be differentially impaired, one must first consider all the ways in which tools and animals might tend to differ. That is, what are the informational and structural differences between the two that may have representational consequences? In terms of low-level vision, there might well be differences between the two in patterns of spatial frequencies, wavelength functions, and in the extent to which contours are constructed by irregularly shaped fractals (presumably, this last alternative would apply more to animals than to tools). At mid-level vision, there are differences in texture, edge junctions, and perhaps even in the distributions of the most typical primitive geons. Furthermore, there are differences between tools and animals in typical colour distributions.

Similarly, at high-level vision, there are a host of possible differences including overall shape, axis of symmetry (for instance, animals might have bilateral symmetry around a vertical axis more frequently than do artefacts), and particular feature configurations (for instance, faces). Furthermore, there could also be statistical differences between animals and tools with regard to how frequently certain types of perceptual features occur in each. Living kinds might tend to have a larger collection of texture types than most artefacts (i.e. an average animal has a larger set of different textures than an average tool) whereas artefacts could have larger set of possible perpendicular surfaces and edges. Such disparities at the perceptual level could form an informational basis for having different categories.

There are also rich interactions between these things that can distinguish the two. One such interaction might be that of colour patches and part boundaries or limb junctions. Colour patches in artefacts are more likely to break neatly at part boundaries than are colour patches in animals. In animals, it is not common for there to be a discrete colour-change line between limbs and body. In contrast, this is quite common for similar limb-like protrusions in vehicles, furniture and tools. Interactions between mid-level and high-level vision could also provide cues to category membership. In the extreme, one might imagine that an animal that did have such distinctive colour changes at its joints and a smooth texture might be mistakenly judged as an artefact (such as a toy or robot) by a naive observer viewing a static display. Similarly, seeing a hairless cat like a sphynx always provokes surprise and indignation, and sometimes complete denial of its membership in the cat category at all, as it violates perceptual "requirements" for animals as having a fuzzy texture that is continuous between the limbs and body. Certainly, when one mixes perceptual features at one level with features at other levels (i.e. functional features), there are vastly more ways to distinguish the two categories.

Thus far, we have described only static perceptual differences, but there are many dynamic ones as well. Cutting (1986) has shown that rigidity of limbs and their motions around joints look very different for moving artefacts and animals, as do the typical centre of gravities as inferred from their motions. If one attaches point lights to various parts of moving artefacts and living kinds, even for relatively small numbers of such dots, there are significant differences in both the patterns and timing parameters of movement (Cutting, 1986). For instance, the time of action and reaction seems different for the two categories. For many mechanical systems, movement of one bounded solid causes immediate consequences when there is contact with another, such as in the launching effects documented by Michotte (1963). In Michotte's experiments, a circular disk approaches another at a constant velocity and then suddenly stops adjacent to a second disk, which then starts moving off along the same path at the same or a somewhat reduced velocity. Adult subjects report not just seeing the contiguity but the powerful impression that the first disk 'launched' the second one by transmitting a force through the collision. The effect disappears, however, when the delay between the stopping of the first disk and the starting of the second becomes appreciable. Subjects still notice the contingency relations just as strongly, but they do not have the compelling phenomenal experience of seeing the first disc causally launch the second.

For animals, there might be much longer delays between cause and effect.

Likewise, categorising simple geometric forms as intentional or agential in Heider and Simmel's (1944) dynamic perceptual arrangements is an almost unavoidable consequence of viewing the display. The Heider and Simmel displays involve plane figures such as circles, squares, and triangles moving in contingent ways that suggest not just social actions in general but specific social roles such as aggression, fear, and friendship. Even 12-month-olds attribute rational action to a ball that they had previously seen expand and contract as though it were respiring, and interact with a second ball in a contingent manner (Gergely, Nadasdy, Csibra, & Biró, 1995). Such compelling dynamic cues involving intricate, and in many ways social, timing might similarly distinguish animals from artefacts or tools. It is at this dynamic perceptual level that considerations of differences between animals and artefacts often stop. There are, however, many more differences that continue at higher levels. These differences could, in fact, be just as salient to very young children as many of the lower-level perceptual ones.

The range of possible higher-level differences is extensive and is discussed in more detail elsewhere (Atran, 1996; Keil & Richardson, 1999), but a few key contrasts here will illustrate the point. Some differences revolve around the relative roles and locations of essences for the two kinds, others around causal patternings among component properties, others centre on paths of origins, and still others around patterns of variation across exemplars. We will consider the first two differences here.

First, consider the notion of essences. The idea of essences seems to be very different for artefacts than for animals. Some have suggested that artefacts do not have any essence at all (Keil, 1989), while others (Bloom, 1996) suggest that there is an essence for artefacts but that it should be understood as one that involves the intention of the creator of the artefacts. Either way, we seem to envision the critical nature of the two kinds as very different. For animals, there is the notion of a fixed kind of substance inside that makes each kind distinct, today frequently conceptualised as DNA. Tiger DNA is the essence of tigers, and wombat DNA the essence of wombats. This folk notion is really a probabilistic distribution of DNA types for natural selection, because the notion is wrong if one thinks of a specific sequence of DNA that spans across all members of a species. Correct or not, however, it could be a foundational way in which we understand living kinds as different from artefacts. Of course, DNA is a recent concept, but essentialism, a belief in some inner fixed entity that is causally responsible for each species, is as old as written history. In other cultures, and in earlier times, the essence of a living kind could have been seen as a vital force or an organ, but the notion of essence itself recurs frequently. In fact, some have argued that humans' naive essentialist bias presented a powerful cognitive bias against coming up with the idea of evolution by natural selection, an idea that only emerged with the writings of Darwin and Wallace in the mid-nineteenth century, despite millennia of selective breeding of plants and animals (Hull, 1965).

The appreciation of essence emerges very early in children as well (Gelman & Hirschfeld, 1999; Keil, 1989). For instance, seven-year olds but not five-year olds know that natural kinds conserve their identity over transformations whereas artefacts can be changed from one kind to another with a few alterations in physical structure (e.g. turning a table into a bookcase; Keil, 1989). Further, by 8 years of age, children come to know that animals and machines have different internal component structures (Simons & Keil, 1995). However, it is not known just how early essentialist realisations emerge. There are, to date, no studies on the expectations of very young infants' about essences of animals versus artefacts, and it is not entirely clear how this understanding could be tested. Likewise, we also do not know whether it is learned at all, or if it appears independent of experience. The important point in highlighting this developmental trend, but also in pointing out the dearth of infant research, is simply to suggest that it could give some insight as to what kinds of information might be more basic than others in structuring categories. This is certainly true in the case of reasoning about essences. Perhaps the key message of late from developmental research is that developmental patterns do not seem to follow a strict progression from perceptual to conceptual (see Keil, Smith, Simons, & Levin [1998] for a recent argument). This, in turn, raises questions about what would be core components of adult knowledge. If the idea of essences is indeed universal across all cultures, then it could well be an intrinsic way in which we organise some concepts. We might (although not necessarily consciously) look for essences in most kinds that we encounter and then, depending on whether we sense one at work, we might organise the relevant category in a distinctive way. Or, to put it another way, we might evaluate the origin of the essence as being internal to the organism or external to it (as might be the case for artefacts) and from this assess its artefact/natural-kind status.

To broaden the discussion, consider a few other alternatives. We could attribute intrinsic, non-intentional needs to all living kinds in ways that we do not to artefacts. A flower needs sun and water to survive, and a person needs food, water and shelter to survive. An artefact, however, does not have intrinsic needs. Rather, an intentional agent needs to supply things to some artifacts to have them perform a needed function. Perhaps the ability to see what entities need in their own right is necessary to having a coherent living kind concept, but not to having a coherent concept of most artefacts. Similarly, one could also consider the significance of teleological or functional characteristics when categorising artefacts and natural kinds. Asking what a particular characteristic is "for", that is, ascertaining the purpose of features such as a pointed surface of a rock versus the hide of a dinosaur, or the green colour of a plant versus that of an emerald, might or might not be appropriate given the domain of reference (Keil, 1994, Kelemen, 1999b). Moreover, such a distinction might further differentiate categories of biological and non-biological natural kinds. Indeed, a debate has arisen regarding the importance of functional relations in reasoning about artefacts and natural kinds, particularly in terms of whether such reasoning spans many domains or is specific to biology and artefacts (Keil, 1994; Kelemen, 1999a). The debate concerns the origins of teleological reasoning and how it is mapped onto domains, with some research (Keil, 1994) suggesting that even four-year olds know that teleological expressions fit better with aspects of biological kinds than with other non-living natural kinds, and other research (Kelemen, 1999a) suggesting a much broader and often inappropriate mapping of teleological explanations onto other natural kinds. As this issue becomes resolved, it will help explain how teleological reasoning comes to be involved in organising natural kind and artefact category membership.

Second, there are more elaborate networks of causal patternings that distinguish living kinds and artefacts. The causal patternings of artefacts and living kinds differ fundamentally in that molecular features tend to cause functional features in living kinds, but functional features tend to cause molecular features in artefacts (Ahn, 1998). For instance, Ahn has used the example that in birds, the feature of "having wings" is what enables the bird "to fly", but in chairs, the feature "you sit on it" is the reason why it is "made of solid material" (and not made of something like gelatin). Differences in causal patternings might also distinguish several other kinds as well, including intentional versus mechanical agents, vehicles versus tools, and predators versus prey. These differences might be located either roughly at the same processing level, or at higher and lower levels.

Furthermore, causal patternings have a significant impact on how we categorise. One specific way in which this occurs has been reported by Ahn and Kim (2000) and Ahn et al. (in press), who demonstrated that the more causally central a feature is, the more important it is in categorisation. For instance, if people think that a novel animal called a rooban eats fruits, has sticky feet, and builds nests in trees, and that these features are not causally connected, they treat each of these features as equally important in categorisation. However, if they are instead told that sugars in the fruits are secreted through the pores of the roobans' feet, giving them sticky feet, and that these sticky feet in turn enable roobans to climb up trees to build their nests, people then treat these features differently in categorisation. Specifically, they treat the most causally central feature (eating fruits) as most important in categorisation, the causally intermediate feature (sticky feet) as next most important, and the terminal effect feature (build nests in trees) as least important. This effect of causal status has been demonstrated robustly in the domains of both novel and real-life animals, plants, artefacts, mental disorders, and other social categories, using a variety of measures including free sorting, categorisation of transfer items after learning novel categories, and judgements of typicality and conceptual centrality (Ahn & Kim, 2000; Ahn et al., in press; Kim & Ahn, in press; Sloman, Love, & Ahn, 1998). Thus, our ability to distinguish general types of causal patternings for different domains significantly influences the way we categorise new exemplars and think about categories.

It is apparent, therefore, that many distinct levels can informationally distinguish categories, ranging from simple sensory properties to richer perceptual structures to complex causal patterns that predominate in a domain. The ability to detect and utilise all (or at least most) of these levels is likely to be present in humans early on in life, suggesting that they might all be fundamental to domain-specific processing. Humans, even very young ones, might be made aware of at least some of these differences and could use them to tell the two classes apart (Mandler, Bauer, & McDonough, 1991; Mandler & McDonough, 1993). Moreover, it is not obvious that the lowest sensory level is privileged either developmentally or in the course of processing (see Chapter 11). That is, to some extent all levels might be present early on (Keil et. al., 1998). Thus, there is a broad continuum of processing levels at which domain-specific specialisations seem to occur early on in development, ranging from low-level percepts to high level cognition. To probe further into our initial question of determining the levels at which domain-specific processing occurs, we turn now to the contributions and impact of nativist and empiricist approaches to developmental examinations of conceptual structure.

NATIVISM, EMPIRICISM, AND CHANNELLING

We have suggested that there seem to be a great many kinds of information that we can use to be far better than chance at telling not only animals and artefacts apart, but also to make distinctions within many other higher level categories, such as intentional agents, plants, and vehicles. Moreover, adult humans probably have access to most or all of these levels. A contentious issue arises, however, when we ask about what kinds of information are central or peripheral to the mental structures and processes that are involved when we think about such categories. The answer to this question is by no means straightforward. It is possible that some informational patterns, which seem, at first glance, distinctively associated with a category, play only a minor role in influencing thought about members of that category. The crucial point here is that we want to ascertain the structural relations between levels of information both in terms of real-time thought and in terms of how developing humans first distinguish animals and artefacts. Lurking beneath the surface of many of these debates is the nativist/empiricist controversy and the ways in which scholars ally themselves with one side of the debate.

First, however, we need to clarify exactly what this debate is about. One way to understand the nativist/empiricist debate is in terms of domain speci-ficity and levels of processing (Cowie, 1999; Keil, 1994, 1999). Both sides agree that humans are biologically endowed with structures and processes that are needed to help them make sense of the world around them. Some-thing intrinsic to us and not to the crib enables us to learn. Moreover, some-thing intrinsic to us enables us to learn differently from other living creatures. Humans learn things that other species either cannot learn at all or learn at a much slower rate. None of this should be the least bit controversial, so it is puzzling to read discussions attacking nativists as arguing that humans are unique and empiricists as arguing that we are just like other species. No one would deny that in some respects we clearly are unique, whereas in others we are not. It is in the details of those dimensions of similarity and detail that the nativist/empiricist debate resides.

The primary difference between the two views involves an interaction between level of psychological operation and specificity for kinds of informa-tion. Again, both nativists and empiricists agree that we come into the world with structures and processes innately tailored to certain patterns of informa-tion. We obviously agree, for example, on the existence of sensory organs, such as eyes and ears, that are clearly structured in ways to be sensitive to only certain kinds of information and not others. We all acknowledge that other species have sensory organs that might differ from others in this respect, whether it be the sensitivity of bees to ultraviolet light, the sensitivity of bats to some sound patterns, or the vomeronasal sensory organ of the rat (Halpern, 1987), which is sensitive to large molecules that seem halfway between taste and smell.

The difference in opinion arises when we move "upstream" from the sens-ory receptors and ask about information specialisations in higher-level struc-tures and processes. The whole notion of upstream is an oversimplification, given the rich feedback connections from "higher" levels back down to lower levels, as well as lateral pathways within a level (Van Essen, Anderson, & Fellemen, 1992; Van Essen, Drury, Joshi, & Miller, 1998). None the less, there is, generally speaking, a hierarchy of higher and higher levels of processing as one moves inwards from the sensory receptors (an extremely simplified example might be the visual information pathway from sensory receptors to the lateral geniculate nucleus (LGN) to primary visual area V1 to the higher-level visual areas of V2, V4, and so on). Nativist/empiricist controversies become intense as theorists try to specify the nature of domain specialisations in terms of level and the kinds of information for which the specialisations exist. Empiricists might argue that sensory levels of processing are most basic, and that there exist early neural specialisations only for more primitive forms of information. Nativists, on the other hand, might argue that higher levels of processing are fundamental, and that there exists early neural specialisations for more complex cognition.

What evidence is there for each side of the debate, framed in this perspective? It seems that at the very least we have specialisations for information that is more high-level than the lowest-level sensory input. For example, specialisations for light-related information continue far up into visual cortex, becoming only questionable when multimodal neurons arise in the neural architecture. There are also specialisations that result in categorical perception, such as those for colour, which are present from at least 4 months of age (Bornstein, Kessen, & Weiskopf, 1976). Thus, we have specialisations not only for a particular form of energy, such as light versus sound, but for particular parts of an energy continuum. Such specialisations result in the ability to categorise or subjectively parse apart colours from an otherwise continuous range of visible wavelengths, speech sounds, and tones, among others. Moreover, it is now widely agreed that information specialisations are often tailored to distal as opposed to proximal patterns in the world. That is, Gibson (1950) argued that we perceive objects, surfaces, and layout, not just stimulations on the retina or eardrum. This requires higher level perceptual processing, which integrates a variety of types data from the sensory environment. This is certainly beyond the functional capacity of retinal ganglion cells in the visual system, for instance. Indeed, evidence suggests that we have neural structures in what is known as mid-level vision, tailored to perceive surfaces, objects, and occlusions (Nakayama, He, & Shimojo, 1995).

In principle, it is possible that specialisations for information might exist at all levels of processing. To return to the example of animals versus artefacts and the role of timing and teleology, it is possible that our ability to tell them apart emerges not just from picking up perceptual differences but also differences in their causal patternings. We might have a collection of expectations about things that act on each other at a distance or with certain time delays characteristic of intentional agents (Csibra et al., 1999; Heider & Simmel, 1944), which are sharply distinct from our expectations concerning the more immediate spatial and temporal continuities of mechanical objects. We might also expect that animals as a whole have no functional purposes, whereas their parts do (except for domesticated animals, which might be viewed as somewhat artefactual). By contrast, we do think that artefacts as a whole have purposes. There is an abundance of such possible expectations, many of which might be interconnected and interdependent, in a network that constitutes an intuitive "theory" of living things. We have been careful not to call this "theory" a network of beliefs, because it is not clear that they are necessarily explicit beliefs so much as they are implicit expectations that guide how we interpret the behaviours of living things. Most adults may have never consciously realised that they do not expect animals as a whole to have a purpose in the ways that artefacts do, but they might nonetheless show that knowledge daily in the ways they ask questions about, and behave towards, the two kinds. In sum, the possibility exists that we may well have information specialisations at all levels of processing.

THE LOW-LEVEL PERCEPTUAL SHUNT AND "ENLIGHTENED EMPIRICISM"

Before speculating further upon this point, however, we must consider an intriguing empiricist argument about the origins of high-level domain-specific circuits (and even discrete areas of neural tissue) dedicated to processing only some kinds of information. Its most explicit form is often discussed in reference to face perception. Here, a "low-level perceptual shunt" is thought to result in higher levels of domain specificity. Moreover, it is proposed that there exists only a low-level perceptual specialisation at birth, which becomes more developed over time and with experience (an example is discussed in detail later). Such accounts are in accord with what some have argued to be the new "enlightened empiricism" (Cowie, 1999). It is useful, therefore, to consider in some detail how this case might be extended to conceptual domains. Ultimately, we want to ask if it is possible empirically to distinguish such enlightened empiricist hypotheses from nativist ones.

As introduced earlier, perhaps the most lucid proposal of a low-level perceptual shunt has been offered for faces (Johnson & Morton, 1991). A young infant is assumed to have a neural circuit that is specialised for faces, but only in the crudest sense. The circuit, in fact, might be little more than a simple detector for three blobs forming an inverted triangle (two eyes and mouth). According to this model, early on, this detector might only be activated when the triangle is moving, as it would be on the face of an infant's caretaker. Empiricists grant that this much must be built in from birth, but their story thereafter diverges dramatically from a nativist view. The infant might have a region of its cortex, perhaps the fusiform gyrus, that is initially organised no differently from many other regions of cortex. This particular region, however, is the only area of cortex to which outputs of the "triangle tracking system" are sent. Over time, because it is receiving visual information about faces and little else, this region of cortex comes to organise itself in ways that are specifically attuned to faces. Eventually, they argue, a specific brain region becomes specialised for face processing. It shows "activation" to face stimuli in fMRI studies, and face processing degenerates if it is damaged.[2]

---

[2] In fact, the literature on face perception has turned out to be much more complex than this account, both in adult neuropsychology studies (Farah, 1994; Kanwisher, Stanley, & Harris, 1999) and in developmental studies in infants (Dannemiller & Stephens, 1988; Easterbrook, Kisilevsky, Muir, & Laplante, 1999). However, the key point here is to show how domain-specific organisation, even to the point of dedicated neural circuits in a certain area of brain tissue, could result from a system whose initial biases were only to track upside-down moving triangles with a certain spatial frequency.

Consider now how this sort of approach might be extended to other areas of perception and, more critically, to cognition. One of the most striking cases involves the category of sentient beings (for most of us, that means other people). What is often called folk psychology or theory of mind is, in adults, a body of knowledge about the category of things with beliefs and desires. Although there might be no cases of adult brain damage that lead to specific deficits in this area, there are clear cases of a selective theory of mind deficit in people who are autistic. There is also a smaller but none the less clear deficit in more verbal individuals with Asperger's syndrome. It is usually supposed that these individuals have a congenital, if not genetic, deficit in a specific brain region or system dedicated to thinking about mental states (Frith & Happé, 1998). There is, however, another possibility that builds on the perceptual shunt idea, taking a developmental perspective. Suppose there is no region of cortex that has any specialisation for mental states from the start, but that there are instead specialisations of simple, perceptual properties that are merely correlated with a goal-directed creature. These simple, perceptual properties might include motions of bounded objects that interact with each other with certain temporal delays, or which emit sounds in an alternating contingent fashion, or objects that move in a way that is contingent on the infant's own actions. The perceptual shunt model assumes that young infants do not "know" that these features are correlated with mental beings. Instead, it assumes that infants simply have a tendency to track these objects and, when they do, information about these objects is shunted either to a particular dedicated piece of neural tissue or a dedicated circuit that is more globally distributed. In this model, evolution did not prewire the child with any notions about beliefs and desires, but it did prewire the infant to track objects that manifest perceptual features correlated with mental entities. It also prewired a disposition to shunt this information to a special neural area and/or circuit, which receives input consisting of only this sort of information, albeit not having any *a priori* specialisation for it.

To date, we do not have enough evidence to tell us if this account is correct, but there are good reasons to believe in the claim that there are specialisations for noticing certain timing contingencies. For instance, if an infant makes a noise and an object makes a noise back in a contingent fashion, the infant will take special notice of the object. By at least 8 months, and possibly earlier, if such an object suddenly turns 90 degrees, infants will turn their heads to see where it is "looking", even though the object has no eyes or face (Johnson, 2000; Watson, 1985). Even the abilities of newborn infants to imitate could be related to the cyclic nature of their having been shown the behaviour by an adult or older child. Sticking out one's tongue once to an infant rarely elicits imitation. Rather, if one shows repeated tongue protrusions while looking at the infant, imitation is much more likely to emerge (Meltzoff & Moore, 1977, 1989). Thus, right from the start, certain contingencies associated with social beings might attract the attention of the young infant.

For such accounts to represent the strongest possible forms of empiricism, one might attribute to the infant a special sensitivity to only the lowest level perceptual cues that are reliably correlated with social beings. To explain any patterns of higher-level specialised brain regions or circuits for thinking about other minds, one might then append the idea that when these low-level perceptual features are noticed, they trigger a shunting of the input to a brain region with no *a priori* specialisation for that information. We can postulate that it might be viable for the case of a naive folk psychology because, as we have been describing, there are now several studies showing a special sensitivity in infants for perceptual information that is distinctively associated with intentional beings. The perceptual shunt and more nativist proposals start to make different predictions here with respect to autistic children. The perceptual shunting view would predict that infants who become autistic would, from the start, have a deficit in the ability to detect perceptual features that are distinctively associated with intentional agents. By contrast, nativist views allow for the possibility that such infants would be completely normal in their sensitivity to the perceptual cues but would have difficulties in making cognitive interpretations of those cues.

Might this shunting account also be viable for the development of different kinds of cognition? It seems plausible to us that it might well be. One might speculate that there are indeed special perceptual triggers for liquids that lead to specialised beliefs about how this set of non-solids behaves. Perhaps there are triggers for artefacts (such as smooth edges or colour junction correlations) that shunt to brain regions that become specialised for them. So also for living kinds. To reiterate, the idea here is that infants could start with unspecialised neural tissue that, in itself, is receptive to many sources of perceptual data. Furthermore, data can only enter the system if it sets off primary perceptual triggers. It is only through the process of funnelling input to specific brain regions that higher-order calculations can be made about the complex relations between the various parts of the entities (whether this be timing, contingencies, or feature arrangement like the colour junction correlations mentioned above). As time and experience progress, similar perceptual data builds upon itself and becomes manifest in increasingly sophisticated "cognitive" category determinations. In this way, perceptual categorisation fosters the growth of conceptual categorisation.

What, then, is a more nativist alternative to such a model? The nativist view might agree that certain perceptual features are especially attractive to infants, but rather than concede that this perceptual input is shunted to a specialised region of the brain, a strong nativist view would have this input "trigger" a set of *a priori* cognitive expectations about relations in a domain. For example, seeing a certain pattern of temporal contingencies might trigger a set of explicit expectations about the object's having goals and desires, and how these goals and desires are related to actions. Alternatively, the strong nativist view might say that when an infant sees that something is graspable and has certain textures, this perception may trigger an artifact/tool set of expectations that leads to questions asking what the object is "for" in a teleological sense. In the extreme, various perceptual triggers might lead to detailed beliefs about objects in a domain, but few such proposals are advanced today.

A somewhat more modest nativist model might also see a rich network of cognitive interconnections that are triggered by perceptual input, but would be more agnostic about how close those interconnections are to beliefs. As we mentioned above, if an object makes responsive beeps to an infant's vocalisations that are contingent in ways that suggest a social interaction, the infant will assume that the object is facing the infant, even though the object has no facial features. When the object then turns 90 degrees, the infants turn in the same direction, as though to follow the object's "gaze" (Johnson, 1998; Watson, 1985). This pattern of "gaze" following has been demonstrated in 8-month-old infants, but could plausibly be shown in much younger children, pending the invention of age-appropriate methodologies. Assume, for a moment, that "gaze" following has been demonstrated in infants so young that it could not plausibly have been learned. In this case, there might exist in the infant a set of expectations that entities respond with certain contingency and timing relations. These expectations might be that the entities have fronts, that those fronts are oriented towards the individual whose sounds are being responded to, and that if the entity rotates, its attention has been shifted in the direction that its front is now facing, presumably to something it has found interesting. Admittedly, that pattern of expectations suggests that an infant has beliefs about other mental entities and their mental states, and the causal consequences of those states—perhaps too much to attribute to someone so extremely young. A third, less potent alternative might be to say that certain contingency and timing relations attract an infant's attention to the side of the entity facing the infant and that, when that side turns, the turning of the facing part of the entity triggers in the infant a routine to look in the direction that is 90 degrees to the face of the object. In short, there might be a rich set of perceptual motor and attentional relationships set off by an object that responds contingently to one's voice, but that rich set of relationships may not be at the level of conscious beliefs.

It might seem implausible to think of the infant's responses as being outside the realm of beliefs, but consider what seem to be contingent non-conscious behaviours in other species. A sheep dog, for example, will actively attend to other animals (such as sheep) that act in a highly specific way contingent to the dog's behaviours. The dog then responds to these animals' behaviours by engaging itself in a set of herding behaviours. Many of the dog's herding behaviours make the dog appear as though it is anticipating, in a very complex manner, where the other animals want to go. Still, we are much more inclined to see the dog's mental states as an intricate mix of perceptual, motor, attentional, and spatial relations than to see them at the level of explicit beliefs. That is, although complex herding behavior emerges, we are reluctant to grant the dog herding "beliefs" or concepts about the sheep it herds. Likewise with infants, the third alternative suggests that infants use a combination of various cues and relations, which include but are not exclusive to perceptual input, to react to stimuli in a seemingly belief-oriented way. Again, it is not necessarily the case that they must possess or use a richly structured set of beliefs about social contingencies.

In short, it seems plausible that rich sets of cognitive interconnections can lead to elaborate expectations about how certain objects will behave, given some initial information and with perhaps little or no prior relevant learning. Such a possibility would conflict with most, if not all, forms of empiricism. However, there is still enormous variety in the possible nature of these expectations, ranging from sets of explicit beliefs to sets of perceptual motor responses. The enlightened empiricist view of perceptual shunting to an all purpose learning circuit differs conceptually and importantly from this view. How might the two views be shown to be different experimentally? To address this issue, we must first consider in more depth what non-perceptual knowledge of categories must look like.

HIGH BUT SPARSE: RETHINKING WHAT IT MEANS TO HAVE HIGH-LEVEL CONCEPTUAL KNOWLEDGE

We have suggested that category knowledge can arise from psychological processes at many levels, ranging from sensory perception to explicit beliefs of the sort found in a detailed theory. In this framework, one might claim that there is a region of neural tissue that contains a theory of the behaviour of physical objects or a theory of biology and is just waiting to be filled with real-world examples. However, such characterisations of the theory-laden aspect of categorisation could be severely misleading. It is now generally acknowledged that much of human categorisation seems to make sense only in terms of explanatory knowledge that the categoriser has (Murphy & Medin, 1985). Consider the well-known example of a category that includes children, money, photograph albums, and pets. This category makes sense only if you know that it represents "things to take out of one's house in case of a fire" (Barsalou, 1983). Furthermore, people readily reject high correlations that make no theoretical sense and will inflate or even create correlations that fit with theoretical relations (Chapman & Chapman, 1969). People routinely weigh features and frequencies in ways that follow from reasonable causal interpretations of what is going on in a domain. For instance, imagine that you were told that most of the athletes who qualified for the Olympic swimming team had certain properties, whereas most of those who did not qualify did not have those properties. Suppose you were further told that the qualifying athletes had broader shoulders, more ear piercings, diets higher in a certain protein, more cars with even numbers in their license plates, and lower resting heart rates than the non-qualifying athletes. No one would pay much attention to some of these properties, because they cannot fit into a coherent theory of what might help athletic performance.

The importance of theory-like relations to categorisation does not necessarily mean, however, that we have comprehensive, detailed theories of why aspects of the world are the way they are. Ask people how specific artefacts work as they do and you will usually find glaring holes in their knowledge, even when they might have previously expressed great confidence that they could answer the question with a high level of accuracy and detail (Rozenblit & Keil, 1999). Such holes, as well as inconsistencies and downright contradictions, are commonplace in folk beliefs about why things in the world around us are as they are (Wilson & Keil, 1998). Some have interpreted such limitations as clear indications that theories do not play any role in concepts at all (Fodor, 1998). Indeed, if our naive "theories" are to be understood as detailed, coherent theories either of the explicit or intuitive sort, then we would not be able to say that category knowledge arises from high level cognition. This would seem to be especially true of children, who have even less systematic knowledge than adults. Indeed, it might be adaptive to be able to reason effectively, and to categorise accurately, with such skeletal knowledge. It is not likely that we would always have a complete data set in front us from which to categorise correctly, or unlimited time to process all the information. In real life, we have limited time to link the parts that we do know about and, from this, make inferences about the missing details. To make an analogy, it is like being able to perceive a whole object in spite of the presence of occluders that chop-up smooth contours and surface textures. It would seem, then, as if category knowledge might have more of a perceptual basis after all.

There is an alternative, however. We can consider the possibility that lay people might have high-level, theory-like knowledge that is quite sparse and skeletal in nature (Wilson & Keil, 1998). A general example of high-level but sparse category knowledge might be having a causal schema of what sorts of patterns go best in a domain without knowing the exact details of how something in that domain works (for instance, knowing how feedback systems work, which is a common principle in applied physics, but not knowing how a digital thermostat regulates system temperature). Similarly, a lay person's explanatory knowledge about the category of living things might include knowing that they reproduce (but not knowing how they do it), knowing that each distinct biological kind has its own unique path of origin (two turtle doves do not grow from hatchling to mature birds by two radically different morphological routes) without knowing the details of those paths of origin, and so on. The point here is that one can know a great deal about members of a category that is by any account high level and abstract, but which is still sparse in terms of not knowing the details. In considering how we acquire category knowledge or in what becomes impaired and spared in neuropsychology cases, therefore, one must allow for this kind of theory-based knowledge without expecting fully worked-out mental models of some aspect of the world.

DISTINGUISHING THE MODELS

We have suggested that the organisation of our knowledge into concepts, including neural instantiations, might arise through specialisations for information at many different levels, ranging from the sensory and psychophysical to the theory-laden and causally interpreted. However, this suggestion is interesting from a developmental standpoint only if there are indeed ways to distinguish these levels of specialisation empirically. We think that there are, but that a substantial array of converging methods will be necessary to make sense of the issues that arise. To illustrate, we will first consider these issues framed as much more specific questions before we return to the broader question of how to differentiate the two accounts. Suppose, for example, that an individual suffered a stroke and has difficulty naming, recognising, and defining living things while keeping his ability to recognise artefacts relatively intact. A number of such cases have been reported in the literature (Humphreys & Forde, in press; Sartori & Job, 1988; Warrington & Shallice, 1984). There has been substantial debate with regard to the basis for such category-specific deficits, often revolving around the question of whether the deficit is that of being able to access such distinctions as functional versus perceptual features. By some accounts, functional features play a more important role for artefacts relative to perceptual features, so an impairment in access to perceptual features could cause a relative impairment in the ability to identify and possibly define living kinds (Farah & McClelland, 1991).

Such dichotomies, however, are inadequate to explain the deficits of all the patients in the literature, and more complex models are needed (Caramazza, 1998; Carmazza & Shelton, 1998; Humphreys & Forde, 2001; Shelton & Caramazza, 1999). In terms of the continuum of domain specificity we have described here, one can envision deficits at levels ranging from problems with certain kinds of visual features to problems in thinking about entities in teleological terms and, indeed, several patterns of neuropsychological data seem to require higher-level broad conceptual deficits that could arise from "a categorical structure for evolutionarily important categories of knowledge"

(Shelton, Fouch, & Carmazza, 1998, p. 339). In addition, various interactions between different kinds of information might be impaired. Indeed, it appears that many of these factors might be at work, and that theories will need to address several of them to be able to account for the full range of clinical cases (Humphreys & Forde, 2001). There is still, however, something of a bias in the literature towards explaining the effects in terms of deficits in feature types, such as perceptual and functional features, and a neglect of possible deficits in what we might call modes of construal—a kind of cognitive system for organising, processing, and interpreting information pertaining to a specific domain. Modes of construal are ways of interpreting or understanding information in a specific domain but also have more of a framework nature than a fully worked-out theory. Thus, a biological mode of construal might involve teleological reasoning, a search for essences and their links to surface phenomena and several other biases concerning the kinds of causal patternings in a domain (see Keil [1994] for a more in-depth look at the idea of modes of construal itself). Certainly, by one interpretation of the autism literature, deficits in such modes might be one factor contributing to a selective theory of mind impairment.

Indeed, it is not at all impossible that deficits might be partially due to damage in such higher-level conceptual systems. Imagine, for instance, that adults have a specialised neural system for thinking about essences. This "essentialist system" might have a complex structure that instigates a continuous search for deeper and deeper causes of surface phenomena. Imagine further that, for our concepts of living kinds, virtually all features of such kinds are linked in some way, perhaps through other features, to the essence of that concept (e.g. DNA). Thus, when our hypothetical neural "essentialist system" for living kinds is defective, the features might be less tightly associated with one another than they would be normally, and are therefore less useful for identifying instances of living things.

It is well known that explanatory schemata can heavily influence the subjective weightings of features (Murphy & Allopena, 1994), so it is not implausible that a missing essentialist bias might cause very different weightings of features for living kinds and result in lowered performance on a wide range of tasks applied to that domain. Furthermore, it might be that an essence bias would be more strongly connected to some kinds of features than to others. Perhaps the essence bias is triggered by salient perceptual features, which then motivate a search for underlying causes and hidden features. In effect, it is conceivable that a problem with such an essentialist bias might cause many of the deficits seen in the neuropsychological literature. Such an account is completely speculative at this time, but it makes a useful point. Neuropsychological data alone might be hard pressed to tease apart quite dramatically different alternatives as to the level of cognitive involvement. Greater insight can be gained from combining lesion studies with imaging studies, and more still will be learned from transcranial magnetic stimulation (TMS) temporary "lesions", but even all of these collectively might have great difficulty distinguishing the levels at which the effects are occurring.

Thus, we must consider addressing the question from several other perspectives as well: chronometric, developmental, crosscultural, comparative across species, and in the normal range of individual differences. When these are combined with data on neuropsychological deficits, the relative importance of the different levels of information in everyday use of categories will become more apparent. Ultimately, then, the goal is not just to understand category-specific deficits in their own right but to understand how such deficits converge with other assessments of category knowledge. In this way, we can better understand how our knowledge of categories originates, functions, and is structured in its mature state. For complex reasons, it might be that lesions result in a much more refined differentiation of perceptual versus functional features than of different essentialist biases or teleological modes of construal. However, until converging evidence from a variety of methodologies is considered, it is risky to assume that perceptual and functional features represent the core basis for differences in knowledge across categories. A case in point, to return to an earlier example, is Ahn's (1998) demonstration that people rely more fundamentally on causal theories than on perceptual versus functional features to identify artifacts and natural kinds.

But, one might argue, consider another way in which perceptual versus functional features might distinguish the two kinds. Perhaps the ratio of functional features to perceptual ones is higher for artefacts than for living kinds (see Humphreys & Forde [2001] for a related discussion). Some patterns of brain damage could then differentially damage access to one of these feature types and thereby produce a deficit biased towards one category over another. Again, even if all of this were the case, even tentative conclusions about how categories are mentally represented should be drawn with great caution. To illustrate the problem, imagine a more extreme example. Presumably, a blind person should have far less access to perceptual features than a sighted individual, even if we allow for some compensation via increased sensitivity to auditory and tactile features. Thus, a blind individual's knowledge of living kind and artefact categories might be expected to be much more similar to each other, relative to a sighted individual, in terms of the relative ratios of perceptual and functional features. If this were the key representational difference between the two categories, one might expect, for instance, more conversational impasses in conversations with blind people about living kinds. However, no such conversational confusions have been reported. Moreover, lesions in regions that cause a deficit in thought about living things for sighted individuals would not be expected to have a comparable effect for blind people. We do not know of any specific cases of this nature, but suspect that no such differences would be present following lesions in blind and sighted people. Thus, simply shifting the discussion to possible interesting scenarios presented by special populations illustrates more clearly the limitations of any one perspective and provides a basis for showing how different theoretical approaches make different predictions.

Indeed, focusing on functional and perceptual features as the critical difference between how the concepts of the two kinds of categories are represented seems less effective than considering a much wider range of perspectives. A look at the developmental literature reveals that even distinguishing perceptual from functional features is a far more tricky affair than it might first seem. Classic claims that children proceed from organising their worlds primarily in terms of perceptual features and only later in terms of functional features have proven to be difficult to support empirically (Keil et al., 1998). Young infants are capable of picking up on some functional features of objects at extremely early ages, such as graspability. Furthermore, the Gibsonian idea of affordances—properties of objects that afford actions—has blurred the perceptual/functional feature distinction almost completely (Adolph, Eppler, & Gibson, 1993; Gibson et al., 1987).

Thus, we have argued here for an approach in which we assume, by default, that all levels of information that could distinguish members of categories are used to make sense of the world, and that no one kind of feature is necessarily privileged, whether in terms of processing speed, neural instantiation, or development. Indeed, just as the classical idea of a perceptual to functional shift in development has foundered in recent years, so has the idea that perceptual features alone must be the first features to affect information processing. Of course, for novel objects out of context, perceptual features must be processed first, but for most things we perceive in the world, prior knowledge at all levels plays a role in constraining what information we pick up. Consider the phenomenon of inattentional blindness (Most et al., 2000; Simons & Levin, 1998). Depending on the task at hand, observers clearly do not see certain objects and/or events, even when they are directly in the centre of the visual field. Higher-level, theory-based expectations about what is being observed can cause "blindness" to that which is not expected. Similarly, in learning to categorise objects, expectations about plausible causal relations among properties will lead observers to more rapidly identify instances with causally plausible properties than those with properties that are less plausible but occur more frequently in training (Murphy, 2000).

When categorisation is viewed from the perspective of just one approach, whether it be category-specific brain damage, developmental change in categorisation, categorisation across species, or speed of access, a single level of analysis (often different depending on the particular approach) might appear to predominate. Only when these various perspectives are taken together can we address the need to synthesise information at all possible levels. Moreover, it might also be of critical importance to consider interactions between these levels. In general, as we have pointed out, there seems to be a general tendency to model the representations subserving categorisation in terms of feature sets and their distributions (often with a bias towards perceptual features). Instead, interactions between features must be considered, especially those that capture causal and temporal relations. Additionally, it is important to note that there is more at work here than simply the notion that every possible bit of relevant information is important to our mental representations of categories. Rather, the argument is that an awareness of the multiple levels and their interactions should motivate studies aimed at unveiling a clearer assessment of what is central in learning, development, and mature functioning.

As a final example of how multiple research perspectives could be combined to gain a fuller view of multilevel categorisation, consider again the nativist–empiricist debate. How might one contrast the perceptual shunt "enlightened empiricist" accounts explaining the origins of our knowledge about living things from the more nativist accounts? The empiricist model would predict that infants who are exposed to very different informational patterns should have more radically different high-level cognitive systems as adults. Thus, one might expect blind and sighted individuals to have markedly different high-level cognitive organisations about living and artefact kinds. A more nativist view that sees rich prior organisation in dedicated neural circuits, even if it is below the level of specific beliefs, would see less variation across individuals with different experiences, assuming that either of these different experiences (i.e. blind and sighted) might be adequate to fill out the organisation in the circuits. Thus, studies in blind and sighted individuals aimed at investigating these hypotheses would be both viable and informative.

Another technique might be to look at normal individual differences, an approach rarely used to ask questions about the organisation of cognition. From the vast literature on intelligence, we know that there are individual differences in subcomponents of cognition such as spatial ability, verbal ability, and processing speed. Analogously, it seems plausible that the different levels of information that could inform categorisation would also show individual differences. As an example, take again the case of autism. There may be a continuum from autistic individuals to Asperger's to socially awkward people to those who are remarkably socially adroit (indeed, some have argued, not in jest, that men generally resemble autistic individuals more so than women do). It is possible, then, that there might be a distinct mental faculty for reasoning about social beings that varies across individuals. The same possibility exists for the ability to handle information at each of the levels that are relevant to categorisation. Some individuals might be better at coding functional features, others at seeing colour distributions, others at encoding action-at-a-distance relations, and still others at making teleological inferences. Such an analysis, especially in conjunction with developmental ones, would help discriminate enlightened empiricist models from more nativist ones.

Recently, the values of an individual differences approach have been illustrated in a research programme examining the degree to which lexical versus syntactic development is associated with genetic variance. If identical (monozyogotic) and fraternal (dizygotic) twins are compared in the developmental trajectories for their lexions and syntactic structures, only the syntactic structures show a stronger correlation among identical twins than fraternal ones, suggesting a more direct role for domain-specific biological specialisations for syntax (Ganger, Pinker, Baker, & Chawla, 1999). This same kind of approach could be extended to many other areas of cognition as well.

One final approach in our multiperspective framework might be to examine comparative work across species. Increasingly, we see evidence of other species' sensitivity to real-world covariation between timing relations and specific domains. The development of taste aversion is the classic example, in which animals such as rats link their feeling of nausea with the taste of a food ingested hours earlier and not with a visual event occurring just prior to the nausea's onset (Garcia & Koelling, 1966; Rozin & Kalat, 1971). More recently, it has been shown that relatively unsophisticated primates, such as cotton top tamarins, assume that colour is more central to similarity of novel foods than it is to similarity of novel artefacts (Santos, Hauser, & Spelke, 2001). Thus, it is plausible that this sort of work could reveal that there are, even in species presumably less sophisticated than humans, the sorts of top-down, theory-influenced expectations about the kinds of correlations, contingencies, and features that are most relevant to a particular domain. Indeed, we have just suggested a variety of research approaches that together might provide insight on the question of whether the nativist and enlightened empiricist approaches are, in fact, distinguishable.

CONCLUSIONS

We have argued that categorisation might rely on information that is processed at many different levels of perception and cognition, and that discussion of the representational basis for categorisation to date has tended to focus solely on relatively low-level perceptual features. Recently, there has been a movement to look more at interactions between different levels of processing (Humphreys & Forde, in press). However, we see many more alternatives when the full range of possibilities is considered. There is an implicit bias in much of the developmental literature to assume that the perceptual is developmentally more basic than the conceptual, and thus more immediately and easily processed. We have, however, found little support for such an assumption, and suggest that such a bias has led to a neglect of the various ways in which cognition about information relevant to category differences might be central to category-based knowledge. We recommend that an integrated perspective that links neuropsychology with several other approaches will bring more clarity to how we might use these different levels of information and how we might distinguish them empirically.

ACKNOWLEDGEMENTS

This project was supported in part by NIH Grant R01-HD23922 to Frank Keil and by a National Science Foundation Graduate Fellowship to Nancy Kim.

REFERENCES

Adolph, K.E., Eppler, M.A., & Gibson, E.J. (1993). Development of perception of affordances. *Advances in Infancy Research, 8*, 51–98.

Ahn, W. (1998). Why are different features central for natural kinds and artifacts? The role of causal status in determining feature centrality. *Cognition, 69*, 135–178.

Ahn, W., & Kim, N.S. (2000). The causal status effect in categorization: An overview. In D.L. Medin (Ed.), *The psychology of learning and motivation* (pp. 23–65). New York: Academic Press.

Ahn, W., Kim, N.S., Lassaline, M.E., & Dennis, M. (in press). Causal status as a determinant of feature centrality. *Cognitive Psychology*.

Atran, S. (1996). Knowledge of living kinds. In D. Sperber, D. Premack, & A. Premack (Eds.), *Causal cognition: A multidisciplinary debate*. New York: Oxford University Press.

Barsalou, L.W. (1983). Ad hoc categories. *Memory & Cognition, 11*, 211–217.

Bloom, P. (1996). Theories of artifact categorization. *Cognition, 66*, 87–93.

Bornstein, M.H., Kessen, W., & Weiskopf, S. (1976). Color vision and hue categorization in young human infants. *Journal of Experimental Psychology: Human Perception and Performance, 2*, 115–129.

Boyd, R. (1999). Homeostasis, species and higher taxa. In R.A. Wilson (Ed.), *Species: New interdisciplinary essays*. Cambridge, MA: MIT Press.

Caramazza, A. (1998). The interpretation of semantic category-specific deficits: What do they reveal about the organization of conceptual knowledge in the brain? *Neurocase, 4*, 265–272.

Caramazza, A., & Shelton, J. (1998). Domain-specific knowledge systems in the brain: The animate/inanimate distinction. *Journal of Cognitive Neuroscience, 10*, 1–34.

Chapman, L.J., & Chapman, J.P. (1969). Illusory correlation as an obstacle to the use of valid psychodiagnostic signs. *Journal of Abnormal Psychology, 74*, 271–280.

Cosmides, L., & Tooby, J. (1994). The evolution of domain specificity: The evolution of functional organization. In L.A. Hirschfeld & S.A. Gelman (Eds.), *Mapping the mind: Domain specificity in cognition and culture*. Cambridge: Cambridge University Press.

Cowie, F. (1999). *What's within? Nativism reconsidered*. New York: Oxford University Press.

Csibra, G., Gergely, G., Biró, S., Kóró, O., & Brockbank, M. (1999). Goal attribution without agency cues: The perception of 'pure reason' in infancy. *Cognition, 72*, 237–267.

Cutting, J.E. (1986). *Perception with an eye for motion*. Cambridge, MA: MIT Press.

Dannemiller, J.L., & Stephens, B.R. (1988). A critical test of infant pattern preference models. *Child Development, 59*, 210–216.

Dunbar, K. (1994). How scientists really reason: Scientific reasoning in real-world laboratories. In R.J. Sternberg & J. Davidson (Eds.), *Mechanisms of insight*. Cambridge, MA: MIT Press.

Easterbrook, M.A., Kisilevsky, B.S., Muir, D.W., & Laplante, D.P. (1999). Newborns discriminate schematic faces from scrambled faces *Canadian Journal of Experimental Psychology, 53*, 231–241.

Farah, M.J. (1994). Neuropsychological inference with an interactive brain: A critique of the 'locality assumption'. *Behavioural and Brain Sciences, 17*, 43–61.

Farah, M.J., & McClelland, J.L. (1991). A computational model of semantic memory impairment: Modality specificity and emergent category specificity. *Journal of Experimental Psychology: General, 120*, 339–357.

Fodor, J.A. (1975). *The language of thought*. New York: Thomas Y. Crowell.

Fodor, J.A. (1998). *Concepts: Where cognitive science went wrong*. Oxford: Oxford University Press.

Frith, U. (1999). Autism. In R.A. Wilson & F.C. Keil (Eds.), *The MIT encyclopedia of the cognitive sciences* (pp. 58–60). Cambridge: MIT Press.

Frith, U., & Happé, F. (1999). Theory of mind and self consciousness: What is it like to be autistic? *Mind and Language, 14*, 1–22.

Ganger, J., Pinker, S., Baker, A., & Chawla, S. (1999) *A twin study of early vocabulary and grammatical development*. Paper presented at the biennial meeting of the Society for Research in Child Development, Albuquerque, NM. We also couldn't find this ref.

Garcia, J., & Koelling, R.A. (1966). Relation of cue to consequence in avoidance learning. *Psychonomic Science, 4*, 123–124.

Gelman, S., & Hirschfeld, J. (1999). How biological is essentialism? In D.L. Medin & S. Atran (Eds.), *Folkbiology*. Cambridge, MA: MIT Press.

Gergely, G., Nadasdy, A., Csibra, G., & Biró, S. (1995). Taking the intentional stance at 12 months of age. *Cognition, 56*, 165–193.

Gibson, J.J. (1950). *Perception of the visual world*. Boston, MA: Houghton Mifflin.

Gibson, E.J., & Adolph, K. (1999). Affordances. In R.A. Wilson & F.C. Keil (Eds.), *The MIT encyclopedia of the cognitive sciences* (pp. 4–6). Cambridge: MIT Press.

Gibson, E.J., Riccio, G., Schmuckler, M.A., Stroffregen, T.A., Rosenberg, D., & Toarmina, J. (1987). Detection of the traversibility of surfaces by crawling and walking infants. *Journal of Experimental Psychology: Human Perception and Performance, 13*, 533–544.

Halpern, M. (1987). The organization and function of the vomeronasal system. *Annual Review of Neuroscience, 10*, 325–362.

Heider, F., & Simmel, M. (1944). An experimental study of apparent behavior. *American Journal of Psychology, 57*, 243–259.

Hull, D. (1965). The effect of essentialism on taxonomy: 2000 years of stasis. *British Journal for the Philosophy of Science, 15, 16*, 314–326, 1–18.

Humphreys, G.W., & Forde, E.M.E. (2001). Category specific impairments: A review and presentation of the hierarchical interactive theory (HIT). *Behavioral and Brain Sciences, 24*, 453–465.

Johnson, S.C. (2000) The recognition of mentalistic agents in infancy. *Trends in Cognitive Sciences, 4*, 22–28.

Johnson, M.H., & Morton, J. (1991). *Biology and cognitive development: The case of face recognition*. Cambridge, MA: Blackwell.

Johnson, S.C., Slaughter, V., & Carey, S. (1998). Whose gaze will infants follow? Features that elicit gaze-following in 12-month-olds, *Developmental Science, 1*, 233–238.

Kanwisher, N., Stanley, D., & Harris, A. (1999) The fusiform face area is selective for faces not animals. *Neuroreport, 10(1)*, 183–187.

Keil, F.C. (1989). *Concepts, kinds and cognitive development*. Cambridge, MA: MIT Press.

Keil, F.C. (1994). The birth and nurturance of concepts by domains: The origins of concepts of living things. In L.A. Hirschfeld & S.A. Gelman (Eds.), *Mapping the Mind: Domain specificity in cognition and culture*. New York: Cambridge University Press.

Keil, F.C. (1999). Nativism. In R.A. Wilson & F.C. Keil (Eds.), *MIT encyclopedia of the cognitive sciences*. Cambridge, MA: MIT Press.

Keil, F.C., Smith, C., Simons, D.J., & Levin, D.T. (1998). Two dogmas of conceptual empiricism: Implications for hybrid models of the structure of knowledge. *Cognition, 65*, 103–135.

Keil, F.C., & Richardson, D.C. (1999). Species, stuff, and patterns of causation. In R.A. Wilson (Ed.), *Species: New interdisciplinary essays*. Cambridge, MA: MIT Press.

Kelemen, D. (1999a). Function, goals and intention: Children's teleological reasoning about objects. *Trends in Cognitive Science, 3*, 461–468.

Kelemen, D. (1999b). Why are rocks pointy? Children's preference for teleological explanations of the natural world. *Developmental Psychology, 35*, 1440–1452.

Kim, N.S., & Ahn, W. (in press). The influence of naive causal theories on lay concepts of mental illness. *American Journal of Psychology*.

Mandler, J.M., Bauer, P.J., & McDonough, L. (1991). Separating the sheep from the goats: Differentiating global categories. *Cognitive Psychology, 23*, 263–298.

Mandler, J.M., & McDonough, L. (1993). Concept formation in infancy. *Cognitive Development, 8*, 291–318.

Medin, D.L., & Shoben, E.J. (1988). Context and structure in conceptual combination. *Cognitive Psychology, 20*, 158–190.

Meltzoff, A.N., & Moore, M.K. (1977) Imitation of facial and manual gestures by human neonates. *Science, 198*, 75–78.

Meltzoff, A.N., & Moore, M.K. (1989). Imitation in newborn infants: Exploring the range of gestures imitated and the underlying mechanims. *Developmental Psychology, 25*, 954–962.

Michotte, A. (1963). *The perception of causality*. London: Methuen.

Most, S.B., Simons, D.J., Scholl, B.J., & Chabris, C.F. (2000). Sustained inattentional blindness: The role of location in the detection of unexpected dynamic events. *Psyche, 6(14)*. http://psyche.cs.monash.edu.au/v6/psyche-6-14-most.html

Murphy, G.L. (2000). Explanatory concepts. In F.C. Keil & R.A. Wilson (Eds.), *Cognition and explanation* (pp. 361–392). Cambridge, MA: MIT Press.

Murphy, G.L., & Allopenna, P.D. (1994). The locus of knowledge effects in concept learning. *Journal of Experimental Psychology: Learning, Memory, and Cognition, 20*, 904–919.

Murphy, G.L., & Medin, D.L. (1985). The role of theories in conceptual coherence. *Psychological Review, 92*, 289–316.

Nakayama, K., He, Z.J., & Shimojo, S. (1995). Visual surface representation: A critical link between lower-level and higher-level vision. In S.M. Kosslyn & D.N. Osherson (Eds.), *Visual cognition: An invitation to cognitive science*, Vol. 2 (2nd ed.). Cambridge, MA: MIT Press.

Rozenblit, L., & Keil, F.C. (November, 1999). *The unbearable lightness of theory? An illusion of explanatory depth*. Paper presented at the annual meeting of the Psychonomic Society, Los Angeles, CA.

Rozin, P., & Kalat, J.W. (1971). Specific hungers and poison avoidance as adaptive specializations of learning. *Psychological Review, 78*, 459–486.

Salmon, W.C. (1989). *Four decades of scientific explanation*. Minneapolis, MN: University of Minnesota Press.

Santos, L.R., Hauser, M.D., & Spelke, E.S. (2001). Representations of food kinds in rhesus monkeys (*Macaca mulatta*) An unexplored domain of knowledge. *Cognition, 82*, 127–155.

Sartori, G., & Job, R. (1988). The oyster with four legs: A neuropsychological study on the interaction of visual and semantic information. *Cognitive Neuropsychology, 5*, 105–132.

Shelton, J., & Caramazza, A. (1999) Deficits in lexical access and semantic processing: Implications for models of normal language. *Psychonomic Bulletin and Review, 6*, 5–27.

Shelton, J., Fouch, E., & Caramazza, A. (1998). The selective sparing of body part knowledge: A case study. *Neurocase, 4*, 339–350.

Simons, D.J., & Keil, F.C. (1995). An abstract to concrete shift in the development of biological thought: The insides story. *Cognition, 56*, 129–163.

Simons, D.J., & Levin, D.T. (1998). Failure to detect changes to people during a real-world interaction. *Psychonomic Bulletin & Review, 5*, 644–649.

Sloman, S., Love, B., & Ahn, W. (1998). Feature centrality and conceptual coherence. *Cognitive Science, 22*, 189–228.

Van Essen, D.C., Anderson, C.H., & Fellemen, D.J. (1992). Information processing in the primate visual system: An integrated systems perspecive. *Science, 255*, 419–423.

Van Essen, D.C., Drury, H.A., Joshi, S., & Miller, M.I. (1998). Functional and structural mapping of human cerebral cortex: Solutions are in the surfaces. *Proceedings of the National Academy of Sciences, 95*, 788–795.

Watson, J.S. (1985). Contingency perception in early social development. In T.M. Field & N.A. Fox (Eds.), *Social perception in infants*. Norwood, NJ: Ablex.

Warrington, E.K., & Shallice, T. (1984). Category-specific semantic impairment. *Brain, 107*, 829–854.

Wilson, R.A., & Keil, F.C. (1998). The shadows and shallows of explanation. *Minds & Machines, 8*, 137–159.

CHAPTER 14

The relationships between anatomical and cognitive locus of lesion in category-specific disorders

Guido Gainotti
Director Neuropsychology Service, Università Cattolica–Policlinico Gemelli, Rome, Italy

INTRODUCTION: THE MAIN MODELS

Three main theoretical accounts have been proposed for category-specific semantic disorders for living and non-living things. The first, and perhaps most influential model, put forward by Warrington and Shallice (1984) in their seminal paper, proposes that the living–non-living distinction could be the by-product of a more basic dichotomy, concerning the differential weighting that visuoperceptual and functional attributes might have in the identification of members of biological and respectively of artefacts categories. This model is often labelled the "sensory/functional" hypothesis.

The second theoretical model, proposed more recently by Caramazza and Shelton (1998), assumes that category-specific defects for living and non-living entities may be due to disruption of different evolutionary-adapted dedicated neural mechanisms for the domains of "animals", "plant life" and "artefacts". This model is usually called the "domain-specific knowledge systems" hypothesis.

The third and last theoretical model, proposed by Gonnerman et al. (1997), assumes that different levels of interconnections might exist within the semantic structure between shared (perceptual and functional) attributes of living and non-living things and that this structural difference might be more important than the differential weighting of these attributes to explain category-specific semantic disorders. This last model is often labelled the "intercorrelations among semantic features" hypothesis.

The main criteria that have been used by various authors to support or disconfirm these theoretical models are: (i) the relative impairment of visual and functional knowledge in patients with selective damage to the living or non-living categories; (ii) the detailed pattern of impaired and spared categories that can be found in these patients; and (iii) the results of computational studies, which have used computer simulations to produce category-specific defects for living or non-living things.

Less frequently considered, although potentially relevant from the theoretical point of view, are the brain correlates of category specificity. To be sure, in recent years some functional neuroimaging studies (Damasio et al., 1996; Martin, Wiggs, Ungerleider, & Heixby, 1996; Moore & Price, 1999; Mummery, Patterson, Hodges, & Wise, 1996; Mummery, Patterson, Hodges, & Price, 1998; Perani et al., 1995, 1999; Spitzer et al., 1995; Thompson-Schill, Aguirre, D'Esposito, & Farah, 1999) have tried to clarify this issue (see Chapter 15). Results of these studies, however, have not been very consistent and only a couple of papers (Gainotti, Silveri, Daniele, & Guistolisi, 1995; Saffran & Schwartz, 1994) have taken the more direct approach of reviewing the neuroanatomical correlates of category-specific disorders. As, even in these articles, only a rather impressionistic survey had been provided, I have recently undertaken a more systematic study of this topic (Gainotti, 2000). A discussion of data gathered in this survey constitutes the specific subject of the present chapter, but some introductory words seem necessary to properly understand the meaning of these neuroanatomical data.

In this chapter, I will first summarise the theoretical and empirical reasons that make it difficult to choose between the alternative models proposed to explain category-specific disorders. I will then analyse the implicit and explicit assumptions that each of these models make for extent and localisation of brain lesions provoking a category-specific disorder. After these preliminary sections, I will proceed to discuss the results of the survey of the neuroropathological data, by taking into account the neuroanatomical correlates of category-specific disorders arising at the semantic, lexical, and visual levels. A short comparison of the anatomical areas damaged in patients with category-specific disorders and activated in normal subjects during neuroimaging studies using specific categories of objects will ensue. Finally, I will conclude with a discussion of the implications of these neuro-anatomical data with respect to the above mentioned theoretical models.

THEORETICAL PROBLEMS AND CONFOUNDING FACTORS IN THE STUDY OF CATEGORY-SPECIFIC DISORDERS

Theoretical problems

Both theoretical and factual reasons make it difficult to choose among the "sensory/functional", the "domains of knowledge", and the "interconnections among semantic features" hypotheses. The first theoretical reason concerns the fact that there are different versions of each of these models and each version can be supported or falsified by a different set of data. Thus, there are at least three versions of the "sensory/functional" hypothesis. The first and most influential version is consistent with the distributed models of semantic representation proposed by Allport (1985), Shallice (1988), and Damasio (1990). These models assume that each object concept can be represented as an autoassociated pattern of activation distributed across different sensory and motor attribute domains, located in different cortical regions. A local lesion of this network should, therefore, preferentially disrupt semantic categories for which the damage falls at the centre of gravity of their pattern of interconnected attributes; nevertheless, other concepts having a similar pattern of autoassociated properties should also be concomitantly damaged. According to this version, category-specific defects for living things should be the result of a lesion impinging upon areas processing and storing visual-perceptual information, whereas defects selectively concerning artefacts should result from lesions encroaching upon areas mainly dealing with functional knowledge.

The second version of the "sensory/functional" hypothesis has been put forward by Sartori and Job (1988), drawing on the distinction proposed by Riddoch and Humphreys (1987) and Humphreys, Riddoch, & Quinlan (1988) between a presemantic "structural description system" that stores the visual properties of objects and a "central semantic memory system" that stores associative and functional knowledge about objects. Sartori and Job (1988) suggested that the problem of their patient, Michelangelo, concerned the presemantic structural description system, rather than the central semantic memory system (see Chapter 2). A similar interpretation of category-specific semantic disorders for living things has been proposed by other authors (Etcoff, Freeman, & Cave, 1991; Arguin, Chapter 4; Arguin, Bub, & Dudech, 1996; Forde et al., 1997).

Finally, a third version of the theory, more consistent with a modular than with a distributed model of semantic representation, has been proposed by McCarthy and Warrington (1988). These authors described two patients, TOB (McCarthy & Warrington, 1988) and DRS (Warrington & McCarthy, 1994) who presented as follows: TOB had a category-specific impairment for living things limited to verbal tasks and DRS had a visual recognition disorder preferentially affecting man-made objects. On the basis of these observations, McCarthy and Warrington proposed that the semantic system might be organised both by category (living versus non-living) and by modality of input (verbal versus visual). It seems clear that each of these versions is consistent with a different model of semantic representation and with a different set of empirical data.

The second theoretical source of confounding stems from the fact that, as already suggested by some authors (Forde et al., 1997; Gainotti & Silveri, 1996; Sheridan & Humphreys, 1993), category-specific disorders for living and non-living things must probably be considered as complex and heterogeneous syndromes, rather than as homogeneous entities. Looking at data reported in the available literature, one notes, in fact, that both the presumable locus of damage within the cognitive system and the pattern of categorical impairment can be different in different patients (see also Chapter 3). For instance, the majority of patients show a category-specific impairment across different verbal and non-verbal tasks, consistent with a semantic locus of defect, but other patients seem to have a purely lexical category-specific disorder and still others a modality-specific category recognition defect. Thus, patients MD (Hart, Berndt, & Caramazza, 1985), AN (Damasio, 1990), TU (Farah & Wallace, 1992), KQU (Goldenberg, 1992), KR (Hart & Gordon, 1992), and SRB (Forde et al., 1997) showed a category-specific impairment for living things on naming tasks, but not on tasks probing the knowledge of the corresponding semantic category. A similar category-specific lexical impairment for artefacts has been described in patients CG (Silveri et al., 1997), GP (Cappa et al., 1998) and IW (Lambon Ralph, Howard, Nightingale, & Ellis, 1998). On the other hand, Damasio (1990) has described two patients (PSD and DBR) who showed a selective defect in recognition of living beings restricted to the visual modality, and an analogous visual recognition disorder preferentially concerning man-made objects has been described by Warrington and McCarthy (1994) in patient DRS.

An equally variegated picture can be observed in the pattern of impaired and spared semantic categories, both inside and outside the broad domains of living and non-living things. On one hand, Caramazza and Shelton (1998) observed that within the biological domain the impairment is sometimes restricted to the narrower categories of "animals" and "plant life". On the other hand, the co-occurrence of selective defects for living things and for categories lying outside the living domain (such as food and musical instruments) has been well documented in some patients and cannot be easily discarded as a simple artefact of uncontrolled stimulus factors (Breedin, Saffran, & Coslett, 1994; De Renzi & Lucchelli, 1994; Fery, 1997; Gainotti & Silveri, 1996; Sheridan & Humphreys, 1993).

Confounding factors

A number of counfounding variables, such as word frequency, stimulus familiarity, age of acquisition of the object's name, and visual complexity, have not
always been properly controlled in studies on category-specific impairments
(for the importance of these variables, see Forde & Humphreys, 1999; Funnell & Sheridan, 1992; Gaffan & Heywood; 1993; Stewart, Parkin, & Hunkin,
1992). Two important points should be taken into account when considering
these confounding factors. The first point is that the exact mechanisms of
these factors in category-specific disorders has been only partly clarified. The
second point is to recognise that other confounding factors must be taken
into account in category-specificity.

As for the first point, Gainotti and Silveri (1996) suggested that it is not
clear whether the influence of the above-mentioned factors is quite aspecific
or if an interaction exists between the impact of these individual variables
and the variety of category-specific impairments. Thus, stimulus familiarity,
which determines the strength of the object's trace in semantic memory,
could play the most important role when the category-specific disorder is
subserved by a defect of memory retrieval, whereas visual complexity could
be the most important factor when the category-specific disorder results from
a visual recognition disorder or from a defect of the structural description
system.

As for the second point, it seems likely that controversies about the (equal
or unequal) level of impairment of visual and functional knowledge in
patients with a category-specific semantic impairment for living things might
in part result from the operational definition of the visual–perceptual and
functional properties of living beings and of man-made objects. Several
reasons seem to support this claim. The first is that there are patients with
category-specific semantic impairments for living things who show very different patterns of performance when studied with different kinds of tests
devised to explore their knowledge of visual–perceptual and functional
knowledge of living and non-living things. For example, patient SE, who had
a category-specific impairment for living things after recovering from herpes
simplex encephalitis (HSE), has shown a deficit for functional attributes of
animals (Laws, Evans, Hodges, & McCarthy, 1995), but the opposite pattern
of results (namely, a selective impairment for the visual properties of living
things) when studied with a different battery of tests (Moss, Tyler, & Jennings, 1997). The second reason is that the term "functional properties" is
often used in different ways when referring to living things and non-living
things. This was explicitly recognised by Moss, Tyler, Durrant-Peatfield, and
Bunn (1998), who maintained that the key functional properties of living
things concern biological actions, such as eating, walking, and growing,
rather than the typical actions accomplished with objects by humans, which

constitute the key functional properties of non-living things. An implicit trend in the same direction, namely to employ a different use of the term "functional" properties when probing the functional knowledge of living and non-living things can also be found in standard batteries, such as the one proposed by Laiacona, Barbarotto, & Capitani (1993, 1997) to study perceptual and functional/associative knowledge in patients with category-specific disorders. This tendency to use a broader definition of the term "functional" knowledge when dealing with living things is probably due to the extreme difficulty that we meet when we try to define many instances of living things in terms of the function that the living thing has for humans. I have personally experienced this difficulty when constructing a naming-to-definition task and a sentence verification task in which the same (living and non-living) stimuli were described with reference once to visuoperceptual and once to functional–encyclopaedic information (Gainotti & Silveri, 1996). It seems clear, however, that it is not possible to compare the "functional" knowledge of living things and of non-living things if the term functional knowledge is used once with a narrow definition (specific function and actions requested to man) and once with a much broader (biological) definition. The significance of the results obtained with various test batteries with respect to the sensory/functional hypothesis must, therefore, be considered very cautiously.

ASSUMPTIONS MADE BY THEORETICAL MODELS CONCERNING NEUROANATOMY

Each of the theoretical models described above explicitly makes (or is consistent with) a different set of predictions about the extent and localisation of the brain pathology provoking category-specific defects for living and non-living things. For example, the sensory/functional hypothesis leads to a rather clear prediction: lesions provoking a category-specific semantic impairment for living things should encroach upon brain structures playing a critical role in processing and storing high level visual knowledge, whereas those provoking a selective deficit for non-living things should impinge upon brain areas involved in manipulation and physical use of objects. Less clear are the predictions made by the "domain-specific knowledge systems" hypothesis, although Caramazza and Shelton (1998) have explicitly claimed that: (i) dedicated neural circuits for domain-specific knowledge systems should not process a specific kind of information, but rather represent all types of perceptual and conceptual information relevant to that category of knowledge; and (ii) because of the "affective/emotional components associated with the flight and feeding responses to animals and plants" (Caramazza & Shelton, 1998), it is not unplausible that the assumed neural circuits for these biological categories involve the limbic system.

The "intercorrelations among semantic features" hypothesis makes different predictions, because this model assumes that the severity of brain damage, rather than its precise anatomical location, should play a major role in provoking a category-specific defect for living or non-living entities. Gonneman et al. (1997) argued that living things, which have many more interconnected features than non-living things in their semantic structure, should be more resistant to a mild diffuse damage of the semantic system. This hypothesis has been validated by a computer simulation study, which has shown that with a small degree of damage to the system there was a greater impairment of non-living things, but that with increasing damage, there was a dramatic decline of the living categories. Following the same line of thought, Moss et al. (1998) have commented on the frequent occurrence of HSE in patients with a category-specific impairment for living things and observed that "the brain damage caused by HSE is often extensive and it is difficult to identify which brain structures are crucially involved in the impairment for living things". If Gonneman et al. (1997) and Moss et al. (1998) are correct, there should be a large variability in the localisation of lesions provoking a category-specific semantic disorder both for living and for non-living things, because the size of lesions should be more important than their exact location.

RESULTS OF THE SURVEY OF THE NEUROANATOMICAL CORRELATES OF CATEGORY-SPECIFIC DISORDERS

My survey has taken into account all instances of category-specific disorders for living or non-living things that I could find in the neuropsychological literature where neuroanatomical data were available. I identified 47 patients who presented with a selective impairment for living beings and 10 who presented with a selective impairments for non-living things. Within the 47 patients showing a selective defect for biological entities, the cognitive impairment was considered to be at the semantic level in 38 patients, at the lexical output level in 8 subjects and at the purely visual level in 1 patient (see Appendix A). Within the 10 subjects with a selective impairment for non-living things, the defect was semantic in nature in 6 patients, lexical in 3 subjects and purely visual in 1 patient. The anatomoclinical correlates of category-specific disorders for living and non-living things arising at the semantic, lexical, and visual levels have been taken into account separately.

Category-specific disorders arising at
the semantic level

The contrast between category-specific semantic disorders for living and non-living things was striking at both the neuropathological and cognitive level of analysis. Aetiology of lesion, anatomical locus of lesion, and pattern of categorical impairment were, in fact, very different (and sometimes even opposite) in patients with a selective impairment for living and non-living categories.

From the aetiological point of view, lesions observed in patients with a category-specific semantic impairment for living things were mainly due to HSE, closed head trauma (CHT) and semantic dementia (these three diseases accounting respectively for 55%, 18%, and 14% of all patients forming this group), whereas only two subjects suffered from a cerebrovascular accident. On the contrary, all the patients with selective semantic disorder for non-living things were affected by large infarcts, in the territory of the left middle cerebral artery. One paradoxical observation was that the more frequent category-specific impairment for living things was usually observed in patients with unfrequent diseases, such as HSE or semantic dementia, and rarely observed in patients with cerebrovascular accidents. This is probably due to the typical distribution of lesions in these various diseases. Lesions are usually bilateral and mainly encroach upon the anterior parts of the temporal lobes in HSE (Esiri, 1982; Kapur et al., 1994), CHT (Adams, 1990), and semantic dementia (Hodges, Garrard, & Patterson 1998), whereas they are generally unilateral and rarely involve the anterior parts of the temporal lobes in cerebrovascular accidents. As a matter of fact, from the anatomical point of view, a more or less severe (and usually bilateral) involvement of the temporal lobe(s) was observed in almost all the patients showing a category-specific semantic impairment for living things (in 36/38 cases). Furthermore, a more detailed analysis of the lesion location within the temporal lobes (conducted in 20 patients with MRI or other high resolution neuroimaging technique) allows the conclusion that, in these patients, the lesions: (i) are usually bilateral, but asymmetrically distributed and often larger on the left side; (ii) selectively involve the anterior, mesial, and inferior parts of the temporal lobes (including the temporal pole, hippocampus and parahippocampal gyri, and the inferior temporal lobe) and generally spare the posterolateral temporal cortices; and (iii) systematically involve the inferior temporal lobe (ITL), which was more or less extensively, and more or less symmetrically, damaged in all patients considered in the survey.

In contrast, in patients with a category-specific semantic impairment for non-living things the lesions were always unilateral, involving the territory of the left middle cerebral artery, and in particular the frontoparietal areas of the dominant hemisphere. Schematic representations of the neuroanatomical correlates of category-specific semantic disorders for living and non-living things, based on data analiticaly reviewed by Gainotti (2000) are reported in Figures 14.1 and 14.2.

Finally, even the pattern of impaired and spared semantic categories was strikingly different in patients with a selective impairment for living and non-living things. In patients with a category-specific semantic impairment for living things both the "animals" and the "plants" categories were often disrupted in association with the (non-living) categories of "food" and "musical instruments", whereas the ("living") category of "body parts" was systematically spared. On the contrary, in patients with a category-specific semantic impairment for non-living things, both animals and plants were usually spared, again in association with the "food" category, whereas "body parts" were frequently impaired. A detailed review of the semantic categories impaired and spared in patients with a selective disorder for "living" or "non-living things" who have been submitted to a detailed categorical assessment can be found in Gainotti (2000), whereas a synthetic survey of this issue is reported in Table 14.1.

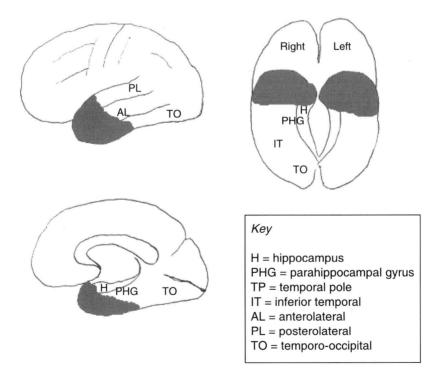

Figure 14.1. Schematic representation of the anatomical locus of lesion usually found in patients with a category-specific semantic impairment for living beings.

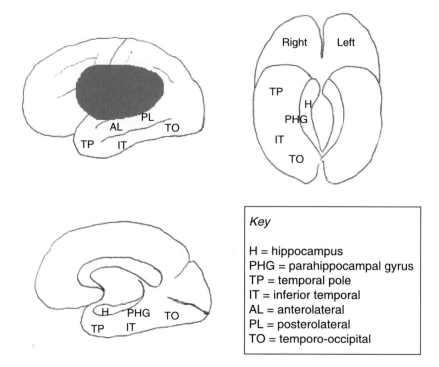

Figure 14.2. Schematic representation of the typical distribution of lesions in patients with a category-specific semantic impairment for non-living things.

TABLE 14.1

Categories impaired and spared in patients with a selective disorder for living and non-living things submitted to a detailed categorical assessment

Frequency of impairment in patients with a selective impairment for	Semantic categories					
	Animals	Vegetables	Food	Musical instruments	Body parts	Artefacts
Living things	19/19	16/18	7/11	8/13	0/14	0/19
(%)	100	90	63	61	0	0
Non-living things	0/7	0/6	1/4	–	5/7	9/9
(%)	0	0	25	–	71	100

These contrasting patterns of anatomoclinical and cognitive data can, in my opinion, be explained if we take into account the main functions of the anteromesial and inferior parts of the temporal lobes and of the fronto-parietal areas of the dominant hemisphere. The anteromedial temporolimbic structures and the inferior temporal lobe (ITL) could, indeed, constitute a cortical network, devised to process and integrate high-level visual–perceptual knowledge with other kinds of information. The ITL is, in fact, the main component of the "ventral stream" of extrastriate visual processing system, which plays a critical role in object recognition (Goodale, Milner, Jakobson, & Carey, 1991; Mishkin, Malamut, & Bachevalier, 1984; Unger-leider & Mishkin, 1982) According to Mishkin et al.(1984), its anterior parts (and in particular area TE) could store the structural description (or the visual templates) of objects. On the other hand, the entorhinal cortex (which is part of the telencephalic temporolimbic structures) receives convergent, integrated input from all the sensory modalities (Jones & Powell, 1970; Mesu-lam, Van Hoesen, Pandya, & Geschwind, 1977; Van Hoesen, 1982) and, through the perforant pathway, transmits all these integrated informations to the hippocampus long-term memory system (Hyman, Van Hoesen, Kromer, & Damasio, 1986). Finally, the temporal pole is considered by Damasio (1989, 1990) as a higher-order "convergence zone", that is, as the densely interconnected top of a cascade of cortical processors that binds together the different components of a concept's distributed representation. The inferior temporal lobe, temporolimbic structures and temporal pole could, therefore, be critically involved in processing, storing, and retrieving the representations of those semantic categories whose knowledge is mainly based upon sensory (and above all upon visual) attributes. It is worth noting that this definition applies not only to the biological categories of animals and plants, but also to the non-biological categories of food and of musical instruments (for a more thorough discussion of this issue, see Gainotti, 2000; Gainotti & Silveri, 1996). A very different set of functions is usually attributed to the dorso-lateral (and in particular to the frontoparietal) areas of the dominant hemisphere. These areas are, in fact, part of the "dorsal system" of visual processing, involved in spatial and action functions (Goodale et al., 1991) and play a very important role both in action planning and in high level somatosensory processing. The frontoparietal areas of the dominant hemi-sphere subserve somatosensory and motor schemata that could have critically contributed (through processes of concrete utilisation and of physical con-tact) to building the semantic representation of non-living things, just as the anteromesial and inferior parts of the temporal lobes provide the con-vergence of sensory (and above all of visual) attributes that form the essence of the semantic representations of living things. From this point of view, the joint impairment of the categories of man-made objects and body parts could be due to the fact that the sensorimotor mechanisms that critically contribute to the construction of the semantic representation of man-made objects are also crucially involved in building the representation of the category of body parts.

Category-specific disorders arising at the lexical level

The results of the neuroanatomical correlates of category-specific semantic disorders for living and non-living things described above have been largely confirmatory. In particular, they confirm the conclusions reached by Saffran and Schwartz (1994) and by Gainotti et al. (1995) in previous surveys of this subject. However, the results for the neuroanatomical correlates of category-specific disorders arising at the lexical level were more surprising. In the current review, we identified a small group of patients with a specific naming defect for living things and these patients showed a very consistent cluster of cognitive and anatomoclinical characteristics.

From the cognitive point of view, these subjects, namely patients TU (Farah & Wallace, 1992), KQU (Goldenberg, 1992), and SRB (Forde et al., 1997) showed a prevalent or selective impairment in naming members of the "plants" category. From the anatomoclinical standpoint, all of them suffered from cerebrovascular accidents located in the territory of the left posterior cerebral artery and encroaching upon the inferomedial and temporo-occipital areas of the left hemisphere (Figure 14.3).

One interpretation of these findings, consistent with the more general model that I have proposed to explain the anatomical correlates of category-specific semantic disorders for living things, is that: (i) in these patients the semantic representation of the "plants" category is disconnected from the mechanisms of lexical output; and (ii) the semantic representation of "plants" might be preferentially stored in rather "pure" visual areas because this category relies even more heavily on purely visual attributes (e.g. colour) than other biological categories. This admittedly speculative hypothesis is consistent with both the anatomoclinical data and cognitive models. From the anatomoclinical point of view, the key mechanism of this posterior disconnection syndrome consists in an inability to connect purely visual attributes, such as colours, with the left hemisphere language areas. It is not unplausible that the same mechanism could also apply to the connections between semantic representations mainly based upon visual properties and lexical output structures. From the cognitive point of view, Humphreys and co-workers (Forde et al., 1997; Price & Humphreys, 1989; Sheridan & Humphreys, 1993) have repeatedly proposed that a loss of stored knowledge about the colour of objects might precipitate deficit in naming categories such as fruit and flowers, whose semantic representation relies heavily upon colour information. This hypothesis is also consistent with results of a computa-

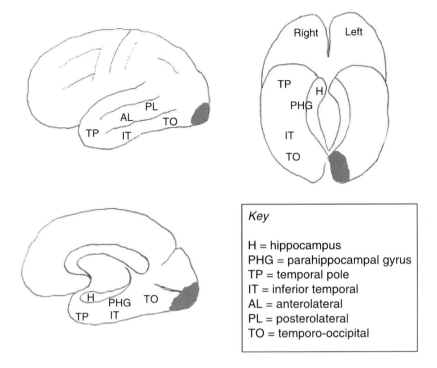

Figure 14.3. Schematic representation of the anatomical locus of lesion found in patients TU (Farah & Wallace, 1992), KQU (Goldenberg, 1992), and SRB (Forde et al., 1997), who showed a selective impairment in naming members of the "plant" category.

tional study recently performed by Small et al. (1995). These authors investigated the significance of some semantic features in performing object identification and demonstrated the relative importance of "colour" features in the identification of fruits and vegetables compared to other kinds of objects.

However, the anatomical correlates of lexical output disorders affecting the artefacts category are less easy to explain, and only three patients showing this pattern of impairment have been identified in our survey. They are patients CG (Silveri et al., 1997), GP (Cappa et al., 1998),and IW (Lambon - Ralph et al., 1998). All three showed a lesion circumscribed to the left temporal lobe, but the intralobar localisation was very variable, concerning the dorsolateral temporoparietal areas in CG, the temporal pole in GP, and the anteroinferior parts of the left temporal lobe in IW. The mild level of discrepancy between living and non-living categories and the inconsistency of the anatomoclinical correlates suggest great caution in interpreting the significance of these findings.

Category-specific disorders arising at the visual level

Only two patients in our review showed a category-specific impairment for living or non-living things restricted to the visual modality. One of them, patient PSD, showed a selective impairment in visual recognition of living categories (Damasio, 1990). In contrast, the other patient (DRS) presented with a category-specific impairment for non-living things (Warrington & McCarthy, 1994). Anatomically, PSD showed bilateral temporo-occipital lesions, mainly involving the inferomesial parts of these lobes, whereas DRS presented with bilateral but asymmetric infarcts in the right parietal lobe and in the left inferior temporo-occipital region. The anatomical data for patient PSD are consistent with the lesion location of another patient (DRB) who had a similar visual recognition disorder selectively affecting living entities (Damasio, 1990) and with the results of a group study recently reported by Tranel, Damasio, and Damasio (1997). These authors have shown that a selective impairment for animals (observed in 19 patients) was associated with lesions involving the mesial occipital or temporo-occipital regions of both the right and the left hemisphere. In contrast, a selective impairment for tools (observed in five patients) was associated with maximal lesion overlap in the dorsolateral left temporoparieto-occipital junction areas. These data are consistent with an exclusive involvement of the ventral stream of visual processing in tasks concerning living categories and a greater involvement of the dorsal stream in those concerning man-made objects.

COMPARISON BETWEEN NEUROPATHOLOGICAL DATA AND FUNCTIONAL NEUROIMAGING RESEARCH

Methodological reasons suggest that great caution should be exerted in drawing a comparison between the anatomical areas damaged in patients with category-specific disorders and those activated in normal subjects during cognitive tasks using specific categories of stimuli. There are often differences in the experimental paradigm, quality of stimuli, and the methods used for data acquisition and analysis, which can lead to significant inconsistencies between different functional imaging studies (see Chapter 15). In addition, only Damasio et al. (1996) have tried to distinguish the areas involved in lexical retrieval from those subserving semantic knowledge in a functional imaging study, and even this attempt has been criticised on methodological grounds (Caramazza & Shelton, 1998).

All these caveats made, some important differences have been observed between the brain areas activated by living things and non-living things in imaging studies and these differences are generally consistent with the neuropathological data. Several authors have, in fact, shown that, with the living things, the brain activation is often bilateral and involves either the inferior parts (Perani et al., 1995) or the anterior portions (Moore & Price, 1999; Mummery et al., 1996;) of the temporal lobes. For non-living things, the brain activation is usually limited to the left hemisphere, involving parts of its lateral convexity, such as the dorsolateral or inferior frontal regions (Martin et al., 1996; Perani et al., 1995, 1999) or the posterior middle portions of the temporal lobe (Damasio et al., 1996; Moore & Price, 1999; Mummery et al., 1998; Perani et al., 1999). An important parallel therefore exists between results of these activation studies and results of our survey of the neuroanatomical correlates of category-specific disorders arising at the semantic level. Both sets of data suggest a bilateral involvement of the inferior and anteromedial parts of the temporal lobes in the semantic representation of living things and a major role of the dorsolateral cortices of the left hemisphere in the semantic representation of man-made artefacts.

IMPLICATIONS OF THE ANATOMICAL DATA WITH RESPECT TO THEORETICAL MODELS

The results of this survey clearly show that the brain lesions provoking category-specific defects for living and non-living things have precise anatomical locations. They are, therefore, at variance with the assumptions made by the "intercorrelations among semantic features hypothesis", which predicted that the severity of brain damage, rather than its exact location, should play the major role in provoking a category-specific defect for living and non-living things. These results also show that the brain areas subserving these different semantic representations are not randomly located at the cortical level, but are part of cortical networks processing just those types of information that play a critical role in the acquisition and organisation of the disrupted semantic category. These findings are inconsistent with the predictions made by the "domain-specific knowledge systems" hypothesis. This hypothesis was, in fact, neutral concerning the anatomical structures subserving the various category-specific knowledge systems and assumed a link only between the limbic system and cortical areas storing the semantic representation of animals and plants. It predicted that these brain structures, far from being linked with the processing of a specific kind of information, should represent all types of perceptual and conceptual information relevant to that category of knowledge.

Several aspects of our results are consistent with the assumptions made by the "sensory/functional" hypothesis, and in particular with those made by the distributed models of semantic representation proposed by Allport (1985), Shallice (1988), and Damasio (1990). The first finding of this survey consistent with the assumptions of these models is the selective bilateral damage of the inferior and anteromesial parts of the temporal lobes in patients with category-specific semantic impairments for living things. The second is the preferential involvement of the inferomesial parts of the temporo-occipital cortices in category-specific disorders arising at the visual and at the lexical (rather than at the semantic) level. The third finding is the preferential encroachement of the brain lesions upon the dorsolateral areas of the left hemisphere in patients with a category-specific semantic impairment for man-made objects.

The neuroanatomical correlates of disorders selectively affecting living things are quite consistent with the assumptions made by the "sensory/functional" hypothesis, as both the inferomesial parts of the occipito-temporal cortices and the anterior structures of the temporal lobe are parts of the ventral stream of visual processing. Furthermore, the observation that a disruption of the upper (occipitotemporal) parts of this stream results in a modality specific (visual or lexical) category-specific disorder, whereas a (bilateral) lesion of the anterior temporal regions is usually required to provoke a properly semantic disorder for living entities is also consistent with the present views about the intrinsic organisation of the ventral stream of visual processing. Results of experimental studies in animals (Iwai, 1985; Tanaka, Fukada, Fukumoto, & Saito, 1987) and of functional brain imaging in humans (Gauthier et al., 1997; Moore & Price, 1999; Vandenberghe et al., 1996) have, in fact, consistently shown that the inferior occipitotemporal cortices subserve complex visuoperceptual activities, whereas the anterior parts of the temporal lobes are mainly involved in mnesic functions and in accessing semantic knowledge. These facts had led Srinivas, Breeding, Coslett, and Saffran (1997) to suggest that lesions limited to the anterior parts of the temporal lobe should provoke category-specific semantic deficits without impairment of the structural description, whereas lesions encroaching on the posterior parts of the inferotemporal cortex should impair the structural description but spare semantic knowledge of living things. Results of our survey are consistent with these suggestions. Equally consistent with the basic assumptions of the sensory/functional hypothesis is the preferential encroachment of the brain lesions upon the dorsolateral areas of the left hemisphere in patients showing a category-specific semantic disorder for non-living things. Indeed, it is possible that the dorso-lateral areas of the left hemisphere process those somatosensory (functional) properties that contribute to the development of the semantic representation of man-made objects, just as inferotemporal cortices process the visuoperceptual properties crucially involved in the semantic representation of living things.

In recent years, some functional neuroimaging studies have shown that the dorsolateral areas of the left hemisphere (and in particular the frontal region) are strongly activated not only by tasks requiring identification and naming of man-made tools (Perani et al., 1995; Martin et al., 1996), but also by other tasks concerned with actions, such as the generation of action words (Martin et al., 1996) or the observation of meaningful actions (Decety et al., 1997). These results provide empirical support for the idea that "the categories of man-made objects may be chiefly subserved by the fronto-parietal regions of the left hemisphere, because knowledge of these categories is at least in part based on handling, manual use or, in any case, physical contact and concrete utilization of objects" (Gainotti et al., 1995). The frequent observation of disorders simultaneously affecting artefacts and body parts could be consistent with this interpretation, because the action schemata and the sensorimotor mechanisms that contribute to the knowledge of the body parts are also in part involved in the construction of the semantic representation of the artefacts category.

REFERENCES

Adams, J.H. (1990). Brain damage in fatal non-missile head injury in man. In P.J. Vinken, G.W. Bruyn & H.L. Klawans (Eds.), *Handbook of Clinical Neurology* (Vol. 13, (57) pp. 43–63). North Holland: Elsevier.

Allport, D.A. (1985). Distributed memory, modular systems and dysphasia. In S.K. Newman & R. Epstein (Eds.), *Current Perspectives in Dysphasia* (pp. 32–60). Edinburgh: Churchill Livingstone.

Arguin, M., Bub D., & Dudeck G. (1996). Shape integration for visual object recognition and its implication in category-specific visual agnosia. *Visual Cognition, 3*, 221–275.

Barbarotto, R., Capitani E., Spinnler H., Trivelli C. (1995). Slowly progressive semantic impairment with category specificy. *Neurocase, 1*, 107–119.

Barbarotto, R., Capitani E., & Laiacona M. (1996). Naming deficit in herpes-simplex encephalitis. *Acta Neurologica Scandinavica, 93*, 272–280.

Basso, A., Capitani E., & Laiacona M. (1988). Progressive language impairment without dementia: A case with isolated category specific semantic defect. *Journal of Neurology, Neurosurgery and Psychiatry, 51*, 1201–1207.

Behrman, M., & Lieberthal T. (1989). Category-specific treatment of a lexical-semantic deficit: A single case study of global aphasia. *The British Journal of Disorders of Communication, 24*, 281–299.

Breedin, S.D., Saffran E.M. & Coslett H.B. (1994). Reversal of concreteness effect in a patient with semantic dementia. *Cognitive Neuropsychology, 11(6)*, 617–660.

Cappa, S.F., Frugoni M., Pasquali P., Perani D., & Zorat F. (1998). Category-specific naming impairment for artefacts: A new case. *Neurocase, 4*, 391–397.

Caramazza, A., & Shelton J.R. (1998). Domain-specific knowledge systems in the brain: the animate-inanimate distinction. *Journal of Cognitive Neuroscience, 10*, 1–34.

Cardebat, D., Demonet J.F., Celsis P., & Puel M. (1996). Living/non-living dissociation in a case of semantic dementia: A SPECT activation study. *Neuropsychologia, 34*, 1175–1179.

Damasio, A.R. (1989). Time-locked multiregional retroactivation: A systems-level proposal for the neural substrates of recall and recognition. *Cognition, 33*, 25–62.

Damasio, A.R. (1990). Category-related recognition defects as a clue to the neural substrates of knowledge. *Trends in Neuroscience, 13*, 95–98.

Damasio, A.R., Damasio H., & Tranel D. (1990a). Impairments of visual recognition as clues to the processes of memory. In G. Edelman, W.A. Gall, & W.M. Cowan (Eds.). *Signal and sense. Local and global order in perceptual maps* (pp. 451–473). New York, NY: Wiley.

Damasio, A.R., Damasio H., Tranel D., & Brandt J.P. (1990b). Neural regionalisation of knowledge access: Preliminary evidence. *Cold Spring Harbor Symposia on Quantitative Biology 55* (pp. 1039–1047). Cold Spring Harbor, NY: Cold Spring Laboratory Press.

Damasio, H., Grabowski T.J., Tranel D., Hitchwa RD., & Damasio AR. (1996). A neural basis for lexical retrieval (see comments) (published erratum appears in Nature; 381:810). *Nature, 380*, 499–505. Comment in: *Nature, 380*, 485–48.

Decety, J., Grezes J., Costes N., Perani D., Jeannerod M., Procyk E., et al. (1997). Brain activity during observation of actions. Influence of action content and subject's strategy. *Brain, 120*, 1763–1777.

De Haan, E.H.F., Young A.W., & Newcombe F. (1992). Neuropsychological impairment of face recognition units. *The Quarterly Journal of Experimental Psychology, 44A*, 141–175.

De Renzi, E., & Lucchelli F. (1994). Are semantic systems seperately represented in the brain? The case of living category impairment. *Cortex, 30*, 3–25.

Esiri, M.M. (1982). Herpes simplex encephalitis: An immunohistological study of the distribution of viral antigen within the brain. *Journal of Neurological Science; 54*, 209–226.

Etcoff, N.L., Freeman R., & Cave K.R. (1991). Can we lose memory of faces? Content specificity and awareness in a prosopagnosic. *Journal of Cognitive Neuroscience, 3*, 25–41.

Farah, M.J., Hammond K.M., Mehta Z., & Radcliff G. (1989). Category-specificity and modality-specificity in semantic memory. *Neuropsychologia, 27*, 193–200.

Farah, M.J., McMullen P.A., & Meyer M.M. (1991). Can recognition of living things be selectively impaired? *Neuropsychology, 29*, 185–193.

Farah, M.J., & Wallace M.A. (1992). Semantically-bounded anomia: implications for the neural implementation of naming. *Neuropsychologia, 30*, 609–621.

Fery, P. (1997). Catégories et modalités en memoire sémantique: Une approche neuropsychologique. Unpublished doctoral thesis. Université Libre de Bruxelles. Bruxelles: Belgium.

Forde, E.M.E., Francis D., Riddoch M.J., Rumiati R.I., & Humphreys G.W. (1997). On the links between visual knowledge and naming: A single case study of a patient with a category-specific impairment for living things. *Cognitive Neuropsychology, 14*, 403–458.

Forde, E.M.E. & Humphreys, G.W. (1999). Category-specific recognition impairments: A review of important case studies and influential theories. *Aphasiology, 13(3)*, 169–193.

Funnell, E., & Sheridan J. (1992). Categories of knowledge: Unfamiliar aspects of living and nonliving things. *Cognitive Neuropsychology, 9*, 135–153.

Gaffan, D., & Heywood CA. (1993). A spurious category-specific visual agnosia for living things in normal human and nonhuman primates. *Journal of Cognitive Neuroscience, 5(1)*, 118–128.

Gainotti, G. (2000). What the locus of brain lesion says about the nature of the cognitive defect in category-specific disorders: A review. *Cortex, 36*, 539–559.

Gainotti, G., Silveri M.C. (1996). Cognitive and anatomical locus of lesion in a patient with a category-specific semantic impairment for living beings. *Cognitive Neuropsychology, 13*, 357–389.

Gainotti, G., Silveri M.C., Daniele A., & Giustolisi L. (1995). Neuroanatomical correlates of category-specific semantic disorders: a critical survey. *Memory, 3*, 247–264.

Gauthier, I., Anderson A.W., Tarr M.J., Skudlarski P., & Gore JC. (1997). Levels of categorization in visual recognition studied using functional magnetic resonance imaging. *Current Biology, 7*, 645–651.

Goldenberg, G. (1992). Loss of visual imagery and loss of visual knowledge. A case study. *Neuropsychologia, 12*, 1081–1099.

Gonnerman, L.M., Anderson E.S., Devlin J.T., Kempler D., & Seidenberg M.S. (1997). Double dissociation of semantic categories in Alzheimer's disease. *Brain and Language, 57*, 254–279.

Goodale, M.A., Milner A.D., Jakobson L.S., Carey D.P. (1991). A neurological dissociation between perceiving objects and grasping them. *Nature, 349*, 154–156.

Hart, J., Berndt R.S., Caramazza A. (1985). Category-specific naming deficit following cerebral infarction. *Nature, 316*, 439–440.

Hart, J. Jr, & Gordon B. (1992). Neural subsystem for object knowledge. *Nature, 359*, 60–64.

Hillis, A.E., & Caramazza A. (1991). Category-specific naming and comprehension impairment: a double dissociation. *Brain, 114*, 2081–2094.

Hillis, A.E., Rapp B., Romani C., & Caramazza A. (1990). Selective impairment of semantic in lexical processing. *Cognitive Neuropsychology, 7*, 191–243.

Hodges, J.R., Garrard P., & Patterson K. (1998); Semantic dementia. In A. Kertesz, & D.G., and Munoz, (Eds.) *Pick's disease and Pick complex*. New York: Wiley–Liss.

Humphreys, G.W., Riddoch M.J., & Price C.J. (1997). Top-down processes in object identification: evidence from experimental psychology, neuropsychology and functional anatomy. *Proceedings of the Royal Society, Series B, 352*, 1275–1282.

Humphreys, G.W., Riddoch M.J., & Quinlan P.T. (1988). Cascade processes in picture identification. *Cognitive Neuropsychology, 5*, 67–104.

Hyman, B.T., Van Hoesen G.W., Kromer L.J., & Damasio A. (1986). Perforant pathway changes and the memory impairment in Alzheimer's disease. *Annals of Neurology, 20*, 472–481.

Iwai, E. (1985). Neurophysiological basis of pattern vision in macaque monkey. *Vision Research, 25*, 425–439.

Jones, E.G., & Powell T.P.S. (1970). An experimental study of converging sensory pathways within the cerebral cortex of the monkey. *Brain, 93*, 793–820.

Kapur, N., Barker S., Burrows E.H., Ellison D., Brice J., Illis L.S., Scholey K., Colbourn C., Wilson B., & Loates M. (1994). Herpes-simplex encephalitis: long-term magnetic-resonance-imaging and neuropsychological profile. *Journal of Neurology, Neurosurgery and Psychiatry, 57*, 1334–1342.

Kolinsky, R., Fery P., Messina D., Evink S., Perez I., & Morais J. (submitted). The fur of the crocodile and the mooing sheep: a longitudinal study of a patient with a category-specific impairment for biological things.

Laiacona, M., Barbarotto R., & Capitani E. (1993). Perceptual and associative knowledge in category specific impairment of semantic memory: A study of two cases. *Cortex, 29*, 727–740.

Laiacona, M., Capitani E., & Barbarotto R. (1997). Semantic category dissociations: a longitudinal study of two cases. *Cortex, 33*, 441–61.

Lambon Ralph, M.A., Howard D., Nightingale G., & Ellis A.W. (1998). Are living and non-living category-specific deficits causally linked to impaired perceptual or associative knowledge ? Evidence from a category-specific double dissociation. *Neurocase, 4, 311–338.*

Laws, K.R., Evans J.J., Hodges J.R., & McCarthy R. (1995). Naming without knowing and appearance without associations: Evidence for constructive processes in semantic memory ? *Memory, 3*, 409–433.

McCarthy, R.A., & Warrington E.K. (1988). Evidence for modality-specific meaning systems in the brain. *Nature, 334*, 428–430.

Martin, A., Wiggs C.L., Ungerleider L.G., & Haxby J.V. (1996). Neural correlates of category-specific knowledge. *Nature, 379*, 649–652.

Mesulam M.M.G., Van Hoesen G.W., Pandya D.N., & Geschwind N. (1977). Limbic and sensory connections of the IPL in the rhesus monkey. *Brain Research*, 136, 393–414.

Mishkin M., Malamut B., & Bachevalier J. (1984). Memories and habits: Two neural systems. In G. Lynch, J.L. McGaugh, & N.M. Weinberger, (Eds.), *Neurobiology of Learning and Memory* (pp. 65–77). New York: The Guilford Press.

Moore, C.J., & Price C.J. (1999). A functional neuroimaging study of the variables that generate category-specific object processing differences. *Brain, 122*, 943–962.

Moss, H.E., Tyler L.K., Durrant-Peatfield M., & Bunn E.M. (1998). Two eyes of a see-through: Impaired and intact semantic knowledge in a case of selective deficit for living things. *Neurocase, 4*, 291–310.

Moss, H.E., Tyler L.K., & Jennings F. (1997). When leopards lose their spots: knowledge of visual properties in category-specific deficits for living things. *Cognitive Neuropsychology, 14*, 901–950.

Mummery, C.J., Patterson K., Hodges J.R., & Price C.J. (1998). Functional neuroanatomy of the semantic system: divisible by what? *Journal of Cognitive Neuroscience, 10*, 766–777.

Mummery, C.J., Patterson K., Hodges J.R., & Wise R.J. (1996). Generating 'tiger' as an animal name or a word beginning with T: Differences in brain activation (published erratum appears in *Proc. R. Soc. Lond. B. Biol. Sci. 1996, 263*, 1755–1756). *Proceedings of the Royal Society of London: Series B, Biological Science, 263*, 989–995.

Perani, D., Cappa S.F., Bettinardi V., Bressi S., Gorno Tempini M., & Matarrese M. (1995). Different neural systems for the recognition of animals and man-made tools. *Neuroreport, 6*, 1637–1641.

Perani, D., Schnur T., Tettamanti M., Gorno-Tempini M., Cappa S.F., & Fazio F. (1999). Word and picture matching: A PET study of semantic category effects. *Neuropsychologia, 37*, 293–306.

Pietrini, V., Nertempi P., Vaglia A., Revello M., Pinna V., & Ferro-Milone F. (1988). Recovery from herpes-simplex encephalitis-selective impairment of specific semantic categories with neuroradiological correlation. *Journal of Neurology, Neurosurgery and Psychiatry, 51*, 1284–1293.

Price, C.J., & Humphreys G.W. (1989). The effects of surface detail on object categorisation and naming. *Quarterly Journal of Experimental Psychology, 41A*, 797–828.

Riddoch, M.J., & Humphreys G.W. (1987). Visual object processing in optic aphasia: A case study of semantic access agnosia. *Cognitive Neuropsychology, 4*, 131–185.

Sacchett, C., & Humphreys G.W. (1992). Calling a squirrel a squirrel but a canoe a wigwam: a category-specific deficit for artefactual objects and body parts. *Cognitive Neuropsychology, 9*, 73–86.

Saffran, E.M., & Schwartz M.F. (1994). Of cabbages and things: Semantic memory from a neuropsychological perspective – A tutorial review. *Attention and Performance, 25*, 507–536.

Samson, D., De Wilde V., & Pillon A. (1998). Impaired knowledge of visual and nonvisual attributes in a patient with a naming impairment for living entities: A case of a true category-specific deficit. *Neurocase, 4*, 273–290.

Sartori, G., & Job R. (1988). The oyster with four legs: A neuropsychological study on the interaction of visual and semantic information. *Cognitive Neuropsychology, 5*, 105–132.

Sartori, G., Miozzo M., & Job R. (1994). Rehabilitation of semantic memory impairments. In E.J. Riddoch, G.W. Humphreys (Eds.), *Cognitive neuropsychology and cognitive rehabilitation* (pp. 103–124). Hove, UK: Lawrence Erlbaum Associates Ltd.

Shallice, T. (1988). *From neuropsychology to mental structure.* Cambridge: Cambridge University Press.

Sheridan, J., & Humphreys G.W. (1993). A verbal–semantic category-specific recognition impairment. *Cognitive Neuropsychology, 10*, 143–184.

Silveri, M.C., Gainotti G., Perani D., Cappelletti J.Y., Carbone G., & Fazio F. (1997). Naming deficit for non-living items: Neuropsychological and PET study. *Neuropsychologia, 35*, 359–367.

Sirigu, A., Duhamel J.R., & Poncet M. (1991). The role of sensorimotor experience in object recognition. A case of multimodal agnosia. *Brain, 114*, 2555–2573.

Small, S.L., Hart J., Nguyen T., & Gordon B. (1995). Distributed representations of semantic knowledge in the brain. *Brain, 118*, 441–453.

Spitzer, M., Kwong K.K., Kebnnedy W., Rosen B.R., & Belliveau J.W. (1995). Category-specific brain activation in fMRI during picture naming. *Neuroreport, 6*, 2109–2112.

Stewart, F., Parkin A.J., & Hunkin N.M. (1992). Naming impairments following recovery from herpes simplex encephalitisi: Category-specific? *Quarterly Journal of Experimental Psychology Human Experimental Psychology, 44a*, 261–284.

Swales, M., & Johnson R. (1992). Patients with semantic memory loss: Can they relearn lost concepts? *Neuropsychological Rehabilitation, 2*, 295–305.

Tanaka, K., Fukada Y., Fukumoto M., & Saito H. (1987). The inferior temporal cortex of the macaque monkey. I: Regional differences in the response properties of cells. *Society of Neuroscience Abstracts, 13*, 627.

Thompson-Schill, S.L., Aguirre G.K., D'Esposito M., & Farah M.G. (1999). A neural basis for category and modality specificity of semantic knowledge. *Neuropsychologia, 37*, 671–676.

Tranel, D., Damasio H., & Damasio A. (1997). A neural basis for the retrieval of conceptual knowledge. *Neuropsychologia, 35*, 1319–1327.

Ungerleider, L.G., & Mishkin M. (1982). Two cortical visual system. In D.J. Ingle, M.A. Goodale, & R.J.W. Mansfield (Eds.), *Analysis of visual behavior*. Cambridge, MA: MIT Press.

Vandenberghe, R., Price C., Wise R., Josephs O., & Frackowiak R.S. (1996). Functional anatomy of a common semantic system for words and picture (see comments). *Nature, 383*, 254–256. Comment in: *Nature, 383*, 216–217.

Van Hoesen, G.W. (1982). The primate parahippocampal gyrus: New insights regarding its cortical connections. *Trends in Neuroscience, 5*, 345–350.

Warrington, E.K., & McCarthy R.A. (1987). Categories of knowledge: Further fractionations and an attempted integration. *Brain, 100*, 1273–1296.

Warrington, E.K., & McCarthy R.A. (1994). Multiple meaning systems in the brain: A case for visual semantics. *Neuropsychologia, 32*, 1465–1473.

Warrington, E.K., & Shallice T. (1984). Category-specific semantic impairment. *Brain, 107*, 829–854.

Wilson, B.A., Baddeley A.D., & Kapur N. (1995). Dense amnesia in a professional musician following herpes simplex virus encephalitis. *Journal of Clinical and Experimental Neuropsychology, 17*, 668–681.

No.	Patient	Author	Aetiology	Anatomical locus of lesion. Side and lobe(s) involved

Living things

Semantic problems (n = 38)

No.	Patient	Author	Aetiology	Anatomical locus of lesion. Side and lobe(s) involved
1	ELM	Arguin et al., 1996	CVA (embolic)	Bilateral temporal (> Right)
2	MF	Barbarotto et al., 1995	Semantic dementia	Bilateral temporal (> Right)
3	FA	Barbarotto et al., 1996	HSE	Left temporal lobe (+ Right frontal)
4	FI	Barbarotto et al., 1996	HSE	Left temporal lobe (+ Right periventricular)
5	NV	Basso et al., 1988	Semantic dementia	Left temporal (+ Left caudate)
6	DM	Breedin et al., 1994	Semantic dementia	Left temporal
7	EW	Caramazza & Shelton, 1998	CVA	Left frontoparietal
8	GC	Cardebat et al., 1996	Semantic dementia	Left temporal
9	Boswell	Damasio et al., 1990a	HSE	Bilateral temporal
10	Felicia	De Renzi & Lucchelli, 1994	HSE	Bilateral temporal (> Left)
11	LH	Farah et al., 1989	Head trauma	Bilateral temporo-occipital (+ Right frontal)
12	MB	Farah et al., 1991	Head trauma	Left temporal
13	VV	Fery, 1997	Cardiac arrest	Right frontal
14	SL	Funnell & Sheridan, 1992	Head trauma	Right temporal (lobectomy)
15	LE	Gainotti & Silveri, 1996	HSE	Bilateral temporal (> Left)
16	PS	Hillis & Caramazza, 1991	Head trauma	Left temporal (+ small right temporal and frontal)
17	ER	Kolinsky et al., submitted	HSE	Temporal bilateral
18	FM	Laiacona et al., 1993	Head trauma	Left temporoparietal + frontal bilateral
19	GR	Laiacona et al., 1993	Head trauma	Left frontal and temporal
20	LF	Laiacona et al., 1993	HSE	Left temporal
21	EA	Laiacona et al., 1993	HSE	Left temporal
22	DB	Lambon Ralph et al., 1998	Alzheimer's disease	Bilateral temporal
23	SE	Laws et al., 1995; Moss et al., 1997	HSE	Bilateral temporal (> Right)
24	TOB	McCarthy & Warrington, 1988	Semantic dementia	Left temporal
25	RC	Moss et al., 1998	HSE	Bilateral temporal (> Left)

APPENDIX—*contd*

No.	Patient	Author	Aetiology	Anatomical locus of lesion. Side and lobe(s) involved
26	RM	Pietrini et al., 1988	HSE	Left temporal + left frontobasal
27	JV	Pietrini et al., 1988	HSE	Left temporal + left frontobasal
28	Jennifer	Samson et al., 1998	Head trauma	Left posterior + left frontal
29	Michelangelo	Sartori & Job, 1988	HSE	Bilateral temporal
30	Giulietta	Sartori et al., 1994	HSE	Temporal bilateral
31	SB	Sheridan & Humphreys, 1993	HSE	Left temporal
32	FB	Sirigu et al., 1991	HSE	Bilateral temporal
33	JH	Swales & Johnson, 1992	HSE	Left temporal
34	KB	Warrington & Shallice, 1984	HSE	Bilateral temporal (> Left)
35	JBR	Warrington & Shallice, 1984	HSE	Bilateral temporal
36	SBY	Warrington & Shallice, 1984	HSE	Bilateral temporal (> Left)
37	ING	Warrington & Shallice, 1984	HSE	Bilateral temporal + diffuse atrophy
38	CW	Wilson et al., 1995	HSE	Bilateral temporal (> Left)

Lexical problems (*n* = 8)

No.	Patient	Author	Aetiology	Anatomical locus of lesion. Side and lobe(s) involved
1	AN	Damasio, 1990; Damasio et al., 1990b	NR	Left temporal
2	TU	Farah & Wallace, 1992	CVA (AVM)	Left occipital
3	SRB	Forde et al., 1997; Humphreys et al., 1997	CVA (AVM)	Left temporo-occipital (+ Right thalamic)
4	KQU	Goldenberg et al., 1992	CVA	Left temporo-occipital (+ Right frontal)
5	NR	DeHaan et al., 1992	Head trauma	Left temporoparietal (+ Right parietal)
6	MD	Hart et al., 1985	CVA	Left frontal and basal ganglia
7	KR	Hart & Gordon, 1992	Paraneoplastic syndrome	Bilateral temporal
8	DM	Humphreys et al., 1997	CVA (AVM)	Left temporo-occipital

Visual problems (*n* = 1)

No.	Patient	Author	Aetiology	Anatomical locus of lesion. Side and lobe(s) involved
1	PSD	Damasio, 1990; Damasio et al., 1990b	NR (CVA?)	Bilateral temporo-occipital

425

Non-living things

Semantic problems (*n* = 6)

1	VER	Warrington & McCarthy, 1983	CVA	Left frontotemporoparietal (Global aphasia)
2	YOT	Warrington & McCarthy, 1987	CVA	Left frontotemporoparietal (Global aphasia)
3	CH	Behrmann & Lieberthal, 1989	CVA	Left frontotemporoparietal (Global aphasia)
4	KE	Hillis et al., 1990	CVA	Left frontoparietal (Broca's aphasia)
5	JJ	Hillis & Caramazza, 1991	CVA	Left temporal and basal ganglia (Wernicke's aphasia)
6	CW	Sacchett & Humphreys, 1992	CVA	Left frontoparietal (Broca's aphasia)

Lexical problems (*n* = 3)

1	CG	Silveri et al., 1997	Semantic dementia	Left temporoparietal
2	GP	Cappa et al., 1998	Haematoma	Left temporal (Polectomy)
3	IW	Lambon Ralph et al., 1998	Semantic dementia	Atrophy of the left temporal lobe

Visual problems (*n* = 1)

1	DRS	Warrington & McCarthy, 1994	CVA	Right parietal + left temporal-occipital

Legend: AVM, arterovenous malformation; NR, not reported; CVA, cerebrovascular accident; HSE, herpes simplex encephalitis.

CHAPTER 15

Functional imaging studies of category specificity

Cathy J. Price and Karl J. Friston
Wellcome Department of Cognitive Neurology, London, UK

INTRODUCTION

Category-specific deficits are intriguing to a wide range of neuroscientists because they illustrate the high degree of cognitive and neuronal specialisation in the human brain. This chapter considers how functional neuroimaging might contribute to understanding the nature of this specialisation and how category specific deficits arise. The first and second sections describe the potential ways that neuroimaging can be used to assess, respectively, the underlying neuronal systems and cognitive models of category specificity. The third section reviews the current functional neuroimaging literature and its implications for cognitive models. Finally, the fourth section discusses future directions for addressing category specificity issues with neuroimaging.

REVEALING THE UNDERLYING NEURONAL SYSTEMS

Double dissociations in category-specific deficits suggest that different categories of items rely on anatomically dissociable neuronal systems that can be selectively damaged following brain injury. One way to identify the different anatomical systems is to link the site of brain damage to the lost functions. For instance, damage to the anterior temporal lobes has been associated with deficits identifying natural kinds of objects and left frontoparietal damage has been associated with deficits identifying man-made objects (for a review

427

see Gainotti, Silveri, Daniele, & Giustolisi, 1995). However, the limitations of this approach are well recognised. For instance, pathological (as opposed to experimental) lesions seldom conform to functionally homogenous neuro-anatomical systems and neuropsychological profiles tend to be complicated, involving more than one cognitive deficit. The full extent of the cognitive deficit might also be obscured by compensatory strategies adopted by the patient to overcome the deficits (cognitive reorganisation) or compensatory changes in functional anatomy (neuronal reorganisation). Another limitation, which is critical to the arguments presented in this chapter, is that most cognitive functions involve the integration of activity in more than one brain area and the different components can be distributed throughout the brain. Damage to one region can disrupt processing in distant undamaged areas that would not be revealed by structural indices of lesions (from the conventional use of computerised tomography [CT] and magnetic resonance imaging [MRI] scanners). It is therefore impossible for the lesion deficit approach to distinguish between loss of a cognitive function due to lesioning of one area or disconnection from an undamaged area. In short, one cannot say that the damaged region was either sufficient for, or uniquely identifiable with, the lost function. All that can be concluded, from a lesion deficit study, is that the neuronal systems intrinsic to the lesioned area, or the connections passing through that area, were necessary for the lost function. This limitation was recognised by the early cognitive neurologists who postulated that cognitive deficits either arose from damage to specialised areas or to the connections between these areas (Golz, 1881; Lichtheim, 1885; Wernicke, 1874).

Functional imaging techniques offer several fundamental advantages over the lesion deficit model. In addition to measuring brain activity non-invasively, *in vivo*, in subjects who have normal psychological and physiological responses, functional imaging can identify the system of distributed cortical areas that sustain a particular sensory, motor, or cognitive task. Unlike the lesion-deficit model, it is not limited to the region of the brain that has been damaged. Furthermore, functional imaging can evaluate two different types of functional specialisation. The most commonly adopted approach is referred to as "functional segregation" when different cortical regions are associated with different cognitive processes in a modular or segregated fashion (e.g. phonological retreival activates posterior temporal and inferior frontal regions). The other approach is not limited to the assumption that cognitive processes or operations are localised in discrete anatomical areas but allows for specialisation that emerges when different cognitive processes depend on the pattern of interactions among a set of regions. This is referred to as "functional integration" because it encompasses changes in the way different areas interact with one another (as discussed later). Segregation and integration are not exclusive, they are complementary, and functional neuroimaging studies need to evaluate their relative contribution to each psychological process.

Functional integration

In the cognitive domain, functional integration is analogous to the functionality described in connectionist models (i.e. some functions arise from slowly acquired changes in the connection strengths between a limited number of specialised components). The emphasis we want to make is that neuronal components are "labile" (context sensitive). This is because the functional role played by any neuronal component (e.g. cortical area, subarea, neuronal population, or neuron) is largely defined by its interactions with other neuronal components. Forward connections (from lower to higher regions) are predominantly driving and excitatory, whereas backward connections (from higher to lower regions) mediate top-down influences. The modulatory effects of the backward connections can be thought of as changing the effective strength of the forward driving connections, which implicitly changes what any neuronal population will respond to. In other words, the responses in any one area depend on activity in all the regions that provide afferents. Thus, the function of a neuronal region depends on which areas it is interacting with. It is in this sense that neuronal representations are "labile" or context sensitive. Another way to appreciate this is to consider that each neuronal area might be part of more than one cortical system. For instance, area A might have function X when it receives inputs from areas B, C, and D but function Y when it receives inputs from areas R, S, and T. The function of A therefore depends on the source of its effective inputs at any particular time.

The implication, highlighted by studies of functional integration, is that representations cannot be divorced from the context in which they occur. They are a function of, and dependent upon, input from distal cortical areas. With respect to functional neuroimaging studies, regionally specific responses to a particular "category" can be detected in one context but not in another. The context in which an effect occurs is unlikely to be answered in a single functional neuroimaging experiment (this is discussed later, see p. 432). It requires multiple experiments to determine: (i) whether category-specific brain activation effects are context sensitive or insensitive; and (ii) an understanding of the underlying neuronal components (e.g. those associated with semantic processing). Thus, the use of functional neuroimaging to investigate category-specific effects depends on the results of many experiments, including some that are not related directly to category specificity. For instance, to evaluate whether there are anatomical regions in the brain that are specialised for different categories, we first need to establish the basic components of object recognition, auditory and visual word processing, the semantic system, and phonological responses. We then need to see how these systems respond when changing only the category. This relates to the experimental designs used in functional neuroimaging studies which we now turn to discuss.

Experimental design in functional imaging

The functional imaging techniques that will be considered in this chapter are positron emission tomography (PET) and functional magnetic resonance imaging (fMRI). Although there are some subtle differences between these techniques (PET measures blood flow, fMRI measures changes in the concentration of deoxyhaemoglobin), they both measure neural activity by detecting locally specific changes in blood composition and flow that accompany neural activity. The response variable in functional neuroimaging is therefore the haemodynamic response. As in the use of reaction times (RTs), the characterisation of the haemodynamic response involves either categorical comparisons (e.g. animal relative to tool naming) or a correlation with a continuous psychological variable (e.g. increasing word frequency). The former approach is referred to as "subtraction" and the second is referred to as "parametric". Parametric designs are limited to those variables that offer a continuous measure, and they have not so far been applied to functional imaging studies of category specificity. In fact, all functional imaging studies of category specificity to date have used cognitive subtraction and this is the technique we will therefore focus on. There are two pitfalls in subtraction that deserve consideration. The first relates to the selection of conditions that differ only in the process of interest. This requires tasks that are matched for every other possible variable (word frequency, word familiarity, auditory or visual features, etc.). Obviously, a complete match is impossible because different categories have, by definition, variable orthographic, structural, semantic, and phonological content. The difficulty matching these variables is particularly relevant to functional neuroimaging studies because even if subtle task differences have little effect on RTs, they can have profound effects on the distribution of brain activity. Additionally, condition specific brain activity can be elicited that is unrelated to the task performance and not predicted by the task analysis. For instance, face naming relative to face viewing could elicit emotional responses that change brain activity but do not affect naming RTs. In brief, functional neuroimaging data might be far more sensitive to subtle changes in conditions that relate to different aspects of processing, particularly those components that might be implicit or indeed incidental.

The second pitfall of subtraction methodology is one that has been acknowledged for decades, perhaps most explicitly by Sternberg's revision of Donder's subtractive method (Sternberg, 1969). It is that the difference between two tasks comprises not only the extra task components but also the integration of the added and shared components (e.g. the integration of phonology and face recognition when face naming is contrasted to face viewing). The solution to this problem, well known to psychologists, is to use multifactorial designs that assess the interactions between different variables. Multifactorial designs are now used almost routinely in functional neuro-imaging. However, it should be noted that the data are much more compli-cated to interpret in functional neuroimaging studies because of the sheer number of observations being made. For instance, whereas RT analyses are based on a single observation per condition (such as the condition mean and variance) and result in a single interaction effect, the haemodynamic response (used in functional neuroimaging studies) has to be measured in tens of thousands of voxels throughout the brain for each condition. Different voxels can express both positive and negative interactions in the context of activa-tions and deactivations.

The use of subtraction methodology is therefore fraught with difficulties particularly for neuroimaging. The key points are that: (i) the experimental task variables have to be as closely matched as possible; and (ii) assessing the interactions between different factors is crucial, although more complicated in neuroimaging than behavioural studies, which have only one dependent variable.

In summary, functional neuroimaging is the only technique currently available that has the potential to characterise the anatomical components of the distributed neuronal systems that engender category-specific effects. By assessing category-specific differences in brain activation over a range of conditions and in different task contexts, functional imaging should be able to distinguish whether there are functionally segregated areas for different categories or whether category-specific effects arise from changes in the pat-tern of interactions among shared cortical regions. The next section considers in more detail the types of experiment that might be relevant for testing current cognitive models.

TESTING COGNITIVE MODELS OF CATEGORY SPECIFICITY

A number of cognitive explanations are available for category-specific effects. These have been summarised by Caramazza (1998) and discussed in detail in the accompanying chapters. Most of these theories do not attempt to make any inferences about the underlying brain systems. Instead, the neuro-psychological inference is purely about the cognitive architecture that might or might not have architectural homologies at a neuronal level. Nevertheless, this section considers how functional neuroimaging might evaluate three of the most popular explanations. The first is the view upheld by Caramazza and his colleagues, which proposes that functional specialisation emerges as a function of the categories themselves because different categories have different biological salience in terms of adaptive responses during neurodevelopment (Caramazza & Shelton, 1998). The second view was proposed by Warrington and Shallice in 1984. It postulates that there are separable systems for perceptual and functional knowledge, identification of natural objects relies more on perceptual features and identification of man-made objects relies more on functional knowledge. The third view is that category-specific effects need not reflect a semantic system that is organised by category or type of knowledge. Rather, specialisation arises from the differential demands on a shared processing system. For example, natural objects tend to share many visual attributes and require more perceptual discrimination than man-made objects (Humphreys, Riddoch, & Quinlan, 1988). These three theories will now be addressed in turn.

Specialisation according to category

If category-specific effects occur because there are category-specific neuronal systems, then these should be revealed when different categories are directly contrasted with one another. Furthermore, the same category-specific responses should: (i) occur in any task that elicits category-specific effects—usually tasks requiring a recognition or identification response (e.g. naming, reading, semantic decision); and (ii) not occur in response to any other effect (e.g. in an area that is sensitive to word frequency, irrespective of category). The latter restriction is obviously one that requires a full exploration of all possible response determinants. Therefore, even if category-specific effects were identified irrespective of task, a range of complementary investigations are then required to assess how the putative category-specific areas are affected by other factors. In short, although functional imaging might generate hypotheses concerning brain regions that underpin category specificity, definitive answers will require extensive experimentation. This problem can be illustrated with an area in the right fusiform that is particularly sensitive to the visual presentation of faces (Kanwisher et al., 1997, 1999). Although it is designated as a face-specific area, other studies have demonstrated that categorisation level, familiarity, and expertise with objects also determine activity (Gauthier et al., 1997, 1999, 2000). Thus, an alternative to face-specific responses is that it is more responsive to faces than any other category of object because of differences in categorisation level and expertise.

Specialisation according to semantic attribute

If category-specific effects occur because different categories place differential demands on the representation and retrieval of perceptual and functional attributes, then activation elicited by natural, relative to man-made, objects should correspond to that elicited when perceptual attributes are accessed relative to functional attributes. This is a simple hypothesis that rests on demonstrating separable neuronal systems for perceptual and functional knowledge and the same anatomical segregation for natural kinds of objects and man-made objects, respectively.

Specialisation arising from the differential demands on a shared processing system

If category-specific effects arise because of differential demands on parts of a shared processing system, then category-specific activation should correspond to specific components of the system. For example, the shared processing system might be composed of components specialised for structural object processing, semantic processing, and phonological processing. If natural kinds of objects place greater demands on structural object processing as suggested by Humphreys et al. (1988), then we would expect greater activation for natural kinds of objects in structural object processing areas. According to this hypothesis, category-specific effects will vary when the stimuli are objects or words because only the former involves object recognition.

Of course, evidence for any of these theories does not exclude the possibility that there is more than one explanation for category-specific effects. The next section discusses the relevant functional neuroimaging data.

REVIEW OF FUNCTIONAL NEUROIMAGING DATA ON CATEGORY-SPECIFIC EFFECTS

To date (early 2000), there have been fourteen published accounts of functional imaging studies that have compared the distribution of neural activity in response to natural kinds of objects (animals, fruit, and vegetables) or man-made kinds of objects (tools and manipulable small objects). The findings are probably as divergent and inconsistent as those reported in the neuropsychological literature. Many factors contribute to the inconsistency. These include the sensitivity of the brain scanner, the type of data analysis applied, and whether the conditions have been matched for variables such as familiarity, word length, or visual complexity. Another critical feature concerns differences in the threshold of the selected significance level. As neuroimaging studies usually involve analyses of effects in tens of thousands of voxels, a correction needs to be made for multiple comparisons. In early PET studies, where sensitivity to activation was less than that of the scanners available now, a $p < 0.001$ level was often considered appropriate to eliminate false positives (Bailey et al., 1991). However, as scanning techniques improved (for both PET and fMRI), the importance of formally correcting for the number of comparisons being made became more appreciated. It is now almost standard practice to use "corrected probability levels" (see Worsley et al., 1996).

The overall point being made is that functional neuroimaging is a relatively new and fast-developing field and the standard of experimental design, data acquisition, and data analysis is improving continuously. In this review it is therefore appropriate to present an overview of each of the relevant fourteen studies in chronological order where the early studies can be considered "pioneering" and the latter studies can be seen as benefitting from hindsight. At the end of this synopsis, we will then consider the implications of these findings for cognitive models of category specificity.

Paper 1, 1995.   Perani et al. (1995) published the first functional imaging study of category specificity. Eleven subjects were scanned with PET while performing a same–different matching task on pairs of line drawings depicting either living (animals) or non-living (man-made tools) items. Occipital and temporal regions were activated for both living and non-living items but there were no significant category differences at the minimum level used to avoid false positives in PET data when no *a priori* hypotheses have been made ($p < 0.001$, uncorrected for multiple comparisons, see Bailey et al., 1991). At a sub-threshold level ($p < 0.01$), living relative to non-living items enhanced activation in two visual processing areas (left fusiform and lingual gyri) and non-living relative to living items enhanced activation in a region of the left inferior frontal gyrus. These findings were interpreted by the authors as "*in vivo* evidence for neural fractionation of semantic knowledge".

Paper 2, 1996.   Martin, Wiggs, Ungerleider, and Haxby (1996) scanned thirty-two subjects using PET while they named either line drawings (sixteen subjects) or silhouettes of the line drawings (sixteen subjects), which depicted either animals or tools. There were many regions (including occipital, temporal, and frontal cortices) that were activated in common to animals and tools relative to viewing nonsense objects. Two category-specific effects were also observed at $p < 0.001$ uncorrected for number of comparisons. The first was in the left lingual gyrus (a visual processing region) for animals relative to tools (an area also identified by Perani et al. [1995] for animals relative to tools). The second was in the left posterior middle temporal cortex for tools relative to animals. As both areas were observed irrespective of whether the stimuli were line drawings or silhouettes, an interpretation in terms of differences in visual input was excluded (although see Moore and Price [1999], paper 10). Instead, activation in the lingual gyrus (for animals relative to tools) was attributed to "top-down modulation, or reactivation, of primary visual areas", which might be necessary "to identify an object uniquely when relatively subtle differences in physical features are the primary means by which the object can be distinguished from other members of its category".

The left posterior middle temporal region, where Martin et al. (1996) found more activation for tools than animals, was "nearly identical to the area activated in a previous study by Martin et al. (1995) in which subjects generated action words associated with objects" (e.g. say "peel" in response to "banana"). Martin et al. (1996) therefore attributed the left posterior middle temporal region to "the site of stored knowledge about patterns of visual action associated with using objects". Thus, the overall conclusions were that tools relied more heavily on functional attributes than animals and animals relied more heavily on visual attributes than tools. Finally, Martin et al., (1996) conclude that their results suggest that "semantic representations of objects are stored as a distributed neural network that includes the ventral regions of the temporal lobe. The location of the other areas recruited as part of this network depend on the intrinsic properties of the object to be identified".

Paper 3, 1996.   Damasio et al. (1996) scanned nine subjects using PET, a naming task, line drawings of animals and tools, and photographs of famous faces. Regions of interest were defined in the ventral temporal cortex on the basis of the authors' analysis of the lesions associated with category-specific deficits (effects seen in the frontal lobe for this study are reported in Grabowski, Damasio, & Damasio [1998], paper 7). The ventral temporal cortex was activated for all categories relative to the control condition (orientation decision on unfamiliar faces) but famous faces (relative to animals and tools) enhanced activation in bilateral anterior temporal cortices and tools (relative to animals) enhanced activation in the left posterior middle temporal cortex (as seen by Martin et al., 1996). There were no animal-specific areas at a corrected level of significance but, below threshold, a medial area of the inferior temporal cortex was more active for animals than for tools.

On the basis of the lesion study, which included only patients who could identify items they could not name, Damasio et al. (1996) attributed the category-specific effects to specialisation at an intermediary level between word form information and conceptual knowledge (perhaps similar to the lemma level; see Levelt, 1989). Importantly, rather than envisage "rigid modules or hard edged centres", Damasio et al. (1996) suggest "interaction, by means of feedforward and feedback projections, between the regions of cerebral cortex which subtend conceptual knowledge and those which can enact lexical knowledge". Furthermore, "distinct kinds of conceptual knowledge lead to the recruitment of distinct intermediary regions".

Paper 4, 1996.   Mummery, Patterson, Hodges, and Wise (1996) scanned six subjects, using PET and auditory presentation of category names that were either natural (vegetables, land animals, fruit, and sea creatures) or manipulable (toys, clothes, tools, and weapons). Subjects were asked to name as many members of each category as they could within 20 seconds. Manipulable relative to natural word generation enhanced activation in the left posterior middle temporal cortex, as seen by Martin et al. (1996) and Damasio et al. (1996). For natural kinds, there was more activation in bilateral, medial, and anterior temporal cortices, and in the right inferior parietal lobe. The bilateral anterior temporal activations for natural kinds were medial to those associated with faces in the Damasio et al. (1996) study, but are consistent with the lesions that result in natural kind deficits (Gainotti et al., 1995), particularly the ability to retrieve visual features defining different members of living categories (Sartori et al., 1993). Mummery et al. (1996) concluded that "objects in various conceptual domains have differential weightings of sensory features within the complex network of semantic knowledge". Notably, the task used by Mummery et al. (1996) was auditory stimulated word production and there was no activation in visual areas for natural kinds as seen when the stimuli were visually presented as drawings (Martin et al., 1996; Perani et al., 1995).

Summary of studies to the end of 1996.   At the end of 1996, the neuroimaging literature on category-specific effects had highlighted the lingual gyrus as important for visually presented pictures of animals, bilateral anterior temporal cortices for generating words depicting natural kinds, and the left posterior middle temporal cortex for naming, matching, or generating manipulable objects.

Paper 5, 1998.   Mummery, Patterson, Hodges, and Price (1998) went on to report a second study in which ten subjects were scanned using PET while visually presented with triads of words (either living things or artefacts) where a target had to be matched to one of two distractors on the basis of semantic association (either location or colour). Irrespective of task (location or colour), artefacts resulted in greater activation in the left posterior middle temporal cortex (as seen by Damasio et al., 1996; Martin et al., 1996; Mummery et al., 1996) and the left parahippocampal gyrus (associated with semantic retrieval in other studies; e.g. Ricci et al., 1999; Vandenberghe et al., 1996). Areas that were more active for living items (the left middle frontal gyrus and the right inferior parietal cortex) were observed only during the location task. No areas were more active for living things across tasks and the authors conclude that when the task demands and stimulus attributes were carefully controlled "there are no areas specific to the semantic processing of words denoting living things".

Paper 6, 1998.   Cappa et al. (1998) scanned thirteen subjects using PET and visually presented words depicting either an animal or a tool. For animal words, the task either tapped visual associations ("Is the tail long or short with respect to the body?") or semantic associations ("Is it from Italy?"). For tools, the task was either visual ("Is it longer than wider or wider than longer?") or functional ("Is it used for food preparation?"). There was no interaction between task and category. Living things (irrespective of task) increased activation in the right middle frontal and right fusiform gyri. Non-living things (irrespective of task) increased activation in the same left posterior middle temporal area seen for tools and inanimate objects by Martin et al. (1996), Damasio et al. (1996), Mummery et al. (1996), and Mummery et al. (1998). Cappa et al. (1998) also observed the left supramarginal gyrus, the right superior temporal gyrus, and the right thalamus for non-living more than living items. None of these regions had previously been associated with category-specific deficits and the effects did not reach a significance level that was corrected for multiple comparisons.

Paper 7, 1998.   Grabowski et al. (1998) report the same experiment as Damasio et al. (1996) and focus on the frontal rather than temporal activations. With respect to differences between tools and animals, Grabowski et al. (1998) do not report direct comparisons. However, activation for tool but not animal naming (relative to orientation decisions on unfamiliar faces) was identified in the anterior bank of the left precentral gyrus, which extended along the left inferior and middle frontal gyri. This region was also found to be more active for tool naming than animal naming by Martin et al. (1996) but is not discussed above because the difference did not reach significance, even at an uncorrected level. Grabowski et al. (1998) and Martin et al. (1996) argue that greater activation in the premotor cortex for tools arises because of the "action" associated with tools. The evidence underlying this argument is that the premotor cortex is activated for generating verbs and actions relative to word repetition (Martin et al., 1995; Petersen et al., 1988) and generating nouns (Warburton et al., 1996). However, activation in the premotor cortex is not restricted to verb generation, it is also activated during letter fluency (Frith, Friston, Liddle, & Frackowiak, 1991) and generating nouns (Warburton et al., 1996). Further experiments are therefore required to confirm that the left premotor activation indicates implicit generation of manual responses rather than verbalisation or other more generalised responses. It should also be emphasised that the differences in activation for tool relative to animal naming in the left premotor cortex were not assessed directly by Grabowski et al. (1998) and were not significant in the Martin et al. (1996) study.

Paper 8, 1998.   Spitzer et al. (1998) were the first to report an fMRI study of category-specific effects but the methods used were not as developed as those used in the PET studies. For instance, only 2cm of brain was imaged (as opposed to 10–15cm in most of the PET studies) and subjects were analysed individually rather than as a group. Twelve subjects were scanned while covertly naming pictures of either animals or household items and differences between these categories revealed "rather little activation. In nine of the 12 subjects, relatively small regions in the middle and inferior frontal gyrus, as well as the superior temporal gyrus and inferior parts of the parietal lobe were identified as showing significant selective activation". However, although there was no apparent consistency across subjects, the authors conclude that "semantic representations in the frontal and temporal areas are, to some degree, localized and possibly implemented as multiple maps".

Summary of studies to the end of 1998.   At the end of 1998, the neuroimaging literature on category-specific effects had strengthened the association of the left posterior middle temporal cortex with tool processing irrespective of stimulus (pictures, visual words, and auditory words) or task (naming, matching, perceptual, and functional). These modality-independent effects suggest that the tool-specific effect is arising at a semantic level. The left posterior middle temporal area is also more active for accessing action than perceptual knowledge (Martin et al., 1995). This suggests that the presentation of stimuli depicting tools enhances activation associated with "actions". The premotor areas reported by Martin et al. (1996) and Grabowski et al. (1998) are also consistent with enhanced activation of "actions" in response to tools. With respect to living items, category-specific effects have been far less consistent. Interestingly, the activations in the lingual gyrus identified by Perani (1995) and Martin et al. (1996) are not replicated when the stimuli are visually or auditorily presented words (Cappa et al., 1998; Mummery et al., 1996, 1998). This suggests that the effect in the lingual gyrus is specific to picture presentation (see Moore & Price [1999], paper 10).

Paper 9, 1999.   Perani et al. (1999) report more details from the study by Perani et al. (1995) and a word version of the same paradigm. The word version involved PET scanning of eight subjects who performed a same–different matching task on visually presented words referring to animals, manipulable objects (tools) or a baseline (legal pseudowords like "tromp"). No areas were identified that were more active for animals (relative to tools and pseudowords) or tools (relative to animals or pseudowords) but when pseudowords were excluded significant activation (at $p < 0.001$ uncorrected) was found for tools in the left posterior middle temporal cortex (as seen for tools by Cappa et al., 1998; Damasio et al., 1996; Martin et al., 1996; Mummery et al., 1996, 1998). Interestingly, for tools relative to animals, there was also more activation in visual processing regions (left lingual, cuneus, and precuneus) although when pictures have been used as stimuli, visual areas tend to be more active for animals (Martin et al., 1996; Perani et al., 1995). The most likely explanation relates to physical differences in the visual configuration of the stimuli (see Moore & Price [1999], paper 10). The only areas found to be significantly more active for animals than tools were the thalamus and the right superior parietal lobule, neither of which was identified in any previous studies of category specificity. These areas add to the growing number of miscellaneous regions that have been associated with animals or living items. As the living specific activations tend to be unique to particular studies and do not withstand a correction for the number of comparisons made, the most likely explanation is one of false positives. Nevertheless, Perani et al. (1999) considered that their results indicated "different brain networks subserving the identification of living and nonliving entities".

Paper 10, 1999. Moore and Price (1999) scanned fourteen subjects using PET and visually presented pictures of animals, tools, vehicles, and fruit. Eight subjects named the pictures and six subjects made same–different decisions on picture–word pairs from the same categories. For man-made (vehicles and tools) relative to natural (animals and fruit) objects, there was increased activation in the left lingual gyrus as previously reported for animals relative to tools (Martin et al., 1996; Perani et al., 1995). Activation in the lingual gyrus was greatest for vehicles but there was also more activation for animals relative to fruit, suggesting that responses in this region might depend on the complexity of the visual configuration rather than the semantic category. With respect to activation in the left posterior middle temporal area for tools (as seen by Cappa et al., 1998; Damasio et al., 1996; Martin et al., 1996; Mummery et al., 1996, 1998; Perani et al., 1999), this effect was only observed by Moore and Price (1999) in the word–picture match and even here activation for tools did not exceed that for non-objects. (Note that in the Perani et al. [1999] study, left posterior middle temporal activation for tools was not above pseudowords either.)

For natural kinds relative to man-made objects, there were no differences in activation when the stimuli were appropriately coloured but, when the stimuli were black and white outline drawings, natural objects (relative to man-made objects) increased activation in bilateral anterior temporal cortices and the right posterior temporal cortex. The left anterior temporal area was also more active for natural kinds relative to non-objects consistent with a semantic role in this region (see also Vandenberghe et al., 1996; Mummery et al., 1996, 1998). The right anterior and posterior temporal regions, by contrast, were not more active for natural kinds than non-objects. Moore and Price (1999) argue that these areas reflect the demands placed on object processing because the same right hemisphere areas activate when: (i) black and white drawings are contrasted to coloured drawings (where object processing is more demanding when it is not facilitated by the presence of colour); and (ii) non-objects are contrasted to pictures of man-made objects (where object processing is more demanding when the stimuli are unfamiliar). These results suggest that differences in the demands placed on structural object processing can generate category-specific differences that cannot be attributed to differences at a semantic level (see Humphreys et al., 1988).

Paper 11, 1999.   Gerlach, Law, Gade, and Paulson (1999) scanned fifteen subjects, using PET and visually presented outline drawings of objects and non-objects during an object decision task. Objects depicted either natural or man-made stimuli. Non-objects were novel in the easy version of the task and composed of parts of the objects in the difficult version of the task. A two-by-two factorial design (object category and type of non-object) revealed no effect of category and no category-by-task interaction using a threshold corrected for the number of comparisons made. *Post hoc* analyses suggested that activation of regions associated with structural object processing (the right inferior and anterior fusiform gyri) was more extensive for natural kinds than man-made kinds but this does not imply segregated cortical structures. The results are simply interpreted as a reflection of the greater perceptual differentiation required for natural kinds of object (see also Humphreys et al., 1988; Moore & Price, 1999).

Paper 12, 1999.   Thompson-Schill, Aguirre, D'Esposito, and Farah (1999) scanned five subjects, using fMRI and auditory presentation of questions concerning the visual or non-visual attributes of living or non-living objects. An example of a visual question is "Do ducks have long ears?". An example of a non-visual question is "Can headphones play stereo music?". A region of interest was proposed in the left fusiform gyrus, which the authors had previously associated with "visual semantics" (D'Esposito et al., 1997). Based on the "interactive modality specific hypothesis of semantic organisation" (Farah & McClelland, 1991), Thompson-Schill et al. (1999) predicted that the left fusiform "visual semantic" area should be activated by living things irrespective of question but only for non-living things when the question was visual (for arguments against this assumption, see Caramazza, 2000). Thompson-Schill et al. then claim to present evidence to confirm their prediction but the critical interaction between visual and non-visual questions to living and non-living items was exceedingly small ($t = 1.9$). This is lower than any of the effects reported in the imaging experiments discussed earlier. It should also be noted that the evidence for the fusiform area being specific to visual semantics is limited to two studies (D'Esposito et al., 1997; Martin et al., 1995) where visual semantics was confounded either by stimuli, type of task, or task difficulty. Furthermore, the same fusiform area responds when congenitally blind subjects read abstract words in Braille (Buechel, Price, & Friston, 1998), a finding that is not consistent with a function related to visual semantic memory.

Paper 13, 1999.   Chao, Haxby, and Martin (1999) scanned 26 subjects using fMRI during object viewing, object matching, object naming, or reading object names. The objects were faces, animals, tools, or houses. Pictures of animals, relative to pictures of tools, increased activation in bilateral medial and inferior occipital, ventral temporal, and superior temporal cortices. In contrast, pictures of tools, relative to animals, increased activation in the medial fusiform gyrus and the lateral middle posterior temporal gyrus. It is not clear, however, whether these effects arise from differences in visual configuration, frequency or other such variables, which are not reported to be controlled. Furthermore, no group analyses were presented. Instead, subjects were analysed as individuals, results were presented as the proportion of subjects showing an effect (at an exceedingly low threshold, $p < 0.05$ uncorrected for the number of comparisons) and there was considerable variability between subjects. For instance, when the stimuli were words, greater activation for animals relative to tools was observed in 0/8 subjects in the medial occipital gyrus (associated with animals when the stimuli are pictures), 2/8 subjects in the left inferior occipital gyrus, 3/8 subjects in the right inferior occipital gyrus, 4/8 in the left lateral fusiform gyrus, 5/8 in the right lateral fusiform gyrus, and 2/8 in the left superior temporal sulcus. The most consistent effect for reading was observed for tools relative to animals in the left posterior middle temporal cortex in 7/8 subjects. This is the area that has been associated with tools in many of the studies reported above.

Paper 14, 2000.   Finally, a recent study by Gorno-Tempini et al. (2000) used eight subjects and PET to look at differences between six different categories of objects during a picture naming and reading task. The categories included were famous faces, animals, manipulable small man-made objects, body parts, maps of countries, and colour patches. The aim was to investigate whether category differences were dependent on the demands placed on lexical retrieval (which was expected to be more involved in picture naming than reading). To exclude perceptual differences between tasks, words in the reading task were presented alongside their corresponding pictures and strings of false fonts (matched to the visual features of words) were presented alongside the pictures in the naming task. This design allowed differences in visual input to be excluded from the interpretation of any task specific category effects. However, no such task specific effects were observed.

Category differences in the Gorno-Tempini et al. (2000) paper were, however, observed across task (when visual input between categories could not be controlled). For instance, the left posterior middle temporal area associated with tools and "action retrieval" (see earlier discussion) was more active for the object and body part conditions relative to the other four categories. As body parts are also associated with self-generated actions, this study provides further support that the left posterior middle temporal cortex is linked to "action" associations. Other category-specific differences observed (at a significance level corrected for multiple comparisons) related to finding more activation in: (i) medial extrastriate visual areas for faces, animals and maps relative to objects and body parts—interpreted as increased visual analysis for the former; (ii) a region of the left ventral anterior temporal cortex for famous faces more than all other categories—consistent with the association of this area with famous relative to unknown faces in a previous study by Gorno-Tempini et al. (1998); and (iii) right superior occipital, right intraparietal, and right parahippocampal areas for maps more than all other categories—consistent with the association of these areas with "spatial topographical processing", which might be required to recognise a topographical illustration of a country's shape in relation to its surroundings.

Summary of the fourteen studies. In summary, none of the fourteen neuroimaging papers discussed above have demonstrated highly significant category-specific effects when visual input is controlled. The most consistent effect is the association of the left posterior middle temporal cortex when objects or words depict tools (Figure 15.1). As already discussed, this area has also been associated with retrieving the actions associated to objects (Martin et al., 1995; see also Phillips, Noppeney, Humphreys, & Price, in press) and was found to be more active for pictures of body parts (Gorno-Tempini et al., 2000). Greater activation in this left posterior middle temporal "action area" for tools and body parts suggests that actions are implicitly activated even when this is not required by the task. On the other hand, there are no areas that were consistently more active for natural kinds relative to man-made objects. Activation for natural kinds has tended to be associated with visual processing areas or areas associated with the demands on structural object processing but only when the stimuli are pictures (Chao et al., 1999; Gerlach et al., 1999; Martin et al., 1996; Moore and Price, 1999; Perani et al., 1995; see Figure 15.2). These results offer no support for any theory proposing specific neural processing at a semantic processing level for natural kinds of objects.

Implications for cognitive models of category specificity

As noted several times earlier, the most consistent finding from the functional neuroimaging literature to date is that a region in the left posterior middle temporal cortex (Figure 15.1) is more active for tools (and body parts) relative to other categories of objects. As there is also some evidence to suggest that this area is more involved in action retrieval than retrieval of other types of semantic attribute (Martin et al., 1995; Phillips et al., in press), the functional neuroimaging results offer some support to the most popularly held

Left hemisphere **Right hemisphere**

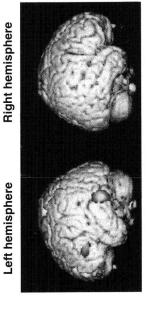

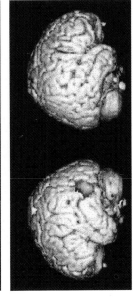

Action (Twist/Pour) > Screen size
decisions on words or pictures of objects
(Phillips et al., 1999)

Man-made and body parts > Natural
during picture naming and reading
(Gorno-Tempini et al., 2000)

Man-made > Natural
during verbal fluency to auditory cues
(Mummery et al., 1996)

Figure 15.1. Left posterior middle temporal "action" area can be more active for man-made objects.

Object processing areas
that are more active for
black/white > coloured
pictures during naming
(Moore and Price, 1999)

Natural kinds > Man-made
during picture naming
(Moore and Price, 1999)

Natural kinds > Man-made
during verbal fluency
to auditory cues
(Mummery et al., 1996)

Left hemisphere   Right hemisphere

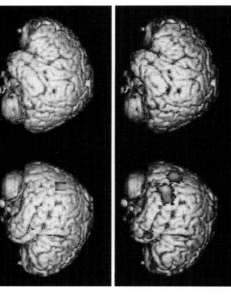

**Horizontal sections showing
anterior temporal activations**

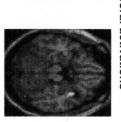

Figure 15.2.   Right hemisphere object processing areas can be more active for natural kinds.

view that identification of man-made objects relies on functional attributes (Warrington & Shallice, 1984).

The other side of the functional–perceptual theory predicts that natural kinds of objects will enhance activation in areas associated with perceptual attributes. This has not been reliably demonstrated in functional neuroimaging because there has been no clear demonstration of which areas might be associated with perceptual semantics *per se* (Cappa et al., 1998; Mummery et al., 1998; Vandenberghe et al., 1996). Furthermore, there are no areas that have been consistently associated with natural kinds of objects when the stimuli are visually or auditorily presented words (see earlier). This might reflect the sensitivity of the techniques currently available. Nevertheless, when the stimuli are pictures rather than words, natural kinds of objects tend to enhance activation in visual or structural processing areas (Chao et al., 1999; Gerlach et al., 1999; Gorno-Tempini et al., 2000; Martin et al., 1996; Moore and Price, 1999; Perani et al., 1995, 1999). In fact, the only studies using pictures that are not included in this list report regions of interest that did not involve visual or structural processing areas. Greater activation for natural kinds of objects in visual and structural processing areas is consistent with the view that natural kinds of objects place greater demands on structural object processing (see Humphreys et al., 1988). This does not imply that deficits with natural kinds of object necessarily result from impaired structural processing. Indeed, selective deficits with natural kinds of objects can occur for visually and auditorily presented words indicating a higher level impairment. Finally, it is interesting to note that, in the neuropsychological literature, deficits with natural kinds are far more prevalent than deficits with man-made objects while functional imaging data has been more consistent at revealing neural specialisation for manmade items.

FUTURE DIRECTIONS FOR NEUROIMAGING STUDIES OF CATEGORY SPECIFICITY

Functional neuroimaging studies have firmly established functional specialisation as a principle of brain organisation in man. The point emphasised throughout the first section of this chapter is that functional specialisation can arise either from selective responses in the component regions (functional segregation) or from changes in the pattern of interactions among the same set of regions (functional integration). The experiments described in the third section focused on identifying segregated subsystems. Although these represent a step in the right direction, they show few consistent effects. The inconsistency suggests that category effects at a neuronal level could be profoundly context sensitive. The hypothesis that now needs addressing is whether functional specialisation subtending category specificity emerges from the integration of activity among distributed brain regions that are shared by all object categories. Future functional neuroimaging experiments therefore need to evaluate the relative contribution of segregation and integration for eliciting category-specific effects. There are two main approaches. The first is multifactorial designs that assess: (i) context-independent effects (e.g. face processing in the right occipitotemporal cortex); (ii) context-sensitive effects (e.g. tool processing in the left posterior middle temporal cortex); and (iii) the contexts that elicit the effects (e.g. naming but not viewing). Multifactorial analyses are required because context-sensitive effects cannot be determined without establishing what the context is. For instance, the above review of the data indicates that the left posterior middle temporal cortex is more active for tools than animals in some studies but not others, and we do not know what the determinants of the context-sensitive responses are. It might be, for instance, that the left posterior middle temporal "tool" area is part of a shared processing system that is differentially engaged by some aspect of tool processing (e.g. implicit activation of associated actions) that occur in some conditions (or subjects) but not others.

A more direct approach to studying the role of functional integration is to assess the effective connectivity among regions (see Friston, 1995). This can be defined as the influence that one area exerts over another and can be assessed by various forms of regression analysis where the activity in one area is modelled as some function of activity in other areas. These correlations imply that activity goes up and down together with a temporal scale in the order of milliseconds for electrophysiological studies (which record spike trains of neural activity) and seconds in functional neuroimaging studies (which measure haemodynamic changes). Effective connectivity measurements can dissociate: (i) correlations where activity changes in one region cause activity changes in another region; and (ii) correlations that do not involve direct connections between the correlated areas but a shared source of input. Critically, a cognitive effect can be realised physiologically in terms of an increase in the coupling or integration of two areas. For instance, animal-specific effects might result from increases in the coupling between two or more regions that also respond (in an uncorrelated way) to other object categories. Conventional subtraction of different conditions cannot reveal such effects. Current work on analytical models for neuroimaging data aims to accommodate these process-specific increases in coupling.

In conclusion, functional neuroimaging is still maturing. It has the potential to provide physiological explanations for long-standing psychological questions but the answers are going to come from a slow synthesis of accumulating results and a proper understanding of functional integration in relation to cognitive processes.

ACKNOWLEDGEMENTS

This work was funded by the Wellcome Trust. We would like to thank Caroline Moore and Joseph Devlin for their helpful comments.

REFERENCES

Bailey, D.L., Jones, T., Spinks, T.J., Gilardi, M.C., & Townsend, D.W. (1991). Noise equivalent count measurements in a neuro-PET scanner with retractable septa. *I.E.E.E. Transactions in Medical Imaging, 10*, 256–260.

Buechel, C., Price, C.J., & Friston, K.J. (1998). A multi-modal language area in the ventral visual pathway. *Nature, 394*, 274–277.

Cappa S.F., Perani D., Schnur T., Tettamanti M., & Fazio F. (1998). The effects of semantic category and knowledge type on lexical-semantic access: A PET study. *Neuroimage, 8(4)*, 350–359.

Caramazza A. (1998). The interpretation of semantic category-specific deficits: What do they reveal about the organization of conceptual knowledge in the brain. *Neurocase, 4*, 265–272.

Caramazza A. (2000). Minding the facts: A comment on Thompson-Schill et al.'s "A neural base for category and modality specificity of semantic knowledge". *Neuropsychologia, 38(7)*, 944–949.

Caramazza A., & Shelton J.R. (1998). Domain-specific knowledge systems in the brain: The animate-inanimate distinction. *Journal of Cognitive Neuroscience, 1*, 1–34.

Chao L.L., Haxby J.V., & Martin A. (1999). Attribute-based neural substrates in temporal cortex for perceiving and knowing about objects. *Nature Neuroscience, 2(10)*, 913–914.

Damasio H., Grabowski T.J., Tranel D., Hitchwa R.D., & Damasio A.R. (1996). A neural basis for lexical retrieval. *Nature, 380*, 499–505.

D'Esposito, M., Detre, J.A., Auguirre, G.K., Stallcup, M., Alsop, D.C., Tippet, L.J., & Farah, M.J. (1997). A functional MRI study of mental image generation. *Neuropsychologia, 35(5)*, 725–730.

Farah M., & McClelland J. (1991). A computational model of semantic memory impairment: Modality specificity and emergent category specificity. *Journal of Experimental Psychology, General, 120*, 339–357.

Friston K.J. (1995). Functional and effective connectivity in neuroimaging: A synthesis. *Human Brain Mapping, 2*, 56–78.

Frith, C.D., Friston, K.J., Liddle, P.F., & Frackowiak, R.S.J. (1991). Willed action and the prefrontal cortex in man. *Proceedings of the Royal Society of London (Biology), 244*, 241–246.

Gainotti, G., Silveri, M.C., Daniele, A., & Giustolisi, L. (1995). Neuroanatomical correlates of category-specific semantic disorders: A critical study. *Memory* 3(3/4), 247–264.

Gauthier, I., Anderson, A.W., Tarr, M.J., Skudlarski, P., & Gore, J.C. (1997). Levels of categorization in visual recognition studies using functional magnetic imaging. *Current Biology, 7(9)*, 645–651.

Gauthier, I., Skudlarski, P., Gore, J.C., & Anderson, A.W. (2000). Expertise for cars and birds recruits brain areas involved in face recognition. *Nature Neuroscience, 3(2)*, 191–197.

Gauthier, I., Tarr, M.J., Anderson, A.W., Skudlarski, P., & Gore, J.C. (1999). Activation of the middle fusiform "Face area" increases with expertise in recognizing novel objects. *Nature Neuroscience, 2(6)*, 568–573.

Gerlach, C., Law, I., Gade, A., & Poulson, O.B. (1999). Perceptual differentiation and category effects in normal object recognition – A PET study. *Brain, 122(11)*, 2159–2170

Goltz, F. (1881) In W. MacCormac (Ed.), *Transactions of the 7th international medical congress* (Vol. 1, pp. 218–228). London: Kolkmann.

Gorno-Tempini, M.L., Cippolotti, L., & Price, C.J. (2000). Category-specific brain activation: Where does it come from? *Proceedings of the Royal Society. London Series B, 267,* 1253–1258.

Gorno-Tempini, M.L., Price, C.J., Josephs, O., Vandenberghe, R., Cappa, S.F., Kapur, N., & Frackowiak, R.S.J (1998). The neural systems sustaining face and proper name processing. *Brain, 121,* 2103–2118.

Grabowski T.J., Damasio H., & Damasio A.R. (1998). Premotor and prefrontal correlates of category-related lexical retrieval. *Neuroimage, 7,* 232–243.

Humphreys, G.W., Riddoch, M.J., & Quinlan, P.T. (1988). Cascade processes in picture identification. *Cognitive Neuropsychology, 5,* 67–103.

Kanwisher, N., McDermott, J., & Chun, M.M. (1997). The fusiform face area: A module in human extrastriate cortex specialized for face perception. *Journal of Neuroscience, 17(11),* 4302–4311.

Kanwisher, N., Stanley, D. & Harris, A. (1999). The fusiform face area is selective for faces not animals. *Neuroreport, 10,* 183–187.

Lichtheim, L. (1885). On aphasia. *Brain, 7,* 433–484.

Levelt, W.J.M. (1989). *Speaking: From intention to articulation.* Cambridge, MA: MIT Press.

Martin, A., Haxby, J.V., Lalonde, F.M., Wiggs, C.L., & Ungerleider, L.G. (1995). Discrete cortical regions associated with knowledge of color and knowledge of action. *Science, 270,* 102–105.

Martin, A., Wiggs, C.L., Ungerleider, L.G., & Haxby, J.V. (1996). Neural correlates of category-specific knowledge. *Nature, 379,* 649–652.

Moore, C.J., & Price, C.J. (1999) A Functional Neuroimaging study of the variables that generate category-specific object processing differences. *Brain, 122,* 943–962.

Mummery, C.J., Patterson, K., Hodges, J.R., & Price, C.J. (1998). Functional neuroanatomy of the semantic system: Divisible by what? *Journal of Cognitive Neuroscience, 10(6),* 766–777.

Mummery, C.J., Patterson, K., Hodges, J.R., & Wise, R.J.S. (1996). Generating 'tiger' as an animal name or a word beginning with T: Differences in brain activation. *Proceedings of the Royal Society London, Biological, 263,* 989–995.

Perani, D., Cappa, S.F., Bettinardi, V., Bressi, S., Gorno-Tempini, M.L., Matarrese, M., & Fazio, F. (1995). Different neural systems for the recognition of animals and manmade tools. *Neuroreport, 6,* 1637–1641.

Perani, D., Schnurt, T., Tettanmanti, M., Gorno-Tempini, M., Cappa, S.E., & Fazio, F. (1999). Word and picture matching: A PET study of semantic category effects. *Neuropsychologia, 37,* 293–306.

Petersen, S.E., Fox, P.T., Posner, M.I., Mintum, M., & Raichle, M.E. (1988). Positron emission tomographic studies of the cortical anatomy of single word processing. *Nature, 331,* 585–589.

Phillips, J., Noppeney, U., Humphreys, G., & Price, C. (in press). Can segregation within the semantic system account for category-specific deficits? *Brain.*

Ricci, P.T., Zelkowicz, B.J., Nebes, R.D., Meltzer, C.C., Mintum, M.A., & Bexker, J.T. (1999). Functional neuroanatomy of semantic memory: Recognition of semnatic associations. *NeuroImage, 9,* 88–96.

Sartori, G., Job, R., Miozzo, M., Zago, S., & Marchiori, G. (1993). Category-specific form-knowledge deficit in a patient with herpes simplex virus encephalitis. *Journal of Clinical Experimental Neuropsychology, 15(2),* 280–299.

Spitzer, M., Kischka, U., Guckel, F., Bellemann, M.E., Kammer, T., Seyyedi, S., Weisbrod, M., Schwartz, A., & Brix, G. (1998). Functional magnetic resonance imaging of category-specific cortical activation: Evidence for semantic maps. *Cognitive Brain Research, 6,* 309–318.

Sternberg S. (1969). The discovery of processing stages: Extension of Donder's method. *Acta Psychology, 18,* 643–662.

Thompson-Schill, S.L., Aguire, G.K., D'Exposito, M.D., & Farah, M.J. (1999) A neural basis for category and modality specificty of semantic knowledge. *Neuropsychologia, 37*, 671–676.

Vandenberghe, R., Price, C., Wise, R., Josephs, O., & Frackowiak, R.S.J. (1996). Functional anatomy of a common semantic system for words and pictures. *Nature, 383*, 254–256.

Warburton, E., Wise, R.J.S., Price, C.J., Weiller, C., Hadar, U., Ramsay, S., & Frackowiak, R.S.J. (1996). Studies with positron emission tomography of noun and verb retrieval by normal subjects. *Brain, 119*, 159–179.

Warrington, E.K., & Shallice, T. (1984). Category-specific impairments. *Brain, 107*, 829–852.

Wernicke, C. (1874). *Der Aphasiche Symptomenkomplex [The aphasias]*. Breslau, Poland: Cohen and Weigert.

Worsley, K.J., Marrett, S., Neelin, P., Vandal, A.C., Friston, K.J., & Evans, A.C. (1996). A unified statistical approach for determining significant signals in images of cerebral activation. *Human Brain Mapping, 4*, 58–83.

Author Index

Subject Index